STUDENT'S BOOK O

College English

Rhetoric, Readings, Handbook

NINTH EDITION

DAVID SKWIRE

HARVEY S. WIENER

MARYMOUNT MANHATTAN COLLEGE

Longman

New York San Francisco Boston
London Toronto Sydney Tokyo Singapore Madrid
Mexico City Munich Paris Cape Town Hong Kong Montreal

Vice President: Eben W. Ludlow
Development Editor: Ellen Darion
Marketing Manager: Carlise Paulson
Senior Production Manager: Eric Jorgensen
Project Coordination, Text Design, and Electronic Page Makeup: Electronic Publishing
Services Inc., NYC
Cover Design Manager: John Callahan
Cover Designer: Maria Ilardi
Cover Photo: © PhotoDisc, Inc.
Photo Researcher: Julie Tesser
Manufacturing Buyer: Al Dorsey
Printer and Binder: Courier, Westford
Cover Printer: Phoenix Color Corp.

For permission to use copyrighted material, grateful acknowledgment is made to the copyright holders on pp. 731– 734, which are hereby made part of this copyright page.

Library of Congress Cataloging-in-Publication Data
Skwire, David.
    Student's book of college English : rhetoric, readings, handbook / David Skwire,
Harvey S. Wiener.—9th ed.
      p.   cm.
    Includes index.
    ISBN 0-205-33623-X
    1. English language—Rhetoric.   2. English language—Grammar—Handbooks,
manuals, etc.   3. College readers.   4. Report writing.   I. Wiener, Harvey S.

PE1408.S546   2002
808′ .0427—dc21   00-054601

Please visit our website at http://www.ablongman.com

ISBN 0-205-33623-X

1 2 3 4 5 6 7 8 9 10—CRW—04 03 02 01

Brief Contents

Detailed Contents

10 Comparison and Contrast   226

Review Checklists

Preface to the Instructor

Changes give life; consistency sustains it. Although few traps are more insidious for an instructor than teaching a book—or a course—from memory, relying on a text's consistent philosophy from edition to edition has many rewards. Our ninth edition has changed and improved, yet the basic appeal of *Student's Book* remains unchanged: It provides in a small package, and at a reasonable cost, thorough instruction on all the issues likely to face students within a full year of Freshman English—and then supplements that instruction with numerous essays as well as with readings in poetry and fiction by student writers and professionals.

One of the special, possibly unique, features of *Student's Book* is the mix wherever practicable of readings for use as models and readings for use as subjects for compositions. We believe that this mix significantly increases the versatility of the book and helps account for its success. We maintain this principle in the ninth edition. Users will find, for example, student and professional models of descriptive writing, but they will also find a short story that students can profitably analyze in writing their own descriptions.

We hope that clear prose and good sense also made their contributions to the success of earlier editions. We have tried to keep them constantly in mind while writing the current one.

Highlights of This Edition

By making additions and improvements in the ninth edition of *Student's Book*, we aim to keep the text fresh and timely. These improvements include:

- **Many new readings,** including new contemporary essays and new poems and short stories.

- An expanded chapter on **classification** as a rhetorical method.
- Continued attention to **learning aids** such as review checklists throughout the text.
- Fresh and lively **student models** at key points in the text.
- Continued focus on writing arguments with "Having Your Say" writing activities throughout Parts One and Two.
- **Collaborative learning** activities as key to understanding and practicing the reading and writing process.
- Expanded instruction and practice in **outlining** (Chapter 3).
- A new chapter on **business writing**, including instructions on preparing résumés and writing business letters.
- An updated section on the **research paper**, now including more information on using and citing electronic sources.
- **Self Tests** throughout Part Six ("Handbook and Glossary") so that students can check their own progress, using the Answer Key provided on pages 721–730.

Plan of the Book

In **Part One, "The Principles of Good Reading and Writing,"** we explore active reading, prewriting strategies, drafting, and revising, and provide extensive practice on drafting and developing a thesis. We show student writing at various stages of development and offer commentary to guide a reader's appreciation of how a paper progresses from start to finish. We continue our full coverage of outlining and instruction in the use of computers as an aid to writing and in peer evaluations.

Part Two, "Methods of Development," contains nine chapters, one devoted to each of the key rhetorical modes, beginning with description and narration, working through example, process, comparison and contrast, classification and division, cause and effect, definition, and ending with argumentation. Each of these chapters contains a discussion of how to write in the particular mode, professional and student examples ("Models of Writing"), readings intended to inspire writing ("Readings for Writing"), and a large number of analytical and generative exercises ("For Writing or Discussion" questions follow every selection). Many readings in Part Two are new. We've tried to incorporate new readings that reflect the cultural diversity of today's student body.

To add to the practicality of the book, all chapters in Part Two end with suggested writing topics and with review checklists to serve as reminders and chapter summaries. Another popular feature in Part Two, "Crosscurrents," points out even more possibilities for writing topics by directing students' attention to thematic parallels between and among writing selections in different parts of the book.

Part Three, "Special Writing," includes a chapter on literary analysis and a chapter on writing essay exams.

Part Four, "Research," gives considerable attention to the essential research instruction. We include computerized research with databases, computerized card catalogs, and significant coverage of writing and revising. The *MLA Handbook for Writers of Research Papers,* Fifth Edition, and the *Publication Manual of the American Psychological Association,* Fourth Edition, guide our instruction in research. As electronic media continue to grow as sources for research papers, we include documentation material relative to electronic sources.

Part Five, "Style," includes three chapters: Chapter 21, on effective sentences, enables us to highlight those stylistic issues directly involved with creation of effective sentences; Chapter 20 on words and Chapter 22 on stylistic problems and solutions continue to offer students practical writing advice, including guidelines for avoiding sexist language. The style chapters are especially noteworthy, we believe, for the great number and variety of exercises.

Part Six, "Handbook and Glossary," is easily accessible through alphabetical arrangement of entries, a colored bar at the edge of all Part Six pages, and tabs with symbols that correspond to the list of Correction Symbols and Abbreviations on the inside front cover. The inside back cover contains guides to the text's planning, writing, and revising coverage, and a guide to the Handbook and Glossary, for quick reference. Student writers can find answers to any questions they have about grammar, sentences, punctuation, and mechanics in the Handbook and Glossary. Extensive exercises in Part Six enable students to demonstrate their command of the basics.

Acknowledgments

We are proud and grateful for the more than twenty years that our textbook has served college writers over the country. Our deepest thanks go to the faculty, students, and, we are certain, some of those students' children who have honored us with their trust and attention.

The planning and preparation of this edition, as well as earlier editions, have benefited enormously from the wise counsel and cultivated palate of Eben W. Ludlow, our editor at Longman Publishers. Thanks also to his assistant, Grace Trudo, whose intelligence and alacrity have moved the book along. And we want to express special appreciation to Ellen Darion, whose good sense and good humor lifted us over the usual (and not so usual!) hurdles of book production.

We are also grateful for the helpful professional advice of the reviewers for this edition: Kristin Brady, Delaware Technical & Community College; Marsula Guarino, Jamestown Community College; Gloria C. Johnson, Tennessee State University; Joe Law, Wright State University; Julian Medina, Mount San Antonio College; and Charles G. Rooney, Northwest State Community College.

Finally, special appreciation is due to Melissa Jacobs for her help with Part Five and with general editorial and clerical burdens.

Preface to the Student

We have written this book for you. We don't say that simply to win your confidence or to make you think well of us. We've felt for a long time that most textbooks are written for your instructor.

Writing textbooks for your instructor instead of for you is natural enough, in a way. Instructors, after all, must teach from the books, and no book that makes them unhappy is going to find its way into the classroom. Still, this book is written for you. Its purpose is to help you become a better writer and a more thoughtful reader than you are now. We believe that if you read this book carefully and ask questions in class whenever there are points you have any trouble with, you can improve your writing significantly. Neither we nor anyone else knows how to teach you to be a great writer, but—with your active participation—we think we can teach you to manage competently any writing assignment you're likely to get.

We've tried to write this book in a straightforward, unfussy fashion. We've concentrated as much as possible on being helpful about writing situations that you'll really face in class. We understand the ups and downs of drafting papers, and we try to guide you through the writing process. We've tried to pick reading selections that will interest you, as they have interested our own students, and that demonstrate writing principles you can apply to your own work. We've included a number of student writings, too, because we feel that comparing your work solely to that of experienced professionals is unprofitable and unfair. These writings were prepared by college students for classes similar to the one you're taking. Most of them are solid, honest pieces of work—but that's all. They are not intended to dazzle you with their genius, and they didn't all get *A*'s in class either. We hope you'll use them as general points of reference, not as supreme models of excellence. We hope that you'll often outdo them in your own writing.

First Lesson

Now for your first lesson.

Although this book will give you a great deal of information about writing, almost all of that information grows out of five simple ideas—ideas that are sufficiently important and usable to be thought of as rules. We're not peddling magic formulas, however, and we're not suggesting that a ready-made list of rules and regulations can substitute for the experiences and discoveries and sheer hard work by which writers educate themselves. No list ever made the pain of having nothing to say less painful. And people—not lists—write dramatic first sentences, come up with fresh insights, and choose the perfect word. Any rules we set down here or elsewhere are useful only because they can give direction and control to the inevitable hard work and thus increase the chances that the hard work will be worth the effort.

Don't approach the five simple ideas that follow, therefore, as representing more than important guidelines. They're starting points, but they're not eternal truths. George Orwell, our lead essayist (Chapter 1), once drew up a list of rules for writing, the last of which was, "Break any of these rules rather than say anything outright barbarous." As a more immediate example, this book will advise you to write well-developed paragraphs and avoid sentences fragments. That's excellent advice, and we take it seriously, but in the first paragraph of this preface we deliberately wrote a five-word paragraph that also happened to be a sentence fragment. Enough said.

Here are the five ideas on which we base much of this book:

1. Except for a few commonsense exceptions such as recipes, technical manuals, encyclopedia articles, and certain kinds of stories, poems, and plays, *writing should state a central idea.* (We call that central idea—or position, or stand, or contention—the *thesis.*)
2. *The primary function of writing is to prove or support its thesis.*
3. *The most effective and interesting way to prove or support the thesis is to use specific details presented in specific language.*
4. *Writing requires organization. Every statement must connect logically to the thesis.*
5. Good writing is the result of an ongoing process. First thoughts and first drafts should lead to second thoughts and second drafts, sometimes third ones and fourth ones. *Revise, revise, revise.*

We'll be repeating and expanding and sometimes strongly qualifying these ideas throughout the book, but they are the heart of what we have to say. They are not obscure secrets or brand new discoveries. They are the assumptions about writing that nearly all good writers make. They are the principles that nearly all good writers try to put into practice in their own work.

In the chapters that follow, we will discuss in detail the full meaning and implications of these ideas and try to show you the most effective ways of applying them to common classroom writing assignments.

David Skwire
Harvey S. Wiener

About the Authors

David Skwire, with degrees from the University of Wisconsin–Madison and Cornell University, taught composition, creative writing, and American literature at Cuyahoga Community College for twenty-five years. He also served on the faculties at Tufts University and Temple University. He acknowledges, however, that his job of most interest to students was a two-year stint as a writer of humorous greeting cards. In addition to his co-authorship of all editions of *Student's Book of College English,* he is author of the successful *Writing with a Thesis* (Harcourt Brace). Now retired, Skwire lives near Cleveland.

Harvey S. Wiener is Associate Vice President at Marymount Manhattan College. Wiener has worked as an educator for over thirty years, including seventeen years as professor of English at LaGuardia Community College. He has directed the basic writing program at Pennsylvania State University and has taught at Teachers College, Columbia University, Brooklyn College, Queensborough Community College, and the State University of New York at Stony Brook. A Phi Beta Kappa graduate of Brooklyn College, Wiener holds a Ph.D. in Renaissance literature from Fordham University. He was founding president of the Council of Writing Program Administrators and was chair of the Teaching of Writing Division of the Modern Language Association (1987).

Wiener is the author of many books on reading and writing for college students and their teachers, including *The Writing Room* (Oxford, 1981). His book for parents, *Any Child Can Write,* was a Book-of-the-Month Club alternate.

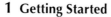

The Principles of Good Reading and Writing

Among the first things you'll do in your college English course is read an essay and write a paper, and the chapters in Part One of *Student's Book of College English* provide important information on how to accomplish those ends with maximum efficiency and success. We look with particular attention at the writing process from start to finish.

Chapter 1 explains how to read an essay intelligently and what to look for as you read. Recognizing the qualities of good writing in your readings will help you become a better writer—one of your main goals for the course. Also in Chapter 1 you will see how to get started by using a variety of prewriting strategies for identifying a topic, organizing your ideas, limiting your topic appropriately, and considering your purpose and audience. A sample draft paper

offers a concrete example of how one student put his ideas on paper. The chapter also includes a section on writing with a computer. Chapter 2 focuses on the all-important thesis; you'll see how to develop a thesis for the topic that interests you and how to support it with details. Chapter 3 deals with planning by showing how to outline your written work. Chapter 4 gives you an overview of the parts of a typical paper—the introduction, the body, and the conclusion—and explores paragraph development. Finally, Chapter 5 explains and demonstrates how to revise and edit a paper. It includes a student's intermediate draft accompanied by an example of a peer evaluation as well as the student's final draft with his teacher's comments; the chapter also provides checklists for revising and proofreading.

Getting Started

Reading and writing well aren't easy. But following some well-chosen advice can make your task easier than you might expect. Too many students we know leap into a reading or writing assignment with insufficient prior thought. Hence, our first piece of advice is *be self-aware.* By this we mean that you should engage the processes of reading and writing as an active—conscious, if you will—learner. In this chapter we address first some specific strategies that can enhance the way you read and understand text. Next, we help you get started as a writer. Since much of what makes any piece of writing good takes place before the writer puts pen to paper, we discuss the kind of thinking that you might do before you begin to write.

Active Reading

The strategies below will help you approach not only the essays and stories you have to read for your English composition class but also the readings required by courses in other college disciplines.

Reading for Best Results

■ *Have a purpose in reading.* A simplistic response to this advice is, "My purpose is to do my assignment." That, of course, is not what we mean. When you define your purpose in reading, you connect it to the intellectual demands of the reading material and your expectations from it. Are you reading to learn new concepts and vocabulary? Are you reading to prepare for a class lecture or discussion? to learn about someone's opinions on a controversial topic? to stimulate your own writing for a required essay? to explore essential scholarship for a research paper? to examine rhetorical and other writing strategies as an aid to honing your own skills? Of course, purposes overlap, and you can change your purpose as you read and reread the text. But the point here is that without a purpose—or purposes—in bringing eye to paper, you risk a passive stance as a reader, and that puts you at risk of never truly interacting with the words before you.

■ *Explore what you know about the topic before you read.*   Prior knowledge dramatically influences a reader's response to a text, in terms of both understanding and appreciation. Yet it is odd that so few students explore what they know about a topic before reading an essay or a chapter of a book. Before you read anything below the title look long and hard at it. What does it mean? What thoughts does it stimulate in your mind? Where have you seen, heard, or read about related information? Look at any subtitles with a similar goal. Always examine photographs, illustrations, graphs, charts—and all the accompanying captions—before you begin reading text of any kind. Think a moment about the author's name and about any information provided about the author. What do these details tell you about the selection? And, when you start reading, stop after you complete the first paragraph or two. Think again about how you can relate what you already know to the topic the writer is investigating.

■ *As you read, record your responses.*   As a way of forcing active reading and interaction with the text, write down your responses to what you read. What does the selection make you think of? What does it make you feel? How do the ideas expressed in the essay confirm or contradict your beliefs? What questions do you have about your reading? What would you like to say to the writer if the two of you could meet and converse? Copy out phrases and sentences that stimulate, challenge, annoy, thrill, puzzle, or ignite you. Think of your written efforts here as an informal entry in a journal; don't worry about form, structure, or correctness. Just put on paper your raw responses to the text.

■ *Determine the writer's thesis.*   What is the main point here? That is the question all good readers engage as they make their way through a text. As you read, as you think about what you are reading, and certainly after you read, answer the question at the head of this paragraph: What is the main point? Sometimes the writer will tell you very directly what her thesis is, and before the end of the first few paragraphs—sometimes at the end of the very first sentence—you'll know exactly where the writer stands on that issue. But in other cases, no single statement or statements will tell you the thesis precisely. Here you have to state the writer's thesis in your own words. The various sentences and paragraphs in an essay will contribute information that you must use to define the thesis yourself.

■ *Pay attention to the language.*   All writers are obsessed about language. Which words to use, and why, fire the writing engine, so to speak, and many writers labor at choosing what Flaubert called *le seul mot juste*, the single right word. As you know, words are alive with both denotative (the dictionary definition) and connotative (implied or suggested definition) meanings. Consider for a moment that a writer naming a person of about thirteen years old can use one of these words that, roughly speaking, would do the job: youngster, child, adolescent, teenager, kid, eighth grader, prepubescent, young adult. Active readers always consider the implications of word choice and think about why a writer selects one word instead of another. Additionally, as you think about language, consider imagery and the writer's power to show you pictures through words. Is the vocabulary, in general, appropriate for the selection? Are the words precise enough for you to understand the points? Has the writer taken too long, used too many words, to make a simple assertion? Are the words deliberately loaded, that is, designed to create an emotional reaction even before you can weigh their meaning in the context of the essay?

■ *Determine the writer's purpose and audience.* As you read pay attention to what you think the writer's reasons are for writing and whom he has targeted as his primary readers. Writers have many reasons for writing: to inform, to entertain, to challenge, to complain, to convince, to describe, to tell a story, to call for action—there are others certainly. Here again, alert reading will help you determine the writer's purpose; don't expect a "This is why I'm writing" sentence. But as you pay attention to the thesis, the various details used to support it, the kind of language the writer uses, you should be able to figure out the intended purpose. Related to the writer's purpose is the audience the writer has in mind for the essay. The intended audience influences the writing markedly. For example, to write about steps for preventing the spread of AIDS, a writer would use wholly different strategies if writing for eighth-grade kids in a suburban classroom or for social workers in Chicago or San Francisco. The language, the thesis, the purpose, the structure of the essay—the audience influences all these elements for the writer.

■ *Consider the structure of the piece.* How has the writer constructed the essay? You want to look at elements like introductions and conclusions, the essay's opening and closing door so to speak. Do they achieve their ends? Do they satisfy you? How do the parts of the essay hold together? Do all the ideas seem to relate to the central point? Do the various sentences connect smoothly with each other? And how has the writer accomplished these near-magical feats? Attending to the structure of what you read will help you learn strategies for your own writing.

■ *Be aware of the writer's tone.* Simply stated, *tone* is the writer's attitude toward her subject. For example, one writer writing about the high incidence of guns in schools could approach the topic with shock and horror; another, with anger; another, analytically, seeking only to understand motives; another, clinically, simply describing, or chronicling events; another, sentimentally, longing for the good old school days with no weapons and with well-behaved kids. Thoughtful readers always keep an eye on the tone; like purpose and audience, it influences word choice, sentence structure, and style. Conscious of tone, you can avoid being manipulated into positions and emotional responses before you bring appropriate thought and analysis to the issues.

REVIEW CHECKLIST: TIPS FOR ACTIVE READING

- Have I established a purpose for reading before I begin?
- Have I explored my prior knowledge on the topic in advance of reading, using titles, subtitles, and other aids as well as the first couple of paragraphs to prod thoughts and ideas before I delve into the selection?
- Am I writing down my responses regularly as I move through a text, recording questions, observations, irritations, and so on, to help me interact with the material?
- Am I reading to determine the writer's thesis, the main idea of the selection to which the sentences and paragraphs all seem to point, remembering that I may have to state the thesis in my own words?
- Am I paying attention to language, particularly word choice, and thinking about what the use of certain words instead of others with similar meanings says about the writer's intentions?
- Am I trying to determine the writer's purpose and audience and to think about how these elements affect language and sentences?
- Am I attentive to the structure of the piece and to how the writer uses structure to advance the points being made?
- Am I trying to determine the tone of the essay, that is, the writer's attitude toward the subject?

EXERCISE

Using what you have learned here about active reading, examine the essay on pages 7–10, "A Hanging," by George Orwell (1903–1950). Orwell, a renowned essay writer, journalist, and social critic, searingly examines the relations between individual rights and oppressive governments in his novels *Animal Farm* and *1984*. Next, answer the questions below.

Before You Read

1. What purpose have you set for yourself before you read the text?
2. Before reading the entire essay, look at the note above about the author, look at the title of the selection, and read only the first two paragraphs. What thoughts are stimulated in your mind? What do you think this essay will be about? Where else have you read about or discussed similar issues?

During and After Your Reading

3. Keep pen and paper handy and write down thoughts as they occur to you. Use the margins if you like. Underline, highlight, copy out challenging phrases and sentences. Raise questions.

4. What is the writer's thesis? State it in your own words. Where in the essay does the writer himself come closest to stating what you think is the thesis?

5. What is your view of the writer's use of language? Where do you find indelible images, snapshots of people and places through the use of color, sound, and action? What is the effect on the reader of the images in the first paragraph? the first sentence?

6. Further about language, Orwell certainly is dealing with an explosive topic here, but his language is not inflammatory. Rather, he proceeds mostly through description, narration, and dialog. Why has he chosen to address his topic in this way? Why does he never directly criticize capital punishment? Nonetheless, you are left with a very clear idea of where Orwell stands on the issue. How does he achieve that end? How does paragraph 10 serve the essay?

7. What is Orwell's purpose in writing this essay? How can you tell? Who do you believe is his intended audience? How can you tell?

8. Comment on the introduction (the first couple of paragraphs). Are they effective in bringing you into the scene as well as in revealing the topic of the essay? Why or why not? What is your reaction to the last paragraph? How does it provide dramatic closure to the essay? What strategies has Orwell used to connect the ideas smoothly from one sentence to the next, from one paragraph to the next?

9. What is the tone of the essay—Orwell's attitude to his subject? Is he indifferent, humorous, melodramatic, astonished, saddened, ironical, sentimental, imperialistic, liberal—or something else? Defend your choice.

GEORGE ORWELL

A Hanging

It was in Burma, a sodden morning of the rains. A sickly light, like yellow tinfoil, was slanting over the high walls into the jail yard. We were waiting outside the condemned cells, a row of sheds fronted with double bars, like small animal cages. Each cell measured about ten feet by ten and was quite bare within except for a plank bed and a pot of drinking water. In some of them brown silent men were squatting at the inner bars, with their blankets draped round them. These were the condemned men, due to be hanged within the next week or two.

One prisoner had been brought out of his cell. He was a Hindu, a puny wisp of a man, with a shaven head and vague liquid eyes. He had a thick, sprouting moustache, absurdly too big for his body, rather like the moustache of a comic man on the films. Six tall Indian warders were guarding him and getting him ready for the gallows. Two of them stood by with rifles with fixed bayonets, while the others handcuffed him, passed a chain through his handcuffs and fixed it to their belts, and lashed his arms tight to his sides. They crowded very close about him, with their hands always on him in a careful, caressing grip, as though all the while feeling him to make sure he was there. It was like men handling a fish which is still alive and may jump back into the water. But he stood quite unresisting, yielding his arms limply to the ropes, as though he hardly noticed what was happening.

3   Eight o'clock struck and a bugle call, desolately thin in the wet air, floated from the distant barracks. The superintendent of the jail, who was standing apart from the rest of us, moodily prodding the gravel with his stick, raised his head at the sound. He was an army doctor, with a grey toothbrush moustache and a gruff voice. "For God's sake hurry up, Francis," he said irritably. "The man ought to have been dead by this time. Aren't you ready yet?"

4   Francis, the head jailer, a fat Dravidian in a white drill suit and gold spectacles, waved his black hand. "Yes sir, yes sir," he bubbled. "All iss satisfactorily prepared. The hangman iss waiting. We shall proceed."

5   "Well, quick march, then. The prisoners can't get their breakfast till this job's over."

6   We set out for the gallows. Two warders marched on either side of the prisoner, with their files at the slope; two others marched close against him, gripping him by arm and shoulder, as though at once pushing and supporting him. The rest of us, magistrates and the like, followed behind. Suddenly, when we had gone ten yards, the procession stopped short without any order or warning. A dreadful thing had happened—a dog, come goodness knows whence, had appeared in the yard. It came bounding among us with a loud volley of barks, and leapt round us wagging its whole body, wild with glee at finding so many human beings together. It was a large woolly dog, half Airedale, half pariah. For a moment it pranced round us, and then, before anyone could stop it, it had made a dash for the prisoner, and jumping up tried to lick his face. Everyone stood aghast, too taken aback even to grab at the dog.

7   "Who let that bloody brute in here?" said the superintendent angrily. "Catch it, someone!"

8   A warder, detached from the escort, charged clumsily after the dog, but it danced and gambolled just out of his reach, taking everything as part of the game. A young Eurasian jailer picked up a handful of gravel and tried to stone the dog away, but it dodged the stones and came after us again. Its yaps echoed from the jail walls. The prisoner, in the grasp of the two warders, looked on incuriously, as though this was another formality of the hanging. It was several minutes before someone managed to catch the dog. Then we put my handkerchief through its collar and moved off once more, with the dog still straining and whimpering.

9   It was about forty yards to the gallows. I watched the bare brown back of the prisoner marching in front of me. He walked clumsily with his bound arms, but quite steadily, with that bobbing gait of the Indian who never straightens his knees. At each step his muscles slid neatly into place, the lock of hair on his scalp danced up and down, his feet printed themselves on the wet gravel. And once, in spite of the men who gripped him by each shoulder, he stepped slightly aside to avoid a puddle on the path.

10   It is curious, but till that moment I had never realised what it means to destroy a healthy, conscious man. When I saw the prisoner step aside to avoid the puddle, I saw the mystery, the unspeakable wrongness, of cutting a life short when it is in full tide. This man was not dying, he was alive just as we were alive. All the organs of his body

were working—bowels digesting food, skin renewing itself, nails growing, tissues forming —all toiling away in solemn foolery. His nails would still be growing when he stood on the drop, when he was falling through the air with a tenth of a second to live. His eyes saw the yellow gravel and the grey walls, and his brain still remembered, foresaw, reasoned—reasoned even about puddles. He and we were a party of men walking together, seeing, hearing, feeling, understanding the same world; and in two minutes, with a sudden snap, one of us would be gone—one mind less, one world less.

The gallows stood in a small yard, separate from the main grounds of the prison, and overgrown with tall prickly weeds. It was a brick erection like three sides of a shed, with planking on top, and above that two beams and a crossbar with the rope dangling. The hangman, a grey-haired convict in the white uniform of the prison, was waiting beside his machine. He greeted us with a servile crouch as we entered. At a word from Francis the two warders, gripping the prisoner more closely than ever, half led, half pushed him to the gallows and helped him clumsily up the ladder. Then the hangman climbed up and fixed the rope round the prisoner's neck.   11

We stood waiting, five yards away. The warders had formed in a rough circle round the gallows. And then, when the noose was fixed, the prisoner began crying out on his god. It was a high, reiterated cry of "Ram! Ram! Ram! Ram!", not urgent and fearful like a prayer or a cry for help, but steady, rhythmical, almost like the tolling of a bell. The dog answered the sound with a whine. The hangman, still standing on the gallows, produced a small cotton bag like a flour bag and drew it down over the prisoner's face. But the sound, muffled by the cloth, still persisted, over and over again: "Ram! Ram! Ram! Ram! Ram!"   12

The hangman climbed down and stood ready, holding the lever. Minutes seemed to pass. The steady, muffled crying from the prisoner went on and on, "Ram! Ram! Ram!" never faltering for an instant. The superintendent, his head on his chest, was slowly poking the ground with his stick; perhaps he was counting the cries, allowing the prisoner a fixed number—fifty, perhaps, or a hundred. Everyone had changed colour. The Indians had gone grey like bad coffee, and one or two of the bayonets were wavering. We looked at the lashed, hooded man on the drop, and listened to his cries—each cry another second of life; the same thought was in all our minds: oh, kill him quickly, get it over, stop that abominable noise!   13

Suddenly the superintendent made up his mind. Throwing up his head he made a swift motion with his stick. "Chalo!" he shouted almost fiercely.   14

There was a clanking noise, and then dead silence. The prisoner had vanished, and the rope was twisting on itself. I let go of the dog, and it galloped immediately to the back of the gallows; but when it got there it stopped short, barked, and then retreated into a corner of the yard, where it stood among the weeds, looking timorously out at us. We went round the gallows to inspect the prisoner's body. He was dangling with his toes pointed straight downwards, very slowly revolving, as dead as a stone.   15

The superintendent reached out with his stick and poked the bare body; it oscillated, slightly. "*He's* all right," said the superintendent. He backed out from under the gallows, and blew out a deep breath. The moody look had gone out of his face quite suddenly. He glanced at his wristwatch. "Eight minutes past eight. Well, that's all for this morning, thank God."   16

17   The warders unfixed bayonets and marched away. The dog, sobered and conscious of having misbehaved itself, slipped after them. We walked out of the gallows yard, past the condemned cells with their waiting prisoners, into the big central yard of the prison. The convicts, under the command of warders armed with lathis, were already receiving their breakfast. They squatted in long rows, each man holding a tin pannikin, while two warders with buckets marched round ladling out rice; it seemed quite a homely, jolly scene, after the hanging. An enormous relief had come upon us now that the job was done. One felt an impulse to sing, to break into a run, to snigger. All at once everyone began chattering gaily.

18   The Eurasian boy walking beside me nodded towards the way we had come, with a knowing smile: "Do you know, sir, our friend (he meant the dead man), when he heard his appeal had been dismissed, he pissed on the floor of his cell. From fright—Kindly take one of my cigarettes, sir. Do you not admire my new silver case, sir? From the boxwallah, two rupees eight annas. Classy European style."

19   Several people laughed—at what, nobody seemed certain.

20   Francis was walking by the superintendent, talking garrulously: "Well, sir, all hass passed off with the utmost satisfactoriness. It was all finished—flick! like that. It iss not always so—oah, no! I have known cases where the doctor wass obliged to go beneath the gallows and pull the prisoner's legs to ensure decease. Most disagreeable!"

21   "Wriggling about, eh? That's bad," said the superintendent.

22   "Ach, sir, it iss worse when they become refractory! One man, I recall, clung to the bars of hiss cage when we went to take him out. You will scarcely credit, sir, that it took six warders to dislodge him, three pulling at each leg. We reasoned with him. 'My dear fellow,' we said, 'think of all the pain and trouble you are causing to us!' But no, he would not listen! Ach, he wass very troublesome!"

23   I found that I was laughing quite loudly. Everyone was laughing. Even the superintendent grinned in a tolerant way. "You'd better all come out and have a drink," he said quite genially. "I've got a bottle of whisky in the car. We could do with it."

24   We went through the big double gates of the prison, into the road. "Pulling at his legs!" exclaimed a Burmese magistrate suddenly, and burst into a loud chuckling. We all began laughing again. At that moment Francis's anecdote seemed extraordinarily funny. We all had a drink together, native and European alike, quite amicably. The dead man was a hundred yards away.

COLLABORATIVE LEARNING

We have pointed out the importance of being an active learner as you approach your reading and writing assignments for this course (and all your courses, for that matter.) One of the best ways to develop an active learning style is to engage regularly in conversation about text—text you read and text you write. Toward that end, we provide throughout Parts One and Two of this book a series of collaborative learning exercises, where you can benefit from the thoughts and ideas of fellow classmates. But collaborative learning is not merely giving everyone a chance to speak. It is an effort to reach consensus on an issue. What is consensus?

Simply, it is collective agreement or accord—a general concurrence after conversational give and take—with necessary acknowledgment of dissenting opinions. Through collaboration, you have a chance to air your thoughts and to shape and reshape them, benefiting from the interactions in a group of people wrestling with a challenging topic or question.

Try this collaborative effort as a result of your reading of "A Hanging." Form groups of five students and discuss the issue of capital punishment. Using Orwell's essay as a springboard for thinking and conversation, make a list of the pros and cons of taking the lives of accused criminals in the name of the state. As a group, try to reach consensus: If your group had the power, would it sustain or eliminate capital punishment? One person from each group should report back to the whole class. What is the general feeling of the class about this issue?

As your instructor directs, after you have heard all the groups' reports, look ahead to "Pro and Con: Arguments on the Death Penalty" in Chapter 14 and write an essay about capital punishment.

Active Writing

Much of what we have suggested for the active reader applies to the active writer; and you can turn several of the questions in the checklist on page 6 easily into a self-critical guide for the writer. But let us begin at the beginning—how to focus your topic so that you can produce a successful paper.

Limiting Your Subject

Many college composition books begin by advising the student to choose a subject, but we won't do that because it's needless advice. After all, no one writes in a vacuum. If you choose to write on your own, you do so because you're so interested in a subject—a sport, a vacation, a candidate, a book, a social issue, a love affair—that you want to share your thoughts with others. Your enthusiasm selects your subject. If you don't actually "choose" to write but are told to do so by an instructor or employer, your general subject will usually be given to you. Your professor of history probably won't tell you simply to write a paper; he will assign a paper on some effects of Islamic culture on the Western world. Your employer won't merely ask for a report; she will ask for an analysis of your office's operations that includes recommendations for cutting costs and increasing productivity. Even when your assignment is an essay based on a personal experience, your instructor will give you a general subject: a memorable journey, an influential person, a goal, a hobby, a favorite newspaper or magazine. Choosing the subject, then, isn't really a big problem.

But most subjects need to be **limited,** and that can be a problem. Suppose, for instance, that your instructor is an old-fashioned type and wants you to write about your vacation. No matter how short your vacation might have been, if you set out to discuss every detail of it, you could fill a book. Because most classroom assignments call for only three hundred to one thousand words, the subject must be limited. You must decide what part of the subject you will write about.

As no doubt you've discovered, your instructors in all disciplines are making demands on you to write. More and more, teachers in all subjects see writing as a key means for learning. "All right," you may protest, "it would be easy enough to settle on a subject if I never had to write about anything but my vacation. But what about my history paper?" As a beginning student of history (or sociology or economics), you may feel that your problem is finding enough to say about any given subject, not simply limiting the subject. Still, we insist that almost every subject can and must be limited, even when some limiting has already been done by the instructor.

Consider an assignment about the effects of Islamic culture on the West, for example. Your first reaction might well be to try to assemble any effects you could come up with, devoting one section of your paper to each effect—but that would lead to a very dull paper. Think a minute. If your instructor expects you to manage some part of that topic, you have had some preparation for it. You've probably read part of a textbook and heard lectures on the subject; you've heard class discussions about it; perhaps you've been asked to do some supplementary reading in the library. From all of these sources, you've already begun to appreciate the vastness of the subject, even before doing any further research.

You must limit the subject. Doing so is, of course, not as easy as limiting subjects like vacations or roommates, but the process is similar. As with your vacation, you can try warm-up activities. Study your notes and then try jotting down everything you can think of about the subject. Talk the topic over with friends. Do brainstorming. Free associate. Make lists and diagrams. You'll soon see one or two groups of ideas or facts dominating your early activities. You could choose one of them as your limited subject.

Or, again, as with your vacation, you can let your special interests determine how you limit the subject. If, for example, you have a good understanding of architecture, you may decide to explain how the Islamic culture, forbidden by its religion to use human images, contributed to modern architecture by exploring the possibilities of geometric forms. Or you might discuss the influence on modern sculpture of geometric form as design. If you're a nursing or pre-med student, you could trace the contributions of the Islamic world to medical science. If you're an interested observer of the political scene, you might discuss the effects on early Islamic cultures of the lack of a centralized government, comparing these cultures with others of the same period that were governed by a pope or emperor. Your interests could lead to other subjects—from military strategies to love poems—and still fulfill the assignment. Any subject, then, can and must be limited before you begin to write, and your personal interests can often determine the way you limit it.

Much of the writing you will do for your college courses, in a wide range of disciplines, will require research. We've taken pains in Chapter 19 to show you how to use sources appropriately. We also show you how to use a few citation systems so that you can adapt your writing and documentation to your teacher's instructions. But remember, all good writing and all good research must begin with a limited topic.

EXERCISE

Limit the following broad topics, drawn from a wide variety of college courses.

Example

Broad topic	More limited	Still more limited
The Middle East	Peace negotiations in the Middle East	Anwar Sadat's efforts to make peace between Egypt and Israel in the 1970s

 1. Food fads
 2. China's future
 3. An embarrassing moment
 4. The Declaration of Independence
 5. Winter blues
 6. Horror movies
 7. American poetry
 8. Men's magazines
 9. Domestic violence
10. Train travel
11. Poverty
12. Adult education
13. Life in the big city
14. Happiness
15. Rock concerts

EXERCISE

Select any three courses (other than this writing course) that you are taking now and list them on a sheet of paper. Beside each one identify a subject that would be appropriate to write about in the course. Drawing on your past interests and experiences, limit the subject to a topic you might develop in an essay.

Determining Your Purpose and Audience

Once you've limited your subject, you need to set your purpose and determine what audience you will write for, and doing so involves some related choices.

■ First, you need to decide how you will treat your limited subject, what you will do with it. Will you explain a process—for example, how to pitch a tent? Will you compare two campsites? Will you report an event—what happened when you unwittingly pitched your tent in a cow pasture? Will you argue that one can have an enjoyable yet inexpensive vacation by camping in state parks?

You can't hope to write a coherent paper until you decide what you will do with your subject, because that decision determines, in large measure, what you include and what you leave out. If, for example, you decide to describe how to pitch a tent, you won't discuss the deep satisfaction that you've gained by sleeping under the stars or the delicious taste of a fish that you've caught yourself and cooked over an open fire. You have decided to give instructions for a particular activity, and you will do just that in the clearest manner possible. If, on the other hand, you choose to argue that camping in state parks is enjoyable, you might very well describe not only the joy of sleeping under the stars and cooking over an open fire, but also the conveniences provided to campers by the park system and the fun of meeting people in the relaxed atmosphere that a campfire creates.

■ A second choice is your *audience*. What kind of reader are you writing for? The answer to that question will affect the style and content of your paper.

Pretend, for a moment, that while driving your father's car to school the other day, you were stopped for speeding but were able to persuade the officer not to give you a ticket. How did you talk to the officer? Later you ran into a good friend at the snack bar. How did you describe the incident to your friend? You hadn't planned to tell your father at all, but at dinner your tongue slipped, the fact was out, and your father demanded an explanation. How did you describe the incident to your father? The kind of language, the tone of voice, even the facts selected were different in each case, weren't they?

That's the way it is with writing. The words a writer chooses and the facts a writer selects are largely determined by who will read the material. One physician writing to another physician may say,

> In the web of the patient's left thumb and forefinger, there is a 1.5-centimeter slightly raised, mildly erythematous and tender, soft furuncle-appearing lesion that blanches with pressure.

The patient, in writing a letter to a close friend, may say,

> I've been in pretty good health lately—except for a little sore on my left hand. It's red and tender and looks like a boil. I suppose I should ask the doctor about it.

The audience makes a difference in what writers say and how they say it. In your process paper about pitching a tent, just imagine how different the paper would look if you wrote it for Cub Scouts planning to sleep in the backyard, troopers training in unfamiliar terrain, sporting goods sales clerks who have to explain a new product to potential buyers, or out-of-shape senior citizens camping for the first time.

You may now be thinking that any discussion of audience is pointless because you know who your reader is—your English professor. In one sense, that's true, of course. But you'll write better papers if, instead of thinking of your English professor every time you begin to write, you imagine other specific kinds of readers. After all, English professors are an adaptable lot, and they can assume the personalities of many different kinds of readers when they pick up your paper. So define a reader. Are you writing for a group of experts on your subject? for your classmates? for the president of your company? for readers of the editorial page of the morning paper? for readers of *Playboy? Good Housekeeping?* for the "general reader"? (See "Miscellaneous Do's and Don'ts," pages 594–596.) It's a good idea to approach these audiences differently. Defining the reader not only helps you decide the style and exact content of your paper but also makes for livelier reading. Writing addressed to no one in particular usually isn't satisfying.

■ A third choice—and one closely related to defining the reader—is the author image you want to present to your reader. This image, this personality, is essential if you want the paper to read as if it were written by a human being, not by a computer. Are you a specialist writing for nonspecialists? Are you an expert writing for other experts? Are you an average citizen writing for other average citizens? Are you an employee suggesting a change in policy to the president of your company? And how do you feel about your subject? Do you love it? Do you hate it? Are you angry? calm and reasonable? mildly amused? detached? delighted? Are you optimistic? pessimistic? In short, what personality do you want to project?

■ The final choice you face is deciding how you want to affect your audience: How do you want to make your appeal? Do you want to amuse as well as persuade? Do you want to move the readers to tears? Do you simply want them to understand your subject more fully? or perhaps to follow your advice? This choice, too, is important to the total effect of your paper.

All these choices—your treatment of the subject, your audience, your author image, your effect on the audience—help determine the purpose of your paper. And the purpose controls the style and content of the paper—its organization, its facts, its diction, its tone.

EXERCISE

For each topic listed here, discuss the purposes you might have for writing about it. Look at the example. You may wish to limit the topic first.

Example

Topic: Teenage drivers

Possible purposes
1. To describe a harrowing drive with "wild man Bob," my sixteen-year-old cousin.
2. To explain how teenagers can save money on driving costs by following a few simple steps.
3. To compare and contrast male and female teenage drivers.

4. To classify types of sports car drivers I've observed in my job as a gas station attendant.
5. To argue in favor of allowing fourteen-year-olds to drive under special circumstances.
6. To convince teenagers of the dangers of drinking and driving.

Topics

1. Child care
2. Outdoor cooking
3. Job hunting
4. Buying a car
5. Drug testing
6. Presidential elections

COLLABORATIVE LEARNING

Divide the class into five groups and examine the topic and audience sets below. Beside each topic is a list of possible audiences a writer could address. What demands do you think each audience would make on the writer? What different issues would the writer have to address for each audience?

Topic	Possible audience
1. The dangers of smoking	a. High school basketball players b. Biology teachers c. Restaurateurs
2. The advantages of airplane travel	a. Travel agents b. Acrophobics c. First-time flyers
3. Relaxation techniques	a. Sixth graders in an inner-city public school b. High-pressured business executives c. Recovering heart attack patients
4. Baking chocolate chip cookies	a. Students at a chef's training school b. First-time homemakers c. Kindergarteners
5. The advantages of swimming in improving fitness	a. Home swimming pool manufacturers b. Physical therapists c. Overweight, sedentary college students

Writing a Thesis

Once you have narrowed your topic and have identified your audience and purpose, you have to develop a **thesis.** Simply put, a thesis is a statement of the main point of your essay. We have much to say about finding and supporting a thesis, so we give the topic a whole chapter, and you might want to look ahead to Chapter 2 for detailed information about thesis development. At this point, as you are preparing the first draft of your first essay in English class, be aware that your reader should know as early as possible just what main point you are trying to make about the topic. From your thesis, your purpose and audience as well as your limited topic should be clear.

Remember that your topic is not your thesis. You have to say something about your topic—express an opinion toward or an attitude about the topic that your essay will attempt to support.

EXERCISE

Look at the thesis sentences below. What is the topic of each? What is the writer's main point—what does he or she want to say about the topic? How do you think each writer will go about supporting the thesis?

1. Despite government and industry support, Health Management Organizations (HMOs) pose many problems for consumers.
2. Many people find writing essays boring, but exotic surroundings and good humor can turn tedium into—yes, fun!
3. Despite the obvious temptations, many respected educators urge parents to avoid teaching their children to read at home.
4. The old house on the corner of Main and Fifth has a deserved reputation as an edifice of weird and unexplained events.
5. Through a variety of creative programs and police vigilance, it is possible to cut down dramatically on drunk driving among teens.

EXERCISE

Look at the topics in the exercise on page 15. What thesis could you develop about each of them?

Prewriting

As we've already suggested, the best way to start limiting your topic is to think carefully about it in advance of putting your ideas on paper. You must spend time sorting out your thoughts before you actually begin writing. Experienced writers use many different **prewriting strategies** to limber up, so to speak, well before they start producing the connected sentences and paragraphs that make up a first draft. Especially if you block on a subject—you just can't seem to come up with any ideas—you should use one of these strategies. Each one can help stimulate your creativity.

PREWRITING STRATEGIES

- As preliminary thoughts start taking shape, **discuss** them with friends, roommates, parents or other relatives, teachers, and fellow classmates or workers at your part-time job. Nothing helps develop an idea as well as hearing someone else react to it. Your own thinking can take new turns as you engage in productive conversation with people you trust.
- As your thoughts form and re-form, **do some leg work in your library.** Check the online and (or) card catalog and a periodical index. What kinds of books and articles are people writing about your topic? Read something in print, watch a videotape, look at some photographs, listen to an audiocassette, or examine a CD-ROM related to your concerns. Watch a talk show or documentary on network or cable television. What kinds of issues have been identified by people who already have examined your topic?
- When you're ready to try some writing, don't rush into a draft unless you're bursting with thoughts and ideas. Begin instead with some warm-up exercises. **Free associate** on the topic—that is, write nonstop for fifteen or twenty minutes without editing a single thought. Let the ideas flow from your mind to your pen, no matter how unfocused or unimportant your thoughts may seem as you're putting them down. Later, you'll return to evaluate the ideas you produced on paper. Which ones might you develop into an essay? Which thoughts connect with each other?
- You might simply **develop an informal list** of ideas that your topic stimulates in your mind.
- You might **brainstorm** on paper—that is, raise question after question about your topic and study your list of questions as a means of finding answers that can help you develop a good essay. The familiar reporter's questions, five *w*'s and an *h* (*who, what, where, when, why,* and *how*), can start off your list of questions.
- You might keep a **journal,** an informal notebook in which you jot down impressions on any matter that comes to mind. Returning to these written impressions, a writer often can identify a topic to develop into a paper.
- Or, you might use some **visual strategy**—a subject map or subject tree, for example (see page 22)—where you track ideas visually by connecting them to lines or shapes that help move your thoughts along.

The convenient label for these warm-up activities—**prewriting**—is one you'll hear often, no doubt, in your college writing courses. It's a useful term: The prefix *pre-* reminds you that you have a good deal to do in advance of writing your paper. Many inexperienced writers fail because they leap too soon into producing their papers and do not take enough time with the various steps that can lead to successful writing.

By practicing the prewriting strategies we're talking about here—thinking and talking about your ideas, free association, list-making, brainstorming, the journal, reporters' questions, subject trees or maps—you'll uncover a surprising number of possibilities for your topic. For example, if you're trying to get started on a paper about some summer vacation topic, your prewriting exercises might stimulate memories of dancing all night and then going for a swim at sunrise, or the day your foreign car broke down in a small town where the only mechanic would service nothing but American products, or eating your first fiery salsa, or meeting a village character, or watching the sun set over the ocean, or sleeping out under the stars, or being confined to a tent for two hours amid torrential rain at a campsite one evening. You might have noticed differences among motels and restaurants, or various accents might have fascinated you. Any one of the memories could make a good paper. But how do you choose?

Often you can let your major interests decide for you. If you have a sense of the comic, you might decide to write about the mechanic who couldn't help you, or about water seeping into your sleeping bag despite your canvas tent, or about your first attempt to chew and swallow a salsa laced with jalapeño peppers. If you like to study people, you might decide to write about the town oddball, or about the people you met when you danced all night, or about the personalities of the waiters who served you. If the way people talk interests you, the accents or colorful expressions of those you met on your journey could make a good subject for a paper. If scenery appeals to you, describe that sunset or sunrise or those stars.

If your major interests don't tell you what your limited subject is, you can limit the subject in other ways. Go back to what your warm-up activities produced and examine them. You may see that one or two groups of ideas or facts dominate your thinking; that is, you may have jotted down more points about, say, the town oddball you met than about any other highlight of your vacation. In that case, your choice should be clear: Write about the village character. If, despite what your early jottings tell you, the subject doesn't strike your fancy, you could even let your mood of the moment determine your limited subject. You may find yourself in a bad mood when you begin planning your paper, and that may cause you to look back on your vacation with a jaundiced eye. In that case, your mood may tell you that the mechanic's refusal to work on your foreign car was unforgivable. Once again, you have a limited subject. If you discover that you have a number of limited subjects you could write about, flip a coin and settle on one so that you can get on with writing the paper. You will probably have other opportunities to write about your other subjects.

ORGANIZING IDEAS

After you've recorded on paper your early unedited thoughts on a topic, try to organize your thinking somewhat. You've thought about your *thesis* (again, look ahead to Chapter 2), and you have considered your *audience* and *purpose*. Now, as you zero in on your central idea, look at your written thoughts and eliminate any that seem off-target. Cluster the thoughts that seem to go together. You might even try a rough outline of main topics as headings and subtopics numbered beneath them. Or, you might draw arrows and make circles to join related ideas or use scissors and paste to lay connected impressions near each other.

Working with a computer can make this part of your writing easier (see page 27). Simply mark passages that you want to move or copy onto another page of your paper, give the computer an appropriate command, and see if your new version of a sentence or paragraph pleases you. Writing with a computer enables you to keep at hand many versions of your sentences and paragraphs. You can refer to often, and perhaps even salvage, thoughts you may have rejected.

Your attempts at grouping related material are important because they can help you develop a formal outline (pages 51–56), a key organizing strategy for many writers. Outlining is especially important when you deal with complex topics or with lots of research materials. Like a road map, your outline can help you find your way through new territory. We'll have more to say about formal outlining in Chapter 3.

Bear in mind that the prewriting activities we've described are not rigid prescriptions. They vary from writer to writer, and they do not necessarily follow each other in an exact sequence. For example, thinking about your topic does not occur only at the beginning of the writing process; obviously, you're thinking about your topic at each stage of your writing. In addition, you might do some prewriting and then decide to do some spadework in the library. You might produce a rough outline and then decide that you need to brainstorm on a feature of the topic that you hadn't considered carefully enough. And some writers produce outlines after, not before, they write drafts. The point we're trying to make is that prewriting is a loosely defined process that you should adapt freely to your own needs as a writer and to the elements of the writing task at hand.

After you produce some prewriting, feel that your topic is reasonably well focused, and do some crucial planning and outlining, you're probably ready to write a first draft. How do you begin?

Writing Drafts

First, you should realize that whatever you put down as a first draft can never serve as the finished product. Writing means rewriting and revising—hammering away at ideas, words, and sentences so that they ultimately have the shape that will satisfy you and your readers. Revision must sit squarely and firmly at the center of your writing activities.

To begin the all-important drafting stage, use your prewriting. Read over your ideas on paper and your efforts at grouping your thoughts. Then, without worrying about spelling, grammar, or punctuation, try to get your ideas down. Remember that you're only exploring here; you're not aiming for perfection. Your first draft is a rough copy that you will revisit later to make changes, additions, and deletions. Cross out words and phrases that are dead ends. Insert new thoughts in the margins. Don't worry here about being neat or correct. Your goal at this stage is to write clear, connected sentences that address your topic. If you're working on a computer, your first draft may look like a finished copy when you print it out. But don't let a neat, clean page lull you into thinking that you've finished working!

Once you've produced a draft, show it to a friend, your roommate, or another member of your writing class. Friendly readers can tell you, among other things, where you've succeeded in making your point, where the ideas are fuzzy or lacking in detail, and where the language hits or misses the mark. Drawing on peer review (see page 93) can provide very useful advice from fellow writers in your class. Sometimes your instructor will read an early draft to help you think about possible approaches to your next draft.

Use the comments made on your papers to help you think about your revision and create your next draft. (Look ahead to Chapter 5.) You don't have to follow all the recommendations you receive or answer all the questions raised—but you must consider them.

As you revise your paper, developing intermediate drafts, you want to change any sentences that are off base, add necessary details to support a point, and fix key errors. Don't concentrate on grammatical errors in early drafts; do address these errors as you move closer to a final copy. Don't shy away from asking your friends to listen to you read from the various stages of your writing: Thoughtful listeners always can help you see where you need to do more work in making your points clearer. By the time you're ready to share your final copy as a completed product, you will have shaped and reshaped your topic many times.

One Student Writing

Let's see how some of this advice works in practice. In this chapter and in Chapter 5, we'll show how one student, John Fousek, went about limiting a subject and developing and revising a paper. Having been told to write a short paper on the topic "a friend," John did lots of advance thinking before he wrote. To explore his thoughts, he made a subject map about the topic (see following page). As he considered this preliminary effort, he finally chose to write about his roommate, Jim, and began jotting down impressions about him. Because he knew his roommate well, however, John soon found that he would have too much material for a short paper and would have to limit his subject to one of Jim's characteristics. That was easy to do because John had argued with his roommate that morning and, still annoyed, could readily identify his major interest of the day: his roommate's irritating habits.

Next, John began to make a list of any of those habits that happened to occur to him. He ended up with quite a list:

```
doesn't empty ashtrays          doesn't tighten cap on shampoo

doesn't put out cigarettes      uses my printer paper without

doesn't take out garbage          replacing

slams doors on mornings I       leaves wet towels on bathroom

  can sleep                       floor
```

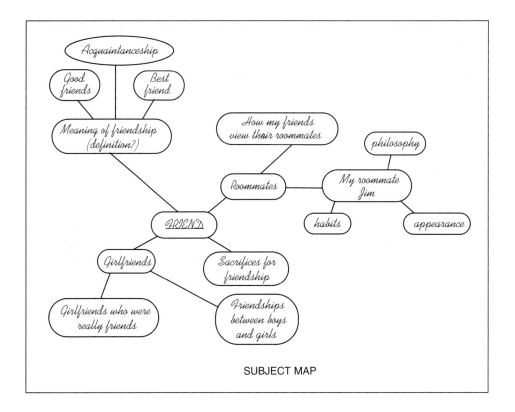

SUBJECT MAP

doesn't rinse dirty dishes	opens bathroom door when I'm
uses my after-shave lotion	showering
wears my socks	leaves drawers open
doesn't write down	never closes closet door
telephone messages	never hangs up his coat
doesn't do his share of	doesn't remove muddy boots
cooking	never empties dishwasher
plays stereo when I'm	reads my mail
studying	

After studying the list, John saw that he could not develop every point; he had to eliminate some items. Thinking more about the list and about his roommate, John concluded that two of Jim's shortcomings bothered him most: Jim's failure to close things and his failure to dispose of things. He eliminated all

items on the list that did not pertain to those two failures and could now group
his ideas:

```
Not closing                 Not disposing

doesn't tighten cap         doesn't put out cigarettes

  on shampoo                doesn't empty ashtrays

doesn't close bathroom door doesn't empty dishwasher

doesn't close drawers       doesn't rinse dishes

doesn't close closet door
```

Then John realized that even this limiting left him with too much to cover; finally,
he decided to discuss in his paper only his roommate's failure to close things.

As John thought about how to organize his paper, he produced this rough
outline:

```
Intro:

1. how much I like Jim--his personality, sharing, funny,

   honest

2. what I don't like: never closes things


Drawers

1. kitchen drawer always messy and left open

2. bedroom drawers and closets

3. I'm embarrassed by it all


Bathroom

1. leaves door open--shower area gets freezing cold

2. forgets to close shampoo bottle--shampoo spills all over

   me, much wasted down drain
```

Note how this informal outline builds on the preceding grouped list titled
"Not closing." The rough outline provides a working plan for the first draft of
John's essay.

With this outline and his prewriting as resources, John was able to
arrange his ideas and write a draft of his paper. His first draft appears on the
next page.

FIRST DRAFT

John Fousek

My friend Jim really irritates me with his habbit of ~~not~~ never closing things that he opens up. Don't get me wrong. As roommates for the last couple of years Jim and I get along real well in our small apartment. As students we don't get to see each other a whole lot. We also both work and this cuts down on the time we spend together too. We share

[margin: Thesis statement OK?]

check spelling
responsibilities in the apartment. I clean and Jim cooks.
has a   *We had a good relationship over the last two years.*
He's generous, ∧good sense of humor and is honest. ∧But boy
his shortcoming of not closing things up burn∧me up. It's a   *Its?*
real pain.

[margin: Show what's in drawers]

For example never closing a drawer. This embarasses
because
me a lot, ∧I am compulsive about being neat, Jim is a
slob. He never thinks of organizing his drawers. He just
dumps everything, into his drawers and, closets. In the
                  ?   ?
kitchen everything is just dumped into the drawers and he's
constantly banging silverware before every meal. This is
when I'm usually studying and I prefer peace and quite to
rattling kitchen items.

Of course he leaves the kitchen drawers open along with
the clothing drawers. Our apartment always looks like a bomb
If he'd only organize the drawer in the first place he
hit it. ∧The appearance irritates my neat soul. I'm   *Trite?*
check spelling   *wouldn't be bothering*
embarassed when friends visit us.   *me with his noise and*

[margin: Fix this? Sounds funny]

I get even madder at Jim's failure to close things in the
                                                           one
bathroom he never closes the shampoo cap. This makes me lose *sentence?*
my cool ~~composure~~ more than anything. ~~I always~~ When I'm in
comma?
the shower/I always grab the shampoo bottle by the cap a
loose cap results in the agravation of shampoo on my toes   *check*
                                                             spelling
instead of my hair. And because I am economically minded,
moneywise, watching shampoo go down the drain really bothers
me.

Jim also often fails to close the bathroom door after
using the facilities while I shower. Since the bathroom has
                                          r
become warm and steamy during the couse of my shower, the
                chills
cold air ~~annoys~~ me, the idea that Jim has been so
thoughtless bothers me.

[margin: Conclusion too short? Expand?]

I try to overlook Jim's bad habbits but when he doesn't
close things up especially when I get a cold blast of morning
air in the shower it really irritates me.

John's rough draft is a good start. He states a thesis early in the paper. He presents concrete examples to support his irritation with Jim. He seems to have a good grasp of his topic. The paper has a beginning, a middle, and an end, and its ideas are related to each other. Note how John has raised questions for himself in the margins and spaces between lines.

But John's paper still needs revising and editing. John notes in the margin some issues he wants to think about when he revises, but there are many others he'll have to consider. His sentences are sometimes rambling and repetitive, and the writing is much too informal in spots. The ideas should be more smoothly connected, and some of the paragraphs should be joined. You no doubt noted errors in spelling and sentence structure. John must address all these issues as he develops successive drafts.

Chapter 5 looks at the critical revision and editing issues you'll need to consider as you write, and you'll see there how John Fousek continued developing his paper.

REVIEW CHECKLIST: TIPS FOR GETTING STARTED

- Did I think carefully about the writing assignment before putting pen to paper or switching on the computer?
- Should I try prewriting strategies to limit my topic?
  (a) Discuss my ideas with friends and fellow students.
  (b) Browse in the library, checking the catalog, magazines, journals, books, and other library resources for approaches to my topic.
  (c) Do free association.
  (d) Develop an informal list of ideas related to the subject.
  (e) Brainstorm.
  (f) Keep a journal.
  (g) Produce a subject tree to help me limit my topic.
- How can I organize my prewriting efforts to help me connect ideas to develop in a draft? Have I thought about my thesis? (Look ahead to pages 32–38.)
- Am I prepared to ignore issues of spelling, grammar, and punctuation as I write my first draft, knowing that I will make revisions and editorial changes later based on comments provided by my classmates, my instructor, or other readers?
- Have I considered my purpose and audience carefully as I write my draft?

EXERCISE

Examine John Fousek's prewriting activities and his first draft and then answer the following questions.

1. How did John's subject map help him limit his topic? Trace what you think were his probable thought processes as he moved from the general topic *friend* to the more limited topic he ultimately chose to write about.
2. How does John's first list compare and contrast with his second list (see pages 21 and 23)? What specific features of the first list has he eliminated in the second? Why has he dropped so many details from the first list?
3. How does John's rough outline build on the list that he prepared, "Not closing"?
4. How does John's rough draft compare with his rough outline? How has he drawn on the outline to create the rough draft of his paper? How has he deviated from his outline?

EXERCISE

Use the prewriting techniques explained on pages 18–19 for one of the following topics that interests you. From these warm-up activities, determine how you would limit the subject.

1. Taking pictures
2. The environment
3. Friendship
4. Fear
5. House repairs
6. Concerts
7. Watching television
8. Computers
9. Going shopping
10. Being a student

COLLABORATIVE LEARNING

Bring to class your prewriting efforts developed from the exercise above. Form groups of three students. In each group examine each other's prewriting. Answer the following questions for each student's work:

- Does the prewriting show evidence of uncensored thought on the topic?
- Has the writer used the prewriting strategies to explore the topic effectively? How?
- What recommendations could you make to the writer so that he or she could get even better results from the prewriting effort?
- Does the prewriting activity help the writer limit the subject? How?

EXERCISE

Using your prewriting efforts, develop a first draft of your paper.

Writing with a Computer

Access to computer technology has revolutionized the way many students write papers for their courses. The computer is a valuable writing tool that can help you write quickly, make revisions easily, examine several drafts of your papers, check your spelling, style, and grammar, and produce near-perfect copy on a printer.

We won't say that using a computer will magically transform all your written efforts into pure gold or that using a computer will be worry-free. Even when you use a computer, you have to attend to all the issues of good writing that we've presented in this section. If you do use a word processor, the following pointers will help keep your problems to a minimum and will ensure that you follow the conventions of computer-generated papers for college courses.

1. *Learn the ins and outs of your computer program and take advantage of all the features.* Be sure you know how to move sentences and paragraphs, insert and delete words, and copy portions of your paper. Make yourself familiar with the keyboard, and be sure to read the instructions that accompany the machine or are available in the computer lab. Use the delete function thoughtfully as you draft because you may want to return to early versions of your sentences. It's often best to *move* unwanted sentences rather than delete them.

2. *Evaluate your writing closely when using the "delete" and "move" functions.* In removing words and sentences or in shifting text around within your draft, reread your work to ensure that what you have moved fits sensibly in its new place. The ease and speed with which we're able to move text around can make us lazy or sloppy or both. This often yields jumbled sentences, incorrectly inserted passages, or empty spaces where words once stood, all of which will easily distract a reader. Remember to proofread your text carefully for these irritants.

3. *Remember two key words:* print *and* save. Before you leave the computer terminal—and especially if the computer is used by many different people—print out a draft of your work and be sure to save what you have written. Generating hard copy, or the printed version of your work, allows you to make changes and revisions when you are away from the computer. You can later incorporate these changes when you return. Storing (saving) your writing involves preserving your document on a disk or on the computer's hard drive so that you always can return to the document without having to start writing from scratch. Most programs create backup files on command; that means it's easy to save the most recent document you have worked on as well as earlier versions of it.

4. *Take care of your disks.* The 3½ or 5¼ inch plastic disk on which you store your work is not indestructible. The electrical and magnetic fields that allow data storage are easily disrupted by other electrical equipment such as radios, televisions, and stereo sets. Keep your disks away from these and other electronic devices. Also, you should guard your disks against food, dust, and any rough handling in general. The hard drive within the computer is considerably less fragile. Nevertheless, both floppy and hard disks can fail without notice, and printing out copies of your work and making backup files on both hard and soft disks are good insurance against potential mishaps.

5. *Follow your instructor's guidelines about using special word processing features.* Your writing instructor may have strong feelings about computer dictionaries (spell checkers) or thesauruses and grammar or style programs—especially if you're in a course designed to teach spelling, vocabulary, grammar, and style. These devices can help you proofread and edit your writing, but they do have limitations. A spell checker wouldn't detect omitted words or incorrectly used but correctly spelled words, for instance. Style checkers—that is, programs that read your pages for repeated words, excessively long or short sentences, too many adjectives, and other stylistic quirks—lack any creative capacity or the ability to reason. And the style checkers may offer advice contrary to your instructor's advice. Ultimately, you alone will have to perform the various checking functions—although these special computer features can be of some assistance. However, be sure to check with your instructor about whether she will sanction your use of these features.

6. *When printing your final document for submission to others, follow the conventions of manuscript preparation.* We want to point out that using a computer is not license for disregarding format considerations. Remember to leave appropriate margins—top, bottom, and sides. Always separate the pages, which sometimes are connected when fed through the printer. Do not leave ragged edges when you separate these pages. Remove carefully the perforated strip of holes down both sides of computer paper. Erase any commands that sometimes print out on your pages. Give appropriate commands to paginate the paper or to provide other key information such as your name and the date at the top or bottom of each page. Avoid using a variety of faces—printing in Roman, italics, boldface, small and large print—in one paper. Readers find so many typefaces distracting. You should resist justifying the right-hand margin in the papers submitted for evaluation because this can result in unusual and distracting spacing within the paper itself.

Now let's look at another student's paper. As you read consider the thesis, and notice how the writer's choices of author image and audience contribute to the development of the paper. Also, before you read, review the checklist "Tips for Active Reading" on page 6.

Clifford Wendell

The Computer and I

Computers were designed to make our lives easier, or so   1
I'm told. Easier? Not in my experience. They tend to put some
challenge into my ordinarily dull life.

For example, upon receiving my usual monthly statement   2
from a local department store, I was a trifle surprised to
find that the ten-dollar gift certificate I had charged had
suddenly turned into a generous one-hundred-dollar gift.
Tucked into the envelope along with my inflated bill was a
gentle reminder from the credit department informing me that
they were happy to serve me but my last charge had put my balance well above my meager limit. My charge card was temporar-
ily suspended, and my account was turned over to their nasty
little collection department. I telephoned to inquire about
this error that was ruining my credit rating and was informed
by a crisp, high-pitched voice that it knew I had purchased a
one-hundred-dollar gift certificate because that's what the
computer said. I was also informed that the computer rarely
made an error. I told the owner of the high-pitched voice that
I am usually the exception to any rule and that her electronic
co-worker had, in fact, made an error on my bill. "Impossible," she said coldly. "The balance is owing."

"And that's exactly how it will remain--owing," I snapped   3
in return. It's cash from now on.

Another example of how the computer has made life more   4
interesting happened at the bank last week. It was a sunny
Friday afternoon, and I was looking forward to a relaxing but
productive weekend. It seemed that nothing could spoil my

light, contented mood. I went into the drab, dark branch to
make a withdrawal from my savings account because I had just
realized that the automobile insurance was due the next day,
the rent the following day, and I desperately needed to put
some groceries in the bare cupboards. I finally made it to the
caged teller and slid my pink withdrawal slip in her direction. Her fat fingers flew over the keyboard of her terminal,
and then with a smug smile she said that I did not have the
funds to cover my withdrawal. Patiently I showed her my
receipt for a deposit made just the day before, my bankbook,
and my displeasure at not being able to get at my own money.
I explained that I would starve, my auto insurance would be
canceled, and I would surely get into an accident the hour
after it was no longer in effect, and I would probably be
evicted from my home. "So," I said, "please check your records;
there's some mistake." She smirked and said that I would have
to wait until Monday for all the transactions to be processed.
I wanted to process her. Instead, I withdrew fifteen of the
twenty dollars she said remained in my account, went to McDonald's instead of the grocery store, took the bus instead of
driving my uninsured car, and didn't answer the door when the
landlord stopped by to collect the rent.

5   Then there was the time. . . . But I won't go into that;
it's too depressing. Sometimes I think computers don't like me.

➤ **FOR WRITING OR DISCUSSION**

1. What is the writer's thesis? Does he state it? If so, where and how? If not, how can you tell what his thesis is?
2. What is the difference here between the thesis and the topic?
3. How does the writer's description of the Friday afternoon as sunny, his mood as light and contented, and the bank as drab and dark (paragraph 4) contribute to the thesis? to the development of the paper?

4. The writer's descriptions of the clerk in the collection department and of the bank teller are not flattering (". . . a crisp, high-pitched voice"; "it knew"; "her fat fingers"; "she smirked"). Do you think he intended these phrases as personal insults? Why, or why not?

5. What is the effect of referring to the computer as "her electronic co-worker"?

6. Who is the audience for this paper? How do you know?

7. What author image does Wendell present? On what specific qualities of the paper do you base your judgment?

COLLABORATIVE LEARNING

Brainstorm in groups about the role of computers in our lives. Ask members of your group to share positive and negative computer experiences. What is the general consensus in each group: Have computers had an unquestionably positive impact on our lives? After one person from each group reports to the full class, write a paper in which you explore computers in your life.

2

Finding and Supporting a Thesis

One of the key steps in writing a successful paper is stating your main point clearly and succinctly. Most good writing benefits from a central idea. The idea unifies the paper.

Think, for example, how dull and rambling a report about spending a day at the nearest shopping mall would be if you covered, hour by hour, everything you did on that day—from waiting for a bus in the morning to opening the door to the mall and so on to returning home by bus in the late afternoon. You could enliven many of the day's details if instead you settled on a central idea: *When I feel blue, I can always cheer myself up, at little expense, by spending the day at my neighborhood shopping mall.* Now you have a focus for the details of the day. You go first to the most exclusive department store and try on designer clothes—everything from blue jeans to fun furs—just for the pleasure of seeing how good you look in them. Then you enter the best jewelry store, letting your sandaled feet sink into the deep-piled carpet, and inspect the gold chains. By now, you have worked up an appetite, so, forgetting about calories, you go to your favorite restaurant where service is quiet, efficient, and courteous and have a hamburger topped with lettuce, tomato, avocado, and sprouts and accompanied by French fries and, for dessert, a banana split. Later, you sit in the mall and enjoy people-watching for a while. Finally, just before you leave, you go to your favorite discount store and buy a new T-shirt as a memento of your happy day. Having a central idea enables you to select the details that make for a lively paper.

The Thesis

To be sure you have the kind of central idea that will lead to an interesting and unified paper, you still have one more step to take in the process of thinking before writing: You must state a thesis and you must consider how to present appropriate and logical support for it.

A **thesis** is the position a writer takes on an arguable point—one on which more than one opinion is possible. It is the main idea that the paper will support. The writer must convince the reader that this position or idea is valid. A thesis statement is a one-sentence summary of the idea the writer will defend: *Students in technical programs should be required to take some courses in the humanities,* for example; or *A few simple changes would improve the registration procedure on our campus.*

With few exceptions, the papers you will be asked to write in college will benefit enormously from a thesis. Your professors will expect you to do more than merely arrange logically the facts you have gleaned from a course; your teachers are interested in what you think about the facts, to show what point you think the facts add up to. A professor of American literature won't ask you to summarize *Huckleberry Finn.* She wants to know what conclusions you reached after a careful reading of the novel: *Mark Twain's* Huckleberry Finn *is an indictment of slavery,* let's say; or *Mark Twain in* Huckleberry Finn *criticizes the violence of the pre–Civil War South.* Until you can make that kind of statement, you aren't ready to write because you don't have clearly in mind the point you will make. And if you aren't certain of what your idea is, you stand little chance of convincing a reader of its validity. It's important, therefore, to spend time thinking your idea through before you start writing. This will save time and grief in the long run.

A good thesis has five characteristics:

1. *It can usually be stated in one complete sentence.* That doesn't mean you must present the thesis statement, word for word, in the paper itself. In fact, once you start writing, you may find that you want to devote a paragraph or more to presenting the idea of your paper. Still, it's good to have a one-sentence statement in mind before you begin writing. Until you can state your main idea in one sentence, you may not have it under control.

2. *A good thesis makes a statement, that is, gives an opinion or attitude about the facts.* To say that Brutus stabbed Shakespeare's Julius Caesar on the Ides of March is to state a fact. A thesis, a statement *about* the fact, might read, *Brutus succeeded in killing Caesar on the Ides of March because Caesar had grown too arrogant and proud to protect himself.*

3. *A good thesis is limited;* that is, the idea stated must be one that can be clearly explained, supported, and illustrated in the space called for. A long magazine article might have this as its thesis:

Although, as a result of a controversial and aggressive promotional campaign, women professional golfers now make more money and receive greater recognition than they did ten years ago, they still do not make as much money, receive as much television coverage, or command as much respect as men professional golfers.

But this won't do for a thousand-word paper; the thesis could not be developed fully in so short a space. A better thesis for a short paper might read, *The promotional campaign for the Women's Professional Golf Association has attracted money and attention for professional female golfers.* An even better thesis would be, *The photographs of golfer Jan Stephenson used in the promotional campaign for the Women's Professional Golf Association may prove harmful to her career.*

4. *A good thesis is appropriately focused.* Consider this thesis: *The reports in* Time *are entertaining and informative, but* Time *slants its reports to suit its political bias, and the vocabulary used by* Time *requires constant trips to the dictionary.* This thesis says three things about *Time:* the magazine's reports are entertaining and informative; the reports are slanted; the vocabulary of *Time* requires constant use of the dictionary. A writer who begins with such a thesis runs the risk of writing a three-part paper that has no central focus. The point of emphasis is not clear. To emphasize that the magazine's reports are entertaining and informative, the writer must subordinate the other points to that idea:

> Although the vocabulary used in Time requires constant trips to the dictionary and the reports are often slanted to suit a political bias, the reports are entertaining and informative.

To emphasize the shortcomings of the magazine, the writer should subordinate the entertaining and informative nature of the reports:

> Although the reports in Time are entertaining and informative, their vocabulary makes them hard to read and the material is often slanted to suit a political bias.

5. *A good thesis is precise.* It lets the reader and the writer know exactly what the paper will contain. Words such as *good, interesting, impressive,* and *many* are too vague to do the job. They say nothing about the subject: What is interesting or good to one person may appear dull or offensive to another. Don't say, "Agatha Christie's detective stories are good." Say, instead, "Agatha Christie's detective stories appeal to those who enjoy solving puzzles." Don't say, "My history class is interesting." Say, "My professor makes history easy to understand."

Stating Your Thesis

Rules, of course, are one thing; applying them is another. You may well ask how one arrives at that perfectly stated thesis. Sometimes, especially in essay examinations, the thesis statement is suggested by the question. Often, all you have to do is think of a one-sentence answer to the question, and you have your thesis statement.

Example question: What is job enrichment? Is job enrichment an attempt by management to exploit workers?

Sample thesis statement: Job enrichment, an effort to increase productivity by making the job more attractive, is an attempt by management to exploit laborers by motivating them to work harder.

In this thesis statement, the writer has both defined *job enrichment* and stated an opinion about the practice. The rest of the essay will give the reasons job enrichment, in this writer's opinion, is an attempt to exploit laborers.

Not all writing assignments are so directed, however. Frequently, you may be given a large-scale subject. As you know, it is up to you to limit the subject and decide what point you want to make about it. On some subjects—subsidizing college athletics, for example—you may already have a strong opinion. If you have information to back up that opinion, you have no problem. Just state your opinion and then begin thinking about how you can back it up. On other subjects, though, you may at first think you have no opinion. But you may have a question. You might have wondered why, for example, Japan seemed in years past to outdistance the United States in the production of everything from television sets to automobiles. Go to the library and do some reading on the subject. You may then decide that one reason Japan became a major industrial power is that the economy had not, since the end of World War II, had to support a military machine. Now you have a thesis.

A valuable way to produce a thesis statement is to review your prewriting activities—free association, brainstorming, lists, and subject maps (see Chapter 1)—with an eye toward a central issue that may be brewing somewhere in your early, unedited thinking on a topic. Suppose that you're considering a paper on the subject of children's toys. It's near holiday time, you're a parent, and you've been giving lots of thought to toys lately. You've used free association to jot down anything that comes to mind on the topic. Your list might look like this:

```
                        Topic: Toys

1. expense of toys

2. shoddy construction: plastic parts don't fit together

3. focus on violence: guns, destructive images

4. too many batteries required

5. sexist toys

6. difficulty in putting together the parts of toys

7. unclear, misleading assembly instructions
```

Considering your list, you note that three items (6, 7, and part of 2) relate to your frustrations at toy assembly. Putting together that kiddie gym really irritated you, didn't it? The more you think about that experience and others like it, the more you realize that item 7 on your list is the heart of the matter. The reason assembling toys is so difficult is that the instructions are unclear and misleading. There's your thesis statement: *Instructions accompanying disassembled toys are misleading.*

Your thesis, then, can originate in many different ways. It may depend on your mood. John, for example, being angry with his roommate, quickly could decide to prove that his roommate's failure to close things is irritating. The thesis may depend on your experience of, let's say, putting toys together. Or you may choose to disprove a point made in an essay you have read, or you may disagree with a point made by a classmate. Or you could pick up on some comment made in class. Or you could disagree with some bit of accepted wisdom—*Never put off until tomorrow what you can do today*, for example. The way you arrive at the thesis statement doesn't matter. The important message is, have a thesis statement clearly in mind as you plan the rest of the paper.

It should be clear by now that a thesis is different from a topic. A topic is simply the subject of your paper, whereas a thesis makes an assertion about the subject. For the topic *toys*, you saw how the writer developed the thesis statement. Having a topic in mind helps you produce a thesis. Merely placing a title on top of your page to reflect your topic does not mean that you have provided a thesis statement.

EXERCISE

Determine which of the following items are thesis statements and which are not. Also determine which thesis statements are too general or too lacking in unity to make a good paper. How does each statement meet the specifications for a thesis as explained on page 33? Revise the unacceptable thesis statements accordingly.

1. In a strong economy employers cannot find quality workers.
2. Teenage drivers are a menace!
3. Americans are saving less and less money each year.
4. Many violent action films appear during summer months.
5. Political candidates use radio and television to earn support from American voters.
6. Asthma affects many inner-city schoolchildren.
7. Curtailing drug use begins with education.
8. Helpful friends and careful planning made the moving of my four thousand books from one apartment to another easier than I had expected.
9. Books are expensive; shelves for books are costly and take up space; owning many books helps the student of literature by saving the time that would otherwise be spent in libraries.
10. The trouble with newspapers is that they never print good news.

EXERCISE

Return to the exercise on page 26. For any five topics that you limited there, develop thesis statements that could be used successfully in a paper.

Supporting Your Thesis: Details

Once you've stated your thesis clearly you need to consider how you will support it. The best way to convince a reader that your idea is worth considering is to offer details that back up your point and to present these details logically.

Chapter 14 presents the topic of logic in some detail, and you no doubt will examine it fully later on. Here, it is important to know that logic involves the relation between the particulars and generalities as you present them in your paper. Logic is the process of reasoning inherent in your writing, and all readers expect a kind of clarity and intelligence that make the points and arguments understandable and easy to follow. Logical writing avoids what we call fallacies, that is, false notions, ideas founded on incorrect perceptions. We'll consider logic and logical fallacies in greater depth later in your course.

In presenting details to support your point, you have many options. If you're drawing on your own personal experience, you can *provide examples* that illustrate your point. Examples drawn from experience rarely prove anything; however, they point out why you've made the generalization put forth in your thesis. When you use personal experiences to support a thesis, you should rely on **concrete sensory details**—colors, actions, sounds, smells, images of taste and touch. Details rooted in the senses make what you've experienced come alive for the reader. If you are narrating an event or describing a scene, concrete imagery will help your readers see things your way. Thus, if you're writing about the misleading instructions for assembling toys, you might show your frustration by describing your efforts to put together the offending kiddie gym—the hunt for an orange plastic tube, the pungent smell of epoxy glue, the rough silver hooks that don't fit the holes made for them, and the diagram labeled in black Japanese characters and no English words.

Other kinds of supporting details draw on **data**—statistics and cases that demonstrate a point. For example, if your thesis is *Driver's education courses have had a dramatic effect on improving the car-safety record of young teenagers,* you'd need to cite comparative data of teens who took the course and those who didn't. You also would need to show the decrease, let us say, in speeding violations, drunk driving, and fatal accidents. Your analysis of the data would help readers see how you interpret the details. You might focus on a particularly illuminating case—the record of a young driver, say, before and after a driver's education course.

In supporting your thesis, you also might want to present expert testimony as supporting details. **Expert testimony** means the words and ideas of respected thinkers on your subject. Depending on your topic, you'll find an array of experts, thoughtful researchers, and other authorities who have considered the same issue and who have shared their observations in print, on the airwaves, or in personal conversation. Thus, the books and magazines you read, the films and television programs you watch, the radio stations you listen to, and the lectures and recitations in which you participate at school are all rich sources for details in an essay. For that thesis on assembling toys at home, for example, you might cite a Taiwanese manufacturer whom you saw on a business news film clip on the Public Broadcasting System and who talked about the problems in producing clear instructions for home toy assembly. You'd certainly want to quote from one or more sets of instructions to highlight their inadequacies. Perhaps an article in your local paper reported on a toy buyers' revolution, where dozens of angry parents dumped parts from unassembled kiddie gyms on the doorstep of a toy store because the parents couldn't figure out how to put the expensive toys together. Citing that article would strengthen your thesis.

Without adequate support, your thesis is merely an assertion—an opinion. Unsupported assertions never win readers' respect.

COLLABORATIVE LEARNING

Form five groups. Ask each group to propose the kinds of details a writer might provide to support the following theses. Have each group report to the whole class.

1. I always worry when my son borrows the car at night.
2. Hispanic Americans have contributed substantially to economic growth in our Southern cities.
3. Textbooks across the elementary school curriculum present women in passive roles.
4. Dawn on the desert is a haunting display of light and shadow.
5. Caring for an aging parent can drain a family's resources.

EXERCISE

For any three thesis statements that you developed for the exercise on page 36, indicate the kinds of details that you might use to support them.

Student Writing: Thesis and Details

Now let's look at a student's paper that illustrates a carefully defined thesis. As you read, see how the writer establishes the thesis and supports it in the essay.

Thomas Healey

"You Must Be Crazy!"   **Title: a phrase from the essay's dialog**

Generalization in first sentence draws reader's attention.

It's easy to note the behavioral dark spots in those around us. My father is a skinflint; when I need a loan or simply extra cash, he turns a deaf ear to my pleading hysterics. Mom is excessively moody. When something bothers her she sulks for hours, never revealing what set her off, and we just have to wait until she gets over it. However, as a fairly normal teenager, I never thought of myself as having any particular character flaws. Yet, as I faced my brother Matthew at his bedroom door one spring afternoon last year, I became aware of the ugly features of anger and temper in my personality.

Introduction builds up to the thesis; Healey will not write about his mother and father anywhere in the essay other than here in the introduction.

1

Thesis sentence states writer's opinion, is well limited, well focused, and precise.

Though he's two years younger than I am, Matt and I share many things, including our clothes sometimes. But this time he had borrowed my new tan sweater and had returned it to my drawer with big grease stains on the sleeve and near the collar. "How did this happen?" I shouted, pointing to a large black spot. "Oh," he said casually, looking up from the Sports Illustrated he was reading on the brown rug near his bed, "I was fooling around with the Chevy. Oil dripped on everything."

Concrete sensory details support point of the paragraph.

Transition: Words "Matt and I" remind readers of previous paragraph content.

2

Realistic dialog enlivens essay.

I couldn't believe my ears. "You wore my good sweater to work on your stupid car? I don't believe you." My neck tightened and my hands grew wet and cold. I felt my eyelid twitch. Matt rubbed the arch of his left foot covered in a white sweat sock. Then he shrugged his shoulders. "Those are the breaks," he said, looking down again at his magazine.

Descriptive details help reader envision Matt.

3

Transition: "that lack of concern"

It was probably that lack of concern that drove me   4
wild. Lunging at him, I pushed him down to the floor.

Words "drove me wild" establish frame for supporting detail in paragraph.

The more I pushed against him, the angrier I felt. Some
strange power had overtaken my body and mind. When I
looked at Matt's face suddenly, I heard him choking, and

Strong sensory details further support thesis.

I realized that I had my elbow pressed against his
throat. What was I doing? I jumped up as Matt lay sput-
tering. "You must be crazy!" he gasped in a voice I
could barely hear. His frightened blue eyes stared at
me in amazement. "You could have killed me."

I remember looking at my hands and then back at   5
Matt. He was right. I was crazy--crazy with anger.
If rage could turn me into such a monster with my own
brother, imagine what it could do under other conditions. "I'm sorry," I said. "I'm really sorry."

Conclusion connects to ideas expressed in thesis sentence.

At that moment I realized the full meaning of   6
anger. It was a strong and dangerous emotion that could
easily overpower a person who did not work to keep it
under control.

HAVING YOUR SAY

Is "sibling rivalry"—the competition between brothers and sisters in the same family for attention and approval by parents and others—an inescapable consequence of living together in a family unit? Write an essay in which you argue for one side or the other on this question. Support your point of view with appropriate detail.

➤ **FOR WRITING OR DISCUSSION**

1. What is the writer's topic? What is his thesis? What is the relation between the topic and the thesis? In what ways is the thesis limited, focused, and precise? What is the writer's opinion or attitude as expressed in the thesis?

2. How do the sentences in the introduction build to the thesis? Has the writer done a satisfactory job in setting up the thesis?

3. How has the writer best used descriptive detail to advantage? How does the description of Matthew contribute to the thesis? How has the writer used narration to advance his essay?

4. What is the writer's purpose in this essay?

5. What is your opinion of the conclusion—the last paragraph of the essay? How might you expand it from its two-sentence structure? Or do you find it satisfying as is? Why, or why not?

6. Write a paper in which you explore anger or some other "dark spot" in your personality or in the personality of someone you know well.

Models of Writing

Read the pieces that follow, which have clearly defined theses and convincing supporting details, and then answer the questions that follow each one. Examine "Review Checklist: Tips for Active Reading" on page 6 before you begin.

ANNA QUINDLEN

Women Are Just Better

My favorite news story so far this year was the one saying that in England scientists are working on a way to allow men to have babies. I'd buy tickets to that. I'd be happy to stand next to any man I know in one of those labor rooms the size of a Volkswagen trunk and whisper "No, dear, you don't really need the Demerol; just relax and do your second-stage breathing." It puts me in mind of an old angry feminist slogan: "If men got pregnant, abortion would be a sacrament." I think this is specious. If men got pregnant, there would be safe, reliable methods of birth control. They'd be inexpensive, too.   1

I can almost hear some of you out there thinking that I do not like men. This isn't true. I have been married for some years to a man and I hope that someday our two sons will grow up to be men. All three of my brothers are men, as is my father. Some of my best friends are men. It is simply that I think women are superior to men. There, I've said it. It is my dirty little secret. We're not supposed to say it because in the old days men used to say that women were superior. What they meant was that we were too wonderful to enter courtrooms, enjoy sex, or worry our minds about money. Obviously, this is not what I mean at all.   2

The other day a very wise friend of mine asked: "Have you ever noticed that what passes as a terrific man would only be an adequate woman?" A Roman candle went off in my head; she was absolutely right. What I expect from my male friends is that they are polite and clean. What I expect from my female friends is unconditional love, the   3 ability to finish my sentences when I am sobbing, a complete and total willingness to pour their hearts out to me, and the ability to tell me why the meat thermometer isn't supposed to touch the bone.

4   The inherent superiority of women came to mind just the other day when I was reading about sanitation workers. New York City has finally hired women to pick up the garbage, which makes sense to me, since, as I discovered, a good bit of being a woman consists of picking up garbage. There was a story about the hiring of these female sanitation workers, and I was struck by the fact that I could have written that story without ever leaving my living room—a reflection not upon the quality of the reporting but the predictability of the male sanitation worker's responses.

5   The story started by describing the event, and then the two women, who were just your average working women trying to make a buck and get by. There was something about all the maneuvering that had to take place before they could be hired, and then there were the obligatory quotes from male sanitation workers about how women were incapable of doing this job. They were similar to quotes I have read over the years suggesting that women are not fit to be rabbis, combat soldiers, astronauts, firefighters, judges, ironworkers, and President of the United States. Chief among them was a comment from one sanitation worker, who said it just wasn't our kind of job, that women were cut out to do dishes and men were cut out to do yard work.

6   As a woman who has done dishes, yard work, and tossed a fair number of Hefty bags, I was peeved—more so because I would fight for the right of any laid-off sanitation man to work, for example, at the gift-wrap counter at Macy's, even though any woman knows that men are hormonally incapable of wrapping packages and tying bows.

7   I simply can't think of any jobs any more that women can't do. Come to think of it, I can't think of any job women don't do. I know lots of men who are full-time lawyers, doctors, editors, and the like. And I know lots of women who are full-time lawyers and part-time interior decorators, pastry chefs, algebra teachers, and garbage slingers. Women are the glue that holds our day-to-day world together.

8   Maybe sanitation workers who talk about the sex division of duties are talking about girls just like the girls that married dear old dad. Their day is done. Now lots of women know that if they don't carry the garbage bag to the curb, it's not going to get carried—either because they're single, or their husband is working a second job, or he's staying at the office until midnight, or he just left them.

9   I keep hearing that there's a new breed of men out there who don't talk about helping a woman as though they're doing you a favor and who do seriously consider leaving the office if a child comes down with a fever at school, rather than assuming that you will leave yours. But from what I've seen, there aren't enough of these men to qualify as a breed, only as a subgroup.

10   This all sounds angry; it is. After a lifetime spent with winds of sexual change buffeting me this way and that, it still makes me angry to read the same dumb quotes with the same dumb stereotypes that I was reading when I was eighteen. It makes me angry to realize that after so much change, very little is different. It makes me angry to think that these two female sanitation workers will spend their days doing a job most of the coworkers think they can't handle, and then they will go home and do another job most of their coworkers don't want.

➤ **FOR WRITING OR DISCUSSION**

1. What is Quindlen's thesis in this selection?
2. What details does the writer provide to support her thesis? Which details are most convincing to you? For example, how effective is the list of jobs Quindlen says women can do?
3. Where has Quindlen used cases effectively?
4. How do quotations serve the selection? Why does the writer draw on quoted information? Why does she not name the people who made the statement in the first place?
5. Who is the audience for this piece? How do you know? Point to specific language, style, and sentence structure that help you respond to this question.
6. How does the story about the two female sanitation workers relate to the thesis?
7. What author image does Quindlen present?
8. Do you find Quindlen's argument convincing? Why, or why not?

HAVING YOUR SAY

Write your own brief essay called "Women Are Just Better"—or, if you prefer, "Men Are Just Better"—in which you argue your point with a strong thesis and convincing detail.

RICHARD RODRIGUEZ

Complexion

Complexion. My first conscious experience of sexual excitement concerns my complexion. One summer weekend, when I was around seven years old, I was at a public swimming pool with the whole family. I remember sitting on the damp pavement next to the pool and seeing my mother, in the spectators' bleachers, holding my younger sister on her lap. My mother, I noticed, was watching my father as he stood on a diving board, waving to her. I watched her wave back. Then I saw her radiant, bashful, astonishing smile. In that second I sensed that my mother and father had a relationship I knew nothing about. A nervous excitement encircled my stomach as I saw my mother's eyes follow my father's figure curving into the water. A second or two later, he emerged. I heard him call out. Smiling, his voice sounded, buoyant, calling me to swim to him. But turning to see him, I caught my mother's eye. I heard her shout over to me. In Spanish she called through the crowd: "Put a towel on over your shoulders." In public, she didn't want to say why. I knew.

That incident anticipates the shame and sexual inferiority I was to feel in later years because of my dark complexion. I was to grow up an ugly child. Or one who thought

1

2

himself ugly. (*Feo.*) One night when I was eleven or twelve years old, I locked myself in the bathroom and carefully regarded my reflection in the mirror over the sink. Without any pleasure I studied my skin. I turned on the faucet. (In my mind I heard the swirling voices of aunts, and even my mother's voice, whispering, whispering incessantly about lemon juice solutions and dark, *feo* children.) With a bar of soap, I fashioned a thick ball of lather. I began soaping my arms, I took my father's straight razor out of the medicine cabinet. Slowly, with steady deliberateness, I put the blade against my flesh, pressed it as close as I could without cutting, and moved it up and down across my skin to see if I could get out, somehow lessen, the dark. All I succeeded in doing, however, was in shaving my arms bare of their hair. For as I noted with disappointment, the dark would not come out. It remained. Trapped. Deep in the cells of my skin.

3   Throughout adolescence, I felt myself mysteriously marked. Nothing else about my appearance would concern me so much as the fact that my complexion was dark. My mother would say how sorry she was that there was not money enough to get braces to straighten my teeth. But I never bothered about my teeth. In three-way mirrors at department stores, I'd see my profile dramatically defined by a long nose, but it was really only the color of my skin that caught my attention.

4   I wasn't afraid that I would become a menial laborer because of my skin. Nor did my complexion make me feel especially vulnerable to racial abuse. (I didn't really consider my dark skin to be a racial characteristic. I would have been only too happy to look as Mexican as my light-skinned older brother.) Simply, I judged myself ugly. And, since the women in my family had been the ones who discussed it in such worried tones, I felt my dark skin made me unattractive to women.

5   Thirteen years old. Fourteen. In a grammar school art class, when the assignment was to draw a self-portrait, I tried and I tried but could not bring myself to shade in the face on the paper to anything like my actual tone. With disgust then I would come face to face with myself in mirrors. With disappointment I located myself in class photographs—my dark face undefined by the camera which had clearly described the white faces of classmates. Or I'd see my dark wrist against my long-sleeved white shirt.

6   I grew divorced from my body. Insecure, overweight, listless. On hot summer days when my rubber-soled shoes soaked up the heat from the sidewalk, I kept my head down. Or walked in the shade. My mother didn't need anymore to tell me to watch out for the sun. I denied myself a sensational life. The normal, extraordinary, animal excitement of feeling my body alive—riding shirtless on a bicycle in the warm wind created by furious self-propelled motion—the sensations that first had excited in me a sense of my maleness, I denied. I was too ashamed of my body. I wanted to forget that I had a body because I had a brown body. I was grateful that none of my classmates ever mentioned the fact.

7   I continued to see the *braceros,* those men I resembled in one way and, in another way, didn't resemble at all. On the watery horizon of a Valley afternoon, I'd see them. And though I feared looking like them, it was with silent envy that I regarded them still. I envied them their physical lives, their freedom to violate the taboo of the sun. Closer to home I would notice the shirtless construction workers, the roofers, the sweating men tarring the street in front of the house. And I'd see the Mexican gardeners. I was unwilling to admit the attraction of their lives. I tried to deny it by looking away. But what was denied became strongly desired.

In high school physical education classes, I withdrew, in the regular company of five or six classmates, to a distant corner of a football field where we smoked and talked. Our company was composed of bodies too short or too tall, all graceless and all— except mine—pale. Our conversation was usually witty. (In fact we were intelligent.) If we referred to the athletic contests around us, it was with sarcasm. With savage scorn I'd refer to the "animals" playing football or baseball. It would have been important for me to have joined them. Or for me to have taken off my shirt, to have let the sun burn dark on my skin, and to have run barefoot on the warm wet grass. It would have been very important. Too important. It would have been too telling a gesture—to admit the desire for sensation, the body, my body.

Fifteen, sixteen. I was a teenager shy in the presence of girls. Never dated. Barely could talk to a girl without stammering. In high school I went to several dances, but I never managed to ask a girl to dance. So I stopped going. I cannot remember high school years now with the parade of typical images: bright drive-ins or gliding blue shadows of a Junior Prom. At home most weekend nights, I would pass evenings read- ing. Like those hidden, precocious adolescents who have no real-life sexual experiences, I read a great deal of romantic fiction. "You won't find it in your books," my brother would playfully taunt me as he prepared to go to a party by freezing the crest of the wave in his hair with sticky pomade. Through my reading, however, I developed a fab- ulous and sophisticated sexual imagination. At seventeen, I may not have known how to engage a girl in small talk, but I had read *Lady Chatterley's Lover*.

It annoyed me to hear my father's teasing: that I would never know what "real work" is; that my hands were so soft. I think I knew it was his way of admitting pleasure and pride in my academic success. But I didn't smile. My mother said she was glad her children were getting their educations and would not be pushed around like *los pobres.* I heard the remark ironically as a reminder of my separation from *los braceros.* At such times I suspected that education was making me effeminate. The odd thing, however, was that I did not judge my classmates so harshly. Nor did I consider my male teachers in high school effeminate. It was only myself I judged against some shadowy, mythical Mexican laborer—dark like me, yet very different.

Language was crucial. I knew that I had violated the ideal of the *macho* by becoming such a dedicated student of language and literature. *Machismo* was a word never exactly defined by the persons who used it. (It was best described in the "proper" behavior of men.) Women at home, nevertheless, would repeat the old Mexican dictum that a man should be *feo, fuerte, y formal.* "The three F's," my mother called them, smiling slyly. *Feo* I took to mean not literally ugly so much as ruggedly handsome. (When my mother and her sisters spent a loud, laughing afternoon determining ideal male good looks, they finally settled on the actor Gilbert Roland, who was neither too pretty nor ugly but had looks "like a man.") *Fuerte,* "strong," seemed to mean not physical strength as much as inner strength, character. A dependable man is *fuerte. Fuerte* for that reason was a characteristic sub- sumed by the last of the three qualities, and the one I most often considered—*formal.* To be *formal* is to be steady. A man of responsibility, a good provider. Someone *formal* is also constant. A person to be relied upon in adversity. A sober man, a man of high seriousness.

I learned a great deal about being *formal* just by listening to the way my father and other male relatives of his generation spoke. A man was not silent necessarily. Nor was he limited in the tones he could sound. For example, he could tell a long, involved, humorous story and laugh at his own humor with high-pitched giggling. But a man was not talkative the way a woman could be. It was permitted a woman to be gossipy and chatty. (When one heard many voices in a room, it was usually women who were talking.) Men spoke much less rapidly. And often men spoke in monologues. (When one voice sounded in a crowded room, it was most often a man's voice one heard.) More important than any of this was the fact that a man never verbally revealed his emotions. Men did not speak about their unease in moments of crisis or danger. It was the woman who worried aloud when her husband got laid off from work. At times of illness or death in the family, a man was usually quiet, even silent. Women spoke up to voice prayers. In distress, women always sounded quick ejaculations to God or the Virgin; women prayed in clearly audible voices at a wake held in a funeral parlor. And on the subject of love, a woman was verbally expansive. She spoke of her yearning and delight. A married man, if he spoke publicly about love, usually did so with playful, mischievous irony. Younger, unmarried men more often were quiet. (The *macho* is a silent suitor. *Formal.*)

13   At home I was quiet, so perhaps I seemed *formal* to my relations and other Spanish-speaking visitors to the house. But outside the house—my God!—I talked. Particularly in class or alone with my teachers, I chattered. (Talking seemed to make teachers think I was bright.) I often was proud of my way with words. Though, on other occasions, for example, when I would hear my mother busily speaking to women, it would occur to me that my attachment to words made me like her. Her son. Not *formal* like my father. At such times I even suspected that my nostalgia for sounds—the noisy, intimate Spanish sounds of my past—was nothing more than effeminate yearning.

14   High school English teachers encouraged me to describe very personal feelings in words. Poems and short stories I wrote, expressing sorrow and loneliness, were awarded high grades. In my bedroom were books by poets and novelists—books that I loved—in which male writers published feelings the men in my family never revealed or acknowledged in words. And it seemed to me that there was something unmanly about my attachment to literature. Even today, when so much about the myth of the *macho* no longer concerns me, I cannot altogether evade such notions. Writing these pages, admitting my embarrassment or my guilt, admitting my sexual anxieties and my physical insecurity, I have not been able to forget that I am not being *formal.*

15   So be it.

➤ FOR WRITING OR DISCUSSION

1. What is Rodriguez's thesis in this selection? State the thesis in your own words. Which sentence best contributes to your idea of the thesis?
2. How does the writer support his thesis?
3. What is the effect of drawing on personal experiences from different periods of Rodriguez's childhood?
4. What is the Mexican dictum about manhood? How does it affect the writer?

5. What stereotypes of men and women did Rodriguez grow up with in his household?
6. Write an essay in which you define "manhood" or "womanhood." Draw on your own experiences to generate and support your definition.

SOPHFRONIA SCOTT GREGORY

Teaching Young Fathers the Ropes

Two years ago, Paul Smalley found himself getting sucked into a stereotype. At 21 he returned home from military prison a frustrated, unemployed young black man who also happened to be a brand-new unmarried father. His son and namesake was already four months old, and Smalley was so unfamiliar with his new role that he thought he could not touch the baby without permission. "I was asking if I could pick him up," he says. "I just didn't feel like a father." 1

Smalley worried because he could see a familiar pattern forming, born of his shame over not being able to support his child, the feeling of inadequacy and the strain of his relationship with the baby's mother. He resisted joining the ranks of young black fathers who cut out on their kids because they will not face the pressures of parent-hood, but he could not see how to break the cycle—until he learned from a friend about the Responsive Fathers Program at the Philadelphia Children's Network. 2

While social-assistance programs have long been available to teenage mothers, lit-tle effort has gone into helping young fathers. The Responsive Fathers Program is one of a growing number of groups across the United States seeking to fill the vacuum. The programs try to help young unmarried men become better fathers, providers, and mates through counseling services, particularly assistance in a job search. The sixty-one par-ticipants in the Philadelphia program, who range in age from 16 to 26, meet in group sessions once a week and discuss child rearing, self-esteem, male-female relationships, and the job market. "The program helped me to open up," says Smalley. "It gave me the drive to want to do things. I've learned how anger affects my child and about how he needs both parents." 3

Fathers come to the program either by referral from a hospital, community center, or probation office or, like Smalley, by word of mouth from a friend. Thomas J. Henry, 47, the program's director, says that many young fathers just need help cutting through the bureaucracy: filling out forms, standing in the correct lines for public assistance, and dealing with unresponsive bureaucrats. "This system encourages fathers not to be there," he says. "You have many fathers declared absent when they are actually present. People think they're just making babies and don't have any feelings attached to that act. Every-one says, 'We want you to be a responsible father,' but we give them nothing to be responsible with." 4

The Responsive Fathers Program is part of a study being conducted by Public/ Private Ventures, a nonprofit public-policy research organization that focuses on youth 5 development. Using five other similar programs from across the country, PPV launched the study last year to try to discover whether it could get young unwed fathers to come forward and seek help, identify their needs, and direct them to the services they require. The group aims to provide information to policymakers responsible for family welfare programs so that as they debate decisions concerning young mothers, they will keep young fathers in mind as well.

6   "It is important for families that we begin to consider the role of fathers," says Bernadine Watson, director of individual and family support at PPV. "Our work has shown that these men, even though they are young and do not have the educational background or employment skills, are very interested in being good parents."

7   Henry believes the Philadelphia program will make a difference because it is willing to take the three to six years needed to "put things right" in a young man's life. Such a philosophy and time frame contrast with government programs offering quick-fix solutions, but Henry believes in taking a pay-now-or-pay-later approach. His goal for the fathers is true self-sufficiency, by training them for jobs in areas such as printing, building maintenance, and computer programming. This is no easy trick; the program has a hard time persuading employers to give the young men a chance. "We go along begging, pleading to anybody to give us jobs," says Henry. The program currently has fathers who have been on the job waiting list for six months. Still, the dads attend the sessions, even though the only thing Henry and his colleagues can give them is carfare home.

8   The young men say they enjoy the sessions because they can vent their feelings of frustration, often born of their sense that society perceives them as bad parents. The black male has become the focal point of blame for the deterioration of the African-American family. But in many cases such blame is misdirected. Devon Shaw, 24, whose three children range in age from six months to four years, was just out of high school when his first child was born. He doesn't like the way the system "lets you know what we're doing wrong, not what they're doing wrong." Smalley, who now works as an animal-care technician and goes to school at night, admits that many of his friends simply cannot function as fathers: "Some don't even try. Some don't care. They just turn to drugs or drug dealing as their way out." But he stresses that there are many more who are trying to be responsible, who want their kids to have two parents, a good education, and a safe place to live. "It's just we have so many obstacles to becoming decent men," he says. "But it is inside of us. It's in the black men out there."

➤ **FOR WRITING OR DISCUSSION**

1. What is Gregory's thesis in this essay?
2. What kinds of details does the writer provide to support the thesis? Which details are most convincing to you and why? What cases and examples help Gregory support her point?
3. What is the Responsive Fathers Program? What pattern does it aim to break? To what group does it address its services?

4. What are some of the difficulties that unwed fathers face? What factors other than youth contribute to these difficulties?
5. Who is the audience for the piece? How do you know?
6. What author image does Gregory present?
7. Write an essay in which you present your views on the roles fathers should play in families, particularly in rearing children. Present a thesis and support it with clear and sufficient details.

REVIEW CHECKLIST: STATING A THESIS

- Have I examined my warm-up activities—free association, brainstorming, and so on—to help me identify my thesis?
- Have I paid appropriate attention to logic in producing my thesis? (See Chapter 14.)
- Have I stated my thesis in a complete sentence?
- Have I made a statement about the topic by sharing an opinion or attitude about it?
- Have I limited my thesis to an idea I can explain, support, and illustrate in the paper I am writing?
- Have I focused my thesis appropriately?
- Have I produced a precise thesis, avoiding vague words like *good* or *interesting?*
- Have I considered how I will support my thesis—concrete sensory details, data, or expert testimony?
- Am I prepared to provide adequate supporting detail? What resources will I have to draw on to support my thesis?
- Have I revised my thesis to suit the developing ideas in my various drafts of the paper?

CHAPTER
3

Planning a Paper: Outlining

Proper planning is a key to writing a successful paper. As we saw in Chapter 1, John Fousek's two planning efforts—grouping related materials in lists and a scratch outline—helped him to produce his drafts. In this chapter, however, we explore a more rigorous kind of planning, **formal outlining.** A formal outline requires clearly defined headings and subheadings, which are arranged in a prescribed format of Roman and Arabic numbers and upper- and lowercase letters.

The Importance of Planning

First let's review briefly the concept of planning as a strategic step in the writing process. Once you have formulated a thesis and determined how you will support it, you need to plan the order of development. What supporting detail will you give first in your paper? What next? Supporting the thesis with adequate detail is critical, and an outline helps you see whether your information backs up the main idea of your essay. Thus, here you should be thinking about your examples. What examples will you use? Where? In some cases, your purpose sets the plan for your paper. If, for example, you plan to describe a process, such as responding to a fire or changing auto plates, you would arrange the steps in the most convenient order for getting the job done. Some reports of events call for chronological order, in which case the planning involves grouping the details under such headings as, for example, discovering the fire, sounding the alarm, fighting the fire, and cleaning up the debris. If, however, your purpose is to convince, to develop a thesis, the plan may not be as obvious, and you will need to think carefully about the order in which you need to arrange the material.

Whatever the case, it's necessary to plan your paper before you begin to write because if you don't, you may get so involved in choosing the right words that you forget where you want to go. Part Two of this text describes many different methods of organization. Here, as we consider outlining, we want you to see the value of making a diagram of your paper before you write it. You've already seen the value of informal outlining as a prewriting strategy (pages 18–23). Let's consider now the general methods of more formal outlining.

The Formal Outline

An outline is a schematic presentation of your paper—a procedural diagram, if you will, in which you show the order of your topics and how they relate to each other. If readers of your papers have told you in the past that your ideas seem disorganized or that their direction is unclear, formal outlining can help you. A formal outline gives a picture of the logical relations between the separate parts of the paper and the thesis or purpose. After your preliminary thinking on your topic and your prewriting in hand, consider the formal outline as a road map to a territory you have just begun exploring but need clearer directions to navigate.

When you produce a formal outline, follow the conventions of its format, as presented on pages 52-53. After your prewriting, you should have an idea of your thesis. Thus, always begin your outline by stating your thesis or purpose. You may want to modify your thesis as your outline takes shape, so don't be concerned if you haven't stated your thesis exactly the way you want it.

After you state your thesis, your next task is to determine the main divisions of the paper as suggested by the thesis. In many cases, your choice of method of development (Part Two of this book) will determine the major sections. For example, if you wanted to write about why your brother decided not to go to college, what he is doing instead, and how his decision affected his personality, the sections of the paper seem clear, and you would use them as main headings in the outline format. Yes, you would still have to decide on what order to use in order to present the points in the paper, and what order to use for the supporting details under each point, but the three major parts of the paper are clear simply from the way you want to develop it.

In other papers, main divisions may not suggest themselves so clearly at the outset. As you examine your prewriting, try to see how some of what you've written falls into large blocks of thought. If you've written preliminary thoughts by hand, circles and arrows or marks in different colored pens or pencils can help you make visual linkages among related ideas that may be spread out over the page.

If you write by computer, you can experiment by grouping different thoughts into blocks, saving your effort, and trying yet another plan. As the related thoughts come together, look at them as main points. If you can create a label for each thought block, you then can convert the label into a main heading. Usually, in papers of the kind you'll be writing in your freshman courses, three to five thought blocks are enough. Thus, the main headings in your outline should match the number of blocks you have identified. If you see that your outline has more than five or so main points, reexamine it: You may be trying to do too much in your paper.

With thought blocks identified and labeled, you need then to think about the supporting details to place under each heading. The supporting points, of course, will pertain clearly to the main thought you stated in the heading. As you group these supporting points—some of which will appear in your prewriting, others to be invented as you produce the outline—they will become subheadings in your outline.

Once you've settled on different thought blocks, you will have to decide how to organize them. In a descriptive essay (Chapter 6), you generally move the reader from one place to the next, and once you decide where to begin (in a room, for example, front, back, sides, or middle) logic of place will assert itself. In a narrative essay (Chapter 7), sequence of events ordinarily will impose an order on your paper. But for most other essays the arrangement of thought blocks is strictly the writer's option, with logic the prevailing factor for appropriate decisions. Without exhausting the numerous possibilities, we try to suggest relevant arrangement schemes in later chapters on essay development, and you may find them helpful as you determine how to oder your main headings.

The Formal Outline Format

Begin by stating the thesis or purpose. Then indicate all major divisions of the paper with Roman numerals. Mark the support for the major divisions with capital letters and additional support for those major divisions with Arabic numerals. If you are planning a very long paper, you may want to make further subdivisions. To do so, next use small letters—*a, b, c*—and then Arabic numerals in parentheses—*(1), (2)*—then lowercase letters in parentheses—*(a), (b)*.

A standard formal outline for a complex paper has the following format:

Thesis or Purpose: [State the thesis or purpose of your paper here.]

    I. Major division
       A. First-level subdivision
          1. Second-level subdivision
          2. Second-level subdivision
             a. Third-level subdivision
             b. Third-level subdivision
                (1) Fourth-level subdivision
                (2) Fourth-level subdivision

     B. First-level subdivision
       1. Second-level subdivision
       2. Second-level subdivision

II. Major division
     A. First-level subdivision
       1. Second-level subdivision
       2. Second-level subdivision
     B. First-level subdivision
       1. Second-level subdivision
         a. Third-level subdivision
         b. Third-level subdivision
       2. Second-level subdivision
         a. Third-level subdivision
         b. Third-level subdivision
           (1) Fourth-level subdivision
           (2) Fourth-level subdivision
              (a) Fifth-level subdivision
              (b) Fifth-level subdivision

Depending on the complexity of your topic, you may find it helpful to develop short papers through the types of informal planning discussed in Chapter 1, such as grouping related material in lists or preparing a rough outline. Yet even short papers may lend themselves to the rigors of formal outlining. The visual scheme of a formal outline helps you see whether the main divisions of your paper advance the thesis and if the subdivisions fall logically under the main divisions.

An outline for a short paper usually includes several major divisions and sometimes two or three subdivisions for each major topic. Remember that a word or a phrase in an outline can be expanded into a sentence—even a paragraph—in your essay.

A typical outline format for a short paper looks like this:

Thesis or Purpose: [State the thesis or purpose of your paper here.]

   I. Major division
     A. Subdivision
     B. Subdivision

  II. Major division
     A. Subdivision
     B. Subdivision
     C. Subdivision

 III. Major division
     A. Subdivision
     B. Subdivision
     C. Subdivision

Topic and Sentence Outlines

Formal outlines are of two types, *topic outlines* or *sentence outlines*. A **topic outline** is one in which the writer uses just a few words or phrases to indicate the topics and subtopics that the paper covers. Topic outlines are sufficient for many short papers, especially for papers that classify or present a process. Longer papers and those that develop theses often profit from sentence outlines.

   Here is a topic outline for a short paper on the sensory experiences surrounding an attempt at doing homework.

Thesis: When I attempt to do homework in the student lounge, my senses are assaulted by sights, smells, and sounds.

  I. Sights   *First major division*
     A. Trash spilling out of garbage containers   *First subdivision*
     B. Trash on tables   *Second subdivision*
 II. Smells   *Second major division*
     A. Cigarette smoke   *First subdivision*
     B. Garbage   *Second subdivision*
III. Sounds   *Last major division*
     A. Vending machines   *First subdivision*
     B. Money changer   *Second subdivision*
     C. Conversations of students   *Third subdivision*

Now look at a topic outline for a short paper on how to change automobile license plates.

Purpose: To show how to change auto license plates.

  I. Assemble materials
     A. Find screwdriver
     B. Find household oil
     C. Buy plastic screws

 II. Remove old plates
     A. Oil screws to loosen rust
     B. Unscrew plates
     C. Discard metal screws

III. Mount new plates
     A. Position plate with screw holes
     B. Screw on plate using plastic screws

 IV. Break and discard old plates

EXERCISE

1. What is the first major division? The second? The third?
2. What supporting information does the outline indicate as subdivisions for the major division, "Remove old plates"?
3. Why does the fourth major division not have any subdivisions under it?
4. What thesis could you propose for the essay that this outline suggests?
5. In what order has the writer chosen to arrange the thought blocks indicated as major divisions?

Longer papers and those that develop theses often benefit from sentence outlines. To write a **sentence outline,** you must sum up in one sentence what you want to say on each topic and subtopic. The sentence doesn't merely indicate the topic; it states what you intend to say about the topic. This kind of outline forces you to think through exactly what you want to say before you begin to write. By constructing a sentence outline, you will find out whether you really have support for your position.

Following is a sentence outline for a paper written by Filippos Georgopoulos, who, having been in America for only six months, explained why his attitude toward the English language has changed.

Thesis: My attitude toward the English language has changed
from loathing to acceptance.
    I. At first, I hated the English language. *First major division*
        A. Knowing very little English, I felt isolated. *First level subdivision*
            1. I could not understand what people said to me. *Second level*
            2. I could not tell others what I thought or felt. *subdivisions*
        B. The isolation I felt made me want to return to Greece. *First level subdivision*
   II. Now, six months later, I like the English language very *Second major division*
      much.
        A. The support of the Greek family I live with has helped *First level subdivision*
        me to accept English.
            1. They gave me courage to try to use the language. *Second level subdivisions*
               a. They proved to me that they had learned the
                   language. *Third level subdivisions*
               b. They proved to me that they could talk with
                   others in English.
            2. They held conversations with me in English.

B. The teachers in my English classes have helped me to accept the language.
  1. They are approachable and helpful outside of class.
  2. They are good instructors in class.
    a. They explain material clearly.
    b. They discuss a variety of subjects.
      (1) The variety increases my vocabulary.
      (2) The discussions improve my comprehension and speech. *} Fourth level subdivisions*

III. I go out of my way now to assure my continuous contact with English.
  A. I study English regularly.
    1. I work with a tutor for one hour every day.
    2. I study grammar and vocabulary two hours every night.
  B. Since I meet few Greeks, I must speak English every day.
    1. I go to the supermarket to read and pronounce the names of consumer products.
      a. I love to say the weird names of candies and cereals.
        (1) Have you ever eaten Fiddle Faddle?
        (2) I have lots of fun with Captain Crunch®, Sugar Frosted Flakes®, and Count Chocula®.
      b. I made friends with one of the stock boys who helps me when my English fails me.
    2. I always accept solicitation calls on the telephone just to practice my English.

EXERCISE

1. What are the major divisions of the outline? Put a checkmark beside each one. How do the major divisions relate to the thesis as stated as the first outline entry?
2. How do the items in I. A. 1. and 2. relate to the item in I. A.? To the item in I.? To the thesis?
3. Look at the various items connected to III in the outline. Label each item appropriately as major division and first-, second-, third-, and fourth-level subdivisions. Be prepared to explain the reasons why you chose the labels you did for the entries.
4. Using any one of the thought blocks labeled as a major division as well as the various subdivisions beneath it, try your hand at writing the paragraph that the outline suggests.

From Outline to Essay: One Student Writing

In a literature class one student, Alan Benjamin, received this assignment: Discuss the implications of the inscription on the pedestal of the statue in Shelley's poem, "Ozymandias." We'll have more to say about approaches to literacy analysis in Chapter 15; here we want to examine how the student developed a formal outline and how that outline led to the production of his essay.

First, read the poem "Ozymandias" so that you'll know what stimulated the assignment.

PERCY BYSSHE SHELLEY

Ozymandias

I met a traveller from an antique land
Who said: Two vast and trunkless legs of stone
Stand in the desert. Near them, on the sand,
Half sunk, a shattered visage lies, whose frown,
And wrinkled lip, and sneer of cold command,
Tell that its sculptor well those passions read
Which yet survive, stamped on these lifeless things,
The hand that mocked them, and the heart that fed:[1]
And on the pedestal these words appear:
"My name is Ozymandias, king of kings:
Look on my works, ye Mighty, and despair!"
Nothing beside remains. Round the decay
Of that colossal wreck, boundless and bare
The lone and level sands stretch far away.

[1] The passions stamped on the broken face of the statue survive the hand (of the sculptor) that mocked them and the heart (of Ozymandias) that fed them.

Initial thinking about the assignment led the writer to this prewriting effort.

PREWRITING

Such arrogance! Oz thinks he'll survive time?

Statue meant to challenge all who saw it — I am mighty, the rest of you puny

How was statue built in the first place?

People today who think they're powerful can learn from Ozy's fate— not from envy

"King of Kings"— Ozymandias thinks a lot of himself

"Sneer of cold command"— poet shows vanity and arrogance in having statue built in the first place

Ozy believes no one else will be able to match the magnificence of his works

Is Ozy a real figure in history?

Vanity today too— all material things crumble and yield disappointment if you put your faith in the material things

Where was Ozymandias' statue erected? Maybe at the gates of his capital city?

Where is this "antique land"?

Time eats away buildings and statues— look what's left of Ozymandias' vain effort to preserve his reputation and instill fear in people

"Despair"— Ozymandias' idea of despair comes from petty and foolish reasons. Now we have more realistic reasons for the origin of despair

Using his prewriting as a record of his preliminary thinking, Alan Benjamin tried to link related ideas visually using lines and boxes. As he considered the thought blocks suggested by his prewriting, he weighed how to organize them. He numbered related points so that he could see their interconnections. He did not link thoughts that did not seem related to each other.

GROUPING THOUGHT BLOCKS

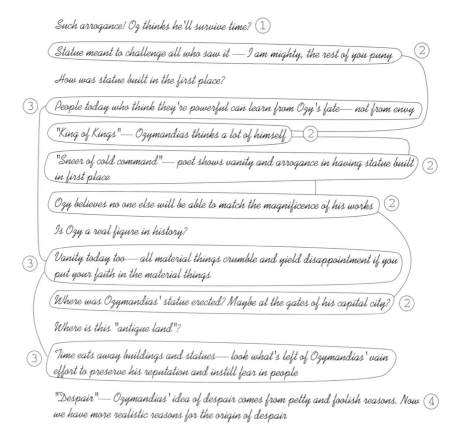

Such arrogance! Oz thinks he'll survive time? ①

Statue meant to challenge all who saw it — I am mighty, the rest of you puny ②

How was statue built in the first place?

③ *People today who think they're powerful can learn from Ozy's fate — not from envy*

"King of Kings"— Ozymandias thinks a lot of himself ②

"Sneer of cold command"— poet shows vanity and arrogance in having statue built in first place ②

Ozy believes no one else will be able to match the magnificence of his works ②

Is Ozy a real figure in history?

③ *Vanity today too— all material things crumble and yield disappointment if you put your faith in the material things*

Where was Ozymandias' statue erected? Maybe at the gates of his capital city? ②

Where is this "antique land"?

③ *Time eats away buildings and statues— look what's left of Ozymandias' vain effort to preserve his reputation and instill fear in people*

"Despair"— Ozymandias' idea of despair comes from petty and foolish reasons. Now ④ *we have more realistic reasons for the origin of despair*

The next step on the road to preparing the outline and then writing the paper was to label the numbered blocks of thought. What words and phrases would best identify each cluster of information? The labels developed are preliminary and subject to considerable change as the outline takes shape; but you can see the first efforts below. The numbers correspond to the numbered thought blocks Benjamin grouped (see page 58).

LABELS FOR THOUGHT BLOCKS

1. Meaning of despair different now from Ozymandias' day

2. Meaning of the statue to Ozymandias and his contemporaries

3. Meaning now

4. The petty and foolish vs. realistic reasons for despair

These labels provided a good start for developing a formal outline. As the writer examined the labels and blocks of thought, he could identify the purpose he had in writing his paper. He wanted to contrast Ozymandias' views of despair as expressed in the poem with the meanings we bring to that word today. And the more he weighed his purpose and the thought blocks he produced, he realized that the numbered clusters suggested the order that he would use. First, he would present the king's notion of despair; then he would present the views we have of the term today based on the poem's assertions.

Here is the outline developed from the preliminary materials you have explored.

OUTLINE

Purpose: To contrast Ozymandias' view of the word *despair* with the meanings we bring to the word as a result of the passage of time.

    I. In the poem "Ozymandias" by Percy Bysshe Shelley, the inscription "My name is Ozymandias, king of kings:/Look on my works, ye Mighty and despair!" appears on a broken statue in the desert.

        A. King Ozymandias had one thing in mind with that inscription.

        B. Today the words take on a dramatically different meaning.

II. Vanity and arrogance motivated Ozymandias to build the statue of himself.

A. The features of his face assert his self-importance.

  1. His "wrinkled lip and sneer of cold command" are apparent.

  2. The size of the statue is "colossal."

  3. He describes himself as "king of kings."

B. We can imagine the site of the statue at the gates of the capital or its central square and people's reactions to it.

  1. Marble buildings gleam in the sunlight.

    a. We can visualize the palace, the treasury, and the temples.

    b. There are monuments to military victories.

  2. "Mighty" people come to see the wonders of Ozymandias' kingdom.

  3. "Look on my works, ye Mighty and despair" the statue sneers.

    a. Despair because your creations will never equal mine.

    b. Despair because my works will make you see the insignificance of your own.

III. The passage of time has given a new dimension to Ozymandias' statement.

A. Ozymandias' kingdom is now a desert.

  1. Time eats away marble.

  2. Buildings and statues crumble.

    a. Little remains of the statue of Ozymandias.

      (1) Two grotesque stone legs stick up in the air.

      (2) The statue has a "shattered visage."

    b. What remains is sand and desolation.

B. The inscription on the pedestal takes on new
   significance.
   1. In one sense it is meaningless.
      a. There are no more "works" left to look on.
      b. Ozymandias was silly in his pomposity.
   2. In another sense the words have stronger and
      truer meaning than Ozymandias dreamed.
      a. Powerful people today can still despair as
         they look at Ozymandias' works.
      b. The despair people face will not be based on
         envy, however.
         (1) They will despair because they can see
             the fate of their own works.
         (2) They will despair because no matter
             how great their works are, the works
             won't matter.
         (3) They will despair because those who put
             their faith in material things are
             doomed to disappointment.
IV. With these contrasting views there is more than enough
    despair to go around.

The paper developed from the formal outline appears next. As you read it, consider how the two relate to each other—and to the prewriting. How has the outline influenced the essay? What differences do you note?

Alan Benjamin

Enough Despair to Go Around

In Percy Bysshe Shelley's "Ozymandias," we are told   1

that the following words are inscribed on the pedestal of

a broken statue in the desert: "My name is Ozymandias,

king of kings: / Look on my works, ye Mighty, and despair!"

What King Ozymandias had in mind when he chose those words
is dramatically different from the meaning they have now.
The new meaning comes not from Ozymandias but from the passage of time.

2   The still visible "wrinkled lip and sneer of cold
command" suggest the vanity and arrogance that motivated
Ozymandias to have his statue built in the first place.
The "colossal" size of the statue and Ozymandias' description of himself as "king of kings" add to the impression
that he thought a great deal of himself and wanted others to
do the same. We can imagine the statue being erected at the
gates or in the central square of King Ozymandias' great
capital city. Marble buildings gleam in the sunlight: the
palace, the treasury, the temples, the monuments to military
victories. Powerful and "mighty" people from all over the
known world come to see the wonders of Ozymandias' kingdom.
"Look on my works, ye Mighty, and despair," sneers Ozymandias. Despair because your creations, your works, will never
be able to equal the magnificence of mine. Despair because
when you look at my works, you can only feel a sense of the
pitiful insignificance of your own.

3   Time passes. Time eats away marble. Buildings and statues crumble. The glorious, thriving kingdom of Ozymandias is
now a desert. Two grotesque stone legs stick up in the air,
and together with a "shattered visage" they are all that is
left of the statue. Everything else is sand and desolation.
In one sense, the inscription on the pedestal has now become
meaningless, for there are no more "works" left to look on,
and we can think only of how silly Ozymandias must have
been. In another sense, the words are filled with a strong
new meaning, stronger and far more true than Ozymandias

ever dreamed. Powerful and mighty people today can look at Ozymandias' works and still despair. This time, however, they will despair not because of envy, but because they can see the eventual fate of all their own works. They will despair because, even if their own works surpass those of Ozymandias, it won't make any difference. They will despair now because they can see that all material things crumble to dust and that people who put their faith in such things are doomed to futility and disappointment.

Ozymandias originally hoped that the despair would come   4
from petty and foolish reasons. Today it can come from more intelligent and realistic reasons. But there is still more than enough despair to go around as "the lone and level sands stretch far away."

EXERCISE

1. How do both the outline and the essay fulfill the writer's statement of purpose? What is the writer's thesis in this essay? Where does the writer state it most clearly?
2. How did the labels for the blocks of thought in the prewriting influence the outline?
3. What three items in the prewriting did Alan Benjamin not include in the thought blocks? Why do you think he excluded these items?
4. The outline is obviously a sentence outline; yet in two places we read not sentences but only fragments. Where? Why does the writer use fragments here? How do the items appear in the essay itself?
5. Look at the four major headings and the various subheadings in the outline. How do they relate to the essay itself? What similarities do you note? How does the essay differ from the section of the outline to which it corresponds?

HAVING YOUR SAY

What do you think the inscription on the pedestal means in Shelley's poem "Ozymandias"? Reread the poem on page 57. Then make an assertion about the inscription and argue for your point with specific detail.

Preparing Your Outline

The outlines you have looked at so far show that whether your outline is a topic or a sentence outline, it should include a statement of the thesis or purpose of the paper (depending on your teacher's instructions) and an indication by means of Roman numerals of the main points to be covered in the paper. Major and minor subdivisions, indicated by letters and Arabic numerals, respectively, should show how the main points will be developed.

Here are other points to observe in preparing an outline:

1. *Do not make single subdivisions.* If you decide to subdivide a point, you must have at least two subdivisions. If there is a I, there must be a II; if there is an A, there must be a B. If you cannot think of two divisions, rephrase the heading so that no division is necessary.

2. *Use parallel grammatical form for headings of equal importance* to show their relation to one another. If heading I reads "Assembling the ingredients," heading II should read "Mixing the ingredients," not "Mix the ingredients."

3. *Make sure the divisions of an outline do not overlap and that you stick to a single principle of division.* You should not, for example, discuss books in terms of fiction, nonfiction, and novels because novels are logically a subdivision of fiction. You should not discuss the branches of government in terms of legislative, judicial, executive, and crooked politicians because one might find crooked politicians in any of the branches. You should not discuss people in terms of overweight, underweight, normal weight, and handsome. Obviously, the topic "handsome" does not belong in a division based on a principle of weight.

4. *Make sure that headings and subheadings show a proper logical relation.* In discussing athletes, you should not establish Babe Ruth as one major division and baseball players as a second. You might, however, treat great home-run hitters as a major division and Babe Ruth and Hank Aaron as subdivisions.

One final note about outlines: They can be as helpful after you've written your paper as they are during the early stages of development. For example, if you choose to use only your prewriting activities as a guide to writing your rough draft, a formal outline at this stage provides a visual scheme of how your ideas relate to each other logically.

As you develop your outline, ask yourself these questions:

REVIEW CHECKLIST: PREPARING AN OUTLINE

- Did I produce prewriting on the topic?
- Did I attempt to identify related blocks of thought in my prewriting?
- Did I group and label the thought blocks?
- Did I use these labels to help me develop the major divisions of my outline?

> ■ Do my major divisions advance my thesis?
> ■ Does each subdivision fit logically under each major division?
> ■ Do further subdivisions grow logically from the divisions under which they appear?

Your answers to these questions can provide guidance as you write and revise your draft. You can determine if your major divisions relate logically to your thesis, and you can shift subdivisions or add new ones as necessary.

EXERCISE

Comment on the following topic outlines. What are their successes? their faults?

1. *Thesis:* All my teachers make me think.

   I. My English teacher
      A. Challenges logic of papers
      B. Relates reading assignments to everyday life
      C. Wears pretty clothes

   II. My history teacher
      A. Gives lectures

   III. My music teacher
      A. Speaks three languages
      B. Has great sense of humor

2. *Purpose:* To classify types of television comedy shows.

   I. Sitcoms
      A. "Typical" family settings
      B. "Atypical" families
         1. single-parent households
         2. unrelated characters in household

   II. Comedy specials
      A. Single-star comedy special
         1. Eddie Murphy
         2. George Carlin
      B. Multiple-star comedy special

   III. Talk shows
      A. Evening talk shows
      B. Daytime talk shows

   IV. Male comedians vs. female comedians
      A. Jay Leno
      B. Rosie O'Donnell

3. *Purpose:* To classify the divisions of the federal government.

    I. The executive
       A. President

   II. Legislative
       A. House of Representatives
       B. Senate
       C. Lawyers

  III. Judicial
       A. Supreme Court
       B. Judges

EXERCISE

What strengths and weaknesses do you see in the following sentence outlines? Revise them so that they are more suitable to the writer's needs.

1. *Thesis:* Both Christmas and Easter are religious holidays that provide an opportunity for secular pleasures.

    I. Both are religious holidays.
       A. Christmas observes the birth of Christ.
       B. Easter observes the Resurrection of Christ.
       C. Halloween is the eve of All Saints' Day.

   II. Both provide opportunities for secular pleasures.
       A. Christmas is a time for parties and gifts.
          1. Families decorate trees.
          2. Children sing carols.
       B. Easter is a time for new clothes and egg hunts.
          1. The bunny rabbit is a symbol of Easter.
          2. Baskets are beautifully decorated.
          3. The president of the United States sponsors an egg roll on the White House lawn.
             a. Many children participate.

2. *Thesis:* Nationalism swept two major countries in Europe through the strength of dynamic leaders.

    I. In the last half of the nineteenth century, nationalism surfaced in Germany and Italy.

   II. Bismarck in Germany, and Cavour, Garibaldi, and Mazzini in Italy were the four key figures in nineteenth-century nationalism.
       A. Cavour, Garibaldi, and Mazzini combined their talents to unify Italy.
          1. Cavour was the "brains" of unification.

    2. Garibaldi was the "sword."

    3. Mazzini was the "spirit" of the revolution.

  B. Otto von Bismarck was the creator of a unified German state.

    1. He used "blood and iron" to unify the separate German states.

    2. He suppressed liberalism and democracy.

    3. His militaristic policies contributed to the outbreak of World War I.

3. *Thesis:* Getting a broken appliance repaired by sending it to a service center requires careful packing and mailing.

  I. Broken appliances can be repaired by service centers.

    A. It's generally easy to bring the appliance to a service unit if one exists in your city.

    B. Often, no such centers exist nearby.

      1. The manufacturer's center may be out of state.

      2. Local repair shops cannot do the work.

      3. Each company has its own designs and required parts.

  II. Mailing the appliance requires attention to important details.

    A. You can find the mailing address easily.

      1. Check the literature that accompanied the object.

      2. Telephone the store where you purchased the object to find out the address.

    B. The biggest job is packing up the object and mailing it off.

      1. Find a strong cardboard box and pack the appliance well in order to prevent shifting and breakage.

      2. Close the carton with strong tape.

      3. Print mailing and home addresses carefully.

      4. Write a letter providing essential information.

        a. Tell what is wrong with the appliance and where you bought it.

        b. Address the envelope correctly and enclose the letter.

        c. Tape the envelope to the outside of the carton.

      5. The post office will weigh the package and tell you costs for mailing and insurance.

EXERCISE

The seven statements that follow, if properly grouped, will develop the thesis *It is unfair to call television "a vast wasteland."* Decide which statements should be indicated by Roman numerals and which by capital letters. Then construct an outline.

1. Television has given Americans vivid close-ups of surgeon and patient in the operating room, of men on the surface of the moon, and of the most exotic specimens in the plant and animal world.

2. "Trashy" magazines and newspapers are much more common on drugstore racks than magazines and newspapers of a better sort.
3. Television has brought Shakespeare to unnumbered thousands who might never have seen a Shakespeare play without it.
4. Tasteless advertisements and advertisements for worthless and even harmful products take up space in newspapers and magazines, just as they take up time on television.
5. Television, more than any other medium, has widened America's consciousness of the major arts and sciences.
6. Television has had a principal part in the recent rise of ballet and modern dance to a top place among the performing arts.
7. Many of the serious failings of television are failings of the media generally.

EXERCISE

Put the following information into a sentence outline that follows the suggested form.

- *First main heading:* Travel throughout America is increasing in popularity with people of all age groups.
- *Subheadings:* College and high school students find travel adds to their education. People with young families feel that their children should experience people in different settings. Old people find travel gives life a sense of purpose.
- *Second main heading:* There are several popular methods of travel.
- *Subheading:* Hitchhiking is frequently used among teenagers.
- *Further divisions:* It allows inexpensive travel. It allows the traveler to meet many people. It is dangerous, however.
- *More subheadings:* Young families still choose small automobiles and camping equipment. Older people often take planes or trains.

EXERCISE

One student jotted down the following information for an essay entitled "Linking Atlantic and Pacific: The Panama Canal." Read all of her data and then choose the two facts that represent the main headings (I and II). Then group the related facts under these headings in order to fill in the outline.

Disease, corruption, and lack of equipment caused the company to go bankrupt.

Actual construction cost $320 million.

The United States government eventually built the canal.

De Lessep's company dug 76 million cubic yards of dirt.

Sanitation cost $20 million.

A French company owned by Ferdinand De Lesseps was the first to try to dig a canal through the Isthmus of Panama.

The United States government removed over 211 million cubic yards of earth.

The original French companies received $40 million.

The canal cost the United States about $390 million.

Ten million dollars was paid to Panama for rights.

EXERCISE

Write a formal topic or sentence outline of John Fousek's paper on his roommate's irritating habits (see Chapter 1, page 24).

EXERCISE

Write a formal topic or sentence outline of Clifford Wendell's paper "The Computer and I" on pages 29–30.

EXERCISE

For the topic you limited in the exercise on page 13, prepare an outline that will help you develop a draft paper.

EXERCISE

Look ahead to the formal outline (pages 223, 228, and 230–231) for the student essays "Life After Death," "Smarter But," and "Shaver's Choice." How do the outlines in each case relate to the essays prepared from them?

EXERCISE
Look ahead to the formal outline (page 531) for the research paper. What does the outline tell you about how the writer will develop the paper?

COLLABORATIVE LEARNING

Bring to class the outline you produced for the preceding exercise, an outline to help you develop a draft of a paper. Form groups of three or four and comment on each other's outlines. As you discuss the work of members in the group, address these questions:

- Does the outline indicate a clear thesis? If not, how can the writer improve it?
- Do the main categories indicate appropriate divisions for the paper?
- Do the subcategories logically support the main categories under which the writer has placed them?
- Does the outline follow the conventions of outline form?

4

Writing a Paper:
An Overview of Parts

Before we proceed in Part Two to developing different kinds of papers—comparison, classification, process, and others—we first need to discuss the characteristics common to almost all types of papers.

The Introduction

To start, you need a beginning, or an **introduction.** The simplest introduction identifies the subject and states the thesis. This is not to say that the thesis statement you produced in your prewriting or placed at the top of your outline must necessarily appear in the same form in the actual introduction. For example, John Fousek's original thesis in Chapter 1, *My friend Jim really irritates me with his habit of never closing things that he opens up,* is stated differently in the introductory paragraph of his final draft in Chapter 5:

```
But Jim has one shortcoming that irritates me: He doesn't

close things.
```

Turn to Fousek's paper on pages 99-101 and note how his introduction builds to the thesis with interesting and pertinent information about his roommate Jim that sets the stage for the main point of the paper.

Similarly, Clifford Wendell's thesis statement for the outline of "The Computer and I" in Chapter 1 read:

```
Instead of making my business transactions simple, computers

sometimes create problems for me.
```

However, in the paper Wendell states his thesis in this way:

```
Computers were designed to make our lives easier, or so I'm

told. Easier? Not in my experience. They tend to put some

challenge into my ordinarily dull life.
```

For yet another example, look ahead to the paper in Chapter 15, "The Beginning of the End" (pages 421–423). Harriet McKay's original thesis statement in her outline for that paper was

```
Although the ending of "Charles" by Shirley Jackson is a

surprise, the author subtly presents clues throughout the

story that enable one, on a second reading, to see that

Jackson does prepare for the ending.
```

As you can see, in the final paper, she writes instead:

```
     Until the last sentence of Shirley Jackson's "Charles,"

I had no idea that Charles, the terror of kindergarten, was

an imaginary person created by Laurie and that Charles's

little monster antics were really Laurie's own antics. The

author fooled me completely, but I have to admit that she

played fair. She gave her readers all the clues they needed

to make a sensible guess about how the story would end.
```

What matters is to present the idea of the thesis in the most interesting manner possible.

Here is a less dramatic example of an introduction that also identifies the subject and states the thesis:

```
Ted Poston's "The Revolt of the Evil Fairies" tells of a

little boy in an all-black school who, because of his ebony

skin, is forced to take the undesirable role of an evil fairy

in his school's annual presentation of Prince Charming and

the Sleeping Beauty; on the night of the production, he gets
```

been busy shoppers, but now they stand transfixed before a
situation comedy without sound.

    And who has not felt the hypnotic power of a wood-burning
fireplace? The flames, now blue, now orange, now red, leap and
fall, and one stares as if fire were new to the planet.

    Movement and color--the combination is compelling. One
may well ask why.

This four-paragraph introduction identifies the subject—the attraction of movement and color—and gives three examples of the attraction, but it doesn't state
the thesis. Instead, it asks a question: Why is the combination of color and
movement so compelling? The answer to the question will make up the body of
the paper. The thesis, the one-sentence answer to the question, need not be
directly stated.

    In other words, many kinds of introductions can be effective. You might, for
example, occasionally try dramatizing a situation:

    Sheila felt light-headed: Her eyes would not focus and
there was a slight hum in her ears. Her hands, wet and
clammy, shook so that she could hardly write. She could not
concentrate. She wanted only to run, to be away from that
terrible scene.

    Sheila had not just witnessed some horrible accident that
she must report. She is a freshman composition student who has
been told to write her first "in-class" composition. Many students will recognize Sheila's symptoms. Perhaps the following
tips about writing a composition under pressure will help
alleviate their pain.

The scene described in the first paragraph attracts the reader's attention. The
second paragraph explains the situation and anticipates the rest of the paper,
which offers tips on writing under pressure. Another option is to use an anecdote to illustrate the subject:

    Mrs. Peters was busily talking to a neighbor over the
telephone one afternoon when she experienced the sudden fear
that her baby son had been hurt. She told her neighbor and

```
ran to check the baby, supposedly napping in his crib

upstairs. To her horror, she found the child unconscious on

the floor. Evidently he had tried to climb out of the crib

but, in the attempt, had fallen on his head. Mrs. Peters's

"knowing" her baby was in danger is the kind of experience

many of us have had at one time or another. Yesterday, for

example, I dialed a friend, and just before his telephone

could ring, he picked up the receiver to call me. Both of

these incidents are illustrations of the kind of thought

transference known as telepathy.
```

The two anecdotes in this introduction show how telepathy, the subject of the paper, functions. The remainder of the paper contains an extended definition of the term.

As you can see, introductions take various forms. In many cases, as in the preceding paragraph, the thesis sentence appears at the end of the introduction. The examples here by no means exhaust the possibilities, but they do illustrate some ways of approaching a subject. Whatever form you choose, it's important to remember that the introduction must interest your readers—after all, you do want them to read the remainder of the paper—and it should in some way prepare readers for what follows.

The Body

The **body** of a paper provides support for the thesis presented in the introduction. Body paragraphs develop the writing plan or outline and should lead readers logically from one section to another without causing confusion.

Topic Sentences

One method of leading your reader is to write clear topic sentences for each paragraph. A **topic sentence** is to a paragraph what a thesis is to a paper: It expresses the central idea of the paragraph. The remainder of the paragraph gives support for the topic sentence. If you use a sentence outline, you may find that the sentences for major divisions serve well as topic sentences. Whether you use sentences from your outline or create new ones, though, the topic sentences should clearly convey to readers the idea of each paragraph.

Topic sentences generally appear at the beginning of a paragraph, as in this example:

Mrs. Jackson, my landlady's mother, is very nosy. Living on the first floor of the building affords her easy knowledge of the comings and goings of everyone living there. No matter how many times I descend the stairs in one day, I always find Mrs. Jackson peeking out of her front door. Usually she makes some statement or asks some question: "You really get around a lot. I guess you're going to the grocery now, huh?" I must give an explanation, denial, or confirmation of her guess, rather loudly, I might add, because of her hearing problem. Whenever company calls, they too are detained and cross-examined on the first floor. "Who are you going to see?" "Are you a relative?" "I guess you've known her a long time." Never does a visitor get up the stairs without first conversing with Mrs. Jackson. She also inspects all deliveries and sometimes confiscates the mail. No harm comes to these things because Mrs. Jackson holds, secures, and delivers them herself. I guess in a way her nosiness is good because she does keep an eye out. Then, too, it gives her something to do because, after all, she is ninety-five years old. We all love her, but her nosiness sometimes burdens us, even though we know she has our best interests at heart.

Sometimes, however, the best place for a topic sentence is at the end of the paragraph:

He drank noisily and chewed with his mouth open. He stuffed food into his mouth with his fingers and wiped his chin with the sleeve of his coat. He made loud, vulgar comments to the waitress, who had difficulty hiding her anger as other customers turned to stare. His idea of conversation was to regale his date with statistics about the World Series or

facts about his expensive new car--especially its expense.
An hour with Bruce in the city's most costly restaurant
made Jane wish she had dined at home alone on a tuna fish
sandwich.

A topic sentence even can appear in the middle of a paragraph:

> A fire-warning detector will "smell" smoke and sound an alarm; a guided mis-
> sile will "see" and pursue a radar echo or the hot engines of a bomber; a speed
> governor will "feel" when a shaft is spinning too fast and act to restrain it.
> *But . . . quotation marks are appropriate in all such cases, because these machines do not
> have minds and they do not perceive the world as human beings do.* Information from
> our eyes, ears, and other senses goes to our brains, and of some of it (by no
> means all) we are aware as a vivid part of our conscious experience, showing us
> the world we inhabit.
>
> *—Nigel Calder,* The Mind of Man

On rare occasions, the topic sentence need not be directly stated at all; instead, it
may be implied:

Often when I find some passage in a book especially
impressive--especially bright, say, or especially moving--
I find myself turning to the dust jacket, if the author's
picture is there, to communicate, to say a kind of "Well
done." Coretta Scott King's photograph, soft, shadowed, and
lovely, is on the jacket of her book My Life with Martin
Luther King, Jr. I must have turned to it a dozen times in
the reading of this book.

Here, the paragraph's central idea—that Coretta Scott King's *My Life with Martin
Luther King, Jr.* is especially impressive—is so clear that a statement of it is
unnecessary; indeed, to state it directly would mar the grace of the paragraph.
Implied topic sentences are tricky, though; use them cautiously. An idea that
seems quite clear to you may not be as clear to your reader.

In summary, a topic sentence states the central idea of the paragraph. Usually the topic sentence appears at the beginning of the paragraph to give the
reader immediate notice of the point being developed. However, a topic sentence also can appear at the end or even in the middle of the paragraph. Once
in a while, you can omit it altogether. Wherever you decide to put your topic
sentence, keep your readers in mind. They should not experience any confusion in
following your thought. The central idea of every paragraph must be clear
enough to lead readers easily from one point of your paper to another.

➤ FOR WRITING OR DISCUSSION

1. Why, according to the writer, must his friends and acquaintances become backyard mechanics?
2. How many types of backyard mechanics does the writer know?
3. What is the thesis of the paper?
4. Do the topic sentences give you a good idea of the nature of each type of mechanic? Why, or why not?
5. Which type of mechanic is the best? In what paragraph is this type described? Should he have been described earlier? Why, or why not?
6. Does the audience for the paper need to know much about cars to appreciate the descriptions of each type? Why, or why not?
7. What does the topic sentence of the last paragraph contribute to your impression of the three types?

COLLABORATIVE LEARNING

Form five groups. Each group should examine one of the following five short paragraphs, all of which lack a topic sentence. As a group, develop a logical topic sentence for your paragraph. Then, report your topic sentence to the whole class.

1. Jason's room is always in a shambles because he never bothers to pick up after himself. His clothes, schoolbooks, and other papers are on the floor, on his bed, and every place else. He never bothers to take dishes back to the kitchen. He just lets them pile up, and he won't lift a finger to tidy up his room until he is literally threatened. Jason is so lazy that when he is watching television, rather than get up and change the channel, he'll just watch the same station all evening, even if he doesn't like the programs. He even walks around with his shoes untied because he is too lazy to bend over and tie them. Sometimes I think he may be too lazy to breathe.

2. Bigfoot, for example, has unusual eating and drinking habits. Instead of eating his own dry cat food, he eats the dog's food. He eats my mother's plants and gets on top of the table to drink tea from a cup when he thinks no one is looking. Besides his peculiar eating and drinking habits, Bigfoot has weird physical features. He has six toes on each of his front paws. He's also cross-eyed. And talk about crazy behavior! Bigfoot behaves more strangely than any other cat I've met. He chases dogs off the porch, wrestles with the family dog, and bites and chases his own tail. The crazy cat can't even climb a tree.

3. Many students enter college with poor reading and writing skills. During their first year of college they need special courses designed to elevate their language competence, although they should have achieved a reasonably high level in high school. In addition, teachers often criticize first-year college students for their inability to think critically. What, college teachers wonder, have students done during four years of high school? What books

have they read? What writing have they done? Have they not analyzed books, films, events?

4. The minute you park the car just outside Ty Park, you can smell mouth-watering food cooking over an open fire. As you approach the stand, you can see barbecued ribs and chicken cooked to a tantalizing brown, then drenched in barbecue sauce until it slowly drips off. The cole slaw and potato salad sit in huge mounds. When you finally sit down with your plate piled high, you sink your teeth into meaty barbecued ribs covered with a tangy sauce. The corn on the cob, dripping with butter and sweet as sugar, is very juicy, and each kernel crunches as you chew. Potato salad, full of hard-boiled eggs, chopped onions, green peppers, and celery, adds to your very fattening meal. For dessert there are ice cold sweet watermelon, caloric apple and cinnamon pastries, and plenty of ice cream rich in butter fat. To wash all this down, you can stand in the shade of a tree and drink cold, refreshing beer until you just about burst open. Just when you feel you can't eat another bite, you hear someone yell, "Get your fresh roasted hot dogs here." On your way to the hot dog stand, you look down at your bulging stomach and say, "Oh, what the heck, a few more pounds won't hurt."

5. First, tiny rays of bright sun slip through the morning fog—a stream of gold here, a circle of yellow there. Still, however, the dominant color is steel gray as mist swirls about the sea, rolling up to the shore like clouds. Little by little the fog separates as streams of ever-lightening sky run between the bands of morning darkness. Suddenly, behind a thick black smudge over the horizon, an orange circle leaps up; beads of color dance on the blue waves; crystals of sand catch fire; the eyes of low-flying gulls glitter like jewels. It is dawn over the Massachusetts coast and the rest of the day will never be the same.

Transitions

Another way to help readers follow your thoughts is to use **transitions,** words or phrases that show the logical connections between ideas. Transitional words like *and, but, however, therefore, next,* and *finally* act as signals. They say to a reader, "Here's an additional point," or "A contrast is coming up," or "Now, I'm drawing a conclusion." Transitions make connections between ideas clear and therefore easy to follow. Consider, for example, the following pairs of sentences.

Awkward: My nephew is a brat. I love him.

Better: My nephew is a brat, *but* I love him.

Awkward: The magician showed the audience that the hat was empty. He pulled a rabbit from it.

Better: *First,* the magician showed the audience that the hat was empty. Then he pulled a rabbit from it.

Among the most natural transitions are the coordinating conjunctions: *and, or, nor, but, yet, for:*

> I do not need to tell you how important the election is. *Nor* do I need to remind you to vote tomorrow.

> Laura is always on one kind of diet or another. *Yet* she never seems to lose any weight.

Here are some other commonly used transitions:

> first, second, third, finally, next
>
> in the first place, in the second place, in addition, besides
>
> furthermore, moreover, again, also, similarly
>
> for example, for instance, to illustrate
>
> on the other hand, nevertheless, conversely, instead, however, still
>
> therefore, consequently, as a result, accordingly
>
> of course, obviously, indeed

> Medicare and Blue Cross can be a blessing to elderly people. The difficulty of filling out all the required forms, however, sometimes makes them wonder how blessed they are.

> I have been a thrifty stay-at-home most of my life. It was a surprise to my children, therefore, when I went off to Europe first class last summer.

Employed sensibly, transitions contribute to the smoothness of your paper. However, too many transitions can be as distressing to a reader as too few. This example overuses transitional words:

> The children wanted to see the animals in my woods. *However,* they made too much noise. *In the first place,* all twenty of them shouted. *Moreover,* they screamed. *Furthermore,* they threw rocks into the streams. *Therefore,* birds, frogs, even bugs went rushing to the hills. *As a result,* the children saw no animals. *Nor* should they have expected to see animals after making so much noise. *Nevertheless,* I was sorry that they thought they might see what only hours of silence and days of watching ever bring to sight.

Now look at how the paragraph actually appears in *The Inland Island* by Josephine Johnson:

> "Where are all your animals?" the little children cried, running . . . through the woods—twenty little children, panting, shouting, screaming, throwing rocks into the streams. Birds, frogs, even bugs went rushing to the hills. How sad that the children thought they might see what only hours of silence, days of watching ever bring to sight.

Clearly, Johnson's paragraph is far better. All those transitions in the first paragraph do not help it flow; rather, they get in the way. Use transitions, then, but use them only to signal a logical connection that would not otherwise be obvious.

In marking connections between ideas, you are not limited to single words and short phrases. Often the topic sentence serves both as a transition and as an indicator of the central idea of a paragraph.

> *Besides making life difficult for his parents,* Charles sent his first-grade teacher home with a nightly headache.

> *Although the Puritans observed a strict code of behavior,* their lives were often filled with great joy.

In sentences of this kind, the introductory adverbial phrase or clause (shown here in italics) points back to the preceding paragraph to provide a transition. At the same time, the rest of the sentence points forward to the subject matter of the paragraph for which it is the topic sentence.

Occasionally, an entire paragraph may serve as a transition. It's sometimes a good idea to stop—at a logical point, of course—and sum up what you've said so far before going on to another point. The good **transitional paragraph**, like the transitional topic sentence, points back to what has gone before and points forward to what is yet to come. Note the successful use of the transitional paragraph in this sequence of paragraphs:

> Thus, granting Professor Maly time to do a thorough and conscientious new edition of her book will add to her professional standing, bring a bit of valuable attention and some money to the college, and result in a book more helpful than ever in teaching students how to write clear English. These considerations are, I think, justification for the professional leave she has requested, but I have other reasons for recommending that her request for leave be granted.

> So much for the preparation of the surface. Now we are ready to paint.

> Thus, Jackie Robinson had to confront a long tradition of bigotry in the major leagues. How did he meet this challenge?

> With all these arguments in favor of state-run lotteries, opponents of such lotteries can still raise some valid points.

EXERCISE

Underline the transitions in the following letter, written by Abraham Lincoln to General Joseph Hooker in 1863.

> I have placed you at the head of the Army of the Potomac. Of course I have done this upon what appears to me to be sufficient reasons. And yet I think it best for you to know that there are some things in regard to which I am not quite satisfied with you. I believe you to be a brave and skillful soldier, which, of course, I like.

Another logical relation that can give coherence to a paragraph is **cause and effect:**

> This sentiment of retaliation is, of course, exactly what impels most offenders to do what they do. Except for racketeers, robbers, and professional criminals, the men who are arrested, convicted, and sentenced are usually out to avenge a wrong, assuage a sense of injury, or correct an injustice as they see it. Their victims are individuals whom they believe to be assailants, false friends, rivals, unfaithful spouses, cruel parents—or symbolic figures representing these individuals.
>
> —*Karl Menninger,* The Crime of Punishment

Perhaps one of the most useful logical relations you can use to achieve coherence within a paragraph is the **comparison** of one thing to another:

> In science fiction, which is the literature of extrapolation, there is to be found the recurrent theme of the omniscient computer which ultimately takes over the ordering of human life and affairs. Is this possible? I believe it is not; but I also believe that the arguments commonly advanced to refute this possibility are the wrong ones. . . . It is said, for example, that computers [unlike humans] "only do what they are told," that they have to be programmed for every computation they undertake. But I do not believe that I was born with an innate ability to solve quadratic equations or to identify common members of the British flora; I, too, had to be programmed for these activities, but I happened to call my programmers by different names, such as "schoolteacher," "lecturer," or "professor."
>
> —*W. T. Williams, "Computers as Botanists"*

Use any of these methods—or any others that work—to achieve coherence. The important thing is to achieve it—to make the relation between and among sentences clear to the reader.

PARAGRAPH COMPLETENESS

A paragraph must be **complete.** Every paragraph in your paper must be adequately developed. This means using enough facts, details, examples, quotations of authorities, or reasons to support the topic sentence. Inadequate development, like lack of unity and coherence, causes confusion for the reader. Consider, for example, the difference between the following two paragraphs.

> Until a few years ago, there was a myth that the divorced woman, because of a generous alimony and child-support check, enjoyed a life of luxury and excitement. I wish that were so.

> The good life is supposed to begin as soon as a woman regains her freedom, or so I've been told. According to the script of the good life, a fat alimony and child-support check will carry the divorcee until she walks into a glamorous new job filled with challenge, excitement, and a fabulous salary. She will enjoy a spacious suite of rooms in an exclusive neighborhood. Her closet will bulge with expensive clothes from the finest boutiques. A classic automobile, perhaps an El Dorado,

will wait for her to turn the key and carry her to exotic places and adventures with exciting new friends. My experience has not quite hit all these high spots.

Obviously, the second paragraph is more fully developed than the first, which contains nothing but a bare statement of the idea. The second paragraph brings the idea to life by spelling out the myth of the divorced woman.

Now consider the following descriptive paragraphs.

Running in the park, first thing in the morning, is a habit I can't quit. I feel excited when I begin to run. A mile later, still feeling good, I begin to perspire. Later, I slip into a trancelike state. At three miles, I am snapped out of the trance by a change of scenery, a path that winds deep into the woods. Twenty-five minutes have passed, and I'm into the final stretch. I feel a great sense of exhilaration. Running five miles lifts my spirit, and I know that tomorrow I'll just have to do it again.

Running in the park, first thing in the morning, is a habit I can't quit. As I make my way to the starting line, a feeling of excitement, like being at a carnival in the summertime, overcomes me. The crisp morning air and a slight breeze bring goose bumps to the uncovered parts of my body. Feeling good, I'm off running. In front and on both sides of me are grass and dead, dried leaves still covered with the morning's glasslike dew. Eight minutes and one mile later, an easy-going stride brings beads of perspiration to my forehead. A sharp turn has me running uphill. The steep, demanding climb takes me to a picturesque scene of sun rays bouncing off the turbulent water of the Rocky River. Refreshed by the scene, I slip into a trancelike state caused by the rhythm of my sneakers pounding the asphalt pavement every half second. At three miles, I am snapped out of the trance as the scenery changes. The path is winding deep into the woods. Sitting and waiting to say hello is a squirrel. I can hear his not-so-bold friend rustling in the brush, afraid to confront the foreigner. Twenty-five minutes have passed and I'm into the final stretch. I feel a great sense of exhilaration as I cross my imaginary finish line. Running five miles lifts my spirit, and I know that tomorrow I'll just have to do it again.

As in the previous example about the myth of the divorced woman, the second paragraph here brings the experience to life by providing specific details. The fully developed second paragraph is more convincing than the first.

Not every paragraph need be so long, of course. The length of a paragraph is determined by its topic sentence. You have to decide how much material you need to develop the idea. Some ideas require more development than others, but in every case, the material should relate to the point and should be as concise as possible. In other words, you should never pad your writing. An intelligent reader can tell immediately if you are using words simply to fill space and will probably reject your arguments, however worthy, because of your manner. You should, then, use as many facts, details, examples, quotations, or reasons as you need to develop your point, but no more. (See pages 37–38, "Supporting Your Thesis: Details.")

CHAPTER
5

Revising and Editing
Your Paper

As good as John Fousek's first draft is (see Chapter 1, page 24), like all papers, it needs revising and editing. These two interrelated terms identify critical stages in the development of a successful paper.

When you **revise,** you rethink the ideas and concepts in your paper and change them to reflect your new thoughts. Revision means literally *looking again.* In revising your paper, you want to present and explore any fresh insights you've developed, make necessary changes in focus and direction for your topic, and add essential details. When you **edit,** you make changes in language and expression. You reshape sentences for clarity and emphasis, you improve the style, you attend to appropriate word choice, diction, and sentence structure. As a specialized part of editing, **proofreading** (see pages 98–99) allows you to concentrate on often overlooked errors in spelling, grammar, and punctuation. Frequently, the efforts work hand in hand, especially as you draw closer to your final draft; you revise and edit at the same time. Developing a new idea may help you clarify a point and change your language and sentences simultaneously; an attempt to edit for improved sentence structure may unlock ideas that send you in an exciting new direction.

In your first effort to produce another draft, you should focus on the content of your essay. Try to make your paper as clear as possible. Check on organization and development of ideas. Examine your introduction and conclusion. Consider the unity, coherence, and completeness of your paragraphs. Where should you add information? What unexplored feature of your topic could you open for your readers' advantage? How could you connect related thoughts in different parts of your paper?

One Student Revising and Editing

John shaped his first draft by working first with another student in a peer-critiquing session in class.

Learning from Other Students: Peer Review

Some teachers now build peer review sessions into regular writing instruction. In **peer review**, you and your classmates comment on each other's drafts. Sometimes you work in small groups and offer comments and suggestions orally. Or, you can write comments directed at specific questions posed by fellow writers or by your teacher on a peer-response checklist.

Following the instructor's guidelines for using a peer-response guide or checklist, the person who read John's paper gave him this written evaluation.

Peer evaluation guide and student response

1. What is the main point of the paper?
   You are trying to show what annoys you about your roommate, that he doesn't close things.

2. What is the best part of the paper?
   The bathroom examples—funny! I've had toe shampoos, too! I also like the open drawers part.

3. What recommendations for improvement can you make?
   a. Add more details. Show some of the stuff in the drawers—how they're dumped in. Maybe describe the bathroom, too?
   b. I agree with your question—watch trite and slang words. "Like a bomb hit it" must go!

These comments from one of John's classmates will be very helpful as John attends to the next draft. Certainly, the paper could benefit from more precisely stated details. And, as the student reviewer suggests, the writing is too conversational. John thought more about his topic and the comments and suggestions his classmate provided. Another friend and John's teacher offered further insights about the first draft.

COLLABORATIVE LEARNING

Exchange drafts with another student in the class and write comments about the student's paper. Ask the other student to write comments on your paper as well. The purpose of your comments is to help the writer produce the next draft.

DRAFT WITH INSTRUCTOR'S COMMENTS

I'm bothered even more by Jim's failure to close
bathroom objects, for example, he never closes the
cs

shampoo cap. This makes me lose my ~~cool~~ composure more
Good change here!

than anything. When I'm showering. I always grab the
frag
sp

shampoo bottle by the cap. A loose cap always results in
Good! You corrected a run-on.

shampoo on my toes and not in my hair, which at this

point is soaking wet. Because I am economically minded,
The "wise" ending is questionable in making adjectives. Do you need "moneywise" at all here?

moneywise watching a green puddle of shampoo going down
the drain wasted every day really upsets me. Jim
forgets to close the bathroom door after using the
facilities while I shower. The bathroom has grown warm
and steamy during the course of my shower, the cold
cs

morning air chills me. Jim's thoughtlessness is very
annoying.

Jim is such a great guy, and I know his failure to
Too much coordination in this sentence. Revise?

close things is a minor bad habit, and I try to
overlook it. However, it does tend to irritate me,
especially when cold air hits me right after I'm out of
the shower.

You've certainly made Jim's habits real for us. Everybody knows an "I don't close things" person. (I admit it—I'm one myself!) Limiting the topic to one specific shortcoming focuses the paper well. I like sensory images like "banging silverware" (par. 2) and "warm and steamy" (next-to-last par.).

Consider these points as you revise:

1. Provide more details in par. 2. Show us the mess in the drawers. What's in them? What do they look like?

2. Slang and colloquial expressions can be bothersome. Don't get too stuffy now, but do strive for a slightly more formal writing style. Look especially at "pretty well" and "fun guy."

3. Smooth out transitions and logic as I've indicated in the margin.

4. Proofread carefully for those run-ons, comma splices, and fragments—these can be major problems on a final draft. See relevant sections in the Handbook (at the end of Student's Book) for review and practice.

5. The conclusion lacks impact. Can you interpret the significance of your experience with Jim? Go beyond the immediate experiences you share with the readers here.

Good try for an intermediate draft, John. Revise! Revise! Revise!

Putting It All Together

In Part One you've examined many key features in developing a paper for your writing course and have done numerous exercises designed to help you produce and revise a draft. Since your revised copy will be the draft you submit for evaluation, take time to review the following checklist as you rework your drafts. The tips are stated as general questions to ask yourself as you revise, edit, and proofread.

We've devised similar checklists, more specific for the focused writing task at hand, for each chapter in Part Two, "Methods of Development."

REVIEW CHECKLIST: REVISING AND EDITING YOUR DRAFTS

Thought and Content Revisions

- Does my thesis state the topic clearly and give my opinion about the topic?
- Is my thesis sufficiently limited?
- Have I provided sufficient details to support my assertions?
- Have I used precise and appropriate language?
- Have I varied my sentence structure? Do my sentences sound right when I read them aloud?
- Have I eliminated unnecessary words?
- Are my thoughts unified: Do my ideas relate to each other?
- Is my writing coherent: Do my ideas flow logically?
- Are my purpose and audience clear? Have I given readers the information they need to understand my points?
- Have I expressed my ideas in a pleasing style?

Revising Essay Form

- Will my introduction engage readers?
- Do my body paragraphs expand on my thesis?
- Does my conclusion grow naturally from the ideas stated in the thesis and developed in the essay?
- Do my transitions logically connect paragraphs and thoughts within paragraphs?

Editing and Proofreading: Grammar, Usage, and Mechanics

- Have I avoided run-on sentence errors and used appropriate end punctuation marks to signal sentence endings?
- Have I checked for sentence fragments by joining them to other sentences or by adding necessary subjects, verbs, or verb helpers?
- Do my subjects and verbs agree?

- Are my verb tenses correct?
- Are my pronoun references clear?
- Have I avoided sexist language?
- Have I used punctuation—commas, colons, semicolons, end marks—to enhance sentence meanings? Have I used uppercase letters correctly?
- Have I checked carefully for appropriate uses of the apostrophe?
- Have I used quotation marks correctly and consistently to indicate someone else's words?
- Have I checked the spelling of any difficult words in a dictionary? If I used a computer spell checker, did I look especially for homonyms and misused (but correctly spelled) words that the computer may have missed?
- Did I check appropriate handbook sections in this book for more detailed explanations of grammar, usage, and mechanics problems in my writing?

Proofreading

Proofreading is a part of the editing process in which you reread your paper particularly for errors. This step in the writing process is best accomplished at two separate stages.

First, proofread your draft after you make revisions and edit but before you produce the final copy for submission. At this point, check for problems in grammar, syntax, spelling, and usage. Proofread the paper a second time just before you turn it in to catch any mistakes you may have overlooked earlier. At this stage, minor revisions can be made neatly on the final copy. However, if you discover major problems that require extensive reworking, you should produce another copy. Do not submit for evaluation a paper containing numerous changes and corrections.

You'll find the following pointers useful as you proofread.

REVIEW CHECKLIST: POINTERS FOR CAREFUL PROOFREADING

- When you proofread, read slowly. Your purpose is to check for errors, and quick readings make errors hard to find.
- Proofread after you have made revisions and editing changes. Do not try to revise and proofread at the same time. Except for glaring errors, which you should correct as you find them, revision and

editing call for concentration on thought and meaning. If you attend to errors when you revise, you won't be focusing on issues related to the content and clarity of your paper. Thus, do proofreading as a separate activity, after you're satisfied with your writing and revising.

- Be familiar with the types of errors that you tend to make and keep them in mind as you proofread. If you tend to write run-on sentences or fragments, proofread your paper for those mistakes especially. Thoughtful students keep a record of their own errors and consult it before proofreading. At the very least, you should look over any comments and corrections that your instructor or your peers have written on other papers that you wrote.

- If you use a computer, be sure to remove wrong words or extra letters when you make spelling changes. Also remember to reformat your text if necessary and to examine your paragraphing: All paragraphs must be indented. Use the cursor as a proofreading aid by moving it from word to word as you proofread; this step will help you slow down your reading.

- If you must make minor revisions on a final copy, use blue or black ink, not pencil. Cross out errors neatly with one line and insert changes directly above the mistake or in the margin if you need more room. Remember, extensive changes on a draft mean that you must do another draft before submitting it. Use a caret (∧) for insertions.

```
                        her
She admonished ∧ brother for being late.
```

After reading his paper over several times, discussing it with friends and his writing teacher, making revisions, and producing new drafts, John finally submitted the following paper to his instructor.

FINAL DRAFT

```
     My roommate, Jim, and I have shared a small apartment        1

for the past two years. On the whole, we get along very well.

We are both students, and we both work, so we don't spend much

time together; but when we do, we cooperate. Jim, who is good

at it, does most of the cooking; I do most of the cleaning.

We find the arrangement satisfactory. And I like Jim. He is
```

generous, witty, honest. Our two-year association has, for the most part, been a good one. But Jim has one shortcoming that irritates me: He doesn't close things.

2   Jim, for example, almost never closes a drawer or a closet door, and his failure to do so is often a source of embarrassment to me. The problem is that I am compulsively neat, and Jim, I'm sorry to say, is a slob. It seems never to have occurred to him that the contents of a drawer could be organized. When he does his laundry, he just empties his bag of clean clothes into a drawer--white tube socks, shorts, a rainbow of T-shirts with college crests, pajamas, graying handkerchiefs. When the drawer is full, he begins filling the next one. Then when he needs clean socks or a shirt, he rolls the contents of the drawer around until he finds what he wants, often leaving rejected items hanging on the edge of the drawer. His clothes closet is just as messy as the drawers. He does the same kinds of things in the kitchen. Spatulas, flat-ware, eggbeaters, knives clink together as he pokes through the nearest open drawer to find his favorite tool for beating eggs or mincing onions. If he'd organized the drawer in the first place, the rattle of kitchenware wouldn't disturb my study time before every meal. Since Jim doesn't close drawers or closets, our apartment usually looks like the site of a rummage sale at closing time. The appearance offends my neat soul and embarrasses me when friends visit us.

3   The irritation I experience because of open drawers and closets, however, is nothing compared with the irritation that Jim's failure to close things in the bathroom produces. Jim's failure to tighten the cap on the shampoo bottle, for example, causes me to completely lose my composure when I am

showering. Because I am in the habit of grasping the shampoo bottle by its cap, a loose cap results in the annoyance of shampoo on my toes instead of in my hair. And because I am a frugal sort, I hate seeing a green puddle of unused shampoo oozing down the drain each day. Jim also often fails to close the bathroom door after using the facilities while I shower. Since the bathroom has become warm and steamy during the course of my shower, the cold draft of morning air chills and distresses me, and the idea that he has been so thoughtless bothers me.

When that frigid air blasts my wet body, my irritation **4** with Jim reaches its peak. Nevertheless, because he is such a great guy and because I know his failure to close things is, in the scheme of human problems, just a minor bad habit, I try to overlook it. I shut my mouth and take a deep breath. In fact, by learning to deal with this annoyance I think I've learned a little about how to handle the frustrations of some of my friends' strange habits in general. I keep a good sense of humor and I hold my temper. After all, I'd rather have opened closets and drawers than a door closed on friendship.

EXERCISE

How does John's intermediate draft compare and contrast with the first draft? What advice did he take from the peer critique? What other changes did he make?

EXERCISE

How does John's final draft compare and contrast with his intermediate draft? What additions has he made? How has he improved the level of detail in the intermediate draft? How has he improved the structure of his paragraphs? Where has he eliminated unnecessary words and sentences?

A Brief Note on Style

Your paper should be readable. We realize, of course, that a polished style doesn't just happen when some English teacher calls for it, and we have devoted Part Five of this book to a lengthy discussion of style. But for starters—even before your teacher subjects you to a rigorous consideration of stylistic elements—you might find it helpful to study the "Miscellaneous Do's and Don'ts" on pages 594–596.

Methods of Development

In Part One we considered the general requirements for a good paper: It must have a limited subject, a purpose, and a thesis; it must support the thesis; and it must be organized. In Part Two we look at the requirements for particular kinds of papers.

Many writing assignments call for specific methods of development. In a psychology class, for example, you might be asked to **compare and contrast** psychosis and neurosis. In a history class, you might be asked to trace the **process** by which the Bolsheviks took power after the Russian Revolution. In a sociology class, you might be asked to **classify** the groups that make up a community, taking into consideration the level of income, education, taste, and social practices of each group. Each of these assignments requires a specific method of development, and Part Two of the text shows you how to meet these requirements.

Other writing assignments, though they may not call for specific methods, profit from an intelligent combination of the methods of development. A definition, for instance, might require the use of comparisons, examples, and cause-and-effect methods. Thus, even though we have, for the purposes of discussion, arbitrarily established separate methods, we recognize that, more often than not, these methods are combined in writing.

We also recognize that our "rules" about methods of development are not sacred, even though we often deliver them as if we believe they are. But we have discovered from our own students that at least some clearly stated guidelines are helpful. As you gain practice, you will discover the exceptions to these guidelines that work for you.

CHAPTER
6

Description

When most students receive an assignment like "Write a **description** of a person, place, or thing" (a car, a wedding, a painting, or a temper tantrum), their first impulse is often to describe what the person, place, or thing looks like. Although many excellent descriptions do just that, in deciding on your subject and how to treat it, you don't need to limit your choices so severely. Most good descriptive writing appeals to the reader's senses, and sight is only one of our five senses. For example, an essay titled "Good Old Franks and Beans" would describe taste; "Nighttime Noises" would describe sound; "Real Men Don't Use Cologne" would describe smell; and "Kids Need Cuddling (and So Do I)" would stress how good it feels to be cuddled—the sense of touch. A piece of descriptive writing also may explore more than one of the senses: The glories of franks and beans could involve sight and smell as well as taste, for example. Good description, moreover, can describe feelings or behavior with little or no direct concentration on the senses as such. You might describe the rudeness of Joe or the snobbishness of Susan, your fear of crowds or your love of travel. Strong specific writing (see pages 37–41) is filled with life, and sensory appeal is likely to be built right in.

But how can you apply the principles of good writing that this book has advocated to a descriptive paper? What special elements characterize a well-written descriptive paper? What special difficulties and temptations do you need to avoid? Although all writing involves an elusive process, the following guidelines for descriptive writing should be helpful.

Writing Your Descriptive Paper

■ *Don't take inventory. You must have a thesis.*   Periodically, shopkeepers need to take inventory. They itemize every article in their store so that they will know which have sold well or poorly and therefore will be able to order future goods intelligently. This procedure is vital to business survival, but if you try to include every piece of information you have on your subject in a descriptive theme, you are inviting disaster.

The writer who takes inventory may begin a theme this way:

```
My friend Judy is twenty years old. She is a solid C student.

She has black hair, brown eyes, and weighs 115 pounds. Her fam-

ily is comfortably middle class. Judy is very nearsighted but is

vain about her appearance and often does not wear her glasses.

She's been my friend for many years, and I like her a lot.
```

This paragraph is simply a random collection of stray facts. No logic, no principle, seems to be at work here except the desire to get everything in—to take inventory. But getting everything in is a task that has no end; if the writer feels Judy's grades are worth mentioning, why decide not to mention the titles of the books she has read over the past year? Why decide that her grades are worth mentioning in the first place—or her weight, or her eyesight, or her family? Why are twenty thousand other facts about Judy not in the paper—the presents she received on her last birthday, her height, the name of her optometrist? If the writer is only taking inventory, all facts are of equal importance, which means in effect that no facts are of any importance.

A descriptive theme needs a thesis. This statement will come as no surprise to you, but it has many specific consequences. It means that you must give up the effort to tell your reader everything. It means that you must think of your paper not as "A Description of Judy," but as an attempt to prove that "Judy is terribly vain," or "Many people think that Judy is self-centered, but she has a lot of fine qualities," or "Judy has no remarkable traits of any kind, and I wonder why she has been my best friend for so many years." It means that you must choose only the descriptive details that are connected to your thesis; if it will break your heart to omit a colorful but irrelevant detail, you must change your thesis to make the detail relevant. Sometimes, of course, a simple change in phrasing can turn a seemingly irrelevant detail into something significant, and your thesis can remain unchanged. Notice how a thesis and a few additional phrases can transform the mess about Judy into a coherent start for a potentially effective paper.

```
There is nothing at all special about my friend Judy.

Judy is such a completely ordinary twenty-year-old woman that
```

I often wonder how our friendship has lasted so long and
stayed so warm.

    Just for starters, consider these totally ordinary facts
about her. Physically, she has absolutely undistinguished
black hair and brown eyes, stands an average 5 feet 4 inches,
and weighs an average 115 pounds. Scholastically, she is a
solid C student. By solid I <u>mean</u> solid. In two years at college, I can't recall her once getting a daring C- or an exciting C+. Her family--you guessed it--is comfortably middle
class, not too rich and not too poor. Even in her little
flaws, Judy is just what you'd expect. Like so many people of
her age, she tends to be vain about personal appearance and
all too frequently tries to get by without her glasses, even
though she's very nearsighted.

■ *Use lively, specific details.*   The most effective way of communicating an
immediate sense of your subject is to use specific details—and a lot of them.
Don't spend as much time telling your reader that a room is old and neglected as
you do telling about the squeaky floorboard next to the door, the lint collected in
the coils of the radiator, the window that needs to be propped up with a sooty
stick of wood. If you do the job with details, the sense of age and neglect will
come through. In many ways, the more precise the detail, the greater its potential for arousing the attention of your reader. Nothing should be beneath your
notice. The condition of a man's fingernails, the name of the store where a
woman buys her clothes, or a broken traffic light on a street corner can convey as
much information about a man, a woman, or a neighborhood—and convey it
more interestingly—than any number of generalized comments.

■ *Choose a principle of organization that presents the descriptive details in a
logical sequence.*   This suggestion means that you should have some way of
determining what comes first and what comes next. The particular organizing
principle you select makes little difference as long as it helps create a coherent
paper. In describing a snowstorm, for instance, you might organize by **time,** presenting the storm from the first hesitant flakes, through the massive downfall,
to the Christmas-card quietness at the end of the storm. In describing a landscape, you might organize by **space,** beginning with the objects farthest from the
observer and working your way closer. A physical description of a person could
go from top to bottom or bottom to top.

Fortunately, not all principles of organization have to be this rigid. A landscape description could be built by progressing from the most ordinary details to the least ordinary details. If the top-to-bottom approach to a description of a person strikes you as dull or inappropriate, you might organize the paper by unattractive features and attractive features or first impressions and second impressions. The important consideration is that some clear principle is needed to give structure to the paper.

Rules mean nothing, of course, until they are applied. What do you think of the student papers that follow?

Student Writing: Description

In the selection below a student uses description to explore the relation between his father's working life and his own. Annotations in the margin point to key features of the essay, particularly the elements of description that enhance the writing.

Nick Fiscina

Dad's Disappointment

As a kid of fifteen, I'll never forget the first time I worked along with my father in the attic of our old house one hot summer afternoon. Dad spent most of his life as a construction worker, and I saw then how disappointing this existence was to him.   1

Thesis statement

As we worked together to finish the attic by putting up insulation on the bare wooden beams of the roof, the smell of dust and perspiration filled the air. In the large gray room bits of paint and plaster hung loose on the walls. As if in another world, Dad lifted a large black bag of insulation onto his left shoulder and lumbered to the wooden ladder. Climbing it, he raised up the insulation in his large hands, brown and scarred, and waited without a word for me to   2

Transition to opening paragraph: "As we worked together to finish the attic"

Sensory details. Examples:
Sight: bare wooden beams; large hands, brown and scarred; snowy white powder
Sound: staples clicked loudly
Smell: dust and perspiration
Touch: burned and scratched

staple the substance in place. His fingers held the material firmly as the staples clicked loudly, joining the insulation to the roof beams. Dad's nails were broken and dirty and small freckles spread beneath the graying hairs on the backs of his hands. As he held the insulation without talking, streams of burning dust fell on us, covering our arms and faces, and in the curly strands of black hair that hung on Dad's forehead there was a snowy-white layer of fine powder. Although it burned and scratched me, nothing bothered Dad's toughened, tanned skin.

Transition to previous paragraph: "grim, silent efforts"

As I watched his grim, silent efforts, it passed through my mind that my father had a teaching degree from a university in the old country, Italy. I asked him, maybe too harshly as I think about this moment so many years ago, why he got into construction work if he had qualifications as a teacher. He remained silent for a long time. His massive arms hung at his sides and circles of sweat stained his brown shirt. After a while a voice filled with defeat broke into the dust-filled air. "Well, you see, Nicola," he said, "in life you make the best you can with what you have. I have to work with my hands to keep the family going." It really surprised me that my father should have such an attitude. This man I often hated for his angry temper and harsh words seemed very human to me. When I looked into his hard brown eyes gazing sadly past me, and watched the crow's feet at the comers wrinkle in a squint, I saw that he had accepted the life of a construction worker with disappointment in spite of success at it.

3

Sensory details communicate an immediate sense of the subject.

Spoken words animate the subject.

Closing sentence to paragraph 3 captures the essence of the moment.

A family man myself with two young boys of my own, I've now had my fill of construction work. I earn a living at it, but I too feel its disappointments. The conditions are harsh, the work is hard, and there is no security. I shudder to think of my sons writing an essay like this about me fifteen years from now. I can't accept my father's view of things: simply making the best you can with what you have. I want something better and more challenging, and I'm willing to sacrifice what I have to achieve it. That's why I'm enrolled in this community college course for medical technology, which, I believe, will be a more fulfilling career. Though I still nail insulation to roofbeams and do other jobs with my hands, I look forward to a better life for my family and me.

4

Conclusion links to introduction and thesis sentence.

➤ **FOR WRITING OR DISCUSSION**

1. What is the writer's thesis? Does he keep the thesis in mind through the body of the paper? How do you know?
2. What details of the writer's father do you find particularly compelling and original? To which senses do the images you like seem to appeal?
3. How has the writer managed to convey his father's disappointment other than in the direct statement in the opening paragraph?
4. How is this essay an example of descriptive detail arranged chronologically?
5. The closing paragraph moves off the topic of the writer's father and focuses on the writer himself. What is your reaction to this conclusion? Does it violate the thesis, or does it apply the thesis to a new frame of reference? Support your opinion.
6. Write a short descriptive paper focusing on some relative who, through his or her words or actions, gave you some special insight into that person's character. Use concrete sensory detail to give the reader a snapshot of your relative.

Rosemary J. Sexton

The Near West Side Way Back When

The most remarkable thing about growing up in our neigh-   1
borhood was that it was so self-contained, so self-sufficient.
Everything we needed was available within two city blocks.

At the center was Rosky and Obert's, a big old-fashioned   2
pharmacy with a real soda fountain. Unfortunately, sodas were
expensive and frivolous. My mother only took us there for
prescription medicines.

Two doors down from the corner was Hanna's Five and Dime,   3
and it literally was a five and dime. Hanna's was a dark,
narrow store jam-packed with all sorts of mysterious little
gadgets, rubber toys, and five-cent candy bars. To a seven-
year-old girl it was the most marvelous place on earth. If I
had a nickel, and occasionally I did, I always spent it at
Hanna's.

A little farther down the street was the bowling alley,   4
situated directly across the street from my house. This bowling alley, along with Joe Peep's Pizzeria, was our neighborhood's version of nightlife. From my bedroom window I could
see guys and girls arriving in their Chevies and Fords. The
girls wore lots of black eyeliner and pale pink lipstick, and
they ratted their hair. The guys wore Banlon shirts, workies
(a kind of Chinos), and wing tip shoes. On summer nights, as I
lay in bed, I would hear them calling to each other across the
parking lot. The sound was at once recklessly exciting, as I
imagined their teenaged lives were, and faintly reassuring--
this night was the same as other nights before it.

5   At the other end of the block was the business district. This area housed a post office, shoe repair, jeweler, dime store, drugstore, dry goods store, antique store, credit union, hardware store, pizzeria, and furrier.

6   A trip to this farther removed section of our neighborhood was like a trip downtown. The dime store here was much bigger than Hanna's Five and Dime. The counters were lower, the goods more carefully displayed. There was even a lunch counter where you could order a grilled cheese sandwich and a soda for a quarter. The dime store was reserved for special shopping such as for birthdays and Christmas.

7   Usually we would go to Haas's Dry Goods Store to buy only one thing at a time: a pair of dark socks for my fourteen-year-old brother, a white blouse with a Peter Pan collar for my sister, a pair of hose for my grandmother. All these mundane items were to be found at Hass's.

8   Wlady's Shoe Repair was always a favorite place of mine because Mr. Wlady had lots of fascinating pictures on the walls of dogs: dogs playing cards, dogs dressed as Keystone Kops, gangster dogs. I never tired of looking at those dogs.

9   The other store that completed our neighborhood was not on our block but two blocks over. For all our everyday needs--Millbrook bread, milk, baloney--White Front's Grocery was the place to go. The store was especially appealing to my mother because they let her buy food on account. The ledger that recorded everyone's account was a small, dirty, gray binder filled with dog-eared pages showing each family's bill. I would always feel nervous when my mother said, "Put it on my bill." As well as I can remember, though, they only refused her once. I liked White Front's because in the summer they sold lemon ice, in the winter Christmas trees.

This once wonderful neighborhood now houses a convenience 10
store, a used-car lot, and an abundance of empty storefronts. I
don't get around there very often anymore. This is not because
I fear the area, which is now overrun with drug addicts and
prostitutes. There is still a familiarity about these streets.
But I feel such an enormous loss and emptiness when I see what
has happened there. The happy little self-supporting community
of my childhood exists only in my memory, and therefore a part
of me has died.

➤ FOR WRITING OR DISCUSSION

1. What principle of organization (see pages 107–108) has the writer followed to present the descriptive details?
2. Where are the details most effective? Where are they least effective? Are there any business establishments we want to know more about?
3. The paper describes a neighborhood as it was about twenty-five years ago. What details dramatize the sense of "times gone by"?
4. Write a descriptive paper based on a past-versus-present topic. You may choose to describe a person, a house, a block, a school, a neighborhood, a holiday, or some similar topic. As an alternative assignment, you may describe a feeling of your own that has changed over time—your attitude toward school, parents, marriage, or religion, for example.

Models of Writing

The examples of description that follow show professional writers at work. Note how description never becomes merely a piece of pretty writing but communicates insights and ideas.

GEORGE EPPLEY

Sister Clarissa

The 100 or more essays I just finished correcting for my English 101 classes are a 1
mixed bag: some outstanding, most average, and the rest fair to poor. I get impatient with students who keep writing run-on sentences and incoherent sentences. Sometimes I have to pause and reflect over a glass of juice or a sip of coffee. I resolve not to bleed so much red ink over their papers. And I remind myself that most of my

students never encountered an English teacher like Sister Clarissa who taught me in the sixth grade at Our Lady of Angels School in the 1930s.

2   She towered only over the runts in the first four grades. Her face was almost chalk white. Beneath her coal-black eyebrows were sunken sockets that housed the most piercing eyes I had ever seen.

3   In those days one did not bring apples to school for the teachers but little hand clickers that were contained in each box of Buster Brown shoes. A school bell signaled the start and end of the school day. But often there were occasions when 700 kids had to move from the school to the church and then back again. This was done efficiently and silently. The only sounds that could be heard were those of the Buster Brown clickers which the sisters held in their hands. One click, march; two clicks, stop; three clicks, genuflect; four clicks, be seated; and five clicks, rise.

4   Had we been the U.S. Army in World War II, we could have marched across the Rhine and surprised the Germans, who would have mistaken those clicks for crickets.

5   Sister Clarissa was good with the clicker, but the grammar book was her forte. She held it in her left hand. In her right hand she usually carried a ruler or a pointer. If someone would say "them books"—"I ain't"—"she don't"—"between you and I"—"that there blackboard"—Sister would come flying down the aisle and rap the barbarian across the knuckles or the back of the head.

6   If a student could not look at a sentence on the blackboard and identify the subject, verb, direct and indirect objects, Sister would sometimes grip the student's jaw with her right hand and the back of his head with the left and then slowly shake it. From experience I know that this maneuver greatly increases the powers of memory. Frequently she kept us after school to go over declensions, conjugations and misspelled words.

7   What happiness was ours when we passed from the sixth to the seventh grade. We were free of Sister Clarissa. That summer, however, she was promoted to teach the seventh grade. We questioned why a merciful and loving God did not take Sister Clarissa to himself.

8   Somehow we survived her seventh grade. Shortly before we began the eighth grade, word spread through the neighborhood that Sister Clarissa was returning as principal. She was relieved of all teaching duties except one. She would teach grammar to students in the eighth grade. We envied our Protestant friends who went to public school.

9   Surprisingly, the eighth grade class with Sister was fun. No one's knuckles were rapped and no one's head was caught in that famous head grip. We thought that Sister had mellowed. Only later did we realize that we had improved.

10   After graduation, seven of us went to Cathedral Latin School for boys. It was on the other side of the city, and it took two long streetcar rides to reach it. But the school had an excellent academic reputation and an outstanding football team and band. On the first day we took the placement tests in English, science and math with 300 freshmen from all parts of the city.

11   A few days later a booming voice came over the public address system: "All freshman boys from Our Lady of Angels School report immediately to the principal's office." We went down to Father Lawrence Yeske's office. In that all-male school, he had the nickname "the Moose." We fully expected him to bellow at us for our disgraceful streetcar behavior. That day, however, the Moose was a lamb.

"Come in, boys," he said. When we were all assembled around his desk, he asked,   12
"Who taught you English at Our Lady of Angels School?"

"Sister Clarissa. Why?"   13

"Well," he said, "Sister Clarissa must be a tremendous teacher because in the Eng-   14
lish exam all of you placed at the top of the freshman class."

We assured him that she was indeed quite a teacher. We had the good grace not to   15
mention the bumps on our heads and the bruised knuckles. We left his office proud and
happy and grateful that in matters grammatical Sister Clarissa had explained it all to us.

➤ **FOR WRITING OR DISCUSSION**

1. What is the primary principle of organization used in "Sister Clarissa"?
2. This essay is concerned mainly with describing how Sister Clarissa taught
   grammar. Is the description of the "clickers" related to the rest of the essay, or
   is it merely an amusing irrelevancy?
3. Write a paper describing the best or worst teacher you ever had.

VIRGINIA WOOLF

The Death of the Moth

Moths that fly by day are not properly to be called moths; they do not excite that   1
pleasant sense of dark autumn nights and ivy-blossom which the commonest yellow underwing asleep in the shadow of the curtain never fails to rouse in us. They are
hybrid creatures, neither gay like butterflies not sombre like their own species. Nevertheless the present specimen, with his narrow hay-coloured wings, fringed with a tassel of
the same colour, seemed to be content with life. It was a pleasant morning, mid-Septem-
ber, mild, benignant, yet with a keener breath than that of the summer months. The
plough was already scoring the field opposite the window, and where the share had
been, the earth was pressed flat and gleamed with moisture. Such vigour came following
in from the fields and the down beyond that it was difficult to keep the eyes strictly turned
upon the book. The rooks too were keeping one of their annual festivities; soaring round
the tree-tops until it looked as if a vast net with thousands of black knots in it has been
cast up into the air; which, after a few moments sank slowly down upon the trees until
every twig seemed to have a knot at the end of it. Then, suddenly, the net would be
thrown into the air again in a wider circle this time, with the utmost clamour and vocifer-
ation, as though to be thrown into the air and settle slowly down upon the tree-tops were
a tremendously exciting experience.

The same energy which inspired the rooks, the ploughmen, the horses, and even, it   2
seemed, the lean bare-backed downs, sent the moth fluttering from side to side of his
square of the window-pane. One could not help watching him. One was, indeed, conscious of a queer feeling of pity for him. The possibilities of pleasure seemed that morning so enormous and so various that to have only a moth's part in life, and a day moth's
at that, appeared a hard fate, and his zest in enjoying his meagre opportunities to the
full, pathetic. He flew vigorously to one corner of his compartment, and, after waiting

there a second, flew across to the other. What remained for him but to fly to a third corner and then to a fourth? That was all he could do, in spite of the size of the downs, the width of the sky, the far-off smoke of the houses, and the romantic voice, now and then, of steamer out at sea. What he could do he did. Watching him, it seemed as if a fibre, very thin but pure, of the enormous energy of the world had been thrust into his frail and diminutive body. As often as he crossed the pane, I could fancy that a thread of vital light became visible. He was little or nothing but life.

3   Yet, because he was so small, and so simple a form of the energy that was rolling in at the open window and driving its way through so many narrow and intricate corridors in my own brain and in those of other human beings, there was something marvelous as well as pathetic about him. It was as if someone had taken a tiny bead of pure life and decking it as lightly as possible with down and feathers, had set it dancing and zigzagging to show us the true nature of life. Thus displayed one could not get over the strangeness of it. One is apt to forget all about life, seeing it humped and bossed and garnished and cumbered so that it has to move with the greatest circumspection and dignity. Again, the thought of all that life might have been had he been born in any other shape caused one to view his simple activities with a kind of pity.

4   After a time, tired by his dancing apparently, he settled on the window ledge in the sun, and the queer spectacle being at an end, I forgot about him. Then, looking up, my eye was caught by him. He was trying to resume his dancing, but seemed either so stiff or so awkward that he could only flutter to the bottom of the window-pane; and when he tried to fly across it he failed. Being intent on other matters I watched these futile attempts for a time without thinking, unconsciously waiting for him to resume his flight, as one waits for a machine, that has stoped momentarily, to start again without considering the reason for its failure. After perhaps a seventh attempt he slipped from the wooden ledge and fell, fluttering his wings, onto his back on the window-sill. The helplessness of his attitude roused me. It flashed upon me that he was in difficulties; he could no longer raise himself, his legs struggled vainly. But, as I stretched out a pencil, meaning to help him to right himself, it came over me that the failure and awkwardness were the approach of death. I laid the pencil down again.

5   The legs agitated themselves once more. I looked as if for the enemy against which he struggled. I looked out of doors. What had happened there? Presumably it was midday, and work in the fields had stopped. Stillness and quiet had replaced the previous animation. The birds had taken themselves off to feed in the brooks. The horses stood still. Yet the power was there all the same, massed outside indifferent, impersonal, not attending to anything in particular. Somehow it was opposed to the little hay-coloured moth. It was useless to try to do anything. One could only watch the extraordinary efforts made by those tiny legs against an oncoming doom which could, had it chosen, have submerged an entire city, not merely a city, but masses of human beings; nothing, I knew, had any chance against death. Nevertheless after a pause of exhaustion the legs fluttered again. It was superb this last protest, and so frantic that he succeeded at last in righting himself. One's sympathies, or course, were all on the side of life. Also, when there was nobody to care or to know, this gigantic effort on the part of an insignificant little moth, against a power of such magnitude, to retain what no one else valued or desired to keep, moved one strangely. Again, somehow, one saw life, a pure bead. I lifted the pencil again, useless though I

knew it to be. But even as I did so, the unmistakable tokens of death showed themselves. The body relaxed, and instantly grew stiff. The struggle was over. The insignificant little creature now knew death. As I looked at the dead moth, this minute wayside triumph of so great a force over so mean an antagonist filled me with wonder. Just as life had been strange a few minutes before, so death was now as strange. The moth having righted himself now lay most decently and uncomplainingly composed. O yes, he seemed to say, death is stronger than I am.

➤ FOR WRITING OR DISCUSSION

1. Woolf's purpose is more than just to describe the moth's death. What is that purpose?
2. Concrete sensory language, down to the minutest detail in some cases, makes the selection come alive for the reader. Which details can you picture most clearly in your mind? Which do you think are most original?
3. What figurative expressions—simile, metaphor, and personification—do you note here? What does the writer achieve by using them? What, for example, is the effect of the comparison between the birds and a net in paragraph 1?
4. What contrast does the writer make in the outdoor scene in paragraphs 1 and 5? What does Woolf achieve with this contrast? How does it connect to the moth's state?
5. Write a description of some element of nature that you have observed close up—for example, an insect, an animal, or a plant—in its environment. Perhaps you too have witnessed the death of a creature, as Woolf has. Use concrete sensory detail to paint a clear scene for your reader.

ROGER ANGELL

On the Ball

It weighs just over five ounces and measures between 2.86 and 2.94 inches in diameter. It is made of a composition-cork nucleus encased in two thin layers of rubber, one black and one red, surrounded by a hundred and twenty-one yards of tightly wrapped blue-gray wool yarn, forty-five yards of white wool yarn, fifty-three more yards of blue-gray wool yarn, a hundred and fifty yards of fine cotton yarn, a coat of rubber cement, and a cowhide (formerly horsehide) exterior, which is held together with two hundred and sixteen slightly raised red cotton stitches. Printed certifications, endorsements, and outdoor advertising spherically attest to its authenticity. Like most institutions, it is considered inferior in its present form to its ancient archetypes, and in this case the complaint is probably justified: on occasion in recent years it has actually been known to come apart under the demands of its brief but rigorous active career. Baseballs are assembled and hand-stitched in Taiwan (before this year the work was done in Haiti, and before 1973 in Chicopee, Massachusetts), and contemporary pitchers claim that there is a tangible variation in the size and feel of the balls that now come into play in a single game; a true peewee is treasured by hurlers, and its departure from the premises, by fair means or foul, is secretly mourned. But never mind: any baseball is beautiful. No other small package comes as close to the ideal in design and utility. It is a perfect object for a man's hand. Pick it up and it instantly suggests its purpose; it is meant to be thrown a considerable distance—thrown hard and with precision. Its feel and heft are the beginning of the sport's critical dimensions; if it were a fraction of an inch larger or smaller, a few centigrams heavier or lighter, the game of baseball would be utterly different. Hold a baseball in your hand. As it happens, this one is not brand new. Here, just to one side of the curved surgical welt of stitches, there is a pale-green grass smudge, darkening on one edge almost to black—the mark of an old infield play, a tough grounder now lost in memory. Feel the ball, turn it over in your hand; hold it across the seam or the other way, with the seam just to the side of your middle finger. Speculation stirs. You want to get outdoors and throw this spare and sensual object to somebody, or, at the very least, watch somebody else throw it. The game has begun. . . .

➤ **FOR WRITING OR DISCUSSION**

1. What are the two meanings of the essay's title, "On the Ball"?
2. When were you certain that the subject being discussed is a baseball?
3. Notice the number of facts in the first two sentences. What purpose do the facts serve in the development of the description?
4. What is meant by the sentence that begins, "Like most institutions, it is considered inferior in its present form . . . "? What does the sentence show about the author's attitude toward contemporary manufacturing techniques? How does the sentence telling where baseballs were once made support that attitude?
5. What is the thesis of the selection?
6. At what point does the selection cease to be factual and become a matter of opinion?
7. At what point does the author bring the reader into the description? Why does he do so?
8. Do the sentences beginning with "Hold a baseball in your hand" make you feel the ball? Why or why not?
9. Write a paper describing a single small object—for example, a football, an ashtray, a kitchen utensil, a wristwatch. Try to use both factual and personal details to make your reader see or feel the object as you do.

ALAN DEVOE

Our Enemy, the Cat

1   We tie bright ribbons around their necks, and occasionally little tinkling bells, and we affect to think that they are as sweet and vapid as the coy name "kitty" by which we call them would imply. It is a curious illusion. For, purring beside our fireplaces and pattering along our back fences, we have got a wild beast as uncowed and uncorrupted as any under heaven.

It is five millenniums since we snared the wild horse and broke his spirit to our whim, and for centuries beyond counting we have been able to persuade the once-free dog to fawn and cringe and lick our hands. But a man must be singularly blind with vanity to fancy that in the three—ten?—thousand years during which we have harbored cats beneath our rooftrees, we have succeeded in reducing them to any such insipid estate. It is not a "pet" (that most degraded of creatures) that we have got in our house, whatever we may like to think. It is a wild beast; and there adheres to its sleek fur no smallest hint of the odor of humanity.

It would be a salutary thing if those who write our simpering verses and tales about "tabby-sit-by-the-fire" could bring themselves to see her honestly, to look into her life with eyes unblurred by wishful sentiment. It would be a good thing—to start at the beginning—to follow her abroad into the moonlight on one of those raw spring evenings when the first skunk cabbages are thrusting their veined tops through the melting snow and when the loins of catdom are hot with lust.

The love-play of domestic creatures is mostly a rather comic thing, and loud are the superior guffaws of rustic humans to see the clumsy, fumbling antics that take place in the kennels and the stockpen. But the man had better not laugh who sees cats in their rut. He is looking upon something very like aboriginal passion, untainted by any of the overlaid refinements, suppressions, and modifications that have been acquired by most of mankind's beasts. The mating of cats has neither the bathetic clumsiness of dogs' nor the lumbering ponderousness of cattle's, but—conducted in a lonely secret place, away from human view—is marked by a quick concentrated intensity of lust that lies not far from the borderline of agony. The female, in the tense moment of the prelude, tears with her teeth at her mate's throat, and, as the climax of the creatures' frenzy comes, the lean silky-furred flanks quiver vibrantly as a taut wire. Then quietly, in the spring night, the two beasts go their ways.

It will be usually May before the kittens come; and that episode, too, will take place secretly, in its ancient feline fashion, where no maudlin human eye may see. Great is the pique in many a house when "pussy," with dragging belly and distended dugs, disappears one night—scorning the cushioned maternity-bed that has been prepared for her—and creeps on silent feet to the dankest cranny of the cellar, there in decent aloneness to void her blood and babies. She does not care, any more than a lynx does, or a puma, to be preyed upon while she licks the birth-hoods from her squirming progeny and cleans away the membrane with her rough pink tongue.

A kitten is not a pretty thing at birth. For many days it is a wriggling mite of lumpy flesh and sinew, blind and unaware, making soft sucking noises with its wet, toothless mouth, and smelling of milk. Daily, hourly, the rough tongue of the tabby ministers to it in its helplessness, glossing the baby-fur with viscid spittle, licking away the uncontrolled dung, cleaning away the crumbly pellet of dried blood from its pointed ears. By that tenth or fourteenth day when its eyes wholly unseal, blue and weak in their newness, the infant cat is clean to immaculateness, and an inalienable fastidiousness is deep-lodged in its spirit.

It is now—when the kitten makes its first rushes and sallies from its birthplace, and, with extraordinary gymnastics of its chubby body, encounters chairlegs and human feet and other curious phenomena—that it elicits from many those particular expressions of gurgling delight which we reserve for very tiny fluffy creatures who act very comically. But the infant cat has no coy intent to be amusing. If he is comic, it is only because of the incongruity of so demure a look and so wild a heart. For in that furry head of his, grim and ancient urges are already dictating.

8   Hardly larger than a powder-puff, he crouches on the rug and watches a fleck of lint. His little blue eyes are bright, and presently his haunches tense and tremble. The tiny body shivers in an ague of excitement. He pounces, a little clumsily perhaps, and pinions the fleeting lint-fleck with his paws. In the fractional second of that lunge, the ten small needles of his claws have shot from their sheaths of flesh and muscle. It is a good game; but it is not an idle one. It is the kitten's introduction into the ancient ritual of the kill. Those queer little stiff-legged rushings and prancings are the heritage of an old death dance, and those jerkings of his hind legs, as he rolls on his back, are the preparation for that day when—in desperate conflict with a beast bigger than himself— he will win the fight by the time-old feline technique of disembowelment. Even now, in his early infancy, he is wholly and inalienably a cat.

9   While he is still young he has already formulated his attitude toward the human race into whose midst he has been born. It is an attitude not easily described, but com- pounded of a great pride, a great reserve, a towering integrity. It is even to be fancied that there is something in it of a sort of bleak contempt. Solemnly the cat watches these great hulking two-legged creatures into whose strange tribe he has unaccountably been born— and who are so clumsy, so noisy, so vexing to his quiet spirit—and in his feline heart is neither love nor gratitude. He learns to take the food which they give him, to relish the warmth and the comfort and the caresses which they can offer, but these profferments do not persuade his wild mistrustful heart to surrender itself. He will not sell himself, as a dog will, for a scrap of meat; he will not enter into an allegiance. He is unchangeably and incorruptibly a cat, and he will accommodate himself to the ways and spirit of mankind no more than the stern necessity of his unnatural environment requires.

10 Quietly he dozes by the fire or on a lap, and purrs in his happiness because he loves the heat. But let him choose to move, and if any human hand tries to restrain him for more than a moment he will struggle and unsheath his claws and lash out with a furi- ous hate. Let a whip touch him and he will slink off in a sullen fury, uncowed and out- raged and unrepenting. For the things which man gives to him are not so precious or essential that he will trade them for his birthright, which is the right to be himself—a furred four-footed being of ancient lineage, loving silence and aloneness and the night, and esteeming the smell of rat's blood above any possible human excellence.

11 He may live for perhaps ten years; occasionally even for twenty. Year after year he drinks the daily milk that is put faithfully before him, dozes in laps whose contours please him, accepts with casual pleasure the rubbing of human fingers under his chin—and with- draws, in every significant hour of his life, as far away from human society as he is able. Far from the house, in a meadow or a woods if he can find one, he crouches immobile for hours, his lithe body flattened concealingly in the grass or ferns, and waits for prey.

12 With a single pounce he can break a rabbit's spine as though it were a brittle twig. When he has caught a tawny meadow mouse or a mole, he has, too, the ancient cat- ecstasy of toying and playing with it, letting it die slowly, in a long agony, for his

amusement. Sometimes, in a dim remembrance from the remote past of his race, he may bring home his kill, but mostly he returns to the house as neat and demure as when he left, with his chops licked clean of blood.

Immaculate, unobtrusive, deep withdrawn into himself, he passes through the long   13
years of his enforced companionship with humanity. He takes from his masters (how absurd a word it is) however much they may care to give him; of himself he surrenders nothing. However often he be decked with ribbons and cuddled and petted and made much over, his cold pride never grows less, and his grave calm gaze—tinged perhaps with a gentle distaste—is never lighted by adoration. To the end he adores only his own gods, the gods of mating, of hunting, and of the lonely darkness.

One day, often with no forewarning whatever, he is gone from the house and never   14
returns. He has felt the presaging shadow of death, and he goes to meet it in the old unchanging way of the wild—alone. A cat does not want to die with the smell of humanity in his nostrils and the noise of humanity in his delicate peaked ears. Unless death strikes very quickly and suddenly, he creeps away to where it is proper that a proud wild beast should die—not on one of man's rugs or cushions, but in a lonely quiet place, with his muzzle pressed against the cold earth.

➤ FOR WRITING OR DISCUSSION

1. "Our Enemy, the Cat" is written with a strong thesis. Express the thesis in your own words.
2. How adequately does the title convey the thesis?
3. How does the author try to refute those who feel that cats are really fond of people?
4. Why does the author appear to despise dogs?
5. What principle of organization determines the order in which the descriptive details are presented?
6. Write an essay called "Our Friend, the Cat" in which you argue the opposite point of view to Devoe's.

HAVING YOUR SAY

Using description, write an essay in which you attack some conventional point of view, as Devoe has. ("Most people think that cats are sweet and cute," he asserts, "but most people are wrong.") You might choose to attack our stereotypical notions of babies, homeless people, a "great" book or movie, dogs, Friday night parties, or cleaning the house—these are just some examples. Pick your own topic and convince your readers that your view is worth attention.

JUDITH ORTIZ COFER

Grandmother's Room

1   My grandmother's house is like a chambered nautilus; it has many rooms, yet it is not a mansion. Its proportions are small and its design simple. It is a house that has grown organically, according to the needs of its inhabitants. To all of us in the family it is known as *la casa de Mamá*. It is the place of our origin; the stage for our memories and dreams of Island life.

2   I remember how in my childhood it sat on stilts; this was before it had a downstairs. It rested on its perch like a great blue bird, not a flying sort of bird, more like a nesting hen, but with spread wings. Grandfather had built it soon after their marriage. He was a painter and housebuilder by trade, a poet and meditative man by nature. As each of their eight children were born, new rooms were added. After a few years, the paint did not exactly match, nor the materials, so that there was a chronology to it, like the rings of a tree, and Mamá could tell you the history of each room in her casa, and thus the genealogy of the family along with it.

3   Her room is the heart of the house. Though I have seen it recently, and both woman and room have diminished in size, changed by the new perspective of my eyes, now capable of looking over countertops and tall beds, it is not this picture I carry in my memory of Mamá's casa. Instead, I see her room as a queen's chamber where a small woman loomed large, a throne-room with a massive four-poster bed in its center which stood taller than a child's head. It was on this bed where her own children had been born that the smallest grandchildren were allowed to take naps in the afternoons; here too was where Mamá secluded herself to dispense private advice to her daughters, sitting on the edge of the bed, looking down at whoever sat on the rocker where generations of babies had been sung to sleep. To me she looked like a wise empress right out of the fairy tales I was addicted to reading.

4   Though the room was dominated by the mahogany four-posters, it also contained all of Mamá's symbols of power. On her dresser instead of cosmetics there were jars filled with herbs: *yerba buena, yerba mala*,[1] the making of purgatives and teas to which we were all subjected during childhood crises. She had a steaming cup for anyone who could not, or would not, get up to face life on any given day. If the acrid aftertaste of her cures for malingering did not get you out of bed, then it was time to call *el doctor*.

5   And there was the monstrous chifforobe she kept locked with a little golden key she did not hide. This was a test of her dominion over us; though my cousins and I wanted a look inside that massive wardrobe more than anything, we never reached for that little key lying on top of her Bible on the dresser. This was also where she placed her earrings and rosary at night. God's word was her security system. This chifforobe was the place where I imagined she kept jewels, satin slippers, and elegant sequined, silk gowns of heart-breaking fineness. I lusted after those imaginary costumes. I had heard that Mamá had been a great beauty in her youth, and the belle of many balls. My

---

[1] Good herbs, bad herbs.

cousins had other ideas as to what she kept in that wooden vault: its secret could be money (Mamá did not hand cash to strangers, banks were out of the question, so there were stories that her mattress was stuffed with dollar bills, and that she buried coins in jars in her garden under rosebushes, or kept them in her inviolate chifforobe); there might be that legendary gun salvaged from the Spanish-American conflict over the Island. We went wild over suspected treasures that we made up simply because children have to fill locked trunks with something wonderful.

On the wall above the bed hung a heavy silver crucifix. Christ's agonized head   6
hung directly over Mamá's pillow. I avoided looking at this weapon suspended over where her head would lay; and on the rare occasions when I was allowed to sleep on that bed, I scooted down to the safe middle of the mattress, where her body's impression took me in like a mother's lap. Having taken care of the obligatory religious decoration with a crucifix, Mamá covered the other walls with objects sent to her over the years by her children in the States. *Los Nueva Yores*[2] were represented by, among other things, a postcard of Niagara Falls from her son Hernán, postmarked, Buffalo, N.Y. In a conspicuous gold frame hung a large color photograph of her daughter Nena, her husband and their five children at the entrance to Disneyland in California. From us she had gotten a black lace fan. Father had brought it to her from a tour of duty with the Navy in Europe (on Sundays she would remove it from its hook on the wall to fan herself at Sunday mass). Each year more items were added as the family grew and dispersed, and every object in the room had a story attached to it, a *cuento* which Mamá would bestow on anyone who received the privilege of a day alone with her. It was almost worth pretending to be sick, though the bitter herb purgatives of the body were a big price to pay for the spirit revivals of her story-telling.

➤ FOR WRITING OR DISCUSSION

1. Ortiz's purpose is more than just to describe her grandmother's room. What is that purpose?
2. Concrete sensory details make the selection come alive for the reader. Which details do you find most vivid and original?
3. The writer uses a number of figurative expressions—similes and metaphors designed to make the scene clear and striking through comparisons. In fact the selection begins with a simile. Why does Ortiz choose the "chambered nautilus" to open the piece? What is a chambered nautilus? What other figures of speech enliven the scene?
4. What do the Spanish words and expressions contribute to the piece?
5. The writer states that her grandmother's room is "the heart of the house." Write a description of a room from your childhood that stands out in your mind as the heart of your house. Make the place come alive to the reader through sensory details.

---

[2] A Puerto Rican expression for the United States.

Readings for Writing

Use the short story and essay that follow as potential topics for descriptive papers of your own.

JOHN COLLIER

The Chaser

1   Alan Austen, as nervous as a kitten, went up certain dark and creaky stairs in the neighborhood of Pell Street, and peered about for a long time on the dim landing before he found the name he wanted written obscurely on one of the doors.

2   He pushed open this door, as he had been told to do, and found himself in a tiny room, which contained no furniture but a plain kitchen table, rocking chair, and an ordinary chair. On one of the dirty buff-colored walls were a couple of shelves, containing in all perhaps a dozen bottles and jars.

3   An old man sat in the rocking chair, reading a newspaper. Alan, without a word, handed him the card he had been given. "Sit down, Mr. Austen," said the old man very politely. "I am glad to make your acquaintance."

4   "Is it true," asked Alan, "that you have a certain mixture that has—er—quite extraordinary effects?"

5   "My dear sir," replied the old man, "my stock in trade is not very large—I don't deal in laxatives and teething mixtures—but such as it is, it is varied. I think nothing I sell has effects which could be precisely described as ordinary."

6   "Well, the fact is—" began Alan.

7   "Here, for example," interrupted the old man, reaching for a bottle from the shelf. "Here is a liquid as colorless as water, almost tasteless, quite imperceptible in coffee, milk, wine, or any other beverage. It is also quite imperceptible to any known method of autopsy."

8   "Do you mean it is a poison?" cried Alan, very much horrified.

9   "Call it cleaning fluid if you like," said the old man indifferently. "Lives need cleaning. Call it a spot-remover. 'Out, damned spot!' Eh? 'Out, brief candle!'"[1]

10   "I want nothing of that sort," said Alan.

11   "Probably it is just as well," said the old man. "Do you know the price of this? For one teaspoonful, which is sufficient, I ask five thousand dollars. Never less. Not a penny less."

12   "I hope all your mixtures are not as expensive," said Alan apprehensively.

---

[1]These lines are from Shakespeare's tragedy *Macbeth*. [Editors' note]

"Oh, dear, no," said the old man. "It would be no good charging that sort of price   13
for a love potion, for example. Young people who need a love potion very seldom have
five thousand dollars. Otherwise they would not need a love potion."

"I'm glad to hear you say so," said Alan.   14

"I look at it like this," said the old man. "Please a customer with one article, and he   15
will come back when he needs another. Even if it is more costly. He will save up for it,
if necessary."

"So," said Alan, "you really do sell love potions?"   16

"If I did not sell love potions," said the old man, reaching for another bottle, "I   17
should not have mentioned the other matter to you. It is only when one is in a position
to oblige that one can afford to be so confidential."

"And these potions," said Alan. "They are not just—just—er—"   18

"Oh, no," said the old man. "Their effects are permanent, and extend far beyond   19
the mere casual impulse. But they include it. Oh, yes, they include it. Bountifully. Insis-
tently. Everlastingly."

"Dear me!" said Alan, attempting a look of scientific detachment. "How very   20
interesting!"

"But consider the spiritual side," said the old man.   21

"I do, indeed," said Alan.   22

"For indifference," said the old man, "they substitute devotion. For scorn, adoration.   23
Give one tiny measure of this to the young lady—its flavor is imperceptible in orange
juice, soup, or cocktails—and however gay and giddy she is, she will change altogether. She'll want nothing but solitude, and you."

"I can hardly believe it," said Alan. "She is so fond of parties."   24

"She will not like them any more," said the old man. "She'll be afraid of the pretty   25
girls you may meet."

"She'll actually be jealous?" cried Alan in a rapture. "Of me?"   26

"Yes, she will want to be everything to you."   27

"She is, already. Only she doesn't care about it."   28

"She will, when she has taken this. She will care intensely. You'll be her sole inter-   29
est in life."

"Wonderful!" cried Alan.   30

"She'll want to know all you do," said the old man. "All that has happened to you   31
during the day. Every word of it. She'll want to know what you are thinking about, why
you smile suddenly, why you are looking sad."

"That is love!" cried Alan.   32

"Yes," said the old man. "How carefully she'll look after you! She'll never allow you   33
to be tired, to sit in a draft, to neglect your food. If you are an hour late, she'll be terrified. She'll think you are killed, or that some siren has caught you."

"I can hardly imagine Diana like that!" cried Alan.   34

"You will not have to use your imagination," said the old man. "And by the way,   35
since there are always sirens, if by any chance you *should*, later on, slip a little, you

need not worry. She will forgive you, in the end. She'll be terribly hurt, of course, but she'll forgive you—in the end."

36   "That will not happen," said Alan fervently.

37   "Of course not," said the old man. "But, if it does, you need not worry. She'll never divorce you. Oh, no! And, of course, she herself will never give you the least grounds for—not divorce, of course—but even uneasiness."

38   "And how much," said Alan, "how much is this wonderful mixture?"

39   "It is not so dear," said the old man, "as the spot remover, as I think we agreed to call it. No. That is five thousand dollars; never a penny less. One has to be older than you are, to indulge in that sort of thing. One has to save up for it."

40   "But the love potion?" said Alan.

41   "Oh, that," said the old man, opening the drawer in the kitchen table, and taking out a tiny, rather dirty-looking phial. "That is just a dollar."

42   "I can't tell you how grateful I am," said Alan, watching him fill it.

43   "I like to oblige," said the old man. "Then customers come back, later in life, when they are rather better off, and want more expensive things. Here you are. You will find it very effective."

44   "Thank you again," said Alan. "Goodbye."

45   "*Au revoir*," said the old man.

➤ FOR WRITING OR DISCUSSION

1. Why does the old man talk about what he calls "cleaning fluid" when Alan is clearly there for something else? Why is the cleaning fluid so expensive? What reason does the old man give for charging so little for the love potion that Alan seeks? Do you believe the old man? Why, or why not?

2. What are some of the predicted effects of the love potion on Alan's beloved, Diana? Why does Collier give us so many details of the potion's outcomes, once applied? How do you think Alan would define love, based on his views expressed here?

3. The old man stresses that "customers come back, later in life" and then finishes the story with, "*Au revoir*," which means "until we meet again." What is the effect of these two statements when taken together? What is the old man suggesting about Alan's love relation with Diana?

4. What are the possible multiple meanings of the title? How do these meanings contribute to the humorous effects of the story?

5. "The Chaser" is written largely in dialog. Description can be your job. Write a paper describing Alan, Diana, or the old man. Show that you have read the story by making use of whatever information is stated or implied. You are free to invent details where the story allows such freedom, but nothing in your paper should contradict clearly established information in the story itself.

DICK FEAGLER

Willie

What do you want to do with Willie Sommervil? His life is in your hands.   1

Obviously, you ought to know a little bit about him before you decide. So let me   2
help you out.

Willie is 36. A black man. A churchgoer. In fact, he sings in the choir. He has three   3
children. They are not with him, but that isn't his fault. That's because of circumstances
beyond his control. He sends them as much money as he can. He hasn't got a lot and
sometimes he works a 15-hour-day to make it.

His work is seasonal. If you want to get fancy about it, you can call him a landscape   4
architect. He cuts lawns and plants flowers. He rakes leaves. He'll do a little painting
for you. He'll clean your gutters. Wash your windows if you want him to.

Most of this is fair-weather work. In the winter, things are leaner for Willie. He'll   5
shovel your driveway or your walk. When he runs short of money, there's a restaurant
that will hire him to wash dishes. Willie won't take a dime of welfare.

He pays his taxes and his Social Security. In the high summer, when work is plenti-   6
ful, he hires neighborhood kids to help him out. Oh, and he worked himself up from
total poverty. He started his business with a borrowed lawn mower. Now he owns a
pickup truck, three lawn mowers and a house.

I feel I'm losing you. Virtue does not hold an audience. The little devices we use to   7
capture your attention are not present, so far, in Willie's story.

So I'll tell you that Willie is in danger. Real and immediate danger. Since I told you   8
he is black, you might be tempted to make certain stereotypical assumptions about the
kind of danger he is in. Stray bullet danger, perhaps. Drug gang danger. And it is true
that once Willie was beaten and burned on the face. But the people who beat him and
burned him are not his worst enemies at the moment.

You are.   9

Maybe you think I'm being melodramatic? Think again. The biggest threat to Willie's   10
future is you and the power you have reposed in the . . . federal immigration judge.

Willie Sommervil is a Haitian refugee. Why didn't I say so in the first place?   11
Because, if I had, you might have said, "The hell with him, then."

Say the words "Haitian refugee" and a little movie starts playing in the mind. A little   12
movie that shows crowds of people, packed in a boat like sardines, some of them AIDS
infected. Threatening to spill out on our shores and jam the welfare rolls and spread
disease and clutter up some vision of what America should be.

Willie Sommervil is all that an American should be and more than many are. When   13
he lived in Haiti, he befriended American missionaries and U.S. Coast Guardsmen.
That's why he was beaten and burned on the face. Government-sanctioned thugs did it
because he was a friend to America.

14   A Methodist clergyman got him out seven years ago and brought him to the community of Lakeside on Marblehead in Ottawa County [Ohio]. That's where Willie pulled himself up by his bootstraps—just like we Americans are always telling the poor to do.

15   I've got a cottage at Lakeside and that's how I happen to know Willie. I happen to be writing this in a room he painted. I see him at least once a week. His English is pretty good and he's working to make it better. Sometimes, in church on Sunday, I watch him in the choir and suspect he's just moving his lips during some of the more arcane passages of the old Wesley hymns.

16   But his spirit is articulate. And when he prays, he prays to stay here. And to bring over his children.

17   I want Willie to stay here. He's the kind of American America needs. So I will be in the federal court at 9 a.m. April 20, along with a lot of my Lakeside neighbors, to urge [the judge] to allow Willie to keep being what he already is. A good American.

18   The problem is you. You don't want him. I admit you probably didn't know that until now. But your government, acting on your behalf, has already denied Willie's earlier request for asylum and ordered him deported. Sent back to the people who burned him and beat him and who still have his name on their list.

19   Karen Meade is Willie's lawyer. She specializes in immigration law. Her case files, she says, are full of deserving people who ought to be allowed their chance at America. People who are working hard and paying taxes and ought to be permitted to stay. People whom we ignore, brush off, because their skin is chocolate brown like Willie's, but who are sweating to make the battered old promise of America live. The way the Irish made it, and the Poles, and the Germans.

20   You hear Meade say that and you ignore it. It is easy to ignore pieces of paper in a file. When you reduce human beings to file folders, they cease to be human. You can issue orders that collapse their worlds and send them off to fates unknown. And assume the country is better for it.

21   I've told you about Willie Sommervil, the man. Willie Sommervil is also a file number. He is an "A" with eights digits after it. He is in a drawer in the immigration office. Probably, these days, he is also in a computer. A couple of key strokes and his American dream will vanish. Maybe there will be one last message on the screen asking if you wish the data to be saved.

22   How about it? Do you?

➤ **FOR WRITING OR DISCUSSION**

1. The essay begins and ends with questions. Which, if any, are traditional questions with the author wondering what the answer will be? Which, if any, are rhetorical questions used primarily for effect with the author knowing what answer he expects or wants?

2. The author has a more important purpose than simply to describe Willie. What is that purpose?

3. Where does the writer attack stereotyped conceptions that he feels his readers are likely to have?

4. "Virtue does not hold an audience," Feagler complains. It's hard to make goodness and decency as interesting as evil. Write a description of a person who is characterized by unspectacular, everyday goodness and decency. Make the goodness come to life through specific details.

WRITING TOPICS

If you cannot easily decide on a topic for your description paper, you might want to try one or more of these suggestions. Note that you can approach many of the suggestions in two different ways. With a subject like "doctors," for example, you could choose to write a description of doctors in general—"Doctors are the people I admire the most," "Doctors are the people who frighten me the most"— or a description of a specific individual—for instance, the doctor who cares for your family.

1. Office workers
2. Priests, nuns, ministers, rabbis
3. Playful pets
4. Taxi drivers
5. An afternoon schoolyard
6. People waiting in a line
7. Sloppy eaters
8. Doctor's waiting room
9. Waiters or waitresses
10. Bad drivers
11. A school cafeteria
12. Beaches, pools, amusement parks
13. A garden
14. The contents of a wallet or pocketbook
15. Summer nights
16. A natural disaster
17. A relative
18. My best friend
19. A bus ride
20. My favorite food

CROSSCURRENTS

1. Both Richard Rodriguez in "Complexion" (page 43) and Judith Ortiz Cofer in "Grandmother's Room" (page 122) provide insights into Hispanic and Latino families and their values. What similarities do you note about the families in the two selections? What differences? Write a brief paper that explores the two essays.
2. Virginia Woolf in "Death of the Moth" (page 115) and Alan Devoe in "Our Enemy, the Cat" (page 118) describe phenomena in the world of nature. What similar strategies have the writers used to present their descriptions? How do the strategies differ?

COLLABORATIVE LEARNING

Form groups of five students and discuss the student models: "Dad's Disappointment" (page 108) and "The Near West Side Way Back When" (page 111). How do the papers demonstrate the principles of descriptive writing? What recommendations would you make for improving the essays? Discuss your group's conclusions with the rest of the class.

REVIEW CHECKLIST: WRITING AND REVISING YOUR DESCRIPTIVE PAPER

- Have I used prewriting to explore ideas for a subject?
- Have I thought carefully about my purpose?
- Have I written for the usual general audience? If I am writing for a special audience, have I made that clear to the reader?
- Have I limited my subject?
- Have I established a clear thesis?
- Do I have enough support for my thesis?
- Do my descriptive details clearly support the thesis?
- Have I used lively, specific details?
- Have I organized the details in a clear, logical sequence?
- Have I proofread for grammar, spelling, and mechanics?

Photo courtesy: © Akos Szilvasi/Stock, Boston

——FROM IMAGE TO WORDS: A PHOTO WRITING ASSIGNMENT ——

Look at the photograph above. Use the picture as the basis for a short descriptive paper.
Be sure that you establish a thesis; and make your description come alive with sensory
detail. Expand the single visual dimension of the photograph by imagining and recording, colors, sounds, smells, and sensations of touch.

7

Narration

"Last night, as I was driving home from work, I stopped for the light at Fifty-fifth and Main. I was just sitting there minding my own business when, all of a sudden. . . ."

"Yesterday I ran into Aunt Myrtle at the grocery, and she told me. . . ."

"You'll never guess what the kids did today."

"That reminds me of the time. . . ."

Think of how often during a conversation you say something like "That reminds me of the time . . . " and then tell a story.

We all tell stories, and for many different reasons. Usually we tell stories just to share our daily experience with others. Frequently, however, we tell stories to make a point. Sometimes the point is simply, "Yes, I've had an experience like that, too. I know how you feel." That kind of story helps establish a bond between people. At other times, we tell stories that illustrate ideas. A pastor, for example, does not merely say that repentance will bring forgiveness; he reads the story of the prodigal son from the Bible. Or we tell stories that support standards of conduct. Remember how your parents used to say, "When I was young . . . ," and you knew that by the time they finished the story you were going to feel guilty about not cleaning your room? Or we tell stories to make people laugh: "Once there was a person named Mike who had a friend named Pat, and. . . ." Sometimes the stories are actual accounts of our own experience or that of someone else, and sometimes they are fictional. Whatever the case, we enjoy telling and hearing stories, and you have been telling and hearing them all your life. So the assignment to write a narrative paper should be one you will enjoy doing.

A **narrative** is a story. To *narrate* means "to tell, to give an account of." Narratives take many forms. A novel is a narrative. So is a short story. A biography is a narrative because it tells the story of a person's life. Often a narrative is a brief story included in a longer work to illustrate an idea. (An argument calling for the enforcement of safety standards in steel mills, for example, might include a story about a worker who lost two fingers because a hot steel bar fell on the worker's hand.) A **narrative paper** tells a story, usually of a personal experience, that makes a point or supports a thesis. The purpose of a narrative paper is to re-create an experience in such a way that your readers can imaginatively participate in it and share it with you. As you plan and write your paper, keep the following principles in mind.

Writing Your Narrative Paper

■ *Limit the subject.*   Almost any experience you have had can serve as subject matter for a narrative paper. You need not have climbed Mount Everest to have a significant tale to tell. You've had thousands of experiences in your life, and any one of them—from getting lost on your way to school to moving into your first apartment—can make good subject matter for a paper if you tell the story well. Most of us, after all, are interested in people and what happens to them.

Any subject, then, any experience you can turn into a story, will work for you. But you must limit the subject, and, in a narrative paper, time usually determines the limits of your subject. Your goal is to tell a story so dramatically and so completely that your readers can share the experience. A subject such as your summer as a camp counselor, therefore, is too broad—unless you want to write a book. But you could tell about the time a skunk got into your tent. A subject such as your two-week vacation in London is too big. But you could tell about the night you were rushing to a theater and a helpful young woman, recognizing you as a lost tourist, showed you a shortcut. Even one day in the country provides too much material for a complete and dramatic story. But some part of that day—the hour you spent watching a pair of cardinals teach their baby how to fly—can make a good story. It's probably no exaggeration to say that the subject cannot be too limited.

■ *Have a thesis.*   The experience you narrate is not as important as its significance to you. Why did the experience matter to you? Why do you want to tell about it? Did it change you in some way? Did it embarrass you? Did it make you happy? Sad? Was it thrilling? Frustrating? Did it lead to a decision? Did you learn something about yourself or about others or about the world around you? Were you disappointed? Did it, perhaps, give you an inkling that it's great to be alive or that your neighborhood has joys you never noticed before? Any little event in your life—even taking out the garbage—can make good subject matter for a narrative paper if you determine the significance of the experience and tell the story well.

The student essay "The Death of Santa Claus" on page 139, for example, tells of the painful way one little girl learned the truth about Santa. As you read the story, you'll surely find it touching, amusing, and sad. You may feel that the older brother, Clay, was unnecessarily cruel. The reason you have these feelings is that the author saw the significance of her experience and narrated it so skillfully that you share it with her. And you enjoy the sharing. No matter how ordinary the experience may seem to you, if you determine its significance, your readers will be able to share it with you and will find it interesting.

The significance of your experience—your interpretation of it, what it meant to you—is your thesis. The thesis of "The Death of Santa Claus," for example, is *Because of the manner in which I learned the truth, Christmas lost its joy and sense of magic when I discovered there is no Santa Claus.* You often don't have to state the thesis directly in your paper, but you should certainly know what it is, because the significance of the experience is exactly what you want to convey to your audience.

The thesis is important, too, because it controls the content of the paper. It helps you decide what to put in the paper and what to leave out. You probably know someone who tells stories that go something like this:

> Yesterday, I decided to go to the shopping center, so I changed clothes and found my car keys and drove up—oh, what *is* the name of that street? Bertha, what's the name of the street I take to go to the shopping center? Taylor? Yes, Taylor. I drove up Taylor Street and parked the car. I went in the west entrance. I think it was the west entrance; no, it was the east; I remember because I decided I wanted to stop and buy some birthday cards on my way in. Anyhow, I went in the east entrance and walked through the men's department and then took the escalator to the mall level. I was just walking along and stopped to look at the dresses in the window at Randall's. My dear, the styles are simply dreadful this year, and so expensive! And right next to me who should I see but Aunt May. And. . . .

Now the point this poor soul wants to make is that Aunt May has lost thirty pounds in three months and has inspired her niece to see a doctor and go on the same sort of diet. But we'll never know that because we stop listening when she gets to the part about the parking lot, if not before, and sit with frozen smiles on our faces until we can make a polite getaway, which is a pity. For suppose we do care about Aunt May's niece and have been concerned about the amount of weight she has gained in recent months. We would be delighted to learn that she has resolved to go on a diet, if only she could get to the point: *Aunt May's fabulous new appearance has inspired me to follow her example and lose weight.* Having that point in mind, the niece could then tell about meeting Aunt May, being surprised and delighted by her new appearance, discovering how this new appearance was achieved, and resolving to imitate Aunt May and thus achieve a similar new appearance. And we would pay attention.

We tolerate rambling spoken narratives, when we must, out of consideration for the speakers' feelings. Even so, we wish they would get to the point. We won't tolerate written narratives that ramble because we don't have to. We can always put the book or paper down. So, have a thesis; it helps keep the narrative under control.

To see how a thesis keeps the narrative under control, turn again to "The Death of Santa Claus." Notice that the writer does not tell everything that happened on Christmas Eve. She doesn't tell her readers that she brushed her teeth, ate breakfast, and put together a jigsaw puzzle or that between ten and eleven o'clock she and her brother enjoyed playing bingo. Such facts do not contribute to her point. But other facts do: Clay is accustomed to deference from the younger children (and they are accustomed to giving it); everyone in the house is irritable, which leads to the author's challenge of her brother's authority and the mother's uncharacteristic rebuke of the boy; and the mother forces Clay to take his little sister with him to the grocery. These facts explain why Clay wants to hurt his sister, and what better way to hurt a seven-year-old on Christmas Eve than to tell her the truth about Santa Claus? These are the facts developed in the narrative, and they are determined by the thesis.

■ *Use specific details.*   In every chapter of this book, we urge you to use specific details because they give life to your writing, and the narrative paper is no exception. If your story is about being frightened out of your wits the first time you spent a night alone in your aunt's hundred-year-old house, it matters that the dark red living room curtains were made of velvet so thick that no light could penetrate them, that cobwebs hung from the ceiling, that the stern eyes in the portrait over the mantel seemed to follow you as you moved about the room, that no lamp in the room was bright enough to illuminate the corners, that the stairs creaked and the wind moaned. Remember, a narrative re-creates an experience for your readers. In most cases, you can make your readers feel what you felt if you use specific details. What you learned in the last chapter about descriptive writing will help you considerably here and elsewhere when you need to marshal concrete sensory language.

A word of caution, however. The details you use, like everything else in your paper, should support your thesis. Consider these details:

> My breakfast consisted of six ounces of freshly squeezed orange juice, two soft-scrambled eggs, three strips of lean, crisp bacon, an English muffin laden with butter and topped with homemade strawberry jam, and two cups of coffee with heavy cream.

The details used here are wonderfully specific, but whether they will work depends on your thesis. If your thesis is *Working at the Brookside hunger center last Thursday made me humble,* the details will work: The contrast between your sumptuous breakfast and the meager bags of food you distributed to the needy should indeed make you humble. On the other hand, if your thesis is *Watching the proceedings in Criminal Court yesterday morning made me realize it's important to vote for good judges,* just reporting that you had breakfast, if you mention it at all, will be sufficient: "Eager to leave on time, I had a quick breakfast and ran to my car."

Indeed, sometimes a narrative paper doesn't even have an introduction. In this case, the writer simply begins with the first event of the story:

> "There's a gun at your back. Raise your hands and don't make a sound," a harsh voice snarled at me. I raised my hands.

The body of the narrative paper also differs from that of most other papers in that its organization can be only chronological. It's possible to begin with the present and then portray an earlier episode:

> As I sit in my soft leather easy chair that I keep in front of the fireplace this time of year and gaze at brightly burning pine logs, I remember a Christmas forty years ago when I was not so comfortable.

But the heart of the narrative—what happened forty years ago—should be arranged chronologically. Since you want your readers to share the events as you experienced them, you must present the events in the order that they occurred: First this, then that, and later something else. And you should let your readers know, by means of transitions, what the chronology is. Transitions are, of course, important to any piece of writing, but the kinds of transitions that indicate the passage of time are essential to a narrative paper:

> then, next, soon, later
>
> at four o'clock, a few minutes later, on the way back, the next morning
>
> After I removed the bullets . . .
>
> I must have been asleep a couple of hours when I was awakened by a shout.

Finally, the narrative's conclusion is different as well. In some narratives, the thesis of the paper appears for the first time in the conclusion. The writer tells a good story in the introduction and body and then states the significance of the story at the end of the paper:

> At last I admitted to myself that the raccoons had won. I was tired of getting up in the middle of the night to gather the garbage they scattered about the backyard. I was tired of trying to find a garbage can that they could not open. I was, in fact, tired of the country. As I crept wearily back to my bedroom, I knew *the raccoons had taught me a valuable lesson: I did not belong in the country; I belonged in a high-rise apartment in the heart of the city.* And that's just where I moved two weeks later.

At other times, when the main point of the narrative is sufficiently clear within the piece, the conclusion may imply the thesis without restating it, or it may take up other ideas stated or hinted at in the narrative. In the essay "Foul Shots" (page 149), one might state writer Rogelio R. Gomez's thesis like this: *Our failure to respond to a slight at a basketball game that we thought would assert our racial superiority instead made us feel worthless and inferior.* The essay's conclusion reads:

> Two decades later, the memory of their gloating lives on in me. When a white person is discourteous, I find myself wondering what I should do, and afterward, if I've done the right thing. Sometimes I argue when a deft comment would suffice. Then I reprimand myself, for I am no longer a boy. But my impulse to argue bears

witness to my ghosts. For, invariably, whenever I feel insulted I'm reminded of that day at Churchill High. And whenever the past encroaches upon the present, I see myself rising boldly, stepping proudly across the years and crushing, underfoot, a silly bag of Fritos.

Since the essay narrative makes the point, Gomez has no need to belabor the obvious. But note how his conclusion reminds readers of the ideas presented in the introduction and helps unify the essay.

In any event, the conclusion for a narrative paper should do what all good conclusions do: give the paper a sense of completeness.

Student Writing: Narration

Following are two narratives, both written by students. See what you think of them. Annotations highlight narrative strategies and essay development.

Alycia Hatten

Limited subject: "one Christmas Eve" confines topic in time and establishes narrative sequence.

The Death of Santa Claus

Introduction: brief (one sentence long), yet clearly implies thesis, which controls contents of paper.

I will never forget that heartbreaking Christmas Eve   1

when my oldest brother murdered Santa Claus.

Clay was eleven that year; I was seven, Brian five,   2

Important background details

and Kevin four. Clay had always been the leader. Brian,

Kevin, and I had always done everything he told us to do,

and we always believed everything he said: If Clay said

it, then it was the gospel truth. Clay, naturally, had

come to expect us to look up to him.

That Christmas Eve was cold and rainy, so we children   3

Narrative chronology begins here.

had been in the house all day. Although we tried to be

good so Santa would visit us that night, we grew restless

and irritable as the day wore on. Our mother, too, became

irritable because, in addition to answering our questions

and trying to think of ways to keep us amused, she had

worked all day preparing for the Christmas feast our three

uncles and four aunts would share with us the next day.

Time transition:
"that after-
noon"; "about
four o'clock."

I don't know where I got the nerve, but that afternoon, for the first time in my life, I challenged Clay's
authority. It was about four o'clock, and, at my mother's
suggestion, I had turned to my coloring book. I had almost
finished coloring the picture of a little girl, and I was
especially proud of the costume I had given her. At that
time, I believed pink and purple to be the two loveliest
colors possible, and I had given the little girl a pink
dress and purple shoes.

4

Specific details
appeal to sense
of sight: "pink
dress and pur-
ple shoes."

Just as I was putting the finishing touches on the
shoes, Clay came into the den from the kitchen and began
to inspect my work. "That's dumb," he said. "Who ever
heard of purple shoes?" And picking up a black crayon, he
began coloring my beautiful purple shoes black.

5

"Mommie," I screamed, "Clay's messin' up my picture
and he says I'm dumb! You can, too, have purple shoes,
can't you?"

6

My mother could usually settle an argument so gently
that we were seldom aware it had been settled. This time,
however, she rushed into the den from the kitchen, wiping
flour dust from her hands, and snapped, "Clay, put that
crayon back where you found it and leave your sister
alone!" To me she said, "There's nothing to cry about.
I've always liked purple shoes."

7

Sharp image
of mother:
Sensory details
appeal to sight,
sound, and
touch.

Clay dropped the crayon and, turning on the TV, sat
down to watch Sesame Street. Since my mother had confirmed
my taste in colors, I finished my picture and forgot
about the incident.

8

Transitions
continue to
advance the
chronological
sequence: "A
few minutes
later."

A few minutes later, my father came home, and we all
had an early supper. My mother resumed her baking and

9

discovered that she would need more candied citrus to finish her last batch of cookies. Perhaps because she knew Clay was hurt and she wanted us to become friends again, she told Clay and me to put on our raincoats and go to the corner store to get the citrus.

"Why does <u>she</u> have to go with me?" Clay whined.   10

"It'll be good for your sister to get out of the house   11
for a while. Besides, she's getting to be a big girl, and you can teach her to count the change," my mother replied.

Clay and I set out on our journey. I babbled all the   12
way. Clay said hardly a word, but I was too happy to be going to the grocery with him to notice. On the way back I said to Clay, "Let's run home so we won't miss any of the 'Santa Claus Is Coming to Town' special."

Clay said, "No, I'm not runnin' home to see that stupid   13
program, and there ain't a Santa Claus anyway."

I stopped dead in my tracks and said, "What do you   14
mean there ain't a Santa Claus? Mommie just took us to Halle's yesterday to see him and we have pictures of him at home, and Mommie and Daddy don't tell lies, and I'm gonna tell on you when we get home." I could hardly wait to get home so I could tell my mother about Clay's awful lie.

"Your brother's just teasing you, and if he doesn't   15
stop, Santa's going to leave him a big bag of ashes," my mother reassured me. Brian, Kevin, and I laughed with relief! I went into the den and started watching "Santa Claus Is Coming to Town."

When the commercial came on, Clay said, "Come on,   16
I'll prove it to you." He went to Daddy's desk and got his flashlight. Then we went downstairs to the basement. Clay

Direct quotations throughout give sense of reality to narrative.

said, "Come over here to this big locker and I'll show you

your toys."

We went to the locker, and Clay pulled open the door   17

while I looked in with the flashlight. And there they were:

Most of the toys I had asked Santa for were in the locker!

I went to bed that night heartbroken. I felt as if   18

someone had died. The next morning, even the presence

of the bicycle I had dreamed of couldn't cheer me up. I

didn't feel the sense of magic and the happiness that

I had come to associate with Christmas morning. And I

haven't ever again, not since Clay killed Santa Claus.

➤ FOR WRITING OR DISCUSSION

1. Do the title and the first paragraph of the narrative reveal too much of the story? Why, or why not?
2. The writer uses strong words like *murdered, died,* and *killed* to suggest the way she felt when learning the truth about Santa. What do these words reveal about her understanding of her brother's behavior?
3. The thesis of the narrative is not directly stated. Should it be?
4. Identify four expressions that indicate the passage of time.
5. What do the direct quotations reveal about Clay and his sister?
6. How do the following details serve the narrative?

   "That Christmas Eve was cold and rainy. . . ." (paragraph 3)

   "I had given the little girl . . . purple shoes." (paragraph 4)

   ". . . [S]he rushed into the den . . . , wiping flour dust from her hands. . . ." (paragraph 7)

7. Write a narrative paper about the time you learned the truth about some myth (Santa Claus, the Easter bunny, the tooth fairy) of your childhood. Or, write a narrative about the difficulty you have or had in giving up some cherished belief.

Mary Nelson

The Big Lie

1   In the summer of my fifth year, I had a number of sore

throats, each requiring a visit to our family doctor, a man I

adored because every time I went to see him, he let me listen
to my own heartbeat with his stethoscope, and he gave me a
lollipop at the close of each visit. By the end of the summer,
I had decided that I, too, would become a doctor. For what
could be more desirable than working in an office that contained so many wonderful, shiny gadgets and an apparently
limitless supply of lollipops?

Imagine my delight, then, when, during one of my frequent   2
visits, Dr. Grover asked, "Mary, how would you like to take a
tour of the hospital where I work?"

During the week between that visit and the date of my   3
tour, I was the happiest five-year-old on the block. I bragged
to every child in the neighborhood that I was to have my very
own tour of the big hospital downtown where my friend Dr.
Grover worked. And I must have asked my mother a hundred times
when we were going to the hospital.

On the morning of the big day, I noticed, as I got in the   4
car, that my mother was putting my small suitcase, the one I
used only when I visited Grandmother, in the trunk of the car.
"What are you doing with my suitcase?" I demanded.

"Sometimes doctors change clothes several times a day when   5
they're working in a hospital," my mother replied, "so I've
packed some extra clothes for you in case you and Dr. Grover
have to change." I had never felt so important or grown-up.

I was somewhat disappointed when, upon our arrival,   6
Dr. Grover was not standing in the doorway waiting for me,
but at a big desk my mother and I were greeted by a nurse who
told us that Dr. Grover was expecting us. My mother told me
to go with the nurse, and I cheerfully obeyed, certain that
she would take me to Dr. Grover and the beginning of my tour.

7   We entered a big room that was filled with baby cribs, but Dr. Grover wasn't there. The nurse told me to get undressed and put on the funny-looking gown she handed me. I knew about changing clothes in the hospital, but I was sorry that I had left my suitcase with my mother, for I was sure she would have packed something much prettier than the gown I was being asked to put on. Yet I had my tour ahead of me, so I did as I was told.

8   Then strange things began to happen. The nurse lifted me into one of the baby cribs. I was unhappy about that because I was a big girl, not a baby. I didn't have time to protest, though, for almost immediately another nurse came into the big room and took my temperature and held my wrist. Being a normal five-year-old, I asked the nurse why she was holding my wrist and looking at her watch. She replied simply, "Doctor's orders." I felt better because if Dr. Grover had ordered these strange goings-on, they must have something to do with my tour. So I sat in my crib inspecting the room as I happily watched the nurses come and go.

9   I wasn't even too unhappy when a nurse approached my crib with a needle. Oh, I cried at first. But the nurse assured me it wouldn't hurt and that I could watch her and learn how to give a shot. She also told me that, soon, someone would come with a big cart to roll me around the hospital.

10   Finally some men did come with the cart, and I was on my way. I sat up on the cart taking everything in--the nurses' station, the blinking lights in the corridors, the nurses running from one room to another. Then the cart was rolled into a huge elevator with lots of buttons, and down we went into another big room where there was what looked like another cart

with a very big, round, bright light over it. The men told me to get on the other cart, and as I did, I noticed a table near the cart that seemed loaded with shiny tools and lots of other things I didn't recognize. This was indeed a grand tour of the hospital.

But then my tour turned into a nightmare. Someone told me   11
to lie down, which I thought was silly because I wanted to get on with my tour. Before I could explain, though, two men pushed me down on the cart and fastened straps around me. Someone put a cloth over my eyes and then a mask over my nose and mouth, and I could smell some awful odor. I screamed for my mother over and over again. I tried to move but was held fast. I screamed and screamed for my mother, but she never came. I couldn't understand why she didn't hear and come help me. I was terrified.

I guess I eventually went to sleep. When I woke up, my   12
tonsils were gone, and I had a terrible sore throat, sorer than the usual discomfort that follows a tonsillectomy because I had inhaled ether fumes while screaming. A worse pain, though, was the feeling that Dr. Grover and my mother had betrayed me. I cried for hours about the betrayal, and there was no way my mother could comfort me, for she had been a part of it.

That was almost forty years ago, but often I still think   13
of the terror and heartbreak I felt and remember that they occurred because the doctor and my mother lied to me.

➤ **FOR WRITING OR DISCUSSION**

1. Why is "The Big Lie" a better title for this narrative than, say, "The Great Deception" or "My Grand Tour"?
2. What is the thesis of the paper? When do you learn what the thesis is?

3. The writer uses deliberately vague expressions—*a big desk, a funny-looking gown, some men*—to suggest the impression the hospital made on a five-year-old girl. Other words—*stethoscope, corridors, tonsillectomy*—are those used by adults. Do the different levels of usage detract from the narrative? Why, or why not?

4. What is the real reason that the mother packed the suitcase? How does her lie about the suitcase contribute to the narrative?

5. You probably found it hard to believe that a child could go on being deceived as long as the narrator did. What details justify her continuing belief that she was going on a tour of the hospital?

6. Write a narrative paper about a time when you made a discovery (pleasant or unpleasant) about a family member or a teacher. Or, write a paper about your first hospital stay.

Models of Writing

These professsional examples of narration are typical of the narratives you will have to write, stories that come directly from the writers' personal experiences. Notice as you read how each selection tells a good story but also makes a significant point.

CAROL K. LITTLEBRANDT

Death Is a Personal Matter

1   My father sleeps. I sit writing…trying to get something on paper I know is there, but which is as elusive and slippery as the life that's ending before me.

2   My father has cancer. Cancer of the sinuses, and as the autopsy will show later, of the left occipital lobe, mastoid, cerebellum.

3   His head lies at an awkward angle on the pillow because of a lump on his neck grown to grapefruit size—the visible sign that, for some reason, was not considered worthy of biopsy for ten doctor-to-doctor-running months. The invisible is worse.

4   My imagination enters the chamber of horrors of overgrown sinus passages, and I wince at the thought of the excruciating pain my father has borne for so long. Occasionally the pain rips through the veil of drugs and, still asleep, he reaches out a skinny white arm and grips the bed railing with a hand, gnarled, but still warm and amazingly strong.

5   I watch his rickety body shudder from the bombarding agonies. I cry and pray and gently wipe the glistening sweat from his forehead, sit again and watch, not quite sure what I am watching for. I have no measure of previous days and nights. I have only been here a few hours.

A Painful Burden

When I came in, he didn't know me. I wrote my name on a card with the words, "I'm   6
here, Dad." And he tried to understand, but couldn't. Later, when a friend arrived, he
managed introductions of the lovely lady "who looks just like my daughter" to "my
good friend, Oskar." Then, joking and being gracious, he made Oskar and me laugh,
enjoy ourselves and feel comfortable. And we felt love. Now it is night, and I do not
know whether the fitful sleep is appropriate and whether tomorrow he will wake and
have time to joke and be gracious again.

I have not seen my father for nine months, when the lump was still a secret below   7
his ear. A few months later I heard about it and headaches, and then from time to time
all the diagnoses of arthritis, a cyst, sinusitis…even senility. Then finally—the lump
now a painful burden to be carried—he was subjected to nine days of tests of bowels,
bladder, blood. And on the last day a hollow needle was inserted into the growth; the
cells gathered, magnified, interpreted and pronounced cancer. Immediate surgery
and/or cobalt treatment indicated.

They were told, my mother and father, the day after his 75th birthday party. Then,   8
after panic and the trauma of an old World War I rifle that would not fire, with my
mother—ordered outside the bedroom—hearing click, click, click…and a plastic bag,
tucked around my father's face in one last act of stricken, singular loyalty and coopera-
tion by my mother, to be clawed away at the last moment…and spilled pills…and
falling…and weeping…and holding each other…and finally giving in, my father reluctantly left his own bed and was taken to the hospital.

"Let Me Alone"

And after the trauma of no dentures, no hearing aid and one unexpected cobalt treat-   9
ment, triumphant that his mind functioned and his voice was firm, he state unfalter-
ingly: "Let me alone. No more treatments. I am 75. I have had an excellent life. It is
time for me to die in my own way." His decision was not met with approval.

These things I learned later, but now I hear him moan and watch his face contort   10
and his bony fingers press his forehead. And I go down the night corridors of the hospital and ask for another shot for my father. All the nurses look at me, and I at them. We
do not speak. It is not necessary. The air is filled with the serene mystery of tacit agreements. Another doctor is in charge now, and the orders written on the chart are clear
and kind.

After the shot is given, my father's breathing changes. There are longer intervals   11
between each breath. I time them with my own breathing, and feel the suspense as I
wait to exhale and take another breath. But even now I do not know I am here for the
end. I am not familiar with dying. I pray again he will not suffer long. I anticipate weeks
because his heart is that of a lion.

I pet him, and hold his hand and kiss it. I wipe away the urine from between his   12
wasted legs, knowing he would be terribly embarrassed if he knew. But I am grateful to
minister to him with love at the end of his life.

13   In the morning, another friend comes in to relieve me. I go for breakfast. A head nurse severely scolds me for wearing a cotton nightgown smock over my slacks as certainly not appropriate to wear in my father's room. I shrug and order coffee.

14   Later on, washed and clean, my father rests peacefully on his side. I take his hand. He wakens, and now with only one eye functioning, but it blue and clear, he smiles a sweet gentle smile, and says, "Holy smokes…it's Carol." The last child has come and he is happy. Then for a moment he looks puzzled…Carol all the way from Buffalo?…and then he understands. He tells me he would like to rest now and squeezes my hand. His eyes close, and as though a shade were being pulled back from his face, the pain moves from chin to nose to forehead and disappears. He sleeps and breathes softly. I smile at his peace. I leave.

15   My mother returns to the hospital to take my place. The phone rings 30 minutes later. Gently and quietly my father has died with her last kiss upon his lips.

Joyous Freedom

16   As the family drives back to the hospital, I sense a great elation as if someone were flying with arms flung out in total freedom. I chuckle because the joyous, almost gleefully alive, feeling, is so strong. Yes, old man…Pop…I'm glad for you. Enjoy, enjoy and Godspeed.

17   Death is not easy under any circumstances, but at least he did not suffer tubes and IVs and false hope, and we did not suffer the play-acting, the helpless agonies of watching a loved one suffer to no purpose, finally growing inured to it all or even becoming irritated with a dying vegetable that one cannot relate to any longer. In the end, I have learned, death is a very personal matter between parent and offspring, husbands and wives, loving neighbors and friends, and between God or symbols of belief and the dying ones and all who care about them.

18   There comes a point where it is no longer the business of the courts, the American Medical Association, the government. It is private business. And I write now publicly only because it needs to be said again, and my father would have agreed.

19   So, Pop, I say it for you, for all of us still here. Wish us well and God bless.

➤ **FOR WRITING OR DISCUSSION**

1. What is the thesis of this piece?
2. Littlebrandt is writing about a complex and controversial subject. Where does she seem to give serious consideration to the position of those who may differ with her views?
3. What is the writer's attitude toward the medical profession? In what ways are her views both positive and negative?
4. What purposes do the many details about the nature of the father's illness serve in the essay?
5. Explain the meaning of "Wish us well…" in paragraph 19.
6. We all celebrate or commemorate the landmarks in our lives—births, marriages, deaths. Write a narrative showing how a person or group of people faced one of these major events.

ROGELIO R. GOMEZ

Foul Shots

Now and then I can still see their faces, snickering and laughing, their eyes mocking me. And it bothers me that I should remember. Time and maturity should have diminished the pain, because the incident happened more than 20 years ago. Occasionally, however, a smug smile triggers the memory, and I think, "I should have done something." Some act of defiance could have killed and buried the memory of the incident. Now it's too late.

In 1969, I was a senior on the Luther Burbank High School basketball team. The school is on the south side of San Antonio, in one of the city's many barrios. After practice one day our coach announced that we were going to spend the following Saturday scrimmaging with the ball club from Winston Churchill High, located in the city's rich, white north side. After the basketball game, we were to select someone from the opposing team and "buddy up"—talk with him, have lunch with him and generally spend the day attempting friendship. By telling us that this experience would do both teams some good, I suspect our well-intentioned coach was thinking about the possible benefits of integration and of learning to appreciate the differences of other people. By integrating us with this more prosperous group, I think he was also trying to inspire us.

But my teammates and I smiled sardonically at one another, and our sneakers squeaked as we nervously rubbed them against the waxed hardwood floor of our gym. The prospect of a full day of unfavorable comparisons drew from us a collective groan. As "barrio boys," we were already acutely aware of the differences between us and them. Churchill meant "white" to us: It meant shiny new cars, two-story homes with fireplaces, pedigreed dogs and manicured hedges. In other words, everything that we did not have. Worse, traveling north meant putting up a front, to ourselves as well as to the Churchill team. We felt we had to pretend that we were cavalier about it all, tough guys who didn't care about "nothin'."

It's clear now that we entered the contest with negative images of ourselves. From childhood, we must have suspected something was inherently wrong with us. The evidence wrapped itself around our collective psyche like a noose. In elementary school, we were not allowed to speak Spanish. The bladed edge of a wooden ruler once came crashing down on my knuckles for violating this dictum. By high school, however, policies had changed, and we could speak Spanish without fear of physical reprisal. Still, speaking our language before whites brought on spasms of shame—for the supposed inferiority of our language and culture—and guilt at feeling shame. That mixture of emotions fueled our burning sense of inferiority.

After all, our mothers in no way resembled the glamorized models of American TV mothers—Donna Reed baking cookies in high heels. My mother's hands were rough and chafed, her wardrobe drab and worn. And my father was preoccupied with making ends meet. His silence starkly contrasted with the glib counsel Jim Anderson offered in "Father Knows Best." And where the Beaver worried about trying to understand some difficult homework assignment, for me it was an altogether different horror, when I was told by my elementary school principal that I did not have the ability to learn.

6   After I failed to pass the first grade, my report card read that I had a "learning disability." What shame and disillusion it brought my parents! To have carried their dream of a better life from Mexico to America, only to have their hopes quashed by having their only son branded inadequate. And so somewhere during my schooling I assumed that saying I had a "learning disability" was just another way of saying that I was "retarded." School administrators didn't care that I could not speak English.

7   As teenagers, of course, my Mexican-American friends and I did not consciously understand why we felt inferior. But we might have understood if we had fathomed our desperate need to trounce Churchill. We viewed the prospect of beating a white, north-side squad as a particularly fine coup. The match was clearly racial, our need to succeed born of a defiance against prejudice. I see now that we used the basketball court to prove our "blood." And who better to confirm us, if not those whom we considered better? In retrospect, I realize the only thing confirmed that day was that we saw ourselves as negatively as they did.

8   After we won the morning scrimmage, both teams were led from the gym into an empty room where everyone sat on a shiny linoleum floor. We were supposed to mingle—rub the colors together. But the teams sat separately, our backs against concrete walls. We faced one another like enemies, the empty floor between us a no man's land. As the coaches walked away, one reminded us to share lunch. God! The mere thought of offering them a taco from our brown bags when they had refrigerated deli lunches horrified us.

9   Then one of their players tossed a bag of Fritos at us. It slid across the slippery floor and stopped in the center of the room. With hearts beating anxiously, we Chicanos stared at the bag as the boy said with a sneer, "Y'all probably like 'em"—the "Frito Bandito" commercial being popular then. And we could see them, smiling at each other, giggling, jabbing their elbows into one another's ribs at the joke. The bag seemed to grow before our eyes like a monstrous symbol of inferiority.

10   We won the afternoon basketball game as well. But winning had accomplished nothing. Though we had wanted to, we couldn't change their perception of us. It seems, in fact, that defeating them made them meaner. Looking back, I feel these young men needed to put us "in our place," to reaffirm the power they felt we had threatened. I think, moreover, that they felt justified, not only because of their inherent sense of superiority, but because our failure to respond to their insult underscored our worthlessness in their eyes.

11   Two decades later, the memory of their gloating lives on in me. When a white person is discourteous, I find myself wondering what I should do, and afterward, if I've done the right thing. Sometimes I argue when a deft comment would suffice. Then I reprimand myself, for I am no longer a boy. But my impulse to argue bears witness to my ghosts. For, invariably, whenever I feel insulted I'm reminded of that day at Churchill High. And whenever the past encroaches upon the present, I see myself rising boldly, stepping proudly across the years and crushing, underfoot, a silly bag of Fritos.

➤ **FOR WRITING OR DISCUSSION**

1. What specific evidence in the narrative shows that the white teammates stereotyped their Hispanic opponents?
2. What specific details are used to embody the white world of the north side of town? Is the author guilty of stereotyping?
3. Why is it significant that the events written about happened "more than 20 years ago"?
4. The good intentions of the coaches appear only to have made matters worse. Write a narrative showing the failure of good intentions.

MAYA ANGELOU

Champion of the World

The last inch of space was filled, yet people continued to wedge themselves along   1
the walls of the Store. Uncle Willie had turned the radio up to its last notch so that
youngsters on the porch wouldn't miss a word. Women sat on kitchen chairs, dining-
room chairs, stools and upturned wooden boxes. Small children and babies perched on
every lap available and men leaned on the shelves or on each other.

The apprehensive mood was shot through with shafts of gaiety, as a black sky is   2
streaked with lightning.

"I ain't worried 'bout this fight. Joe's gonna whip that cracker like it's open season."   3

"He's gone whip him till that white boy call him Momma."   4

At last the talking was finished and the string-along songs about razor blades were   5
over and the fight began.

"A quick jab to the head." In the Store the crowd grunted. "A left to the head and a   6
right and another left." One of the listeners cackled like a hen and was quieted.

"They're in a clinch, Louis is trying to fight his way out."   7

Some bitter comedian on the porch said, "That white man don't mind hugging that   8
niggah now, I betcha."

"The referee is moving in to break them up, but Louis finally pushed the contender   9
away and it's an uppercut to the chin. The contender is hanging on, now he's backing
away. Louis catches him with a short left to the jaw."

A tide of murmuring assent poured out the doors and into the yard.   10

"Another left and another left. Louis is saving that mighty right . . ." The mutter in   11
the Store had grown into a baby roar and it was pierced by the clang of a bell and the
announcer's "That's the bell for round three, ladies and gentlemen."

As I pushed my way into the Store I wondered if the announcer gave any thought to   12
the fact that he was addressing as "ladies and gentlemen" all the Negroes around the
world who sat sweating and praying, glued to their "master's voice."

13   There were only a few calls for R.C. Colas, Dr Peppers, and Hires root beer. The real festivities would begin after the fight. Then even the old Christian ladies who taught their children and tried themselves to practice turning the other cheek would buy soft drinks, and if the Brown Bomber's victory was a particularly bloody one they would order peanut patties and Baby Ruths also.

14   Bailey and I laid the coins on top of the cash register. Uncle Willie didn't allow us to ring up sales during a fight. It was too noisy and might shake up the atmosphere. When the gong rang for the next round we pushed through the near-sacred quiet into the herd of children outside.

15   "He's got Louis against the ropes and now it's a left to the body and a right to the ribs. Another right to the body, it looks like it was low . . . Yes, ladies and gentlemen, the referee is signaling but the contender keeps raining the blows on Louis. It's another to the body, and it looks like Louis is going down."

16   My race groaned. It was our people falling. It was another lynching, yet another Black man hanging on a tree. One more woman ambushed and raped. A Black boy whipped and maimed. It was hounds on the trail of a man running through slimy swamps. It was a white woman slapping her maid for being forgetful.

17   The men in the Store stood away from the walls and at attention. Women greedily clutched the babes on their laps while on the porch the shufflings and smiles, flirtings and pinching of a few minutes before were gone. This might be the end of the world. If Joe lost we were back in slavery and beyond help. It would all be true, the accusations that we were lower types of human beings. Only a little higher than apes. True that we were stupid and ugly and lazy and dirty and unlucky and, worst of all, that God Himself hated us and ordained us to be hewers of wood and drawers of water, forever and ever, world without end.

18   We didn't breathe. We didn't hope. We waited.

19   "He's off the ropes, ladies and gentlemen. He's moving towards the center of the ring." There was no time to be relieved. The worst might still happen.

20   "And now it looks like Joe is mad. He's caught Carnera with a left hook to the head and a right to the head. It's a left jab to the body and another left to the head. There's a left cross and a right to the head. The contender's right eye is bleeding and he can't seem to keep his block up. Louis is penetrating every block. The referee is moving in, but Louis sends a left to the body and it's an uppercut to the chin and the contender is dropping. He's on the canvas, ladies and gentlemen."

21   Babies slid to the floor as women stood up and men leaned toward the radio.

22   "Here's the referee. He's counting. One, two, three, four, five, six, seven . . . Is the contender trying to get up again?"

23   All the men in the store shouted, "NO."

24   "—eight, nine, ten." There were a few sounds from the audience, but they seemed to be holding themselves in against tremendous pressure.

25   "The fight is all over, ladies and gentlemen. Let's get the microphone over to the referee . . . Here he is. He's got the Brown Bomber's hand, he's holding it up . . . Here he is . . ."

26   Then the voice, husky and familiar, came to wash over us—"The winnah, and still heavyweight champeen of the world . . . Joe Louis."

Champion of the world. A Black boy. Some Black mother's son. He was the   27
strongest man in the world. People drank Coca-Colas like ambrosia and ate candy
bars like Christmas. Some of the men went behind the Store and poured white lightning in their soft-drink bottles, and a few of the bigger boys followed them. Those who
were not chased away came back blowing their breath in front of themselves like
proud smokers.

It would take an hour or more before the people would leave the Store and head for   28
home. Those who lived too far had made arrangements to stay in town. It wouldn't do
for a Black man and his family to be caught on a lonely country road on a night when
Joe Louis had proved that we were the strongest people in the world.

➤ FOR WRITING OR DISCUSSION

1. Why does Angelou, in paragraph 2, characterize the mood of the people gathered at the store as apprehensive?
2. How many stories does this narrative contain?
3. In what ways does the author achieve suspense about the outcome of the
   fight? When did you know how the fight would end?
4. Angelou uses many direct quotations. How do they contribute to the narrative?
5. Angelou says, "This might be the end of the world. If Joe lost we were back in
   slavery and beyond help. It would all be true, the accusations that we were
   lower types of human beings. . . ." Do you think she actually believes her race
   would be "lower types . . . , stupid and ugly and lazy and dirty . . ." if Louis
   lost his title? If not, why does she say so?
6. What connection do those listening to the fight make between its outcome
   and their own lives?
7. What is the thesis of the narrative?
8. Write a narrative about your participation in some athletic or cultural event
   and the importance of its outcome to you. Or, write a narrative about a gathering of people (perhaps for Superbowl Sunday) that makes a point.

J. S. MARCUS

Crash

Last fall, I wanted to get away. I was staying in suburban Milwaukee at the time, in the   1
house I had grown up in. I had left New York, where I live, in August, when my
mother went to the hospital for what turned out to be the final time—she had been ill
for years, though her death, at the beginning of September, was relatively unexpected.
Now it was Thanksgiving. I had spent week after week wandering around the house in
a state of cool confusion, a wakeful sleepiness that I now recognize as what the mind
does to itself when it gets bored with grieving.

I couldn't return to New York, and I couldn't stay in Milwaukee. After several car   2
trips to towns in northern Wisconsin—towns with paper mills and bait-and-tackle

shops and gas stations selling cheese curds at the cash register—I rented a house on a lake in Waupaca, not far from Appleton, where Kleenex and Joe McCarthy and Harry Houdini come from. This is what I need, I thought. I would go for long walks. I would work on my next book. I would sort things out.

3   I ended up spending a lot of time in the car. I drove back and forth between Appleton and Waupaca, between Appleton and Green Bay, between Waupaca and what I now think of as my father's house. The car became a kind of house; I piled the seats with tapes and maps and empty soda bottles. There wasn't any snow yet—the winter was stalling—but I had two scrapers and a bottle of antifreeze on the floor, hat and gloves and scarf on the front passenger seat, like throw pillows. I could feel it all shifting when I made sudden stops.

4   I didn't much care for the house I had rented; it was dusty and dark. I liked to drive back and forth on Highway 10, through little towns, passing other cars in no-passing zones, on hills, around turns. Those little towns had speed limits of 25 or 35 miles per hour, I went through them at 70, 75. This, I thought, is saving me; I love this car; I love to drive.

5   · One night toward the end of December, coming back from Appleton after hanging out at a bar across from the Houdini Historical Center, I noticed that wet snow was falling. I could feel my tires resist the road, slide a little, and I was mildly excited. The car and the empty landscape and the towns had begun to bore me; my mind or my soul or whatever I should call it had been slipping back into sleep. The snow stopped. Good, I thought, and I went faster.

6   Sometimes Highway 10 is two lanes and sometimes it is four lanes; it widens and narrows unexpectedly; it dips, seems to disappear from itself; it is, as highways go, very dangerous. A 10-mile stretch near Waupaca, I later learned, accounts for a significant proportion of Wisconsin's traffic deaths.

7   I was in the middle of that stretch, at the top of a brief hill, when I saw two semis approaching. There were only two lanes and I instinctively put on my brakes; suddenly the road seemed to buckle. I was skidding; I slid into the other lane and saw the first semi speeding toward me. Then, somehow, I was back in my lane, and the first semi had just missed me. I could feel my car swerve back again toward the other lane as the second semi approached; I wasn't able to steer, I guess. I don't remember the second semi passing; I remember putting my arms over my face. I ended up in a ditch, with my back wheels in the air, the tapes and the maps and gloves in an exact pile on the floor.

8   I undid my seat belt—I remember smiling uncontrollably, shaking a little. I was fine. Soon I was standing behind the car, admiring the angle of the tires, the ice-covered grass. It was all a sort of miracle, or a dream.

9   Later I read in the local paper that there had been two other accidents that night in nearly the same spot and that both drivers had ended up in the hospital. I ended up in a bar down the road, waiting for a tow truck, listening to locals talk about wrecks on Highway 10; they sounded like sailors, or survivors.

10   For a while after that, I was, in some sense, elated—no longer mourning my mother but celebrating the fact of my survival. The few seconds of accident replaced the months of grinding grief. When I closed my eyes, I saw the semi, the angle of the tires, the pile of tapes, remembered the icy grass. I dreamed of car accidents instead of my mother.

There are many things in life that you want to go through only once, small and large   11
things that may be necessary, inevitable in retrospect, but upsetting, literally, as though
something inside you has been tossed in the air. I am back in New York now. It has been
a cold spring. There are often winter temperatures but spring light; the blooming trees
seem a little like miracles. Of course I still think about my mother but not as much. In
the past few weeks, when I closed my eyes, I would think about the cold white air and
about the sun, about things getting warmer, about one step following another.

➤ FOR WRITING OR DISCUSSION

1. What is the thesis of Marcus's essay?
2. How does the death of his mother affect the writer?
3. What purposes do the many details of the drives serve, particularly the drive
   on the night of the accident?
4. How do you account for the fact that an accident with potentially dire consequences (which, of course, were avoided) has had such a positive effect on the
   writer?
5. Explain the meaning of the first sentence of the final paragraph. What life
   event that you recognize as necessary and inevitable but upsetting are you
   glad to have gone through only once?
6. The narrative structure of this piece is pretty clear. Make an outline of the
   essay that shows the clear sequence of events in Marcus's narrative.
7. Write a narrative about some serious event you witnessed or lived through in
   or with an automobile.

LANGSTON HUGHES

Salvation

I was saved from sin when I was going on thirteen. But not really saved. It happened like   1
this. There was a big revival at my Auntie Reed's church. Every night for weeks there
had been much preaching, singing, praying, and shouting, and some very hardened
sinners had been brought to Christ, and the membership of the church had grown by
leaps and bounds. Then just before the revival ended, they held a special meeting for
children, "to bring the young lambs to the fold." My aunt spoke of it for days ahead.
That night I was escorted to the front row and placed on the mourners' bench with all
the other young sinners, who had not yet been brought to Jesus.

My aunt told me that when you were saved you saw a light, and something hap-   2
pened to you inside! And Jesus came into your life! And God was with you from then
on! She said you could see and hear and feel Jesus in your soul. I believed her. I had
heard a great many old people say the same thing and it seemed to me they out to know.
So I sat there calmly in the hot, crowded church, waiting for Jesus to come to me.

The preacher preached a wonderful rhythmical sermon, all moans and shouts and   3
lonely cries and dire pictures of hell, and then he sang a song about the ninety and

nine safe in the fold, but one little lamb was left out in the cold. Then he said: "Won't you come? Won't you come to Jesus? Young lambs, won't you come?" And he held out his arms to all us young sinners there on the mourner's bench. And the little girls cried. And some of them jumped up and went to Jesus right away. But most of us just sat there.

4   A great many old people came and knelt around us and prayed, old women with jet-black faces and braided hair, old me with work-gnarled hands. And the church sang a song about the lower lights are burning, some poor sinners to be saved. And the whole building rocked with prayer and song.

5   Still I kept waiting to *see* Jesus.

6   Finally all the young people had gone to the altar and were saved, but one boy and me. He was a rounder's son named Westley. Westley and I were surrounded by sisters and deacons praying. It was very hot in the church, and getting late now. Finally Westley said to me in a whisper: "God damn! I'm tired o' sitting here. Let's get up and be saved." So he got up and was saved.

7   Then I was left all alone on the mourners' bench. My aunt came and knelt at my knees and cried, while prayers and songs swirled all around me in the little church. The whole congregation prayed for me alone, in a mighty wail of moans and voices. And I kept waiting serenely for Jesus, waiting, waiting—but he didn't come. I wanted to see him, but nothing happened to me. Nothing! I wanted something to happen to me, but nothing happened.

8   I heard the songs and the minister saying: "Why don't you come? My dear child, why don't you come to Jesus? Jesus is waiting for you. He wants you. Why don't you come? Sister Reed, what is this child's name?"

9   "Langston," my aunt sobbed.

10   "Langston, why don't you come? Why don't you come and be saved? Oh, Lamb of God! Why don't you come?"

11   Now it was really getting late. I began to be ashamed of myself, holding everything up so long. I began to wonder what God thought about Westley, who certainly hadn't seen Jesus either, but who was now sitting proudly on the platform, swinging his knickerbockered legs and grinning down at me, surrounded by deacons and old women on their knees praying. God had not struck Westley dead for taking his name in vain or for lying in the temple. So I decided that maybe to save further trouble, I'd better lie, too, and say that Jesus had come, and get up and be saved.

12   So I got up.

13   Suddenly the whole room broke into a sea of shouting, as they saw me rise. Waves of rejoicing swept the place. Women leaped in the air. My aunt threw her arms around me. The minister took me by the hand and led me to the platform.

14   When things quieted down, in a hushed silence, punctuated by a few ecstatic "Amens," all the new young lambs were blessed in the name of God. Then joyous singing filled the room.

15   That night, for the last time in my life but one—for I was a big boy twelve years old—I cried. I cried, in bed alone, and couldn't stop. I buried my head under the quilts, but my aunt heard me. She woke up and told my uncle I was crying because the Holy Ghost

had come into my life, and because I had seen Jesus. But I was really crying because I couldn't bear to tell her that I had lied, that I had deceived everybody in the church, that I hadn't seen Jesus, and that now I didn't believe there was a Jesus any more, since he didn't come to help me.

➤ FOR WRITING OR DISCUSSION

1. The first instruction this chapter gives about writing narration is to limit the subject. How has Hughes followed this instruction?
2. What is the thesis of this selection? State it in your own words.
3. What is the chronology of events in this narration? Make a list of them. What transitions help the writer link the various events?
4. What specific sensory details enliven the narrative for the reader?
5. Why does the narrator not stand as he was expected to early in the narrative? Why at the end does he in fact rise? How do the people around him react when he finally stands? Why? Why does the narrator cry at night?
6. Write a narrative essay about how people pressured you (or someone you know) to do something you weren't sure was right. Or, perhaps you would prefer to write a narrative essay about a religious experience that you had.

HAVING YOUR SAY

Hughes implies that we sometimes lie to make others happy or pleased with us. Is such an action defensible? Write an essay in which you argue one side or the other of this question.

Readings for Writing

The two essays that follow can provide you with strong subjects for your own narrative paper.

GREG SARRIS

"You Don't Look Indian"

I have heard that someone said to American Indian writer Louise Erdrich, "You don't look Indian." It was at a reading she gave, or perhaps when she received an award of some kind for her writing. Undoubtedly, whoever said this noted Erdrich's very white skin, her green eyes and her red hair. She retorted, "Gee, you don't look rude."   1

2   You don't look Indian.

3   How often I too have heard that. But unlike Erdrich, I never returned the insult, or challenged my interlocutors. Not with words anyway. I arranged the facts of my life to fit others' conceptions of what it is to be Indian. I used others' words, others' definitions. That way, if I didn't look Indian, I might still be Indian.

4   Well, I don't know if I am Indian, I said, or if I am, how much. I was adopted. I know my mother was white—Jewish, German, Irish. I was illegitimate. Father unknown. It was back in the fifties when having a baby without being married was shameful. My mother uttered something on the delivery table about the father being Spanish. Mexican maybe. Anyway, I was given up and adopted, which is how I got a name. For awhile things went well. Then they didn't. I found myself with other families, mostly on small ranches where I milked cows and worked with horses. I met a lot of Indians—Pomo Indians—and was taken in by one of the families. I learned bits and pieces of two Pomo languages. So if you ask, I call myself Pomo. But I don't know . . . My mother isn't around to ask. After she had me, she needed blood. The hospital gave her the wrong type and it killed her.

5   The story always went something like that. It is true, all of it, but arranged so that people might see how I fit. The last lines—about my mother—awe people and cause them to forget, or to be momentarily distracted, from their original concern about my not looking Indian. And I am illegitimate. That explains any crossing of borders, anything beyond the confines of definition. That is how I fit.

6   Last year I found my father. Well, I found out his name—Emilio. My mother's younger brother, my uncle, whom I met recently, remembered taking notes from his sister to a "big Hawaiian type" on the football field. "I would go after school while the team was practicing," my uncle said. "The dude was big, dark. They called him Meatloaf. I think his name though was Emilio. Try Emilio."

7   To have a name, even a nickname, seemed unfathomable. To be thirty-six years old and for the first time to have a lead about a father somehow frightened me. You imagine all your life; you find ways to account for that which is missing, you tell stories, and now all that is leveled by a name.

8   In Laguna Beach I contacted the high school librarian and made arrangements to look through old yearbooks. It was just after a conference there in Southern California, where I had finished delivering a paper on American Indian education. I found my mother immediately, and while I was staring for the first time at an adult picture of my mother, a friend who was with me scanned other yearbooks for an Emilio. Already we knew by looking at the rows and rows of white faces, there wouldn't be too many Emilios. I was still gazing at the picture of my mother when my friend jumped. "Look," she said. She was tilting the book, pointing to a name. But already, even as I looked, a dark face caught my attention, and it was a face I saw myself in. Without a doubt. Darker, yes. But me nonetheless.

9   I interviewed several of my mother's and father's classmates. It was my mother's friends who verified what I suspected. Emilio Hilario was my father. They also told me that he had died, that I missed him by about five years.

I had to find out from others what he couldn't tell me. I wanted to know about his   10
life. Did he have a family? What was his ethnicity? Luckily I obtained the names of several relatives, including a half-brother and a grandfather. People were quick about that,
much more so than about the ethnicity question. They often circumvented the question
by telling stories about my father's athletic prowess and about how popular he was. A
few, however, were more candid. His father, my grandfather, is Filipino. "A short Filipino man," they said. "Your father got his height from his mother. She was fairer."
Some people said my grandmother was Spanish, others said she was Mexican or
Indian. Even within the family, there is discrepancy about her ethnicity. Her mother
was definitely Indian, however. Coast Miwok from Tomales Bay just north of San Francisco, and just south of Santa Rosa, where I grew up. Her name was Rienette.

During the time my grandmother was growing up, probably when her mother—   11
Rienette—was growing up too, even until quite recently, when it became popular to
be Indian, Indians in California sometimes claimed they were Spanish. And for good
reason. The prejudice against Indians was intolerable, and often only remnants of
tribes, or even families, remained to face the hatred and discrimination. My grandmother spoke Spanish. Her sister, Juanita, married a Mexican and her children's children are proud *Chicanos* living in East Los Angeles. Rienette's first husband, my
grandmother and her sister's father, was probably part Mexican or Portuguese—I'm
not sure.

The story is far from complete. But how much Indian I am by blood is not the ques-   12
tion whose answer concerns me now. Oh, I qualify for certain grants, and that is important. But knowing about my blood heritage will not change my complexion any more
than it will my experience.

In school I was called the white beaner. This was not because some of my friends   13
happened to be Mexican, but because the white population had little sense of the local
Indians. Anyone with dark hair and skin was thought to be Mexican. A counselor once
called me in and asked if my family knew I went around with Mexicans. "Yes," I said.
"They're used to it." At the time, I was staying with an Indian family—the McKays—and
Mrs. McKay was a mother to me. But I said nothing more then. I never informed the
counselor that most of my friends, the people she was referring to, were Indian—Pomo
Indian. Kashaya Pomo Indian. Sulfur Bank Pomo Indian. Coyote Valley Pomo Indian.
Yokaya Pomo Indian. Point Arena Pomo Indian. Bodega Bay Miwok Indian. Tomales
Bay Miwok Indian. And never mind that names such as Smith and Pinola are not Span-
ish (or Mexican) names.

As I think back, I said nothing more to the counselor not because I didn't want to   14
cause trouble (I did plenty of that), but because, like most other kids, I never really
knew a way to tamper with how the authorities—counselors, teachers, social workers,
police—categorized us. We talked about our ethnicity amongst ourselves, often specu-
lating who was more or less this or that. So many of us are mixed with other groups—
white, Mexican, Spanish, Portuguese, Filipino. I know of an Indian family who is half
Mexican and they identify themselves as Mexicans. In another family of the same
admixture just the opposite is true. Yet for most of the larger white community, we were
Mexican, or something.

15   And here I am with blue eyes and fair skin. If I was a white beaner, I was, more generally, a kid from the wrong side of the tracks. Hood. Greaser. Low Brow. Santa Rosa was a much smaller town then, the lines more clearly drawn between the haves and the have-nots, the non-colored and the colored. Suburban sprawl was just beginning; there was still the old downtown with its stone library and old Roman-columned courthouse. On the fringes of town lived the poorer folk. The civil rights movement had not yet engendered the ethnic pride typical of the late sixties and early seventies.

16   I remember the two guys who taught me to box, Manual and Robert. They said they were Portuguese, Robert part Indian. People whispered that they were black. I didn't care. They picked me out, taught me to box. That was when I was fourteen. By the time I was sixteen, I beat heads everywhere and every time I could. I looked for fights and felt free somehow in the fight. I say I looked for fights, but really, as I think about it, fights seemed to find me. People said things, they didn't like me, they invaded my space. I had reason. So I fought. And afterwards I was somebody. Manny said I had a chip on my shoulder, which is an asset for a good fighter. "Hate in your eyes, brother," he told me. "You got hate in your eyes."

17   I heard a lot of "Indian" stories too. We used to call them old-time stories, those about Coyote and the creation. Then there were the spook stories about spook men and women and evil doings. I knew of a spook man, an old guy who would be sitting on his family's front porch one minute and then five minutes later, just as you were driving uptown, there he'd be sitting on the old courthouse steps. The woman whose son I spent so much time with was an Indian doctor. She healed the sick with songs and prayer; she sucked pains from people's bodies. These are the things my professors and colleagues wanted to hear about.

18   I was different here too. I read books, which had something to do with my getting into college. But when I started reading seriously—about the middle of my junior year in high school—I used what I read to explain the world; I never engaged my experience to inform what I was reading. Again, I was editing my experience, and, not so ironically, I found meaning that way. And, not so ironically, the more I read the more I became separated from the world of my friends and what I had lived. So in college when I found people interested in my Indian experience as it related to issues of ecology, personal empowerment, and other worldviews, I complied and told them what I "knew" of these things. In essence I shaped what I knew to fit the books and read the books to shape what I knew. The woman who was a mother to me came off as Castaneda's Don Juan. Think of the "separate reality" of her dream world, never mind what I remember about her—the long hours in the apple cannery, her tired face, her clothes smelling of rotten apples.

19   Now, as I sort through things, I am beginning to understand why I hated myself and those people at the university; how by sculpting my experience to their interests, I denied so much of my life, including the anger and self-hatred that seeps up from such denial. I wanted to strike back, beat the hell out of them; I imagined them angering me in some way I could recognize—maybe an insult, a push or shove—so that I could hurt them. Other times I just wanted them to be somewhere, perhaps outside the classroom, on a street, in a bar, where they came suddenly upon me and saw me fighting, pummelling somebody. Anger is like a cork in water. Push it down, push it down, and still it keeps coming to the surface.

➤ **FOR WRITING OR DISCUSSION**

1. How does the writer's illegitimacy explain "any crossing of borders, anything beyond the confines of definition"?
2. What stereotypes did Sarris have to endure as he was growing up?
3. What steps does the writer take to uncover his personal family history? How do you explain his efforts?
4. Assume that Sarris could have one meeting with his father or mother. Write a narrative about that meeting. Or, as an alternate assignment, write a narrative about the first meeting between a child and a long-lost parent.

WILLARD GAYLIN

What You See Is the Real You

It was, I believe, the distinguished Nebraska financier Father Edward J. Flanagan who professed to having "never met a bad boy."[1] Having, myself, met a remarkable number of bad boys, it might seem that either our experiences were drastically different or we were using the word "bad" differently. I suspect neither is true, but rather that the Father was appraising the "inner man," while I, in fact, do not acknowledge the existence of inner people.   1

Since we psychoanalysts have unwittingly contributed to this confusion, let one, at least, attempt a small rectifying effort. Psychoanalytic data—which should be viewed as supplementary information—is, unfortunately, often viewed as alternative (and superior) explanation. This has led to the prevalent tendency to think of the "inner" man as the real man and the outer man as an illusion or pretender.   2

While psychoanalysis supplies us with an incredibly useful tool for explaining the motives and purposes underlying human behavior, most of this has little bearing on the moral nature of that behavior.   3

Like roentgenology, psychoanalysis is a fascinating, but relatively new, means of illuminating the person. But few of us are prepared to substitute an X-ray of Grandfather's head for the portrait that hangs in the parlor. The inside of the man represents another view, not a truer one. A man may not always be what he appears to be, but what he appears to be is always a significant part of what he is. A man is the sum total of *all* his behavior. To probe for unconscious determinants of behavior and then define *him* in their terms exclusively, ignoring his overt behavior altogether, is a greater distortion than ignoring the unconscious completely.   4

Kurt Vonnegut has said, "You are what you pretend to be," which is simply another way of saying, you are what we (all of us) perceive you to be, not what you think you are.   5

Consider for a moment the case of the ninety-year-old man on his deathbed (surely the Talmud must deal with this?) joyous and relieved over the success of his deception. For ninety years he has shielded his evil nature from public observation. For ninety years he has affected courtesy, kindness, and generosity—suppressing all the malice he

---

[1]Father Flanagan, the founder of Boys Town for delinquent youths, was an accomplished fund-raiser.

knew was within him while he calculatedly and artificially substituted grace and charity. All his life he had been fooling the world into believing he was a good man. This "evil" man will, I predict, be welcomed into the Kingdom of Heaven.

7   Similarly, I will not be told that the young man who earns his pocket money by mugging old ladies is "really" a good boy. Even my generous and expansive definition of goodness will not accommodate that particular form of self-advancement.

8   It does not count that beneath the rough exterior he has a heart—or, for that matter, an entire innards—of purest gold, locked away from human perception. You are for the most part what you seem to be, not what you would wish to be, nor, indeed, what you believe yourself to be.

9   Spare me, therefore, your good intentions, your inner sensitivities, your unarticulated and unexpressed love. And spare me also those tedious psychohistories which—by exposing the goodness inside the bad man, and the evil in the good—invariably establish a vulgar and perverse egalitarianism, as if the arrangement of what is outside and what inside makes no moral difference.

10 Saint Francis may, in his unconscious, indeed have been compensating for, and denying, destructive, unconscious Oedipal impulses identical to those which Attila projected and acted on.[2] But the similarity of the unconscious constellations in the two men matters precious little, if it does not distinguish between them.

11 I do not care to learn that Hitler's heart was in the right place. A knowledge of the unconscious life of the man may be an adjunct to understanding his behavior. It is *not* a substitute for his behavior in describing him.

12 The inner man is a fantasy. If it helps you to identify with one, by all means, do so; preserve it, cherish it, embrace it, but do not present it to others for evaluation or consideration, for excuse or exculpation, or, for that matter, for punishment or disapproval.

13 Like any fantasy, it serves your purposes alone. It has no standing in the real world which we share with each other. Those character traits, those attitudes, that behavior—that strange and alien stuff sticking out all over you—*that's the real you!*

➤ **FOR WRITING OR DISCUSSION**

1. Why, according to Gaylin, will the ninety-year-old man go to heaven (paragraph 6)? Do you agree that he should? Why, or why not?
2. Describe what you think Gaylin's reactions to these people would be:
   a. A person who claims to have the soul of a great poet but who has never written any great poetry and hardly ever writes poetry of any kind.
   b. A man who abuses his wife and children but insists that he loves them.
3. Does the author deny the existence of an inner self?
4. Write a narrative about a person who tries to justify his or her bad or stupid behavior. Or, write a narrative showing conflict within a person, a person at war with himself or herself.

[2]Saint Francis of Assisi is considered a model of Christian humility and love. Attila the Hun is a model of brutal military conquest.

WRITING TOPICS

If you are having trouble deciding on a topic for your narration paper, you might find it helpful simply to choose one of the following proverbs, quotations, or commonsense statements and then write a narration supporting or attacking it.

1. Money can't buy happiness.
2. Fools and their money are soon parted.
3. The love of money is the root of all evil.
4. I never met a man I didn't like.
5. Luck is the residue of design.
6. When the going gets tough, the tough get going.
7. You can't tell a book by its cover.
8. If at first you don't succeed, try, try again.
9. Marry in haste, repent in leisure.
10. Be brave, young lovers.
11. Absence makes the heart grow fonder.
12. There's no such thing as a bad boy.
13. Nobody knows the trouble I've seen.
14. The Lord will provide.
15. A penny saved is a penny earned.
16. Small children, small problems; big children, big problems.
17. Spare the rod and spoil the child.
18. Hell hath no fury like a woman scorned.
19. Good fences make good neighbors.
20. A stich in time saves nine.

CROSSCURRENTS

1. Sports and prejudice are central elements in both "Foul Shots" (page 149) and "Champion of the World" (page 151); yet the essays are dramatically different in thesis, style, and purpose. Write an essay in which you discuss these two selections together. What similarities do you see? What differences? Provide specific examples to support your views.
2. Both "'You Don't Look Indian'" by Greg Sarris (page 157) and "The Big Lie" by Mary Nelson (page 142) deal with relations between parents and children. How do the ideas in the selections relate to each other? What do you think Nelson would have said to Sarris?

COLLABORATIVE LEARNING

In groups of five students each, compare and contrast the two student pieces "The Death of Santa Claus" (page 139) and "The Big Lie" (page 142) as models of narrative essays. Use the "Review Checklist: Writing and Revising Your Narrative Paper" as a touchstone for your comments.

REVIEW CHECKLIST: WRITING AND REVISING YOUR NARRATIVE PAPER

- Have I used prewriting to explore ideas for a subject?
- Have I thought carefully about my purpose?
- Have I written for the usual general audience? If I am writing for a special audience, have I made that clear to the reader?
- Have I limited my subject?
- Have I established a clear thesis?
- Do I have enough support for my thesis?
- Have I brought my subject to life with specific details?
- Have I used natural, conversational language? Have I checked the punctuation of any dialogue?
- Have I given order to the narration?
- Have I proofread for grammar, spelling, and mechanics?

Photo courtesy: © Tony Stone Images

──────── **FROM IMAGE TO WORDS: A PHOTO WRITING ASSIGNMENT** ────────
Examine the photograph above. Write a short narrative paper to tell the story that to your mind emerges from the picture. Be sure to write a thesis that establishes both the topic and your opinion about it. Make the narrative come alive with sensory detail. Be sure that the sequence of events that you propose is clear to your readers.

CHAPTER

8

Example

An **example** is something selected to represent, or sometimes to show the primary nature of, the larger group to which it belongs: a rattlesnake is an example of a reptile; kidnapping is an example of crime; a Pontiac is an example of General Motors products. Put another way, an example is one of many specific instances in which a generalization can prove to be true: A package delivered two months late could be an example of the generalization that the post office provides poor service. An **example paper** relies almost solely on examples for support of the thesis, and learning to handle it well will help prepare you for all the kinds of papers you will be called on to write.

Nearly all good writing depends heavily on examples as an important means of supporting ideas—and for sound reasons. Examples give concreteness and, therefore, clarity to ideas. A magazine writer may say, for instance, that going to school can be frustrating, and, as a student, you nod your head in agreement. But how can you be sure that you and the writer have the same understanding of frustration? To you, frustration may result from the long reading assignments you find yourself plodding through, or from the difficulty of finding in the library just the right piece of information with which to finish your term paper. But when the writer goes on to tell stories about the causes of her frustration—when she writes about her inability to stand on her head in her physical education class, or her ineptness at dissecting a cat in her anatomy class, or her habitual failure to recharge the batteries of her calculator before going to her math class—you understand what the writer

EXAMPLE   167

means by frustration. The examples give to the abstract idea *frustration* not only clarity but concreteness, and the concreteness does much to make the idea interesting.

Because concreteness and clarity are essential to good writing, example often shapes even the smallest sentence sequence:

> To convince a reader, good writers usually offer support for their generalizations. In the Declaration of Independence, for example, Thomas Jefferson cited twenty-eight violations of basic human rights to support his assertion that George III was a tyrant.

Similarly, examples can develop an entire paragraph, sometimes in a chatty and informal manner:

> I can do almost anything to keep myself from writing. I can sharpen pencils. I can dust my desk. I can consider whether to use white or yellow paper. I can arrange my dictionary at a neat 45-degree angle to the wall. I can stare vacantly out the window, praying for inspiration. I can sharpen my pencils all over again.

The same principle can apply in a more formal paragraph:

> History and legend tell us that some of the greatest scientific discoveries are the result of inspirations caused by chance occurrences. Three brief examples can demonstrate this point. First, Archimedes' noticing the rise of the water level as he submerged himself in a tub led to the formulation of the laws of liquid displacement, the foundation of many of the laws of modern physics. Second, Sir Isaac Newton discovered the law of gravity because an apple fell on his head while he was sitting under a tree. Third, after being caught in a strong current of hot rising air while flying his gas balloon, George Alexander Whitehead thought about the occurrence and developed the fundamental principles of meteorology. These and other incidents show that many of the greatest scientific developments spring from lucky accidents that stimulate work in a specific direction.

Writing Your Example Paper

Sentences and paragraphs may be shaped by example, but our concern in this chapter is to look at an entire paper developed by example. In such a paper, the writer offers well-developed examples to support a thesis. The success of the paper will depend largely on the quality of these illustrations and on their arrangement. We have some suggestions.

■ *Be specific.*   Remember, the purpose of an example is to give concreteness and clarity to an idea, and you won't get either with vague language (see page

556). Notice the concrete language and the specific details in the following passage from Eric Hoffer's "Cities and Nature":

> I spent a good part of my life close to nature as a migratory worker, lumberjack, and placer miner. Mother Nature was breathing down my neck, so to speak, and I had the feeling that she did not want me around. I was bitten by every sort of insect, and scratched by burrs, foxtails and thorns. My clothes were torn by buckbrush and tangled manzanita. Hard clods pushed against my ribs when I lay down to rest, and grime ate its way into every pore of my body. Everything around me was telling me all the time to roll up and be gone. I was an unwanted intruder. I could never be at home in nature the way trees, flowers and birds are at home . . . in the city. I did not feel at ease until my feet touched the paved road.
>
> The road led to the city, and I knew with every fiber of my being that the manmade world of the city was man's only home on this planet, his refuge from an inhospitable nonhuman cosmos.

Now, consider how much less vivid and therefore less interesting is the following version of Hoffer's passage:

> I lived and worked outdoors for several years, and the experience taught me that the city is the preferable habitat for man. In nature, I always felt dirty and uncomfortable. Nature was inhospitable to me. I was an alien there and never felt comfortable until I turned again toward the city, the only appropriate environment for man.

Obviously, good examples use specific details expressed in concrete language.

■ *Make certain that your examples are examples, and that your generalization, or thesis, is one that examples can support.* As noted earlier, an example is a single item selected from many to show the nature or character of the group, or it is one of many specific instances in which a generalization proves to be true. If Suzy is the only woman in your school who has dyed her hair green, you cannot generalize that green hair is a fad in your school and then cite the one case as an example, no matter how vividly you describe Suzy's new hair color. You can, however, use Suzy's green hair as an example of her eccentricity if she really is eccentric—if she exhibits several other odd characteristics. An example is one of many, and a generalization is that which is usually or frequently or generally true of its subject.

■ *Play fair.* When the subject allows, you should try to select examples that represent an honest cross section of your subject. If you want to show, for instance, that most of the teachers in a particular school are boring lecturers, try to find examples of some who are young, some who are middle-age, and some who are nearing retirement. Again, some of your examples should be women and some men, some perhaps single teachers and some married. Your examples should also indicate a fair distribution among departments. You don't want your examples to suggest that all boring lecturers are middle-age, married men who wear glasses and teach English. Rather, you want to show that boring teachers pop up everywhere and too often in this particular school, reflecting many different ages and backgrounds and subject areas—and even ways of being boring.

EXAMPLE   **169**

Of course, you don't always have to use several examples to make your point. Often, the best way to develop a thesis is to use one extended example. Even so, the example should be selected according to the same rules of fairness that apply to the selection of numerous examples. It must truly represent an honest cross section of the subject. The following passage from Annie Dillard's "Heaven and Earth in Jest" does just that. In it, Dillard illustrates the mindless cruelty of nature with an unforgettable story about the death of a frog.

A couple of summers ago I was walking along the edge of the island to see what I could see in the water, and mainly to scare frogs. Frogs have an inelegant way of taking off from invisible positions on the bank just ahead of your feet, in dire panic, emitting a froggy "Yike!" and splashing into the water. Incredibly, this amused me, and, incredibly, it amuses me still. As I walked along the grassy edge of the island, I got better and better at seeing frogs both in and out of the water. I learned to recognize, slowing down, the difference in texture of the light reflected from mud-bank, water, grass, or frog. Frogs were flying all around me. At the end of the island I noticed a small green frog. He was exactly half in and half out of the water, looking like a schematic diagram of an amphibian, and he didn't jump.

He didn't jump; I crept closer. At last I knelt on the island's winter-killed grass, lost, dumbstruck, staring at the frog in the creek just four feet away. He was a very small frog with wide, dull eyes. And just as I looked at him, he slowly crumpled and began to sag. The spirit vanished from his eyes as if snuffed. His skin emptied and drooped; his very skull seemed to collapse and settle like a kicked tent. He was shrinking before my eyes like a deflating football. I watched the taut, glistening skin on his shoulders ruck, and rumple, and fall. Soon, part of his skin, formless as a pricked balloon, lay in floating folds like bright scum on top of the water: it was a monstrous and terrifying thing. I gaped bewildered, appalled. An oval shadow hung in the water behind the drained frog; then the shadow glided away. The frog skin bag started to sink.

I had read about the giant water bug, but never seen one. "Giant water bug" is really the name of the creature, which is an enormous, heavy-bodied brown beetle. It eats insects, tadpoles, fish, and frogs. Its grasping forelegs are mighty and hooked inward. It seizes a victim with these legs, hugs it tight, and paralyzes it with enzymes injected during a vicious bite. That one bite is the only bite it ever takes. Through the puncture shoot the poisons that dissolve the victim's muscles and bones and organs—all but the skin—and through it the giant water bug sucks out the victim's body, reduced to a juice. This event is quite common in warm fresh water. The frog I saw was being sucked by a giant water bug. I had been kneeling on the island grass, when the unrecognizable flap of frog skin settled on the creek bottom; swaying, I stood up and brushed the knees of my pants. I couldn't catch my breath.

Of course, many carnivorous animals devour their prey alive. The usual method seems to be to subdue the victim by downing or grasping it so it can't flee, then eating it whole or in a series of bloody bites. Frogs eat everything whole, stuffing prey into their mouths with their thumbs. People have seen frogs with their wide jaws so full of live dragonflies they couldn't close them. Ants don't even have to catch their prey; in the spring they swarm over newly hatched, featherless birds in the nest and eat them tiny bite by bite.

On reading this passage, we accept Dillard's generalization not only because the story of the frog's death is vividly told but also because it is representative of the mindless cruelty of nature. The author uses one extended example to make her point. The last paragraph, with its few, quick additional examples, merely confirms what the reader has already accepted.

One extended example, then, can serve to support a thesis if the example is fully and convincingly developed. More often than not, however, you can build a stronger argument with several short examples. In this case, you need to give order to your examples, and this brings us to our last tip on writing an example paper.

■ *Think about the arrangement of your examples.*   Sometimes the best arrangement is chronological. The examples in the paragraph on page 167 about scientific discoveries, for instance, are presented in chronological order—from the ancient to the modern world. At other times, a spatial order works best. In supporting a thesis about the restaurants in your town, you might offer examples from several sections of the town, and those examples could be arranged geographically from north to south, east to west.

Or consider this: Many writers like to save their best example for last in order to achieve a dramatic conclusion. Others like to use their best example first to awaken interest. Certainly, the first and last are likely to get the most attention from a reader. Since some examples are more dramatic and convincing than others, you would do well to bury any weaker ones in the middle of the paper. Of course, if all your examples are equally excellent, you have nothing to worry about.

Student Writing: Example

See what you think of the quality and arrangement of examples in the following student papers. Annotations for the first paper will help focus your attention on key elements in writing example essays.

Monica Branch

Keep It Simple

Introduction: provides background information that builds to the thesis. Paper is not about "incredible food," yet with this information writer establishes reason for choosing her thesis.

I have eaten some incredible food in my time. My family has always liked to celebrate important occasions by going out to fancy restaurants, so graduations, engagements, college acceptances, anniversaries, and so on are times to try venison with cranberry gravy, or lobster Newburg, or pasta with a cream sauce and seven

EXAMPLE   171

different kinds of unpronounceable mushrooms. So, I have eaten some fabulous meals over the years, and I have loved virtually all of them. But the more gourmet food I sample, the more I become convinced that the very best food is the simplest.

Thesis presents generalization that examples can illustrate.

Consider barbecued spareribs. They are simple, unassuming, messy finger food. But purchased from the smoke-filled corner rib joint, served over a slice of white bread to catch the sauce, with a side of fries and a paper cup of soggy coleslaw, dripping with fat, calories, and character, there is absolutely nothing better.

Transition: "Consider . . ." links first body paragraph to thesis.

2

First example to support thesis. Concrete details provide sensory image for reader.

There is nothing better except for maybe real, home-made macaroni and cheese (not the kind that comes in a box with a packet of orange powder). Give me a brutally cold winter day. Let me feast my eyes on that beautiful, crunchy, brown top, fresh from the oven. We're talking joy. We're talking peace. We're talking love.

Second example

3

Sensory appeals to sight and sound

And then there's the fluffernutter! A huge glob of peanut butter and a huger glob of marshmallow fluff on the softest white bread around--it sounds like nothing, but it is the perfect sandwich. It wraps sweet, salty, crunchy, and smooth into one convenient package. The incredible stickiness is a delight as well.

Third example: Examples represent a good cross section of the subject.

4

More specific language to provide images for reader

There are Oreo cookies, ants on a log (celery sticks decorated with cream cheese and raisins), packaged chicken soup with ring-shaped noodles, southern fried steak, cold leftover pizza, bright orange French dressing, cinnamon toast, oatmeal with brown sugar, dill pickles, and a thousand other marvelous, simple foods. I love them all.

Last body paragraph lists other examples to supplement three examples developed in previous body paragraphs.

5

6

Conclusion: Returns to the idea of the thesis and reminds reader of "incredible food" introduction.

So, the next time my family and I have something special to celebrate, I will happily go to the fanciest restaurant they can find, but my love and respect for simple, ordinary, better-than-anything foods will never cease. And I'll be down at the rib joint when they're ready to go.

➤ FOR WRITING OR DISCUSSION

1. Where does the writer first present the thesis statement? Where does she repeat it?
2. Instead of providing an additional lengthy example, the next-to-last paragraph lists a number of short examples. What is gained by this change in strategy?
3. Where are definitions provided for foods with which some readers may be unfamiliar?
4. Use the title "Keep It Simple" for an example paper of your own celebrating simplicity in a subject of your choice, such as clothing, cars, weddings, laws, music, movies, and so on.

Denise Bornszkowski

Children Don't Need Toys

1   I suppose it started when my daughter was about six months old. That was when I brought home the bunny. This soft, pink-cloth bunny was both adorable and washable. It also acted as a puppet. It came practically guaranteed to chase away nighttime fears and eliminate the need for a security blanket. It would also encourage imaginative play and interaction between parent and child. I approached my daughter with this very important toy (VIT) as she lay in her crib, happily play-ing with her toes. I slipped the rabbit on my hand, wiggled its ears, and in my best bunny voice said, "Hi, Michelle." My child stared at this VIT with absolutely no reaction. I slid the bunny over her little clenched fist. She shook it off and turned her head. I demonstrated the art of snuggling this VIT and handed it back. Perhaps just to please me, she let it rest

EXAMPLE   **173**

against her body and fell asleep. In the morning I found the bunny pushed halfway through the crib rails and my little one clutching her blanket. For the next two weeks, I played with the bunny at night and then gave it to her. By morning I would find it pushed farther and farther from her. By the third week it was all the way to the floor. It lay alongside another VIT: a soft ball with bells inside that was supposed to teach color recognition and the basic principles of cause and effect. Every morning my baby awoke holding that meaningless blanket. It was then that I first began to suspect that children really don't need toys.

2   I am told that most of you who are parents have had the following experience: It's Christmas morning and your child is very young. You have carefully selected all of the most popular and life-enriching playthings for your youngster. You have invested much time and money in anticipation of this great day. Your little one toddles out of the bedroom, warm and sleepy. You point out all of the brightly wrapped packages and hand them to the child. Within moments the big event has arrived. You are watching your bright and creative child play on Christmas morning. But it is the ribbons and bows, wrapping paper and boxes that have caught your child's fancy. The beautiful puzzles and books, building blocks and talking dolls, remote-controlled cars and other VITs lie in a disregarded heap under the tree. All you can do is shake your head and begin to plan the child's birthday. Then you can start over, and this time buy the right toys.

3   From my own childhood I remember sticks being swords, unless a string was tied on one end. They then became fishing rods. A tree was a fort. A bed was a boat. A blanket between

two chairs was a tent, and several chairs placed in a row became a train. And I did not suffer from a lack of toys.

4   A friend of mine invested in a toy sink for her son. This included a complete set of dishes and two tubs for holding water. It qualified as a VIT. The idea was that, in addition to encouraging nonsexist values, the sink would give the boy something to do while his mother was working in the kitchen. A month has gone by, and this child is still pushing a chair up to the "real sink" to do the "real dishes." He mops the floor and tries to help his mother cook. My friend has resigned herself to her son's being underfoot in the kitchen. When she's cleaning the house, she dutifully removes the dust that has gathered on the shiny new toy sink with the complete set of dishes and the two little tubs.

5   Recently my daughter celebrated her fourth birthday. Ten small children sang "Happy Birthday." Ten small children ate hot dogs and cake. Most of the ten presented my child with little dolls and ponies and crayons, enough little VITs for all to play with. Ten little figures, alone or in twos and threes, slipped away into the bedroom, leaving the baubles and trinkets behind. Soon enough, standing in the toy-laden room, I heard my child's voice: "Mommy, can we clear off the bed and jump on it?"

6   I ask you, do children really need toys?

➤ **FOR WRITING OR DISCUSSION**

1. Is the title "Children Don't Need Toys" a full statement of the writer's thesis or mostly an attention-grabbing phrase? If you feel it is not a full thesis statement, devise a more accurate one in your own words.
2. What does the writer give examples of in paragraph 3? Why are these examples important to the paper as a whole?

EXAMPLE   175

3. This essay's introductory material is presented in a single long example. The student paper that precedes it, "Keep It Simple," uses a more conventional introduction. Which introduction do you find superior? Does either one violate the principles of writing a good introduction discussed on pages 70–75?

4. In contrast to Bornszkowski's lengthy introduction, her conclusion (paragraph 6) consists of a mere eight words. Is the conclusion effective or too abrupt? Explain.

5. Write an example paper supporting one of the following theses:
   a. Parents worry too much.
   b. There are exceptions to all good rules.
   c. Children always find a way to surprise you.

Models of Writing

The four selections that follow demonstrate how effective examples can be in making a point.

ANDY ROONEY

In and of Ourselves We Trust

Last night I was driving from Harrisburg to Lewisburg, Pa., a distance of about 80 miles. It was late, I was late, and if anyone asked me how fast I was driving, I'd have to plead the Fifth Amendment to avoid self-incrimination.   1

At one point along an open highway, I came to a crossroads with a traffic light. I was alone on the road by now, but as I approached the light, it turned red, and I braked to a halt. I looked left, right, and behind me. Nothing. Not a car, no suggestion of headlights, but there I sat, waiting for the light to change, the only human being for at least a mile in any direction.   2

I started wondering why I refused to run the light. I was not afraid of being arrested, because there was obviously no cop anywhere around and there certainly would have been no danger in going through it.   3

Much later that night, after I'd met with a group in Lewisburg and had climbed into bed near midnight, the question of why I'd stopped for that light came back to me. I think I stopped because it's part of a contract we all have with each other. It's not only the law, but it's an agreement we have, and we trust each other to honor it: We don't go through red lights. Like most of us, I'm more apt to be restrained from doing something bad by the social convention that disapproves of it than by any law against it.   4

It's amazing that we ever trust each other to do the right thing, isn't it? And we do, too. Trust is our first inclination. We have to make a deliberate decision to mistrust someone or to be suspicious or skeptical.   5

6   It's a darn good thing, too, because the whole structure of our society depends on mutual trust, not distrust. This whole thing we have going for us would fall apart if we didn't trust each other most of the time. In Italy they have an awful time getting any money for the government because many people just plain don't pay their income tax. Here, the Internal Revenue Service makes some gestures toward enforcing the law, but mostly they just have to trust that we'll pay what we owe. There has often been talk of a tax revolt in this country, most recently among unemployed auto workers in Michigan, and our government pretty much admits that if there were a widespread tax revolt here, they wouldn't be able to do anything about it.

7   We do what we say we'll do. We show up when we say we'll show up.

8   I was so proud of myself for stopping for that red light. And inasmuch as no one would ever have known what a good person I was on the road from Harrisburg to Lewisburg, I had to tell someone.

➤ FOR WRITING OR DISCUSSION

1. What is meant by "a contract we all have with each other" (paragraph 4)?
2. What is the thesis of the article?
3. How many examples does Rooney use to support his thesis? Are they equally convincing?
4. Does the "we" that Rooney uses ("we trust each other to honor it") refer to all humanity or to Americans only? How do you know?
5. Do you agree that "most of us [are] more apt to be restrained from doing something bad by the social convention that disapproves of it than by any law against it" (paragraph 4)?
6. Write a paper containing two or three well-developed examples with the thesis "People will bend or break rules if they know they can get away with it."

JOHN UPDIKE

Still Afraid of Being Caught

1   In a sense, all of life—every action—is a transgression. A child's undulled sensitivity picks up the cosmic background of danger and guilt. A child is in constant danger of doing something wrong. I was most severely punished, as I fallibly recall it, for being late in getting back home. At least once and perhaps several times my mother, her face red with fury, pulled a switch from the stand of suckers at the base of the backyard pear tree and whipped me on the backs of the calves with it, when I had been, let's say, a half-hour late in returning from the playground or some friend's house a few blocks away. Fear for my safety was, I suppose now, behind this stinging discipline, but at the time it seemed mixed up with her fear that, by playing late with some other boy, I would be on the road to homosexuality. She didn't like to see me wrestling with other boys, even on our own property. No doubt she was right, taking "homosexual" in its

EXAMPLE   **177**

broadest meaning, about young male roughhousing, but to my prepubescent self her anxieties seemed exaggerated. She didn't like to see my father, a 6-foot-2 schoolteacher with, as far as I could see, normal tendencies, put his hand on his hip either. But whatever the psychological roots of her (as I saw it, with eyes full of tears) overreaction, it did its work on my superego. I have an unconquerable dread of being late for appointments or returning home later than promised, and what modest heterosexual adventures were mine in adulthood received the slight extra boost, from deep in my subconscious, of my mother's blessing. Better this than one more game of Parcheesi over at Freddy Schreuer's, as the clock ticked sinfully toward 5:30.

We were Lutherans, and, as American Protestant denominations go, Lutherans were rather soft on transgression. In Luther's combative, constipated sense of the human condition, there was not much for it but to pray for faith and have another beer. This side of the cosmic background and of my mother's sexual preferences, I didn't really think I could do much wrong. Normal childhood sadisms—bug torture, teasing, fishing—repelled me, and I was all too thoroughly inclined to believe the best of my cultural-political context, from President Roosevelt down.

A child's transgressions are often, I believe, simple misunderstandings of how the world is put together. Once, attending a movie with my parents, I took the chewing gum from my mouth and put it on the seat where my father, a second later, sat, ruining forever (my impression was) the trousers of his new suit. The sense of a grievous financial mishap, verging on ruin, permeated the days afterward, and I had no answer to the question, *Why did I do it?* The answer seemed to be that I had wanted to get the chewing gum out of my mouth and had no sense of the consequences of my placing it on the seat beside me. I certainly meant my father no harm; he was mildness itself toward me, and an awareness of his financial fragility dominated our threadbare household.

Yet the other transgression that comes to mind also threatened him, though remotely, it appears now. Shillington, Pa, was a small town, where everything impinged. My father was a schoolteacher, and his domain began just beyond our backyard, across an alley and a narrow cornfield. The school grounds included the yellow-brick high school, several accessory buildings, a football field encircled by a cinder track, a baseball diamond with grass and wire backstop and bleachers, and a softball field that was little more, off season, than a flat piece of dirt with a scruffy grass outfield. Early one spring, exulting perhaps in my March birthday, I was riding my fat-tired Elgin bicycle in this familiar terrain, alone, and thought to pedal across the dirt infield. I was stupidly slow to realize that the thawing earth was mud and that I was sinking inches down with every turn of the wheel. Within some yards, I could pedal no farther, and dismounted and walked the bike back to firmer terra; only then did I see, with a dull thud of the stomach, that I had left a profound, insolently wandering gouge in the infield, from beyond third base to behind the pitcher's mound. It looked as if a malevolent giant had run his thumb through the clay. I sneaked home, scraped the dried crust from my tires and hoped it would all be as a dream. Instead, my father began to bring home from school news of this scandal, the vandalized softball field. The higher-ups were incensed and the search for the culprit was on. He would be fired, I reasoned, if the culprit were revealed as his son, and we would all go to the county poorhouse—which, conveniently, was situated only two blocks away.

5   I forget how it turned out—my best memory is that I never confessed, and that the atrocious scar remained on the softball field until the advent of summer. How old was I? Old enough to propel a bicycle with some force, and yet so young that I did not grasp the elemental fact of spring mud. How blind we are, as we awkwardly push outward into the world! Such a sense of transgression and fatal sin clings to this (in its way, innocent) incident that I set down my confession with trepidation, fearful that the Shillington authorities will at last catch up to me, though I live hundreds of miles away, my father has been dead for more than 20 years and the last time I looked at the softball field it was covered with Astroturf.

➤ FOR WRITING OR DISCUSSION

1. What is the thesis of Updike's essay?
2. What examples does Updike provide to illustrate his point about transgression and punishment?
3. What is your response to the explanation Updike gives for his mother's anxieties about his lateness? In what ways is she merely being protective of her son's well-being? In what ways is she being homophobic? Looking back, is he tolerant or critical of her behavior? How do attitudes toward homosexuality today compare and contrast with the attitude Updike reveals in his mother?
4. Write an example paper about misdeeds and misbehaviors and the ensuing punishments, real or perceived, in your childhood or the childhood of someone you know. Develop a thesis that finds some central thread in or that proposes an interesting generalization from these examples.

BARBARA EHRENREICH

What I've Learned from Men

1   For many years I believed that women had only one thing to learn from men: how to get the attention of a waiter by some means short of kicking over the table and shrieking. Never in my life have I gotten the attention of a waiter, unless it was an off-duty waiter whose car I'd accidentally scraped in a parking lot somewhere. Men, however, can summon a maître d' just by thinking the word "coffee," and this is a power women would be well advised to study. What else would we possibly want to learn from them? How to interrupt someone in mid-sentence as if you were performing an act of conversational euthanasia? How to drop a pair of socks three feet from an open hamper and keep right on walking? How to make those weird guttural gargling sounds in the bathroom?

2   But now, at mid-life, I am willing to admit there are some real and useful things to learn from men. Not from all men—in fact, we may have the most to learn from some of the men we like the least. This realization does not mean that my feminist principles have gone soft with age: what I think women could learn from men is how to get *tough*.

EXAMPLE   179

After more than a decade of consciousness-raising, assertiveness training, and hand-to-hand combat in the battle of the sexes, we're still too ladylike. Let me try that again—we're just too *damn* ladylike.

Here is an example from my own experience, a story that I blush to recount. A few years ago, at an international conference held in an exotic and luxurious setting, a prestigious professor invited me to his room for what he said would be an intellectual discussion on matters of theoretical importance. So far, so good. I showed up promptly. But only minutes into the conversation—held in all-too-adjacent chairs—it emerged that he was interested in something more substantial than a meeting of minds. I was disgusted, but not enough to overcome 30-odd years of programming in ladylikeness. Every time his comments took a lecherous turn, I chattered distractingly; every time his hand found its way to my knee, I returned it as if it were something he had misplaced. This went on for an unconscionable period (as much as 20 minutes); then there was a minor scuffle, a dash for the door, and I was out—with nothing violated but my self-esteem. I, a full-grown feminist, conversant with such matters as rape crisis counseling and sexual harassment at the workplace, had behaved like a ninny—or, as I now understand it, like a lady.

The essence of ladylikeness is a persistent servility masked as "niceness." For example, we (women) tend to assume that it is our responsibility to keep everything "nice" even when the person we are with is rude, aggressive, or emotionally AWOL. (In the above example, I was so busy taking responsibility for preserving the veneer of "niceness" that I almost forgot to take responsibility for myself.) In conversations with men, we do almost all the work: sociologists have observed that in male–female social interactions it's the woman who throws out leading questions and verbal encouragements ("So how did you *feel* about that?" and so on) while the man, typically, says "Hmmmm." Wherever we go, we're perpetually smiling—the on-cue smile, like the now-outmoded curtsy, being one of our culture's little rituals of submission. We're trained to feel embarrassed if we're praised, but if we see a criticism coming at us from miles down the road, we rush to acknowledge it. And when we're feeling aggressive or angry or resentful, we just tighten up our smiles or turn them into rueful little moues. In short, we spend a great deal of time acting like wimps.

For contrast, think of the macho stars we love to watch. Think, for example, of Mel Gibson facing down punk marauders in "The Road Warrior" . . . John Travolta swaggering his way through the early scenes of "Saturday Night Fever" . . . or Marlon Brando shrugging off the local law in "The Wild One." Would they simper their way through tight spots? Chatter aimlessly to keep the conversation going? Get all clutched up whenever they think they might—just might—have hurt someone's feelings? No, of course not, and therein, I think, lies their fascination for us.

The attraction of the "tough guy" is that he has—or at least seems to have—what most of us lack, and that is an aura of power and control. In an article, feminist psychiatrist Jean Baker Miller writes that "a woman's using self-determined power for herself is equivalent to selfishness [and] destructiveness"—an equation that makes us want to avoid even the appearance of power. Miller cites cases of women who get depressed just when they're on the verge of success—and of women who do succeed and then bury their achievement in self-deprecation. As an example, she describes one company's periodic meetings to recognize outstanding salespeople: when a woman is asked to say a few words about her achievement, she tends to say something like, "Well, I really don't know how it happened. I guess I was just lucky this time." In contrast, the men will cheerfully own up to the hard work, intelligence, and so on, to which they owe their success. By putting herself down, a woman avoids feeling brazenly powerful and potentially "selfish"; she also does the traditional lady's work of trying to make everyone else feel better ("She's not really so smart, after all, just lucky").

7   So we might as well get a little tougher. And a good place to start is by cutting back on the small acts of deference that we've been programmed to perform since girlhood. Like unnecessary smiling. For many women—waitresses, flight attendants, receptionists—smiling is an occupational requirement, but there's no reason for anyone to go around grinning when she's not being paid for it. I'd suggest that we save our off-duty smiles for when we truly feel like sharing them, and if you're not sure what to do with your face in the meantime, study Clint Eastwood's expressions—both of them.

8   Along the same lines, I think women should stop taking responsibility for every human interaction we engage in. In a social encounter with a woman, the average man can go 25 minutes saying nothing more than "You don't say?" "Izzat so?" and, of course, "Hmmmm." Why should we do all the work? By taking so much responsibility for making conversations go well, we act as if we had much more at stake in the encounter than the other party—and that gives him (or her) the power advantage. Every now and then, we deserve to get more out of a conversation than we put into it: I'd suggest not offering information you'd rather not share ("I'm really terrified that my sales plan won't work") and not, out of sheer politeness, soliciting information you don't really want ("Wherever did you get that lovely tie?"). There will be pauses, but they don't have to be awkward for *you.*

9   It is true that some, perhaps most, men will interpret any decrease in female deference as a deliberate act of hostility. Omit the free smiles and perky conversation-boosters and someone is bound to ask, "Well, what's come over *you* today?" For most of us, the first impulse is to stare at our feet and make vague references to a terminally ill aunt in Atlanta, but we should have as much right to be taciturn as the average (male) taxi driver. If you're taking a vacation from smiles and small talk and some fellow is moved to inquire about what's "bothering" you, just stare back levelly and say, the international debt crisis, the arms race, or the death of God.

10 There are all kinds of ways to toughen up—and potentially move up—at work, and I leave the details to the purveyors of assertiveness training. But Jean Baker Miller's study underscores a fundamental principle that anyone can master on her own. We can stop acting less capable than we actually are. For example, in the matter of taking credit when credit is due, there's a key difference between saying "I was just lucky" and saying "I had a plan and it worked." If you take the credit you deserve, you're letting people know that you were confident you'd succeed all along, and that you fully intend to do so again.

11 Finally, we may be able to learn something from men about what to do with anger. As a general rule, women get irritated: men get *mad.* We make tight little smiles of ladylike exasperation; they pound on desks and roar. I wouldn't recommend emulating the full basso profundo male tantrum, but women do need ways of expressing justified

EXAMPLE   181

anger clearly, colorfully, and, when necessary, crudely. If you're not just irritated, but *pissed off,* it might help to say so.

I, for example, have rerun the scene with the prestigious professor many times in my mind. And in my mind, I play it like Bogart. I start by moving my chair over to where I can look the professor full in the face. I let him do the chattering, and when it becomes evident that he has nothing serious to say, I lean back and cross my arms, just to let him know that he's wasting my time. I do not smile, neither do I nod encouragement. Nor, of course, do I respond to his blandishments with apologetic shrugs and blushes. Then, at the first flicker of lechery, I stand up and announce coolly, "All right, I've had enough of this crap." Then I walk out—slowly, deliberately, confidently. Just like a man.   12

Or—now that I think of it—just like a woman.   13

> ## ➤ FOR WRITING OR DISCUSSION

1. Specifically, what changes in their usual behavior does the author think would be beneficial for women?
2. Is the author guilty of stereotyping men and women?
3. Why is the frequent use of humor so effective?
4. Write a paper using examples either to describe or to demonstrate the falsity of a common male or female stereotype (the "strong, silent type," the "jock," the "dumb blonde," the "schoolmarm," and so on).

BRENT STAPLES

Just Walk On By: A Black Man Ponders His Power to Alter Public Space

My first victim was a woman—white, well dressed, probably in her early twenties. I came upon her late one evening on a deserted street in Hyde Park, a relatively affluent neighborhood in an otherwise mean, impoverished section of Chicago. As I swung onto the avenue behind her, there seemed to be a discreet, uninflammatory distance between us. Not so. She cast back a worried glance. To her, the youngish black man—a broad six feet two inches with a beard and billowing hair, both hands shoved into the pockets of a bulky military jacket—seemed menacingly close. After a few more quick glimpses, she picked up her pace and was soon running in earnest. Within seconds she disappeared into a cross street.   1

That was more than a decade ago. I was twenty-two years old, a graduate student newly arrived at the University of Chicago. It was in the echo of that terrified woman's footfalls that I first began to know the unwieldy inheritance I'd come into—the ability to alter public space in ugly ways. It was clear that she thought herself the quarry of a mugger, a rapist, or worse. Suffering a bout of insomnia, however, I was stalking sleep, not defenseless wayfarers. As a softy who is scarcely able to take a knife to a raw chicken—let alone hold it to a person's throat—I was surprised, embarrassed, and   2 dismayed all at once. Her flight made me feel like an accomplice in tyranny. It also made it clear that I was indistinguishable from the muggers who occasionally seeped into the area from the surrounding ghetto. That first encounter, and those that followed, signified that a vast, unnerving gulf lay between nighttime pedestrians—particularly women—and me. And I soon gathered that being perceived as dangerous is a hazard in itself. I only needed to turn a corner into a dicey situation, or crowd some frightened, armed person in a foyer somewhere, or make an errant move after being pulled over by a policeman. Where fear and weapons meet—and they often do in urban America—there is always the possibility of death.

3   In that first year, my first away from my hometown, I was to become thoroughly familiar with the language of fear. At dark, shadowy intersections in Chicago, I could cross in front of a car stopped at a traffic light and elicit the *thunk, thunk, thunk, thunk* of the driver—black, white, male, or female—hammering down the door locks. On less traveled streets after dark, I grew accustomed to but never comfortable with people who crossed to the other side of the street rather than pass me. Then there were the standard unpleasantries with police, doormen, bouncers, cab drivers, and others whose business it is to screen out troublesome individuals *before* there is any nastiness.

4   I moved to New York nearly two years ago and I have remained an avid night walker. In central Manhattan, the near-constant crowd cover minimizes tense one-on-one street encounters. Elsewhere—visiting friends in SoHo,[1] where sidewalks are narrow and tightly spaced buildings shut out the sky—things can get very taut indeed.

5   Black men have a firm place in New York mugging literature. Norman Podhoretz[2] in his famed (or infamous) 1963 essay, "My Negro Problem—And Ours," recalls growing up in terror of black males; they "were tougher than we were, more ruthless," he writes—and as an adult on the Upper West Side of Manhattan, he continues, he cannot constrain his nervousness when he meets black men on certain streets. Similarly, a decade later, the essayist and novelist Edward Hoagland extols a New York where once "Negro bitterness bore down mainly on other Negroes." Where some see mere panhandlers, Hoagland sees "a mugger who is clearly screwing up his nerve to do more than just *ask* for money." But Hoagland has "the New Yorker's quick-hunch posture for broken-field maneuvering," and the bad guy swerves away.

6   I often witness that "hunch posture," from women after dark on the warrrenlike streets of Brooklyn where I live. They seem to set their faces on neutral and, with their purse straps strung across their chests bandolier style, they forge ahead as though bracing themselves against being tackled. I understand, of course, that the danger they perceive is not a hallucination. Women are particularly vulnerable to street violence, and young black males are drastically overrepresented among the perpetrators of that violence. Yet these truths are no solace against the kind of alienation that comes of being ever the suspect, against being set apart, a fearsome entity with whom pedestrians avoid making eye contact.

7   It is not altogether clear to me how I reached the ripe old age of twenty-two without being conscious of the lethality nighttime pedestrians attributed to me. Perhaps it was

[1]A district of lower Manhattan.
[2]A well-known author, literary critic, and former editor of *Commentary* magazine.

EXAMPLE   **183**

because in Chester, Pennsylvania, the small, angry industrial town where I came of age in the 1960s, I was scarcely noticeable against a backdrop of gang warfare, street knifings, and murders. I grew up one of the good boys, had perhaps a half-dozen fist fights. In retrospect, my shyness of combat has clear sources.

Many things go into the making of a young thug. One of those things is the consummation of the male romance with the power to intimidate. An infant discovers that random flailings send the baby bottle flying out of the crib and crashing to the floor. Delighted, the joyful babe repeats those motions again and again, seeking to duplicate the feat. Just so, I recall the points at which some of my boyhood friends were finally seduced by the perception of themselves as tough guys. When a mark cowered and surrendered his money without resistance, myth and reality merged—and paid off. It is, after all, only manly to embrace the power to frighten and intimidate. We, as men, are not supposed to give an inch of our lane on the highway; we are to seize the fighter's edge in work and in play and even in love; we are to be valiant in the face of hostile forces.

Unfortunately, poor and powerless young men seem to take all this nonsense literally. As a boy, I saw countless tough guys locked away; I have since buried several, too. They were babies, really—a teenage cousin, a brother of twenty-two, a childhood friend in his mid-twenties—all gone down in episodes of bravado played out in the streets. I came to doubt the virtues of intimidation early on. I chose, perhaps even unconsciously, to remain a shadow—timid, but a survivor.

The fearsomeness mistakenly attributed to me in public places often has a perilous flavor. The most frightening of these confusions occurred in the late 1970s and early 1980s when I worked as a journalist in Chicago. One day, rushing into the office of a magazine I was writing for with a deadline story in hand, I was mistaken for a burglar. The office manager called security and, with an ad hoc posse, pursued me through the labyrinthine halls, nearly to my editor's door. I had no way of proving who I was. I could only move briskly toward the company of someone who knew me.

Another time I was on assignment for a local paper and killing time before an interview. I entered a jewelry store on the city's affluent Near North Side. The proprietor excused herself and returned with an enormous red Doberman pinscher straining at the end of a leash. She stood, the dog extended toward me, silent to my questions, her eyes bulging nearly out of her head. I took a cursory look around, nodded, and bade her good night. Relatively speaking, however, I never fared as badly as another black male journalist. He went to nearby Waukegan, Illinois, a couple of summers ago to work on a story about a murderer who was born there. Mistaking the reporter for the killer, police hauled him from his car at gunpoint and but for his press credentials would probably have tried to book him. Such episodes are not uncommon. Black men trade tales like this all the time.

In "My Negro Problem—And Ours," Podhoretz writes that the hatred he feels for blacks makes itself known to him through a variety of avenues—one being his discomfort with that "special brand of paranoid touchiness" to which he says blacks are prone. No doubt he is speaking here of black men. In time, I learned to smother the rage I felt at so often being taken for a criminal. Not to do so would surely have led to madness—via that special "paranoid touchiness" that so annoyed Podhoretz at the time he wrote the essay.

13   I began to take precautions to make myself less threatening. I moved about with care, particularly late in the evening. I give a wide berth to nervous people on subway platforms during the wee hours, particularly when I have exchanged business clothes for jeans. If I happen to be entering a building behind some people who appear skittish, I may walk by, letting them clear the lobby before I return, so as not to seem to be following them. I have been calm and extremely congenial on those rare occasions when I've been pulled over by the police.

14   And on late-evening constitutionals along streets less traveled by, I employ what has proved to be an excellent tension-reducing measure: I whistle melodies from Beethoven and Vivaldi and the more popular classical composers. Even steely New Yorkers hunching toward nighttime destinations seem to relax, and occasionally they even join in the tune. Virtually everybody seems to sense that a mugger wouldn't be warbling bright, sunny selections from Vivaldi's *Four Seasons.* It is my equivalent of the cowbell that hikers wear when they know they are in bear country.

➤ **FOR WRITING OR DISCUSSION**

1. What is the thesis of Staples's essay? Is it implied or expressed directly?
2. Which examples does the writer provide to support the thesis? In what way do the examples differ sufficiently from one another to represent an honest cross section of experiences?
3. How much does the author blame the individual Chicago woman in his first example for her reaction to him (paragraphs 1–2)?
4. Write an example paper showing that prejudice—racism, sexism, ageism, prejudice because of religion or ethnic background—is still very much present today. Or, use examples to show that prejudice of a particular kind is practiced less often today than in the past.

Readings for Writing

A short, humorous article on a serious topic, a short story about finding a job, and a well-known essay on wanting a wife provide you with possible subject matter for an example paper.

MILOS VAMOS

How I'll Become an American

1   I have been Hungarian for 38 years. I'll try something else for the next 38. I'll try to be American, for instance. North American, I mean. As an American, I'll speak English fluently. I'll make American mistakes instead of Hungarian mistakes and I'll call them slang.

EXAMPLE   **185**

As an American, I'll have a credit card. Or two. I'll use and misuse them and have   2
to pay the fees. I'll apply for other cards right away. Golden Visa. Golden American.
Golden Gate. And I'll buy a car, a great American car. Then I'll sell my car and buy a
smaller West German car because it's reliable and doesn't use so much gasoline. Later,
I'll sell it and buy a smaller Japanese car with a computer aboard. Then I'll sell it and
buy a camper. When I sell the camper I'll buy a bicycle.

As an American, I'll buy a dog. And a cat. And a goat. And a white whale. And also   3
some big stones as pets.

I'll live in my own house. It will be mine, except for the 99 percent mortgage. I'll   4
sell my house and buy a condo. I'll sell my condo and buy a mobile home. I'll sell my
mobile home and buy an igloo. I'll sell my igloo and buy a tent. As an American, I'll be
clever: I'll sell my igloo and buy a tent when I move to Florida from Alaska.

Anyway, I'll move a lot. And I'll buy the best dishwasher, microwave, dryer and hi-   5
fi in the world—that is, the U.S.A. I'll have warranty for all—or my money back. I'll use
automatic toothbrushes, egg boilers and garage doors. I'll call every single phone number starting 1-800.

I'll buy the fastest food I can get and I'll eat it very slowly because I'll watch TV dur-   6
ing the meals. Of course, I'll buy a VCR. I'll watch the taped programs and then retape.
Sometimes I'll retape first.

As an American, I'll have an answering machine, too. My outgoing message will   7
promise that I'll call you back as soon as possible, but it won't be possible soon.

If I answer the phone as an exception, I'll tell you that I can't talk now because I   8
have a long-distance call on the other line, but I'll call you back as soon as possible
(see above).

And I'll get a job. I'll always be looking for a better job, but I won't get the job I   9
want. I'll work really hard since as an American I wanna be rich. I'll be always in a
hurry: Time Is Money. Unfortunately, my time won't be worth as much money as my
bosses' time. Sometimes I will have some time and I still won't have enough money.
Then I'll start to hate the wisdom of this saying.

As an American, sometimes I'll be badly depressed. I'll be the patient of 12 psychia-   10
trists, and I'll be disappointed with all of them. I'll try to change my life a little bit. I'll try to
exchange my wives, my cars, my lovers, my houses, my children, my jobs and my pets.

Sometimes, I'll exchange a few dollars into other currencies and I'll travel to   11
Europe, Hawaii, Tunisia, Martinique and Japan. I'll be happy to see that people all over
the world are jealous of us Americans.

I'll take at least 2,000 snapshots on each trip. I'll also buy a video camera and shoot   12
everywhere. I'll look at the tapes, photos and slides, and I'll try to remember my experiences when I have time and am in the mood. But I won't have time or be in the mood
because I'll get depressed again and again.

I'll smoke cigarettes. Then I'll be afraid of cancer and I'll stop. I'll smoke cigars. And   13
opium. I'll take a breather and then try LSD and heroin and cocaine and marijuana. To
top it all off: crack. I'll try to stop then but I won't be able.

I'll call 1-800-222-HELP. If nothing helps, I'll have some gay experiences. And   14
swing. And if I am still unhappy, I'll make a final effort: I'll try to read a book. I'll buy

15   I'll always be concerned about my health as an American. I won't eat anything but health food until I get ill. From time to time, I'll read in the paper that I should stop eating meat, sugar, bread, fiber, grains, iron, toothpaste, and that I should stop drinking milk, soda, water, acid rain. I'll try to follow this advice, but then I'll read in the paper that I should do it the other way around.

some best sellers. I'll prefer James A. Michener. My second favorite will be the "How to Be Rich in Seven Weeks." I'll try to follow this advice in seven years.

16   I'll be puzzled. "Hey, I don't even know what cholesterol is!" Yet I'll stick to decaf coffee, sugar-free cookies, salt-free butter and lead-free gasoline. I'll believe that proper diet and exercise make life longer. I'll go jogging every day until I am mugged twice and knocked down three times. Then I'll just exercise in my room, but it will also increase my appetite. I'll go on several diets, and little by little I'll reach 200 pounds.

17   As an American, I'll buy a new TV every time a larger screen appears on the market. In the end, the screen will be larger than the room. It will be difficult to put this enormous TV into my living room; thus, I will put my living room into the TV. Anyway, my living room will look very much like the living rooms you can see on the screen. My life won't differ from the lives you can see in the soaps: nobody will complain. I won't complain either. I'll always smile.

18   After all, we are Americans, aren't we?

> ## FOR WRITING OR DISCUSSION

1. How does the writer produce the obviously humorous effects in this essay? What elements of being an American does this Hungarian writer hold up for us to look at?
2. From your point of view, which features of Americanism presented in Vamos's essay strike closest to home? Do you recognize yourself, your relatives, or your friends in these details? Which ones? Give some examples of the Americanism you observe in yourself and others.
3. Write an example paper on what qualities you think someone wanting to be an American should adopt. Make your paper humorous, like Vamos's, or serious if you prefer.

GARY SOTO

Looking for Work

1   One July, while killing ants on the kitchen sink with a rolled newspaper, I had a nine-year-old's vision of wealth that would save us from ourselves. For weeks I had drunk Kool-Aid and watched morning reruns of *Father Knows Best,* whose family was so uncomplicated in its routine that I very much wanted to imitate it. The first step was to get my brother and sister to wear shoes at dinner.

EXAMPLE   **187**

"Come on, Rick—come on, Deb," I whined. But Rick mimicked me and the same   2
day that I asked him to wear shoes he came to the dinner table in only his swim trunks.
My mother didn't notice, nor did my sister, as we sat to eat our beans and tortillas in the
stifling heat of our kitchen. We all gleamed like cellophane, wiping the sweat from our
brows with the backs of our hands as we talked about the day: Frankie our neighbor was
beat up by Faustino; the swimming pool at the playground would be closed for a day
because the pump was broken.

Such was our life. So that morning, while doing-in the train of ants which arrived   3
each day, I decided to become wealthy, and right away! After downing a bowl of cereal,
I took a rake from the garage and started up the block to look for work.

We lived on an ordinary block of mostly working class people: warehousemen,   4
egg candlers, welders, mechanics, and a union plumber. And there were many retired
people who kept their lawns green and the gutters uncluttered of the chewing gum
wrappers we dropped as we rode by on our bikes. They bent down to gather our litter,
muttering at our evilness.

At the corner house I rapped the screen door and a very large woman in a muu-muu   5
answered. She sized me up and then asked what I could do.

"Rake leaves," I answered, smiling.   6

"It's summer, and there ain't no leaves," she countered. Her face was pinched with   7
lines; fat jiggled under her chin. She pointed to the lawn, then the flower bed, and said:
"You see any leaves there—or there?" I followed her pointing arm, stupidly. But she had
a job for me and that was to get her a Coke at the liquor store. She gave me twenty cents,
and after ditching my rake in a bush, off I ran. I returned with an unbagged Pepsi, for
which she thanked me and gave me a nickel from her apron.

I skipped off her porch, fetched my rake, and crossed the street to the next block where   8
Mrs. Moore, mother of Earl the retarded man, let me weed a flower bed. She handed me a
trowel and for a good part of the morning my fingers dipped into the moist dirt, ripping up
runners of Bermuda grass. Worms surfaced in my search for deep roots, and I cut them in
halves, tossing them to Mrs. Moore's cat who pawed them playfully as they dried in the
sun. I made out Earl whose face was pressed to the back window of the house, and
although he was calling to me I couldn't understand what he was trying to say. Embarrassed, I worked without looking up, but I imagined his contorted mouth and the ring of
keys attached to his belt—keys that jingled with each palsied step. He scared me and I
worked quickly to finish the flower bed. When I did finish Mrs. Moore gave me a quarter
and two peaches from her tree, which I washed there but ate in the alley behind my house.

I was sucking on the second one, a bit of juice staining the front of my T-shirt, when   9
Little John, my best friend, came walking down the alley with a baseball bat over his
shoulder, knocking over trash cans as he made his way toward me.

Little John and I went to St. John's Catholic School, where we sat among the "stu-   10
pids." Miss Marino, our teacher, alternated the rows of good students with the bad, hoping that by sitting side-by-side with the bright students the stupids might become more
intelligent, as though intelligence were contagious. But we didn't progress as she had
hoped. She grew frustrated when one day, while dismissing class for recess, Little John
couldn't get up because his arms were stuck in the slats of the chair's backrest. She
scolded us with a shaking finger when we knocked over the globe, denting the already

troubled Africa. She muttered curses when Leroy White, a real stupid but a great soft-ball player with the gift to hit to all fields, openly chewed his host when he made his First Communion; his hands swung at his sides as he returned to the pew looking around with a big smile.

11   Little John asked what I was doing, and I told him that I was taking a break from work, as I sat comfortably among high weeds. He wanted to join me, but I reminded him that the last time he'd gone door-to-door asking for work his mother had whipped him. I was with him when his mother, a New Jersey Italian who could rise up in anger one moment and love the next, told me in a polite but matter-of-fact voice that I had to leave because she was going to beat her son. She gave me a homemade popsicle, ush-ered me to the door, and said that I could see Little John the next day. But it was sooner than that I went around to his bedroom window to suck my popsicle and watch Little John dodge his mother's blows, a few hitting their mark but many whirring air.

12   It was midday when Little John and I converged in the alley, the sun blazing in the high nineties, and he suggested that we go to Roosevelt High School to swim. He needed five cents to make fifteen, the cost of admission, and I lent him a nickel. We ran home for my bike and when my sister found out that we were going swimming she started to cry because she didn't have the fifteen cents but only an empty Coke bottle. I waved for her to come and three of us mounted the bike—Debra on the cross bar, Little John on the handle bars and holding the Coke bottle which we would cash for a nickel and make up the difference that would allow all of us to get in, and me pumping up the crooked streets, dodging cars and pot holes. We spent the day swimming in the after-noon sun, so that when we got home our mom asked us what was darker, the floor or us? She feigned a stern posture, her hands on her hips and her mouth puckered. We played along. Looking down, Debbie and I said in unison, "Us."

13   That evening at dinner we all sat down in our bathing suits to eat our beans, laugh-ing and chewing loudly. Our mom was in a good mood, so I took a risk and asked her if sometime we could have turtle soup. A few days before I had watched a television pro-gram in which a Polynesian tribe killed a large turtle, gutted it, and then stewed it over an open fire. The turtle, basted in a sugary sauce, looked delicious as I ate an afternoon bowl of cereal, but my sister, who was watching the program with a glass of Kool-Aid between her knees, said, "Caca."

14   My mother looked at me in bewilderment. "Boy, are you a crazy Mexican. Where did you get the idea that people eat turtles?"

15   "On television," I said, explaining the program. Then I took it a step further. "Mom, do you think we could get dressed up for dinner one of these days? David King does."

16   "*Ay, Dios,*" my mother laughed. She started collecting the dinner plates, but my brother wouldn't let go of his. He was still drawing a picture in the bean sauce. Gig-gling, he said it was me, but I didn't want to listen because I wanted an answer from Mom. This was the summer when I spent the mornings in front of the television that showed the comfortable lives of white kids. There were no beatings, no rifts in the fam-ily. They wore bright clothes; toys tumbled from their closets. They hopped into bed with kisses and woke to glasses of fresh orange juice, and to a father sitting before his morning coffee while the mother buttered his toast. They hurried through the day mak-ing friends and gobs of money, returning home to a warmly lit living room, and then dinner. *Leave It to Beaver* was the program I replayed in my mind:

EXAMPLE   **189**

"May I have the mashed potatoes?" asks Beaver with a smile.   17

"Sure, Beav," replies Wally as he taps the corners of his mouth with a starched napkin.   18

The father looks on in his suit. The mother, decked out in earrings and a pearl neck-   19
lace, cuts into her steak and blushes. Their conversation is politely clipped.

"Swell," says Beaver, his cheeks puffed with food.   20

Our own talk at dinner was loud with belly laughs and marked by our pointing forks   21
at one another. The subjects were commonplace.

"Gary, let's go to the ditch tomorrow," my brother suggests. He explains that he has   22
made a life preserver out of four empty detergent bottles strung together with twine and
that he will make me one if I can find more bottles. "No way are we going to drown."

"Yeah, then we could have a dirt clod fight," I reply, so happy to be alive.   23

Whereas the Beaver's family enjoyed dessert in dishes at the table, our mom sent us   24
outside, and more often than not I went into the alley to peer over the neighbor's fences
and spy out fruit, apricots, or peaches.

I had asked my mom and again she laughed that I was a crazy *chavalo* as she stood   25
in front of the sink, her arms rising and falling with suds, face glistening from the heat.
She sent me outside where my brother and sister were sitting in the shade that the fence
threw out like a blanket. They were talking about me when I plopped down next to
them. They looked at one another and then Debbie, my eight-year-old sister, started in.

"What's this crap about getting dressed up?"   26

She had entered her profanity stage. A year later she would give up such words and   27
slip into her Catholic uniform, and into squealing on my brother and me when we
"cussed this" and "cussed that."

I tried to convince them that if we improved the way we looked we might get along   28
better in life. White people would like us more. They might invite us to places, like
their homes or front yards. They might not hate us so much.

My sister called me a "craphead," and got up to leave with a stalk of grass dangling   29
from her mouth. "They'll never like us."

My brother's mood lightened as he talked about the ditch—the white water, the   30
broken pieces of glass, and the rusted car fenders that awaited our knees. There would
be toads, and rocks to smash them.

David King, the only person we know who resembled the middle class, called   31
from over the fence. David was Catholic, of Armenian and French descent, and his
closet was filled with toys. A bear-shaped cookie jar, like the ones on television, sat on
the kitchen counter. His mother was remarkably kind while she put up with the racket
we made on the street. Evenings, she often watered the front yard and it must have
upset her to see us—my brother and I and others—jump from trees laughing, the
unkillable kids of the very poor, who got up unshaken, brushed off, and climbed into
another one to try again.

David called again. Rick got up and slapped grass from his pants. When I asked if I   32
could come along he said no. David said no. They were two years older so their affairs
were different from mine. They greeted one another with foul names and took off down
the alley to look for trouble.

I went inside the house, turned on the television, and was about to sit down with a   33
glass of Kool-Aid when Mom shooed me outside.

"It's still light," she said. "Later you'll bug me to let you stay out longer. So go on."   34

35   I downed my Kool-Aid and went outside to the front yard. No one was around. The day had cooled and a breeze rustled the trees. Mr. Jackson, the plumber, was watering his lawn and when he saw me he turned away to wash off his front steps. There was more than an hour of light left, so I took advantage of it and decided to look for work. I felt suddenly alive as I skipped down the block in search of an overgrown flower bed and the dime that would end the day right.

➤ **FOR WRITING OR DISCUSSION**

1. What vision does the narrator have that would save his family from themselves? What does his television watching have to do with this vision?
2. What do the shows *Father Knows Best* and *Leave It to Beaver* portray? How does the narrator feel about them? What is the relation between the narrator's life and the life shown on these television programs?
3. What jobs does the narrator describe? How did Mrs. Moore reward him for his work? Why do you think work is so important to the narrator? What sensory details make the scene come alive for you?
4. What does the information about the teacher, Mrs. Marino, and how she treats the narrator and his friend, Little John, contribute to the story?
5. Write an example paper about your reactions toward your first job. Once you establish your attitude toward it in your thesis, provide specific examples from your job experience to support that attitude. Be sure to describe your physical surroundings and your employer and (or) the people you worked with. Use concrete sensory detail in the way that Soto has to help readers picture the scene.

HAVING YOUR SAY

Soto's young narrator thinks that work will change his life for the better, but many people argue that work is not right for children: In fact, we have laws that prevent young children from working. Write a paper in which you argue for or against the value of work for young people. Give examples to support your position.

JUDY BRADY

I Want a Wife

1   I belong to that classification of people knows as wives. I am A Wife. And, not altogether incidentally, I am a mother.

2   Not too long ago a male friend of mine appeared on the scene fresh from a recent divorce. He had one child, who is, of course, with his ex-wife. He is obviously looking

EXAMPLE   191

for another wife. As I thought about him while I was ironing one evening, it suddenly occurred to me that I, too, would like to have a wife. Why do I want a wife?

I would like to go back to school so that I can become economically independent, support myself, and, if need be, support those dependent upon me. I want a wife who will work and send me to school. And while I am going to school I want a wife to keep track of the children's doctor and dentist appointments. And to keep track of mine, too. I want a wife to make sure my children eat properly and are kept clean. I want a wife who will wash the children's clothes and keep them mended. I want a wife who is a good nurturant attendant to my children, who arranges for their schooling, makes sure that they have an adequate social life with their peers, takes them to the park, the zoo, etc. I want a wife who takes care of the children when they are sick, a wife who arranges to be around when the children need special care, because, of course, I cannot miss classes at school. My wife must arrange to lose time at work and not lose the job. It may mean a small cut in my wife's income from time to time, but I guess I can tolerate that. Needless to say, my wife will arrange and pay for the care of the children while my wife is working.

I want a wife who will take care of *my* physical needs. I want a wife who will keep my house clean. A wife who will pick up after me. I want a wife who will keep my clothes clean, ironed, mended, replaced when need be, and who will see to it that my personal things are kept in their proper place so that I can find what I need the minute I need it. I want a wife who cooks the meals, a wife who is a *good* cook. I want a wife who will plan the menus, do the necessary grocery shopping, prepare the meals, serve them pleasantly, and then do the cleaning up while I do my studying. I want a wife who will care for me when I am sick and sympathize with my pain and loss of time from school. I want a wife to go along when our family takes a vacation so that someone can continue to care for me and my children when I need a rest and change of scene.

I want a wife who will not bother me with rambling complaints about a wife's duties. But I want a wife who will listen to me when I feel the need to explain a rather difficult point I have come across in my course of studies. And I want a wife who will type my papers for me when I have written them.

I want a wife who will take care of the details of my social life. When my wife and I are invited out by my friends, I want a wife who will take care of the babysitting arrangements. When I meet people at school that I like and want to entertain, I want a wife who will have the house clean, will prepare a special meal, serve it to me and my friends, and not interrupt when I talk about the things that interest me and my friends. I want a wife who will have arranged that the children are fed and ready for bed before my guests arrive so that the children do not bother us. I want a wife who takes care of the needs of my guests so that they feel comfortable, who makes sure that they have an ashtray, that they are passed the hors d'oeuvres, that they are offered a second helping of the food, that their wine glasses are replenished when necessary, that their coffee is served to them as they like it.

And I want a wife who knows that sometimes I need a night out by myself.

I want a wife who is sensitive to my sexual needs, a wife who makes love passionately and eagerly when I feel like it, a wife who makes sure that I am satisfied. And, of course, I want a wife who will not demand sexual attention when I am not in the mood for it. I want a wife who assumes the complete responsibility for birth control, because I do not want more children. I want a wife who will remain sexually faithful to me so that I do not have to clutter up my intellectual life with jealousies. And I want a wife who understands that *my* sexual needs may entail more than strict adherence to monogamy. I must, after all, be able to relate to people as fully as possible.

9   If, by chance, I find another person more suitable as a wife than the wife I already have, I want the liberty to replace my present wife with another one. Naturally, I will expect a fresh, new life; my wife will take the children and be solely responsible for them so that I am left free.

10   When I am through with school and have a job, I want my wife to quit working and remain at home so that my wife can more fully and completely take care of a wife's duties.

11   My God, who *wouldn't* want a wife?

➤ **FOR WRITING OR DISCUSSION**

1. What is the thesis of this essay?
2. How does Brady use the rhetorical strategy of example? Which examples do you find most compelling in support of Brady's argument?
3. What is the effect on the reader of the multiple examples Brady provides? How successful is she in supporting her argument?
3. How has the writer achieved a humorous effect in the essay? In what ways do you detect anger or frustration beneath the surface of the humor?
3. Write an essay called "I Want a Husband." Write the essay from the point of view of a *male* seeking a husband, and provide examples in the way that Brady has. You can choose a humorous or a serious tone, based on your purpose.

HAVING YOUR SAY

Brady wrote this essay in 1970. Have demands on women in our society changed or remained the same from those indicated in the essay? Select one side or the other and write an argumentative paper in which you support your point with specific details.

WRITING TOPICS

If you are having difficulty deciding on a topic for your example paper, you might find some help among our suggestions. Use examples to support or attack one of the following statements.

1. One can tell a great deal about people from the way they dress.
2. I've learned to "eat healthy."
3. Some television commercials are more entertaining than most of the programs.

EXAMPLE   193

4. My senior year in high school was a waste.
5. Many dangers await the desert hiker.
6. Teenagers are the worst conformists of all.
7. Student government teaches important values.
8. Religion leaves many serious problems unsolved.
9. Most of what I enjoy is bad for me.
10. The dating game annoys me.
11. Who needs friends?
12. The chores on a farm are endless!
13. Not all problems can be solved—we just have to live with them.
14. Some modern conveniences have turned out to be very inconvenient.
15. If you can keep your head when all about you are losing theirs, you probably don't understand the seriousness of the situation.

CROSSCURRENTS

1. Andy Rooney writes in "In and of Ourselves We Trust" (page 175): "the whole structure of our society depends on mutual trust, not distrust." Based on your reading of "Just Walk On By: A Black Man Ponders His Power to Alter Public Space" (page 181), what do you think Brent Staples would say in response to Rooney's statement and other relevant ideas in Rooney's essay? Write a letter from Staples to Rooney in which you make your point.
2. One of the main premises in Barbara Ehrenreich's "What I've Learned from Men" (page 178) is that what women could learn from men is "how to get *tough*" and that the tough guy's attraction is that he seems to have, or does have, "an aura of power and control." How would Ehrenreich react to John Updike in "Still Afraid of Being Caught" (page 176)? Does the kind of trepidation he shows in confessing his sins make him weak, or does he maintain "an aura of power and control"? Are Updike's comments related to gender or to something else, do you think? Could a woman have written a piece like "Still Afraid of Being Caught"? Explain your answer.

COLLABORATIVE LEARNING

In groups of five discuss the student essays "Keep It Simple" (page 170) and "Children Don't Need Toys" (page 172) as models of example essays. Comment on the thesis, the quality of the examples (are they specific, fair, and arranged in a clear and effective order, for instance), the introduction and the conclusion, and any other elements that draw your attention. Also consider the audiences to whom the writers have directed their papers. Do thesis, purpose, and details make the point successfully? What recommendations could you make to improve the essays?

REVIEW CHECKLIST: WRITING AND REVISING YOUR EXAMPLE PAPER

- Have I used prewriting to explore ideas for a subject?
- Have I thought carefully about my purpose?
- Have I written for the usual general audience? If I am writing for a special audience, have I made that clear to the reader?
- Have I limited my subject?
- Have I established a clear thesis?
- Do I have enough support for my thesis?
- Are my examples specific?
- Have I selected fair examples?
- Have I arranged my examples in a clear and effective order?
- Have I proofread for grammar, spelling, and mechanics?

EXAMPLE   195

Photo courtesy: © Alden Pellett/The Image Works

——— **FROM IMAGE TO WORDS: A PHOTO WRITING ASSIGNMENT** ———

Use the photograph above as the basis of an essay that you develop by examples. First, decide on a topic that the photograph suggests and your attitude towards it. For example, you might propose a thesis like one of these:

- It's easy to tell the sure signs of spring.
- A Saturday morning in June at the park is filled with people having a good time.

Feel free to use one of these; or develop a thesis sentence of your own. Whatever your thesis sentence, be sure that you support it with examples drawn from the photograph. Feel free to expand and embellish details through concrete sensory language.

Process

The **process** paper describes a series of actions, changes, or functions that bring about an end or a result. The most familiar kind of process paper is the "how-to" paper, a step-by-step set of instructions on how to complete a particular task—how to change a tire, how to bake a cake, how to do aerobic exercise, how to assemble a bicycle.

Writing Your Process Paper

Here are some guidelines for writing process papers:

■ *Make certain that the explanation is complete and accurate.* If, for example, you want to describe the process for baking a cake, you would mislead your reader if you omitted the instruction to grease and flour the pan. It's surprisingly easy to leave out important steps. You will be writing about a process you know extremely well, and you probably perform some steps—such as greasing a pan—without consciously thinking about them.

■ *Maintain strict chronological order.* Tell your reader what to do first, what to do second, and so on. Once the cake is in the oven, it is too late to say that one must stir walnuts into the batter.

■ *If a particular kind of performance is called for in any part of the process, indicate its nature.* Should the batter be stirred vigorously or gently? Should an applicant for a job approach the interviewer humbly, aggressively, nonchalantly? Besides indicating the nature of the action, you should also tell the reader why such action is called for. Readers are more likely to follow instructions if they understand the reasons for them.

■ *Group the steps in the process.*   A process may include many steps, but you usually can group them in their chronological order, under logical headings.

Suppose you want to explain how to make a favorite dish—stir-fried shrimp, for example. You could develop paragraphs around two headings as part of a rough outline as shown here. Because they often require such precise steps in strict order, process papers lend themselves to outlining. You should develop an outline (see Chapter 3) as a check on the accuracy of your presentation.

A. Assembling ingredients

   1. Raw shrimp

   2. Oil

   3. Red and green peppers

   4. Almonds

   5. Hot chiles

   6. Orange rind

   7. Orange juice

   8. Corn starch

B. Assembling utensils

   1. Wok

   2. Sharp kitchen knife with small blade

   3. Cooking fork

   4. Wooden spoon

   5. Measuring cup and measuring spoons

Other headings to organize steps logically for this topic might include "C. Mixing ingredients" and "D. Cooking ingredients." A number of steps may be involved in each of the divisions A, B, C, and D, but reading the steps in paragraphs that address the groups separately is far less overwhelming and confusing to readers than beginning with step 1 and ending with step 19. What steps would you include under the "C" and "D" headings for a process paper on making stir-fried shrimp?

■ *Pay careful attention to your audience.*   Who will read your process paper? Who do you anticipate as your main audience? For example, a paper explaining a quick way to change the oil in a car would use one approach to address a group of experienced auto mechanics but quite another one to address homemakers eager to save on repair costs but unfamiliar with the parts of an automobile.

■ *Define any terms that might be unfamiliar to the reader or that have more than one meaning.*   To most of us, *conceit* means extreme self-love, but to a literary scholar, it means an elaborate and extended metaphor. The scholar, when writing instructions for first-year students on analyzing a poem, would have to define the term for readers.

■ *Have a thesis.*   It's possible just to present a clear set of instructions and stop. But the most interesting process papers do have theses. Few of us read car manuals or recipe books for pleasure, but we might well read the student paper "Porch Scrubbing with the Best" (page 202) more than once, just for the fun of it. Part of the fun comes from the thesis that gives the paper focus and charm. It's a good idea, then, to try for a thesis.

■ *Anticipate difficulties.*   One way to prevent difficulties for your readers is to warn them in advance when to expect problems:

> This step requires your constant attention.
>
> Now you will need all the strength you can muster.
>
> You'd better have a friend handy to help with this step.

Another way to anticipate difficulties is to give readers advice on how to make the process easier or more pleasant. You're the authority on the subject, and you want to pass on to the novice any helpful tips you've gained from experience. Wearing old clothes isn't essential to the process of shampooing a carpet, of course, but you've learned from experience that dirty suds can fly and soil clothing, and you want to pass that information on. Similarly, it's possible to apply organic garden insecticides without using a face mask, but you've learned that the unpleasant odors can cause severe coughing and sneezing even if the products are considered harmless. Naturally, you want to warn your readers about how to avoid possible side effects.

■ *Tell the reader what to do if something goes wrong.*   In many processes, one can follow the instructions faithfully and still encounter problems. Prepare your reader for such cases.

> If, at this point, the pecan pie is not firm when you test the center, reduce the heat to 250 degrees and cook it fifteen minutes longer.
>
> If, even after careful proofreading, you find a misspelled word at the last minute, carefully erase the word and neatly print the correction by hand.

An introduction to a how-to paper, in addition to presenting the thesis, might state when and by whom the process would be performed. It could also list any equipment needed for performing the process, and it might briefly list the major headings or divisions of the process. Don't forget about the need for a conclusion. You want the last thought in your reader's mind to be about the process as a whole, not about the comparatively trivial final step.

Student Writing: Process

Following are student process papers. Study them and determine how the writers have given clear instructions on performing the task. The annotations on the first paper highlight key features of this process essay.

Vicki Schott

Painting a Room

You've heard the expression "About as interesting as watching paint dry"? Although I would never advocate spending time staring at wet paint, the expression gives painting a bad name. Now, I'm not talking about the kind of painting that takes place on canvas in art studios and ultimately winds up in a frame. I am talking about painting rooms in the house or apartment. True, the process of painting a room can be tedious, but if you follow some simple steps carefully, you can feel a great sense of satisfaction and pride at a well-done job.

1

Thesis stated clearly in introductory paragraph

To begin, remove all furniture or, more easily, pile it in the center of the room and cover it with a large drop cloth to prevent bits of plaster and drips of paint from ruining your possessions. Next, spread old newspapers over the floor, or use another drop cloth. Inspect the walls and ceiling for cracks and holes, which require the use of spackling compound. (For really large ruts in the surface of the room you may need some spackling tape as well.) You can mix your own spackle or purchase the premixed variety. Using a trowel or knife, apply the spackle. It will have the consistency of mashed potatoes. Be sure to smooth the substance so that it is flush with the wall. If you create a bulge at a

2

Transition "To begin" starts the chronological arrangement and serves as a transition to the previous paragraph.

Spackling steps grouped together in this paragraph

Specific details to support the steps and enliven the explanation

Definition of spackle implied for readers who do not know about the material

large rut in the surface, sand it lightly after it dries.

Next step in the process. Transition "Once all the spackle dries" moves the process along.

Once all the spackle dries, start your paint preparations. Pry open the paint can with a screwdriver or knife. The contents will look thick as syrup, and you should stir it carefully with a piece of wood until the paint is smooth and creamy. Pour the paint slowly (to avoid air bubbles) into a roller tray, then move the roller gradually back and forth until the paint covers it evenly. Press down on the roller to squeeze out any excess paint.

3

Simile "thick as syrup" helps reader envision the step and contributes important information to the process.

Now you are ready to begin painting. Always paint the ceiling first. While standing on a sturdy ladder, move the roller gently back and forth. It will make a soft squishing sound as it glides over the surface of the ceiling. If paint oozes from the roller or drips from the ceiling, you have too much paint on the roller or you are pressing too hard. Also, be careful not to move the roller too quickly or else it will spit at you, splattering your face with a fine mist of paint.

4

The writer anticipates difficulties: If you move the roller too quickly, you risk being splattered with paint.

When you finish the ceiling, you are then ready to paint the walls. Always start from the top of the wall. In this way, you eventually can cover any dripping. Work the roller from side to side or from top to bottom, whichever makes you more comfortable. The point is to use even strokes and cover the area completely with a smooth coat. You don't want any color showing through from the previous paint job.

5

Once you finish the walls, use a small sash brush to paint the corners of the room and the moldings. Avoid

6

the temptation to touch the tacky surfaces for at least

an hour, even with quick-drying paint varieties. I've

had to repaint too many fingerprint spots because of

my eagerness. And although the pungent smell of paint

will linger for a while, the brief discomfort soon

will pass.

     I certainly don't see a career for myself in room   7

painting, but I don't mind freshening up a room with

Conclusion returns readers to the introduction, maintaining the light mood and reinforcing the gratification in painting a room.   new paint. I can let my mind wander as I pull the roller

back and forth over the walls and ceiling, and I enjoy

the slow repetition of the roller and brush. I can clear

my mind of any problems or anxieties that may be hound-

ing me. Also, I feel a true sense of accomplishment

when I look at a clean, bright room that my work has

spruced up.

➤ FOR WRITING OR DISCUSSION

1. What is the thesis of Schott's essay? How does the introduction help to introduce the thesis?
2. How does the writer observe the requirement of a good process paper?
3. The process of spackling is complicated, yet only a few sentences explain it. Why has Schott treated spackling in this way?
4. Perhaps you too have found a way to accomplish a tedious or difficult task—putting the kids to bed, doing homework under tight deadlines—that others might like to know about. If so, write a process paper telling how to perform the task.

Not all process papers simply give instructions. Some tell "how it works." Such papers explain the functioning of anything from an electric blender to the system by which Congress passes legislation. Still other process papers describe "how it is or was done." This kind of paper could trace the process by which Walter Reed discovered the cause of yellow fever or, as in the popular *Making of the President* books, how a man came to be president. A how-it-was-done paper could even trace the process by which a person achieved a certain kind of awareness, as is the case in the following student paper.

Shirley Lytton-Cannon

Porch Scrubbing with the Best

1   If you want to know about scrubbing porches, your best bet is to take on-the-job training with Elizabeth Lytton. Now, I know that as far as the media are concerned, Elizabeth Lytton doesn't even exist. But when you live in a mining camp such as National, West Virginia, it's darn hard to make a name for yourself, especially if you come from a family of twelve children, have only a fourth-grade education, and don't know much about anything except hard work and empty cupboards. Nonetheless, make a name for herself she did. Everyone in National, as well as in the surrounding mining camps like Flaggy Meadow and Harmony Grove, knows that Elizabeth Lytton has the house with the cleanest porches.

2   At twelve years old I had my first porch-scrubbing lesson with her, and realized why clean porches were so highly respected. We were cleaning our big gray-painted cement porch with the white enamel banisters and green enamel flower boxes. The houses in the camps all have coal furnaces, so between the soot and gritty dirt pouring out of the chimneys, and the smoke seeping out of the mine's slate dump burning nearby, a person really has to know what he's doing if he expects to sit on a porch and not feel as if he'll have to take a bath afterward.

3   We began by dragging the glider, chaise lounge, rocking chair, grass rug, and a couple of miscellaneous tables out into the backyard, during which time Elizabeth told me exactly what she thought of people who merely smear dirt around with a damp mop and call a porch clean.

In the basement for cleaning supplies, I expected her to   4
mix her own magical cleaning concoction. Instead, she opened a
giant-sized box of Spic-n-Span and then added triple the
amount called for on the label to the biggest, hottest bucket
of water into which I ever have had the ill fortune of dunking
my hands. I asked her if she wanted rubber gloves, but she
said that cracks and grooves weren't about to move aside for
fat rubber fingers! I think I began suspecting then that this
would be no ordinary cleaning day.

We carried the bucket of Spic-n-Span water outside to   5
the porch, along with two stiff-bristled scrub brushes, two
mops, two brooms, and two old towels for scrub rags. She
hooked up the garden hose nearby, turned on the faucet, and
we were ready to begin.

I guess at that point your average, everyday porch   6
scrubber would have cleaned the floor of the porch after having wiped off the banisters a little, and then been done with
it. But not Elizabeth. She had a reputation to uphold! She
told me to dip my brush into the bucket and bring as much hot
cleaning water up with it as possible. I was to scrub
the ceiling boards of the porch first, continuing to dip the
brush into the bucket often enough to keep plenty of water on
the boards. Well, we dipped and scrubbed until we cleaned not
only the ceiling boards, but also the side of the house leading from the porch to the inside, as well as the carved ban-
nister posts. That's a lot of dunking and scrubbing! We used
our brooms and what was left of the water to scrub the floor
of the porch. My hands grew accustomed to the water temperature
just as the skin between my fingers felt cracked and flaky.

7   Then we used the hose for rinsing, and the icy water soaked my socks right through my old black loafers! Just about the time I thought we had finished, Elizabeth brought out another huge bucket of plain hot water, and we began to dip the towels into the bucket, squeeze the water out of them, and then wipe each board clean and dry, making sure, if you please, to get all the cracks, grooves and crannies clean also. We used our mops as towels to finish cleaning the floor.

8   Finally, we repeated the whole ritual on the porch furniture and then put everything back in its proper place.

9   We sat down together for a while on the glider, just talking about how nice everything looked and how hard we had worked. I sensed that she felt more pleased with the work we had done than with the fact that it was finally finished.

10   I had always noticed that Elizabeth never did anything half-way--whether it was sewing a dress, growing a garden, caring for a lawn, or scrubbing a porch. It was just her way to do the best she could, no matter how menial the task. She thrived on the pride that came from being the best at it. Maybe that's the secret of all experts such as Elizabeth.

➤ FOR WRITING OR DISCUSSION

1. Besides learning how to scrub a porch, what is the more important lesson the writer learned?
2. Considering the lesson the writer learned, discuss the importance of paragraph 1.
3. How does the first sentence in paragraph 5 help characterize the writer? What other sentences support this characteristic?
4. Perhaps you have had an experience that taught you something about how a friend or a family member approaches work, play, or life in general. Trace the process, by which you made the discovery, in a paper.

Models of Writing

The four selections that follow can help you to develop your process paper. As you read them, keep in mind the guidelines that you examined on pages 167–170. For example, are the explanations clear, complete, and accurate, and how do the writers achieve these goals? Is the order of activities easy to follow? How are the steps in the process grouped for easier understanding? What terms do the writers define? What terms should they have defined? And, perhaps most important, what is the thesis in each case? What does the writer intend for the instructions to demonstrate? The questions after each reading ask you to address these issues.

The selections are good examples of process writing by professionals. The first writer takes a straightforward, no-nonsense, how-to-do-it approach. The next two writers infuse two fairly familiar processes with strong personal views. The last writer proceeds through negative examples to arrive at a definition of clear thinking. See which of the four you like best.

R. H. KAUFFMAN

How to Survive a Hotel Fire

As a firefighter, I have seen many people die in hotel fires. Most could have saved themselves had they been prepared. There are *over 10,000 hotel fires per year* in the United States. In 1979, the latest year for which figures are available, there were 11,500 such fires, resulting in 140 deaths and 1225 injuries. 1

Contrary to what you have seen in the movies, fire is not likely to chase you down and burn you to death. It's the byproducts of fire—smoke and panic—that are almost always the causes of death. 2

For example, a man wakes up at 2:30 A.M. to the smell of smoke. He pulls on his pants and runs into the hallway—to be greeted by heavy smoke. He has no idea where the exit is, so he runs first to the right. No exit. Where is it? Panic sets in. He's coughing and gagging now; his eyes hurt. He can't see his way back to his room. His chest hurts; he needs oxygen desperately. He runs in the other direction, completely disoriented. At 2:50 A.M. we find him . . . dead of smoke inhalation. 3

Remember, the presence of smoke doesn't necessarily mean that the hotel will burn down. Air-conditioning and air-exchange systems will sometimes pick up smoke from one room and carry it to other rooms or floors. 4

Smoke, because it is warmer than air, will start accumulating at the ceiling and work its way down. The fresh air you should breathe is near the floor. What's more, smoke is extremely irritating to the eyes. Your eyes will take only so much irritation, then they will close and you won't be able to open them. 5

Your other enemy, panic—a contagious, overpowering terror—can make you do things that could kill you. The man in the foregoing example would not have died if he 6

PAM KRUGER

How to Talk to Anyone about Anything

1   My former boss, whom I hadn't seen in years, had found fame and fortune as a television personality. We ran into each other during intermission at a play. Naturally, I wanted to make a good impression.

2   Instead of saying something witty, intelligent and original, I asked him about the weather in Los Angeles. Then, inexplicably, I launched into a diatribe against L.A. (using words like "shallow" and "morally reprehensible," even though he said he liked living there). Finally, right after I told him "Your show is much better than I thought it would be," I panicked, asked where the restroom was and made my exit.

3   Whether you run into an ex-boss or a PTA mom, all that's usually required is light, casual conversation. Yet for many of us, small talk is hard work. And there are times when we fail miserably.

4   If you have comforted yourself by saying small talk doesn't matter, think again. It builds rapport and often leads to bigger things, like friendships and new jobs. " 'Small talk' is a misnomer," says Laurie Chock of Chock & Goldberg, a communications consulting firm in New York City. "Those little conversations probably have more impact than any other."

5   In fact, people who know what to say and when to say it are viewed as friendly, gracious and interesting. While some seem to be born with this gift, it can be developed through practice. "Most of us are shy," says Helen Gurley Brown, editor-in-chief of *Cosmopolitan.* "But that doesn't get you off the hook. You have to make the effort—it's part of being a decent, polite human being."

6   Here are the ten secrets of talking to anyone about anything:

7   **1. Silence Your Inner Critic.**   In the classic movie *Annie Hall,* the characters played by Diane Keaton and Woody Allen have just met, and they're eager to impress each other. While the two converse, subtitles flash across the screen, revealing the fears racing through their minds: "Listen to me—what a jerk," "He probably thinks I'm a yo-yo," "She senses I'm shallow."

8   Judith Sills, a Philadelphia-based clinical psychologist, says such harsh self-criticism is the most common obstacle to successful small talk. "If you feel there is nothing to lose—there's no agenda—then you can relax and suspend that fear of judgment," says Sills. That's why many of us who are able to chat easily with a stranger on an airplane draw a blank when it comes to exchanging a few words with our spouse's boss.

9   **2. Begin with the Obvious.**   Your neighbor recently had a child: ask her how she is enjoying motherhood. Your boss's boss was just promoted: congratulate him or her and ask about the new job.

10   You don't have to be clever. Just show you'd like to talk by commenting on the person's interests or whatever it is you have in common—no matter how tenuous it may be.

When you don't have anything in common, or you're both just killing time—waiting for the elevator or for your child to show up from Little League practice—it is perfectly acceptable to discuss the weather. Linda Godawa, office manager for a Chicago dentist, has calmed many nervous patients with such chitchat.   11

What if the person gives only grudging one-word responses? Take the hint. "That means he or she wants to be left alone," says Godawa, "but don't take it personally."   12

3. Compliment—Carefully.   Television journalist Barbara Walters was introduced to Truman Capote at a party soon after his book *In Cold Blood* had been published. She wanted to tell Capote how much she admired it. But worried that he might be tired of hearing praise, she simply mumbled "How do you do" and turned away.   13

"I'm older and wiser now," she wrote years later. "I've learned that authors are almost never bored by praise and sincere questions about their work."   14

Neither are the rest of us. If you follow up a compliment with an easy-to-answer question—"I love your daughter's costume; where did you find it?"—even the most modest person will appreciate the attention, as long as it is sincere.   15

Avoid potentially troublesome areas, such as a person's physical appearance. Your comments, however well-intended, may sting and, worse, there's usually no appropriate comeback. "When someone says 'Gee, you look much prettier in real life than you do on camera,' what am I supposed to say?" asks Sally Jessy Raphaël, the talk-show host. "'Oh, thanks, now I'll shoot my cameraman'?" Instead, just say the person looks terrific and leave it at that.   16

4. Use Friendly Body Language.   A quick way to end a conversation before it even starts is to fold your arms, dart your eyes and lock your face into a grim expression. Whether you mean to or not, you appear uninterested or aloof.   17

Instead, make eye contact, keep an open posture and smile. "Body language speaks before you do," says Don Gabor, author of *Speaking Your Mind in 101 Difficult Situations*. "If you send out friendly messages, you get back friendly messages."   18

5. Turn the Spotlight on Others.   We've all been bored by the proud parents who talk on and on about their wonderfully talented son, never bothering to ask us about our equally special child. At some point the person who is talking has an obligation to turn the conversation around and ask, "How are your children?"   19

"People will think you're fascinating," says Chock, "if you get them to talk about themselves." Ask questions. Discover the person's interests. If you don't understand what he or she is talking about, say so. People are usually so flattered by your interest that they don't notice if your questions aren't brilliant.   20

6. Listen.   You're at a barbecue, trapped in conversation with a bore. What do you do?   21

Listen closely for a nugget to explore. Even boring people have a passion that you   22
can learn from. If that fails, small-talk veterans ask "What do you mean by that?" to encourage the other person. Or they nod in agreement and say "Oh, that must have been very exciting," or "It sounds as if that was tough for you."

7. Keep it Light.   Traditionally, etiquette mavens have warned against controversial   23
topics. While talk of personal illnesses, money woes and marital problems should still be avoided, nowadays politics is usually considered standard small-talk fare.

24   Voice your opinion, yet avoid "I'm right, you're wrong" statements. Soften your disagreement by prefacing your remarks with comments such as "I can see we regard this differently."

25   **8. Give Equal Time.**   You're at a dinner party and have spoken with the man on your left for ten minutes. Do you owe the woman on your right equal time? If she looks bored, common courtesy requires that you involve her in your conversation, says Helen Gurley Brown.

26   "We've all been in that uncomfortable situation of being ignored," Brown explains. "Even if you want to continue talking to someone, you have to be considerate of the other person beside you. I might say something to the first person such as 'I'm sorry I've been monopolizing you. Your other dinner companion should have the chance to talk to you too.'"

27   **9. Have a Sense of Humor.**   Barbie Barna meets dozens of agents, publicists and talent representatives in her work as an executive in New York City. Frequently she runs across the joker who, when learning her name, says "Hey, where's Ken, Barbie?" "Each time, I want to say 'Oh, *you're* original!'"

28   Even the most gracious, considerate people sometimes say stupid, offensive or insensitive things. If you're the butt of such "humor," shrug it off. "The person is probably not mean spirited, just unaware," says Gabor.

29   **10. Make Your Exit.**   You've suffered through that description of her kitchen renovation. Or the conversation has simply wound down. How do you move on without being insulting?

30   Simply excuse yourself during a lull, saying you need a drink or want to say hello to someone else. The more you practice small talk, the better you'll get at sensing what's appropriate.

31   And that, the experts say, is the real secret to small talk. "Very often people who avoid small talk imagine that everyone else is a sparkling conversationalist," says Sills. "Everyone else is not sparkling. They're just connecting." And so can you.

➤ FOR WRITING OR DISCUSSION

1. What, according to Kruger, is the value of small talk? Do you agree? Why, or why not?
2. Which of the ten ways enumerated here to start a conversation and keep it going do you find most effective? Which have you already used? Which do you think could be used in a situation demanding small talk?
3. What is the effect on the reader of the numbered steps in the process? Why has the writer chosen this strategy? Does it oversimplify the process? Make it clearer? Or both? Explain your answer.
4. What elements of writing a process paper (pages 196–198) does Kruger include in her essay?

5. Imagine that you meet a celebrity at a party or some other intimate setting and then you find yourself alone with the person. Write a process paper in which you explain how you would go about starting and sustaining a conversation with the person. Draw on some of the points made in Kruger's essay but feel free to define your own "secrets of talking to anyone about anything."

JACK TRUEBLOOD

For a Love of Fishing

Johnson Creek, where it flows into the North Fork of the Boise River, was about three times as wide as a boy is tall when I discovered it. It is a fast creek, cutting its path through granite mountains as it descends from lakes high in Idaho's Sawtooth Wilderness. There are log jams there that have made a great array of holes, pools, backwaters, and riffles, all hiding trout. 1

One day when we were about fourteen a friend and I fished our way up Johnson Creek, working alternate pools and not concerned with much of anything except the absolute freedom of our situation and the knowledge that we had the ability to catch the wild little cutthroats. When the day was about half used we decided that lunch was in order, so we kept the next four fish and cleaned them while a smokeless willow-twig fire burned to coals on a gravel bar beside the water. Fresh coals were occasionally added from a small fire next to the broiling bed, and the trout we cooked on green willow branches were as good as any fine restaurant could serve. This was an annual event for several years, and the reason it became such a good memory, I think, was not because we could catch the fish, but because we didn't have to. 2

My parents provided me with the opportunity to be near fishing water from an early age. If you would teach a child to love fishing, do *not* put a rod in his hand and insist that he follow along and imitate you. All too often you find that you have moved into water too rough for the kid to handle, or that the casts required are too long, or that there is nothing for him to do but watch. 3

Setting is the first necessity in helping a child learn to love fishing. If you live in an area where camping requires a considerable amount of time, perhaps you can find a pond, lake, or creek nearby to use when teaching the elements of casting. If not, a big lawn will do, but a youngster is likely to become impatient and fiddle with the dandelions instead of the rod. Kids usually want to learn to fish, and the value of learning to cast well becomes obvious only after they need the skill. 4

I've used a fly rod from as early as I can remember, and learned how to handle it while catching crappies from a lake with shores clear of brush. Crappies in season will keep even a novice interested, and it's easy to catch enough to build your confidence. By the time I started fishing seriously on mountain streams I could cast a fly well enough to get by, knew what a strike felt like and how to set up my own tackle. In short, I had passed the primer course in fly fishing before I ever attempted fishing in rough terrain. 5

6   My introduction to trout was in places like Granite Creek on the Boise River in Idaho. As trout streams go, Granite isn't much. It wouldn't get mentioned by most of the people who haunt Silver Creek or Henry's Fork of the Snake. But if you and your old man are crouched under willow branches at the edge of a tiny creek while he quietly explains where the trout will be and how to gently flip a fly so that it will pass over them, then Granite Creek is Henry's Fork. Or Silver Creek. Or the Madison. At that moment you are at the center of the world, and all things come to you.

7   There was a log bridge on Granite Creek, and it was possible for a greenhorn boy to catch wriggling cutthroats just by lying on the bridge and sneaking the tip of his rod over the edge, then easing line out until the fly danced on the water. I soon learned that the same type of sneaking will score on trout from streamside.

8   A prime ingredient of setting is what the child can do when he tires of fishing. Logging hadn't reached Granite Creek yet, so the road was primitive and there was no traffic. My brother Dan and I were great explorers when we weren't fishing, and an old sheep corral near camp lent itself to all types of boyhood adventures.

9   My father, who had experience at being a boy, didn't get upset when we wanted to go climbing around the fences rather than fish. Instead he went with us, explaining where the truck had unloaded the sheep and pointing out the trail they had taken into the high country. We were intrigued by his explanation of the nomadic life of a sheepherder and his pack string. The success of his teaching was in letting us pursue our interests.

10   My age at the time of that trip was less than nine. When I got tired of fishing, there was always something else to do. The point is that you can't teach a kid to love fishing by taking him to a place that is desolate or boring or cold. Go to places that would be good to visit with your kids even if there were no fishing, because he or she is going to be a kid first and then a fisherman.

11   The abundance of fish is another big factor. Getting enough pan-sized trout for a meal was no problem where we kids fished. In the summertime they weren't finicky feeders, and by the time I was fourteen and needed a license, I knew enough about flies to do quite well. It takes only a few times up a stream with an experienced fisherman for a youngster to learn the basics, and long before I learned about hatches and fly colors I knew that I should carry a few of different types: Black Gnat and Brown Hackle for the times when dark colors were winners, Renegade and Royal Coachman when a splash of white was important, a couple of light-colored dry flies, and a few wet flies. Armed with this selection of a dozen or so, a pocketknife, and a light rod, I soon learned that every likely looking spot usually does hold a trout.

12   The streams I fished as a boy were not too big to wade, and that's the kind I take my kids to. Pick streams gentle enough that a child can wade across in most places. Of course there will be deep holes or rapids that might be dangerous, but most youngsters won't get foolhardy in these places if the rest of the stream is something they can handle.

13   Brush is a thing you should consider too. A kid will be slapped in the face by brush adults can push aside. Streams completely enclosed by brush should be avoided because they are too hard for a youngster to approach or to fish.

14   The tackle a beginner uses is most often like that of his teacher. I was brought up to use a fly rod, though most of my friends used spinning tackle. Whatever you decide to start your student with, a few general guidelines are in order.

To begin with, make it light. This will usually mean that it will be more his or her   15
size and less awkward or burdensome to carry, and that it will transmit the feel of the
fish better than a heavy outfit. Next, make it durable. Kids often forget about stubbing
the rod tip when walking, or laying the rod down in a careless place. Also, keep it simple. This will help avoid backlash and tangle problems, and make it easier to sort out
those that do occur. And finally, buy quality. A nice, well-balanced outfit purchased
when a kid is twelve can be used for the rest of his life, whereas an awkward, poorly
made one may discourage the beginner, and in any case, will have to be upgraded as
he becomes a better caster.

When I was a youngster, my folks took my brother and me on a camping vacation   16
every summer. The "boy trips," as they came to be called, were two weeks to a month
and in some of the most scenic places imaginable. It was on these summertime trips that
we both learned about trout fishing, with camping and mountain lore as an added bonus.

Our favorite stream meandered through willows and provided a multitude of good   17
pools and cut banks in addition to beaver ponds. Kids can learn a lot about trout from
beaver ponds because they can see the fish. I can remember finding out that trout are
frightened by footsteps on quaky ground. Although it had been explained before, it
wasn't quite believable until I could actually see them dart for cover.

Another thing you can teach a beginner on a beaver pond is how well trout can see.   18
In still water you can point out how fish are frightened by the shadow of a line, and the
impact of a heavy-handed cast is obvious. Kids learn how to make a fly drift gently to
the water, or if spinning, how to cast beyond fish and bring the bait or lure to them
instead of bonking them on the head with it. The novice soon realizes that fish can see
better through and out of water than people can into it, and the lessons will carry over
whether the water is rough or smooth.

After the beginner has learned the mechanics of using his tackle, about the best way   19
to help is by leaving yours in camp. Now you have made him the center of attention,
and he knows that you are really interested. When the youngster shows signs of tired-
ness or is catching so many trout that you just can't stand it, ask if you might use his
gear to fish the next hole. This makes a kid feel important—after all, the adult wants
what he has for a change, instead of the other way around.

Another advantage of leaving your tackle is that you can give hands-on aid to the   20
beginner. Stand (kneel if your student is short) immediately behind the learner and
grasp the rod grip just ahead of his hand. You do the work of casting and the learner just
sort of coasts along and learns from the feel of your cast things that are difficult to put
into words, like the amount of force used and the timing. The beginner should control
the line, letting it out as you instruct him to. Soon you apply less and less force and he
naturally puts a little more effort into it, until you just step back and leave him in control. This often works better than the clearest of instructions.

Children have an attention span that shortens in direct proportion to their frustra-   21
tion. Probably the greatest frustration to a child is a forceful, nagging, angry teacher.
Enjoyment, after all, is the basic reason for sport fishing, and you have to enjoy your
companions as well as your sport.

You can't teach kids to appreciate fishing if you isolate yourself in the adult world   22
and leave them in the child's world. You must remember that you, too, have experience

at being a boy or girl, and use that experience to communicate the quality of life that is available to you and your kids somewhere along the creek.

➤ **FOR WRITING OR DISCUSSION**

1. What is Trueblood's thesis here? his purpose? How does the title of the essay help you understand both thesis and purpose?
2. Who is the audience Trueblood is addressing? The title of the magazine in which the essay first appeared, *Field and Stream,* provides a strong hint. Still, Trueblood is interested not just in people who fish but in a particular subset of that group of readers. What is the subset? How do you know?
3. What are the key steps to take in helping a child fish and learn to love fishing? List them and explain how Trueblood defends these steps.
4. Explain the last sentence in paragraph 6. How does it provide support for the thesis? The writer repeats a phrase from that sentence in paragraph 19. Why?
5. How do the last two paragraphs serve as a conclusion to the essay? How do they reinforce the thesis and purpose of the essay?
6. Write an essay in which you explain how to teach a child some activity you know well—playing baseball, making cookies, planting a vegetable garden, for example. Your audience should be the child's parents or extended family. Or, you may wish to write directly for the child; in that case, you should define the age group carefully and tailor your prose to suit that group.

EARL UBELL

How to Think Clearly

Sally: "Judy is five minutes late."
Jean: "Yeah, Judy is always late."

Bill: "That's a pretty nice tie, Harry."
Harry thinks: "Bill has no taste. This tie must be terrible. I'll throw it away."

1   Jean and Harry are thinking illogically. Just because Judy may have been late once or twice, Jean jumps to the conclusion that Judy is *always* late. And Harry does not know how to accept a compliment—he sees only the negative side.

2   Jean's and Harry's twisted logic provides only two examples of a dozen kinds of distorted thoughts that hold us in their grip, producing depression, anxiety, and frustration, ruining our relationships with others, and making it difficult for us to think, to work, to love.

3   I call them the "dirty dozen of distorted thinking." Psychologists call them *cognitive distortions.* The word *cognitive* comes from the Latin *cognoscere,* which means "to know." *Cognitive* refers to what you know and believe rather than how you feel, your emotions.

Psychologists say that almost no one escapes cognitive distortions. If twisted logic is   4
giving you trouble with your spouse, your children, your friends, or your boss, or if you
are ever anxious, depressed, or puzzled over emotional problems, you too may be a
victim of one or more of these "dirty dozen."

The "Every" Distortion   Although psychologists call the first distortion *overgeneral-*   5
ization, I call it the *"every" distortion.* After only one or two instances of an event,
you leap to the conclusions that it happens *every* time or to *every*body or *every-*
where. A prime example of the "every" distortion is Jean's twisted thinking at the
beginning of this article. Jean thinks her friend is *always* late even though Judy may
have been late only once before. And Harry, when one dog growls at him, leaps to
the conclusion, "Dogs hate me." But what if the next dog he meets wags its tail at
Harry and licks his hand?

Poisoning the Positive   Like Harry at the beginning of this article, you find reasons to   6
distrust and dismiss compliments or friendly moves. Such poisoned thinking discour-
ages friendships and undermines intimacy. A man says to Jean, "I like you." Jean says to
herself, "Ha! Sure he 'likes me.' I bet. Ha! He can't really mean that. Ha!" Will Jean
ever be able to accept signs of his regard as genuine?

The Shoulds   You set up impossible standards of behavior for yourself or for others,   7
telling yourself and others what *should* or *must* be done. It's easy to fail this way. Reasonable people make suggestions more tentatively. "Such and such *might* be better,"
they say.

All or Nothing   Some of us see everything in terms of one extreme or the other; there   8
is no in-between. For example, we either love or hate something; or we think everybody is either good or bad. We view everything in stringent black-and-white terms
when, figuratively speaking, real life is shades of gray.

No! No! No!   If there is something even remotely negative in another person's actions   9
or words, you will find it and harp on it.

Mind Reading   You really believe that you know what another person is thinking. (*"I*   10
know my boss likes long memos—even though he says he doesn't.") Then when you
act on your beliefs, you get into trouble. The success rate of all mind reading is low, no
matter what you've seen in the movies or on television. Harry thinks, "Maybe Mabel
will think my necktie is terrible; I'd better take it off." What if, before he has a chance to
take it off, Mabel comes along and says, "Nice tie"?

Catastrophizing   If you suffer from this distortion, you view everything as a cata-   11
strophe. One gray hair on your head means that you are old. One lost sale signals
the end of your job. Catastrophizing paralyzes action; if you fear the worst, you
won't make a move.

I! I! I!   You think that everything happens because of you or to you. If your best friend   12
gets the flu, you think it's because you served her iced tea on the rainy afternoon that she
visited—and then you fret that you're sure to catch an even worse case. Most such
occurrences have more than one cause, the least of which is probably your contribution.

13   **Mislabeling**   With mislabeling, you tend to paint a picture of reality that you want or fear rather than what exists. You may say, "I'm a failure," and think that you really are, when all you actually did was make a mistake.

14   **Thoughts as Things**   You take something that exists only in your head and you make it real. This, in turn, leads to a form of mislabeling. You *think* you're being given all the bad jobs in the office when in fact you are not.

15   **Emotional Reasoning**   Essentially, you think, "I feel it, therefore it must be true." For example, you feel anxious, so you conclude that something terrible will happen to you.

16   **Magnify-Minimize**   You either exaggerate or downplay a situation, depending on your needs rather than the reality. If you have a pimple, you may say it's skin cancer. Or you insult someone and minimize the effect by saying, "I was only joking."

17   As you read about the twelve types of warped thought, did you recognize some of your own? If so, you may be a victim of cognitive distortions. And as a result you may be anxious, depressed, or puzzled over your emotional problems.

18   Dr. Aaron T. Beck, professor of psychiatry at the University of Pennsylvania, identified many of these cognitive distortions. He says that unless cognitive distortions are caught early, they can mushroom.

19   "They are particularly deadly in marriage," Dr. Beck says. "You get a couple who have a controversy about a minor point. Instead of seeking a common ground, they begin to look at each other as adversaries and look at their differences. The husband thinks the wife is just being 'hysterical'; the wife sees the husband as 'tyrannical.' "

20   Then one or more of the dirty dozen will take over. First, the "every" distortion. The wife—after one or two battles—thinks the husband is *always* tyrannical; the husband sees the wife as *always* hysterical. From then on, the relationship spirals downward.

21   Enter the second distortion: "poisoning the positive." When the wife cozies up to the husband in an attempt to make up, the husband thinks: "She's manipulating me." And when he rejects her overture, she thinks: "He's trying to control me." And they are trapped.

22   People troubled by illogical thinking often need the help of a psychologist or psychiatrist who is trained in recognizing cognitive distortions. The expert can point out illogical thinking and actually train a couple to think clearly.

23   You also can train yourself. The primary rule for clear thinking is to confront your belief with *reality,* that is, with real evidence. For example, what are the real chances that something you do will end in catastrophe? How many catastrophes have you actually had? Are you really ugly? Or do you have nice features, such as eyes or hair?

24   Therapists often ask their clients to make lists of good or bad things about themselves. This exercise shows patients that reality is different from their negative ideas. (Likewise, if you believe that nobody likes you, try writing down the names of people with whom you are friendly.)

25   Dr. Beck has shown that many depressed individuals owe their conditions to cognitive distortions. By removing the distortions, Dr. Beck and his colleagues say, they have been able to clear up depressive symptoms as effectively as drugs do.

In depressed patients, cognitive distortions foster a sense of worthlessness. For   26
example, the patient thinks, "If *everybody* hates me" or "if I am ugly" or "if *everything* I
do is a catastrophe"—"then I must be worthless." A feeling of worthlessness often
attacks nondepressed people who think this way too.

Dr. Albert Ellis of the Institute for Rational Emotive Therapy in New York City thinks   27
the tendency to distort is built into the human brain.

"When the human race was running through the jungle, thinking that a lion was   28
around the corner was not unreasonable," Dr. Ellis says lightheartedly. "Even if your
perception was distorted—that is, there was no lion—you could live to run another
day. Today, perceiving danger where there is none can be crippling."

Much illogical thinking, he says, also comes from copying the thinking style of   29
one's parents, teachers, and peers, many of whom may have been trapped by their own
distortions.

Dr. Beck reports that, once your thinking is crooked, you will distort what you see   30
and hear and not know you've done so. As evidence, he videotaped confrontations
between spouses. Later, he asked them to list the good things said. Couples in trouble
could not list any. Yet when the videotape revealed otherwise, neither the husbands nor
the wives could remember having heard anything positive. Such distorted perceptions
reinforce our mental distortions.

Dr. Ellis says many of the distortions come from unrealistic needs to be totally loved   31
by everyone. Other unrealistic needs include: "I must be 100 percent right all the
time." "I must have adoring, well-behaved children." "I must be fashionably dressed all
the time." "Nobody matters but me."

The bottom line is that the outside cannot *make* you feel bad. Unbelievable as it   32
sounds, it isn't the actual loss of money, fame, or loved ones that affects your feelings. It is
what you believe that counts.

Dr. Ellis cites the Roman philosopher Epictetus, who said: "What disturbs men's   33
minds is not events but their judgments on events."

➤ FOR WRITING OR DISCUSSION

1. What is the thesis of this essay? How does the essay qualify as a process paper?
2. Who is Ubell's audience? How do you know?
3. Why does the writer take up about half the essay with negative examples,
   telling us, in effect, how *not* to think clearly? Would you change the title of the
   essay to reflect this strategy used by the writer? Or is the reader able to use
   the negatives by turning them into positives? Explain.
4. Ubell uses the term *cognitive distortion*. How does he define the phrase? How
   does he explain people's tendency toward it?
5. What steps should we take to train ourselves to think clearly?
6. What is the effect of the one-sentence final paragraph (paragraph 33)? How
   effective is it as a conclusion to the selection?
7. Write a process essay about how to deliver a talk successfully in class. Like
   Ubell, use negative indicators at the start of the essay—that is, give an
   example of what a good oral presentation is not.

Readings for Writing

The selections that follow are useful in stimulating your thinking about process analysis. The first is an explanation of how a young woman works undercover to investigate men and woman who distrust their partners in romance skills. The second selection, by Shirley Jackson, is a short story.

INDIA, AS TOLD TO ROBERT MACKEY

"You Don't Have to Take the Bait"

1   I've done decoy work for about five years now. I started out doing it as a favor for my friends, to see if their boyfriends were worth their time. I would try to talk to them, just socialize. If I could get the guy's phone number, I would tell my friend: "I don't think he's worth your time. I think he's really a player." Then I saw Jerry Palace on TV talking about Check-a-Mate. I said, "Wow, I can get paid for this?"

2   How it works is, women who are suspicious of their husbands or boyfriends go to Jerry. He asks them what their story is—are they married or engaged or dating? What kind of women is the guy attracted to? They might see a photo of me to see if I'm the right type. The wives tell us if there's a regular club he goes to; if she doesn't know, we'll follow him and see where he heads.

3   I just walk in there, I try to make myself visible, maybe smile, have eye contact, let him know that I'm interested. Physically, I have gone as far as kissing, but I don't think there's a need to go that far. I don't do it the way the other girls do—I don't go in for the kill. I don't think that's fair, because a lot of these guys are in their 40's or 50's, they've been married for God knows how long and here's a woman who's attractive coming on to them. They're like: "Man, I never got an opportunity like this. Let's go for it." I may just be a one-night thing, and he may really not be a cheater.

4   I have a recorder hidden in my purse. I put it right on top of the bar, or wherever I am, and we can record both of us talking. We go for different kinds of proof, that depends on the wife. We had one at a restaurant where the wife walked in while her husband and I were hugging and I had my head on his shoulder. She wanted to catch him right in the act. I remember looking in his eyes when he got up. You could tell that he felt bad for me, and I felt bad for him, but I knew it was the right thing to do. It's a very strange thing: you know you're doing the right thing, but it's an uncomfortable feeling.

5   You can definitely tell which man is just flirting and which man wants to get in your pants. And I can also distinguish between a sleezeball and the guy who took the opportunity because he never thought he'd get one again. Those are the ones I'm a little bit iffy about. I feel bad because I know it was just the moment; they didn't think of what the repercussions would be. But still, what's done is done.

6   I've had more than 100 cases, and I would say out of 100, about 98 fall for it. The main question that people ask me is, Don't you feel bad that you're ruining marriages? And I always say, Well, I didn't ruin it; he did. I don't think it's a trap. A trap takes you in

whether you like it or not. I think I am bait. You don't have to take the bait; you have the freedom to walk away. So do I feel bad that he got caught? And his marriage is ruined? No, I don't. Not at all. I feel bad that this woman had to put her life into this man and then realize he's not at all what she thought he was. That's what I feel bad about. And I'm not knocking men—this goes for both genders. If this person is misleading you, you should know, and get out, and go pursue your life with someone who can offer you a little bit more.

Do I believe in love? I think it's still out there somewhere—I don't know, I'd like to   7
think it is. But I'm not looking for it, because people play too many head games nowadays. And most people don't know who they are, so they're constantly being something they're not, trying to be everything you want them to be. And then you see the true colors too many years later, and then you've wasted all those years on someone. I can't do that. It's sad, it really is. If you think you're settling, you're better off alone.

➤ **FOR WRITING OR DISCUSSION**

1. How did India get into the decoy business? What is Check-a-Mate?
2. What exactly does India do on her job? What is your reaction to her work? How would you feel if a woman you know enlisted India's services?
3. How does she deal with the moral issues? How does the title "You Don't Have to Take the Bait" reflect her position on the job she does?
4. How would you characterize India: heroic, betrayer, self-righteous, dangerous, helpful? Or would you use some other words? Explain your response.
5. Write a process essay in which you explain how you or someone you know might go about discovering whether a romantic partner was faithful. Assume that a service like India's was *not* available to you.

HAVING YOUR SAY

What is your reaction to India's line of work? Is it moral? Necessary in a world with poor values? Opportunistic? Evil? Write an argumentative essay in which you state and support your point of view.

SHIRLEY JACKSON

Charles

The day my son Laurie started kindergarten he renounced corduroy overalls with bibs   1
and began wearing blue jeans with a belt; I watched him go off the first morning with the older girl next door, seeing clearly that an era of my life was ended, my sweet-voiced nursery-school tot replaced by a long-trousered, swaggering character who forgot to stop at the corner and wave good-bye to me.

2   He came home the same way, the front door slamming open, his cap on the floor, and the voice suddenly become raucous shouting, "Isn't anybody *here?*"

3   At lunch he spoke insolently to his father, spilled his baby sister's milk, and remarked that his teacher said we were not to take the name of the Lord in vain.

4   "How *was* school today?" I asked, elaborately casual.

5   "All right," he said.

6   "Did you learn anything?" his father asked.

7   Laurie regarded his father coldly. "I didn't learn nothing," he said.

8   "Anything," I said. "Didn't learn anything."

9   "The teacher spanked a boy, though," Laurie said, addressing his bread and butter. "For being fresh," he added, with his mouth full.

10   "What did he do?" I asked. "Who was it?"

11   Laurie thought. "It was Charles," he said. "He was fresh. The teacher spanked him and made him stand in a corner. He was awfully fresh."

12   "What did he do?" I asked again, but Laurie slid off his chair, took a cookie, and left, while his father was still saying, "See here, young man."

13   The next day Laurie remarked at lunch, as soon as we sat down, "Well, Charles was bad again today." He grinned enormously and said, "Today Charles hit the teacher."

14   "Good heavens," I said, mindful of the Lord's name, "I suppose he got spanked again?"

15   "He sure did," Laurie said. "Look up," he said to his father.

16   "What?" his father said, looking up.

17   "Look down," Laurie said. "Look at my thumb. Gee you're dumb." He began to laugh insanely.

18   "Why did Charles hit the teacher?" I asked quickly.

19   "Because she tried to make him color with red crayons," Laurie said. "Charles wanted to color with green crayons so he hit the teacher and she spanked him and said nobody play with Charles but everybody did."

20   The third day—it was Wednesday of the first week—Charles bounced a see-saw on to the head of a little girl and made her bleed, and the teacher made him stay inside all during recess. Thursday Charles had to stand in a corner during story-time because he kept pounding his feet on the floor. Friday Charles was deprived of blackboard privileges because he threw chalk.

21   On Saturday I remarked to my husband, "Do you think kindergarten is too unsettling for Laurie? All this toughness, and bad grammar, and this Charles boy sounds like such a bad influence."

22   "It'll be all right," my husband said reassuringly. "Bound to be people like Charles in the world. Might as well meet them now as later."

23   On Monday Laurie came home late, full of news. "Charles," he shouted as he came up the hill; I was waiting anxiously on the front steps. "Charles," Laurie yelled all the way up the hill, "Charles was bad again."

24   "Come right in," I said, as soon as he came close enough. "Lunch is waiting."

25   "You know what Charles did?" he demanded, following me through the door. "Charles yelled so in school they sent a boy in from first grade to tell the teacher she

had to make Charles keep quiet, and so Charles had to stay after school. And so all the children stayed to watch him."

"What did he do?" I asked. 26

"He just sat there," Laurie said, climbing into his chair at the table. "Hi, Pop, y'old dust mop." 27

"Charles had to stay after school today," I told my husband. "Everyone stayed with him." 28

"What does Charles look like?" my husband asked Laurie. "What's his other name?" 29

"He's bigger than me," Laurie said. "And he doesn't have any rubbers and he doesn't ever wear a jacket." 30

Monday night was the first Parent-Teachers meeting, and only the fact that the baby had a cold kept me from going; I wanted passionately to meet Charles's mother. On Tuesday Laurie remarked suddenly, "Our teacher had a friend come to see her in school today." 31

"Charles's mother?" my husband and I asked simultaneously. 32

"Naaah," Laurie said scornfully. "It was a man who came and made us do exercises, we had to touch our toes. Look." He climbed down from his chair and squatted down and touched his toes. "Like this," he said. He got solemnly back into his chair and said, picking up his fork, "Charles didn't even *do* exercises." 33

"That's fine," I said heartily. "Didn't Charles want to do exercises?" 34

"Naaah," Laurie said. "Charles was so fresh to the teacher's friend he wasn't *let* do exercises." 35

"Fresh again?" I said. 36

"He kicked the teacher's friend," Laurie said. "The teacher's friend told Charles to touch his toes like I just did and Charles kicked him." 37

"What are they going to do about Charles, do you suppose?" Laurie's father asked him. 38

Laurie shrugged elaborately. "Throw him out of school, I guess," he said. 39

Wednesday and Thursday were routine; Charles yelled during story hour and hit a boy in the stomach and made him cry. On Friday Charles stayed after school again and so did all the other children. 40

With the third week of kindergarten Charles was an institution in our family; the baby was being a Charles when she cried all afternoon; Laurie did a Charles when he filled his wagon full of mud and pulled it through the kitchen; even my husband, when he caught his elbow in the telephone cord and pulled telephone, ashtray, and a bowl of flowers off the table, said, after the first minute, "Looks like Charles." 41

During the third and fourth weeks it looked like a reformation in Charles; Laurie reported grimly at lunch on Tuesday of the third week, "Charles was so good today the teacher gave him an apple." 42

"What?" I said, and my husband added warily, "You mean Charles?" 43

"Charles," Laurie said. "He gave the crayons around and he picked up the books afterward and the teacher said he was her helper." 44

"What happened?" I asked incredulously. 45

"He was her helper, that's all," Laurie said, and shrugged. 46

47   "Can this be true, about Charles?" I asked my husband that night. "Can something like this happen?"

48   "Wait and see," my husband said cynically. "When you've got a Charles to deal with, this may mean he's only plotting."

49   He seemed to be wrong. For over a week Charles was the teacher's helper; each day he handed things out and he picked things up; no one had to stay after school.

50   "The P.T.A. meeting's next week again," I told my husband one evening. "I'm going to find Charles's mother there."

51   "Ask her what happened to Charles," my husband said. "I'd like to know."

52   "I'd like to know myself," I said.

53   On Friday of that week things were back to normal. "You know what Charles did today?" Laurie demanded at the lunch table, in a voice slightly awed. "He told a little girl to say a word and she said it and the teacher washed her mouth out with soap and Charles laughed."

54   "What word?" his father asked unwisely, and Laurie said, "I'll have to whisper it to you, it's so bad." He got down off his chair and went around to his father. His father bent his head down and Laurie whispered joyfully. His father's eyes widened.

55   "Did Charles tell the little girl to say *that?*" he asked respectfully.

56   "She said it *twice,*" Laurie said. "Charles told her to say it *twice.*"

57   "What happened to Charles?" my husband asked.

58   "Nothing," Laurie said. "He was passing out the crayons."

59   Monday morning Charles abandoned the little girl and said the evil word himself three or four times, getting his mouth washed out with soap each time. He also threw chalk.

60   My husband came to the door with me that evening as I set out for the P.T.A. meeting. "Invite her over for a cup of tea after the meeting," he said. "I want to get a look at her."

61   "If only she's there," I said prayerfully.

62   "She'll be there," my husband said. "I don't see how they could hold a P.T.A. meeting without Charles's mother."

63   At the meeting I sat restlessly, scanning each comfortable matronly face, trying to determine which one hid the secret of Charles. None of them looked to me haggard enough. No one stood up in the meeting and apologized for the way her son had been acting. No one mentioned Charles.

64   After the meeting I identified and sought out Laurie's kindergarten teacher. She had a plate with a cup of tea and a piece of chocolate cake; I had a plate with a cup of tea and a piece of marshmallow cake. We maneuvered up to one another cautiously, and smiled.

65   "I've been so anxious to meet you," I said. "I'm Laurie's mother."

66   "We're all so interested in Laurie," she said.

67   "Well, he certainly likes kindergarten," I said. "He talks about it all the time."

68   "We had a little trouble adjusting, the first week or so," she said primly, "but now he's a fine little helper. With occasional lapses, of course."

69   "Laurie adjusts very quickly," I said. "I suppose this time it's Charles's influence."

70   "Charles?"

71   "Yes," I said laughing, "you must have your hands full in that kindergarten, with Charles."

72   "Charles?" she said. "We don't have any Charles in the kindergarten."

➤ **FOR WRITING OR DISCUSSION**

1. Does the story provide any indications of why Laurie invents the character of Charles?
2. How are Laurie's parents supposed to strike the reader? Are they good, bad, or in between? Are they too permissive?
3. How does the response of Laurie's parents help perpetuate the existence of Charles?
4. In what ways did you suspect the truth about Charles before the end of the story? What started your suspicion?
5. Good writers of stories with surprise endings always play fair. They give plenty of clues, which readers tend to overlook, about the outcome of the story. Write a paper in which you trace the process by which Shirley Jackson prepares the alert reader for the outcome of "Charles." Look at Harriet McKay's essay in Chapter 15 on page 421.

WRITING TOPICS

If you cannot easily decide on a topic for your process paper, you might want to use one of these suggestions as a topic idea:

1. How to be a working mother
2. How to use the Internet
3. How to deal with sibling rivalry
4. How to teach math concepts to preschoolers
5. How to adopt a child in your city or state
6. How a steam engine works
7. How to shampoo a rug
8. How to make your favorite sandwich
9. How to do supermarket shopping
10. How beer is made
11. How to give a party
12. How a lightbulb works
13. How to play softball
14. How to waste time
15. How to revise a piece of writing
16. How World War II began
17. How to clean the basement
18. How to knit a sweater
19. How to talk on the telephone
20. How to fix a flat tire

CROSSCURRENTS

1. Earl Ubell in "How to Think Clearly" (page 214) and Pam Kruger in "How to Talk to Anyone about Anything" (page 208) use similar strategies in their pieces. Write an essay in which you analyze these two essays. Explain how they are alike and different in technique. Then suggest which is more successful and why.

2. Both "For a Love of Fishing" (page 211) by Jack Trueblood and "Teaching Young Fathers the Ropes" (page 47) by Sophfronia Scott Gregory provide advice for parents on rearing children. What generalizations can you draw from the two pieces about the appropriate relations between parents and children? How are the selections alike? How are they different?

COLLABORATIVE LEARNING

Develop an outline for the topic you will write about for your process paper. In groups of three students, read each other's outlines. What suggestions can the group make about the development of each paper? Use the outlines to comment on the thesis, purpose, and details. What suggestions can you make for improving the outlines and, therefore, the draft that should follow?

REVIEW CHECKLIST: WRITING AND REVISING YOUR PROCESS PAPER

- Have I done prewriting in an effort to identify some limited task about which I can provide step-by-step instructions for a "how-to" paper?
- Have I thought carefully about my purpose? Am I explaining how to do something or how something works or how something is done?
- Have I considered my audience? Am I writing for beginners or those completely unfamiliar with the process? or am I writing for those somewhat familiar with the topic but who need some further information?
- Have I thought about vocabulary? Which unfamiliar terms should I define?
- Have I developed a thesis? In other words, do I make a statement about or offer an opinion or attitude on the process?
- Have I outlined my paper to help me organize my ideas?
- Have I provided adequate supporting details? Are my explanations clear, complete, and accurate?
- In explaining the steps of a process, did I maintain strict chronological order? Did I indicate the nature of any performance required to carry out the process? Did I group the steps logically?
- Have I warned my reader about any possible problems and indicated what to do if anything goes wrong?
- Have I proofread for grammar, punctuation, and mechanics?

Photo courtesy: © Judy Gelles/Stock, Boston

─────── **FROM IMAGE TO WORDS: A PHOTO WRITING ASSIGNMENT** ───────

Look at the photograph above. Assume the point of view of the man in the picture and in a short paper explain the process shown there to the young girl looking over your shoulder. Be sure that the sequence of steps is clear and that you explain any difficult vocabulary.

CHAPTER
10

Comparison and Contrast

A comparison shows the similarities between two or more things; a contrast shows the differences between two or more things; a **comparison–contrast** shows both similarities and differences. The most common kind of essay question on examinations calls for comparison–contrast. It is important, then, to master the techniques of this method of development.

Comparisons and contrasts are also useful because they enable us to comprehend our world. A small boy asks his parents what an apartment is. The parents respond, "It's like our house. It has a living room, kitchen, bathroom, and bedroom. Some apartments have dining rooms and more than one bedroom—just as we do. But it's not exactly like our house. You wouldn't have your own yard to play in. And there are lots of apartments in one building, so many families live close together. An apartment is usually much smaller than a house. And you are not as free in an apartment as in a house. You wouldn't be able to run in the living room because you might bother the neighbors beneath you." The parents, by comparing and contrasting the familiar with the unfamiliar, are able to give the child some idea of what an apartment is; they have enlarged his comprehension of the world.

Everyone uses comparisons, sometimes to explain the unfamiliar, and sometimes just to establish a superficial similarity: "He is as slow as a snail," for example. But to produce a good comparison–contrast paper, the writer must apply logical principles to the consideration of similarities and differences.

Writing Your Comparison–Contrast Paper

■ *Compare and contrast according to a single principle.*   You might compare automobiles and airplanes as means of transportation, or you might compare them as causes of air pollution. The principle in the first instance might be ease of travel; in the second, pollution. In each case, the principle determines the similarities and differences discussed in the paper. If you're concerned with ease of travel, you won't mention the variety of colors that both airplanes and automobiles can be painted. If you're concerned with pollution, you won't mention the comfort of adjustable seats.

In a sense, this means developing a thesis. However, a principle for comparison–contrast usually needs to be established before you can arrive at a thesis: the meaning of the similarities and differences. Having examined the similarities and differences according to the principle of ease of travel, you might establish as a thesis that travel by air is more convenient than travel by automobile.

■ *Compare and contrast according to a single purpose.*   One useful purpose is to clarify. For an audience that knows little about soccer, for example, you could make the game understandable by comparing it with football, a game with which most American audiences are familiar. A foreign student might explain the courtship and wedding customs of his or her country by contrasting them to their American equivalents.

A second purpose of comparison–contrast is to show the superiority of one thing over another: Spiffy Peanut Butter is a better buy than Spunky Peanut Butter, say; or living in a high-rise apartment is easier than living in a house; or travel by air is more convenient than travel by automobile.

A third purpose of comparison–contrast is to use the two items as examples of a generalization: for instance, "That African Americans want to be thought of as individuals rather than as stereotyped representatives of causes or groups is shown in the writings of Toni Cade Bambara and Toni Morrison."

■ *Be fair with your comparison–contrasts.*   If you see an exception to the comparison you have made, mention it. This is known as qualification, and often can be an effective means of winning the reader's respect and confidence.

■ *Follow an established pattern of organization.*   A comparison–contrast paper can be organized in one of three ways: subject by subject, point by point, or a combination of the two.

Student Writing: Comparison–Contrast

Subject-by-Subject

For short papers, one of the clearest patterns of organization—for comparison *or* contrast—is the **subject-by-subject pattern.** If you select this pattern, you first discuss one side of the subject completely, and then you discuss the other side. You must, of course, stress the same points in discussing each side of the subject; otherwise there will be no comparison. The following student outline and paper use the subject-by-subject pattern of organization.

[handwritten note in margin: Same order at one and then to the other? Looks at one side then to the other]

Lea Fasolo

Life after Death

<u>Thesis</u>: Mrs. Caruso's character underwent a dramatic change for the worse after the death of her husband.

I. Before husband's death

    A. Neighborhood children

    B. Grandsons

    C. Shopping

    D. Church

II. After husband's death

    A. Neighborhood children

    B. Grandsons

    C. Shopping

    D. Church

1   The death of one's spouse can sometimes bring about severe personality changes, particularly in the elderly.

2   I've lived in the house next to the Carusos for twenty years, since I was three. I remember fondly the sweet old couple who used to live next door. George Caruso was a shy, quiet man who kept mostly to himself. His wife, Assunta, on the other hand, was full of life and great fun to be around.

And we were around quite a bit. Many an afternoon there would
be half a dozen kids in her backyard, helping her pull weeds,
pick grapes, or shell peas. We used to take turns mowing her
lawn and trimming her hedges. On days when her grandsons,
Rodney and David, would visit, she'd have us all in the
kitchen for homemade pizza and lemonade. She never seemed to
get tired of us, and we felt the same about her. In fact, she
got along great with all the neighbors. There were a lot of
old couples on the street then, and they used to walk to
church together on Sundays. The women often took shopping
trips together to Shaker Square. Mrs. Caruso was always
involved with some activity in the neighborhood. But most
important in her life was Mr. Caruso, her silent partner.

George died suddenly one day in 1983. From that time on, **3**
Mrs. Caruso was like a different woman. For a while, she
simply shut herself off from everyone around her. But soon
she became known as the "Witch of East 115th Street."

All of a sudden, or so it seemed, the kids were like **4**
poison to her. Even when they offered help, she just yelled at
them to get away from her yard. She was very self-sufficient
now. She mowed the lawn and pulled the weeds with a devilish
passion. Not even in the dead of winter would she let her
grandsons help her. They used to come over and volunteer to
do her shopping and shovel the walk. She would send them away
and go out herself and shovel until the concrete shone through.
As one would guess, visits from her family became less and
less frequent.

It was about this time that she also began doing her **5**
own shopping alone, ignoring the long friendships she had
with the other elderly women on the street, who were now,

like herself, widows also. She no longer went to church,
either. She had grown bitter and cold, but most of all
she just wanted to be alone.

6   And that's how she died last fall--alone. It was a
Tuesday evening, and her garbage cans weren't out front.
That's when I got suspicious. She was very meticulous about
her trash, hauling it from her garage to the lawn every week
without fail. I ran to her back porch to find only the screen
door closed. I yelled and banged, then went home and called
her on the phone. After five tries and no answer, I called the
police. They arrived just as her daughter was making her bian-
nual visit. Minutes later, Lydia's screams confirmed my suspi-
cions. And I cried, because once I had loved Mrs. Caruso as if
she were my grandmother, and it hurt to remember the day I
began to hate her.

Point-by-Point

A second pattern of development is the **point-by-point pattern.** Although this
pattern is most frequently used in writing long papers, it is by no means restricted
to them. In this pattern, the writer establishes one or more points of comparison or
contrast and then applies those points to each side of a subject. The following student outline and essay use the point-by-point method of organization.

                         Barry Barnett

                          Smarter But

Thesis: Over the past ten years, I have become smarter but not
happier.

     I. Food

        A. Ten years ago

        B. Today

II. Exercise

    A. Ten years ago

    B. Today

III. Money

    A. Ten years ago

    B. Today

I'm thirty-two, and I finally had the sense to go to college. All my courses may still have the words "Introduction to" in them, but at least I'm getting decent grades. Yes, I'm a lot smarter than I was at twenty-two, that's for sure. I'm a lot smarter, but . . . [1]

For instance, I'm a lot smarter about food. When I was twenty-two, I was eating my way to an early grave and an even earlier pot belly. Fat and cholesterol were the only things that tasted good. The perfect breakfast consisted of fried eggs, bacon, English muffins lavishly coated with butter, and home fries. For lunch, a king-size corned beef sandwich and a chocolate milkshake would usually be enough. The perfect dinner would be either sirloin steak or barbecued spare ribs--French fries on the side, of course. Any between-meal hunger pangs could be taken care of with a can of beer and a few fistfuls of peanuts. Today I plan to live forever because today it's Total and skim milk for breakfast, a salad with diet dressing for lunch. Dinner is a glorious festival of choices--broiled fish or broiled chicken (no skin, please) or pasta primavera or a microwave special (two whole plastic bags and less than 300 calories). Snack time means veggies and diet Coke. I'm a lot smarter about food, but . . . [2]

3   I'm a lot smarter about exercise, too. When I was twenty-two, exercise generally was limited to unavoidable physical chores like climbing stairs, washing the car, and carrying out the trash. Once in a while I'd engage in a rousing game of ping-pong. Now that I'm ten years older, I try to jog every other day. When it's too cold or wet for jogging, I get on my in-place bicycle and pedal for a half hour. I may easily die of boredom but never of a circulatory disease. I'm a lot smarter about exercise, but . . .

4   Finally, I'm a lot smarter about money than I was at twenty-two. Why have a bad time when I could always buy a good time? All that food and liquid refreshment cost money. Concerts and athletic events cost money. I had a job, and life was for living, and you only go around once. Today I budget my money, and most of it gets spent on rent and utilities and the wife and child who have become the biggest part of my life. I still have a job, but I know too many people who have been laid off, and most of what's left of my money goes to the bank, not to living it up. I'm a lot smarter about money, but . . .

5   So I'm smarter about eating, but eating's no real fun any more. I'm smarter about exercise, but exercise is a bore. I'm smarter about money, but managing money is a major burden. How much have I gained from becoming so smart? Are there any courses on the advantages of staying young and stupid?

HAVING YOUR SAY

Write an essay in which you argue about the advantages of "staying young and stupid" over "becoming so smart." Or, reverse the terms and argue about the advantages of "becoming so smart" over "staying young and stupid."

Combined Patterns

The point-by-point pattern and the subject-by-subject pattern are most useful for stressing only the similarities between two items *or* only the differences between two items. Sometimes, however, you may want to give approximately equal weight to similarities and differences. To do so, the two patterns can be combined, as in the following student outline and paper.

Theodore Sands

Shaver's Choice

<u>Thesis</u>: There are not as many differences between electric shavers and traditional shaving as most people think.

I. Similarities
  A. Closeness
    1. Electric
    2. Traditional
  B. Time
    1. Electric
    2. Traditional

II. Differences
  A. Safety
    1. Electric
    2. Traditional
  B. Convenience
    1. Electric
    2. Traditional

The glories of electric shavers are much advertised,   1
especially around Father's Day and Christmas. Anyone impressed
by the ads and contemplating the purchase of an electric shaver
as a gift or for personal use should probably be prepared for a
few surprises. There are some significant differences between
electrics and the traditional blades and shaving cream, but not
nearly as many as most people think.

Take the closeness of the shave, for instance. Most men   2
probably assume that no electric shaver is a match for their

trusty old Gillette, but those ads for electrics that promise exceptional closeness don't exaggerate by much. Electric shavers truly are more efficient than they used to be, and remember how much more pressure can be applied against the skin with electrics. The same pressure with a blade would create a bloodbath. A bit more effort may be involved with electrics, but closeness is about the same.

3   Most men also imagine that shaving electrically will be much faster than shaving with blade and cream. Time turns out to be very similar, however. Electric shaver manufacturers advise washing the face before shaving, just as with traditional shaving. Application of a pre-electric lotion--unknown to traditionalists--is also highly recommended to get a better shave and to avoid irritation. The extra pressure required for closeness takes time, too, and electric shavers need to be cleaned every so often instead of merely being thrown away when they get dull. It's true that users of electrics don't have to bother with shaving cream, but very few, if any, precious minutes are saved by switching to an electric shaver.

4   The only big difference between electrics and razor blades is safety. Users of electrics do not have to worry about cutting themselves. They do not have to worry about shaving around old cuts or reopening the cuts. They do not have to seal wounds with painful styptic pencils or comical dabs of bathroom tissue. The more sensitive or blemished the skin, the greater the advantage of electric shavers.

5   Electric shavers may also be more convenient in some respects. It's impossible to run out of shaving cream or blades if you never use any. There's a bit more room available on bathroom shelves and in suitcases. Many electric shavers

can also be charged to run for about a week without a cord, so a former inconvenience has pretty much been eliminated.

My overall view is that if you get an electric shaver for a present, you can say "Thank you" and sincerely mean it. Electric shavers won't change your life--or even your shaving--in revolutionary ways, but they can be nice to have around. Whether they are so much nicer than blades that you might want to pay for one with your own money is a more difficult decision.

6

Writing about Literature

The comparison–contrast paper is especially effective as a means of writing about literature. When you examine one literary work along with another, the comparison often provides fresh insights into both works. If, for example, you read the following two poems separately, you would probably not derive the same meaning from them as did the student who compares them in "Two Kinds of Love." The annotations on the student's essay will help you see the pattern at work.

WILLIAM SHAKESPEARE

Sonnet 29

When, in disgrace with Fortune and men's eyes,
I all alone beweep my outcast state,
And trouble deaf heaven with my bootless[1] cries,
And look upon myself and curse my fate,
Wishing me like to one more rich in hope,
Featured like him, like him with friends possessed,
Desiring this man's art, and that man's scope,
With what I most enjoy contented least;
Yet in these thoughts myself almost despising,
Haply[2] I think on thee, and then my state,
Like to the lark at break of day arising
From sullen earth, sings hymns at heaven's gate;
    For thy sweet love remembered such wealth brings
    That then I scorn to change my state with kings.

[1]Futile.
[2]By chance.

WILLIAM SHAKESPEARE

Sonnet 130

My mistress' eyes are nothing like the sun;
Coral is far more red than her lips' red;
If snow be white, why then her breasts are dun;
If hairs be wires, black wires grow on her head.
I have seen roses damasked, red and white,
But no such roses see I in her cheeks;
And in some perfumes is there more delight
Than in the breath that from my mistress reeks.
I love to hear her speak; yet well I know
That music hath a far more pleasing sound.
I grant I never saw a goddess go:
My mistress, when she walks, treads on the ground.
    And yet, by heaven, I think my love as rare
    As any she belied with false compare.

Julie Olivera

Two Kinds of Love

Introduction and thesis: Writer establishes framework for comparison–contrast.

Shakespeare's Sonnet 29, "When, in disgrace with Fortune and men's eyes," and Sonnet 130, "My mistress' eyes are nothing like the sun," both strike me as very fine love poems. Both offer great tributes to the loved person. Love comes in all shapes and sizes, however, and I think the feelings expressed in "My mistress' eyes" are more realistic and more trustworthy. I'd rather be the woman that poem was written for than the other woman. [1]

Purpose clear: to show superiority of one poem over the other

Transition and introduction to first subject in comparison

"When, in disgrace," begins by describing a situation in which the poet feels totally depressed. Totally is no exaggeration. He hasn't had any good "fortune," people look down on him, he is jealous of other people, heaven is "deaf" to his prayers. He has little or no hope. He has [2] few, if any, friends. The things he enjoys most mean noth-

ing to him. He even comes close to hating himself. The

Fair explana-
tions: Writer
identifies son-
net's strengths
even though
she likes this
poem less than
the other poem
she will discuss.
second part of the poem very beautifully says that even in

a foul mood like that if he just happens to "think on

thee," he cheers up. He realizes, in fact, that he is one

of the luckiest men in the world. He has her love, and her

love makes him richer than a king in all that really mat-

Quotations
from poem
advance brief
summary of
Sonnet 29.

ters. "For thy sweet love remembered such wealth brings /

That then I scorn to change my state with kings."

Well, I'd be flattered, of course, and I might even   3

wipe away a tear, but I'm not sure how much I would trust

him. Love is a great inspiration to fall back on if one's

Writer's
interpretation
of "When in
disgrace"
life starts going to pieces, but it also has to exist on

a day-to-day basis, through all the normal wear and tear,

through all the boredom and nothing-special times. If I

save a drowning person, he might say with complete sin-

Analogy helps
writer support
her point about
love as defined
in the poem.

cerity that he loves and adores me, but that is no real

basis for a lifelong relationship. If it takes bad times

to make the poet realize how much he loves his lady, what

starts happening to the love when times aren't so bad?   4

Transition to
second subject
of comparison
and clear
pattern of
organization
In "My mistress' eyes," the poet is not depressed,

but confident and cheerful. He is in love just as much,

but this time with a real person, not a goddess or mira-

cle worker. If anything bothers him, it is people who

have to depend on illusions and lies to make their loves

Summary and
interpretation
of Sonnet 130

seem worthwhile. He still wouldn't trade places with a

king, yet he knows and gladly accepts that other women

are better-looking, and that they have nicer voices, and

even that they have sweeter-smelling breath. He doesn't

have to turn his lady into something she isn't in order
to love her.

I think this expression of love is by far the more   5
valid one. People want to be loved for what they are,
imperfections and all. If someone says he loves me,
I want to feel he loves <u>me</u> rather than an unrealistic
mental image he has of me. If all he loves is the image,
the love is an insult. In direct contrast, the poet in
"When, in disgrace" seems to love the woman for what she
does for him, while the poet in "My mistress' eyes"
loves her simply for what she is.

In this paragraph, writer develops contrast between the two poems.

Between the stickiness and sweetness of the first   6
poem and the realism of the second, I have to choose the
second. Both poems are fine, but one is written for rare
moods, and the other is written for a lifetime.

Conclusion: a strong restatement of the thesis

➤ FOR WRITING OR DISCUSSION

1. The writer depends on the poems to communicate her own feelings about love. Are her summaries of the poems accurate and complete?
2. What pattern of development does the writer use? Can you outline the paper?
3. Has the writer produced a unified comparison–contrast paper, or has she written two separate essays on two separate poems?
4. In your view, do the poems present two opposing attitudes? The writer assumes they were written about two different women. Could they have been written about the same woman?
5. Write a comparison–contrast paper demonstrating the superiority of one film or television program to another. Be sure your two choices have enough in common to be worth comparing and contrasting (for example, two sitcoms, two soap operas, or two horror movies).

Models of Writing

As you read the selections that follow, notice the comparison–contrast patterns at work in each one.

MARK TWAIN (SAMUEL L. CLEMENS)

The Professional

The face of the water [of the Mississippi River where the author was a steamboat pilot] 1
in time became a wonderful book—a book that was a dead language to the unedu-
cated passenger but which told its mind to me without reserve, delivering its most cherished secrets as clearly as if it uttered them with a voice. And it was not a book to be
read once and thrown aside, for it had a new story to tell every day. Throughout the long
twelve hundred miles there was never a page that was void of interest, never one that
you could leave unread without loss, never one that you would want to skip, thinking
you could find higher enjoyment in some other thing. There never was so wonderful a
book written by man, never one whose interest was so absorbing, so unflagging, so
sparklingly renewed with every reperusal. The passenger who could not read it was
charmed with a peculiar sort of faint dimple on its surface (on the rare occasions when
he did not overlook it altogether) but to the pilot that was an *italicized* passage; indeed it
was more than that, it was a legend of the largest capitals with a string of shouting excla-
mation-points at the end of it, for it meant that a wreck or a rock was buried there that
could tear the life out of the strongest vessel that ever floated. It is the faintest and simplest expression the water ever makes, and the most hideous to a pilot's eye. In truth, the
passenger who could not read this book saw nothing but all manner of pretty pictures in
it, painted by the sun and shaded by the clouds, whereas to the trained eye these were
not pictures at all, but the grimmest and most dead-earnest of reading matter.

Now when I had mastered the language of this water, and had come to know every tri- 2
fling feature that bordered the great river as familiarly as I knew the letters of the alphabet,
I had made a valuable acquisition. But I had lost something, too. I had lost something
which could never be restored to me while I lived. All the grace, the beauty, the poetry,
had gone out of the majestic river! I still keep in mind a certain wonderful sunset which I
witnessed when steamboating was new to me. A broad expanse of the river was turned to
blood; in the middle distance the red hue brightened into gold, through which a solitary
log came floating, black and conspicuous; in one place a long, slanting mark lay sparkling
upon the water; in another the surface was broken by boiling, tumbling rings, that were as
many-tinted as an opal; where the ruddy flush was faintest, was a smooth spot that was
covered with graceful circles and radiating lines, ever so delicately traced; the shore on
our left was densely wooded, and the somber shadow that fell from this forest was broken
in one place by a long, ruffled trail that shone like silver; and high above the forest wall a
clean-stemmed dead tree waved a single leafy bough that glowed like a flame in the unob-
structed splendor that was flowing from the sun. There were graceful curves, reflected
images, woody heights, soft distances; and over the whole scene, far and near, the dissolving lights drifted steadily, enriching it every passing moment with new marvels of coloring.

I stood like one bewitched. I drank it in, in a speechless rapture. The world was new 3
to me, and I had never seen anything like this at home. But as I've said, a day came
when I began to cease from noting the glories and the charms which the moon and the
sun and the twilight wrought upon the river's face; another day came when I ceased

altogether to note them. Then, if that sunset scene had been repeated, I should have looked upon it without rapture, and should have commented upon it, inwardly, after this fashion: "This sun means that we are going to have wind tomorrow; that floating log means that the river is rising, small thanks to it; that slanting mark on the water refers to a bluff reef which is going to kill somebody's steamboat one of these nights, if it keeps on stretching out like that; those tumbling 'boils' show a dissolving bar and a changing channel there; the lines and circles in the slick water over yonder are a warning that that troublesome place is shoaling up dangerously; that silver streak in the shadow of the forest is the 'break' from a new snag, and he has located himself in the very best place he could have found to fish for steamboats; that tall dead tree, with a single living branch, is not going to last long, and then how is a body ever going to get through this blind place at night without the friendly old landmark?"

4   No, the romance and beauty were all gone from the river. All the value any feature of it had for me now was the amount of usefulness it could furnish toward compassing the safe piloting of a steamboat. Since those days, I have pitied doctors from my heart. What does the lovely flush in a beauty's cheek mean to a doctor but a "break" that ripples above some deadly disease? Are not all her visible charms sown thick with what are to him the signs and symbols of hidden decay? Does he ever see her beauty at all, or doesn't he simply view her professionally and comment upon her unwholesome condition all to himself? And doesn't he sometimes wonder whether he has gained most or lost most by learning his trade?

➤ **FOR WRITING OR DISCUSSION**

1. What pattern of development does Twain use to contrast the beginner's view of the river to the seasoned professional's view?
2. In paragraph 1, Twain uses analogy—a special kind of comparison—to describe the river as if it were a book. Identify the words and phrases used to show this analogy.
3. In which sentence or sentences does Twain first state the thesis? Where does he restate the thesis?
4. Do you agree with the author that increased knowledge interferes with simple emotional pleasure? Why, or why not?
5. Write a paper about how you once felt about some person, place, or idea, emphasizing the contrast between past and present.

WILLIAM ZINSSER

Speaking of Writing

1   A school in Connecticut once held "a day devoted to the arts," and I was asked if I would come and talk about writing as a vocation. When I arrived I found that a second speaker had been invited—Dr. Brock (as I'll call him), a surgeon who had

recently begun to write and had sold some stories to magazines. He was going to talk about writing as an avocation. That made us a panel, and we sat down to face a crowd of students and teachers and parents, all eager to learn the secrets of our glamorous work.

Dr. Brock was dressed in a bright red jacket, looking vaguely bohemian, as authors are supposed to look, and the first question went to him. What was it like to be a writer?   2

He said it was tremendous fun. Coming home from an arduous day at the hospital, he would go straight to his yellow pad and write his tensions away. The words just flowed. It was easy. I then said that writing wasn't easy and wasn't fun. It was hard and lonely, and the words seldom just flowed.   3

Next Dr. Brock was asked if it was important to rewrite. Absolutely not, he said. "Let it all hang out," he told us, and whatever form the sentences take will reflect the writer at his most natural. I then said that rewriting is the essence of writing. I pointed out that professional writers rewrite their sentences over and over and then rewrite what they have rewritten.   4

"What do you do on days when it isn't going well?" Dr. Brock was asked. He said he just stopped writing and put the work aside for a day when it would go better. I then said that the professional writer must establish a daily schedule and stick to it. I said that writing is a craft, not an art, and that the man who runs away from his craft because he lacks inspiration is fooling himself. He is also going broke.   5

"What if you're feeling depressed or unhappy?" a student asked. "Won't that affect your writing?"   6

Probably it will, Dr. Brock replied. Go fishing. Take a walk. Probably it won't, I said. If your job is to write every day, you learn to do it like any other job.   7

A student asked if we found it useful to circulate in the literary world. Dr. Brock said he was greatly enjoying his new life as a man of letters, and he told several stories of being taken to lunch by his publisher and his agent at Manhattan restaurants where writers and editors gather. I said that professional writers are solitary drudges who seldom see other writers.   8

"Do you put symbolism in your writing?" a student asked me.   9

"Not if I can help it," I replied. I have an unbroken record of missing the deeper meaning in any story, play or movie, and as for dance and mime, I have never had any idea of what is being conveyed.   10

"I *love* symbols!" Dr. Brock exclaimed, and he described with gusto the joys of weaving them through his work.   11

So the morning went, and it was a revelation to all of us. At the end Dr. Brock told me he was enormously interested in my answers—it had never occurred to him that writing could be hard. I told him I was just as interested in *his* answers—it had never occurred to me that writing could be easy. Maybe I should take up surgery on the side.   12

As for the students, anyone might think we left them bewildered. But in fact we gave them a broader glimpse of the writing process than if only one of us had talked. For there isn't any "right" way to do such personal work. There are all kinds of writers and all kinds of methods, and any method that helps you to say what you want to say is the right method for you. Some people write by day, others by night. Some people need silence, others turn on the radio. Some write by hand, some by word processor, some by talking   13 into a tape recorder. Some people write their first draft in one long burst and then revise; others can't write the second paragraph until they have fiddled endlessly with the first.

14   But all of them are vulnerable and all of them are tense. They are driven by a compulsion to put some part of themselves on paper, and yet they don't just write what comes naturally. They sit down to commit an act of literature, and the self who emerges on paper is far stiffer than the person who sat down to write. The problem is to find the real man or woman behind the tension.

➤ **FOR WRITING OR DISCUSSION**

1. What pattern of organization does Zinsser use to present the contrasting approaches to writing?
2. Where does the writer state the thesis of the essay?
3. Although Dr. Brock's approach to writing may be the best method for him, how does Zinsser indicate that he is skeptical of Brock's approach?
4. In paragraph 1, how would Zinsser define the difference between a vocation and an avocation? How does this difference help account for the different attitudes toward writing?
5. Choose some activity other than writing—anything from decorating for a holiday to studying for an examination—and write a paper contrasting the easygoing versus the more difficult approach to completing it.

SUZANNE BRITT

That Lean and Hungry Look

1   Caesar was right. Thin people need watching. I've been watching them for most of my adult life, and I don't like what I see. When these narrow fellows spring at me, I quiver to my toes. Thin people come in all personalities, most of them menacing. You've got your "together" thin person, your mechanical thin person, your condescending thin person, your tsk-tsk thin person, your efficiency-expert thin person. All of them are dangerous.

2   In the first place, thin people aren't fun. They don't know how to goof off, at least in the best, fat sense of the word. They've always got to be doing. Give them a coffee break, and they'll jog around the block. Supply them with a quiet evening at home, and they'll fix the screen door and lick S & H green stamps. They say things like "there aren't enough hours in the day." Fat people never say that. Fat people think the day is too damn long already.

3   Thin people make me tired. They've got speedy little metabolisms that cause them to bustle briskly. They're forever rubbing their bony hands together and eyeing new problems to "tackle." I like to surround myself with sluggish, inert, easygoing fat people, the kind who believe that if you clean it up today, it'll just get dirty again tomorrow.

Some people say the business about the jolly fat person is a myth, that all of us chubbies are neurotic, sick, sad people. I disagree. Fat people may not be chortling all day long, but they're a hell of a lot *nicer* than the wizened and shriveled. Thin people turn surly, mean and hard at a young age because they never learn the value of a hot-fudge sundae for easing tension. Thin people don't like gooey soft things because they themselves are neither gooey nor soft. They are crunchy and dull, like carrots. They go straight to the heart of the matter while fat people let things stay all blurry and hazy and vague, the way things actually are. Thin people want to face the truth. Fat people know there is no truth. One of my thin friends is always staring at complex, unsolvable problems and saying, "The key thing is . . ." Fat people never say that. They know there isn't any such thing as the key thing about anything.   4

Thin people believe in logic. Fat people see all sides. The sides fat people see are rounded blobs, usually gray, always nebulous and truly not worth worrying about. But the thin person persists. "If you consume more calories than you burn," says one of my thin friends, "you will gain weight. It's that simple." Fat people always grin when they hear statements like that. They know better.   5

Fat people realize that life is illogical and unfair. They know very well that God is not in his heaven and all is not right with the world. If God was up there, fat people could have two doughnuts and a big orange drink anytime they wanted it.   6

Thin people have a long list of logical things they are always spouting off to me. They hold up one finger at a time as they reel off these things, so I won't lose track. They speak slowly as if to a young child. The list is long and full of holes. It contains tidbits like "get a grip on yourself," "cigarettes kill," "cholesterol clogs," "fit as a fiddle," "ducks in a row," "organize" and "sound fiscal management." Phrases like that.   7

They think these 2,000-point plans lead to happiness. Fat people know happiness is elusive at best and even if they could get the kind thin people talk about, they wouldn't want it. Wisely, fat people see that such programs are too dull, too hard, too off the mark. They are never better than a whole cheesecake.   8

Fat people know all about the mystery of life. They are the ones acquainted with the night, with luck, with fate, with playing it by ear. One thin person I know once suggested that we arrange all the parts of a jigsaw puzzle into groups according to size, shape and color. He figured this would cut the time needed to complete the puzzle at least by 50 percent. I said I wouldn't do it. One, I like to muddle through. Two, what good would it do to finish early? Three, the jigsaw puzzle isn't the important thing. The important thing is the fun of four people (one thin person included) sitting around a card table, working a jigsaw puzzle. My thin friend had no use for my list. Instead of joining us, he went outside and mulched the boxwoods. The three remaining fat people finished the puzzle and made chocolate, double-fudged brownies to celebrate.   9

The main problem with thin people is they oppress. Their good intentions, bony torsos, tight ships, neat corners, cerebral machinations and pat solutions loom like dark clouds over the loose, comfortable, spread-out, soft world of the fat. Long after fat people have removed their coats and shoes and put their feet up on the coffee table, thin people are still sitting on the edge of the sofa, looking neat as a pin, discussing rutabagas. Fat people are heavily into fits of laughter, slapping their thighs and whooping it up, while thin people are still politely waiting for the punch line.   10

11   Thin people are downers. They like math and morality and reasoned evaluation of the limitations of human beings. They have their skinny little acts together. They expound, prognose, probe and prick.

12   Fat people are convivial. They will like you even if you're irregular and have acne. They will come up with a good reason why you never wrote the great American novel. They will cry in your beer with you. They will put your name in the pot. They will let you off the hook. Fat people will gab, giggle, guffaw, gallumph, gyrate and gossip. They are generous, giving and gallant. They are gluttonous and goodly and great. What you want when you're down is soft and jiggly, not muscled and stable. Fat people know this. Fat people have plenty of room. Fat people will take you in.

➤ **FOR WRITING OR DISCUSSION**

1. Tell why you agree or disagree with this statement: "In 'That Lean and Hungry Look,' Britt is mostly contrasting fat and thin people just for laughs. She is a good deal more serious, however, about contrasting two opposing philosophies of life."
2. What pattern of organization does Britt use to make the contrasts?
3. Using the comparison–contrast technique of Britt's essay, write a paper in which you attempt to refute the author's position; that is, defend the thin person's view.

HAVING YOUR SAY

What is your view of the effects of being thin or being fat on a person's personality? Write an argumentative essay, supporting your point with specifics.

BRUCE CATTON

Grant and Lee: A Study in Contrasts

1   When Ulysses S. Grant and Robert E. Lee met in the parlor of a modest house at Appomattox Court House, Virginia, on April 9, 1865, to work out the terms for the surrender of Lee's Army of Northern Virginia, a great chapter in American life came to a close, and a great new chapter began.

2   These men were bringing the Civil War to its virtual finish. To be sure, other armies had yet to surrender, and for a few days the fugitive Confederate government would struggle desperately and vainly, trying to find some way to go on living now that its

chief support was gone. But in effect it was all over when Grant and Lee signed the papers. And the little room where they wrote out the terms was the scene of one of the poignant, dramatic contrasts in American History.

They were two strong men these oddly different generals, and they represented the strengths of two conflicting currents that, through them, had come into final collision. 3

Back of Robert E. Lee was the notion that the old aristocratic concept might some-how survive and be dominant in American life. 4

Lee was tidewater Virginia, and in his background were family, culture, and tradi-tion . . . the age of chivalry transplanted to a New World which was making its own legends and its own myths. He embodied a way of life that had come down through the age of knighthood and the English country squire. America was a land that was begin-ning all over again, dedicated to nothing much more complicated than the rather hazy belief that all men had equal rights and should have an equal chance in the world. In such a land Lee stood for the feeling that it was somehow of advantage to human soci-ety to have a pronounced inequality in the social structure. There should be a leisure class, backed by ownership of land; in turn, society itself should be keyed to the land as the chief source of wealth and influence. It would bring forth (according to this ideal) a class of men with a strong sense of obligation to the community; men who lived not to gain advantage for themselves, but to meet the solemn obligations which had been laid on them by the very fact that they were privileged. From them the country would get its leadership; to them it could look for the higher values—of thought, of conduct, or per-sonal deportment—to give it strength and virtue. 5

Lee embodied the noblest elements of this aristocratic ideal. Through him, the landed nobility justified itself. For four years, the Southern states had fought a desperate war to uphold the ideals for which Lee stood. In the end, it almost seemed as if the Confederacy fought for Lee; as if he himself was the Confederacy . . . the best thing that the way of life for which the Confederacy stood could ever have to offer. He had passed into legend before Appomattox. Thousands of tired, underfed, poorly clothed Confederate soldiers, long since past the simple enthusiasm of the early days of the struggle, somehow consid-ered Lee the symbol of everything for which they had been willing to die. But they could not quite put this feeling into words. If the Lost Cause, sanctified by so much heroism and so many deaths, had a living justification, its justification was General Lee. 6

Grant, the son of a tanner on the Western frontier, was everything Lee was not. He had come up the hard way and embodied nothing in particular except the eternal toughness and sinewy fiber of the men who grew up beyond the mountains. He was one of a body of men who owed reverence and obeisance to no one, who were self-reliant to a fault, who cared hardly anything for the past but who had a sharp eye for the future. 7

These frontier men were the precise opposites of the tidewater aristocrats. Back of them, in the great surge that had taken people over the Alleghenies and into the open-ing Western country, there was a deep, implicit dissatisfaction with a past that had set-tled into grooves. They stood for democracy, not from any reasoned conclusion about the proper ordering of human society, but simply because they had grown up in the middle of democracy and knew how it worked. Their society might have privileges, but they would be privileges each man had won for himself. Forms and patterns meant 8 nothing. No man was born to anything, except perhaps to a chance to show how far he could rise. Life was competition.

9   Yet along with this feeling had come a deep sense of belonging to a national community. The Westerner who developed a farm, opened a shop, or set up in business as a trader could hope to prosper only as his own community prospered—and his community ran from the Atlantic to the Pacific and from Canada down to Mexico. If the land was settled, with towns and highways and accessible markets, he could better himself. He saw his fate in terms of the nation's own destiny. As its horizons expanded, so did his. He had, in other words an acute dollars-and-cents stake in the continued growth and development of his country.

10   And that, perhaps, is where the contrast between Grant and Lee becomes most striking. The Virginia aristocrat, inevitably, saw himself in relation to his own region. He lived in a static society which could endure almost anything except change. Instinctively, his first loyalty would go to the locality in which that society existed. He would fight to the limit of endurance to defend it, because in defending it he was defending everything that gave his own life its deepest meaning.

11   The Westerner, on the other hand, would fight with an equal tenacity for the broader concept of society. He fought so because everything he lived by was tied to growth, expansion, and a constantly widening horizon. What he lived by would survive or fall with the nation itself. He could not possibly stand by unmoved in the face of an attempt to destroy the Union. He would combat it with everything he had, because he could only see it as an effort to cut the ground out from under his feet.

12   So Grant and Lee were in complete contrast, representing two diametrically opposed elements in American life. Grant was the modern man emerging; beyond him, ready to come on the stage, was the great age of steel and machinery, of crowded cities and a restless burgeoning vitality. Lee might have ridden down from the old age of chivalry, lance in hand, silken banner fluttering over his head. Each man was the perfect champion of his cause, drawing both his strengths and his weaknesses from the people he led.

13   Yet it was not all contrast, after all. Different as they were—in background, in personality, in underlying aspiration—these two great soldiers had much in common. Under everything else, they were marvelous fighters. Furthermore, their fighting qualities were really very much alike.

14   Each man had, to begin with, the great virtue of utter tenacity and fidelity. Grant fought his way down the Mississippi Valley in spite of acute personal discouragement and profound military handicaps. Lee hung on in the trenches at Petersburg after hope itself had died. In each man there was an indomitable quality . . . the born fighter's refusal to give up as long as he can still remain on his feet and lift his two fists.

15   Daring and resourcefulness they had, too: the ability to think faster and move faster than the enemy. These were the qualities which gave Lee the dazzling campaigns of Second Manassas and Chancellorsville and won Vicksburg for Grant.

16   Lastly, and perhaps greatest of all, there was the ability, at the end, to turn quickly from war to peace once the fighting was over. Out of the way these two men behaved at Appomattox came the possibility of a peace of reconciliation. It was a possibility not wholly realized, in the years to come, but which did, in the end, help the two sections to become one nation again . . . after a war whose bitterness might have seemed to

make such a reunion wholly impossible. No part of either man's life became him more than the part he played in their brief meeting in the McLean house at Appomattox. Their behavior there put all succeeding generations of Americans in their debt. Two great Americans, Grant and Lee—very different, yet under everything very much alike. Their encounter at Appomattox was one of the great moments of American history.

> ## ➤ FOR WRITING OR DISCUSSION

1. What is Catton's thesis? Which sentence in the essay best states the thesis?
2. What pattern of organization does Catton use to advance the comparison and contrast? Point to specific paragraphs and sentences to support your view.
3. Which of Lee's qualities do you find most impressive? which of Grant's? Which leader would you rather spend an hour with? Why?
4. Comment on the introduction (paragraphs 1 and 2) and the conclusion (paragraph 16). How do they help create the important sense of unity in the essay?
5. Write a comparison and contrast essay in which you present two public figures—in the military, in government, in the arts, for example. Choose people who have something in common (perhaps their field of interest is enough of a linkage), and explain to readers what makes the two people similar to yet different from each other.

J.E. LIGHTER

Say What?

"Do you *love* it," a sassy Bravo journalist cries at the annual Art Car Weekend in Houston, *"or what?"* Weeks later, in Boston, one of National Public Radio's *Car Talk* hosts says, "Hey, Mabel! Can I have some hash with those eggs, *or what?"* In an episode of *The Simpsons* some years ago Homer asked God, "Are we the most pathetic family on the planet, *or what?"* The *or what?* inventory could go on and on, but if you've been following trends in pop rhetoric, you already know what we're dealing with. 1

There's an old-model *or what?* and a sporty new *or what?* In a diary entry in 1766 the old-model New Englander John Adams asked himself, "In what is this man conspicuous?—in reasoning, in imagination, in painting, in the pathetic [that is 'sympathetic feeling or expression'], *or what?"* That is the classic *or what?* A sniffy schoolmaster of the time might have taken Adams to task for failing to keep his phrases quite parallel ("You mean, sir, '*or in what?*'!"), but that particular quibble would occur to few of us today. For well over two centuries *or what?* has served the useful purpose in English of eliciting a concrete answer from a wide-open range of unspecified choices. ("Hey, Mabel! Are we having eggs or hash or Danish, *or what?"*) The new *or what?* is decidedly more aggressive. 2

"Is this a great idea, *or what?"* "Was that her best performance ever, *or what?"* These new-school *or what?*s get tacked on to semi-rhetorical yes-or-no questions with the 3 not-very-ulterior motive of commanding total agreement. They're "peremptory *or what?*s," in contrast to "inquisitive *or what?*s"—both terms being ad hoc additions to the vocabulary of micro-semantic description. Any sensible reply to Adams ("Sir, he is conspicuous in his mediocrity") would be broadly informative rather than merely affirmative. Peremptory *or what?*s can embellish yes-or-no questions alone. The peremptory "Do you love it, *or what?*" implies that *of course* you love it, and if you don't, you'd better get ready to explain yourself.

4   Whence came the peremptory *or what?*—from Hawaiian pidgin (as one correspondent suggests)? Yiddish (always a handy hypothesis)? *Or what?* There is no real need to search far afield: English, like every other living language, often reinvents itself on its own inspiration. Lots of little idioms are generated almost unconsciously. *Y'know? Yeah, right! Sez who? Uh-hunh. Izzat so? And how! Say what? Duh.*

5   Under just-right conditions even the old-model inquisitive *or what?* can imbue a yes-or-no question with a degree of irony or sarcasm. For example, the nineteenth-century poet Edward FitzGerald, who translated Omar Khayyám's *Rubáiyát* into English, once impatiently inquired of an acquaintance, "Have you supposed me dead *or what?*" Surely that *or what?* effectively plays up the absurdity of any notion that FitzGerald was dead. The current peremptory *or what?* may have battened on this well-established tendency toward irony. (The faded craze for what might be called the accentuated postpositive *not,* repopularized by Mike Myers and *Wayne's World* after decades of dormancy, plays with an even more heavy-handed irony: It's really subtle. *Not!*)

6   And here's another angle. The peremptory *or what?* most typically features a pause before the *or* and emphatic stress on the *what.* The earliest example I am aware of with the current stress came in a 1964 episode of TV's *The Dick Van Dyke Show,* when a self-assured moron asked Laura Petrie, "You wanna go *out* Sataday night—*aw what?*" (The laugh track really appreciated this no-nonsense approach.) That cheeky *or what?* presupposes a "yes" and forestalls any other answer, at least in theory—a rhetorical feat pretty much beyond the reach of traditional *or what?* questions. Maybe it occupies a niche in Broca's area of the brain—that is, the speech area—near the one filled by an equally forceful phrase that crept into English in the nineteenth century, and with just as little fanfare: the ever useful *or else!*

➤ **FOR WRITING OR DISCUSSION**

1. What is the thesis of this essay? Where does the writer come closest to stating it in his own words?
2. What is the purpose of the three examples in the introduction?
3. How does Lighter distinguish between the two elements of the comparison? What label does he give to each?
4. How do the uses of the term *or what?* as compared and contrasted here relate to the way you and your friends use the words?
5. Write an essay in which you compare and contrast the different uses of some popular word or phrase. You might want to use the word *cool,* for example, or *hip hop, dude, gay, awesome*—any word or phrase for which you can make a

usage distinction and write an interesting essay about how the word means different things to different people in different times. You might want to refer to a usage dictionary for help. J.E. Lighter, who wrote the piece you have just read, is the editor of the *Random House Historical Dictionary of American Slang:* You might want to examine this resource.

Readings for Writing

The two short stories that follow can provide you with subject matter for a comparison-and-contrast paper of your own. Questions and possible assignments appear at the end of the second story.

The Battle of the Sexes: Two Stories for Comparison and Contrast

JAMES THURBER

A Couple of Hamburgers

It had been raining for a long time, a slow, cold rain falling out of iron-colored clouds. They had been driving since morning and they still had a hundred and thirty miles to go. It was about three o'clock in the afternoon. "I'm getting hungry," she said. He took his eyes off the wet, winding road for a fraction of a second and said, "We'll stop at a dog-wagon." She shifted her position irritably. "I wish you wouldn't call them *dog*-wagons," she said. He pressed the klaxon button and went around a slow car. "That's what they are," he said. "Dog-wagons." She waited a few seconds. "*Decent* people call them *diners*," she told him, and added, "Even if you call them diners, I don't like them." He speeded up a hill. "They have better stuff than most restaurants," he said. "Anyway, I want to get home before dark and it takes too long in a restaurant. We can stay our stomachs with a couple hamburgers." She lighted a cigarette and he asked her to light one for him. She lighted one deliberately and handed it to him. "I wish you wouldn't say 'stay our stomachs,' " she said. "You know I hate that. It's like 'sticking to your ribs.' You say that all the time." He grinned. "Good old American expressions, both of them," he said. "Like sow belly. Old pioneer term, sow belly." She sniffed. "My ancestors were pioneers, too. You don't have to be vulgar just because you were a pioneer." "Your ancestors never got as far west as mine did," he said. "The real pioneers travelled on their sow belly and got somewhere." He laughed loudly at that. She looked out at the wet trees and signs and telephone poles going by. They drove on for several miles without a word; he kept chortling every now and then.

1

2 "What's that funny sound?" she asked, suddenly. It invariably made him angry when she heard a funny sound. "What funny sound?" he demanded. "You're always hearing funny sounds." She laughed briefly. "That's what you said when the bearing burned out," she reminded him. "You'd never have noticed it if it hadn't been for me." "I noticed it, all right," he said. "Yes," she said. "When it was too late." She enjoyed bringing up the subject of the burned-out bearing whenever he got to chortling. "It was too late when *you* noticed it, as far as that goes," he said. Then, after a pause, "Well, what does it sound like *this* time? All engines make a noise running, you know." "I know all about that," she answered. "It sounds like—it sounds like a lot of safety pins being jiggled around in a tumbler." He snorted. "That's your imagination. Nothing gets the matter with a car that sounds like a lot of safety pins. I happen to know that." She tossed away her cigarette. "Oh, sure," she said. "You always happen to know everything." They drove on in silence.

3 "I want to stop somewhere and get something to *eat*!" she said loudly. "All right, all right!" he said. "I been watching for a dog-wagon, haven't I? There hasn't been any. I can't make you a dog-wagon." The wind blew rain in on her and she put up the window on her side all the way. "I won't stop at just any old diner," she said. "I won't stop unless it's a cute one." He looked around at her. "Unless it's a *what* one?" he shouted. "You know what I mean," she said. "I mean a decent, clean one where they don't slosh things at you. I hate to have a lot of milky coffee sloshed at me." "All right," he said. "We'll find a cute one, then. You pick it out. I wouldn't know. I might find one that was cunning but not cute." That struck him as funny and he began to chortle again. "Oh, shut up," she said.

4 Five miles farther along they came to a place called Sam's Diner. "Here's one," he said, slowing down. She looked it over. "I don't want to stop there," she said. "I don't like the ones that have nicknames." He brought the car to a stop at one side of the road. "Just what's the matter with the ones that have nicknames?" he asked with edgy, mock interest. "They're always Greek ones," she told him. "They're always Greek ones," he repeated after her. He set his teeth firmly together and started up again. After a time, "Good old Sam, the Greek," he said, in a singsong. "Good old Connecticut Sam Beardsley, the Greek." "You didn't see his name," she snapped. "Winthrop, then," he said. "Old Samuel Cabot Winthrop, the Greek dog-wagon man." He was getting hungry.

5 On the outskirts of the next town she said, as he slowed down, "It looks like a factory kind of town." He knew that she meant she wouldn't stop there. He drove on through the place. She lighted a cigarette as they pulled out into the open again. He slowed down and lighted a cigarette for himself. "Factory kind of town that *I* am!" he snarled. It was ten miles before they came to another town. "Torrington," he growled. "Happen to know there's a dog-wagon here because I stopped in it once with Bob Combs. Damn cute place, too, if you ask me." "I'm not asking you anything," she said, coldly. "You think you're so funny. I think I know the one you mean," she said, after a moment. "It's right in the town and it sits at an angle from the road. They're never so good, for some reason." He glared at her and almost ran up against the curb. "What

the hell do you mean 'sits at an angle from the road'?" he cried. He was very hungry now. "Well, it isn't silly," she said, calmly. "I've noticed the ones that sit at an angle. They're cheaper, because they fitted them into funny little pieces of ground. The big ones parallel to the road are the best." He drove right through Torrington, his lips compressed. "Angle from the road, for God's sake!" he snarled, finally. She was looking out her window.

On the outskirts of the next town there was a diner called The Elite Diner. "This looks—" she began. "I see it, I see it!" he said. "It doesn't happen to look any cuter to me than any goddam—" She cut him off. "Don't be such a sorehead, for Lord's sake," she said. He pulled up and stopped beside the diner, and turned on her. "Listen," he said, grittingly, "I'm going to put down a couple of hamburgers in this place even if there isn't one single inch of chintz or cretonne in the whole—" "Oh, be still," she said. "You're just hungry and mean like a child. Eat your old hamburgers, what do I care?" Inside the place they sat down on stools and the counterman walked over to them, wiping up the counter top with a cloth as he did so. "What'll it be, folks?" he said. "Bad day, ain't it? Except for ducks." "I'll have a couple of—" began the husband, but his wife cut in. "I just want a pack of cigarettes," she said. He turned around slowly on his stool and stared at her as she put a dime and a nickel in the cigarette machine and ejected a package of Lucky Strikes. He turned to the counterman again. "I want a couple of hamburgers," he said. "With mustard and lots of onion. *Lots* of onion!" She hated onions. "I'll wait for you in the car," she said. He didn't answer and she went out.

He finished his hamburgers and his coffee slowly. It was terrible coffee. Then he went out to the car and got in and drove off, slowly humming "Who's Afraid of the Big Bad Wolf?" After a mile or so, "Well," he said, "what was the matter with the Elite Diner, milady?" "Didn't you *see* that cloth the man was wiping the counter with?" she demanded. "Ugh!" She shuddered. "I didn't happen to want to eat any of the counter," he said. He laughed at that comeback. "You didn't even notice," she said. "You never notice anything. It was filthy." "I noticed they had some damn fine coffee in there," he said. "It was swell." He knew she loved good coffee. He began to hum his tune again; then he whistled it; then he began to sing it. She did not show her annoyance, but she knew that he knew she was annoyed. "Will you be kind enough to tell me what time it is?" she asked. "Big *bad* wolf, big *bad* wolf—five minutes o' five—tum-dee-*doo*-dee-dum-m-m." She settled back in her seat and took a cigarette from her case and tapped it on the case. "I'll wait till we get home," she said. "If you'll be kind enough to speed up a little." He drove on at the same speed. After a time he gave up the "Big Bad Wolf" and there was deep silence for two miles. Then suddenly he began to sing, very loudly, "*H-A-double-R-I-G-A-N spells Harrr-i-gan—*" She gritted her teeth. She hated that worse than any of his songs except "Barney Google." He would go on to "Barney Google" pretty soon, she knew. Suddenly she leaned slightly forward. The straight line of her lips began to curve up ever so slightly. She heard the safety pins in the tumbler again. Only now they were louder, more insistent, ominous. He was singing too loud to hear them. "Is a *name* that *shame* has never been con-*nec*-ted with—*Harrr*-i-gan, that's *me!*" She relaxed against the back of the seat content to wait.

6

7

MARY WILKINS FREEMAN

The Revolt of "Mother"

1   "Father!"

2   "What is it?"

3   "What are them men diggin' over there in the field for?"

4   There was a sudden dropping and enlarging of the lower part of the old man's face, as if some heavy weight had settled therein; he shut his mouth tight, and went on harnessing the great bay mare. He hustled the collar on to her neck with a jerk.

5   "Father!"

6   The old man slapped the saddle upon the mare's back.

7   "Look here, father, I want to know what them men are diggin' over in the field for, an' I'm goin' to know."

8   "I wish you'd go into the house, mother, an' 'tend to your own affairs," the old man said then. He ran his words together, and his speech was almost as inarticulate as a growl.

9   But the woman understood; it was her most native tongue.

10   "I ain't goin' into the house till you tell me what them men are doin' over there in the field," said she.

11   Then she stood waiting. She was a small woman, short and straight-waisted like a child in her brown cotton gown. Her forehead was mild and benevolent between the smooth curves of gray hair; there were meek downward lines about her nose and mouth; but her eyes, fixed upon the old man, looked as if the meekness had been the result of her own will, never of the will of another.

12   They were in the barn, standing before the wide open doors. The spring air, full of the smell of growing grass and unseen blossoms, came in their faces. The deep yard in front was littered with farm wagons and piles of wood; on the edges, close to the fence and the house, the grass was a vivid green, and there were some dandelions.

13   The old man glanced doggedly at his wife as he tightened the last buckles on the harness. She looked as immovable to him as one of the rocks in his pasture-land, bound to the earth with generations of blackberry vines. He slapped the reins over the horse, and started forth from the barn.

14   "*Father!*" said she.

15   The old man pulled up. "What is it?"

16   "I want to know what them men are diggin' over there in that field for."

17   "They're diggin' a cellar, I s'pose, if you've got to know."

18   "A cellar for what?"

19   "A barn."

20   "A barn? You ain't goin' to build a barn over there where we was goin' to have a house, father?"

21   The old man said not another word. He hurried the horse into the farm wagon, and clattered out of the yard, jouncing as sturdily on his seat as a boy.

22   The woman stood a moment looking after him, then she went out of the barn across a corner of the yard to the house. The house, standing at right angles with the great

barn and a long reach of sheds and out-buildings, was infinitesimal compared with them. It was scarcely as commodious for people as the little boxes under the barn eaves were for doves.

A pretty girl's face, pink and delicate as a flower, was looking out of one of the house windows. She was watching three men who were digging over in the field which bounded the yard near the road line. She turned quietly when the woman entered.   23

"What are they digging for, mother?" said she. "Did he tell you?"   24

"They're diggin' for—a cellar for a new barn."   25

"Oh, mother, he ain't going to build another barn?"   26

"That's what he says."   27

A boy stood before the kitchen glass combing his hair. He combed slowly and painstakingly, arranging his brown hair in a smooth hillock over his forehead. He did not seem to pay any attention to the conversation.   28

"Sammy, did you know father was going to build a new barn?" asked the girl.   29

The boy combed assiduously.   30

"Sammy!"   31

He turned, and showed a face like his father's under his smooth crest of hair. "Yes, I s'pose I did," he said, reluctantly.   32

"How long have you known it?" asked his mother.   33

"'Bout three months, I guess."   34

"Why didn't you tell of it?"   35

"Didn't think 'twould do no good."   36

"I don't see what father wants another barn for," said the girl, in her sweet, slow voice. She turned again to the window, and stared out at the digging men in the field. Her tender, sweet face was full of a gentle distress. Her forehead was as bald and innocent as a baby's, with the light hair strained back from it in a row of curl-papers. She was quite large, but her soft curves did not look as if they covered muscles.   37

Her mother looked sternly at the boy. "Is he goin' to buy more cows?" said she.   38

The boy did not reply; he was tying his shoes.   39

"Sammy, I want you to tell me if he's goin' to buy more cows."   40

"I s'pose he is."   41

"How many?"   42

"Four, I guess."   43

His mother said nothing more. She went into the pantry, and there was a clatter of dishes. The boy got his cap from a nail behind the door, took an old arithmetic from the shelf, and started for school. He was lightly built, but clumsy. He went out of the yard with a curious spring in the hips, that made his loose home-made jacket tilt up in the rear.   44

The girl went to the sink, and began to wash the dishes that were piled up there. Her mother came promptly out of the pantry, and shoved her aside. "You wipe 'em," said she; "I'll wash. There's a good many this mornin'."   45

The mother plunged her hands vigorously into the water, the girl wiped the plates slowly and dreamily. "Mother," said she, "don't you think it's too bad father's going to build that new barn, much as we need a decent house to live in?"   46

Her mother scrubbed a dish fiercely. "You ain't found out yet we're women-folks, Nanny Penn," said she. "You ain't seen enough of men-folks yet to. One of these days   47 you'll find it out, an' then you'll know that we know only what men-folks think we do, so far as any use of it goes, an' how we'd ought to reckon men-folks in with Providence, an' not complain of what they do any more than we do of the weather."

48   "I don't care; I don't believe George is anything like that, anyhow," said Nanny. Her delicate face flushed pink, her lips pouted softly, as if she were going to cry.

49   "You wait an' see. I guess George Eastman ain't no better than other men. You hadn't ought to judge father, though. He can't help it, 'cause he don't look at things jest the way we do. An' we've been pretty comfortable here, after all. The roof don't leak—ain't never but once—that's one thing. Father's kept it shingled right up."

50   "I do wish we had a parlor."

51   "I guess it won't hurt George Eastman any to come to see you in a nice clean kitchen. I guess a good many girls don't have as good a place as this. Nobody's ever heard me complain."

52   "I ain't complained either, mother."

53   "Well, I don't think you'd better, a good father an' a good home as you've got. S'pose your father made you go out an' work for your livin'? Lots of girls have to that ain't no stronger an' better able to than you be."

54   Sarah Penn washed the frying-pan with a conclusive air. She scrubbed the outside of it as faithfully as the inside. She was a masterly keeper of her box of a house. Her one living-room never seemed to have in it any of the dust which the friction of life with inanimate matter produces. She swept, and there seemed to be no dirt to go before the broom; she cleaned, and one could see no difference. She was like an artist so perfect that he has apparently no art. To-day she got out a mixing bowl and a board, and rolled some pies, and there was no more flour upon her than upon her daughter who was doing finer work. Nanny was to be married in the fall, and she was sewing on some white cambric and embroidery. She sewed industriously while her mother cooked, her soft milk-white hands and wrists showed whiter than her delicate work.

55   "We must have the stove moved out in the shed before long," said Mrs. Penn. "Talk about not havin' things, it's been a real blessin' to be able to put a stove up in that shed in hot weather. Father did one good thing when he fixed that stove-pipe out there."

56   Sarah Penn's face as she rolled her pies had that expression of meek vigor which might have characterized one of the New Testament saints. She was making mince-pies. Her husband, Adoniram Penn, liked them better than any other kind. She baked twice a week. Adoniram often liked a piece of pie between meals. She hurried this morning. It had been later than usual when she began, and she wanted to have a pie baked for dinner. However deep a resentment she might be forced to hold against her husband, she would never fail in sedulous attention to his wants.

57   Nobility of character manifests itself at loop-holes when it is not provided with large doors. Sarah Penn's showed itself to-day in flaky dishes of pastry. So she made the pies faithfully, while across the table she could see, when she glanced up from her work, the sight that rankled in her patient and steadfast soul—the digging of the cellar of the new barn in the place where Adoniram forty years ago had promised her their new house should stand.

58   The pies were done for dinner. Adoniram and Sammy were home a few minutes after twelve o'clock. The dinner was eaten with serious haste. There was never much

conversation at the table in the Penn family. Adoniram asked a blessing, and they ate promptly, then rose up and went about their work.

Sammy went back to school, taking soft sly lopes out of the yard like a rabbit. He wanted a game of marbles before school, and feared his father would give him some chores to do. Adoniram hastened to the door and called after him, but he was out of sight.   59

"I don't see what you let him go for, mother," said he. "I wanted him to help me unload that wood."   60

Adoniram went to work out in the yard unloading wood from the wagon. Sarah put away the dinner dishes, while Nanny took down her curl-papers and changed her dress. She was going down to the store to buy some more embroidery and thread.   61

When Nanny was gone, Mrs. Penn went to the door. "Father!" she called.   62

"Well, what is it!"   63

"I want to see you jest a minute, father."   64

"I can't leave this wood nohow. I've got to get it unloaded an' go for a load of gravel afore two o'clock. Sammy had ought to helped me. You hadn't ought to let him go to school so early."   65

"I want to see you jest a minute."   66

"I tell ye I can't, nohow, mother."   67

"Father, you come here." Sarah Penn stood in the door like a queen; she held her head as if it bore a crown; there was that patience which makes authority royal in her voice. Adoniram went.   68

Mrs. Penn led the way into the kitchen, and pointed to a chair. "Sit down, father," said she; "I've got somethin' I want to say to you."   69

He sat down heavily; his face was quite stolid, but he looked at her with restive eyes. "Well, what is it, mother?"   70

"I want to know what you're buildin' that new barn for, father?"   71

"I ain't got nothin' to say about it."   72

"It can't be you think you need another barn?"   73

"I tell ye I ain't got nothin' to say about it, mother; an' I ain't goin' to say nothin'."   74

"Be you goin' to buy more cows?"   75

Adoniram did not reply; he shut his mouth tight.   76

"I know you be, as well as I want to. Now, father, look here"—Sarah Penn had not sat down; she stood before her husband in the humble fashion of a Scripture woman— "I'm goin' to talk real plain to you; I never have since I married you, but I'm goin' to now. I ain't never complained, an' I ain't goin' to complain now, but I'm goin' to talk plain. You see this room here, father; you look at it well. You see there ain't no carpet on the floor, an' you see the paper is all dirty, an' droppin' off the walls. We ain't had no new paper on it for ten year, an' then I put it on myself, an' it didn't cost but ninepence a roll. You see this room, father; it's all the one I've had to work in an' eat in an' sit in since we was married. There ain't another woman in the whole town whose husband ain't got half the means you have but what's got better. It's all the room Nanny's got to have her company in; an' there ain't one of her mates but what's got better, an' their fathers not so able as hers is. It's all the room she'll have to be married in. What would you have thought, father, if we had had our weddin' in a room no better than this? I was married in my mother's parlor, with a carpet on the floor, an' stuffed furniture, an' a   77 mahogany card-table. An' this is all the room my daughter will have to be married in. Look here, father!"

78   Sarah Penn went across the room as though it were a tragic stage. She flung open a door and disclosed a tiny bedroom, only large enough for a bed and bureau, with a path between. "There, father," said she—"there's all the room I've had to sleep in forty year. All my children were born there—the two that died, an' the two that's livin'. I was sick with a fever there."

79   She stepped to another door and opened it. It led into the small, ill-lighted pantry. "Here," said she, "is all the buttery I've got—every place I've got for my dishes, to set away my victuals in, an' to keep my milkpans in. Father, I've been takin' care of the milk of six cows in this place an' now you're goin' to build a new barn, an' keep more cows, an' give me more to do in it."

80   She threw open another door. A narrow crooked flight of stairs wound upward from it. "There, father," said she, "I want you to look at the stairs that go up to them two unfinished chambers that are all the places our son an' daughter have had to sleep in all their lives. There ain't a prettier girl in town nor a more ladylike one than Nanny, an' that's the place she has to sleep in. It ain't so good as your horse's stall; it ain't so warm an' tight."

81   Sarah Penn went back and stood before her husband. "Now, father," said she, "I want to know if you think you're doin' right an' accordin' to what you profess. Here, when we was married, forty year ago, you promised me faithful that we should have a new house built in that lot over in the field before the year was out. You said you had money enough, an' you wouldn't ask me to live in no such place as this. It is forty year now, an' you've been makin' more money, an' I've been savin' of it for you ever since, an' you ain't built no house yet. You've built sheds an' cow-houses an' one new barn, an' now you're goin' to build another. Father, I want to know if you think it's right. You're lodgin' your dumb beasts better than you are your own flesh an' blood. I want to know if you think it's right."

82   "I ain't got nothin' to say."

83   "You can't say nothin' without ownin' it ain't right, father. An' there's another thing—I ain't complained; I've got along forty year, an' I s'pose I should forty more, if it wa'n't for that—if we don't have another house. Nanny she can't live with us after she's married. She'll have to go somewheres else to live away from us, an' it don't seem as if I could have it so, noways, father. She wa'n't ever strong. She's got considerable color, but there wa'n't never any backbone to her. I've always took the heft of everything off her, an' she ain't fit to keep house an' do everything herself. She'll be all worn out inside of a year. Think of her doin' all the washin' an' ironin' an' bakin' with them soft white hands an' arms, an' sweepin'! I can't have it so, noways, father."

84   Mrs. Penn's face was burning; her mild eyes gleamed. She had pleaded her little cause like a Webster; she had ranged from severity to pathos; but her opponent employed that obstinate silence which makes eloquence futile with mocking echoes. Adoniram arose clumsily.

85   "Father, ain't you got nothin' to say?" said Mrs. Penn.

86   "I've got to go off after that load of gravel. I can't stan' here talkin' all day."

87   "Father, won't you think it over, an' have a house built there instead of a barn?"

88   "I ain't got nothin' to say."

Adoniram shuffled out. Mrs. Penn went into her bedroom. When she came out, her   89
eyes were red. She had a roll of unbleached cotton cloth. She spread it out on the
kitchen table, and began cutting out some shirts for her husband. The men over in the
field had a team to help them this afternoon; she could hear their halloos. She had a
scanty pattern for the shirts; she had to plan and piece the sleeves.

Nanny came home with her embroidery, and sat down with her needle-work. She   90
had taken down her curl-papers, and there was a soft roll of fair hair like an aureole
over her forehead; her face was as delicately fine and clear as porcelain. Suddenly she
looked up, and the tender red flamed all over her face and neck. "Mother," said she.

"What say?"   91

"I've been thinking—I don't see how we're goin' to have any—wedding in this   92
room. I'd be ashamed to have his folks come if we didn't have anybody else."

"Mebbe we can have some new paper before then; I can put it on. I guess you won't   93
have no call to be ashamed of your belongin's."

"We might have the wedding in the new barn," said Nanny, with gentle pettishness.   94
"Why, mother, what makes you look so?"

Mrs. Penn had started, and was staring at her with a curious expression. She turned 95
again to her work, and spread out a pattern carefully on the cloth. "Nothin'," said she.

Presently Adoniram clattered out of the yard in his two-wheeled dump cart, stand-   96
ing as proudly upright as a Roman charioteer. Mrs. Penn opened the door and stood
there a minute looking out; the halloos of the men sounded louder.

It seemed to her all through the spring months that she heard nothing but the hal-   97
loos and the noises of saws and hammers. The new barn grew fast. It was a fine edifice
for this little village. Men came on pleasant Sundays, in their meeting suits and clean
shirt bosoms, and stood around it admiringly. Mrs. Penn did not speak of it, and
Adoniram did not mention it to her, although sometimes, upon a return from inspecting
it, he bore himself with injured dignity.

"It's a strange thing how your mother feels about the new barn," he said, confiden- 98
tially, to Sammy one day.

Sammy only grunted after an odd fashion for a boy; he had learned it from his   99
father.

The barn was all completed ready for use by the third week in July. Adoniram had   100
planned to move his stock in on Wednesday; on Tuesday he received a letter which
changed his plans. He came in with it early in the morning. "Sammy's been to the post-
office," said he, "an' I've got a letter from Hiram." Hiram was Mrs. Penn's brother, who
lived in Vermont.

"Well," said Mrs. Penn, "what does he say about the folks?"   101

"I guess they're all right. He says he thinks if I come up country right off there's a 102
chance to buy jest the kind of a horse I want." He stared reflectively out of the window
at the new barn.

Mrs. Penn was making pies. She went on clapping the rolling-pin into the crust,   103
although she was very pale, and her heart beat loudly.

"I dun' know but what I'd better go," said Adoniram. "I hate to go off jest now, right 104
in the midst of hayin', but the ten-acre lot's cut, an' I guess Rufus an' the others can git
along without me three or four days. I can't get a horse around here to suit me, nohow,

an' I've got to have another for all that wood-haulin' in the fall. I told Hiram to watch out, an' if he got wind of a good horse to let me know. I guess I'd better go."

105   "I'll get out your clean shirt an' collar," said Mrs. Penn calmly.

106   She laid out Adoniram's Sunday suit and his clean clothes on the bed in the little bedroom. She got his shaving-water and razor ready. At last she buttoned on his collar and fastened his black cravat.

107   Adoniram never wore his collar and cravat except on extra occasions. He held his head high, with a rasped dignity. When he was all ready, with his coat and hat brushed, and a lunch of pie and cheese in a paper bag, he hesitated on the threshold of the door. He looked at his wife, and his manner was defiantly apologetic. "*If* them cows come to-day, Sammy can drive 'em into the new barn," said he; "an' when they bring the hay up, they can pitch it in there."

108   "Well," replied Mrs. Penn.

109   Adoniram set his shaven face ahead and started. When he had cleared the door-step, he turned and looked back with a kind of nervous solemnity. "I shall be back by Saturday if nothin' happens," said he.

110   "Do be careful, father," returned his wife.

111   She stood in the door with Nanny at her elbow and watched him out of sight. Her eyes had a strange, doubtful expression in them; her peaceful forehead was contracted. She went in, and about her baking again. Nanny sat sewing. Her wedding-day was drawing nearer, and she was getting pale and thin with her steady sewing. Her mother kept glancing at her.

112   "Have you got that pain in your side this mornin'?" she asked.

113   "A little."

114   Mrs. Penn's face, as she worked, changed, her perplexed forehead smoothed, her eyes were steady, her lips firmly set. She formed a maxim for herself, although incoherently with her unlettered thoughts. "Unsolicited opportunities are the guide-posts of the Lord to the new roads of life," she repeated in effect, and she made up her mind to her course of action.

115   "S'posin' I *had* wrote to Hiram," she muttered once, when she was in the pantry— s'posin' I had wrote, an' asked him if he knew of any horse? But I didn't, an' father's goin' wa'n't none of my doin'. It looks like a providence." Her voice rang out quite loud at the last.

116   "What you talkin' about, mother?" called Nanny.

117   "Nothin'."

118   Mrs. Penn hurried her baking; at eleven o'clock it was all done. The load of hay from the west field came slowly down the cart track, and drew up at the new barn. Mrs. Penn ran out. "Stop!" she screamed—"stop!"

119   The men stopped and looked; Sammy upreared from the top of the load, and stared at his mother.

120   "Stop!" she cried out again. "Don't you put the hay in that barn; put it in the old one."

121   "Why, he said to put it in here," returned one of the haymakers, wonderingly. He was a young man, a neighbor's son, whom Adoniram hired by the year to help on the farm.

"Don't you put the hay in the new barn; there's room enough in the old one, ain't   122
there?" said Mrs. Penn

"Room enough," returned the hired man, in his thick, rustic tones. "Didn't need the   123
new barn, nohow, far as room's concerned. Well, I s'pose he changed his mind." He
took hold of the horses' bridles.

Mrs. Penn went back to the house. Soon the kitchen windows were darkened, and a   124
fragrance like warm honey came into the room.

Nanny laid down her work. "I thought father wanted them to put the hay into the   125
new barn?" she said, wonderingly.

"It's all right," replied her mother.   126

Sammy slid down from the load of hay, and came in to see if dinner was ready.   127

"I ain't goin' to get a regular dinner to-day, as long as father's gone," said his   128
mother. "I've let the fire go out. You can have some bread an' milk an' pie. I thought we
could get along." She set out some bowls of milk, some bread, and a pie on the kitchen
table. "You'd better eat your dinner now," said she. "You might jest as well get through
with it. I want you to help me afterward."

Nanny and Sammy stared at each other. There was something strange in their   129
mother's manner. Mrs. Penn did not eat anything herself. She went into the pantry, and
they heard her moving dishes while they ate. Presently she came out with a pile of
plates. She got the clothes-basket out of the shed, and packed them in it. Nanny and
Sammy watched. She brought out cups and saucers, and put them in with the plates.

"What you goin' to do, mother?" inquired Nanny, in a timid voice. A sense of some-   130
thing unusual made her tremble, as if it were a ghost. Sammy rolled his eyes over his pie.

"You'll see what I'm goin' to do," replied Mrs. Penn.   131

"If you're through, Nanny, I want you to go up-stairs an' pack up your things; an' I   132
want you, Sammy, to help me take down the bed in the bedroom."

"Oh mother, what for?" gasped Nanny.   133

"You'll see."   134

During the next few hours a feat was performed by this simple, pious New England   135
mother which was equal in its way to Wolfe's storming of the Heights of Abraham. It
took no more genius and audacity of bravery for Wolfe to cheer his wondering soldiers
up those steep precipices, under the sleeping eyes of the enemy, than for Sarah Penn, at
the head of her children, to move all their little household goods into the new barn
while her husband was away.

Nanny and Sammy followed their mother's instructions without a murmur; indeed,   136
they were overawed. There is a certain uncanny and superhuman quality about all
such purely original undertakings as their mother's was to them. Nanny went back and
forth with her light loads, and Sammy tugged with sober energy.

At five o'clock in the afternoon the little house in which the Penns had lived for   137
forty years had emptied itself into the new barn.

Every builder builds somewhat for unknown purposes, and is in a measure a   138
prophet. The architect of Adoniram Penn's barn, while he designed it for the comfort
of four-footed animals, had planned better than he knew for the comfort of humans.

Sarah Penn saw at a glance its possibilities. Those great box-stalls, with quilts hung before them, would make better bedrooms than the one she had occupied for forty years, and there was a tight carriage-room. The harness-room, with its chimney and shelves, would make a kitchen of her dreams. The great middle-space would make a parlor, by-and-by, fit for a palace. Up stairs there was as much room as down. With partitions and windows, what a house would there be! Sarah looked at the row of stanchions before the allotted space for cows, and reflected that she would have her front entry there.

139   At six o'clock the stove was up in the harness-room, the kettle was boiling, and the table set for tea. It looked almost as home-like as the abandoned house across the yard had ever done. The young hired man milked, and Sarah directed him calmly to bring the milk to the new barn. He came gaping, dropping little blots of foam from the brimming pails on the grass. Before the next morning he had spread the story of Adoniram Penn's wife moving into the new barn all over the little village. Men assembled in the store and talked it over, women with shawls over their heads scuttled into each other's houses before their work was done. Any deviation from the ordinary course of life in this quiet town was enough to stop all progress in it. Everybody paused to look at the staid, independent figure on the side track. There was a difference of opinion with regard to her. Some held her to be insane; some, of a lawless and rebellious spirit.

140   Friday the minister went to see her. It was in the forenoon, and she was at the barn door shelling peas for dinner. She looked up and returned his salutation with dignity, then she went on with her work. She did not invite him in. The saintly expression of her face remained fixed, but there was an angry flush over it.

141   The minister stood awkwardly before her, and talked. She handled the peas as if they were bullets. At last she looked up, and her eyes showed the spirit that her meek front had covered for a lifetime.

142   "There ain't no use talkin', Mr. Hersey," said she. "I've thought it all over an' over, an' I believe I'm doin' what's right. I've made it the subject of prayer, an' it's betwixt me an' the Lord an' Adoniram. There ain't no call for nobody else to worry about it."

143   "Well, of course, if you have brought it to the Lord in prayer, and feel satisfied that you are doing right, Mrs. Penn," said the minister, helplessly. His thin gray-bearded face was pathetic. He was a sickly man; his youthful confidence had cooled; he had to scourge himself up to some of his pastoral duties as relentlessly as a Catholic ascetic, and then he was prostrated by the smart.

144   "I think it's right jest as much as I think it was right for our forefathers to come over from the old country 'cause they didn't have what belonged to 'em," said Mrs. Penn. She arose. The barn threshold might have been Plymouth Rock from her bearing. "I don't doubt you mean well, Mr. Hersey," said she, "but there are things people hadn't ought to interfere with. I've been a member of the church for over forty year. I've got my own mind an' my own feet, an' I'm goin' to think my own thoughts an' go my own ways, an' nobody but the Lord is goin' to dictate to me unless I've a mind to have him. Won't you come in an' set down? How is Mis' Hersey?"

145   "She is well, I thank you," replied the minister. He added some more perplexed apologetic remarks; then he retreated.

He could expound the intricacies of every character study in the Scriptures, he was   146
competent to grasp the Pilgrim Fathers and all historical innovators, but Sarah Penn
was beyond him. He could deal with primal cases, but parallel ones worsted him. But,
after all, although it was aside from his province, he wondered more how Adoniram
Penn would deal with his wife than how the Lord would. Everybody shared the wonder. When Adoniram's four new cows arrived, Sarah ordered three to be put in the old
barn, the other in the house shed where the cooking-stove had stood. That added to the
excitement. It was whispered that all four cows were domiciled in the house.

Towards sunset on Saturday, when Adoniram was expected home, there was a knot   147
of men in the road near the new barn. The hired man had milked, but he still hung
around the premises. Sarah Penn had supper all ready. There were brown-bread and
baked beans and a custard pie; it was the supper that Adoniram loved on a Saturday
night. She had on a clean calico, and she bore herself imperturbably. Nanny and
Sammy kept close at her heels. Their eyes were large, and Nanny was full of nervous
tremors. Still there was to them more pleasant excitement than anything else. An inborn
confidence in their mother over their father asserted itself.

Sammy looked out of the harness-room window. "There he is," he announced, in   148
an awed whisper. He and Nanny peeped around the casing. Mrs. Penn kept on about
her work. The children watched Adoniram leave the new horse standing in the drive
while he went to the house door. It was fastened. Then he went around to the shed.
That door was seldom locked, even when the family was away. The thought how her
father would be confronted by the cow flashed upon Nanny. There was a hysterical
sob in her throat. Adoniram emerged from the shed and stood looking about in a
dazed fashion. His lips moved; he was saying something, but they could not hear
what it was. The hired man was peeping around a corner of the old barn, but nobody
saw him.

Adoniram took the new horse by the bridle and led him across the yard to the new   149
barn. Nanny and Sammy slunk close to their mother. The barn doors rolled back, and
there stood Adoniram, with the long mild face of the great Canadian farm horse looking
over his shoulder.

Nanny kept behind her mother, but Sammy stepped suddenly forward, and stood in   150
front of her.

Adoniram stared at the group. "What on airth you all down here for?" said he.   151
"What's the matter over to the house?"

"We've come here to live, father," said Sammy. His shrill voice quavered out   152
bravely.

"What"—Adoniram sniffed—"what is it smells like cookin?" said he. He stepped   153
forward and looked in the open door of the harness-room. Then he turned to his wife.
His old bristling face was pale and frightened. "What on airth does this mean, mother?"
he gasped.

"You come in here, father," said Sarah. She led the way into the harness-room and   154
shut the door. "Now, father," said she, "you needn't be scared. I ain't crazy. There ain't
nothin' to be upset over. But we've come here to live, an' we're goin' to live here.
We've got jest as good a right here as new horses an' cows. The house wa'n't fit for us

to live in any longer, an' I made up my mind I wa'n't goin' to stay there. I've done my duty by you forty year, an' I'm goin' to do it now; but I'm goin' to live here. You've got to put in some windows and partitions; an' you'll have to buy some furniture."

155   "Why, mother!" the old man gasped.

156   "You'd better take your coat off an' get washed—there's the wash-basin—an' then we'll have supper."

157   "Why, mother!"

158   Sammy went past the window, leading the new horse to the old barn. The old man saw him, and shook his head speechlessly. He tried to take off his coat, but his arms seemed to lack the power. His wife helped him. She poured some water into the tin basin, and put in a piece of soap. She got the comb and brush, and smoothed his thin gray hair after he had washed. Then she put the beans, hot bread, and tea on the table. Sammy came in and the family drew up. Adoniram sat looking dazedly at his plate, and they waited.

159   "Ain't you goin' to ask a blessin', father?" said Sarah.

160   And the old man bent his head and mumbled.

161   All through the meal he stopped eating at intervals, and stared furtively at his wife; but he ate well. The home food tasted good to him, and his old frame was too sturdily healthy to be affected by his mind. But after supper he went out, and sat down on the step of the smaller door at the right of the barn, through which he had meant his Jerseys to pass in stately file, but which Sarah designed for her front house door, and he leaned his head on his hands.

162   After the supper dishes were cleared away and the milk-pans washed, Sarah went out to him. The twilight was deepening. There was a clear green glow in the sky. Before them stretched the smooth level of field; in the distance was a cluster of hay-stacks like the huts of a village; the air was very cool and calm and sweet. The landscape might have been an ideal one of peace.

163   Sarah bent over and touched her husband on one of his thin, sinewy shoulders. "Father!"

164   The old man's shoulders heaved: he was weeping.

165   "Why, don't do so, father," said Sarah.

166   "I'll—put up the—partitions, an'—everything you—want, mother."

167   Sarah put her apron up to her face; she was overcome by her own triumph.

168   Adoniram was like a fortress whose walls had no active resistance, and went down the instant the right besieging tools were used. "Why, mother," he said, hoarsely, "I hadn't no idee you was so set on't as all this comes to."

➤ FOR WRITING OR DISCUSSION

1. Almost every marriage has some underlying tensions. What are the underlying tensions in the marriages treated in these two stories?
2. In which marriage are the tensions more serious?
3. How are the tensions resolved in each marriage? Which way is better? Why?

4. Is either marriage in danger of breaking up? If so, which? Why?
5. If you had to choose one of these couples as friends, which would you choose? Why?
6. Which couple is more admirable?
7. Write a paper comparing or contrasting Freeman's short story with Thurber's. You may use one or more of the preceding questions to guide you in limiting your subject.

WRITING TOPICS

If you are having difficulty deciding on a topic for your comparison-and-contrast paper, some of the following suggestions for topics might be helpful. Bear in mind that the number of comparison-and-contrast topics is almost infinite, and ours just begin to scratch the surface. Our suggestions are intended more to start your own thoughts flowing than to be specific, final topics.

1. Any past versus present topic: cars, sports teams or athletes, girlfriends or boyfriends, movie stars, musical styles, clothes, ways of celebrating a holiday, a change in your attitude toward someone or something.
2. What you thought something was going to be like and what it was actually like: a country, a town, college life, a job, a book, a romantic attachment, a marriage, a divorce, a tourist attraction.
3. A which-is-better topic: two competing products, places to live, newscasters, restaurants, television sitcoms, business establishments, seasons of the year, cats versus dogs, breeds of dog, methods of disciplining children.
4. Two contrasting types of people: teachers, police officers, drivers, salespeople, politicians, "dates," hairstylists, servers at restaurants.
5. Two contrasting (but sometimes confused) emotions or character traits: love and infatuation, courage and recklessness, pride and arrogance, snobbery and good taste, fear and terror.

CROSSCURRENTS

1. In a short essay, compare the views of writing and learning to write as indicated in Zinsser's "Speaking of Writing" (page 240) and George Eppley's "Sister Clarissa" (page 113).
2. Judy Brady and Barbara Ehrenreich present views on the relations between men and women and the differences between the sexes. Write an essay in which you compare and contrast the essential points in "I Want a Wife" (page 190) and "What I've Learned from Men" (page 178).

COLLABORATIVE LEARNING

In groups of three to five students, discuss the student essays "Life after Death" (page 228), "Smarter But" (page 230), and "Shaver's Choice" (page 233). Look particularly at the relations between the outlines presented and the essays themselves. In what ways did the writers use the outlines successfully in developing the papers? What suggestions can the group make for improving the outlines? the essays?

REVIEW CHECKLIST: WRITING AND REVISING YOUR COMPARISON-AND-CONTRAST PAPER

- Have I done prewriting to explore ideas for a subject?
- Have I thought carefully about my purpose?
- Have I written for the usual general audience? If I am writing for a special audience, have I made that clear to the reader?
- Have I limited my subject?
- Have I established a clear thesis?
- Do I have enough support for my thesis?
- Have I compared and contrasted according to a single principle?
- Have I compared and contrasted according to a single purpose?
- Have I been fair with comparisons and contrasts?
- Have I followed an established pattern of organization?
- Have I proofread for grammar, spelling, and mechanics?

Photo courtesy: © Joe Carini/The Image Works

―――――― FROM IMAGE TO WORDS: A PHOTO WRITING ASSIGNMENT ――――――
Use the photograph above to write a brief essay that compares and contrasts the two
women you see there. Consider not only the obvious differences—their age, appearance,
and so on—but also what you think both of their objectives are.

11

Classification and Division

Saturday night is just around the corner, and you've decided to spend a quiet evening at home—cook some spaghetti, make a salad, get a movie from the video rental shop not far from your dorm, and pick up the latest Steven King book for a little nighttime terror before bed. If you're biking, driving, or taking the bus, you're already plotting the most efficient route to get around your town or city. Maybe it's Blockbuster's video rental first, Pathmark Supermarket second, and the local library last.

At Blockbuster's, you try to decide what movie you want. Signs direct you to different groups of films—new releases (a grab bag, really, of movies out in the last year or so), comedies, adventure classics, romances, and others. You decide on *There's Something About Mary*—you've seen it at least twice before—but its raunchy antics seem to be the perfect antidote to what Stephen King will no doubt provide. So you head over to the comedies section and take what you want from the shelf. There's a two-for-one special tonight—well, maybe you'll be bored the third time around with Mary and company—so you head over to the adventure classics section: Your friend Consuelo has been raving about *The Thin Red Line*, a World War II film set in the Pacific that she calls beautiful poetry, and you find your way to the right shelf for that film too.

At Pathmark, your first stop is at the fruits and vegetables area for the makings of a small salad, then to the boxes of macaroni and spaghetti piled high in the pasta section (it's linguine tonight, you've decided), and then over to the shelves marked "Sauces" for a jar of Ronzoni's meat sauce. Finally, you go to the frozen food section, check out the ice-cream bin, and pick Ben and Jerry's Cherry Garcia.

Off to the library then; inside you ask the librarian where to find the new Stephen King book. Ordinarily, she says, she'd direct you to the Library of Congress classification letters and numbers; but this branch has a section called New Releases near the check-out desk. You look for the King book and note that one copy is in the group of books to rent with a daily fee and another copy in the group of free books—from which you grab your copy and head home.

Classification and Division as Modes of Thought

In these acts to settle your Saturday night plan you've taken advantage of a couple of humankind's most advanced modes of thought, division and classification. These higher order thinking skills allow us to see relations among parts and hence make the world around us more comprehensible and less disparate.

When you established your route for picking up the various items you needed for Saturday night at home, you used *division*, maybe even unconsciously. You considered the whole map of your town or neighborhood and divided it into separate units to make your trip easier. The video shop, the supermarket, the library—these are the sections of your larger surrounding geography. When you divide, you break down something (here, your town or neighborhood) into parts or sections. Your purpose in dividing was for ease of transport and so you divided the entity into units that served your purpose. Clearly, many other possibilities exist for dividing the neighborhood you live in, all depending on the purpose for the division. You could separate the neighborhood by the way people vote in elections; by the ethnic makeup of various sections; by the architectural varieties of buildings; by the lawns and flower gardens and what they look like; and by the school districts and the businesses—the options are numerous.

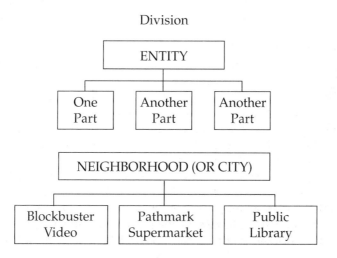

Division

In the process of division—which, incidentally, many people call *analysis*—you break down an entity into its discrete parts, all based on some organizing principle. Division moves from the general to the specific: You look at a large category and try to understand it better by seeing what makes it up. When you analyze a Big Mac, a rock song, a television program, a magazine ad, or a poem, you divide it into distinct elements in order to understand the parts and how they contribute to the whole.

As you scooted around town to the video shop, the supermarket, and the library, you used a different, but related, thinking skill. As you searched for movies, pasta, vegetables, ice cream, and a King thriller, you relied on *classification*. To locate specific items, you had to identify the large group into which someone had placed them. Classification creates large entities from discrete components.

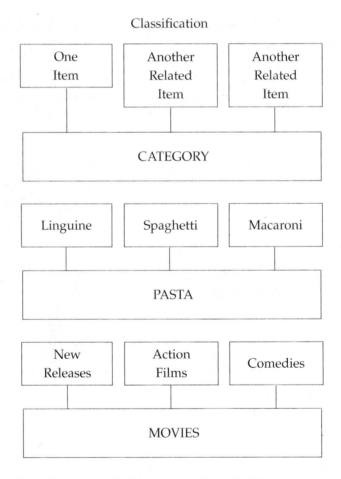

Classification

Do you see the differences? *Division* moves from the larger group to the smaller parts. *Classification* moves from the smaller parts to the larger group. Division and classification as rhetorical strategies often work hand in hand and overlap considerably. If you wanted to write about preparing for your Saturday night at home, as we've revealed it here, you might explain how you *divided* your neighborhood into entities that let you move easily from one stop to the other. Then you'd explain how *classification* at your various stops helped you set up an evening of leisure according to your own design. To take another example, if you wanted to write about violence on television, you might *divide* the topic into news shows, day-time soap operas, and children's programs. Selecting one or more of these, you might then *classify* the soaps, for example. You might identify categories of violence that you saw on the soap operas, such as violence against children, violence among husbands, wives and lovers, and violence at the workplace. Each category would require supporting detail to make you classification stick— but we'll have more to say later about how to write your classification essay.

Photo courtesy: © Lee Synder/Photo Researchers, Inc.

———— FROM IMAGE TO WORDS: A PHOTO WRITING ASSIGNMENT ————

To classify the items in the photograph above, what categories or groups could you establish? How many classification schemes could you suggest as a way of organizing the objects? Indicate at least two ways that you could classify the objects and list several items that you would include in each group. Create a chart and fill in your own responses.

Reviewing Division Strategies

Another name for division is *analysis:* When you analyze—a poem or short story, a process or procedure, or the reasons for some behavior or action—you divide the issue into components. In analysis by *division,* a subject usually thought of as a single unit is broken down into each one of its parts. An analysis of a stereo system, for example, requires naming and describing each of its components. An analysis of a breakfast cereal requires a listing of the number of calories and the grams of protein, carbohydrates, fat, and sodium in a single serving. An analysis of a process—how to change a light bulb or how to make iron ore into steel—requires discussing the separate steps of the process. So, in fact, if you have written a process paper, you have already used one major form of division.

If you wrote a literary analysis using comparison-and-contrast strategies (see pages 235–238), you used division to break the piece of literature into the components that concerned you before you showed similarities and differences.

When you write a cause-and-effect paper, often called *causal analysis* (see Chapter 12), division will help you separate an entity—an event, an action, or a consequence—into separate components.

We deal, therefore, with analysis (division) in other sections of this book. This chapter focuses on *classification.*

Writing Your Classification Paper

As you have seen, **classification** is the process by which members of a large group—ideas, people, plants, animals, books, pasta, films, and so on—are categorized on the basis of a single principle. A credit office, for example, might assign all applicants for credit (large group) to one of three categories: excellent risk, fair risk, poor risk. The assignment would be made on the basis of each applicant's ability and readiness to pay the bills when they come due (the principle of classification in this case). Clearly, classification is essential to the credit office if the company is to remain in business. Classification is useful to others, too, because it enables them to cope with a large body of material by organizing it into smaller, more workable categories. Besides, we all like to classify. We do it naturally. Students classify their professors as boring or stimulating. Homemakers classify their cooking utensils, perhaps as those used often and those used occasionally, and place them in drawers and cupboards accordingly. But whether used for fun or for profit, classification has certain requirements, many of which you have already used in developing outlines.

■ *Determine the basis for classification and then apply it consistently.* To classify automobiles, you would not want to establish as the categories "foreign cars," "expensive cars," and "sedans" because these classes do not have the same basis of classification. The first class is based on country of origin, the second on price, and the third on body style. A member of one class would be likely to overlap into others. A Rolls-Royce or a Mercedes, for example, could fit into any of the three classes. Logic would require selection of a single basis of classification such as price and then sticking to the issue of price with subclasses like "expensive," "medium-priced," and "low-priced." Likewise, if you were going to classify the courses you are taking according to level of interest, you shouldn't establish as the categories "dull," "moderately interesting," and "difficult." The class "difficult" violates the principle of classification—level of interest, in this case.

■ *Define any terms that might be unfamiliar to your audience or that are used in a special way.*   A writer using technical terms like *mesomorphs, ectomorphs,* and *endomorphs* to describe human body types would need to define those terms. Even familiar terms like *mature* and *immature* or *realistic* and *unrealistic* may often require definitions because they can be interpreted in many different ways. Similarly, suppose you invent names for your categories. You might, for instance, classify joggers as red-faced wobblers, short-legged two-steppers, and long-legged striders. You must share with your reader your understanding of these made-up terms.

■ *Decide whether you need only describe each category fully or whether you need to add clarifying examples.*   A classification of people as overweight, underweight, and normal, for example, would require merely a complete description of each type. Readers could, on the basis of the description, decide which category the various people they meet belong to. On the other hand, a classification of the present Supreme Court justices as liberals or conservatives, besides giving the characteristics of liberal and conservative justices, should also give the names of the justices who belong to each category and some explanation of why they have been placed there.

■ *Have a thesis.*   In one sense, of course, the classification itself provides the basis for a thesis. If you assert that there are three classes of teachers or four classes of pet owners or five classes of social drinkers and can support your assertion, you have a thesis. But you should, with certain subjects, take even stronger positions. You could show, for example, that one of the categories is preferable to the others, or that all the categories are silly or despicable or admirable. Having a thesis gives force and interest to your categories.

■ *Establish some kind of order.*   In some cases, you can order your categories according to time, from earliest to latest. Or, depending on your thesis, several other possibilities for ordering the categories present themselves. You might order the categories from worst to best, best to worst, least enjoyable to most enjoyable, or weakest to strongest, for example. In most listings, you may have more interesting comments to make about some classes than about others. Arrange your classes so that the less interesting ones are in the middle of your paper. Hook your readers with a strong first category and leave them satisfied with an even stronger last category. The practice of ordering categories will make an important contribution to your classification papers.

Student Writing: Classification

See what you think of this student's effort at classification; use the annotations to guide your reading.

Yvonne C. Younger

Tomorrow, Tomorrow

Introduction: begins to establish the context for classification

Up and at 'em. Make hay while the sun shines. Seize the bull by the horns. Never put off 'til tomorrow what can be done today. Just do it. There are scores of ways for people to tell others to get up, get out, and get going. Fortunately, there are just as many ways to completely avoid doing anything at all.   1

Over the past few years I have made a serious and concentrated study of the varied ways to procrastinate. I have discovered that there are as many ways to avoid work as there are people who wish to avoid working.   2

Thesis includes writer's assertion and purpose.

Happily for the length of this essay, however, I have determined that all kinds of procrastination can be divided into four major groups: the classic, the childish, the responsible, and the artistic.

Topic divided; categories identified indicate basis for classification.

First category includes example to explain "classic" procrastination.

The classic type of procrastination is particularly typical of teenagers. It involves lying face up on a flat surface of the procrastinator's choice--beds, sofas, and floors are popular. The procrastinator then proceeds to count ceiling tiles, trace the path of a wandering spider, or simply gaze at a fixed point off in the distance. The advantage of this procrastination style is that it requires no effort. The disadvantage is that there is nothing to distract the work-avoider from the guilt he or she feels at not doing what must be done.   3

Second category and examples

Procrastinating in the childish style is standard for college students. Faced with an essay to write, a problem set to complete, or a stack of bills to pay, childish procrastinators are overcome with the desire to play. Koosh balls, Slinkies, Legos, and Silly Putty are the major tools of this method. The popularity of this style is at least partly due to its ability to convince others that deep down the procrastinator is amusing and energetic, not lazy. Its single drawback is the expense of equipping oneself with enough Legos and toy knights to have a really good battle.

4

Those who procrastinate responsibly are liable to be adults with a reputation for being organized and "together." Their approach to avoiding work is to find

5

Third category: "responsible" procrastination with illustrative examples

other, different, less unappealing work to do. To put off filing their taxes, followers of this style will scrub floors, bake endless batches of cookies, alphabetize their CD collections, and even color-code their sock drawers. The advantage of this style is that one is simply too busy to be working at unpleasant chores. The grave disadvantage is that one ends up working anyway.

Last category: most interesting group placed last in the essay

Artistic procrastination is for the creative spirit. On the surface it resembles classic procrastination almost exactly. The work-avoider lies on the couch all day, staring into the distance. However, when accused of procrastinating, the artistic procrastinator looks offended and either explains that he or she is waiting for inspiration to strike, or looks tortured and complains that no one understands artistic struggle and true suffering. The best part of this procrastination method is how impressive it can be if done properly.

6

The worst part is that, no matter how convincingly it is
done, one will always be suspected of simply lying on
the couch.

Conclusion
links to
introduction
and thesis.
    Each type of procrastination has its advantages and   7
disadvantages. Each style is also remarkably good for
ignoring and avoiding work. Try them all; perfect your
favorite, and never work again.

➤ **FOR WRITING OR DISCUSSION**

1. What determines the order in which the first three classes are presented?
2. Should the fourth class have been saved for last, or should it have been presented earlier?
3. Which classes make most effective use of specific details? Which class uses
   specific details least effectively?
4. Where does the essay briefly turn to comparison–contrast writing? Why?
5. Does the author seem to favor any one class above the others? Is there a thesis?
6. Write a classification paper choosing an undesirable type or person or practice
   as your subject: spoiled brats, incompetent parents, nags, worriers, bigots,
   drinkers, smokers, and so on.

Models of Writing

As you read the following models of classification essays, consider whether the
writers have observed the rules of classification discussed in this chapter.

GLEN WAGGONER

Shaking Hands

1   A handshake tells you a lot about a man. For one thing, it tells you that he's probably
an American. Europeans hug when they greet each other, the English nod, the
Japanese bow, but Americans shake hands. And that's the way it is.

2   Extending an empty hand to show that you have no weapon, grasping another's hand
to signify your human bond—you have to admit the handshake has impeccable symbolic
credentials. Too bad that it has become so commonplace as to have lost much of its original meaning. Anyway, it's our way of saying hello, so we might as well get straight once
and for all the main kinds of handshake, especially the only one that is correct.

The Politician's Pump. A familiar face with a toothy grin that materializes out of a 3
crowd as its owner grabs your right hand in a firm grip, while simultaneously seizing
your right forearm in his left hand. Two short, strong shakes and you find yourself being
moved sideways as Teeth swivels to mug the next voter. (Also known as the Receiving-
Line Two-Hand when practiced by college presidents.)

The Preemptive Squeeze. All fingers and thumb. Your extended hand is caught 4
just short of its target by a set of pincers that encloses your four fingers at the second
knuckle and leaves your thumb pointing west. No palm contact whatsoever. One quick
squeeze, a side-to-side waggle, and your hand is unceremoniously dropped, leaving it
utterly frustrated.

The Limp Fish. The most hated of all. Someone puts his fingers in your hand and 5
leaves them there. Excusable in foreigners, who are still grappling with a language
where *gh* and *f* sound alike (as in "tough fish"). For others, unacceptable.

The Macho Man. The old bone-crusher, the familiar signature of the emotionally 6
insecure but physically strong. If you're alert, you can see this one coming in time to
take countermeasures. The best defense is a good offense: grab his hand toward the
base of the palm, cutting down on his fingers' leverage, and start your grip before he
starts his. Of course, if he's strong enough and macho enough, it won't work, and he'll
bond your individual digits into a single flipper for trying to thwart him.

The Preacher's Clasp. As your right hands join, his left folds over the top and 7
immobilizes them both (okay, all three, but who's counting?). Always accompanied by
steady eye contact (no way you won't be the first to blink), and usually by a monologue
delivered two inches closer to your face than is really necessary. Once the exclusive
province of Presbyterian ministers, the Clasp is now practiced by a broad spectrum of
the relentlessly sincere, including motivational speakers and honors graduates of
weekend-therapy marathons. The worst thing about it is that it makes your hand sweat.

The Right Way. A firm, full-handed grip, a steady squeeze, and a definite but 8
understated downward snap (but no up-and-down pumping, unless you're contemplating a disabling karate move), followed at once by a decisive release accompanied by
eye contact and performed only if both parties are standing (the ritual implies mutual
respect and equality, after all). Sounds easy enough, but how frequently do you
encounter a really good one?

Footnote: Shaking Hands with Women. No difference in grip (the Right Way is 9
always right), but convention has it that you should wait for her to extend her hand first.
These days, chances are good she will.

➤ FOR WRITING OR DISCUSSION

1. Originally published in the "Man at His Best" section of *Esquire* magazine,
   Waggoner's primary intended audience in "Shaking Hands" is male. Do the
   classifications of handshakes apply to women as well as men? Explain.
2. The author invents terms to label each class. How effective are the terms in
   suggesting the nature of each type of handshake? Is each handshake clearly
   defined or described?

3. The author's thesis is: Of the six classes of handshakes only one is "right." In supporting the thesis, does Waggoner clearly express or imply his scorn for the five bad classes and his approval for the one good class?

4. Write a paper classifying kisses, laughs, coughs, or handwaves.

KENNETH H. COOPER

How Fit Are You?

1   I was visiting a colleague [like Cooper, a doctor in the U.S. Air Force] who was testing volunteers for a special project that would require men in the best possible condition. I passed three of the volunteers in the hall. Two had normal builds, but the third was definitely muscular.

2   "Which of the three do you think will get our recommendation?" my friend asked, tossing their medical records across the desk. I skimmed over the physiological data until I came to the slot where it asked, "Regular exercise?"

3   One wrote, candidly, "None."

4   The second, "Nothing regular. Just ride my bike to the base and back every day. About three miles one way."

5   The third, "Isometrics and weight lifting, one hour a day, five days a week." The muscular one!

6   I glanced back over each of the records. All pilots, all in their early 30s, none with any history of illness.

7   "Well?" asked my friend.

8   "I'd bet on the cyclist."

9   "Not the weight lifter?"

10   "Not if that's all he does."

11   My friend smiled. "I think you're right."

12   Next day he proved it. The three came back for their treadmill tests and the non-exerciser and the weight lifter were completely fatigued within the first five minutes. The cyclist was still going strong 10 minutes later, running uphill at a 6½ mph clip. He was recommended for the project. The other two weren't.

13   This story, when I use it in my lectures, always surprises people. The nonexerciser they can believe. The cyclist, maybe. But the weight lifter, or anyone who does strictly isometrics or calisthenics, they all *look* in such good condition!

14   In my business, looks are deceitful. Some exceptionally physically fit men tested in our laboratory were middle-aged types with slight builds, including an occasional one with a paunch. Some of the most unfit we've ever seen were husky young men with cardiac conditions.

15   If this shatters any illusions about slim waistlines and large biceps being the key to good health, I'm sorry. They're not a deterrent, but they're no guarantee either. They're mostly a byproduct. The real key is elsewhere.

16   Take those three volunteers. By ordinary standards, all three should have been accepted. None of them had any physical defects, or ever had any. Why the discrimination?

For special projects, the military services can afford to be discriminate. They can   17
afford to classify the physically fit into their three classic categories and choose only
the most fit.

The nonexerciser represents passive fitness. There's nothing wrong with him—not   18
yet anyway—but there's nothing really right with him either. If he's lucky, he can coast
like that for years. But, without any activity, his body is essentially deteriorating.

The weight lifter, or those who emphasize isometrics or calisthenics, represent mus-   19
cular fitness. These types, who have the right motives but the wrong approach, are
stuck with the myth that muscular strength or agility means physical fitness. This is one
of the great misconceptions in the field of exercise. The muscles that show—the skeletal muscles—are just one system in the body, and by no means the most important. If
your exercise program is directed only at the skeletal muscles, you'll never achieve real
physical fitness.

The cyclist, whether he knew it or not, had found one of the most basic means to   20
overall fitness. . . . By riding three miles to work, six miles round trip, he was earning
more than enough points to answer the question, "How much exercise?"[1] and he
proved it on the treadmill.

The cyclist represents the third, and best, kind of fitness, overall fitness. We call it   21
endurance fitness, or working capacity, the ability to do prolonged work without
undue fatigue. It assumes the absence of any ailment, and it has little to do with pure
muscular strength or agility. It has very much to do with the body's *overall* health, the
health of the heart, the lungs, the entire cardiovascular system and the other organs, *as
well as* the muscles.

➤ **FOR WRITING OR DISCUSSION**

1. What are the names given by the author to each kind of physical fitness?
2. The thesis is *not* "There are three kinds of physical fitness." What is the thesis?
3. Where is the thesis expressed directly?
4. Why does the "story," rather than the actual classifications, occupy so large a
   portion of this essay?
5. Write a paper that classifies people to decide which class is best for a particular purpose or occasion: bosses, teachers, parents, athletes, potential spouses,
   and so on.

SCOTT RUSSELL SANDERS

The Men We Carry in Our Minds

"This must be a hard time for women," I say to my friend Anneke. "They have so   1
many paths to choose from, and so many voices calling them."

"I think it's a lot harder for men," she replies.   2

"How do you figure that?"   3

---

[1]Cooper had worked out a point system to evaluate physical fitness.

4   "The women I know feel excited, innocent, like crusaders in a just cause. The men I know are eaten up with guilt."

5   We are sitting at the kitchen table drinking sassafras tea, our hands wrapped around the mugs because this April morning is cool and drizzly. "Like a Dutch morning," Anneke told me earlier. She is Dutch herself, a writer and midwife and peacemaker, with the round face and sad eyes of a woman in a Vermeer painting who might be waiting for the rain to stop, for a door to open. She leans over to sniff a sprig of lilac, pale lavender, that rises from a vase of cobalt blue.

6   "Women feel such pressure to be everything, do everything," I say. "Career, kids, art, politics. Have their babies and get back to the office a week later. It's as if they're trying to overcome a million years' worth of evolution in one lifetime."

7   "But we help one another. We don't try to lumber on alone, like so many wounded grizzly bears, the way men do." Anneke sips her tea. I gave her the mug with the owls on it, for wisdom. "And we have this deep-down sense that we're in the right—we've been held back, passed over, used—while men feel they're in the wrong. Men are the ones who've been discredited, who have to search their souls."

8   I search my soul. I discover guilty feelings aplenty—toward the poor, the Vietnamese, Native Americans, the whales, an endless list of debts—a guilt in each case that is as bright and unambiguous as a neon sign. But toward women I feel something more confused, a snarl of shame, envy, wary tenderness, and amazement. This muddle troubles me. To hide my unease I say, "You're right, it's tough being a man these days."

9   "Don't laugh." Anneke frowns at me, mournful-eyed, through the sassafras steam. "I wouldn't be a man for anything. It's much easier being the victim. All the victim has to do is break free. The persecutor has to live with his past."

10   How deep is that past? I find myself wondering after Anneke has left. How much of an inheritance do I have to throw off? Is it just the beliefs I breathed in as a child? Do I have to scour memory back through father and grandfather? Through St. Paul? Beyond Stonehenge and into the twilit caves? I'm convinced the past we must contend with is deeper even than speech. When I think back on my childhood, on how I learned to see men and women, I have a sense of ancient, dizzying depths. The back roads of Tennessee and Ohio where I grew up were probably closer, in their sexual patterns, to the campsites of Stone Age hunters than to the genderless cities of the future into which we are rushing.

11   The first men, besides my father, I remember seeing were black convicts and white guards, in the cottonfield across the road from our farm on the outskirts of Memphis. I must have been three or four. The prisoners wore dingy gray-and-black zebra suits, heavy as canvas, sodden with sweat. Hatless, stooped, they chopped weeds in the fierce heat, row after row, breathing the acrid dust of boll-weevil poison. The overseers wore dazzling white shirts and broad shadowy hats. The oiled barrels of their shotguns flashed in the sunlight. Their faces in memory are utterly blank. Of course those men, white and black, have become for me an emblem of racial hatred. But they have also come to stand for the twin poles of my early vision of manhood—the brute toiling animal and the boss.

12   When I was a boy, the men I knew labored with their bodies. They were marginal farmers, just scraping by, or welders, steelworkers, carpenters; they swept floors, dug ditches, mined coal, or drove trucks, their forearms ropy with muscle; they trained horses, stoked furnaces, built tires, stood on assembly lines wrestling parts onto cars

and refrigerators. They got up before light, worked all day long whatever the weather, and when they came home at night they looked as though somebody had been whipping them. In the evenings and on weekends they worked on their own places, tilling gardens that were lumpy with clay, fixing broken-down cars, hammering on houses that were always too drafty, too leaky, too small.

The bodies of the men I knew were twisted and maimed in ways visible and invisible. 13 The nails of their hands were black and split, the hands tattooed with scars. Some had lost fingers. Heavy lifting had given many of them finicky backs and guts weak from hernias. Racing against conveyor belts had given them ulcers. Their ankles and knees ached from years of standing on concrete. Anyone who had worked for long around machines was hard of hearing. They squinted, and the skin of their faces was creased like the leather of old work gloves. There were times, studying them, when I dreaded growing up. Most of them coughed, from dust or cigarettes, and most of them drank cheap wine or whiskey, so their eyes looked bloodshot and bruised. The fathers of my friends always seemed older than the mothers. Men wore out sooner. Only women lived into old age.

As a boy I also knew another sort of men, who did not sweat and break down like 14 mules. They were soldiers, and so far as I could tell they scarcely worked at all. During my early school years we lived on a military base, an arsenal in Ohio, and every day I saw GIs in the guardshacks, on the stoops of barracks, at the wheels of olive drab Chevrolets. The chief fact of their lives was boredom. Long after I left the Arsenal I came to recognize the sour smell the soldiers gave off as that of souls in limbo. They were all waiting—for wars, for transfers, for leaves, for promotions, for the end of their hitch—like so many braves waiting for the hunt to begin. Unlike the warriors of older tribes, however, they would have no say about when the battle would start or how it would be waged. Their waiting was broken only when they practiced for war. They fired guns at targets, drove tanks across the churned-up fields of the military reservation, set off bombs in the wrecks of old fighter planes. I knew this was all play. But I also felt certain that when the hour for killing arrived, they would kill. When the real shooting started, many of them would die. This was what soldiers were *for*, just as a hammer was for driving nails.

Warriors and toilers: those seemed, in my boyhood vision, to be the chief destinies 15 for men. They weren't the only destinies, as I learned from having a few male teachers, from reading books, and from watching television. But the men on television—the politicians, the astronauts, the generals, the savvy lawyers, the philosophical doctors, the bosses who gave orders to both soldiers and laborers—seemed as remote and unreal to me as the figures in tapestries. I could no more imagine growing up to become one of these cool, potent creatures than I could imagine becoming a prince.

A nearer and more hopeful example was that of my father, who had escaped from a 16 red-dirt farm to a tire factory, and from the assembly line to the front office. Eventually he dressed in a white shirt and tie. He carried himself as if he had been born to work with his mind. But his body, remembering the earlier years of slogging work, began to give out on him in his fifties, and it quit on him entirely before he turned sixty-five. Even such a partial escape from man's fate as he had accomplished did not seem possible for most of the boys I knew. They joined the army, stood in line for jobs in the smoky plants, helped build highways. They were bound to work as their fathers had worked, killing themselves or preparing to kill others.

17   A scholarship enabled me not only to attend college, a rare enough feat in my circle, but even to study in a university meant for the children of the rich. Here I met for the first time young men who had assumed from birth that they would lead lives of comfort and power. And for the first time I met women who told me that men were guilty of having kept all the joys and privileges of the earth for themselves. I was baffled. What privileges? What joys? I thought about the maimed, dismal lives of most of the men back home. What had they stolen from their wives and daughters? The right to go five days a week, twelve months a year, for thirty or forty years to a steel mill or a coal mine? The right to drop bombs and die in war? The right to feel every leak in the roof, every gap in the fence, every cough in the engine, as a wound they must mend? The right to feel, when the lay-off comes or the plant shuts down, not only afraid but ashamed?

18   I was slow to understand the deep grievances of women. This was because, as a boy, I had envied them. Before college, the only people I had ever known who were interested in art or music or literature, the only ones who read books, the only ones who ever seemed to enjoy a sense of ease and grace were the mothers and daughters. Like the menfolk, they fretted about money, they scrimped and made-do. But, when the pay stopped coming in, they were not the ones who had failed. Nor did they have to go to war, and that seemed to me a blessed fact. By comparison with the narrow, ironclad days of fathers, there was an expansiveness, I thought, in the days of mothers. They went to see neighbors, to shop in town, to run errands at school, at the library, at church. No doubt, had I looked harder at their lives, I would have envied them less. It was not my fate to become a woman, so it was easier for me to see the graces. Few of them held jobs outside the home, and those who did filled thankless roles as clerks and waitresses. I didn't see, then, what a prison a house could be, since houses seemed to me brighter, handsomer places than any factory. I did not realize—because such things were never spoken of—how often women suffered from men's bullying. I did learn about the wretchedness of abandoned wives, single mothers, widows; but I also learned about the wretchedness of lone men. Even then I could see how exhausting it was for a mother to cater all day to the needs of young children. But if I had been asked, as a boy, to choose between tending a baby and tending a machine, I think I would have chosen the baby. (Having now tended both, I know I would choose the baby.)

19   So I was baffled when the women at college accused me and my sex of having cornered the world's pleasures. I think something like my bafflement has been felt by other boys (and by girls as well) who grew up in dirt-poor farm country, in mining country, in black ghettos, in Hispanic barrios, in the shadows of factories, in Third World nations— any place where the fate of men is as grim and bleak as the fate of women. Toilers and warriors. I realize now how ancient these identities are, how deep the tug they exert on men, the undertow of a thousand generations. The miseries I saw, as a boy, in the lives of nearly all men I continue to see in the lives of many—the body-breaking toil, the tedium, the call to be tough, the humiliating powerlessness, the battle for a living and for territory.

20   When the women I met at college thought about the joys and privileges of men, they did not carry in their minds the sort of men I had known in my childhood. They thought of their fathers, who were bankers, physicians, architects, stockbrokers, the big wheels of the big cities. These fathers rode the train to work or drove cars that cost

more than any of my childhood houses. They were attended from morning to night by female helpers, wives, and nurses and secretaries. They were never laid off, never short of cash at month's end, never lined up for welfare. These fathers made decisions that mattered. They ran the world.

The daughters of such men wanted to share in this power, this glory. So did I. They 21 yearned for a say over their future, for jobs worthy of their abilities, for the right to live at peace, unmolested, whole. Yes, I thought, yes yes. The difference between me and these daughters was that they saw me, because of my sex, as destined from birth to be like their fathers, and therefore as an enemy to their desires. But I knew better. I wasn't an enemy, in fact or in feeling. I was an ally. If I had known, then, how to tell them so, would they have believed me? Would they now?

➤ **FOR WRITING OR DISCUSSION**

1. What is the impact of opening this essay with dialog?
2. What categories of men does the writer say he carries in his mind? Which details does he provide to show you these groups clearly?
3. What elements of comparison and contrast do you find in this essay? In what way does the last paragraph challenge the assumptions that emerge from the dialog between the writer and his friend Anneke?
4. Why does Sanders end the essay with two questions? How do you feel about this conclusion to the piece? Answer the two questions Sanders raises.
5. Write a paper in which you classify the men, women, or children that you carry in your mind. Like Sanders, draw on personal experience for details. If your groups are rooted in what you have read or seen in the movies or television, be sure to provide specific examples for the reader.

JOHN HOLT

Three Kinds of Discipline

A child, in growing up, may meet and learn from three different kinds of disciplines. 1 The first and most important is what we might call the Discipline of Nature or of Reality. When he is trying to do something real, if he does the wrong thing or doesn't do the right one, he doesn't get the result he wants. If he doesn't pile one block right on top of another, or tries to build on a slanting surface, his tower falls down. If he hits the wrong key, he hears the wrong note. If he doesn't hit the nail squarely on the head, it bends, and he has to pull it out and start with another. If he doesn't measure properly what he is trying to build, it won't open, close, fit, stand up, fly, float, whistle, or do whatever he wants it to do. If he closes his eyes when he swings, he doesn't hit the ball. A child meets this kind of discipline every time he tries to *do* something, which is why it is so important in school to give children more chances to do things, instead of just reading or listening to someone talk (or pretending to). This discipline is a great teacher.

The learner never has to wait long for his answer; it usually comes quickly, often instantly. Also it is clear, and very often points toward the needed correction; from what happened he can not only see that what he did was wrong, but also why, and what he needs to do instead. Finally, and most important, the giver of the answer, call it Nature, is impersonal, impartial, and indifferent. She does not give opinions, or make judgments; she cannot be wheedled, bullied, or fooled; she does not get angry or disappointed; she does not praise or blame; she does not remember past failures or hold grudges; with her one always gets a fresh start, this time is the one that counts.

2   The next discipline we might call the Discipline of Culture, of Society, of What People Really Do. Man is a social, a cultural animal. Children sense around them this culture, this network of agreements, customs, habits, and rules binding the adults together. They want to understand it and be a part of it. They watch very carefully what people around them are doing and want to do the same. They want to do right, unless they become convinced they can't do right. Thus children rarely misbehave seriously in church, but sit as quietly as they can. The example of all those grownups is contagious. Some mysterious ritual is going on, and children, who like rituals, want to be part of it. In the same way, the little children that I see at concerts or operas, though they may fidget a little, or perhaps take a nap now and then, rarely make any disturbance. With all those grownups sitting there, neither moving nor talking, it is the most natural thing in the world to imitate them. Children who live among adults who are habitually courteous to each other, and to them, will soon learn to be courteous. Children who live surrounded by people who speak a certain way will speak that way, however much we may try to tell them that speaking that way is bad or wrong.

3   The third discipline is the one most people mean when they speak of discipline—the Discipline of Superior Force, of sergeant to private, of "You do what I tell you or I'll make you wish you had." There is bound to be some of this in a child's life. Living as we do surrounded by things that can hurt children, or that children can hurt, we cannot avoid it. We can't afford to let a small child find out from experience the danger of playing in a busy street, or of fooling with the pots on the top of a stove, or of eating up the pills in the medicine cabinet. So, along with other precautions, we say to him, "Don't play in the street, or touch things on the stove, or go into the medicine cabinet, or I'll punish you." Between him and the danger too great for him to imagine we put a lesser danger, but one he can imagine and maybe therefore wants to avoid. He can have no idea of what it would be like to be hit by a car, but he can imagine being shouted at, or spanked, or sent to his room. He avoids these substitutes for the greater danger until he can understand it and avoid it for its own sake. But we ought to use this discipline only when it is necessary to protect the life, health, safety, or well-being of people or other living creatures, or to prevent destruction of things that people care about. We ought not to assume too long, as we usually do, that a child cannot understand the real nature of the danger from which we want to protect him. The sooner he avoids the danger, not to escape our punishment, but as a matter of good sense, the better. He can learn that faster than we think. In Mexico, for example, where people drive their cars with a good deal of spirit, I saw many children no older than five or four walking unattached on the streets. They understood about cars, they knew what to do. A child whose life is full of the threat

and fear of punishment is locked into babyhood. There is no way for him to grow up, to learn to take responsibility for his life and acts. Most important of all, we should not assume that having to yield to the threat of our superior force is good for the child's character. It is never good for *anyone's* character. To bow to superior force makes us feel impotent and cowardly for not having had the strength or courage to resist. Worse, it makes us resentful and vengeful. We can hardly wait to make someone pay for our humiliation, yield to us as we were once made to yield. No, if we cannot always avoid using the Discipline of Superior Force, we should at least use it as seldom as we can.

There are places where all three disciplines overlap. Any very demanding human   4
activity combines in it the disciplines of Superior Force, of Culture, and of Nature. The novice will be told, "Do it this way, never mind asking why, just do it that way, that is the way we always do it." But it probably *is* just the way they always do it, and usually for the very good reason that it is a way that has been found to work. Think, for example, of ballet training. The student in a class is told to do this exercise, or that; to stand so; to do this or that with his head, arms, shoulders, abdomen, hips, legs, feet. He is constantly corrected. There is no argument. But behind these seemingly autocratic demands by the teacher lie many decades of custom and tradition, and behind that, the necessities of dancing itself. You cannot make the moves of classical ballet unless over many years you have acquired, and renewed every day, the needed strength and suppleness in scores of muscles and joints. Nor can you do the difficult motions, making them look easy, unless you have learned hundreds of easier ones first. Dance teachers may not always agree on all the details of teaching these strengths and skills. But no novice could learn them all by himself. You could not go for a night or two to watch the ballet and then, without any other knowledge at all, teach yourself how to do it. In the same way, you would be unlikely to learn any complicated and difficult human activity without drawing heavily on the experience of those who know it better. But the point is that the authority of these experts or teachers stems from, grows out of their greater competence and experience, the fact that what they do *works,* not the fact that they happen to be the teacher and as such have the power to kick a student out of the class. And the further point is that children are always and everywhere attracted to that competence, and ready and eager to submit themselves to a discipline that grows out of it. We hear constantly that children will never do anything unless compelled to by bribes or threats. But in their private lives, or in extracurricular activities in school, in sports, music, drama, art, running a newspaper, and so on, they often submit themselves willingly and wholeheartedly to very intense disciplines, simply because they want to learn to do a given thing well. Our Little-Napoleon football coaches, of whom we have too many and hear far too much, blind us to the fact that millions of children work hard every year getting better at sports and games without coaches barking and yelling at them.

➤ FOR WRITING OR DISCUSSION

1. What are the names of the three kinds of discipline?
2. Identify the topic sentence in each paragraph.

3. In what kinds of discipline are parents and teachers least active? Why?
4. What kind of discipline does the author like least? What are the reasons for his dislike? Is he completely opposed to it?
5. What is the purpose of the last paragraph?
6. Choose some kind of behavior as your subject and write a classification paper titled "Three Kinds of _____ ." Possible subjects could be nervousness, exercise, studying, arguing, driving, shopping, praying, and so on.

Readings for Writing

These selections will stimulate your thinking on division and classification. The first is an essay by Arthur Levine, the president of Teachers' College, Columbia University. The second is a well-known short story by Irwin Shaw.

ARTHUR LEVINE

The Campus Divided, and Divided Again

1   Nowhere do you hear the word "diversity" more than on college campuses. Yet ask for a definition and you will get a reply entombed in ideology and obfuscating rhetoric. At the same time, the students, the engine for action on diversity at most colleges, are making finer and finer distinctions among themselves. It is a generation that defines itself more by its differences than its similarities.

2   No type of organization is growing more quickly on campuses today than advocacy groups focused on particular student populations, according to a 1997 study of chief student affairs officers at a sample of 270 colleges and universities conducted by Jeanette Cureton, an independent researcher, and me. The larger and more selective the college, the greater the number of such groups. Each campus activity, said one administrator, "appeals to smaller pockets of students."

3   In a 1979 study, when I asked undergraduates to describe themselves, they focused on the commonalities their generation shared, like being materialistic or career oriented. By contrast, current students, when asked the same question, emphasized the things that made them unique. A Korean student said he never thought about the fact that he was Asian until he came to college. In his freshman year, he though being Asian was the most important aspect of his being. By his junior year, being Korean became his primary self-descriptor. On one campus I visited, a business club was divided into more than a dozen different groups—a women's business club, a Latino business club, a disabled-student business club, a gay-student business club and so on.

4   This voluntary segregation on campus, while real, is systematically overestimated by students, according to our research. We attended campus parties and then asked

white students how many black students had attended. They made comments like "black students don't attend our events." We asked them to guess the number who attended anyway. The guess was 10; the reality was closer to 50.

At an event sponsored by an Asian student association, we asked how many white students attended. Once again the guess was a handful and the reality was that about a third of the audience was Caucasian. What could explain the discrepancy? Either students do not socialize even when in close proximity or they are so used to segregation they do not even perceive cross-socializing when it occurs.

A related characteristic is a sense of victimization. Men and women, majorities and minorities, rich and poor all think that someone else on campus is getting something they are not, and that they are forced to pay the cost. Our surveys showed a majority of four-year colleges (54 percent) reporting that during the late 1980's and early to mid-1990's students felt more and more victimized, a trend that has only intensified.

Today diversity is the largest cause of student unrest on campus, accounting for 39 percent of student protests, according to our study. Discourse is dominated by two small, but vociferous groups—one yelling that diversity has eclipsed all other aspects of college life and the other shouting that colleges remain impervious to diversity. Meanwhile, the rest of the campus community tries to avoid the issue.

At best, our survey shows a balkanized campus, in which the zone of tolerance or indifference to offense grows increasingly small. At worst, our survey shows a more and more Hobbesian world, where each group battles against others for resources inside and outside the classroom.

In this environment, a climate of political correctness prevails. Diversity frightens university administrators. For several years in the early 90's, I directed a training program for senior administrators. Each summer I presented 100 or so presidents, vice presidents and deans a case study on student efforts to get a women's studies program adopted at a small liberal arts college. I divided the class into three groups—one played the student leader, another played a faculty opponent and the final group played the academic dean on whose desk the problem landed. Year after year, those playing the administrator, regardless of race, gender or age, would say the same thing: "I just want the issue to go away."

Interviews I have had with 14 college presidents in the intervening years produced much the same response. The reason is not that they are trying to shirk responsibility. The reason is that college presidents are hired to solve problems, not to create them. But diversity is a Pandora's box. Solving one problem inevitably leads to another.

If the Bosnian students want Bosnian food in the cafeteria, this can be done. If the Croatian students want a wing in a residence hall, theme dorms are certainly an option. If the Slovenian students want a Slovenian studies program, a committee can be created to study the subject.

The problem is this. At one campus, there was a Puerto Rican studies program. The Dominican students wanted a Dominican studies program. The president proposed a Caribbean studies program. It was flatly rejected by all quarters.

Nonetheless, colleges and universities are making real progress in diversifying their curriculums. In another study of 196 colleges, Jeanette Cureton and I learned that more

14   than a third of all colleges had a diversity requirement. At least a third offered course work in ethnic and gender studies. More than half of all institutions introduced diversity into their departmental offerings. A majority sought to increase the diversity of their faculty.

15   But sheer quantity of activity hides the character of the changes, which are by accretion rather than by design. The result is a grab bag of diversity initiatives in which the whole may be less than the parts.

16   The issue cannot be handled problem by problem, Band-Aid by Band-Aid. if colleges don't set specific and reasonable goals, the poisoned atmosphere will continue to degrade higher education, harming the interests of everyone. Colleges must confront the diversity issue with candor, and not hide behind programs that placate groups but divide the campus.

➤ FOR WRITING OR DISCUSSION

1. What is Levine's thesis in this essay?
2. What kinds of details does the writer provide to support his thesis? Which details are most convincing to you?
3. What differences does Levine note between undergraduates in 1979 and undergraduates today? Why might you agree or disagree with his views of today's students? How do students today perceive the "voluntary segregation" on campus, according to the writer?
4. What, according to Levine, is the largest cause for campus unrest today?
5. In developing his essay, how does Levine use classification strategies? What role does the naming of various groups play in advancing his thesis?
6. Write an essay in which you classify various groups of students on your campus. Decide first on your purpose for classifying them—perhaps to categorize ethnic, social, or economic groups; to group students by the way they study, read, or eat; or to establish categories for the way they participate in class, serve the school in extracurricular ways, or attempt to get dates. These are only suggestions, of course. Once you decide on your reason for classification, write a thesis and develop your paper by identifying the qualities of each group you've established.

HAVING YOUR SAY

Write an argumentative essay in which you explain what you think is the major cause for unrest on campuses today.

IRWIN SHAW

The Girls in Their Summer Dresses

Fifth Avenue was shining in the sun when they left the Brevoort. The sun was warm, even though it was February, and everything looked like Sunday morning—the buses and the well-dressed people walking slowly in couples and the quiet buildings with the windows closed.

Michael held Frances' arm tightly as they walked toward Washington Square in the sunlight. They walked lightly, almost smiling, because they had slept late and had a good breakfast and it was Sunday. Michael unbuttoned his coat and let it flap around him in the mild wind.

"Look out," Frances said as they crossed Eighth Street. "You'll break your neck." Michael laughed and Frances laughed with him.

"She's not so pretty," Frances said. "Anyway, not pretty enough to take a chance of breaking your neck."

Michael laughed again. "How did you know I was looking at her?"

Frances cocked her head to one side and smiled at her husband under the brim of her hat. "Mike, darling," she said.

"O.K." he said. "Excuse me."

Frances patted his arm lightly and pulled him along a little faster toward Washington Square. "Let's not see anybody all day," she said. "Let's just hang around with each other. You and me. We're always up to our neck in people, drinking their Scotch or drinking our Scotch; we only see each other in bed. I want to go out with my husband all day long. I want him to talk only to me and listen only to me."

"What's to stop us?" Michael asked.

"The Stevensons. They want us to drop by around one o'clock and they'll drive us into the country."

"The cunning Stevensons," Mike said. "Transparent. They can whistle. They can go driving in the country by themselves."

"Is it a date?"

"It's a date."

Frances leaned over and kissed him on the tip of the ear.

"Darling," Michael said, "this is Fifth Avenue."

"Let me arrange a program," Frances said. "A planned Sunday in New York for a young couple with money to throw away."

"Go easy."

"First let's go to the Metropolitan Museum of Art," Frances suggested, because Michael had said during the week he wanted to go. "I haven't been there in three years and there're at least ten pictures I want to see again. Then we can take the bus down to Radio City and watch them skate. And later we'll go down to Cavanaugh's and get a steak as big as a blacksmith's apron, with a bottle of wine, and after that there's a French picture at the Filmarte that everybody says—say, are you listening to me?"

19   "Sure," he said. He took his eyes off the hatless girl with the dark hair, cut dancer-style like a helmet, who was walking past him.

20   "That's the program for the day," Frances said flatly. "Or maybe you'd just rather walk up and down Fifth Avenue."

21   "No," Michael said. "Not at all."

22   "You always look at other women," Frances said. "Everywhere. Every damned place we go."

23   "No, darling," Michael said, "I look at everything. God gave me eyes and I look at women and men in subway excavations and moving pictures and the little flowers of the field. I casually inspect the universe."

24   "You ought to see the look in your eye," Frances said, "as you casually inspect the universe on Fifth Avenue."

25   "I'm a happily married man." Michael pressed her elbow tenderly. "Example for the whole twentieth century—Mr. and Mrs. Mike Loomis. Hey, let's have a drink," he said, stopping.

26   "We just had breakfast."

27   "Now listen, darling," Mike said, choosing his words with care, "it's a nice day and we both felt good and there's no reason why we have to break it up. Let's have a nice Sunday."

28   "All right. I don't know why I started this. Let's drop it. Let's have a good time."

29   They joined hands consciously and walked without talking among the baby carriages and the old Italian men in their Sunday clothes and the young women with Scotties in Washington Square Park.

30   "At least once a year everyone should go to the Metropolitan Museum of Art," Frances said after a while, her tone a good imitation of the tone she had used at breakfast and at the beginning of their walk. "And it's nice on Sunday. There're a lot of people looking at the pictures and you get the feeling maybe art isn't on the decline in New York City, after all—"

31   "I want to tell you something," Michael said very seriously. "I have not touched another woman. Not once. In all the five years."

32   "All right," Frances said.

33   "You believe that, don't you?"

34   "All right."

35   They walked between the crowded benches, under the scrubby city-park trees.

36   "I try not to notice it," Frances said, "but I feel rotten inside, in my stomach, when we pass a woman and you look at her and I see that look in your eye and that's the way you looked at me the first time. In Alice Maxwell's house. Standing there in the living room, next to the radio, with a green hat on and all those people."

37   "I remember the hat," Michael said.

38   "The same look," Frances said. "And it makes me feel bad. It makes me feel terrible."

39   "Sh-h-h, please, darling, sh-h-h."

40   "I think I would like a drink now," Frances said.

41   They walked over to a bar on Eighth Street, not saying anything, Mike automatically helping her over curbstones and guiding her past automobiles. They sat near a

window in the bar and the sun streamed in and there was a small, cheerful fire in the fireplace. A little Japanese waiter came over and put down some pretzels and smiled happily at them.

"What do you order after breakfast?" Michael asked. 42

"Brandy, I suppose," Frances said. 43

"Courvoisier," Michael told the waiter. "Two Courvoisiers." 44

The waiter came with the glasses and they sat drinking the brandy in the sunlight. Michael finished his and drank a little water. 45

"I look at women," he said. "Correct. I don't say it's wrong or right. I look at them. If I pass them on the street and I don't look at them, I'm fooling you, I'm fooling myself." 46

"You look at them as though you want them," Frances said, playing with her brandy glass. "Every one of them." 47

"In a way," Michael said, speaking softly and not to his wife, "in a way, that's true. I don't do anything about it, but it's true." 48

"I know it. That's why I feel bad." 49

"Another brandy," Michael called. "Waiter, two more brandies." 50

He sighed and closed his eyes and rubbed them gently with his fingertips. "I love the way women look. One of the things I like best about New York is the battalions of women. When I first came to New York from Ohio that was the first thing I noticed, the million wonderful women, all over the city. I walked around with my heart in my throat." 51

"A kid," Frances said. "That's a kid's feeling." 52

"Guess again," Michael said. "Guess again. I'm older now. I'm a man getting near middle age, putting on a little fat, and I still love to walk along Fifth Avenue at three o'clock on the east side of the street between Fiftieth and Fifty-seventh Streets. They're all out then, shopping, in their furs and their crazy hats, everything all concentrated from all over the world into seven blocks—the best furs, the best clothes, the handsomest women, out to spend money and feeling good about it." 53

The Japanese waiter put the two drinks down, smiling with great happiness. 54

"Everything is all right?" he asked. 55

"Everything is wonderful," Michael said. 56

"If it's just a couple of fur coats," Frances said, "and forty-five dollar hats—" 57

"It's not the fur coats. Or the hats. That's just the scenery for that particular kind of women. Understand," he said, "you don't have to listen to this." 58

"I want to listen." 59

"I like the girls in the offices. Neat, with their eyeglasses, smart, chipper, knowing what everything is about. I like the girls on Forty-fourth Street at lunchtime, the actresses, all dressed up on nothing a week. I like the salesgirls in the stores, paying attention to you first because you're a man, leaving lady customers waiting. I got all this stuff accumulated in me because I've been thinking about it for ten years and now you've asked for it and here it is." 60

"Go ahead," Frances said. 61

"When I think of New York City, I think of all the girls on parade in the city. I don't know whether it's something special with me or whether every man in the city walks 62 around with the same feeling inside him, but I feel as though I'm at a picnic in this city. I like to sit near the women in the theaters, the famous beauties who've taken six hours to get ready and look it. And the young girls at the football games, with the red cheeks, and when the warm weather comes, the girls in their summer dresses." He finished his drink. "That's the story."

63   Frances finished her drink and swallowed two or three times extra. "You say you love me?"

64   "I love you."

65   "I'm pretty, too," Frances said. "As pretty as any of them."

66   "You're beautiful," Michael said.

67   "I'm good for you," Frances said, pleading. "I've made you a good wife, a good housekeeper, a good friend. I'd do any damn thing for you."

68   "I know," Michael said. He put his hand out and grasped hers.

69   "You'd like to be free to—" Frances said.

70   "Sh-h-h."

71   "Tell the truth." She took her hand away from under his.

72   Michael flicked the edge of his glass with his finger. "O.K.," he said gently. "Sometimes I feel I would like to be free."

73   "Well," Frances said, "any time you say."

74   "Don't be foolish." Michael swung his chair around to her side of the table and patted her thigh.

75   She began to cry silently into her handkerchief, bent over just enough so that nobody else in the bar would notice. "Someday," she said, crying, "you're going to make a move."

76   Michael didn't say anything. He sat watching the bartender slowly peel a lemon.

77   "Aren't you?" Frances asked harshly. "Come on, tell me. Talk. Aren't you?"

78   "Maybe," Michael said. He moved his chair back again. "How the hell do I know?"

79   "You know," Frances persisted. "Don't you know?"

80   "Yes," Michael said after a while, "I know."

81   Frances stopped crying then. Two or three snuffles into the handkerchief and she put it away and her face didn't tell anything to anybody. "At least do me one favor," she said.

82   "Sure."

83   "Stop talking about how pretty this woman is or that one. Nice eyes, nice breasts, a pretty figure, good voice." She mimicked his voice, "Keep it to yourself. I'm not interested."

84   Michael waved to the waiter. "I'll keep it to myself," he said.

85   Frances flicked the corners of her eyes. "Another brandy," she told the waiter.

86   "Two," Michael said.

87   "Yes, ma'am, yes, sir," said the waiter, backing away.

88   Frances regarded Michael coolly across the table. "Do you want me to call the Stevensons?" she asked. "It'll be nice in the country."

89   "Sure," Michael said. "Call them."

90   She got up from the table and walked across the room toward the telephone. Michael watched her walk, thinking what a pretty girl, what nice legs.

➤ FOR WRITING OR DISCUSSION

1. How does Michael classify women? What method or system underlies his classification?

2. In your opinion, to what extent is the conflict in the story not just between two individuals but between male and female temperaments or between different types of social conditioning?

3. Do you think Michael loves Frances? Why, or why not? Explain what Shaw means to convey in the last sentence of the story (paragraph 90).

4. Shaw's use of dialog is exceptionally convincing. Is Michael's long speech about the women of New York (paragraphs 60–62) an exception to this statement?

5. Does Shaw want us to take the side of either Michael or Frances? Are we meant to sympathize more with one than the other? Explain.

6. What decision shows that Michael and Frances have given up their illusions about having a near-perfect marriage?

7. Some readers of the story may feel that Michael and Frances have marital problems that cannot be solved, whereas others may feel their marriage is still salvageable. What is your view on the matter? Explain your position.

8. Consider the members of the opposite sex as you have observed them and shared experiences. If you're a man, how would you classify women? If you're a woman, how would you classify men? Determine a basis for grouping the opposite sex and write a classifiction essay identifying and explaining each category you establish.

WRITING TOPICS

The following list of subjects may offer you some ideas for a topic for your classification paper. Notice how some subjects can easily be limited further than they are: "Summer jobs" could be limited to summer jobs at resorts, "outstanding teachers" to outstanding physical education teachers, and so on.

1. Computer users
2. Attitudes toward Christmas
3. Campus parties
4. Outstanding teachers
5. Summer jobs
6. Major classes of love
7. Automobiles
8. Male chauvinists
9. Female chauvinists
10. Clothing
11. People at a sporting event
12. Adventure films
13. Spoiled children
14. Concert goers
15. Poor drivers
16. Garden flowers
17. Family outings
18. Shoppers
19. The contents of my pocketbook (or bookbag or briefcase)
20. Weddings

CROSSCURRENTS

1. Rodriguez's "Complexion" (page 43) and Soto's "Looking for Work" (page 186) deal with the family values issue in distinctly different ways. How do family values affect the lives of the two writers? Which set of values is more conventional? eccentric? closer to your own or those of your friends and family?

2. Collier in "The Chaser" (page 124) and Shaw's "The Girls in Their Summer Dresses" (page 287) deal with unusual features of courtship. In what ways do the selections treat the subject of men and women building relationships? What similarities of theme and attitude do you note in these stories?

COLLABORATIVE LEARNING

Read or reread the essays included in this chapter under "Models of Writing"—"Shaking Hands," "How Fit Are You?" "The Men We Carry in Our Minds," and "Three Kinds of Discipline." Which of the essays does your group think best embodies the principles of good classification papers? What elements do you point to as contributing to the success of the essays? In what ways do the best of the essays reflect the points on pages 270–271?

REVIEW CHECKLIST: WRITING AND REVISING YOUR CLASSIFICATION OR DIVISION PAPER

- Have I used the prewriting process, as necessary, to explore ideas for a subject?
- Have I thought carefully about my purpose?
- Have I written for the usual general audience? If I am writing for a special audience, have I made that clear to the reader?
- Have I limited my subject?
- Have I established a clear thesis?
- Do I have enough support for my thesis?
- Have I determined a basis for classification and applied it consistently?
- Have I defined any unfamiliar terms?
- Have I decided whether I need to give examples for each class?
- Have I established a logical and effective order in which to present the classes?
- Have I proofread for grammar, spelling, and mechanics?

─────── FROM IMAGE TO WORDS: A PHOTO WRITING ASSIGNMENT ───────

Return to the From Image to Words exercise on page 269. Using one of the organizing schemes that you identified there (or some other that you may think of), write a brief paper in which you classify the objects in the photograph on page 269. Be sure that you develop a thesis: make some assertion about the objects that you will classify and provide details from the picture to support your point. Of course, you may expand on any details that the photograph suggests—colors, for example, or smells that are relevant to your classification scheme.

Cause and Effect

Many of the papers you write in college will require analysis of causes or circumstances that lead to a given result: Why does the cost of living continue to rise? Why do people with symptoms of cancer or heart disease put off consulting a doctor? Why is the sky blue? In questions of this type, the **effect** or result is given, at least briefly. Your job is to analyze the causes that produce the effect.

Other assignments will require that you discuss the results of a particular case: What are the positive and negative effects of legalizing lotteries? Discuss the effects of giving direct legislative power to the people. What is the effect of noise pollution on our bodies? In questions of this type, the **cause** is given, and you must determine the effects that might result or have resulted from the cause.

Cause-and-effect papers do not call for the rigid structure demanded of classification and process papers. Nevertheless, some logical demands must be met.

Writing Your Cause-and-Effect Paper

■ *Do not confuse cause with process.* A process paper tells *how* an event or product came about; a cause-and-effect paper tells *why* something happened.
■ *Avoid the* post hoc *fallacy.* That a man lost his billfold shortly after walking under a ladder does not mean that walking under the ladder caused his loss.

Similarly, that a woman lost her hearing shortly after attending a loud rock concert does not prove that her deafness is a direct result of the band's decibel level. (See the discussion of *post hoc* fallacies in Chapter 14 on page 359.)

■ *Do not oversimplify causes.* Getting a good night's sleep before an exam doesn't cause a student to receive the highest grade in the class. The rest certainly won't do any harm, but familiarity with the material covered on the exam, intelligence, and an ability to write also have something to do with the grade. Almost all effects worth writing about have more than one cause.

■ *Do not oversimplify effects.* Even though it may be true that many people lose money by gambling on lotteries, that does not mean legalizing lotteries will result in nationwide bankruptcy.

■ *Follow an established pattern of organization.* Once you have determined the causes or effects you wish to discuss, you can organize your paper in several ways. In a paper devoted primarily to cause, the simplest way to open is to describe the effect in the introduction, then to develop the reasons for that effect in the body of the paper. If, for example, you want to explain a recent rise in the cost of living, you might begin with a description of the rise (effect)—the cost of living has risen dramatically during the past three years and promises to go even higher in the coming year—before dealing with the causes. Similarly, a paper devoted primarily to effect usually begins with a description of the cause. If your subject is the probable effects of a proposed tax increase, you might begin with a description of the proposal itself (cause) before discussing effects.

In some cases, as when cause and effect are of approximately equal concern, you may want to present one dramatic instance of an effect to open the paper. For example, you might begin a paper on ocean pollution with a description of the infamous 1989 oil spill in Alaska, a striking example of oil pollution. The rest of the introduction would lead into the causes, or sources, of ocean pollution in general. The first major division of what follows might list several important causes other than oil spillage, and the second major division might detail the effects of those causes: extermination of sea life, danger to public health, and so on.

Student Writing: Cause and Effect

Now let's take a look at two student papers and see how the authors manage cause-and-effect relation. Annotations on the first paper point to key features of this cause-and-effect essay.

Richard S. Smith

Cause for Failure

I was never a good student and never thought twice   1

about it until I had to face the reality of putting

Introductory
paragraph
presents
thesis.
together a life for myself. When I try now to understand my years of failure in school, I can come up with some answers, now that I'm finally in college and serious about my work. External factors as well as some bad personal decisions all contributed to my problems.

Transition
opens second
paragraph as
writer states
the first cause.
In the first place, things were not easy at home. I'm not trying to lay the blame of my past failures on my home life--I hate people who are constantly making excuses for themselves because other people created trouble for them. Nevertheless, I know that family tensions didn't help my school record. For much of my childhood five of us lived in a small, dark apartment on Sutter Avenue. My father died when I was five, and my mother's energy after a day of packing chemicals at a local factory was too low for her to keep after me. After dinner, her eyelids drooping with exhaustion, she would stretch out on an old brown sofa before the television, and my sisters and I would sit beside her. We never heard a word about doing homework or opening our books. At report card time she was always furious with our failures, but I think she knew that she just had no strength to push us forward. She couldn't even find the strength to push herself.

2

Cause
developed with
images and
explanation

Next cause
introduced.
Word "either"
serves as
transition
that lends
coherence
to paper.
My friends were no help either. They certainly were not the studying kind. On spring afternoons we would cut high school classes regularly, smoking and rapping in my friend Jerry's old Ford or dribbling lay-ups at the basketball courts in Hillcrest Park. I read a survey by the U.S. Department of Education that showed that fewer than two-thirds of my generation's high school students ever

3

Cause
developed
with details

graduated, but in my group of eight students not one of us received a diploma. And we couldn't have cared less!

Another cause
identified:
"most
important
reason"
establishes
principle of
arrangement
in essay.

Perhaps the most important reason for my failures, though, was that I never saw (or maybe it's more accurate to say that I never allowed myself to see) a connection between what we did at our scratched wooden desks and what was waiting for us beyond our high school days. I don't think that I ever believed Mrs. Allen's pages of algebra homework or Mr. Delaney's boring lectures on the Civil War had any real meaning for me. What did this have to do with my life? I had no concept then of what an educated person was supposed to know or understand. Everything to me had to have an immediate payoff. What good would knowing an equation or the Emancipation Proclamation do for me?

4

And then I tried to find a job. I worked for a few years as a stockboy without getting anywhere. Lugging up cartons of Coke and boxes of toilet tissue from the basement of Foodtown was not my idea of a future. I tried finding other jobs without success. In my case, I suppose it was both the lack of a diploma and the lack of an education that held me back. I started studying for the high school equivalency exam and passed it on the first try.

5

Writer
identifies
effects of his
failure in
school as he
builds toward
conclusion.

As a business major now at my community college, I know that there are no guarantees about my life from now on, but at least a college degree may open doors that people slammed in my face before. And I'm trying to see myself as getting educated. Maybe those courses in social science and literature will shape my thinking and help me later on.

6

➤ FOR WRITING OR DISCUSSION

1. What is the thesis of Smith's paper?
2. What pattern of organization does the writer use in this essay?
3. Are the causes the writer gives reasonable explanations for his school failures? Defend your response.
4. What images does the writer provide to help you envision the scene?
5. Think of your own pattern of successes and failures at school and write a paper that analyzes its causes.

Phil Rosetti

Getting Organized

1   I come from a family of date-book addicts. My mother believes that unless each coming event has been written on the calendar it cannot possibly exist. My father has a huge desk calendar, a smaller pocket calendar, and an absurdly high-tech computerized diary and organizer. My sister, whose birthday is right around the New Year, never fails to be made blissful by the gift of a new date book. Me, I never write anything down.

2   Not writing things down wasn't a problem for me for years. When I was a kid, there wasn't really anything to remember. Sandbox, cartoons, dinner, bed. Nothing really complicated. Lately, however, I have begun to realize that the inevitable consequence of my hatred of lists is chaos.

3   The chaos began simply. I noticed that I was making about thirty separate trips out of my apartment each day to run errands. Sometimes, I made three trips to the same place in as many hours. I just couldn't remember all the things I needed.

4   Things rapidly became worse. An old high school friend probably hates me by now because I never call him anymore. You see, I never wrote down his number. Naturally, it's unlisted, so it is completely impossible for me to look him up. My girl-friend isn't speaking to me anymore, either. See, I forgot to

write down when her plane was arriving. She got to the airport, and I wasn't there. She waited, and I still wasn't there. She called, and I was out with the guys. I wanted to make it up to her, of course. So I went to the grocery store to get the ingredients for my famous and irresistible beef stroganoff. I didn't bring a list, and when I got to the store, I completely forgot to buy the essential sour cream. When I served my sweetie peanut butter and jelly sandwiches, she was not impressed.

My social life is a shambles, and my academic life is   5
no better. I recently missed the first meeting of a very important class because I could have sworn it was at 1:30. I didn't write it down, but I could have sworn. . . Well, the class met at 10:30. The professor was not happy. A little later that term, I somehow managed to volunteer to deliver two oral presentations in two different classes on the same day that I had a major paper due in a third class. None of the professors were happy.

Now, I am not an idiot. I understand the principle of   6
learning from experience. I realize that not writing anything down has caused me nothing but chaos and disaster. So I bit the bullet and bought a date book yesterday. Tomorrow I might even write something in it.

➤ FOR WRITING OR DISCUSSION

1. What does the body of this student essay deal with—causes or effects?
2. Into what two groups does the writer organize the many consequences of his lack of organization?
3. Discuss the use of the term *sweetie* in paragraph 4. Is it humorous? Natural? Condescending? Sexist?
4. Do you feel the writer himself believes he has solved his problem? Explain.
5. Write a cause or effect paper on one of your character failings. If you have no failings, you may write about a friend or relative.

You may also find that cause-and-effect analysis is a useful tool for writing about literature. You look at a character and say, "Why is he like that, exactly?" Then you examine the work to discover the causes for the character traits you have observed. Or you may trace the causes that lead to a crisis in a work of literature.

Writing about Literature

Following is a famous poem by Edwin Arlington Robinson, "Richard Cory." After you have read the poem, study the student paper that follows it.

EDWIN ARLINGTON ROBINSON

Richard Cory

1
Whenever Richard Cory went down town,
    We people on the pavement looked at him:
He was a gentleman from sole to crown,
    Clean favored, and imperially slim.

2
And he was always quietly arrayed,
    And he was always human when he talked;
But still he fluttered pulses when he said,
    "Good morning," and he glittered when he walked.

3
And he was rich—yes, richer than a king,
    And admirably schooled in every grace:
In fine, we thought that he was everything
    To make us wish that we were in his place.

4
So on we worked, and waited for the light,
    And went without the meat, and cursed the bread;
And Richard Cory, one calm summer night,
    Went home and put a bullet through his head.

Craig Anders

We and He

1
What caused Richard Cory to "put a bullet through his head"? It is impossible, upon reading the last line of "Richard Cory" by Edwin Arlington Robinson, to say that the poem concludes with a clever surprise ending and then dismiss

it from our minds. The poem does not end with the last line.
Imagine the suicide of a friend or relative. Assuming the
person did not suffer from a painful terminal illness, we
would be stunned with surprise and sadness for a while, but we
would soon begin to ask ourselves and each other the big
question: Why? We will probably never get any certain answers,
but with the knowledge of the suicide, we may think back to
what we imagined were minor events or comments or moods of
daily life and see some of them in a new light. We may, "in
fine," be able to make an intelligent guess about the causes
of the suicide. There are no certain answers about Richard
Cory's death, either, but if we take every word of the poem
seriously, we have a better basis for making an intelligent
guess than we usually find in the world around us.

We certainly will not get very far if we settle for the   2
most obvious explanation and say that Richard Cory killed
himself because money can't buy happiness. First, the poem
concentrates on more about Cory than money alone: his
slimness, his manners, his way of talking, his way of
dressing. Second, the poem makes it clear that poverty
can't buy happiness any more than wealth can. The "people on
the pavement" are extremely unhappy: They envy Cory, resent
having to work, wish vainly for better times, "curse" the
cheap things they have to make do with, and long for the
expensive things they must do without. "Richard Cory" is no
poem about the spiritual rewards of being poor.

At the same time, we need to recognize that with all   3
their unhappiness, the poor people <u>are</u> better off than Richard
Cory. Hating every minute of their lives--or thinking that
they do--they still get up each morning. The simplest, most

inescapable fact of the poem is that Cory killed himself and the people on the pavement went on living. What made their lives more worth living than his?

4   One possible answer is that the poor people's envy keeps them going. They have desires and they have hopes. They want to ride into town like Richard Cory instead of walking on the pavement. They want all that money can buy. It can't buy happiness, but the poor people don't know that yet. Until they find out, they have something to live for. Cory has all that life can offer. But isn't that just another way of saying that life can now no longer offer anything else to Cory? And if that is the case, what point is there to continuing one's life?

5   An even better answer is that what the poor people have that Cory does not have is each other. Cory is a man alone. At one point, the poem expresses amazement at Cory's even being human. When he is acknowledged to be human, he is seen as the most special, most isolated kind of human--a king. He is "richer than a king"; he is not merely slim but "imperially slim"; his head is not an everyday human head but a "crown." The people look up to Cory so much that he might as well inhabit another galaxy, and it's lonely being an alien. Cory comes to town and says, "Good morning," for example, perhaps hoping for a friendly conversation, a little human contact. But Cory does not get conversation. When he says, "Good morning," pulses flutter and hearts skip a bit. "Richard Cory talked to me today. Isn't that fantastic?"

6   The people on the pavement have each other. Cory has no one. The speaker in the poem is a "we," not an "I." We looked at him, we wished we were in his place, we "waited for the light, / And went without the meat, and cursed the bread." The speaker knows more deeply than any conscious thought that he

is part of a "we"--that his feelings, his aspirations, his
resentments are shared by others. It may not be a happy life
or even a good life, but it is a life that is shared, a life
of community and communion. Cory's money, manners, and position not only can't buy that but make it impossible for him to
buy, no matter how "human" he may truly be or want to be.

Richard Cory dies of loneliness. The people on the pavement find the strength to go on living because loneliness is
the only problem they do not have.

➤ FOR WRITING OR DISCUSSION

1. What causes does the writer give for Richard Cory's suicide? Do you have
   some other explanation?
2. Where is the thesis of the paper stated?
3. Does the introduction clearly call for an analysis of causes?
4. Does the author's use of quotations from the poem help prove the thesis?
5. Write a paper on the causes of the "people on the pavement's" envy of
   Richard Cory or on the probable effects of his suicide on them.

Models of Writing

The four readings that follow illustrate different cause-and-effect combinations.
Nathan Cobb's "The Whoomper Factor," and Betty Rollin's "The Best Years of
My Life" deal with effects. Mohan Sivanand deals mainly with causes. In "On
Splitting," Carll Tucker analyzes both causes and effects. As you read the selec-
tions, note the great diversity of subjects that lend themselves to the cause-
and-effect pattern.

NATHAN COBB

The Whoomper Factor

As this is being written, snow is falling in the streets of Boston in what weather fore-   1
casters like to call "record amounts." I would guess by looking out the window that
we are only a few hours from that magic moment of paralysis, as in *Storm Paralyzes
Hub.* Perhaps we are even due for an *Entire Region Engulfed* or a *Northeast Blanketed,*
but I will happily settle for mere local disablement. And the more the merrier.

2   Some people call them blizzards, others nor'easters. My own term is whoompers, and I freely admit looking forward to them as does a baseball fan to April. Usually I am disappointed, however, because tonight's storm warnings too often turn into tomorrow's light flurries.

3   Well, flurries be damned. I want the real thing, complete with Volkswagens turned into drifts along Commonwealth Avenue and the MBTA's third rail frozen like a hunk of raw meat. A storm does not even begin to qualify as a whoomper unless Logan Airport is shut down for a minimum of six hours.

4   The point is, whoompers teach us a lesson. Or rather several lessons. For one thing, here are all these city folk who pride themselves on their instinct for survival, and suddenly they cannot bear to venture into the streets because they are afraid of being swallowed up. Virtual prisoners in their own houses is what they are. In northern New England, the natives view nights such as this with casual indifference, but let a whoomper hit Boston and the locals are not only knee deep in snow but also in befuddlement and disarray.

5   The lesson? That there is something more powerful out there than the sacred metropolis. It is not unlike the message we can read into the debacle of the windows falling out of the John Hancock Tower; just when we think we've got the upper hand on the elements, we find out we are flies and someone else is holding the swatter. Whoompers keep us in our place.

6   They also slow us down, which is not a bad thing for urbania these days. Frankly, I'm of the opinion Logan should be closed periodically, snow or not, in tribute to the lurking suspicion that it may not be all that necessary for a man to travel at a speed of 600 miles per hour. In a little while I shall go forth into the streets and I know what I will find. People will actually be *walking,* and the avenues will be bereft of cars. It will be something like those marvelous photographs of Back Bay during the nineteenth century, wherein the lack of clutter and traffic makes it seem as if someone has selectively airbrushed the scene.

7   And, of course, there will be the sound of silence tonight. It will be almost deafening. I know city people who have trouble sleeping in the country because of the lack of noise, and I suspect this is what bothers many of them about whoompers. Icy sidewalks and even fewer parking spaces we can handle, but please, God, turn up the volume. City folks tend not to believe in anything they can't hear with their own ears.

8   It should also be noted that nights such as this are obviously quite pretty, hiding the city's wounds beneath a clean white dressing. But it is their effect on the way people suddenly treat each other that is most fascinating, coming as it does when city dwellers are depicted as people of the same general variety as those New Yorkers who stood by when Kitty Genovese was murdered back in 1964.

9   There's nothing like a good whoomper to get people thinking that everyone walking towards them on the sidewalk might not be a mugger, or that saying hello is not necessarily a sign of perversion. You would think that city people, more than any other, would have a strong sense of being in the same rough seas together, yet it is not until a quasi catastrophe hits that many of them stop being lone sharks.

10   But enough of this. There's a whoomper outside tonight, and it requires my presence.

➤ **FOR WRITING OR DISCUSSION**

1. Cobb identifies the first lesson—the result or effect—of blizzards as the sense of human littleness and the last effect as people's sense of friendliness and community. Among the other effects he discusses are silence and prettiness. Why does this order of discussion make sense?
2. Why does the author use the term *whoomper* rather than *snowstorm* or *blizzard* in the essay?
3. Write a paper discussing the effects of some element of nature on you, such as thunderstorms, heat waves, springtime, insects, or snakes.

CARLL TUCKER

On Splitting

One afternoon recently, two unrelated friends called to tell me that, well, their marriages hadn't made it. One was leaving his wife for another woman. The other was leaving her husband because "we thought it best."   1

As always after such increasingly common calls, I felt helpless and angry. What had happened to those solemn vows that one of the couples had stammered on a steamy August afternoon three years earlier? And what had happened to the joy my wife and I had sensed when we visited the other couple and their two children last year, the feeling they gave us that here, in this increasingly fractionated world, was a constructive union?   2

I did not feel anger at my friends personally: Given the era and their feelings, their decisions probably made sense. What angered me was the loss of years and energy. It was an anger similar to that I feel when I see abandoned foundations of building projects—piled bricks and girders and a gash in the ground left to depress the passerby.   3

When our grandparents married, nobody except scandalous eccentrics divorced. "As long as we both shall live" was no joke. Neither was the trepidation brides felt on the eves of their wedding days. After their vows, couples learned to live with each other—not necessarily because they loved each other, but because they were stuck, and it was better to be stuck comfortably than otherwise.   4

Most of the external pressures that helped to enforce our grandparents' vows have dissolved. Women can earn money and may enjoy sex, even bear children, without marrying. As divorce becomes more common, the shame attendant on it dissipates. Some divorcés even argue that divorce is beneficial, educational; that the second or third or fifth marriage is "the best." The only reasons left to marry are love, tax advantages, and, for those old-fashioned enough to care about such things, to silence parental kvetching.[1]   5

In some respects, this freedom can be seen as social progress. Modern couples can flee the corrosive bitterness that made Strindberg's marriages nightmares.[2] Dreiser's Clyde Griffiths might have abandoned his Roberta instead of drowning her.[3]

[1]Complaining.
[2]August Strindberg (1849–1912) was a Swedish dramatist.
[3]The reference is to Dreiser's 1925 novel, *An American Tragedy.*

7   In other respects, our rapidly rising divorce rate and the declining marriage rate (as more and more couples opt to forgo legalities and simply live together) represent a loss. One advantage of spending a lifetime with a person is seeing each other grow and change. For most of us, it is not possible to see history in the bathroom mirror—gray hairs, crow's feet, yes, but not a change of mind or temperament. Yet, living with another person, it is impossible not to notice how patterns and attitudes change and not to learn—about yourself and about time—from those perceptions.

8   Perhaps the most poignant victim of the twentieth century is our sense of continuity. People used to grow up with trees, watch them evolve from saplings to fruit bearers to gnarled and unproductive grandfathers. Now, unless one is a farmer or a forester, there is almost no point to planting trees because one is not likely to be there to enjoy their maturity. We change addresses and occupations and hobbies and lifestyles and spouses rapidly and readily, much as we change TV channels. In our grandparents' day one committed oneself to certain skills and disciplines and developed them. Carpenters spent lifetimes learning their craft; critics spent lifetimes learning literature. Today, the question often is not "What do you do?" but "What are you into?" Macrame one week, astrology the next, health food, philosophy, history, jogging, movies, EST—we flit from "commitment" to "commitment" like bees among flowers because it is easier to test something than to master it, easier to buy a new toy than to repair an old one.

9   I feel sorry for what my divorced friends have lost. No matter how earnestly the former spouses try to "keep in touch," no matter how generous the visiting privileges for the parent who does not win custody of the children, the continuity of their lives has been broken. The years they spent together have been cut off from the rest of their lives; they are an isolated memory, no more integral to their past than a snapshot. Intelligent people, they will compare their next marriages—if they have them—to their first. They may even, despite not having a long shared past, notice growth. What I pray, though, is that they do not delude themselves into believing, like so many Americans today, that happiness is only measurable moment to moment and, in their pursuit of momentary contentment, forsake the perspectives and consolation of history.

10   There is great joy in watching a tree grow.

➤ FOR WRITING OR DISCUSSION

1. What causes does Tucker give for the increase in divorce? Does the author clearly approve or disapprove of any of these causes?
2. According to Tucker, what are the most negative effects of divorce? Are there any possible good effects?
3. Explain how the author tries to link the rise in divorce rates to general trends in American lifestyles.
4. Explain what Tucker means in the last sentence of the essay.
5. Write a paper analyzing the effects of some major decision you've made in your life, such as marriage, divorce, or choice of school, job, or place of residence.

MOHAN SIVANAND

Why I Write Wrong

The day I discovered Grammar Check in my new word processor, I was delighted. Grammar Check (GC) is supposed to help you guard against making mistakes in English, including those that would make the best of writers blush.

Oops. I can already see a wiggly green line under *writers* in my previous sentence. That's Grammar Check at work. The green wiggly underline is the digital equivalent of a referee throwing a flag.

Let's see what's wrong. GC suggests that I change *writers* to *writer's*. As in *writer's block,* I suppose—and that's not much help, is it? Meanwhile, I spot a curvaceous red line under *wiggly* itself. This time it's GC's cousin Spell Check blowing the whistle. Suggested change: *wiggle.*

But back to the causes of writer's blush. Grammar Check is very precise. By pressing F7 on the keyboard and clicking on Options then Settings, you can instruct your machine to watch out for Commonly Confused Words, Clichés, Contractions, Jargon, Wordiness, Gender-Specific Words and much, much more.

Strange. Not a single wiggle line appeared in the previous sentence despite the wordiness and all those capitals. GC, however, is not happy with my beginning that paragraph with *But,* and recommends I change it to *Nevertheless.*

"If you're so smart," I say aloud to GC, "here's something you can't mess around with." I type in a well-known line from Shakespeare: "Friends, Romans, countrymen, lend me your ears; I come to bury Caesar, not to praise him."

Oh, dear! GC suggests I change *countrymen* to *fellow citizens*. Friends, Romans, fellow citizens? That is an unkind cut.

Maybe I've been unfair. Shakespeare, after all, was a poet. I try a line of prose: "Sorrow came—a gentle sorrow—but not at all in the shape of any disagreeable consciousness."

Problem again: wiggle line under *came.* "Verb confusion (no suggestions)," says GC's warning box. "You're the one who is confused," I type. "Jane Austen was the most clearheaded of writers, and she never needed no Grammar Check or Microsoft Word." (Know something? GC hasn't yet spotted my double negative. But cousin SC wants me to change *Austen* to *Austin.* Ah, man, that's smart!)

Wait a second. I see a new green wiggle line under *man.* "Gender-Specific Language," I'm warned. The alternatives suggested in place of *man* are *operate* or *staff.*

If grammar is a tricky thing, Grammar Check is a downright booby trap. GC must be at a very early stage in its evolution. Something like jellyfish on the scale of living things. ("Likes jellyfish," GC insists.)

Nevertheless—although you've paid good money for it—you can always switch off Grammar Check. Better still, throw it out the Windows.

➤ **FOR WRITING OR DISCUSSION**

1. In what ways is this a cause-and-effect essay?
2. What author image does Sivanand project?

3. What, according to the writer, is the effect of Grammar Check and Spell Check on his prose? What would result if the writer followed the instructions of these two language helpers that are part of his word processing program?
4. How does the writer achieve humor in his piece?
5. Write your own short, humorous cause-and-effect essay called "Why I _____ Wrong." Fill in the blank with a word or phrase of your choice. For example, you might consider using a word like *eat, sing, talk, dance, drive,* or *do home-work.* Explain the cause of your "wrong" act and indicate some of the consequences of your behavior. Keep a light and humorous tone.

HAVING YOUR SAY

Have computers made our lives simpler or more complicated? Choose one side of the issue and write an essay to support your point of view.

BETTY ROLLIN

The Best Years of My Life

1   I am about to celebrate an anniversary. Not that there will be a party with funny hats. Nor do I expect any greetings in the mail. Hallmark, with its infinite variety of occasions about which to fashion a 50-cent card, has skipped this one. This, you see, is my cancer anniversary. Five years ago tomorrow, at Beth Israel Hospital in New York City, a malignant tumor was removed from my left breast and, along with the tumor, my left breast. To be alive five years later means something in cancer circles. There is nothing intrinsically magical about the figure five, but the numbers show that if you have survived that many years after cancer has been diagnosed, you have an 80 percent shot at living out a normal life span.

2   Still, you probably think Hallmark is right not to sell a card, and that it's weird to "celebrate" such a terrible thing as cancer. It's even weirder than you imagine. Because not only do I feel good about (probably) having escaped a recurrence of cancer, I also feel good about having gotten cancer in the first place. Here is the paradox: although cancer was the worst thing that ever happened to me, it was also the best. Cancer (the kind I had, with no spread and no need of chemotherapy, with its often harrowing side effects) enriched my life, made me wiser, made me happier. Another paradox: although I would do everything possible to avoid getting cancer again, I am glad I had it.

3   There is a theory about people who have a life-and-death scare that goes something like this: for about six months after surviving the scare, you feel shaken and grateful. Armed with a keen sense of what was almost The End, you begin to live your life differently. You pause during the race to notice the foliage, you pay more attention to the people you love—maybe you even move to Vermont. You have gained, as they say, a "new

perspective." But then, according to this theory, when the six months are over, the "new perspective" fades, you sell the house in Vermont and go back to the same craziness that was your life before the car crash or whatever it was. What has happened is that you've stopped feeling afraid. The crash is in the past. The it-can't-happen-to-me feelings that were dashed by the accident reemerge, after six months, as it-can't-happen-to-me-*again*.

It's different for people whose crash is cancer. You can stay off the freeways, but you can't do much about preventing whatever went wrong in your own body from going wrong again. Unless your head is buried deep in the sand, you know damn well it *can* happen again. Even though, in my case, the doctors say it isn't likely, the possibility of recurrence is very real to me. Passing the five-year mark is reassuring, but I know I will be a little bit afraid for the rest of my life. But—ready for another paradox?—certain poisons are medicinal in small doses. To be a little bit afraid of dying can do wonders for your life. It has done wonders for mine. That's because, unlike the way most people feel, my sense of death is not an intellectual concept. It's a lively presence in my gut. It affects me daily—for the better.

First, when you're even slightly afraid of death, you're less afraid of other things— e.g., bosses, spouses, plumbers, rape, bankruptcy, failure, not being liked, the flu, aging. Next to the Grim Reaper, how ferocious can even the most ferocious boss be? How dire the direst household calamity? In my own professional life, I have lost not only some big fears, but most of the small ones. I used to be nervous in front of television cameras. That kind of nervousness was a fear of not being thought attractive, smart and winning. It still pleases me greatly if someone besides my husband and mother thinks I'm attractive, smart and winning; but I am no longer afraid that someone won't. Cancer made me less worried about what people think of me, both professionally and socially. I am less concerned about where my career is going. I don't know where it's going. I don't think about that. I think about where I am and what I'm doing and whether I like it. The result is that these days I continually seem to be doing what I like. And probably I'm more successful than when I aimed to please.

My book *First, You Cry,* which has given me more pleasure than anything else in my professional life, is a good example of this. As a career move, leaving television for six months to write a book about a cancer operation seemed less than sensible. But as soon as I got cancer, I stopped being "sensible." I wanted to write the book. And, just in case I croaked, I wanted to write it the way that was right for me, not necessarily for the market. So I turned down the publisher who wanted it to be a "how-to" book. I like to think I would have done that, cancer or not, but had it not been for cancer, I probably wouldn't have written a book at all, because I would have been too afraid to drop out of television even for six months. And if I had written a book, I doubt that I would have been so open about my life and honest about my less-than-heroic feelings. But, as I wrote, I remember thinking, "I might die, so what does it matter what anyone thinks of me?" A lot of people write honestly and openly without having had a disease, but I don't think I would have. I hadn't done it before.

A touch of cancer turns you into a hypochondriac. You get a sore throat and you think you've got cancer of the throat; you get a corn from a pair of shoes that are too tight and you're sure it's a malignant tumor. But—here's the bright side—cancer hypochondria is so compelling it never occurs to you that you could get anything *else.*

And, when you do, you're so glad it's not cancer that you feel like celebrating. "Goody, it's the flu!" I heard myself say to myself a couple of weeks ago.

8   Some physicians are more sensitive than others to cancer anxiety. My gynecologist prattled on once about some menstrual irregularity without noticing that, as he spoke, I had turned to stone. "Is it cancer?" I finally whispered. He looked dumbfounded and said, "Of course not!" As if to say, "How could you think such a thing?" But an orthopedist I saw about a knee problem took an X-ray and, before saying a word about what it was (a torn cartilage), told me what it wasn't. I limped home joyously.

9   I never went to Vermont because I can't stand that much fresh air; but in my own fashion, I sop up pleasure where and when I can, sometimes at the risk of professional advancement and sometimes at the risk of bankruptcy. An exaggeration, perhaps, but there's no question about it: since cancer, I spend more money than I used to. (True, I have more to spend, but that's mostly because of the book, which is also thanks to cancer.) I had always been parsimonious—some would say cheap—and I'm not anymore. The thinking is, "Just in case I do get a recurrence, won't I feel like a fool for having flown coach to Seattle?" (I like to think I'm more generous with others as well. It seems to me that, since having cancer, I give better presents.)

10   Cancer kills guilt. You not only take a vacation now because next year you might be dead, but you take a *better* vacation because, even if you don't die soon, after what you've been through, you feel you deserve it. In my own case, I wouldn't have expected that feeling to survive six months because, once those months passed, I realized that, compared to some people, I had not been through much at all. But my hedonism continues to flourish. Maybe it was just a question of changing a habit.

11   My girlish masochism didn't resurface, either. Most women I know go through at least a phase of needing punishment from men. Not physical punishment, just all the rest: indifference, harshness, coldness, rudeness or some neat combination. In the past, my own appetite for this sort of treatment was voracious. Conversely, if I happened to connect with a man who was nice to me, I felt like that song: "This can't be love because I feel so well." The difference was that, in the song, it really *was* love, and with me, it really *wasn't*. Only when I was miserable did I know I really cared.

12   The minute I got cancer, my taste in men improved. It's not that my first husband was a beast. I'm fond of him, but even he would admit he was very hard on me. Maybe I asked for it. Well, once you've been deftly kicked in the pants by God (or whoever distributes cancer), you stop wanting kicks from mortals. Everyone who knows the man I married a year ago thinks I'm lucky—even my mother!—and I do, too. But I know it wasn't only luck. It was that cancer made me want someone wonderful. I wasn't ready for him before. I was so struck by this apparent change in me that I checked it out with a psychoanalyst, who assured me that I was not imagining things—that the damage to my body had, indeed, done wonders for my head.

13   Happiness is probably something that shouldn't be talked about too much, but I can't help it. Anyway, I find the more I carry on about it, the better it gets. A big part of happiness is noticing it. It's trite to say, but if you've never been ill, you don't notice—or enjoy—not being ill. I even notice my husband's good health. (He doesn't, but how could he?)

14   I haven't mentioned losing that breast, have I? That's because, in spite of the fuss I made about it five years ago, that loss now seems almost not worth mentioning. Five

years ago, I felt sorry for myself that I could no longer keep a strapless dress up. Today I feel that losing a breast saved my life, and wasn't I lucky. And when I think of all the other good things that have come from that loss, I just look at that flat place on my body and think: small price.

Most of my friends who are past 40 shudder on their birthdays. Not me. They feel a year closer to death, I suppose. I feel a year further from it.   15

O.K., what if I get a recurrence? I'm not so jolly all the time that I haven't given this some serious thought. If it happens, I'm sure I won't be a good sport about it—especially if my life is cut short. But even if it is, I will look back at the years since the surgery and know I got the best from them. And I will be forced to admit that the disease that is ending my life is the very thing that made it so good.   16

> **FOR WRITING OR DISCUSSION**

1. In your own words, what is the thesis about the effects of cancer on the author's life?
2. How many effects does the author discuss to support her thesis? Are all the effects separate, or are some interconnected?
3. Do you think the author's cheerfulness is excessive? Does she mention any unpleasant effects?
4. Write a paper analyzing the good results of a bad experience—a sickness, a poor grade, a divorce, a death, getting fired from a job, and so on.

Readings for Writing

The satirical short story and the humorous essay that follow may provide you with subject matter for writing an analysis of a cause-and-effect relationship.

TED POSTON

The Revolt of the Evil Fairies

The grand dramatic offering of the Booker T. Washington Colored Grammar School was the biggest event of the year in our social life in Hopkinsville, Kentucky. It was the one occasion on which they let us use the old Cooper Opera House, and even some of the white folks came out yearly to applaud our presentation. The first two rows of the orchestra were always reserved for our white friends, and our leading colored citizens sat right behind them—with an empty row intervening, of course.   1

Mr. Ed Smith, our local undertaker, invariably occupied a box to the left of the house and wore his cutaway coat and striped breeches. This distinctive garb was usually reserved for those rare occasions when he officiated at the funerals of our most prominent   2 colored citizens. Mr. Thaddeus Long, our colored mailman, once rented a tuxedo and bought a box too. But nobody paid him much mind. We knew he was just showing off.

3   The title of our play never varied. It was always Prince Charming and the Sleeping Beauty, but no two presentations were ever the same. Miss H. Belle LaPrade, our sixth-grade teacher, rewrote the script every season, and it was never like anything you read in the storybooks.

4   Miss LaPrade called it "a modern morality play of conflict between the forces of good and evil." And the forces of evil, of course, always came off second best.

5   The Booker T. Washington Colored Grammar School was in a state of ferment from Christmas until February, for this was the period when parts were assigned. First there was the selection of the Good Fairies and the Evil Fairies. This was very important, because the Good Fairies wore white costumes and the Evil Fairies black. And strangely enough most of the Good Fairies usually turned out to be extremely light in complexion, with straight hair and white folks' features. On rare occasions a darkskinned girl might be lucky enough to be a Good Fairy, but not one with a speaking part.

6   There never was any doubt about Prince Charming and the Sleeping Beauty. They were always lightskinned. And though nobody ever discussed those things openly, it was an accepted fact that a lack of pigmentation was a decided advantage in the Prince Charming and Sleeping Beauty sweepstakes.

7   And therein lay my personal tragedy. I made the best grades in my class, I was the leading debater, and the scion of a respected family in the community. But I could never be Prince Charming, because I was black.

8   In fact, every year when they started casting our grand dramatic offering my family started pricing black cheesecloth at Franklin's Department Store. For they knew that I would be leading the forces of darkness and skulking back in the shadows—waiting to be vanquished in the third act. Mamma had experience with this sort of thing. All my brothers had finished Booker T. before me.

9   Not that I was alone in my disappointment. Many of my classmates felt it too. I probably just took it more to heart. Rat Joiner, for instance, could rationalize the situation. Rat was not only black; he lived on Billy Goat Hill. But Rat summed it up like this:

10   "If you black, you black."

11   I should have been able to regard the matter calmly too. For our grand dramatic offering was only a reflection of our daily community life in Hopkinsville. The yallers had the best of everything. They held most of the teaching jobs in Booker T. Washington Colored Grammar School. They were the Negro doctors, the lawyers, the insurance men. They even had a "Blue Vein Society," and if your dark skin obscured your throbbing pulse you were hardly a member of the elite.

12   Yet I was inconsolable the first time they turned me down for Prince Charming. That was the year they picked Roger Jackson. Roger was not only dumb; he stuttered. But he was light enough to pass for white, and that was apparently sufficient.

13   In all fairness, however, it must be admitted that Roger had other qualifications. His father owned the only colored saloon in town and was quite a power in local politics. In fact, Mr. Clinton Jackson had a lot to say about just who taught in the Booker T. Washington Colored Grammar School. So it was understandable that Roger should have been picked for Prince Charming.

My real heartbreak, however, came the year they picked Sarah Williams for Sleeping Beauty. I had been in love with Sarah since kindergarten. She had soft light hair, bluish-gray eyes, and a dimple which stayed in her left cheek whether she was smiling or not.   14

Of course Sarah never encouraged me much. She never answered any of my fervent love letters, and Rat was very scornful of my one-sided love affairs. "As long as she don't call you a black baboon," he sneered, "you'll keep on hanging around."   15

After Sarah was chosen for Sleeping Beauty, I went out for the Prince Charming role with all my heart. If I had declaimed boldly in previous contests, I was matchless now. If I had bothered Mamma with rehearsals at home before, I pestered her to death this time. Yes, and I purloined my sister's can of Palmer's Skin Success.   16

I knew the Prince's role from start to finish, having played the Head Evil Fairy opposite it for two seasons. And Prince Charming was one character whose lines Miss LaPrade never varied much in her many versions. But although I never admitted it, even to myself, I knew I was doomed from the start. They gave the part to Leonardius Wright. Leonardius, of course, was yaller.   17

The teachers sensed my resentment. They were most apologetic. They pointed out that I had been such a splendid Head Evil Fairy for two seasons that it would be a crime to let anybody else try the role. They reminded me that Mamma wouldn't have to buy any more cheesecloth because I could use my same old costume. They insisted that the Head Evil Fairy was even more important than Prince Charming because he was the one who cast the spell on Sleeping Beauty. So what could I do but accept?   18

I had never liked Leonardius Wright. He was a goody-goody, and even Mamma was always throwing him up to me. But, above all, he too was in love with Sarah Williams. And now he got a chance to kiss Sarah every day in rehearsing the awakening scene.   19

Well, the show must go on, even for little black boys. So I threw my soul into my part and made the Head Evil Fairy a character to be remembered. When I drew back from the couch of Sleeping Beauty and slunk away into the shadows at the approach of Prince Charming, my facial expression was indeed something to behold. When I was vanquished by the shining sword of Prince Charming in the last act, I was a little hammy perhaps—but terrific!   20

The attendance at our grand dramatic offering that year was the best in its history. Even the white folks overflowed the two rows reserved for them, and a few were forced to sit in the intervening one. This created a delicate situation, but everybody tactfully ignored it.   21

When the curtain went up on the last act, the audience was in fine fettle. Everything had gone well for me too—except for one spot in the second act. That was where Leonardius unexpectedly rapped me over the head with his sword as I slunk off into the shadows. That was not in the script, but Miss LaPrade quieted me down by saying it made a nice touch anyway. Rat said Leonardius did it on purpose.   22

The third act went on smoothly, though, until we came to the vanquishing scene. That was where I slunk from the shadows for the last time and challenged Prince Charming to mortal combat. The hero reached for his shining sword—a bit unsportsmanlike, I always thought, since Miss LaPrade consistently left the Head Evil Fairy unarmed—and then it happened!   23

Later I protested loudly—but in vain—that it was a case of self-defense. I pointed out that Leonardius had a mean look in his eye. I cited the impromptu rapping he had   24 given my head in the second act. But nobody would listen. They just wouldn't believe that Leonardius really intended to brain me when he reached for his sword.

25   Anyway, he didn't succeed. For the minute I saw that evil gleam in his eye—or was it my own?—I cut loose with a right to the chin, and Prince Charming dropped his shining sword and staggered back. His astonishment lasted only a minute, though, for he lowered his head and came charging in, fists flailing. There was nothing yellow about Leonardius but his skin.

26   The audience thought the scrap was something new Miss LaPrade had written in. They might have kept on thinking so if Miss LaPrade hadn't been screaming so hysterically from the sidelines. And if Rat Joiner hadn't decided that this was as good a time as any to settle old scores. So he turned around and took a sock at the male Good Fairy nearest him.

27   When the curtain rang down, the forces of Good and Evil were locked in combat. And Sleeping Beauty was wide awake and streaking for the wings.

28   They rang the curtain back up fifteen minutes later, and we finished the play. I lay down and expired according to specifications but Prince Charming will probably remember my sneering corpse to his dying day. They wouldn't let me appear in the grand dramatic offering at all the next year. But I didn't care. I couldn't have been Prince Charming anyway.

➤ **FOR WRITING OR DISCUSSION**

1. To what race does Miss LaPrade belong?
2. Why is it significant that the narrator made the best grades, was the leading debater, and was the son of a respected family?
3. Why do the "yallers" have the best of everything in the community?
4. Why is the Head Evil Fairy unarmed?
5. Write a paper in which you explain why the narrator of the story "couldn't have been Prince Charming anyway."

GEORGE KOCH

Naked in Orlando

1   I was scheduled recently to introduce the president of my company to a large group of customers meeting at our annual convention in Orlando, Fla. I was late, and didn't show up until long after he had given up on me and introduced himself. My excuse? I was somewhere else. In a hotel, locked alone in a room, naked.

2   I woke up in plenty of time that morning, sailed into the bathroom, closed the door but didn't lock it. I was alone and the outer hotel-room door was deadbolted against overeager housekeepers. I showered, dried myself off and headed out the door. But when I turned the bathroom doorknob it did not budge.

3   There I was, and I was stuck. The room, at the end of the hallway at the end of the hotel, faced nothing—just outside air, 20 stories up. And I'd hung the "Do Not Disturb" sign on the deadbolted door. I was booked for a one-week stay. No reason for anyone

to come by until it was time to check out. Under the circumstances, I asked the question any seasoned executive would: "What would MacGyver do?"

Of course! I could blow the door off. I looked around for some charcoal, sulfur and potassium nitrate to make gunpowder. None. Nor was there a magnesium pipe to file into shavings to make into a blowtorch—as there would be for MacGyver.   4

I poked through my travel kit and finally found . . . a fingernail clipper. I wedged the clipper into the doorjamb and scraped the bolt to slide it out. But the bolt had broken off in place. Rats! I searched the room again: useless towels, soap, little plastic bottles of shampoo, conditioner, moisturizing lotion, a plastic shower cap. Hmm . . . metal towel bars. I yanked one off the wall and was able to hammer the hollow end flat using the thick bottom of a drinking glass and the marble sink top. A pry bar! The stuff of legends. I pushed it into the jamb and pried. The towel bar bent. The door frame was steel and solid wood, nearly two inches thick. A strong door.   5

Valiantly, I tried my pry bar on the hinge pins, again using the drinking glass for a hammer. I'd removed plenty of doors at home this way: Pop the pins out, pull the door. Freedom! But this time the glass broke and the pins didn't budge. On inspection I saw they were welded in place. Next I examined the doorknob and pushed on its own clip to pull the knob off. Hah! Progress! But this only exposed the knob mechanism screwed tightly into the door. So I tried the fingernail clipper as a screwdriver. Too soft, it bent.   6

And I started to sweat. The mirrors, with many high-wattage lights, were turning the room into an oven. I unscrewed most of the bulbs. No need to cook my goose in more ways than one. By now I was glad to be working in the buff. I made a halfhearted effort at tapping out an SOS on the wall and shouting, "Help! Help!" I began dismantling the bathroom looking for a makeshift screwdriver. I took apart the tiny TV, toilet and a wall plug to find a right-angled piece of steel to use on the screws. All were soft metal and plastic. I unplugged the cable and power to the TV, hoping for security devices there to alert the front desk that they were being stolen. For naught.   7

My MacGyver bravado was beginning to wane. How long before I got out? And if I didn't, how would the obituary read? ("Naked man wrecks hotel bathroom, starves to death.")   8

Will renewed, I began to chop up the wooden door around the lock to pull out the mechanism. I used the sharp end of my homemade pry bar and began hacking away. This was slow going, but I was out of clever stratagem. I remembered horror stories of people being buried alive and trying to scrape their way out of wooden caskets with their fingernails. At least I had a towel bar.   9

And then I heard a tiny, distant voice. It was a security guard, outside my room. Someone had heard my SOSs, and reported them to the front desk, not sure if they were real or a prank. (I don't know who you are, but if you're reading this, thank you.)   10

The maintenance guy couldn't get the door loose either, and he couldn't get the lock mechanism out because it was screwed in from my side. He slid a small screwdriver through the narrow space under the door so I could undo the screws, but it was too small, and it bent. Finally, he pounded a larger screwdriver under the door with a hammer. I removed the screws, and he pulled the main mechanism from the door. There was a three-inch peephole now; he could see a whole lot more of me than I could of him.   11

Still, the broken bolt remained in the jamb. The door stayed shut. Now he passed me a very large, flathead screwdriver through the circular hole. I stood in the bathtub,   12 out of the way, trying to use it as a pry bar to pull the door away from the jamb. Then, as I pried, he threw his shoulder into the door, and it thumped open. I emerged at last.

13   I finally made it to the auditorium, an hour late, but with the single-best hotel story anyone had ever heard. The group nicknamed me "MacGyver."

14   The hotel did not apologize. Nor did it send me a bill for the bathroom damages. At least not yet.

➤ FOR WRITING OR DISCUSSION

1. Does this essay deal mostly with causes, effects, or both? Explain.
2. Were any of the author's actions unclear to you?
3. What was the only action that worked? How much luck was involved?
4. Write an essay with the thesis that there was no real need for alarm and tell what the author could have done to be released more quickly and easily. As an alternative assignment, write a paper about the causes or effects of an embarrassing predicament you were once in: finding your car towed, getting lost on a trip, forgetting someone's identity, losing a wallet or purse, being caught telling a lie, and so on.

WRITING TOPICS

If you cannot easily decide on a topic for your cause-and-effect paper, you might want to try one or more of the following suggestions. Most of the subjects can be treated as material for a cause only, effect only, or cause-and-effect papers.

1. One of your personality quirks
2. Passing a test
3. Romance
4. A change of mind about something or someone
5. A strong like or dislike of a particular movie or TV show
6. A strong like or dislike of a particular food or beverage
7. Growth or decrease in the popularity of a style of music
8. Growth or decrease in the popularity of a hairstyle
9. Growth or decrease in the popularity of a clothing style
10. Spending money
11. A major decision in your life
12. An astonishing success
13. A major purchase
14. Emphasis on computers in American schools
15. Effects of an experience with racial or religious prejudice
16. Effects of violence in children's cartoons
17. Excessively strict or lenient parents
18. Excessively strict or lenient teachers
19. Weather and people's moods
20. Making a boss angry

CROSSCURRENTS

1. Reread Maya Angelou's "Champion of the World" (page 151) and Ted Poston's "The Revolt of the Evil Fairies" (page 311). How accurately do these pieces reflect the modern African American experience? How are the pieces alike? different? What fascination does boxing have for each writer?
2. Robinson's "Richard Corey" (page 300), Orwell's "A Hanging" (page 7), Rollin's "The Best Years of My Life" (page 308), and Littlebrandt's "Death is a Personal Matter" (page 146) all treat the issue of death from a variety of perspectives. What social and moral considerations arise in these pieces? What philosophy of living and dying emerges in each essay?

COLLABORATIVE LEARNING

After each student in the class has produced a rough draft for the cause-and-effect essay, form groups of three to discuss the papers at this stage. As each student reads aloud, listen for the logical development of ideas and take notes so that you can provide useful comments. (You may find it helpful to have each student read his or her paper twice.) Have the writers avoided oversimplifying causes and effects? Are the patterns of development clear and easy to follow?

REVIEW CHECKLIST: WRITING AND REVISING YOUR CAUSE-AND-EFFECT PAPER

- Have I done prewriting to explore ideas for a subject?
- Have I thought carefully about my purpose?
- Have I written for the usual general audience? If I am writing for a special audience, have I made that clear to the reader?
- Have I limited my subject?
- Have I established a clear thesis?
- Do I have enough support for my thesis?
- Have I been careful to avoid logical fallacies, especially the *post hoc* fallacy?
- Have I been careful to avoid oversimplifying causes and effects?
- Have I followed an established pattern of organization?
- Have I proofread for grammar, spelling, and mechanics?

Photo courtesy: © Owen Franken/Stock, Boston

————FROM IMAGE TO WORDS: A PHOTO WRITING ASSIGNMENT ————

Look at the photograph above. Write a cause and effect paper that the picture suggests to you. Be sure that your thesis makes some assertion about the topic that you see emerging from the scene. Provide appropriate details to support the causes and (or) effects that you establish.

CHAPTER
13

Definition

From time to time, you've probably found yourself in a shouting match with friends over a question such as, which is the better concert group—U2 or Pfish. Eventually, some wise soul says, "Hey, wait a minute. What's your idea of a good concert group?" The speaker has demanded a **definition** of the term that has sparked the debate. When you and your friends begin to explain what you're shouting about, you may find that one person's standard for "good" is how loud the drums play. Another may appreciate how the lead guitarist subtly improvises on a theme. Then you realize, perhaps, either that your respective ideas of a good group are so different that you can't have a discussion or that, once you understand each other's terms, you have no real disagreement.

When writing, you won't have the advantage of another person's saying, "Hey, wait a minute. Don't you think you'd better define your terms?" If you want to appear reasonable when you present an idea, you sometimes have to define terms. Often, a dictionary won't be much help. It may be a good place to start, but at times a dictionary definition won't explain a term fully. Take that word *good*, for example. A dictionary tells you that it means "having positive or desirable qualities," and so it does; but how does such a definition help you distinguish between one rock group and another? To do so, you could begin with a dictionary definition, to be sure, but you must let your reader know what you believe the positive or desirable qualities of a rock group are. You must write an **extended definition.**

No matter how solid your reasons for approving or disapproving of a person, place, thing, group, or idea, those reasons are unlikely to find acceptance with a reader if you don't define your terms. In writing the Declaration of Independence, for example, Thomas Jefferson clearly understood the need to define a *good* government—one that secures the natural rights of "life, liberty, and the pursuit of happiness" and that derives its powers "from the consent of the governed"—before arguing that George III's government failed to meet those standards. Without the carefully stated definition of a good government, the long list of complaints against the British government might well have been viewed as merely an expression of dissatisfaction by a group of malcontents.

Certain terms, then, require a more extended definition than a dictionary gives. The burden is on you to explain what you mean by the term. Sometimes this extended definition may occupy one or two paragraphs of a long paper. Occasionally, a definition can become the paper itself.

The following kinds of terms often need defining:

- *Judgmental words*—words that reflect opinions—need definition. Whether subjects being discussed are *good, better, best; bad, worse, worst; beautiful, ugly; friendly, unfriendly; wise, foolish; fair, unfair;* and so on, is a matter of opinion.
- *Specialized terms*—terms with a special meaning to a given group—need definition. Almost every professional or occupational group uses terms that the members of the group understand but that require explanation for those outside the group—for example, *psychosis,* a psychological term; *neoclassicism,* a literary term; *writ,* a legal term; and *gig,* a show-business term.
- *Abstractions*—general words like *love, democracy, justice, freedom,* and *quality*—need definition.
- *Controversial terms* like *male chauvinist, nuclear build-up,* and *affirmative action* need definition.
- *Slang terms* like *right on, with it, cool,* and *hot* may need definition for many audiences.

Writing Your Definition Paper

You can present your extended definition in one of two ways—formally or informally.

A **formal definition** contains the three parts of a dictionary definition: (1) the term itself—the word or phrase to be defined; (2) the class—the large group to which the object or concept belongs; and (3) the differentiation—those characteristics that distinguish it from all others in its class.

Term	Class	Differentiation
A garden	is a small plot of land	used for the cultivation of flowers, vegetables, or fruits.

Term	Class	Differentiation
Beer	is a fermented alcoholic beverage	brewed from malt and flavored with hops.
Lunch	is a meal	eaten at midday.

To write an extended formal definition, you need to develop a one-sentence definition of the term. Keep the following cautions in mind:

- *Restrict the class.* Speak of a sonnet not as a kind of literature, but as a kind of poem.
- *Include no important part of the term itself or its derivatives in the class or differentiation.* Don't say that "a definition is that which defines."
- *Make certain that the sentence defines and does not simply make a statement about the term.* "Happiness is a Madonna concert" doesn't have the essential parts of a definition of happiness.
- *Provide adequate differentiation to clarify the meaning.* Don't define a traitor as "one who opposes the best interests of his or her country." That definition doesn't exclude the well-meaning person who misunderstands the country's best interests and opposes from ignorance. Try instead, "A traitor is one who opposes the best interests of his or her country with malicious intent."
- *Don't make the definition too restrictive.* Don't define a matinee as "a drama presented during the day." That definition doesn't include other forms of entertainment, such as ballets or concerts, which could also be held in daytime.
- *Make sure to include the class.* Don't write, "Baseball is when nine players. . . ." Write instead, "Baseball is a *sport* in which nine players. . . ."

EXERCISE

Using a dictionary whenever necessary, write one-sentence formal definitions for the following terms.

1.	Politics	**6.**	Terrorist
2.	Joy	**7.**	Cold fusion
3.	Intelligence	**8.**	Asset
4.	Poker	**9.**	Hanukkah
5.	Bok choy	**10.**	Recession

Once you have composed a one-sentence formal definition, its three parts can become the major divisions of your paper. The introduction to your paper might contain the term and its one-sentence definition. That sentence could become the thesis for your paper. Or, in addition to providing a one-sentence definition, you could also express an attitude toward the term. In the paper on pages 323–324, student writer Frederick Spense expresses his attitude in this way: "Equality *ought to be* a philosophy and set of laws in which all people are given the same opportunity to achieve their own individual potential."

The next division of your paper could discuss the class, and the final division, the differentiation. In these discussions, you can make your idea clear by using specific details, by making comparisons and using analogies, by giving examples or telling anecdotes, and sometimes by tracing the history of the term. Often you will be able to quote or refer to the definitions others have given the term. This technique is particularly useful if experts disagree over the meaning of the term. An especially effective tool is exclusion, showing what the term is *not:*

> *Gourmet* cooking does not mean to me the preparation of food in expensive wines; it does not mean the preparation of exotic dishes like octopus or rattlesnake; it does not mean the smothering of meat with highly caloric sauces. *Gourmet* cooking to me means the preparation of any food—whether black-eyed peas or hollandaise sauce—in such a way that the dish will be as tasty and attractive as it can be made.

In advancing your discussion of class and differentiation, you can use any method or combination of methods of development you have studied. In fact, what makes definition such an interesting rhetorical challenge is that you can draw on most of the familiar patterns of essay development you have studied. For example, suppose you wanted to define the term *happiness.* You could use a variety of approaches as indicated here.

Essay topic: Defining the term *happiness*

Possible approach	Mode of development
Provide accurate sensory details to describe the face and actions of a happy person you know.	Description (Chapter 6)
Tell a story about a moment when you were truly happy.	Narration (Chapter 7)
Provide several illustrations (examples) of happiness.	Example (Chapter 8)
Explain how to be happy or unhappy.	Process (Chapter 9)
Compare one state of happiness with another; contrast happiness with sadness.	Comparison–Contrast (Chapter 10)
Divide happy people into groups or categories.	Classification (Chapter 11)
Explain the conditions necessary for true happiness or the outcomes of happiness in a person's life.	Cause and Effect (Chapter 12)
Argue that happiness is not achievable in America today.	Argumentation (Chapter 14)

Student Writing: Formal Definition

In the paper that follows, the student writer derives a formal definition of the term *equality* from his reading of "Harrison Bergeron." (Vonnegut's short story appears later in the chapter, page 348.) Mr. Spense contrasts his understanding of *equality* with that of the futuristic society represented in Vonnegut's story.

Frederick Spense

Everyone Is Equal in the Grave

Kurt Vonnegut, Jr.'s short story "Harrison Bergeron" contrasts the misunderstanding and perversion of equality with the true meaning of the word. Equality ought to be a philosophy and set of laws in which all people are given the same opportunity to achieve their own individual potential. In the U.S.A. of 2081, equality has become a philosophy and set of laws in which everyone is forced to be the same. 1

The Declaration of Independence presents the principle that "all men are created equal," and various laws attempt to put the principle into practice--laws about voting, employment, housing, and so on. "Equal before God and the law" in the second sentence of the story seems to show Vonnegut's approval of this approach. "Equal every which way" is another problem, though, and the story attempts to show that a government that interprets equality in that manner is going to be a slave state. 2

Giving people an equal opportunity to be the best they can be is not the same as forcing people to be like everyone else. Any person who wants to should have the chance to study ballet. That represents equality. Letting poor dancers join 3

the ballet company and "handicapping" good dancers so everyone
will be the same is the corruption of equality that has taken
place in 2081.

4   Instead of everyone with a good voice having the same
chance to become an announcer if he or she wants to, all
the announcers in the world of 2081 have speech impedi-
ments. Instead of the most skilled technicians competing
for jobs on the television crews so that the best person
will be chosen, the crews consist of people who cannot even
hold cards right side up. Instead of admitting that smart
people and dumb people are different even though they have
the same worth as human beings, the government installs
electronic equipment to prevent the smart people from using
their brains for more than a few seconds at a time. Good-
looking people wear masks to make them "equal" to ugly people. Strong people wear weights to make them "equal" to
weak people.

5   Vonnegut's point is that this is not true equality, but
tyranny. It is not just stupid to stifle exceptional people
and create a world where being outstanding is a sin, but to
do so requires a tremendous government agency whose job is to
snoop and to control the smallest aspects of people's private
lives. The Constitution has to be amended to make all this
possible, and the Handicapper General has the authority to
shoot criminals--that is, individuals--on sight.

6   Equality is and ought to be one of our most precious
ideals. If it ever comes to mean sameness and conformity,
it will not really be equality at all, only obedience
and regimentation. Equality like that is the equality of
the grave.

➤ **FOR WRITING OR DISCUSSION**

1. What is the thesis of this paper?
2. Does Spense successfully achieve a one-sentence formal definition of the term? If so, what is it?
3. What methods of development does the writer use in advancing his definition? How do they help him make his idea clear?
4. From your reading of Vonnegut's story (page 348), do you believe that the definition of *equality* presented in this paper is one of which Vonnegut would approve? Why, or why not?
5. Write your own definition of the term *equality*. You may draw on "Harrison Bergeron," some other story, or your own experience.

Here is another formal definition paper. See what you think of this student's one-paragraph effort.

Shirley Marlyne

Discipline

Human discipline is the setting of boundaries within which a person's actions may range. The foregoing broad definition may be subdivided into two categories: (1) the training intended to produce a specified character or pattern of behavior, juvenile discipline, and (2) the controlled behavior resulting from such training, adult discipline. Throughout their lives, human beings are subject to juvenile discipline--a spanking, the withholding of privileges, a stay in the detention room, a speeding ticket, a chiding for increased girth, a reminder to take the pills before meals. Of far greater importance is adult discipline because it is an internal quality, derived from an intellectual and emotional reservoir. Adult discipline allows a driver to move slowly through a traffic pinch so that other cars can get into line before him. It provides the courage to deliver a message to a crowd while suffering from terrible stage fright. The strength

```
that comes through adult discipline permits the toiler to

perform an overwhelming task in small increments and to be

satisfied with the lesser rewards of gaining each subgoal. It

leads one not to seek revenge or even immediate redress for

injustice. Juvenile discipline, then, is direction from out-

side, but adult discipline is the schooling of self.
```

➤ **FOR WRITING OR DISCUSSION**

1. What is the formal, one-sentence definition of the term *discipline* as the writer sees it?
2. Does the writer favor one form of discipline over the other? Why do you think so? Do you agree with her choice? Why, or why not?
3. What methods of development does the writer use in defining the chosen term?
4. Could you give examples—other than those used by the author—of two kinds of discipline? Explain your response.
5. Write your own brief definition of the word *discipline.*

Although many terms lend themselves to the three-part formal definition, some are better explained by **informal definition.** What is a good teacher, for example? or a bad marriage? or an ideal home? Clearly, such topics can be defined only in a subjective or personal way; your purpose is to show what the term means to you. In such instances, it is probably wise to avoid a rigid formal definition. Make your conception of the term clear by describing the subject as fully as you can. By the time readers finish the paper, they should understand what the term means to you.

As with formal definitions, you can employ any method or combination of methods of development you have studied to create an informal definition. Examples and anecdotes are especially good for explaining a term. So are comparison, process, classification, and cause and effect. The idea is to use whatever techniques come in handy to put the idea across. One good subject for an informal definition is a word or phrase used by a group or a region of the country.

Student Writing: Informal Definition

In the following student paper, the writer explains a term used only by members of her family.

Helen Fleming

The Grinnies

1

Until I was twelve years old, I thought everyone in
the world knew about the grinnies, if I thought about the
term at all--which is unlikely. After all, everyone in my
family used the word quite naturally, and we understood
each other. So far as I knew, it was a word like any
other word--like <u>bath</u>, or <u>chocolate</u>, or <u>homework</u>. But it
was my homework which led to my discovery that <u>grinnies</u>
was a word not known outside my family.

My last report card had said that I was a "C" student in English, and my parents, both teachers, decided
that no child of theirs would be just an average student
of anything. So nightly I spelled words aloud and
answered questions about the fine points of grammar. I
wrote and rewrote and rewrote every composition until
I convinced my mother that I could make no more improvements. And the hard work paid off. One day the teacher
returned compositions, and there it was--a big fat,
bright red "A" on the top of my paper. Naturally, I was
delighted, but I didn't know I was attracting attention
until the teacher snapped, "Helen, what <u>are</u> you doing?"

Called suddenly out of my happy thoughts, I said
"Oh, I've got the grinnies!" The teacher and my classmates burst into laughter, and then I understood that
grinnies were confined to my family. Other people were
not so privileged.

And it is a privilege to have the grinnies, an
uncontrollable, spontaneous state of ecstasy. Grinnies

Introduction provides necessary background as writer presents the term being defined.

Personal experience narrative helps reader see the word "grinnies" in action.

Transition paragraph links personal narrative with explanations and further examples.

Word "And" at beginning of paragraph serves as a transition and helps promote essay coherence.

1

2

3

4

Formal one-sentence definition, even though the essay itself is an *informal* definition

are demonstrated on the outside by sparkling eyes and a wide, wide smile--not just any smile, but one that shows the teeth and stretches the mouth to its limits. A person experiencing the grinnies appears to be all mouth. On the inside, grinnies are characterized by a feeling of joyful agitation, almost a bubbly sensation. Grinnies usually last just a few seconds, but they can come and go. Sometimes, when life seems just perfect, I have intermittent attacks of the grinnies for a whole day.

Further details differentiate the term with precise characteristics.

The term originated in my mother's family. Her younger sister, Rose, who had deep dimples, often expressed her pleasure with such a grin that the dimples appeared to become permanent. When Rose was about four, she started explaining her funny look by saying, "I have the grinnies." The term caught on, and it has been an important word in our family now for two generations.

Historical information further explains the term.

5

The occasion doesn't matter. Anything can bring on the grinnies--just so long as one feels great delight. When my brother finally pumped his bicycle--without training wheels--from our house to the corner and back, he came home with the grinnies. When I was little, my mother's announcement that we would have homemade ice cream for dessert always gave me the grinnies. My father had the grinnies when I was valedictorian. Grinnies can be brought on by a good meal, a sense of pride, a new friend, a telephone call from someone special, an accomplishment. Or sometimes one gets the grinnies for no reason at all: just a sudden sense of well-being can bring on a case. Whatever brings them on, an attack of the grinnies is among life's greatest pleasures.

More examples to clarify the use of the term

6

Conclusion links to previous paragraph through transition "In fact" and to paragraph 2, contributing to the unity in the essay.

In fact, now that I look back on the experience, I feel sorry for my seventh-grade teacher. I think it's a pity that she didn't know the word <u>grinnies</u>. It's such a useful term for saying, "I'm really, really pleased!"

7

➤ **FOR WRITING OR DISCUSSION**

1. What is the author's attitude toward her subject?
2. What is the writer's thesis in the essay? What transitions does the writer use to create coherence?
3. What methods of development does the writer use in defining the term?
4. What examples could you give—other than those used by the author—of situations that could produce the grinnies?
5. Write an informal definition of a word or term used by some particular group or in a special region of the country. You might select a word like *wannabe, dude, honcho, hack,* or *dweeb*—or another of your own choosing.

In another informal definition paper, the next writer uses a humorous analogy to explain a term with which most of us are too familiar—the *gimmies.* Although the word sounds like grinnies, the papers about the two words are quite different.

Devra Danforth

Gimmies: The Unrecognized Disease

Millions of Americans are suffering from a disease that, although it has reached epidemic proportions, is not even recognized by the American Medical Association. There are no telethons to raise money for research and no government-funded programs searching for a cure.

1

This disease does not attack the muscles or bones, and it doesn't leave its victims bedridden or physically deformed. It doesn't limit itself to a specific age: Children, teenagers, and adults are frequent victims. It gives no advance warning, yet it can turn a smiling, normal person into a howling banshee or

2

a whining wimp in a matter of minutes. The illness I speak of is the <u>gimmies</u>, a group of related diseases characterized by uncontrollable expressions of desire and demands for immediate gratification.

3   All of us have seen the gimmies, and most of us recognize them. Picture the small child, standing quietly with his mother in a checkout line, who suddenly spies a toy and is instantly struck down with a case of Infantile Gimmies. He is so overcome by his desire for the toy that he grabs for it. As his mother tries to stop him, the secondary stage of the gimmies strikes, causing him to whine, pout, pull away, and stomp his foot.

4   Teenagers are frequently overcome by a recurring form of Peer Gimmies. Parents can cite repeated cases of hearing, "But everyone else has one, why can't I?" The secondary stage of Peer Gimmies includes pleading, sulking, tirades, and, often, the slamming of doors.

5   The most virulent type of the disease, and the one least subject to cure, is the Adult Gimmies. The dominant symptom of Adult Gimmies is dissatisfaction, often revealed by such expressions as "gimmie love," "gimmie a pat on the back," "gimmie a break," "gimmie fulfillment," "gimmie peace of mind," "gimmie a meaningful relationship," and "gimmie satisfying and worthwhile work." In the secondary stage of the disease, the victim often experiences divorce, macramé classes, and consciousness-raising groups. During this stage, the victim may frequently utter the expression, "gimmie a drink."

6   The gimmies are widespread, and as each new fad breaks, or whenever some new status gizmo comes on the market, there is a fresh outbreak. Medical technology is so advanced that it is on

```
the verge of giving people artificial hearts, but, to date, no
one has even come close to finding a cure for the gimmies.
```

➤ **FOR WRITING OR DISCUSSION**

1. Give a one-sentence definition of the *gimmies.*
2. What method of development does the writer use in defining the discussed term?
3. Think of a current fad or trend that you can characterize by one word and write an informal definition of the word.

Models of Writing

The reading selections that follow provide examples of extended definitions. As you study them, see if you can identify the methods of development that help make them good definitions.

DAVID OWEN
―――――――――――
The Perfect Job

The perfect job—the one you would have if you could have any job in the world— what would it be?

The most nearly perfect part of any less-than-perfect job is usually the occasional hou in which you are able to pretend that you are doing the job when in fact you are reading a magazine and eating candy. The rest of the office is throbbing frantically, but you are sitting quietly at your desk and learning interesting facts about Fergie and that guy who put his wife in the wood chipper. The perfect job would feel like that, but all the time.

The trouble with less-than-perfect jobs is that they usually don't swoop you up and   3
fling you through your day. That is, you don't very often look up at the clock to find out how many minutes past eleven it is and discover that it's five and time to go home. That's what the perfect job would be like. The time would zoom by, the way it does when you are going through some old boxes and suddenly discover that they are filled with artifacts from the Pilgrim days.

Well, I've thought about this a lot (while I was supposed to be doing something   4
else), and I've narrowed down my choice of the perfect job to five possibilities:

- Doing an unbelievably great cleanup of my basement, and organizing my workshop   5
  so that I know exactly where everything is, and drawing up a lot of plans to show
  how I might expand my workshop so that it would fill the entire basement instead of
  only the third that it fills now, and buying every conceivable kind of woodworking

tool and finding exactly the perfect place to keep each one, but never actually getting around to doing any woodworking projects.

6   • Doing the *Times* crossword puzzle and watching MTV while listening to people I knew in college discuss their marital problems on the other side of a one-way mirror.

7   • Sorting my children's vast Lego collection—by type, size, and color—into muffin tins and other containers while my children nearby happily build small vehicles and structures without hitting each other or asking me for something to eat.

8   • Setting the prison sentences of criminals convicted in highly publicized court cases; making all parole decisions for these people; receiving daily updates on how they spend their time in jail.

9   • Touring the houses of strangers and looking through their stuff while they're not there. If I were driving along and happened to see a house that looked interesting, I could pull over and let myself in with a set of master keys. If the people happened to be there, I could spray them with a harmless paralyzing gas that would prevent them from remembering that I had read their diaries and checked to see whether they were making efficient use of their limited amount of storage space, which they probably wouldn't have been.

10   All these jobs, as I see them, would require a full complement of office supplies: every conceivable kind of clip and clasp, name-brand ball-point pens, ungunked-up bottles of correction fluid, ammo-like refills for various desktop mechanisms, and cool, smooth, hard pads of narrow-lined paper. I guess I would also need a fax machine and a staff of cheerful recent college graduates eager to do my bidding. Plus a really great benefits program that would pay not only for doctors and prescription drugs but also for things like deodorant.

11   Recently I've begun to think that my *real* perfect job would probably consist of all five of my *possible* perfect jobs, one for each weekday. That way I would never have to lie awake at night wondering whether sorting my children's Legos would have made me happier than snooping through people's tax returns. Then, on weekends, I could hang around my house, drinking beer and watching golf tournaments on TV. I would seem to be having a really great time, but in reality I would be counting the hours until Monday and just itching to get back to work.

➤ **FOR WRITING OR DISCUSSION**

1. How does paragraph 2 establish the humorous context of the essay? What other elements of humor do you find?
2. What important element of the perfect job does Owen establish in paragraph 3? Do you agree that for a job to be perfect, the time ought to "zoom by"? Why, or why not?
3. Outline the five possibilities in Owen's choice of the perfect job. You know that the writer is not serious about these elements. What, then, is he trying to accomplish?
4. Write a definition essay in which you answer the question posed in the first paragraph.

ROBERT KEITH MILLER

Discrimination Is a Virtue

When I was a child, my grandmother used to tell me a story about a king who had   1
three daughters and decided to test their love. He asked each of them, "How
much do you love me?" The first replied that she loved him as much as all the diamonds and pearls in the world. The second said that she loved him more than life itself.
The third replied, "I love you as much as fresh meat loves salt."

This answer enraged the king; he was convinced that his youngest daughter was   2
making fun of him. So he banished her from his realm and left all of his property to her
elder sisters.

As the story unfolded it became clear, even to a 6-year-old, that the king had made   3
a terrible mistake. The two older girls were hypocrites, and as soon as they had profited
from their father's generosity, they began to treat him very badly. A wiser man would
have realized that the youngest daughter was the truest. Without attempting to flatter,
she had said, in effect, "We go together naturally; we are a perfect team."

Years later, when I came to read Shakespeare, I realized that my grandmother's   4
story was loosely based upon the story of King Lear, who put his daughters to a similar test and did not know how to judge the results. Attempting to save the king from
the consequences of his foolishness, a loyal friend pleads, "Come, sir, arise, away! I'll
teach you differences." Unfortunately, the lesson comes too late. Because Lear could
not tell the difference between true love and false, he loses his kingdom and eventually his life.

We have a word in English which means "the ability to tell differences." That word   5
is *discrimination.* But within the last twenty years, this word has been so frequently
misused that an entire generation has grown up believing that "discrimination" means
"racism." People are always proclaiming that "discrimination" is something that should
be done away with. Should that ever happen, it would prove to be our undoing.

Discrimination means discernment; it means the ability to perceive the truth, to use   6
good judgment and to profit accordingly. *The Oxford English Dictionary* traces this
understanding of the word back to 1648 and demonstrates that for the next 300 years,
"discrimination" was a virtue, not a vice. Thus, when a character in a nineteenth-
century novel makes a happy marriage, Dickens has another character remark, "It does
credit to your discrimination that you should have found such a very excellent young
woman."

Of course, "the ability to tell differences" assumes that differences exist, and this is   7
unsettling for a culture obsessed with the notion of equality. The contemporary belief
that discrimination is a vice stems from the compound "discriminate against." What we
need to remember, however, is that some things deserve to be judged harshly: we
should not leave our kingdoms to the selfish and the wicked.

Discrimination is wrong only when someone or something is discriminated against   8
because of prejudice. But to use the word in this sense, as so many people do, is to destroy
its true meaning. If you discriminate against something because of general preconceptions

rather than particular insights, then you are not discriminating—bias has clouded the clarity of vision which discrimination demands.

9   One of the great ironies of American life is that we manage to discriminate in the practical decisions of daily life, but usually fail to discriminate when we make public policies. Most people are very discriminating when it comes to buying a car, for example, because they realize that cars have differences. Similarly, an increasing number of people have learned to discriminate in what they eat. Some foods are better than others—and indiscriminate eating can undermine one's health.

10   Yet in public affairs, good judgment is depressingly rare. In many areas which involve the common good, we see a failure to tell differences.

11   Consider, for example, some of the thinking behind modern education. On the one hand, there is a refreshing realization that there are differences among children, and some children—be they gifted or handicapped—require special education. On the other hand, we are politically unable to accept the consequences of this perception. The trend in recent years has been to group together students of radically different ability. We call this process "mainstreaming," and it strikes me as a characteristically American response to the discovery of differences: we try to pretend that differences do not matter.

12   Similarly, we try to pretend that there is little difference between the sane and the insane. A fashionable line for argument is that "everybody is a little mad" and that few mental patients deserve long-term hospitalization. As a consequence of such reasoning, thousands of seriously ill men and women have been evicted from their hospital beds and returned to what is euphemistically called "the community" which often means being left to sleep on city streets, where confused and helpless people now live out of paper bags as the direct result of our refusal to discriminate.

13   Or to choose a final example from a different area: how many recent elections reflect thoughtful consideration of the genuine differences among candidates? Benumbed by television commercials that market aspiring officeholders as if they were a new brand of toothpaste or hair spray, too many Americans vote with only a fuzzy understanding of the issues in question. Like Lear, we seem too eager to leave the responsibility of government to others and too ready to trust those who tell us whatever we want to hear.

14   So as we look around us, we should recognize that "discrimination" is a virtue which we desperately need. We must try to avoid making unfair and arbitrary distinctions, but we must not go to the other extreme and pretend that there are no distinctions to be made. The ability to make intelligent judgments is essential both for the success of one's personal life and for the functioning of society as a whole. Let us be open-minded by all means, but not so open-minded that our brains fall out.

➤ **FOR WRITING OR DISCUSSION**

1. What is the thesis of Miller's essay? How is it related to the title? Why would someone who hasn't read the essay find the title surprising?
2. What author image does Miller project?

3. What methods of development does the author use? What is the point of the King Lear story? Of the quote from Dickens?
4. How does Miller try to refine our definition of *discrimination?* Is he successful? Why, or why not?
5. Why does the author believe that good judgment is "depressingly rare" in public affairs? What examples does he provide to support this point?
6. Choose a term that usually has a negative connotation but that you believe is wrongly or inadequately used because people do not acknowledge its positive meaning. (For example, *fear, aggression, hunger for power,* or *shyness* might have unrecognized positive qualities.) Write a definition essay for the term you select.

ELLEN GOODMAN

The New Ambidexters

The political expert explained it carefully over dinner. The country, he said, is turning to the right, but the New Right is farther to the left than it used to be. At the same time, the Left is farther to the right than it was in the Old Days when it was called the New Left.   1

By the time he was through chronicling the evolution of politics in America, I was totally unable to remember which hand I was supposed to cut my food with. Was it the right or the left, and was it important?   2

Now, I had read the Gallup poll, which said that 47 percent of the American people consider themselves to be right of center, and I had heard the accounts of the new conservative bash at the St. Regis hotel in New York last week. But, to be perfectly frank about it, I don't think that we can understand what's going on in politics in the classical terms of political anatomy. I don't think we are turning to the right, or the left, for that matter. I think most of us are turning ambidextrous.   3

To sound more trendy about the whole thing, we seem to have become The New Ambidexters.   4

There is much more widespread uncertainty, often a frustrating sense of the complexity of social issues. Every time someone offers a solution someone else offers a criticism. Most of us have become walking dialecticians, carrying our own debates in our arms. We are constantly arguing with ourselves—"on the one hand . . . on the other hand. . . ." We are, in short, card-carrying members of the New Ambidextrous Party.   5

The New Ambidexters believe, for example, that on the one hand, government should provide services and, on the other hand, government should keep out of our lives. The New Ambidexters believe that the corporations have murderously gunked up the environment and put ruinous chemicals in our food, but that government regulations interfere too much with business.   6

The New Ambidexters believe that welfare mothers should get off the dole and go to work, and that mothers of small children should stay home with them. They believe that we've all become far too selfish, too "me-first," but that individuals have the right to lead their lives as they choose.   7

8   The Ambidexters simply hold onto a wide range of opinions simultaneously, without always seeing them as contradictory. They want government to provide more and cost less. They want security and independence. They believe in responsibility and freedom.

9   The same people who rue the disruption of the family don't believe that people should be forced to stay in rotten marriages. The same people who believe in roots and community believe—on the other hand—in mobility and adventure.

10   Most of them, of course, weren't born ambidextrous. They have lived long enough to see the cost accounting of change.

11   They have seen that change, even the solutions, comes with a full attachment of new problems. When the government sets up a program to help those who can't work, they end up also helping those who won't work. When the government helps the aged who don't have families to depend on, they end up with more aged depending on the government instead of families. As divorce becomes more acceptable in society, there are more divorces for society to accept.

12   The Ambidexters don't want to go back to the thirties or the fifties. Few people want to remove the Social Security system or take away compensation for unemployment. They have no interest in returning to desperation. But when they look ahead to the future they weigh the issues in both hands.

13   The Ambidexters are aware that there are still serious social problems. They believe that government should Do Something. National health care. Day care. Welfare reform. But there are the other problems. Big government. Family responsibility. Taxes.

14   So, in view of the complexity of the situation, the one solution the Ambidexters seem to have agreed upon for the moment is to sit on their hands. The right hand, and the left.

➤ FOR WRITING OR DISCUSSION

1. What is Goodman's thesis in the essay? What sentences best describe the subject?
2. Who do you think is Goodman's audience? In what kind of publication do you think this essay first appeared? How can you tell? What is the author's tone—her attitude toward the subject?
3. What methods of development does Goodman use to define *ambidextrous* in a new way? Where do comparison and contrast serve? Illustration?
4. What do you think of the final paragraph? How does it relate to the thesis? How does it contribute to the overall humor of the essay?
5. Are you or your friends or relatives part of the "New Ambidexters"? Explain why, or why not.
6. Write a definition paper called "The New _____ ," filling in the blank with a term that helps you define some political, social, or economic situation in today's world. You might want to define terms like *The New Generation X, The New Volunteers, The New Travelers, The New Writers, The New Managers, The New Poor,* or *The New Consumer.*

JANICE CASTRO, WITH DAN COOK AND CRISTINA GARCIA

Spanglish

In Manhattan a first-grader greets her visiting grandparents, happily exclaiming, "Come   1
here, *siéntate!*" Her bemused grandfather, who does not speak Spanish, nevertheless
knows she is asking him to sit down. A Miami personnel officer understands what a job
applicant means when he says, "*Quiero un* part time." Nor do drivers miss a beat reading a billboard alongside a Los Angeles street advertising CERVEZA—SIX PACK!

This free-form blend of Spanish and English, known as Spanglish, is common lin-   2
guistic currency wherever concentrations of Hispanic Americans are found in the U.S.
In Los Angeles, where 55% of the city's 3 million inhabitants speak Spanish, Spanglish
is as much a part of daily life as sunglasses. Unlike the broken-English efforts of earlier
immigrants from Europe, Asia and other regions, Spanglish has become a widely
accepted conversational mode used casually—even playfully—by Spanish-speaking
immigrants and native-born Americans alike.

Consisting of one part Hispanicized English, one part Americanized Spanish and   3
more than a little fractured syntax, Spanglish is a bit like a Robin Williams comedy routine: a crackling line of cross-cultural patter straight from the melting pot. Often it
enters Anglo homes and families through the children, who pick it up at school or at
play with their young Hispanic contemporaries. In other cases, it comes from watching
TV; many an Anglo child watching *Sesame Street* has learned *uno dos tres* almost as
quickly as one two three.

Spanglish takes a variety of forms, from the Southern California Anglos who bid   4
farewell with the utterly silly "*hasta la* bye-bye" to the Cuban-American drivers in
Miami who *parquean* their *carros*. Some Spanglish sentences are mostly Spanish, with
a quick detour for an English word or two. A Latino friend may cut short a conversation
by glancing at his watch and excusing himself with the explanation that he must "*ir al*
supermarket."

Many of the English words transplanted in this way are simply handier than their   5
Spanish counterparts. No matter how distasteful the subject, for example, it is still easier to say "income tax" than *impuesto sobre la renta*. At the same time, many Spanish-
speaking immigrants have adopted such terms as VCR, microwave and dishwasher for
what they view as largely American phenomena. Still other English words convey a
cultural context that is not implicit in the Spanish. A friend who invites you to a *lonche*
most likely has in mind the brisk American custom of "doing lunch" rather than the lan-
guorous afternoon break traditionally implied by *almuerzo*.

Mainstream Americans exposed to similar hybrids of German, Chinese or Hindi   6
might be mystified. But even Anglos who speak little or no Spanish are somewhat
familiar with Spanglish. Living among them, for one thing, are 19 million Hispanics. In
addition, more American high school and university students sign up for Spanish than
for any other foreign language.

Only in the past ten years, though, has Spanglish begun to turn into a national   7
slang. Its popularity has grown with the explosive increases in U.S. immigration from

Latin American countries. English has increasingly collided with Spanish in retail stores, offices and classrooms, in pop music and on street corners. Anglos whose ancestors picked up such Spanish words as *rancho, bronco, tornado* and *incommunicado,* for instance, now freely use such Spanish words as *gracias, bueno, amigo* and *por favor.*

8   Among Latinos, Spanglish conversations often flow more easily from Spanish into several sentences of English and back.

9   Spanglish is a sort of code for Latinos: the speakers know Spanish, but their hybrid language reflects the American culture in which they live. Many lean to shorter, clipped phrases in place of the longer, more graceful expressions their parents used. Says Leonel de la Cuesta, an assistant professor of modern languages at Florida International University in Miami: "In the U.S., time is money, and that is showing up in Spanglish as an economy of language." Conversational examples: *taipiar* (type) and *winshi-wiper* (windshield wiper) replace *escribir a máquina* and *limpiaparabrisas.*

10   Major advertisers, eager to tap the estimated $134 billion in spending power wielded by Spanish-speaking Americans, have ventured into Spanglish to promote their products. In some cases, attempts to sprinkle Spanish through commercials have produced embarrassing gaffes. A Braniff airlines ad that sought to tell Spanish-speaking audiences they could settle back *en* (in) luxuriant *cuero* (leather) seats, for example, inadvertently said they could fly without clothes (*encuero*). A fractured translation of the Miller Lite slogan told readers the beer was "Filling, and less delicious." Similar blunders are often made by Anglos trying to impress Spanish-speaking pals. But if Latinos are amused by mangled Spanglish, they also recognize these goofs as a sort of friendly acceptance. As they might put it, *no problema.*

➤ FOR WRITING OR DISCUSSION

1. What is the thesis of Castro's essay?
2. What is the writer's purpose? Who is her audience?
3. Why is the use of Spanglish confined pretty much to cities? Why is it a relatively new phenomenon?
4. What kinds of words do English speakers borrow from Spanish speakers? Spanish speakers from English speakers? Why does each group take words from the other?
5. Many linguistic purists abhor the infusion of other languages into their language. In France, for example, government agencies have directed tirades against words like *le weekend* or *le drugstore.* What is your opinion about absorbing words from one language into another?
6. Write an essay to explore how another group has infused the English language with new words or with fresh meanings for old words. You might want to write about military language, adolescent language, rock language, or the language of the drug culture, among others. Give this effect a catchy name (as Castro has used the word *Spanglish*), and provide examples as you define the phenomenon.

ANDREW DELBANCO

Are You Happy Yet?

A couple of weeks ago, I picked up a new magazine called Simplicity, whose pre-
miere issue features "a quiz to test your happiness quotient." To help improve your
score, it offers a Web site, www.simplicityonline.com, dedicated to creating "a virtual
universe that's not just about making your life easier, but also more euphoric." When I
got home and checked the mail, I found another interesting artifact: a brochure promising happiness from a few spurts of a new "stud spray" (derived from "bushy herbs"
favored by Bulgarians and Brazilian tribesmen). Pump some under the tongue, and—
presto!—you'll "Go From Zero to Hero."

    The happiness business is booming in America, and it seems to have entered a new
phase of hype and strain. Driven, like every going concern, by consumer demand, it
has been a big business at least since Thomas Jefferson dropped the final term from
John Locke's enumeration of human rights—"life, liberty, and ... property"—and
replaced it with what would become the motto of the new nation: "the pursuit of happiness." But even though Jefferson proclaimed the truths of the Declaration of Independence to be "self-evident," it has never been entirely clear what Americans mean by
happiness. Like love, it is a word that evokes for each of us some private memory or
hope that cannot be fully disclosed to others. Yet it is also a word with a public history,
one worth retrieving.

    Lately the pursuit of happiness has become a mainly private activity. Americans
take mood drugs to fire up the happiness circuits of the brain and go to the gym to
release happiness endorphins. Phrases like "job satisfaction" and "personal growth," by
which we assess our careers and marriages, have become part of the language, while
terms like commonweal, and even citizenship—in which there lingers a residual sense
of public goo and private obligation—sound archaic.

    This succession from public to private notions of happiness is the culmination of a
long historical process. In early America, especially in New England, the idea of personal
happiness was close to incomprehensible. Even the word itself was rare, except in its
adverbial form, as in "happily humbled"; expressions like "peace of conscience" or "comfort of heart" were more common. Happiness required deferral. It waited for death to dis-
pel the sorrows of life. The place where it would be fulfilled was heaven, where petty
rivalries would be swept away by the flood of God's love, and where human souls,
released from mutable bodies, would achieve perfect harmony through a kind of tele-
pathic closeness with one another. Certain experiences in this world, like communal wor-
ship or spousal love, might afford a foretaste of happiness, but it was only in the next world
that it could fully be known, and it was always envisioned as a profoundly social emotion.

    The exile of happiness to the future life could not, and did not, last. Under pressure
from Enlightenment rationality, religion acceded slowly (more slowly than in Europe)
to what Garry Wills has called the "displacement of man's hopes from the hereafter" to
the here and now. As a result, "a note of possible heresy in the way men had begun
to talk of happiness" crept into public discourse. Locke used the term in a spirit of
lamentation rather than commendation, as if he were describing creatures no more

likely to reach their goals than dogs chasing their tails: we "think ourselves happy... But as soon as any new uneasiness comes in, this happiness is disturbed and we are set afresh on work in the pursuit of happiness." This was an arduous, treadmill idea of happiness by which human beings are eternally condemned to anticipate the loss of present pleasures and to live in a perpetual state of craving. "Our desires," Locke wrote, always "look beyond our present enjoyments and carry the mind out to absent *good*." Earthly delights like sex, good food or pleasing circumstances merely taunt us with their brevity and give way to renewed longing. Yet by the time Jefferson included "the pursuit of happiness" among the rights of man, the phrase had become a psychological and a political, rather than a theological, term.

6   But if the consolatory force of religion had diminished, the need for some conception of happiness that was immune to time had not. What could take its place? The Scottish moralist Francis Hutcheson—another influence on Jefferson—stated in a sentence the consensual answer to this question: "The surest way to promote his private happiness" is for a man "to do publicly useful actions." Jefferson and his contemporaries believed that happiness could be attained only if and when one could look back on one's life and see that it had had good effects on the lives of others.

7   To believe this was not merely to wish that virtue should be its own reward. It was to make a universal claim that human beings are born with a "moral sense," an impulse to altruism that atrophies if it is not exercised. People, as the cybernetic metaphor now has it, are "hard wired" to do good in order to enhance their own happiness. In its 18th-century version, this theory about the inner life paralleled emerging scientific theories about the outer world: it said that a happy person existing alone without exchanging the energy of benevolence with other people is inconceivable, like a celestial body orbiting around nothing.

8   As expansive as it may have been in some respects, this neoclassic ideal of virtuous citizenship was also scandalously limited. Despite Jefferson's revision of Locke, property (which chiefly meant land) remained the precondition for happiness: it protected against the temptations of corruption, freed the self for inquiry and contemplation and, through the mechanisms of inheritance, fostered a sense of connection to the past and to posterity. Most Americans were simply left out—city dwellers, wage earners, debtors and men of commerce who depended on what Jefferson called the "caprice of customers" for their livelihood. Women did not qualify because they were barely allowed to own anything. And slaves, by definition, were forbidden to own even themselves.

9   Aware that these restrictions posed a threat to their egalitarian ideals, Jefferson and his successors spoke of women and slaves as if they, too, were capable of a certain kind of happiness—but it was an inferior type akin to the frivolity of childhood. Slaves, as one United States senator later put it, are "happy, content, unaspiring and utterly incapable, from intellectual weakness, ever to give us any trouble by their aspirations." After slavery had been forcibly abolished, a Georgia editor remarked without compunction about improverished rural blacks, "I do not think that poverty disturbs their happiness at all." One of the startling features of the history of happiness is the brazenness with which people in power have assured themselves of the happiness of the powerless.

10   Ultimately, the Jeffersonian ideal of what might be called landed happiness could not be reconciled with the deprivations of those on whose labor and service it depended.

Once the Civil War had destroyed what remained of the landed gentry, old civic and paternalistic notions of happiness gave way before the new spirit of free-market capitalism. In many respects, this system proved a boon to happiness, by creating a society of previously unimaginable prosperity. But based on the idea that self-interest ultimately works for the collective good, it reversed the relation between self and community with which the country began. Public happiness was once deemed necessary for private happiness; today, private wants come first, and public needs have become an afterthought.

This modern idea of happiness had been presciently described by Alexis de Tocqueville, who toured the United States early in the 19th century. Well aware that the Old World's static class structure could stifle human aspirations, Tocqueville admired the zeal with which Americans sought to achieve whatever material comforts they witnessed their friends and neighbors enjoying.   11

But as Tocqueville saw, the competitive pursuit of wealth requires the stamina of youth and can be haunted by the fear of age and death. "Men easily attain a certain equality of condition," he wrote, "but they can never attain as much as they desire....They are near enough to see its charms, but too far off to enjoy them; and before they have fully tasted its delights, they die." Americans, he found, were afflicted by a "strange melancholy...in the midst of their abundance."   12

Today the notion that "abundance" and freedom ensure happiness no longer meets much articulate resistance. Of the few remaining countercurrents of discontent, some take the form of bitter irony. An example is Todd Solondz's deliberately repugnant 1998 movie "Happiness" (shelved in the Dysfunctional Families section of my local video store), in which men live miserably from ejaculation to ejaculation while women torment themselves in the frantic pursuit of love. Or they take the form of New Age therapies like those recommended in the Dalai Lama's book "The Art of Happiness," which shares the best-seller lists with the latest manuals for achieving hot sex and renovating the weekend house. Or—as in the Simplicity Web site—they take the form of a technologically assisted return to pastoral purity. The old imperative that personal fulfillment depends on active engagement with helping others also survives—in families, churches, charities, service professions like medicine and teaching and support organizations like Alcoholics Anonymous. And now and then it flares up in the words of a maverick politician. But in most forms of public discourse it has become a muted platitude.   13

Achieving happiness has become an overwhelmingly personal, private, even solitary undertaking. It is understood to require an infinite array of choices and the power to move among them as if you were sampling or grazing your way through life. But abundance and freedom can bewilder as well as liberate, and many Americans—not just evangelicals—are reverting to Williams James's view that "happiness in the absolute and everlasting is what we find nowhere but in religion." And while the premise on which Jefferson's pursuit of happiness was based—that some human beings must be masters and others slaves—has properly become outrageous to us, his conviction that happiness can best be found in selfless service remains a driving motive in many lives.   14

Religious and civic pieties have often cloaked cruelty and hatred, and there is no reason to believe that people in the past lived consistently by the principles they avowed. But it is not merely nostalgic to respect earlier conceptions of happiness. Maybe those who held them were onto something in suspecting that when people spin   15 faster and faster in the pursuit of merely personal happiness, they become exhausted in the futile effort of chasing themselves.

➤ FOR WRITING OR DISCUSSION

1. What definition of *happiness* does Delbanco support?
2. What author image does he project?
3. What audience is the writer attempting to reach? How do you know?
4. Where does Delbanco use comparison-and-contrast strategies in his essay? Who do you think he uses them?
5. How has he used expert testimony in this essay? What effect do the quotations and paraphrases from historical figures contribute to the essay?
6. What does Jefferson's idea of virtuous citizenship have to do with happiness?
7. What, according to Delbanco, is our notion of happiness today?
8. Write your own definition of happiness. How does your definition compare with Delbanco's?

HAVING YOUR SAY

Write an essay in which you argue for or against the value of abundance and freedom as opposed to selfless service (see Delbanco's essay to review the meaning of these terms) as the key to happiness. Draw on Delbanco's essay as well as your other reading, films or television programs you've seen, and (or) your own experience.

Readings for Writing

Use the two stories that follow as the basis of a definition paper of your own. As you read the first story, try to decide what word the title "A Tree. A Rock. A Cloud." is trying to define.

CARSON McCULLERS

A Tree. A Rock. A Cloud.

It was raining that morning, and still very dark. When the boy reached the streetcar café he had almost finished his route and he went in for a cup of coffee. The place was an all-night café owned by a bitter and stingy man called Leo. After the raw, empty

street the café seemed friendly and bright: along the counter there were a couple of soldiers, three spinners from the cotton mill, and in a corner a man who sat hunched over
with his nose and his face down in a beer mug. The boy wore a helmet such as aviators
wear. When he went into the café he unbuckled the chin strap and raised the right flap
up over his pink little ear; often as he drank his coffee someone would speak to him in
a friendly way. But this morning Leo did not look into his face and none of the men
were talking. He paid and was leaving the café when a voice called out to him:

'Son! Hey Son!'   2

He turned back and the man in the corner was crooking his finger and nodding to   3
him. He had brought his face out of the beer mug and he seemed suddenly very happy.
The man was long and pale, with a big nose and faded orange hair.

'Hey Son!'   4

The boy went toward him. He was an undersized boy of about twelve, with one   5
shoulder drawn higher than the other because of the weight of the paper sack. His face
was shallow, freckled, and his eyes were round child eyes.

'Yeah Mister?'   6

The man laid one hand on the paper boy's shoulders, then grasped the boy's chin   7
and turned his face slowly from one side to the other. The boy shrank back uneasily.

'Say! What's the big idea?'   8

The boy's voice was shrill; inside the café it was suddenly very quiet.   9

The man said slowly: 'I love you.'   10

All along the counter the men laughed. The boy, who had scowled and sidled away,   11
did not know what to do. He looked over the counter at Leo, and Leo watched him
with a weary, brittle jeer. The boy tried to laugh also. But the man was serious and sad.

'I did not mean to tease you, Son,' he said. 'Sit down and have a beer with me.   12
There is something I have to explain.'

Cautiously, out of the corner of his eye, the paper boy questioned the men along   13
the counter to see what he should do. But they had gone back to their beer or their
breakfast and did not notice him. Leo put a cup of coffee on the counter and a little jug
of cream.

'He is a minor,' Leo said.   14

The paper boy slid himself up onto the stool. His ear beneath the upturned flap of   15
the helmet was very small and red. The man was nodding at him soberly. 'It is important,' he said. Then he reached in his hip pocket and brought out something which he
held up in the palm of his hand for the boy to see.

'Look very carefully,' he said.   16

The boy stared, but there was nothing to look at very carefully. The man held in his 17
big, grimy palm a photograph. It was the face of a woman, but blurred, so that only the
hat and dress she was wearing stood out clearly.

'See?' the man asked.   18

The boy nodded and the man placed another picture in his palm. The woman was   19
standing on a beach in a bathing suit. The suit made her stomach look very big, and
that was the main thing you noticed.

'Got a good look?' He leaned over closer and finally asked: 'You ever seen her   20
before?'

21   The boy sat motionless, staring slantwise at the man. 'Not so I know of.'

22   'Very well.' The man blew on the photographs and put them back into his pocket. 'That was my wife.'

23   'Dead?' the boy asked.

24   Slowly the man shook his head. He pursed his lips as though about to whistle and answered in a long-drawn way: 'Nuuu—' he said. 'I will explain.'

25   The beer on the counter before the man was in a large brown mug. He did not pick it up to drink. Instead he bent down and, putting his face over the rim, he rested there for a moment. Then with both hands he tilted the mug and sipped.

26   'Some night you'll go to sleep with your nose in a mug and drown,' said Leo. 'Prominent transient drowns in beer. That would be a cute death.'

27   The paper boy tried to signal to Leo. While the man was not looking he screwed up his face and worked his mouth to question soundlessly: 'Drunk?' But Leo only raised his eyebrows and turned away to put some pink strips of bacon on the grill. The man pushed the mug away from him, straightened himself, and folded his loose crooked hands on the counter. His face was sad as he looked at the paper boy. He did not blink, but from time to time the lids closed down with delicate gravity over his pale green eyes. It was nearing dawn and the boy shifted the weight of the paper sack.

28   'I am talking about love,' the man said. 'With me it is a science.'

29   The boy half slid down from the stool. But the man raised his forefinger, and there was something about him that held the boy and would not let him go away.

30   'Twelve years ago I married the woman in the photograph. She was my wife for one year, nine months, three days, and two nights. I loved her. Yes . . . ' He tightened his blurred, rambling voice and said again: 'I loved her. I thought also that she loved me. I was a railroad engineer. She had all home comforts and luxuries. It never crept into my brain that she was not satisfied. But do you know what happened?'

31   'Mgneeow!' said Leo.

32   The man did not take his eyes from the boy's face. 'She left me. I came in one night and the house was empty and she was gone. She left me.'

33   'With a fellow?' the boy asked.

34   Gently the man placed his palm down on the counter. 'Why naturally, Son. A woman does not run off like that alone.'

35   The café was quiet, the soft rain black and endless in the street outside. Leo pressed down the frying bacon with the prongs of his long fork. 'So you have been chasing the floozie for eleven years. You frazzled old rascal.'

36   For the first time the man glanced at Leo. 'Please don't be vulgar. Besides, I was not speaking to you.' He turned back to the boy and said in a trusting and secretive undertone: 'Let's not pay any attention to him. O.K.?'

37   The paper boy nodded doubtfully.

38   'It was like this,' the man continued. 'I am a person who feels many things. All my life one thing after another. But the point is that when I had enjoyed anything there was a peculiar sensation as though it was laying around loose in me. Nothing seemed to finish up or fit in with the other things. Women? I had my portion of them. The same. Afterwards laying around loose in me. I was a man who never loved.'

Very slowly he closed his eyelids, and the gesture was like a curtain drawn at the   39
end of a scene in a play. When he spoke again his voice was excited and the words
came fast—the lobes of his large, loose ears seemed to tremble.

'Then I met this woman. I was fifty-one and she always said she was thirty. I met her   40
at a filling station and we were married within three days. And do you know what it
was like? I just can't tell you. All I had ever felt was gathered together around this
woman. Nothing lay loose in me any more but was finished up by her.'

The man stopped suddenly and stroked his long nose. His voice sank down to a   41
steady and reproachful undertone: 'I'm not explaining this right. What happened was
this. There were these beautiful feelings and loose little pleasures inside me. And this
woman was something like an assembly line for my soul. I run these little pieces of
myself through her and I come out complete. Now do you follow me?'

'What was her name?' the boy asked.   42

'Oh,' he said. 'I called her Dodo. But that is immaterial.'   43

'Did you try to make her come back?'   44

The man did not seem to hear. 'Under the circumstances you can imagine how I felt   45
when she left me.'

Leo took the bacon from the grill and folded two strips of it between a bun. He had a   46
gray face, with slitted eyes, and a pinched nose saddled by faint blue shadows. One of the
mill workers signaled for more coffee and Leo poured it. He did not give refills on coffee
free. The spinner ate breakfast there every morning, but the better Leo knew his customers
the stingier he treated them. He nibbled his own bun as though he grudged it to himself.

'And you never got hold of her again?'   47

The boy did not know what to think of the man, and his child's face was uncertain   48
with mingled curiosity and doubt. He was new on the paper route; it was still strange to
him to be out on the town on the black, queer early morning.

'Yes,' the man said. 'I took a number of steps to get her back. I went around trying to   49
locate her. I went to Tulsa where she had folks. And to Mobile. I went to every town she
had ever mentioned to me, and I hunted down every man she had formerly been connected with. Tulsa, Atlanta, Chicago, Cheehaw, Memphis . . . For the better part of two
years I chased around the country trying to lay hold of her.'

'But the pair of them had vanished from the face of the earth!' said Leo.   50

'Don't listen to him,' the man said confidentially. 'And also just forget those two   51
years. They are not important. What matters is that around the third year a curious thing
began to happen to me.'

'What?' the boy asked.   52

The man leaned down and tilted his mug to take a sip of beer. But as he hovered   53
over the mug his nostrils fluttered slightly; he sniffed the staleness of the beer and did
not drink. 'Love is a curious thing to begin with. At first I thought only of getting her
back. It was a kind of mania. But then as time went on I tried to remember her. But do
you know what happened?'

'No,' the boy said.   54

'When I laid myself down on a bed and tried to think about her my mind became a   55
blank. I couldn't see her. I would take out her pictures and look. No good. Nothing
doing. A blank. Can you imagine it?'

56   'Say Mac!' Leo called down the counter. 'Can you imagine this bozo's mind a blank!'

57   Slowly, as though fanning away flies, the man waved his hand. His green eyes were concentrated and fixed on the shallow little face of the paper boy.

58   'But a sudden piece of glass on a sidewalk. Or a nickel tune in a music box. A shadow on a wall at night. And I would remember. It might happen in a street and I would cry or bang my head against a lamppost. You follow me?'

59   'A piece of glass . . . ' the boy said.

60   'Anything. I would walk around and I had no power of how and when to remember her. You think you can put up a kind of shield. But remembering don't come to a man face forward—it corners around sideways. I was at the mercy of everything I saw and heard. Suddenly instead of me combing the countryside to find her she begun to chase me around in my very soul. *She* chasing *me,* mind you! And in my soul.'

61   The boy asked finally: 'What part of the country were you in then?'

62   'Ooh,' the man groaned. 'I was a sick mortal. It was like smallpox. I confess, Son, that I boozed. I fornicated. I committed any sin that suddenly appealed to me. I am loath to confess it but I will do so. When I recall that period it is all curdled in my mind, it was so terrible.'

63   The man leaned his head down and tapped his forehead on the counter. For a few seconds he stayed bowed over in this position, the back of his stringy neck covered with orange furze, his hands with their long warped fingers held palm to palm in an attitude of prayer. Then the man straightened himself; he was smiling and suddenly his face was bright and tremulous and old.

64   'It was in the fifth year that it happened,' he said. 'And with it I started my science.'

65   Leo's mouth jerked with a pale, quick grin. 'Well none of we boys are getting any younger,' he said. Then with a sudden anger he balled up a dishcloth he was holding and threw it down hard on the floor. 'You draggle-tailed old Romeo!'

66   'What happened?' the boy asked.

67   The old man's voice was high and clear: 'Peace,' he answered.

68   'Huh?'

69   'It is hard to explain scientifically, Son,' he said. 'I guess the logical explanation is that she and I had fleed around from each other for so long that finally we just got tangled up together and lay down and quit. Peace. A queer and beautiful blankness. It was spring in Portland and the rain came every afternoon. All evening I just stayed there on my bed in the dark. And that is how the science come to me.'

70   The windows in the streetcar were pale blue with light. The two soldiers paid for their beers and opened the door—one of the soldiers combed his hair and wiped off his muddy puttees before they went outside. The three mill workers bent silently over their breakfasts. Leo's clock was ticking on the wall.

71   'It is this. And listen carefully. I meditated on love and reasoned it out. I reasoned it out. I realized what is wrong with us. Men fall in love for the first time. And what do they fall in love with?'

72   The boy's soft mouth was partly open and he did not answer.

73   'A woman,' the old man said. 'Without science, with nothing to go by, they undertake the most dangerous and sacred experience in God's earth. They fall in love with a woman. Is that correct, Son?'

'Yeah,' the boy said faintly.   74

'They start at the wrong end of love. They begin at the climax. Can you wonder it is   75
so miserable? Do you know how men should love?'

The old man reached over and grasped the boy by the collar of his leather jacket.   76
He gave him a gentle little shake and his green eyes gazed down unblinking and grave.

'Son, do you know how love should be begun?'   77

The boy sat small and listening and still. Slowly he shook his head. The old man   78
leaned closer and whispered:

'A tree. A rock. A cloud.'   79

It was still raining outside in the street: a mild, gray, endless rain. The mill whistle   80
blew for the six o'clock shift and the three spinners paid and went away. There was no
one in the café but Leo, the old man, and the little paper boy.

'The weather was like this in Portland,' he said. 'At the time my science was begun.   81
I meditated and I started very cautious. I would pick up something from the street and
take it home with me. I bought a goldfish and I concentrated on the goldfish and I loved
it. I graduated from one thing to another. Day by day I was getting this technique. On
the road from Portland to San Diego———'

'Aw shut up!' screamed Leo suddenly. 'Shut up! Shut up!'   82

The old man still held the collar of the boy's jacket; he was trembling and his   83
face was earnest and bright and wild. 'For six years now I have gone around by
myself and built up my science. And now I am a master. Son. I can love anything.
No longer do I have to think about it even. I see a street full of people and a beautiful light comes in me. I watch a bird in the sky. Or I meet a traveler on the road.
Everything, Son. And anybody. All stranger and all loved! Do you realize what a science like mine can mean?'

The boy held himself stiffly, his hands curled tight around the counter edge. Finally   84
he asked: 'Did you ever really find that lady?'

'What? What say, Son?'   85

'I mean,' the boy asked timidly, 'have you fallen in love with a woman again?'   86

The old man loosened his grasp on the boy's collar. He turned away and for the first   87
time his green eyes had a vague and scattered look. He lifted the mug from the counter,
drank down the yellow beer. His head was shaking slowly from side to side. Then
finally he answered: 'No, Son. You see that is the last step in my science. I go cautious.
And I am not quite ready yet.'

'Well!,' said Leo. 'Well well well!'   88

The old man stood in the open doorway. 'Remember,' he said. Framed there in the   89
gray damp light of the early morning he looked shrunken and seedy and frail. But his
smile was bright. 'Remember I love you,' he said with a last nod. And the door closed
quietly behind him.

The boy did not speak for a long time. He pulled down the bangs on his forehead   90
and slid his grimy little forefinger around the rim of his empty cup. Then without looking at Leo he finally asked:

'Was he drunk?'   91

'No,' said Leo shortly.   92

The boy raised his clear voice higher. 'Then was he a dope fiend?'   93

'No.'   94

95   The boy looked up at Leo, and his flat little face was desperate, his voice urgent and shrill. 'Was he crazy? Do you think he was a lunatic?' The paper boy's voice dropped suddenly with doubt. 'Leo? Or not?'

96   But Leo would not answer him. Leo had run a night café for fourteen years, and he held himself to be a critic of craziness. There were the town characters and also the transients who roamed in from the night. He knew the manias of all of them. But he did not want to satisfy the questions of the waiting child. He tightened his pale face and was silent.

97   So the boy pulled down the right flap of his helmet and as he turned to leave he made the only comment that seemed safe to him, the only remark that could not be laughed down and despised:

98   'He sure has done a lot of traveling.'

➤ **FOR WRITING OR DISCUSSION**

1. What is the main point of the story?
2. What kind of place is the café? McCullers fills it with oddball people. Why has she offered characters who seem so strange?
3. What has happened in the life of the man drinking the beer?
4. What is being defined here? How do "A tree. A rock. A cloud." establish the terms of the definition? The old man claims that he reasoned out the definition and that with him "it is a science." What does he mean? Do you accept the premises of his definition?
5. Why does the café owner refuse to answer the last questions put to him by the boy about the old man?
6. How do you think the old man truly feels about the woman who left him?
7. Write an essay in which you define *love*.

KURT VONNEGUT, JR.

Harrison Bergeron

1   The year was 2081, and everybody was finally equal. They weren't only equal before God and the law. They were equal every which way. Nobody was smarter than anybody else. Nobody was better looking than anybody else. Nobody was stronger or quicker than anybody else. All this equality was due to the 211th, 212th, and 213th Amendments to the Constitution, and to the unceasing vigilance of agents of the United States Handicapper General.

2   Some things about living still weren't quite right, though. April, for instance, still drove people crazy by not being springtime. And it was in that clammy month that the H-G men took George and Hazel Bergeron's fourteen-year-old son, Harrison, away.

3   It was tragic, all right, but George and Hazel couldn't think about it very hard. Hazel had a perfectly average intelligence, which meant she couldn't think about anything except in short bursts. And George, while his intelligence was way above normal, had a little mental handicap radio in his ear. He was required by law to wear it at all times. It was turned to

a government transmitter. Every twenty seconds or so, the transmitter would send out some sharp noise to keep people like George from taking unfair advantage of their brains.

George and Hazel were watching television. There were tears on Hazel's cheeks, but she'd forgotten for the moment what they were about.   4

On the television screen were ballerinas.   5

A buzzer sounded in George's head. His thoughts fled in panic, like bandits from a burglar alarm.   6

"That was a real pretty dance, that dance they just did," said Hazel.   7

"Huh?" said George.   8

"That dance—it was nice," said Hazel.   9

"Yup," said George. He tried to think a little about the ballerinas. They weren't   10
really very good—no better than anybody else would have been, anyway. They were burdened with sashweights and bags of birdshot, and their faces were masked, so that no one, seeing a free and graceful gesture or a pretty face, would feel like something the cat drug in. George was toying with the vague notion that maybe dancers shouldn't be handicapped. But he didn't get very far with it before another noise in his ear radio scattered his thoughts.

George winced. So did two out of the eight ballerinas.   11

Hazel saw him wince. Having no mental handicap herself, she had to ask George   12
what the latest sound had been.

"Sounded like somebody hitting a milk bottle with a ball peen hammer," said George.   13

"I'd think it would be real interesting, hearing all the different sounds," said Hazel,   14
a little envious. "All the things they think up."

"Um," said George.   15

"Only, if I was Handicapper General, you know what I would do?" said Hazel.   16
Hazel, as a matter of fact, bore a strong resemblance to the Handicapper General, a woman named Diana Moon Glampers. "If I was Diana Moon Glampers," said Hazel, "I'd have chimes on Sunday—just chimes. Kind of in honor of religion."

"I could think, if it was just chimes," said George.   17

"Well—maybe make 'em real loud," said Hazel. "I think I'd make a good Handi-   18
capper General."

"Good as anybody else," said George.   19

"Who knows better'n I do what normal is?" said Hazel.   20

"Right," said George. He began to think glimmeringly about his abnormal son who   21
was now in jail, about Harrison, but a twenty-one-gun salute in his head stopped that.

"Boy!" said Hazel, "that was a doozy, wasn't it?"   22

It was such a doozy that George was white and trembling, and tears stood on the   23
rims of his red eyes. Two of the eight ballerinas had collapsed to the studio floor, were holding their temples.

"All of a sudden you look so tired," said Hazel. "Why don't you stretch out on the   24
sofa, so's you can rest your handicap bag on the pillows, honeybunch." She was refer-ring to the forty-seven pounds of birdshot in a canvas bag, which was padlocked around George's neck. "Go on and rest the bag for a little while," she said. "I don't care if you're not equal to me for a while."

George weighed the bag with his hands. "I don't mind it," he said, "I don't notice it   25
anymore. It's just a part of me."

26 "You been so tired lately—kind of wore out," said Hazel. "If there was just some way we could make a little hole in the bottom of the bag, and just take out a few of them lead balls. Just a few."

27 "Two years in prison and two thousand dollars fine for every ball I took out." said George. "I don't call that a bargain."

28 "If you could take a few out when you came home from work," said Hazel. "I mean—you don't compete with anybody around here. You just set around."

29 "If I tried to get away with it," said George, "then other people'd get away with it— and pretty soon we'd be right back to the dark ages again, with everybody competing against everybody else. You wouldn't like that, would you?"

30 "I'd hate it," said Hazel.

31 "There you are," said George. "The minute people start cheating on laws, what do you think happens to society?"

32 If Hazel hadn't been able to come up with an answer to this question, George couldn't have supplied one. A siren was going off in his head.

33 "Reckon it'd fall all apart," said Hazel.

34 "What would?" said George blankly.

35 "Society," said Hazel uncertainly. "Wasn't that what you just said?"

36 "Who knows?" said George.

37 The television program was suddenly interrupted for a news bulletin. It wasn't clear at first as to what the bulletin was about, since the announcer like all announcers, had a serious speech impediment. For about half a minute, and in a state of high excitement, the announcer tried to say, "Ladies and gentlemen—"

38 He finally gave up, handed the bulletin to a ballerina to read.

39 "That's all right—" Hazel said of the announcer, "he tried. That's the big thing. He tried to do the best he could with what God gave him. He should get a nice raise for trying so hard."

40 "Ladies and gentlemen—" said the ballerina, reading the bulletin. She must have been extraordinarily beautiful, because the mask she wore was hideous. And it was easy to see that she was the strongest and most graceful of all the dancers, for her handicap bags were as big as those worn by two-hundred-pound men.

41 And she had to apologize at once for her voice, which was a very unfair voice for a woman to use. Her voice was a warm, luminous, timeless melody. "Excuse me—" she said, and she began again, making her voice absolutely uncompetitive.

42 "Harrison Bergeron, age fourteen," she said in a grackle squawk, "has just escaped from jail, where he was held on suspicion of plotting to over-throw the government. He is a genius and an athlete, is under-handicapped, and should be regarded as extremely dangerous."

43 A police photograph of Harrison Bergeron was flashed on the screen upside down, then sideways, upside down again, then right side up. The picture showed the full length of Harrison against a background calibrated in feet and inches. He was exactly seven feet tall.

44 The rest of Harrison's appearance was Halloween and hardware. Nobody had ever borne heavier handicaps. He had outgrown hindrances faster than the H-G men could think them up. Instead of a little ear radio for a mental handicap, he wore a tremendous pair of earphones, and spectacles with thick wavy lenses. The spectacles

were intended to make him not only half blind, but to give him whanging headaches besides.

Scrap metal was hung all over him. Ordinarily, there was a certain symmetry, a military neatness to the handicaps issued to strong people, but Harrison looked like a walking junkyard. In the face of life, Harrison carried three hundred pounds.   45

And to offset his good looks, the H-G men required that he wear at all times a red rubber ball for a nose, keep his eyebrows shaved off, and cover his even white teeth with black caps at snaggle-tooth random.   46

"If you see this boy," said the ballerina, "do not—I repeat, do not—try to reason with him."   47

There was a shriek of a door being torn from its hinges.   48

Screams and barking cries of consternation came from the television set. The photograph of Harrison Bergeron on the screen jumped again and again, as though dancing to the tune of an earthquake.   49

George Bergeron correctly identified the earthquake, and well he might have—for many was the time his own home had danced to the same crashing tune. "My God—" said George, "that must be Harrison!"   50

The realization was blasted from his mind instantly by the sound of an automobile collision in his head.   51

When George could open his eyes again, the photograph of Harrison was gone. A living, breathing Harrison filled the screen.   52

Clanking, clownish, and huge, Harrison stood in the center of the studio. The knob of the uprooted studio door was still in his hand. Ballerinas, technicians, musicians, and announcers cowered on their knees before him, expecting to die.   53

"I am the Emperor!" cried Harrison. "Do you hear! I am the Emperor! Everybody must do what I say at once!" He stamped his foot and the studio shook.   54

"Even as I stand here—" he bellowed, "crippled, hobbled, sickened—I am a greater ruler than any man who ever lived! Now watch me become what I *can* become!"   55

Harrison tore the straps of his handicap harness like wet tissue paper, tore straps guaranteed to support five thousand pounds.   56

Harrison's scrap-iron handicaps crashed to the floor.   57

Harrison thrust his thumbs under the bar of the padlock that secured his head harness. The bar snapped like celery. Harrison smashed his headphones and spectacles against the wall.   58

He flung away his rubber-ball nose, revealed a man that would have awed Thor, the god of thunder.   59

"I shall now select my Empress!" he said, looking down on the cowering people. "Let the first woman who dares rise to her feet claim her mate and her throne!"   60

A moment passed, and then a ballerina arose, swaying like a willow.   61

Harrison plucked the mental handicap from her ear, snapped off her physical handicaps with marvelous delicacy. Last of all, he removed her mask.   62

She was blindingly beautiful.   63

"Now—" said Harrison, taking her hand, "shall we show the people the meaning of the word dance? Music!" he commanded.   64

65   The musicians scrambled back into their chairs, and Harrison stripped them of their handicaps, too. "Play your best," he told them, "and I'll make you barons and dukes and earls."

66   The music began. It was normal at first—cheap, silly, false. But Harrison snatched two musicians from their chairs, waved them like batons as he sang the music as he wanted it played. He slammed them back into their chairs.

67   The music began again and was much improved.

68   Harrison and his Empress merely listened to the music for a while—listened gravely, as though synchronizing their heartbeats with it.

69   They shifted their weights to their toes.

70   Harrison placed his big hands on the girl's tiny waist, letting her sense the weightlessness that would soon be hers.

71   And then in an explosion of joy and grace, into the air they sprang!

72   Not only were the laws of the land abandoned, but the law of gravity and the laws of motion as well.

73   They reeled, whirled, swiveled, flounced, capered, gamboled, and spun.

74   They leaped like deer on the moon.

75   The studio ceiling was thirty feet high, but each leap brought the dancers nearer to it.

76   It became their obvious intention to kiss the ceiling.

77   They kissed it.

78   And then, neutralizing gravity with love and pure will, they remained suspended in air inches below the ceiling, and they kissed each other for a long, long time.

79   It was then that Diana Moon Glampers, the Handicapper General, came into the studio with a double-barreled ten-gauge shotgun. She fired twice, and the Emperor and the Empress were dead before they hit the floor.

80   Diana Moon Glampers loaded the gun again. She aimed it at the musicians and told them they had ten seconds to get their handicaps back on.

81   It was then that the Bergerons' television tube burned out.

82   Hazel turned to comment about the blackout to George. But George had gone out into the kitchen for a can of beer.

83   George came back in with the beer, paused while a handicap signal shook him up. And then he sat down again.

84   "You been crying?" he said to Hazel.

85   "Yup," she said.

86   "What about?" he said.

87   "I forget," she said. "Something real sad on television."

88   "What was it?" he said.

89   "It's all kind of mixed up in my mind," said Hazel.

90   "Forget sad things," said George.

91   "I always do," said Hazel.

92   "That's my girl," said George. He winced. There was the sound of a riveting gun in his head.

93   "Gee—I could tell that one was a doozy," said Hazel.

94   "You can say that again," said George.

95   "Gee—" said Hazel, "I could tell that one was a doozy."

➤ **FOR WRITING OR DISCUSSION**

1. Vonnegut's story is one of the future in which he looks at trends today that disturb him and asks what life would be like if they continue for a hundred years or so. What other stories, novels, movies, and television programs can you think of that use the same approach?

2. What specifically is the author satirizing in modern America? Do you feel he has good cause to be upset?

3. What would the author feel is a correct definition of *equality?* How would Diana Moon Glampers define *equality?*

4. Why is the name Harrison Bergeron a better choice than a name such as John Smith or Bill Jones?

5. Name the different kinds of handicaps in the story. Does each attempt to solve a different problem?

6. Specifically, what are the bad results of the misunderstanding of equality?

7. What is symbolized by the soaring of Harrison and the ballerina to the ceiling?

8. Does the fact that Harrison declares himself an emperor justify the society's fear of him?

9. Write a paper in which you define *equality.*

WRITING TOPICS

Consider these words and terms as possible topics for your extended definition paper.

1. Puppy love	11. Joy
2. Happiness	12. Political correctness
3. Homelessness	13. Forgiveness
4. Optimist	14. Hope
5. Shopping malls	15. Flight
6. Laziness	16. Evil
7. Wealth	17. Religion
8. Grunge	18. America
9. Astrology	19. "Wannabes"
10. Matchmaker	20. Fun

CROSSCURRENTS

1. What relation do you perceive between the essential points in Miller's "Discrimination Is a Virtue" (page 333) and Sarris' "You Don't Look Indian" (page 157)? Imagine a conversation between the two writers. On what would they agree? disagree?

2. Reread James Thurber's "A Couple of Hamburgers" (page 249). How does the diner in Thurber's story compare and contrast with the streetcar café in "A Tree. A Rock. A Cloud." (page 342)? How does each writer use the setting to advance the story line? the thesis? Why are these two places essential to their respective stories?

COLLABORATIVE LEARNING

Once you decide on a topic, do prewriting (see pages 17–20) before you draft your definition essay. Come to class with your prewriting efforts and form groups of three to examine the work of each student in the group. Has each writer selected a term rich in meaning? What suggestions can you make about how to develop the thesis? Which patterns of essay development do you think will help each writer best define the word of choice? Where do you think the writer needs to provide details? Is the writer's intended purpose clear? What audience should the essay aim for, in your opinion?

When you produce the draft of your essay, take into account the comments you received from group members.

REVIEW CHECKLIST: WRITING AND REVISING YOUR DEFINITION PAPER

- Did I think carefully about some word or term rich in meaning for me, and did I use prewriting strategies to stimulate ideas on the topic?
- Did I state clearly in a thesis sentence the word or term I am attempting to define?
- Did I express my attitude and purpose early in the essay?
- Did I use an outline to help me organize my thinking on the topic?
- Did I consider the various options for developing an essay on definition, and did I choose a pattern of development most appropriate to my topic?
- Did I provide adequate detail to support the meanings I ascribe to the word or term?
- Where appropriate, did I use a formal three-part definition? Or, did my topic lend itself more to development in an informal definition?
- Did I carefully consider my audience and the image I intend to project?
- Have I proofread for grammar, spelling, and mechanics?

Photo courtesy: © Laurence Monneret/Tony Stone Images

——— FROM IMAGE TO WORDS: A PHOTO WRITING ASSIGNMENT ———

Look at the photograph above. To your way of thinking, what word does the picture serve to define? Select one word or phrase—*happiness,* perhaps, or *tranquility* or *reflection* or *autumn*, for example—or some other word of your choosing. Then, write an essay in which you define that word. Draw on elements in the photograph for supporting details. Use your imagination to fill in or develop any details not explicit in the photograph. For instance, you might want to pursue the man's state of mind or fill in concrete sensory details of color, sound, smell and touch.

14

Argumentation

An **argumentation** paper attempts to strengthen or change an attitude of the reader, or to persuade the reader to a particular point of view by means of logic. Although writers of argumentation papers may employ emotional appeals, they place their principal faith in appealing to the intellects of their readers.

Argumentation has probably too often been viewed in the combative context of a courtroom or debating society: Right and wrong confront each other; one side wins, and one side loses. The victors gloat over the demolished points of their opponents or graciously accept their opponents' concessions of defeat and apologies for being so wrong. Many writers still do strive for total victory of this sort, of course, but argument can also be a matter of bringing opposing parties together, of showing the strengths and weaknesses of all points of view, of building consensus among former enemies. Argumentation can involve making peace as much as waging war.

Although lengthy books have been written about logic, we believe that the subject doesn't need to be as intimidating as these elaborate treatments suggest. Common sense and fair play are the basic tools—and sometimes the only tools—that conscientious writers need. As far as possible, then, we avoid fine philosophical distinctions and concentrate on the most common logical pitfalls—the basic errors in thinking that can turn up in anyone's writing. You may also find it valuable, after studying our comments, to read or reread Earl Ubell's insights on logic in "How to Think Clearly" (pages 214–217).

Using Logic

To check your own logic and that of others, a knowledge of the two kinds of logical thinking, *induction* and *deduction,* and of the errors in logic, the *fallacies,* will be helpful.

Induction

Induction is the process of reasoning from the particular to the general. It is the process of arriving at a general conclusion about all the members of a class. Induction is a useful tool because it isn't always practical or possible to check every member of a class before drawing your conclusion. If, for example, you develop a stomach ache every time you eat green apples, you may, without sampling every green apple in the world, safely conclude that green apples give you a stomach ache. You've made a generalization about all the members of the class *green apples* after examining some of its members. Or maybe you've noticed that for three Fridays in a row, Professor Hadley has given a pop quiz. You may draw the useful conclusion that Professor Hadley is likely to give pop quizzes on Fridays without waiting until the end of the term to see if you're right.

But induction is useful only if the conclusion about a class is drawn from a fair sampling of that class. What's fair depends on the class. You needn't stick your hand into twenty fires to conclude that fire burns; one or two fires will do. Other classes should be sampled more broadly. Conclusions about groups of people, for example, should be drawn from a large representative sampling and even then should usually be qualified with words like *tend, may, are likely,* and so on. (See "Hasty Generalization" and "Overgeneralization," page 360; see also Chapter 8, "Example.")

Deduction

Deduction is the process of reasoning from the general to the particular. A generalization already established—by oneself or by someone else—is applied to a specific case. Deduction, like induction, is a useful tool. You've concluded, for example, that Professor Hadley is likely to give pop quizzes on Fridays. When your roommate suggests one Friday morning that you cut classes and spend the day in the park, you say, "No, I can't go today. Professor Hadley may give a pop quiz, and my average can't stand a zero." You've applied your generalization (Fridays are likely days for quizzes) to a specific case (this Friday) and just may have assured yourself a passing grade in Professor Hadley's class.

In its simplest form, the deductive process is stated as a syllogism: an argument consisting of a major premise, a minor premise, and a conclusion.

Major premise: Fridays are likely days for pop quizzes.

Minor premise: Today is Friday.

Conclusion: Therefore, today is a likely day for a pop quiz.

Perhaps a more sophisticated example is the syllogism implicit in the Declaration of Independence:

Major premise: Rulers who violate basic human rights should be overthrown.

Minor premise: King George III has violated basic human rights.

Conclusion: Therefore, King George III should be overthrown.

Syllogisms rarely appear in writing or conversation in their pure three-part form. It is far more common to find enthymemes, condensed syllogisms in which one or more parts are missing, the writer assuming that the missing parts are clearly understood and don't need to be stated directly.

It's Friday, so I'd better go to Professor Hadley's class. (*Missing premise:* Fridays are likely days for quizzes in Professor Hadley's class.)

I don't trust him because he's sneaky. (*Missing premise:* Sneaky people should not be trusted.)

I hate movies with violence, and this movie is teeming with violence. (*Missing conclusion:* Therefore, I hate this movie.)

Syllogisms are worth serious study primarily because they enable readers and writers to examine the often unstated, and sometimes shaky, assumptions behind otherwise convincing arguments.

For a syllogism to be taken seriously, of course, both premises must be true. It's hard to imagine a syllogism that begins with the premise "The earth is flat" leading to any valid conclusion. But even if both premises are true, the reasoning process itself may be faulty and the conclusion invalid. Consider this syllogism:

Major premise: English majors read lots of books.

Minor premise: David reads lots of books.

Conclusion: Therefore, David is an English major.

Despite the true premises, the conclusion still doesn't follow. The major premise merely says, "English majors read lots of books"; it says nothing about other people who may also read books. Logically, David may be an English major, but he may also be a merchant marine who spends time on shipboard by reading, an invalid who doesn't enjoy television, a desk clerk whose job is boring, or just someone who likes to read for no particular reason. The logical structure of the argument makes no more sense than this syllogism: Grass is green; her hat is green; therefore, her hat is grass.

Using Induction and Deduction

So far, we have talked about induction and deduction as if the processes were mutually exclusive, but, in practice, they aren't. You will seldom engage in one kind of thought without using the other. When you use induction, you usually have a hunch about what generalization the facts will add up to. If you didn't, you wouldn't have a guideline for handling the facts. Consider, for example, that observation about Professor Hadley's quiz-giving tendency. If you hadn't already suspected that Hadley was a Friday quiz-giver, you might not have noticed that the pop quizzes did occur on Friday. Some deduction, therefore, was involved in the process of reaching the generalization about pop quizzes on Friday.

Similarly, in deductive reasoning you must also employ induction. A syllogism is only as valid as both its premises. To ensure sound premises, you must be sure that your evidence is both adequate and fair, and that involves induction. Induction is important, too, when you present your material. Even if yours is the best of syllogisms, you probably won't convince a reader of its worth unless you offer support for it—reasons, statistics, facts, opinions of authorities, examples. The reader's agreement or approval depends on the case you build; it depends on evidence. In the Declaration of Independence, for example, Thomas Jefferson supported his case against George III by citing twenty-eight instances in which the king had violated basic human rights. The instances came from induction.

Avoiding Logical Fallacies

Whether your primary tool is induction or deduction, you need to make certain that the evidence you offer isn't based on errors in logic. In other words, you should avoid the following fallacies.

POST HOC, ERGO PROPTER HOC

This impressive Latin phrase means, "after this, therefore because of this." This fallacy takes for a cause an event that merely happened earlier: for example, *A black cat crossed my path and ten minutes later I broke my ankle; therefore, the black cat caused my broken ankle.* Unless the speaker tripped over the cat, such a statement is as unreasonable as *Night follows day; therefore, day causes night.*

The *post hoc* **fallacy** often appears in political discussions. Haven't you heard people say things like, "The crime rate has increased since the governor took office; I'm certainly not going to vote for him again"? Possibly the governor could be held responsible for the increased crime, but before he could logically be blamed for it, a direct connection between his policies and the crime rate would have to be proved.

CARD STACKING

Card stacking means using only the evidence that supports a thesis and ignoring that which contradicts or weakens it. Card stacking is dishonest and can sometimes do serious damage. Suppose, for instance, that a popular newspaper columnist dislikes the mayor of the city. The columnist could prevent the mayor's reelection simply by emphasizing the administration's mistakes and playing down its accomplishments. Soon, the readers of the newspaper would begin to think of the mayor as a bungler who shouldn't be reelected.

Unfair? Of course. It's also unnecessary. A reasonable thesis doesn't require card stacking. A writer can make concessions and still advance the argument: *Although the mayor has made some attempts to attract convention business, the efforts have been too few and too late,* for example. If a thesis isn't reasonable, if it requires card stacking for support, it probably isn't worth defending and should be changed.

SLANTING

A variation of card stacking is **slanting**, systematically using words whose connotations suggest extreme approval or disapproval of the subject. A person may be "a bag of bones" or have "a model's figure." In either case, the weight is the same, but one term suggests scorn and the other approval. Similarly, George Washington may be described as "a militant revolutionary responsible for the death of many people." Or he may be "a great military genius who led his freedom-loving people in a victorious battle against tyranny." The conscious use of slanting to sway opinion usually occurs when a writer lacks enough logical evidence to support the thesis. Used this way, it is, like card stacking, quite dishonest. But slanting should not be confused with a writer's legitimate efforts to convey admittedly personal impressions and emotions.

HASTY GENERALIZATION

One snowflake doesn't make a blizzard, nor does one experience make a universal law. That one student has cheated on the last five psychology quizzes doesn't mean that all psychology students in the school are cheaters; to say so is to make a **hasty generalization**, to draw a conclusion about a group that is based on insufficient evidence.

OVERGENERALIZATION

Overgeneralizations are similar to hasty generalizations. A hasty generalization results from drawing a conclusion about a large number on the basis of very limited evidence. Overgeneralization occurs, regardless of how much "evidence" is available, when one assumes that all members of a group, nationality, race, or sex have the characteristics observed in some members of that group: "all feminists hate housework"; "all blacks love music"; "all Italians like spaghetti"; "the English are always cold and reserved"; "never trust a used-car salesperson." Surely it's possible that some feminists like to cook, that some blacks are tonedeaf, that some Italians prefer green salads, that some English people are volatile, and that at least one or two used-car salespersons are trustworthy. Words such as *all, never, always, every, true,* and *untrue* are seldom justified when dealing with the complexities of human beings and human institutions. You would do well in writing your papers to qualify potentially troublesome generalizations with words such as *some, seldom, tend, sometimes, frequently, seem, appear, often, perhaps,* and *many.* Both hasty generalizations and overgeneralizations lead to prejudice and superstition and to theses that cannot be developed logically or effectively.

NON SEQUITUR

Meaning "It does not follow," a ***non sequitur*** is a conclusion that does not follow from the premises. For example:

> I was a volunteer worker this summer so now I am saving to go to medical school.

Usually, *non sequiturs* occur because the writer or speaker neglects to make the connection between the premise and the conclusion clear to readers. In the preceding example, the writer's thinking probably resembles this:

1. I worked as a volunteer this summer for an organization that served men and women with serious diseases.
2. These people suffered greatly.
3. I felt that I was able to bring them some comfort from their pain and that this work gave me great satisfaction.
4. I'd like to be able to help ill people.
5. Therefore, I am saving to go to medical school so that I can become a physician and bring even more comfort to the sick.

Although the writer sees the connection easily, the writer's thought processes must be revealed so that the audience may also see the connection.

Another kind of *non sequitur* occurs because the writer or speaker draws an incorrect or debatable conclusion:

> Jack is 6 feet, 7 inches tall; I want him on my basketball team.

The unstated syllogism that leads to the conclusion is

> Successful basketball players tend to be very tall.
>
> Jack is very tall.
>
> Therefore, Jack will be a successful basketball player.

Although both the major premise and the minor premise are true, the conclusion does not necessarily follow. Jack may be so awkward that he trips over his own feet; thus, not all tall people make good basketball players. The writer's conclusion is, therefore, questionable and perhaps should be rejected.

IGNORING THE QUESTION

In **ignoring the question,** the writer or speaker deliberately or unintentionally shifts emphasis from the topic under discussion. A question can be ignored in several ways.

Ad Hominem *Argument.*   Arguing *ad hominem* (literally, "against the man") means making an irrelevant attack on a person rather than dealing with the actual issue under discussion. Suppose, for example, that Senator Goodfellow, who has admitted to cheating on his income tax for the past five years, proposes a bill for welfare reform. It would be a fallacy to attack the bill by arguing that its proponent is guilty of tax evasion. The bill may be logical, humane, and in the best interest of the country. If it is not, what are its weaknesses? The bill, not Senator Goodfellow's problems with the Internal Revenue Service, should be the subject of discussion.

Not all personal attacks, of course, are necessarily irrelevant. If Senator Goodfellow were seeking reelection, one could logically approve of his ideas and still vote against him because his character defects indicate the danger of trusting him in a position of power and responsibility.

Inexperienced writers sometimes employ the *ad hominem* fallacy in discussing literary works by rejecting a work whose author does not fulfill their idea of a good person:

> One cannot be expected to take "Kubla Khan" seriously. Coleridge admitted to writing it after he had taken drugs.

> Hemingway was a notorious womanizer. How can we value any of his ideas on morality and fidelity?

Such a practice indicates little understanding of the artistic process or of human nature. Writers, like all people, have human quirks and illnesses; yet such writers have produced inspiring works that affirm the highest values of civilization, and those affirmations deserve consideration. After all, most of us are a mixture of good and evil, wisdom and folly, generosity and greed; if we waited until we found a good idea proposed by a perfect person, we might wait forever.

Straw Man Argument.   The writer or speaker attributes to the opposition actions or beliefs of which the opposition is not guilty and then attacks the opposition for those actions or beliefs.

> Parents who boast of never having to spank their children should feel shame instead of pride. Discipline and socially responsible behavior are vitally important, and people who sneer at such things deserve the condemnation of all concerned citizens.

Some parents might very well be able to boast of not having to spank their children and yet also demand of their children discipline and socially responsible behavior.

Begging the Question.   The writer or speaker assumes in the thesis something that really needs to be proved.

> Since students learn to write in high school, the college composition course is a waste of time and should be replaced by a more useful and stimulating course.

One who chooses to write a paper with that thesis has the obligation to prove that students do learn how to write in high school—a source of great controversy in all discussions of American education.

Shifting the Burden of Proof.   Logic requires that *whoever asserts must prove.* It is not logical to say,

> I believe the flu epidemic was caused by a conspiracy of large drug companies, and you can't prove it wasn't.

For the assertion to be taken seriously, reasonable proof of a conspiracy must be offered.

Circular Argument.   Arguing in a circle means simply restating the premise instead of giving a reason for holding the premise.

> I like detective novels because mystery stories always give me great pleasure.

All that sentence says is, "I like detective novels because I like detective novels." One who begins a paper this way will be hard pressed to continue. Of greater interest would be the characteristics of the detective novels the speaker does like. Some readers like Agatha Christie's novels. How do her works differ from, say, Elmore Leonard's detective novels? Or P. D. James's? Surely one's taste for detective novels isn't indiscriminate. In other words, one needs a reason for liking detective novels, and to say that one likes them because they give pleasure is not to give a reason. Why do the novels give pleasure? An honest answer to that question will provide a workable thesis and prevent a circular argument.

EITHER/OR

In the **either/or fallacy,** the writer or speaker suggests that there are only two alternatives when, in fact, there may be more.

> Although I am quite ill, I must turn my term paper in tomorrow, or I will fail the course.

The writer presents only two alternatives; however, it is also possible that the instructor, recognizing the student's illness, might accept a late paper. Of course, if one is cursed with a professor who does not accept late papers, regardless of circumstances, then one actually has only two alternatives, and no fallacy exists.

ARGUMENT BY ANALOGY

An **analogy** is an extended comparison. It can clarify a difficult concept or dramatize an abstraction by comparing the unfamiliar with the familiar. But an analogy doesn't prove anything because, regardless of the number of similarities between two things, there are always some differences. One can't assume that because two things are alike in some respects, they are alike in all respects. Consider the following example.

> Learning to write a good essay is like learning to drive a car. Beginning drivers feel overwhelmed by the number of operations they must perform to keep a car moving—controlling the brake and the accelerator, staying in their lane, watching the cars in front of them while keeping an eye on the rear-view mirror. In addition, they must observe all traffic laws. The tasks seem insurmountable. Yet, in time, some of the operations become almost automatic and the drivers relax enough so that they can even look at the scenery now and then. So it is with beginning writers. At first, they wonder how they can make an outline for a paper, write clear topic sentences, develop paragraphs, provide transitions, write good introductions and conclusions, and still observe all the rules of English grammar. As with driving, part of the process eventually becomes automatic, and the writers relax enough to concentrate primarily on the ideas they wish to develop.

The comparison deals only with the similarities of feelings in the two experiences and is a successful analogy because it clarifies the experience of writing for the beginner. But if one extends the comparison to encompass other demands on drivers—checking antifreeze, acquiring new windshield wipers, renewing license plates, repairing flats, maintaining brake fluid—the analogy falls apart.

Historical analogies present a similar problem. We can't assume that because two historical events are alike in some respects, the outcomes will inevitably be the same. You have probably heard the argument that the United States is on the verge of collapse because some conditions here—relaxed sexual mores, widespread demand for immediate pleasure, and political cynicism and corruption—parallel those of the Roman Empire just before its fall. The argument doesn't consider, among other things, that the forms of government differ, that the bases for the economy differ, or that the means of educating the population differ. The two societies are not alike in every respect, and one cannot assume that because one society fell, the other also will fall.

Analogy can be useful for clarifying an idea, but argument by analogy can be dangerous.

EXERCISE

Following are examples of logical fallacies. Read them, and determine what type of fallacy each most strongly represents.

1. I lost my wallet yesterday. I knew that walking under that ladder in the morning would be trouble!
2. Yesterday, my neighbor's sixteen-year-old son zoomed out of the driveway in his new car and barely missed my daughter, who was riding her tricycle on the sidewalk. Last week, a seventeen-year-old girl hit the rear of my car

when I had to stop suddenly for a traffic light. When are we going to come to our senses and raise the legal driving age to twenty-one?

3. How can she be guilty of that crime? She has such a lovely family—they go to church regularly and are such friendly people.

4. Of course she's poor. Look at that old torn coat she's wearing!

5. How can Senator O'Malley speak for labor? What does he know about the needs of the average worker? He was born rich.

6. I love visiting Wyoming because I really enjoy traveling out West.

7. This unfair method of selecting police cadets must be changed.

8. We should either pay our teachers better salaries or admit that we don't care about the quality of our children's education.

9. I don't understand why Abraham Lincoln is considered a great president. He was a warmonger who, by government proclamation, took away the property of a large number of citizens.

10. How do *you* know that life does not exist on other planets?

Writing Your Argumentation Paper

The subject matter for argumentation papers must be controversial; that is, there must be the possibility for a difference of opinion on the subject. Otherwise, there would be no need for persuasion. That does not mean, however, that the subject matter need be earthshaking. Writers differ on how poems should be interpreted or on how cakes should be baked. In the sense that the purpose of an argumentation paper is to persuade a reader to a point of view, you have been writing argumentation papers since you began your study of English composition. In every paper you have written, you have taken a position on a subject and have offered logical reasons for holding that position.

A formal argumentation paper, however, has its own specific requirements.

- The writer states the problem or issue, sometimes tracing its causes.
- In some cases the writer states the possible positions to be taken on the problem.
- The writer states the position that the paper will take.
- The writer offers proof that the position taken is the reasonable one to hold.
- The writer anticipates objections to the position and refutes them.
- The writer affirms the position and makes a final appeal.

All these requirements are important, but we want especially to note here—and later, when we offer our pro and con essays on a single topic for you to examine—the importance of the next to the last point. Anticipating objections to your position, presenting them in your paper, and admitting or refuting them are key features of the strong argumentative essay.

Student Writing: Argumentation

Examine these student argumentation papers, the first of several that we present in this chapter. The first essay attacks a commonly accepted institution, the second a commonly accepted opinion, and the third an educational practice that the writer finds shocking.

Mary Ann Martin

Self-Serve Is No Serve

1   Filling your gas tank at a self-service station saves some money compared to having the tank filled for you at a traditional service station. That is the single good point about a self-service station. And while nobody has the right to sneer at the idea of saving money, saving a dime or two per gallon is not one of life's major thrills. It's certainly not worth the price the self-service customer pays in all kinds of other ways.

2   As one who neither knows much nor cares much about mechanical operations, I <u>need</u> to have someone check the oil, battery, radiator, and tires. Those services are, or used to be, routine at traditional stations, and they're worth far more than some loose change. Security is at stake as well as convenience, after all. If I'm charged with being lazy or incompetent, I may have to plead guilty, but people who make the accusation miss the point. There are millions of other drivers in as sad a state as I, and self-service stations make their lives more dangerous. Our local AAA just recently, in fact, attributed the record increase in calls for emergency road assistance to the growing number of self-service stations.

Of course, I don't argue that the actual pumping of gas   3
by oneself is a serious safety problem, though I always feel a
touch of fear when I'm forced to do it. But it certainly causes
real problems in grooming. Try to pump your own gas, especially
in winter, without getting dirt smudges from the outside of the
car all over your clothing. (If you have to wash your own windows, too, keeping your clothes clean becomes downright impossible.) And try to pump gasoline without having at least a faint
smell of gas on your hands when you get back into the car. Anyone who thinks these issues of grooming concern only women like
me must know more men than I do who enjoy being dirty and smelly.

The list of inconveniences, irritations, and outrages   4
doesn't stop here, by any means. Self-service stations make
life grossly more difficult for handicapped drivers than it
already is. The insistence of many stations on being paid in
cash in advance of pumping gas is a bother and an insult.
Finally, self-service stations have cut down drastically on
what used to be a major employment opportunity for teenagers,
worsening immeasurably an already serious national problem.

If you're wondering why, instead of complaining, I don't   5
just avoid self-service stations and take my car to a
traditional station instead, I can only say that there aren't
many traditional stations left, and they get harder to find
all the time. Those that are still open tend foolishly to keep
"banker's hours," too, and it's often hard for working people
and students to patronize them.

If the self-service station is anyone's idea of   6
worthwhile economy, call me a spendthrift. If it's anyone's
idea of progress, call me a reactionary.

➤ **FOR WRITING OR DISCUSSION**

1. In the opening paragraph, the writer gives two positions one might take toward self-service gas stations. What are they? Can you think of another position—a reason to approve of self-service stations, perhaps?
2. What is the writer's position on the subject? Where is it stated?
3. What arguments does the writer offer to support her position? Are some arguments stronger than others? Do any need fuller development?
4. Does the writer show an awareness of the arguments that can be offered against her position?
5. Does the concluding paragraph (6) affirm the writer's position?
6. Think of some other emerging trend or some service that seems to be disappearing and write an argumentation paper about it.

Sandra Travis-Edwards

The Right Not to Vote

1   I believe that the right to vote is one of the most important parts of being an American citizen. Our right to participate in choosing the leaders of our country ensures the continuance of our democratic system, and has protected this democracy and allowed it to flourish over the past two centuries. But, although I believe all this as firmly as it is possible to believe anything, I believe just as strongly in a citizen's right not to vote.

2   Many people argue that not voting is sheer foolishness. They believe that not voting is a way of avoiding the responsibility of having a political opinion. They say that it is proof that a person has absolutely no interest in politics, and that a person who doesn't vote just doesn't care. While this may often be true, it is not always the case.

3   I have chosen not to vote twice in my life, both times for different, yet valid reasons. The first time I chose not to vote was when I was going through a three-year period in which I moved three separate times. I came into one community

just in time to register for an extremely important and hotly
contested mayoral election. Needless to say I was flooded with
canvassers from various candidates, with flyers on my car's
windshield, and with advice from my new neighbors. There were
only a few short weeks until the election, and with a new job
and a new apartment to get used to, I knew I would never have
time to catch up with all the election details I needed.
Instead of desperately attempting to become informed about
my new neighborhood, its needs, and how each of the many
candidates might or might not meet them, I chose not to vote.
I believe that when one must choose between casting an
ignorant, uninterested vote and casting no vote at all, the
latter is the only responsible choice.

The second time I decided not to vote was a little later.   4
I had finally gotten settled in the town which is still my home,
and I had had time to get to know the community well enough
to be an interested and excited participant in the various elections that had been held since I moved in. The most recent school
board election was different, however. I hated the candidates.
Everything I saw, heard, and read caused me to distrust their
motives, suspect their honesty, and question their competence.
The campaign was generally referred to as an attempt to determine the lesser of two evils. I was disgusted, as I believe
that voting should be a matter of making a positive choice for
a candidate, not being forced to choose between ineptness and
idiocy. I chose, once again, not to vote. And when I was
asked by anyone--friend, neighbor, or candidate--where my vote
would be going, I explained that it would be staying home with
me, and I explained why. Sometimes, the action of not voting
is a stronger political move than voting is.

5   The right not to vote is as important as the right to
vote. Properly thought out, in situations where it is logically
seen to be the best possible option instead of the easy way out
of an important responsibility, it can be a way of avoiding
casting an ill-informed vote or a way of preserving one's
personal integrity and making one's opinions known when faced
with a bad slate of candidates.

➤ FOR WRITING OR DISCUSSION

1. Of the two examples of deciding not to vote, which strikes you as more justified? Explain.
2. Does the author try to consider possible arguments against her position? Are
   there reasonable and effective arguments that she does not consider? Explain
   your answer.
3. What other situations in addition to those mentioned might support the idea
   that not voting could be the correct decision?
4. Think of a current candidate or proposed law and write an argumentative
   paper expressing your support or opposition.

Michael Weissinger

Abortion Crusade Isn't Educational

1   Coming soon to a high school near you, the battle over
the hearts and minds of America's youth on the volatile issue
of abortion. At least, that would appear to be the plan of
Operation Rescue, an anti-abortion-rights organization, in
its crusade against abortion. A few weeks ago, they began a
campaign in which pictures of dismembered fetuses are held in
front of high schools across the country, inevitably for
teenagers and all to see.

2   Obviously, the point of this dramatic, if not gruesome,
campaign is to discourage teenagers from having abortions, but
when did the sidewalk in front of a school become the proper
forum for such an issue? If abortion is really a question of

life or death, which I'm sure is a statement abortion opponents, including the demonstrators in front of high schools,
would agree with, then why is such an important issue being
argued in the streets?

Pictures do not provide the guidance, education, support,   3
or reason necessary for a young person to make such a significant decision. Pictures do not incorporate these things, but a
moderated discussion that presents both sides of the issue to
teenagers in a controlled environment like school, church, or
the local community center most certainly does. Education is
the key, not shock value.

Of course, the campaign by Operation Rescue is assuming   4
that kids in high school can understand and make a rational
judgment based on these pictures of bloody fetuses; but
according to the laws and community standards, most teenagers
can't understand or make a rational judgment about anything
deemed slightly offensive by adults.

Teenagers under 17 couldn't possibly be able to differen-   5
tiate the violence or sex seen on a movie screen from reality
without the supervision of an adult. They most assuredly
aren't mature enough to listen to offensive words in rap or
alternative-rock songs. Novels like Catcher in the Rye are
much too offensive and dangerous to be left in libraries where
teenagers can read them.

If the majority of adults in America believe violence in   6
movies and lyrics in songs are inappropriate for teenagers,
then how can pictures of dismembered fetuses be appropriate
without proper supervision and guidance?

The whole campaign might be acceptable if it were just   7
kids in high school who saw these pictures. It is quite common, though, that the buildings next door to the local high

school happen to be the local elementary and junior-high schools.

8   At least teenagers are most likely aware of the issue of abortion before they see these pictures, but it is safe to say that most elementary-school children have no idea what abortion is, and many junior-high kids have only heard the word and are not aware of what is really behind it.

9   A person's position on either side of the abortion issue doesn't matter when confronted with the ramifications to a child under the age of say, 10, seeing pictures of dismembered fetuses.

10   The consequences to this child's life could be catastrophic, and all for the sake of shocking high-school kids rather than trying to educate them.

11   For many abortion opponents, I'm sure this seems justifiable when children's lives are at stake, but there are other means, just as effective if not more so, to make their point. Pamphlets passed out in front of high schools by demonstrators would be just as effective as gruesome pictures. Offering classes that contain both sides of the issue would prove to be even better for the future of America's teenagers.

12   In our spirited support for either side of the issue of abortion, let us not sacrifice our sense of decency or the need to explain all sides of this very divisive issue.

➤ FOR WRITING OR DISCUSSION

1. The thesis does not appear in this essay until the third paragraph. State the thesis in your own words. What is your reaction to the paragraphs that precede it?
2. What is the writer's opinion on abortion—is he in favor of it or against it? How can you tell?

3. What point is the writer trying to make about "the rational judgment of teenagers"? Who questions this ability? How is Weissinger being ironic here? How might this element of his argument backfire?

4. Write an essay in which you reflect on the issue of abortion. You might want to deal with the tactics of one side or the other, in the way that Michael Weissinger has, and avoid stating your own views on the issue. Or, remembering to draw on the standards of good written argument, take a position on the issue and defend it.

Mixing Methods of Development

Writers of argument often draw on a wide range of strategies to convince readers of the argument's validity. The methods of development that you have explored throughout this book can help you think through your argumentative paper; with options like description, narration, example, process, comparison and contrast, classification and division, cause and effect, and definition you can draw on one or more of the appropriate strategies to make your argument clear and forceful. As we pointed out at the start of Part Two of this book, many writing efforts profit from an intelligent combination of the methods of development presented here. This observation is particularly true in writing arguments, where combining methods of development can enhance your presentation and help convince your reader that your point is the one to reckon with.

As you plan to write, consider which modes of development might help you best convince your readers. Do you want to write about free speech? Perhaps you will start with an extended definition of the term and then provide examples of the major crises that arose in the course of maintaining that right. Depending on your purpose, you might choose to compare and contrast two particular crises in order to show the complexity of the issue. Do you want to write in support of one candidate for office over another? Here, too, comparison and contrast would come into play, but, in considering actions taken by each candidate, you might explain the causes and effects of such actions. Drawing on sensory detail to describe the candidates might help you offer snapshots of the personalities with which your readers may be unfamiliar. Do you want to argue for a humane setting for emergency room care in local hospitals? Description would certainly come into play here, but you might also want to narrate the events during one evening that you spent at the emergency room. Again, depending on your purpose, you might want to classify the patients and the kinds of services offered to them, and (or) you might want to explain the process by which hospital staff admit patients and establish treatment programs.

Student Writing: Mixing Methods in Writing an Argument

In this annotated paper by student writer Brian Jarvis, who wrote this essay for *Newsweek,* note the mixed modes of development in service of the writer's thesis. Answer the questions after the piece.

Brian Jarvis

Against the Great Divide

I always notice one thing when I walk through the commons at my high school: the whites are on one side of the room and the blacks are on the other. When I enter the room, I think I'm at an African nationalist meeting. The atmosphere is lively, the clothes are colorful, the voices are loud, the students are up and about, the language is different, and there's not a white face to be seen. But the moment I cross the invisible line to the other side, I feel I've moved to another country. There are three times as many people, the voices are softer, the clothes more subdued. Everyone's sitting or lying down, and one has as much chance of seeing a black student as a Martian.

1

Description: **Helps establish details of the moment in the introduction to the essay and frames the problem that the writer will address in his paper.**

Definition: **Here, Jarvis defines "commons" as it applies to the essay. Note the repetition of the word "commons" here as a transition to the first paragraph, where we read the word for the first time in the essay.**

The commons is a gathering spot where students relax on benches and talk with friends. They also buy candy and soda, watch TV, and make phone calls. It's a place where all sorts of things happen. But you'll never find a white student and a black student talking to each other.

2

After three years, I still feel uncomfortable when I have to walk through the "black" side to get to class. It's not that any black students threaten or harass me. They just quietly ignore me and look in the other direc-

3

tion, and I do the same. But there's one who sometimes catches my eye, and I can't help feeling awkward when I see him. He was a close friend from childhood.

Transition: "Ten years ago" helps lend coherence to essay.

Ten years ago, we played catch in our backyards, went bike riding, and slept over at one another's houses. By the fifth grade, we went to movies and amusement parks and bunked together at the same summer camps. We met while playing on the same Little League team, though we attended different grade schools. We're both juniors now at the same high school. We usually don't say anything when we see each other, except maybe a polite "Hi" or "Hey." I can't remember the last time we talked on the phone, much less got together outside of school.

4

Example: From personal experience, writer presents example of a different kind of relation between blacks and whites from relations identified at the writer's school.

Since entering high school, we haven't shared a single class or sport. He plays football, a black-dominated sport, while I play tennis, which is, with rare exception, an all-white team. It's as if fate has kept us apart; though, more likely, it's peer pressure.

5

Comparison and contrast: In paragraphs 5 and 6, Jarvis shows similarities and differences between friend and him.

In the lunchroom, I sit with my white friends and my childhood friend sits with his black ones. It's the same when we walk through the hallways or sit in the library. If Michael Jackson thinks, "It don't matter if you're black or white," he should visit my high school.

6

I wonder if proponents of desegregation realized that even if schools were integrated, students would choose to remain apart. It wasn't until 1983 that St. Louis's voluntary city-suburban desegregation program was approved. Today, my school has 25 percent black students. While this has given many young people the chance

7

for a better education, it hasn't brought the two races closer together.

In high school, I've become friends with Vietnamese Americans, Korean Americans, Iranian Americans, Indian Americans, Russian Americans, and exchange students from France and Sweden. The only group that remains at a distance is the African Americans. I've had only a handful of black students in all my classes and only one black teacher (from Haiti).

Classification: Jarvis lists the groups with whom he has made friends at school.

8

In its effort to put students through as many academic classes as possible and prepare them for college, my school seems to have overlooked one crucial course: teaching black and white students how to get along, which in my opinion, would be more valuable than all the others. It's not that there haven't been efforts to improve race relations. Last fall, a group of black and white students established a program called Students Organized Against Racism. But at a recent meeting, SOAR members decided that the separation of blacks and whites was largely voluntary and there was little they could do about it. Another youth group tried to help by moving the soda machine from the "white" side of the commons to the "black" side, so that white students would have to cross the line to get a Coke. But all that's happened is that students buy their sodas, then return to their own territory.

9

Cause and effect: Here the writer explains the results of efforts to improve race relations at his high school.

Last summer, at a youth camp called Miniwanca in Michigan, I did see black and white teens get along. I don't mean just tolerate one another. I mean play sports together, dance together, walk on the beach together,

10

Example:
Jarvis
proposes a way
to improve race
relations and
draws on
examples from
personal
experience to
support his
point.

and become friends. The students came from all races and backgrounds, as well as from overseas. Camp organizers purposely placed me in a cabin and activity group that included whites, blacks, Southerners, Northerners, and foreigners, none of whom I'd met before.

For 10 days, I became great friends with a group of strangers, at least half of whom were black. One wouldn't know that racism existed at that idyllic place, where we told stories around campfires, acted in plays, and shared our deepest thoughts about AIDS, parents, abortion, and dating. Everyone got along so well there that it was depressing for me to return to high school. But at the same time, it made me hopeful. If black and white teenagers could be friends at leadership camp, couldn't they mix in school as well?

11

Narrative: The
writer provides
a sequence of
events at
leadership
camp to show
how "everyone
got along so
well."

Example: The
illustrations
continue as
the writer
suggests ways
to get "whites
and blacks
together as
much as
possible."

Schools need to make it a real priority to involve whites and blacks together as much as possible. This would mean more multicultural activities, mandatory classes that teach black history, and discussions of today's racial controversies. Teachers should mix whites and blacks more in study groups so they <u>have</u> to work together in and out of school. (Students won't do it on their own.) And most important, all students should get a chance to attend a camp like Miniwanca. Maybe the Clinton administration could find a way to help finance other camps like it.

12

Conclusion:
Provides a
bird's-eye view
of the problem
and the writer's
reaction to it.

As it is now, black and white teenagers just don't know one another. I think a lot about my friend from childhood--what he does on weekends, what he thinks about college, what he wants to do with his life. I have no answers, and it saddens me.

13

➤ **FOR WRITING OR DISCUSSION**

1. What is Jarvis's thesis?
2. Which details convince you most that the races do not get along harmoniously at Jarvis's school? Does Jarvis report any open conflict? Why, then, is he concerned?
3. What transitions can you identify (other than those in the annotations) that lend coherence to the essay?
4. One of the weaknesses in the essay, some might argue, is that the writer does not present any arguments opposed to his position, arguments that he then might refute. What arguments against Jarvis's thesis can you suggest? How would you refute them?
5. What is your reaction to the use of multiple modes of development in this essay?
6. Write an argumentative essay about race relations in your school, neighborhood, or place of business.

Pro and Con: Arguments on Controversial Topics

Examining essays that take opposite positions on a controversial topic can give you many useful insights into writing strong arguments. As we've already pointed out, one of the most helpful strategies as you write your argumentative essay is to consider very carefully the arguments that others might use against your position so that you can refute them. As you read essays that take an opposite position on a single issue, you can see the magnitude of opinions on the matter that can stimulate you to discover the opposition on a topic you choose to write about. Marshaling evidence, presenting details, and avoiding logic traps are not always enough if someone else can make a stronger case from an opposing stance. When you anticipate objections to your position and consider them thoughtfully in your essay, you improve your chances of convincing the reader that your position is the right one.

Student Writing: Opposing Views on the Death Penalty

In the two student essays that follow—both, incidentally, published in the same college newspaper—you can see the argumentative expanse from which one can draw for either side of the death penalty issue. As you read these essays, note the range of positions. Also, note how each writer identifies opposing arguments and deals with them intelligently. Suspend your own beliefs on the death penalty as you read these essays. Which student most convinces you on the strength of the issues addressed in his or her paper?

1.

Lauren Heist

Capital Punishment: An Example for Criminals

A child looks around to see if anyone is watching him. 1
When he's sure that the kitchen is empty, he opens up the
cookie jar and smuggles a cookie up to his room. When his
mother confronts him about the missing cookie, she tells him
taking cookies is not very nice and says if he does it again
he will be in trouble. A little while later the child sees the
cookie jar again. Not seeing anyone around, he again takes a
cookie. The mother tells him taking cookies is wrong again but
does not punish him. Soon the child learns that because he
hasn't gotten in trouble, taking cookies must not be that bad.
Because the mother did not follow through on her threat, the
child begins to take advantage of the mother, and the child
gets away with whatever he wants.

That is what has happened to our police force today. 2
Criminals do not take the law seriously. They do not fear the
government. Criminals are taking advantage of us, and they are
getting away with murder, literally.

The bottom line is people need to respect the law. With- 3
out laws, we would live in anarchy. But too many people feel
that they are above the law and it does not apply to them.
Because people feel alienated from the bureaucrats who make
the laws, they simply choose to ignore the laws.

If we want to live in a peaceful society, we must enforce 4
the laws, and that includes using the death penalty. Every
criminal who commits a first degree murder should receive the
death penalty. The problem with the way the death penalty is
used now is not that it is used too often, but rather that it
is not used enough.

5   How many muggers actually think, "Man, I hope I don't get the death penalty," before they decide to hold a gun to the head of a person getting money out of an ATM machine? I can assure you that is not a thought that often crosses their minds. The death penalty is only used in extreme cases for infamous psychopaths and serial killers. The average run-of-the-mill killer can get out of jail in no time flat. If the death penalty were employed more frequently, killers might actually take it into consideration before shooting someone.

6   The most common argument against the death penalty is that it is hypocritical. Critics ask, how can we claim that murder is wrong and then kill the killer? What most critics do not understand is that governments do not live by the same rules that individual people live by. Governments have powers that people do not have because people concede power to the government.

7   For example, governments have the power to confiscate houses by eminent domain if they are in the way of a road that is going to be built. An individual citizen cannot arbitrarily destroy a house or confiscate property, but governments can do these things because people entrust the government to act in the best interest of the majority of its citizens. The government has the right to use the death penalty because it has a responsibility to keep order in the society.

8   The other argument that people use to oppose the death penalty is that there is always a chance that an innocent person could be executed because the justice system is not perfect. Yes, it is true that the justice system is not entirely foolproof. Nothing is entirely foolproof. The founding fathers

tried to ensure that the justice system would be fair by requiring all murder cases to be decided by a jury. People must have faith that their own peers will make fair, logical decisions. In addition, just as critics of the death penalty fear that innocent people might be executed, there is also the possibility that criminals will be set free and will endanger other innocent people.

Claiming insanity is no excuse for sparing someone from the death penalty. A murderer is a murderer, no matter who commits it or what mental state they claim to be in at the time. Milwaukee's Jeffrey Dahmer, who killed multiple victims and even admitted to practicing cannibalism, was not sentenced to the death penalty. Instead, he was sentenced to life imprisonment and was killed by a fellow inmate. Why was Dahmer not given the death penalty? Because he was determined to be insane. Susan Smith, the mother who drowned her two young sons in a car, also received life imprisonment instead of the death penalty because she pleaded temporary insanity. People who are clearly guilty of murder should be made examples. If Jeffrey Dahmer and Susan Smith do not receive the death penalty, why would any person ever have to fear the death penalty?

9

Finally, the death penalty should be used more often than it is today because it is economical. Keeping someone in a jail cell for years requires that taxpayers pay for that criminal's food and shelter for the rest of the criminal's life, while he takes up a space that could be used by another criminal. Every day, guilty criminals leave the courthouse and head back out onto the street because the prisons and jails are overcrowded. Meanwhile, other criminals sit on death row, eating up the taxpayers' money and not contributing anything to society.

10

11   If we want to take this country back from the mobsters
and the drug lords and put the power back in the people and
the police, we need to use the death penalty. Using the death
penalty will not only be economical for all taxpayers, but it
will also deter future criminals from killing, which will make
us all safer.

2.

Alex Shalom

Abolish the Death Penalty

1   When a convicted murderer's head burst into flames in
Florida's electric chair a few weeks ago, reactions varied.
The state's Attorney General boasted that, due to problems
with the lethal contraption, murderers should be particularly
wary if they commit their crimes in Florida because they will
suffer greatly before their lives are terminated by the state.
Others reacted with disgust and concluded that the United
States should abolish the death penalty. The latter is the
appropriate response.

2   The U.S. would hardly be breaking ground by abolishing
the death penalty. None of the nations of Western Europe practice capital punishment, nor do most of our Latin American
neighbors. The reasons for the abolition of the death penalty
are many; there are reasons why capital punishment is inherently unjust and there are also reasons why the death penalty,
as practiced in the United States, is especially so. I will
briefly address both of these categories of reasons. First,
however, it will be useful to examine the problems with common
justifications for state-sponsored killing.

3   Death penalty proponents generally extend support for
capital punishment from both moral and practical perspectives.

The pragmatic capital punishment advocates contend that the
death penalty deters murder and that it costs less then keeping murderers incarcerated. The appropriate question, however, should not be whether or not the death penalty deters
murder; surely it does. Rather, we should ask whether the
death penalty deters murder better than life imprisonment, for
no death penalty opponent advocates letting murderers walk
free on the street.

Levels of deterrence are difficult to measure, but there   4
are some ways to do so. If one examines the states of Michigan
and Illinois--two states with very similar population, land,
and demographic make-ups--one discovers something very interesting. Michigan has not executed anyone since it became a
state over 150 years ago, while Illinois has actively used the
death penalty over the last 20 years. If the death penalty
were, in fact, a better deterrent than life imprisonment, then
Illinois should have a lower murder rate than Michigan. In
reality, Michigan has a lower murder rate than its southwest-
ern neighbor.

Though it is ridiculous to put a price on human life, some   5
people argue that because prisons are too costly, murderers
should be executed. This is a simplistic answer. While the
actual cost of a lethal injection is clearly cheaper than the
cost of a lengthy imprisonment, because death is the ultimate
punishment, those facing the death penalty are always entitled
to many legal appeals. Oftentimes, because those on death row
are predominantly indigent, the state is forced to pay for
both sides of the appeals process. When the cost of appeals is
factored into the equation, it becomes evident that capital
punishment is not a cost effective solution.

6   All facts and figures aside, many people still attempt to justify the continued practice of capital punishment, arguing both that the punishment should fit the crime--that is, "an eye for an eye"--and that the families of the victims deserve the peace of mind of having the murderer killed. Coretta Scott King, who lost both a husband and a mother-in-law to assassination, offers an answer to both of these statements: "I stand firmly and unequivocally opposed to the death penalty for those convicted of capital offenses. An evil deed is not redeemed by an evil deed of retaliation. Justice is never advanced by the taking of a human life. Morality is never upheld by legalized murder."

7   In the United States, no crimes other than murder are met with punishments that imitate the crime; they are answered with punishments that fit the crime. The government does not burn the homes of arsonists nor does it rape rapists. That simply would not make for a just penal system.

8   There is no reason, moral or practical, to support the death penalty; there are, however, several reasons why it should be abolished. Perhaps the best reason is that no system of justice is infallible. As long as a state practices capital punishment, there is always the possibility that an innocent person will be executed. A 1987 study published by the Stanford Law Review showed that, despite our elaborate appeals system, at least 23 innocent people have been executed in the United States in this century.

9   Colonial Massachusetts is possibly best known for the numerous executions of the innocent during the Salem Witch Trials. The judge in many of those cases, Judge Suel, eventually realized the error of his ways. He made a public statement saying that it was wrong to execute the people that he

had sentenced to death. I hope no more judges are forced to come to the dreadful conclusion that they are responsible for the murder of an innocent person.

Even when the question of innocence does not loom over a judge's head, there are still factors that make the death penalty inequitable and cruelly administered. The death penalty is a racist institution that disproportionately kills the poor. African Americans receive the death penalty somewhat more often than whites. However, the real injustice of capital punishment is that blacks who kill whites are more likely to receive the death penalty than whites who kill blacks. A study presented in front of the Supreme Court showed that murderers whose victims are white are 139 percent more likely to receive the death penalty than if their victim was black. Though it is clearly not the case that the life of a white person is more valuable than that of a black person, this is what our current system of capital punishment is saying.

10

Murderers who are unable to afford to pay for their own defense are far more likely to be executed than those who can afford a lawyer. In Texas, 75 percent of convicted murderers who had court-appointed attorneys received the death penalty, while only 33 of those with private attorneys were killed. According to former Supreme Court Justice Thurgood Marshall, "the burden of capital punishment falls upon the poor, the ignorant, and the underprivileged members of society." This is simply unfair, particularly when lives are at stake.

11

While the United States does not stand alone in the international community in continuing to practice capital pun-ishment, the other countries that practice it are far from world leaders in the area of human rights. Only five countries execute criminals who committed their crimes while under the

12

```
age of 18: Yemen, Saudi Arabia, Iran, Pakistan, and the United
States. Strange bedfellows, indeed. Much of the rest of the
world has realized the inhumanity of capital punishment and
abolished it. How many more people will die at the hands of
the state before the United States follows suit?
```

➤ **FOR WRITING OR DISCUSSION**

1. What is the thesis of each paper? Where is each thesis most clearly stated?
2. How does each writer treat the issue of the economics of the death penalty? In what ways do the presentations on the issue deal with opposing points of view? Where else do the writers treat opposing points of view?
3. In your opinion, which essay makes the more convincing argument about capital punishment?
4. Write your own essay on the death penalty. You might read or reread George Orwell's essay "A Hanging" (page 7) as another example of writing on capital punishment.

Student Writing: Opposing Views on Conditions in the Workplace

In these two student essays, both published on the op-ed page of the *New York Times*, the writers examine the decision by the president of the Nike Corporation to withdraw a grant to the University of Oregon because of the University's activist role in improving worldwide working conditions. The first paper is from a senior at the University who supports United Students Against Sweatshops; the second paper is from the editorial page editor of the *Columbia Daily Spectator*, a publication of Columbia University.

SARAH EDITH JACOBSON

Nike's Power Game

1 When Phil Knight, the chief executive of Nike, withdrew a promised $30 million donation to the University of Oregon last month, his announcement had the tone of an angry parent. He chastised the university for joining the Worker Rights Consortium, a group that monitors conditions in factories that make clothing with college logos. He accused the university of "inserting itself into the new global economy where I make my living" and doing so "on the wrong side, fumbling a teachable moment."

Mr. Knight, an Oregon graduate, was angry that the university had joined the consortium rather than the Fair Labor Association, a group that includes as members the same industries that have profited from sweatshop conditions in their production plants. The Worker Rights Consortium is based on the premise that work conditions will not be changed by codes and monitors that come from industry, but by involvement of workers, through collective bargaining with management. 2

In joining the consortium, the University of Oregon pledged to use its influence to improve conditions at factories producing clothes with the university logo. Mr. Knight, accusing his alma mater of shredding it's "bonds of trust" with him, seemed offended that it had not asked his permission. 3

The university's decision was not made lightly. In March, a referendum sponsored by the student government yielded a three-fourths majority vote in support of membership. A committee accountable to the university president, David B. Frohnmayer, and made up of students, faculty, administrators and alumni, voted unanimously the same month in favor of joining. Then the University Senate, composed of faculty and students, passed a resolution calling for membership. It was only after all these steps that President Frohnmayer signed the university into membership. 4

Mr. Knight's punitive reaction really questions the autonomy of the university itself. If the voice of one alumnus held more weight than a year of university-wide deliberation, what role would there be for shared governance on campus? If donations from corporate America depended on toeing a corporate line, the university would be better off without the money. 5

The goal of students across the country who are organizing around sweatshop issues is to create widespread change in an industry where insufficient wages and mandatory overtime are common. In many third world and American apparel factories, there have been reports of intimidation of workers who try to speak out. And because it is easy for these factories to cut and run, vanishing across national borders and abandoning workers, many people are hesitant to organize unions or demand a living wage. 6

The Worker Rights Consortium and the student anti-sweatshop campaign challenge companies like Nike not only to let the public know the conditions in apparel factories, but to begin long-term change. 7

Will the debate about sweatshop conditions move beyond the specifics of monitoring and toward establishing the right to organize? Phil Knight's withdrawal of money from the University of Oregon sends the signal that his company is resisting a move in that direction. 8

JAIME SNEIDER

Good Propaganda, Bad Economics

College students continue to propagate the myth that Nike and other apparel companies contract out to foreign "sweatshops" where overworked and underpaid workers toil in unhealthful conditions. They are especially outraged by the recent decision by Phil Knight of Nike to withdraw a promised $30 million donation to the University 1 of Oregon in protest of the school's decision to join the Worker Rights Consortium, a labor rights group.

2   Rather than condemn Mr. Knight, students should commend him.

3   The Worker Rights Consortium, which was established last fall by students, unions, and human rights groups, accuses Nike of failing to pay its workers a "living wage," ignoring safety concerns, and forcing employees to work overtime. But, comparatively speaking, conditions at third world factories where Nike goods are made are remarkably benevolent. For example, a number of the plants have air conditioning in countries where it is a rarity. Some factories also have clinics that can be used by employees' families, who otherwise would have little if any medical care. Several others even have schools where workers' children can learn everything from reading and writing to biology and physics.

4   A typical worker in a Nike factory in Vietnam makes about $564 a year, which may not seem like much, but is more than twice the country's average annual income. The employee turnover rate in Nike's factories in Indonesia is consistently below 2 percent, low even by American standards. Such loyalty suggests that workers do not have better prospects.

5   Many statistics cited by student activists are misleading and originate with the A.F.L.-C.I.O., which has endorsed the Worker Rights Consortium. The A.F.L.-C.I.O. has a direct economic interest: the regulations advocated by the consortium would increase American companies' foreign manufacturing costs, thus encouraging them to abandon their operations abroad and manufacture products domestically instead—employing union labor.

6   Phil Knight has agreed to an open monitoring of Nike factories through the Fair Labor Association, a group composed of consumer groups, corporations and universities that has been endorsed by the White House. Nike has said that many students have genuine concerns about working conditions abroad, and that the company recognizes that there is always room for improvement.

7   But, according to a Nike spokeswoman, "the way to get true reform is to have all the players at the table." The Worker Rights Consortium, on the other hand, has not prescribed clear goals or monitoring procedures, and does not yet have legal status as a nonprofit organization. It has been reluctant to include companies like Nike in the dialogue, claiming that corporate participation of any kind threatens workers' rights.

8   While many students uncritically believe the Worker Rights Consortium, they ignore the fact that Phil Knight and Nike have championed the well-being of workers internationally. By trying to punish Nike, these students threaten to impoverish the workers they claim to protect.

➤ **FOR WRITING OR DISCUSSION**

1. What is Jacobson's thesis?
2. How does each writer use the action by Nike Corporation's president as the springboard for the argument?
3. Which writer convinces you more on the strength of the writing? Why? Which details in each do you find most convincing?

4. Write an essay on what you think should be the appropriate relation between universities and private corporations. Should universities accept gifts only if they come without conditions, thereby allowing the university to follow its conscience in all matters? Should corporations insists on particular courses of action if they are to make monetary gifts to universities?

HAVING YOUR SAY

Write an argumentative essay about how Americans should deal with the issues of sweatshops around the world that supply us with clothing and other merchandise. Be sure to present opposing arguments fairly before arguing your own position. Use information from the essays by Jacobson and Sneider, if you wish, to help you make your point.

Models of Writing

The selections that follow are solid examples of argumentative writing. The first three, drawn from popular magazines, demonstrate argumentative writing on serious public issues. The last is one of the most famous and influential arguments ever written, the Declaration of Independence.

MICHAEL E. LEVIN

The Case for Torture

It is generally assumed that torture is impermissible, a throwback to a more brutal age. Enlightened societies reject it outright, and regimes suspected of using it risk the wrath of the United States.   1

I believe this attitude is unwise. There are situations in which torture is not merely permissible but morally mandatory. Moreover, these situations are moving from the realm of imagination to fact.   2

Suppose a terrorist has hidden an atomic bomb on Manhattan Island which will detonate at noon on July 4 unless . . . (here follow the usual demands for money and release of his friends from jail). Suppose, further, that he is caught at 10 A.M. of the fateful day, but—preferring death to failure—won't disclose where the bomb is. What do we do? If we follow due process—wait for his lawyer, arraign him—millions of people will die. If the only way to save those lives is to subject the terrorist to the most excruciating possible pain, what grounds can there be for not doing so? I suggest there are none. In any case, I ask you to face the question with an open mind.   3

4   Torturing the terrorist is unconstitutional? Probably. But millions of lives surely out-weigh constitutionality. Torture is barbaric? Mass murder is far more barbaric. Indeed, letting millions of innocents die in deference to one who flaunts his guilt is moral cow-ardice, an unwillingness to dirty one's hands. If *you* caught the terrorist, could you sleep nights knowing that millions died because you couldn't bring yourself to apply the electrodes?

5   Once you concede that torture is justified in extreme cases, you have admitted that the decision to use torture is a matter of balancing innocent lives against the means needed to save them. You must now face more realistic cases involving more modest numbers. Someone plants a bomb on a jumbo jet. He alone can disarm it, and his demands cannot be met (or if they can, we refuse to set a precedent by yielding to his threats). Surely we can, we must, do anything to the extortionist to save the passengers. How can we tell 300, or 100, or 10 people who never asked to be put in danger, "I'm sorry, you'll have to die in agony, we just couldn't bring ourselves to. . . ."

6   Here are the results of an informal poll about a third, hypothetical, case. Suppose a terrorist group kidnapped a newborn baby from a hospital. I asked four mothers if they would approve of torturing kidnappers if that were necessary to get their own newborns back. All said yes, the most "liberal" adding that she would administer it herself.

7   I am not advocating torture as punishment. Punishment is addressed to deeds irrev-ocably past. Rather, I am advocating torture as an acceptable measure for preventing future evils. So understood, it is far less objectionable than many extant punishments. Opponents of the death penalty, for example, are forever insisting that executing a mur-derer will not bring back his victim (as if the purpose of capital punishment were sup-posed to be resurrection, not deterrence or retribution). But torture, in the cases described, is intended not to bring anyone back but to keep innocents from being dis-patched. The most powerful argument against using torture as a punishment or to secure confessions is that such practices disregard the rights of the individual. Well, if the individual is all that important—and he is—it is correspondingly important to pro-tect the rights of individuals threatened by terrorists. If life is so valuable that it must never be taken, the lives of the innocents must be saved even at the price of hurting the one who endangers them.

8   Better precedents for torture are assassination and preemptive attack. No Allied leader would have flinched at assassinating Hitler, had that been possible. (The Allies did assassinate Heydrich.) Americans would be angered to learn that Roosevelt could have had Hitler killed in 1943—thereby shortening the war and saving millions of lives—but refused on moral grounds. Similarly, if nation A learns that nation B is about to launch an unprovoked attack, A has a right to save itself by destroying B's military capability first. In the same way, if the police can by torture save those who would otherwise die at the hands of kidnappers or terrorists, they must.

9   There is an important difference between terrorists and their victims that should mute talk of the terrorists' "rights." The terrorist's victims are at risk unintentionally, not having asked to be endangered. But the terrorist knowingly initiated his actions. Unlike his victims, he volunteered for the risks of his deed. By threatening to kill for profit or idealism, he renounces civilized standards, and he can have no complaint if civiliza-tion tries to thwart him by whatever means necessary.

Just as torture is justified only to save lives (not extort confessions or recantations), it   10
is justifiably administered only to those *known* to hold innocent lives in their hands.
Ah, but how can the authorities ever be sure they have the right malefactor? Isn't there
a danger of error and abuse? Won't We turn into Them?

Questions like these are disingenuous in a world in which terrorists proclaim them-   11
selves and perform for television. The name of their game is public recognition. After
all, you can't very well intimidate a government into releasing your freedom fighters
unless you announce that it is your group that has seized its embassy. "Clear guilt" is difficult to define, but when 40 million people see a group of masked gunmen seize an airplane on the evening news, there is not much question about who the perpetrators are.
There will be hard cases where the situation is murkier. Nonetheless, a line demarcating
the legitimate use of torture can be drawn. Torture only the obviously guilty, and only
for the sake of saving innocents, and the line between Us and Them will remain clear.

There is little danger that the Western democracies will lose their way if they   12
choose to inflict pain as one way of preserving order. Paralysis in the face of evil is the
greater danger. Some day soon a terrorist will threaten tens of thousands of lives, and
torture will be the only way to save them. We had better start thinking about this.

➤ FOR WRITING OR DISCUSSION

1. According to Levin, torture is permissible only in special circumstances.
   What are those circumstances?
2. In such special circumstances, the author maintains that torture is "not
   merely permissible but morally mandatory." Explain the difference.
3. The author uses only three major examples to support his thesis. Would the
   thesis be more convincing with more examples?
4. What principle determines the order in which the three examples are
   presented?
5. Choose something you would like to see done away with, and write an
   argumentation paper advocating its legal banning. Some possible topics are
   cigarettes, alcohol, divorce, *F* grades, seat-belt requirements, and professional boxing.

BERNARD SLOAN

Old Folks at Home

I once felt sorry for people in old-age homes. I accepted their portrayal on television   1
specials as helpless innocents cast aside by their young, paying the price of growing
old in America. I thought all these lonely old men and women were victims of the indifference and selfishness of the younger generation.

No more.   2

3   I have learned through personal experience why so many grandmothers and grand-fathers end up in institutions for the aged, unwanted and unvisited. It isn't always their children who put them there. Sometimes they put themselves there.

4   These are the selfish, demanding elderly who are impossible to live with. Often they are people who were difficult to live with when they were younger, but now they have age on their side. Their families, torn with pain and guilt, spend months or years struggling to do "the right thing." Finally, they give up.

5   I have been through it. I have friends who are going through it. Caring, concerned sons and daughters who try, God knows they try, but the harder they try the harder it gets. Their elderly parents who should know better carp and criticize and complain. Instead of compromising, they constantly test their children, forever setting up new challenges for them to meet, assuming the one-sided game can go on forever.

6   **A Nightmare**   It comes as a shock to them when the special privileges conferred by their age and relationship run out, and their son or daughter tolerates their tyranny no longer. "How can you do this to me?" the parent cries, bags packed.

7   It is not easy.

8   We have friends who spent a fortune remodeling their home to provide an apartment for the wife's aging mother. The daughter was determined to overcome their differences for the chance to be close to her mother, to give her mother the love of a family rather than the services of a mercenary. Instead, she provided herself and her family with a three-year nightmare, the old woman seizing every opportunity to demean her daughter's husband, criticize the children and turn every family argument into a screaming fight.

9   "She's tearing our family apart," the daughter cries. "I'm going to be the villain by casting her out, but she has to go, or it's the end of my marriage."

10   Our friend is now searching for a suitable home. In her desperation she will settle for the best home available, which will not necessarily be the best home.

11   Another friend not only brings her father-in-law cooked meals, she cleans his apart-ment every week. Not once has he thanked her. But he has managed to find fault with everything she does. How long will he be able to live by himself? Another year, perhaps. And then what? Who will he blame when he winds up in an institution? Not himself.

12   A business acquaintance makes solitary visits to his angry mother in her lonely apartment. His wife will no longer submit to the old woman's hostility. The old woman, an Italian Catholic, cannot forgive her son for marrying a French Catholic. Mixed mar-riages, she still proclaims regularly, don't work. Twenty-five years and three delightful children don't count.

13   Can't she read the handwriting on the wall? She is busy writing her own future.

14   When my mother became ill, I moved her from her Sun Belt apartment to our home so that she could spend her remaining time with her own family, her only grand-children. Although she never approved of my wife (the wrong religion again), we were positive she would relinquish her prejudices in exchange for love and care. No such luck. Instead of making an attempt to adjust to our household, my mother tried to manipulate the four of us to center our lives around her.

15   My wife took her to the doctor regularly, supervised her medication, bought and prepared special foods for her—all while working full time—yet my mother found

nothing right about anything she did. Our refrigerator could be bulging, but my mother managed to crave the one thing missing. We were made to feel guilty if we left her alone for an evening, and were maneuvered into quarrels if we stayed. After five months of this, we began to investigate "homes."

The Life of a Family   Even the most relentlessly cheerful were depressing. Amidst flowered walls and piped-in music ("Heaven, I'm in Heaven") old people stared at television or gathered in activity rooms where they were kept busy with the arts and crafts taught in the third grade. They were not bedridden, these people; they required no nursing, no special care. Although unable to shop, cook and take care of a home of their own, they were quite capable of participating in the life of a family. Yet they were separated from their families.   16

How many of these people had driven their families to drive them out? How many felt that reaching 60 or 70 or 80 entitled them to behave in a manner that would never be tolerated in the young? As if the very fact of being old excused them from the rules of common decency. As if the right to be demanding and complaining was conferred upon them along with half fares on buses and discount days at the market.   17

That cantankerous old man may be a laugh riot on the stage as he sends comic characters scurrying at his every command, but he is hell to live with. That feisty old lady may be hilarious when company comes, but she can drive a family crazy. They are candidates for being "put away" as soon as the family being destroyed gets up the courage.   18

I don't mean to suggest that there are not great numbers of old people who must live in institutions because they are victims—victims of infirmity and, yes, victims of callous, selfish children. But for our own sakes, and for our children, it is pointless to ignore the fact that many of the elderly bear some responsibility for their fate. After all, warm, loving, sharing people are a joy to live with whatever their age.   19

➤ **FOR WRITING OR DISCUSSION**

1. What kind of proof does Sloan use to back up his assertion that many elderly parents, because of their behavior, put themselves in nursing homes? How convincing is his proof?
2. What, according to Sloan, do elderly parents do that makes them candidates for a nursing home?
3. Sloan concludes that "warm, loving, sharing people are a joy to live with whatever their age" (paragraph 19). Should everyone who is not warm, loving, and sharing be placed in an institution?
4. Does the author show an awareness of opposing arguments? Where?
5. Write an argumentation paper using Sloan's approach of attacking a position with which most people agree. Here are some possible topics:

   The nation needs to provide more jobs for teenagers.

   An adopted child has the right to find out the identity of his or her natural parents.

   Nuclear disarmament will decrease the chances of war.

Violence in cartoons is a bad influence on children.

Big-time football and basketball in our colleges have corrupted American education.

Wilderness areas must be preserved.

Let's encourage censorship of any writing that offends moral or religious values.

JAMES Q. WILSON

Just Take Away Their Guns

1. The President wants still tougher gun control legislation and thinks it will work. The public supports more gun control laws but suspects they won't work. The public is right.

2. Legal restraints on the lawful purchase of guns will have little effect on the illegal use of guns. There are some 200 million guns in private ownership, about one-third of them handguns. Only about 2 percent of the latter are employed to commit crimes. It would take a Draconian, and politically impossible, confiscation of legally purchased guns to make much of a difference in the number used by criminals. Moreover, only about one-sixth of the handguns used by serious criminals are purchased from a gun shop or pawnshop. Most of these handguns are stolen, borrowed, or obtained through private purchases that wouldn't be affected by gun laws.

3. What is worse, any successful effort to shrink the stock of legally purchased guns (or of ammunition) would reduce the capacity of law-abiding people to defend themselves. Gun control advocates scoff at the importance of self-defense, but they are wrong to do so. Based on a household survey, Gary Kleck, a criminologist at Florida State University, has estimated that every year, guns are used—that is, displayed or fired—for defensive purposes more than a million times, not counting their use by the police. If his estimate is correct, this means that the number of people who defend themselves with a gun exceeds the number of arrests for violent crimes and burglaries.

4. Our goal should not be the disarming of law-abiding citizens. It should be to reduce the number of people who carry guns unlawfully, especially in places—on streets, in taverns—where the mere presence of a gun can increase the hazards we all face. The most effective way to reduce illegal gun-carrying is to encourage the police to take guns away from people who carry them without a permit. This means encouraging the police to make street frisks.

5. The Fourth Amendment to the Constitution bans "unreasonable searches and seizures." In 1968 the Supreme Court decided (*Terry v. Ohio*) that a frisk—patting down a person's outer clothing—is proper if the officer has a "reasonable suspicion" that the person is armed and dangerous. If a pat-down reveals an object that might be a gun, the officer can enter the suspect's pocket to remove it. If the gun is being carried illegally, the suspect can be arrested.

The reasonable-suspicion test is much less stringent than the probable-cause standard   6
the police must meet in order to make an arrest. A reasonable suspicion, however, is more
than just a hunch; it must be supported by specific facts. The courts have held, not always
consistently, that these facts include someone acting in a way that leads an experienced
officer to conclude criminal activity may be afoot; someone fleeing at the approach of an
officer; a person who fits a drug courier profile; a motorist stopped for a traffic violation
who has a suspicious bulge in his pocket; a suspect identified by a reliable informant as
carrying a gun. The Supreme Court has also upheld frisking people on probation or parole.

Some police departments frisk a lot of people, but usually the police frisk rather   7
few, at least for the purpose of detecting illegal guns. In 1992 the police arrested about
240,000 people for illegally possessing or carrying a weapon. This is only about one-
fourth as many as were arrested for public drunkenness. The average police officer
will make *no* weapons arrests and confiscate *no* guns during any given year. Mark
Moore, a professor of public policy at Harvard University, found that most weapons
arrests were made because a citizen complained, not because the police were out
looking for guns.

It is easy to see why. Many cities suffer from a shortage of officers, and even those   8
with ample law-enforcement personnel worry about having their cases thrown out for
constitutional reasons or being accused of police harassment. But the risk of violating
the Constitution or engaging in actual, as opposed to perceived, harassment can be
substantially reduced.

Each patrol officer can be given a list of people on probation or parole who live on   9
that officer's beat and be rewarded for making frequent stops to insure that they are not
carrying guns. Officers can be trained to recognize the kinds of actions that the Court
will accept as providing the "reasonable suspicion" necessary for a stop and frisk.
Membership in a gang known for assaults and drug dealing could be made the basis, by
statute or Court precedent, for gun frisks.

The available evidence supports the claim that self-defense is a legitimate form of   10
deterrence. People who report to the National Crime Survey that they defended themselves with a weapon were less likely to lose property in a robbery or be injured in an
assault than those who did not defend themselves. Statistics have shown that would-be
burglars are threatened by gun-wielding victims about as many times a year as they are
arrested (and much more often than they are sent to prison) and that the chances of a
burglar being shot are about the same as his chances of going to jail. Criminals know
these facts even if gun control advocates do not and so are less likely to burgle occupied
homes in America than occupied ones in Europe, where the residents rarely have guns.

Some gun control advocates may concede these points but rejoin that the cost of   11
self-defense is self-injury: Handgun owners are more likely to shoot themselves or their
loved ones than a criminal. Not quite. Most gun accidents involve rifles and shotguns,
not handguns. Moreover, the rate of fatal gun accidents has been declining while the
level of gun ownership has been rising. There are fatal gun accidents just as there are
fatal car accidents, but in fewer than 2 percent of the gun fatalities was the victim someone mistaken for an intruder.

Those who urge us to forbid or severely restrict the sale of guns ignore these   12
facts. Worse, they adopt a position that is politically absurd. In effect, they say, "Your

government, having failed to protect your person and your property from criminal assault, now intends to deprive you of the opportunity to protect yourself."

13   Opponents of gun control make a different mistake. The National Rifle Association and its allies tell us that "guns don't kill, people kill" and urge the Government to punish more severely people who use guns to commit crimes. Locking up criminals does protect society from future crimes, and the prospect of being locked up may deter criminals. But our experience with meting out tougher sentences is mixed. The tougher the prospective sentence the less likely it is to be imposed, or at least to be imposed swiftly. If the Legislature adds on time for crimes committed with a gun, prosecutors often bargain away the add-ons; even when they do not, the judges in many states are reluctant to impose add-ons.

14   Worse, the presence of a gun can contribute to the magnitude of the crime even on the part of those who worry about serving a long prison sentence. Many criminals carry guns not to rob stores but to protect themselves from other armed criminals. Gang violence has become more threatening to bystanders as gang members have begun to arm themselves. People may commit crimes, but guns make some crimes worse. Guns often convert spontaneous outbursts of anger into fatal encounters. When some people carry them on the streets, others will want to carry them to protect themselves, and an urban arms race will be underway.

15   And modern science can be enlisted to help. Metal detectors at airports have reduced the number of airplane bombings and skyjackings to nearly zero. But these detectors only work at very close range. What is needed is a device that will enable the police to detect the presence of a large lump of metal in someone's pocket from a distance of ten or fifteen feet. Receiving such a signal could supply the officer with reasonable grounds for a pat-down. Underemployed nuclear physicists and electronics engineers in the post-cold-war era surely have the talents for designing a better gun detector.

16   Even if we do all these things, there will still be complaints. Innocent people will be stopped. Young black and Hispanic men will probably be stopped more often than older white Anglo males or women of any race. But if we are serious about reducing drive-by shootings, fatal gang wars and lethal quarrels in public places, we must get illegal guns off the street. We cannot do this by multiplying the forms one fills out at gun shops or by pretending that guns are not a problem until a criminal uses one.

➤ FOR WRITING OR DISCUSSION

1. What is the thesis of Wilson's essay? Where does he state it most directly?
2. What advantage does Wilson see in the police's using the "reasonable-suspicion test" over the "probable-cause standard"?
3. Why does Wilson support the value of self-defense with weapons? What arguments does he provide in opposition to his own point? Why does he use this strategy of presenting opposing arguments?
4. Write an argumentative essay in which you present your own views on gun control and the right to self-defense with weapons. Support your points with evidence drawn from your own experience or from what you have read or heard as part of this ongoing discussion in American society. Make no empty claims: Support your points with clear reasons for your assertions.

THOMAS JEFFERSON

Declaration of Independence

In Congress, July 4, 1776
The unanimous Declaration of the thirteen
United States of America

When in the course of human events, it becomes necessary for one people to dis-   1
solve the political bands which have connected them with another, and to assume among the powers of the earth, the separate and equal station to which the Laws of Nature and of Nature's God entitle them, a decent respect to the opinions of mankind requires that they should declare the causes which impel them to the separation.

We hold these truths to be self-evident, that all men are created equal, that they   2
are endowed by their Creator with certain unalienable rights, that among these are life, liberty and the pursuit of happiness. That to secure these rights, governments are instituted among men, deriving their just powers from the consent of the governed. That whenever any form of government becomes destructive of these ends, it is the right of the people to alter or to abolish it, and to institute new government, laying its foundation on such principles and organizing its powers in such form, as to them shall seem most likely to effect their safety and happiness. Prudence, indeed, will dictate that governments long established should not be changed for light and transient causes; and accordingly all experience hath shown, that mankind are more disposed to suffer, while evils are sufferable, than to right themselves by abolishing the forms to which they are accustomed. But when a long train of abuses and usurpations, pursuing invariably the same object evinces a design to reduce them under absolute despotism, it is their right, it is their duty, to throw off such government, and to provide new guards for their future security. Such has been the patient sufferance of these colonies; and such is now the necessity which constrains them to alter their former systems of government. The history of the present King of Great Britain is a history of repeated injuries and usurpations, all having in direct object the establishment of an absolute tyranny over these States. To prove this, let facts be submitted to a candid world.

He has refused his assent to laws, the most wholesome and necessary for the   3
public good.

He has forbidden his Governors to pass laws of immediate and pressing impor-   4
tance, unless suspended in their operation till his assent should be obtained; and when so suspended, he has utterly neglected to attend to them.

He has refused to pass other laws for the accommodation of large districts of peo-   5
ple, unless those people would relinquish the right of representation in the Legislature, a right inestimable to them and formidable to tyrants only.

He has called together legislative bodies at places unusual, uncomfortable, and dis-   6
tant from the depository of their public records, for the sole purpose of fatiguing them into compliance with his measures.

7   He has dissolved representative houses repeatedly, for opposing with manly firmness his invasions on the rights of the people.

8   He has refused for a long time, after such dissolutions, to cause others to be elected; whereby the legislative powers, incapable of annihilation, have returned to the people at large for their exercise; the State remaining in the meantime exposed to all the dangers of invasion from without and convulsions within.

9   He has endeavored to prevent the population of these states; for that purpose obstructing the laws of naturalization of foreigners; refusing to pass others to encourage their migration hither, and raising the conditions of new appropriations of lands.

10   He has obstructed the administration of justice, by refusing his assent to laws for establishing judiciary powers.

11   He has made judges dependent on his will alone, for the tenure of their offices, and the amount and payment of their salaries.

12   He has erected a multitude of new offices, and sent hither swarms of officers to harass our people, and eat out their substance.

13   He has kept among us, in times of peace, standing armies without the consent of our legislatures.

14   He has affected to render the military independent of and superior to the civil power. He has combined with others to subject us to a jurisdiction foreign to our constitution, and unacknowledged by our laws; giving his assent to their acts of pretended legislation:

15   For quartering large bodies of armed troops among us:

16   For protecting them, by a mock trial, from punishment for any murders which they should commit on the inhabitants of these States:

17   For cutting off our trade with all parts of the world:

18   For imposing taxes on us without our consent:

19   For depriving us in many cases, of the benefits of trial by jury:

20   For transporting us beyond seas to be tried for pretended offenses:

21   For abolishing the free system of English laws in a neighboring Province, establishing therein an arbitrary government, and enlarging its boundaries so as to render it at once an example and fit instrument for introducing the same absolute rule into these Colonies:

22   For taking away our charters, abolishing our most valuable laws, and altering fundamentally the forms of our governments:

23   For suspending our own Legislatures, and declaring themselves invested with power to legislate for us in all cases whatsoever.

24   He has abdicated government here, by declaring us out of his protection and waging war against us.

25   He has plundered our seas, ravaged our coasts, burnt our towns, and destroyed the lives of our people.

26   He is at this time transporting large armies of foreign mercenaries to complete the works of death, desolation and tyranny, already begun with circumstances of cruelty and perfidy scarcely paralleled in the most barbarous ages, and totally unworthy the head of a civilized nation.

He has constrained our fellow citizens taken captive on the high seas to bear arms   27
against their country, to become the executioners of their friends and brethren, or to fall
themselves by their hands.

He has excited domestic insurrections amongst us, and has endeavoured to bring   28
on the inhabitants of our frontiers, the merciless Indian savages, whose known rule of
warfare, is an undistinguished destruction of all ages, sexes and conditions.

In every stage of these oppressions we have petitioned for redress in the most hum-   29
ble terms: our repeated petitions have been answered only by repeated injury. A prince
whose character is thus marked by every act which may define a tyrant is unfit to be the
ruler of a free people.

Nor have we been wanting in attention to our British brethren. We have warned   30
them from time to time of attempts by their legislature to extend an unwarrantable jurisdiction over us. We have reminded them of the circumstances of our emigration and
settlement here. We have appealed to their native justice and magnanimity, and we
have conjured them by the ties of our common kindred to disavow these usurpations,
which would inevitably interrupt our connections and correspondence. They too have
been deaf to the voices of justice and of consanguinity. We must, therefore acquiesce
in the necessity, which denounces our separation, and hold them as we hold the rest of
mankind, enemies in war, in peace friends.

We, therefore, the Representatives of the United States of America, in General   31
Congress assembled, appealing to the Supreme Judge of the world for the rectitude
of our intentions, do, in the name, and by authority of the good people of these
Colonies, solemnly publish and declare, That these United Colonies are, and of right
ought to be Free and Independent States; that they are absolved from all allegiance
to the British Crown, and that all political connection between them and the state of
Great Britain, is and ought to be totally dissolved; and that as Free and Independent
States, they have full power to levy war, conclude peace, contract alliances, establish commerce, and to do all other acts and things which Independent States may of
right do. And for the support of this declaration, with a firm reliance on the protection of Divine Providence, we mutually pledge to each other our lives, our fortunes,
and our sacred honor.

➤ **FOR WRITING OR DISCUSSION**

1. What does the Declaration of Independence devote most of its efforts
   to proving?
2. What basic assumptions does it make that do not need to be proved?
3. How does the Declaration of Independence take special pains to show that it
   is the product of rational, responsible people rather than hotheads? (This
   question could make a good subject for a paper.)
4. Where does the language become most emotional? Is this emotion justified
   where it occurs, and, if so, why?

5. Write an argumentation paper calling for a major change in government or legislation, such as making voting compulsory, limiting a president to a single term, forcing Supreme Court justices to run for office, or abolishing political parties.

Readings for Writing

Where do you stand? In our first selection, a priest unexpectedly defends the "commercialization" of Christmas and even defends it on religious grounds. Our second selection includes a newspaper editorial on the murder of a child by a paroled sex offender and a writer's angry denunciation of the editorial.

ROBERT A. SIRICO

God's Gift, a Commercial Christmas

1   This holiday season, like every other in memory, we will hear calls to take "commercialism" out of Christmas. The National Council of Churches has already issued a press release to encourage us to "forgo the secular, commercialized frenzy of Christmas" in favor of "genuine charity." "Only those who sit in darkness believe that love can be bought and sold," intoned the Rev. Joan Brown, top executive of the council.

2   These warnings against money and materialism will inspire guilt and conflict, but not much goodness and clarity. The critics of holiday "materialism" forget that commerce during this season is inspired primarily by the desire to give to others. And what other season of the year inspires commercial activity organized around such altruistic themes?

3   The denunciations of commerce at Christmas are usually issued by the same people who castigate capitalism year 'round. In doing so, they offer a new gnosticism; the view that the material world is fundamentally suspect, even evil, and that the possession of material goods, beyond the "essentials," is in itself sinful. To modern gnostics, the ultimate goal of each person's life should be overcoming the fact of material reality. And because the season does indeed remind us of how fortunate we are, the anticommerce message resonates.

4   But often forgotten in the annual screeds against materialism is that both the Jewish and Christian traditions, which embrace the goodness of the physical world, reject the gnostic heresy. The Book of Genesis teaches us that the Earth is a gift from God for our use and that it was created good (Gen. 1:25). To Christians, the Incarnation of the Savior affirms the moral legitimacy of our own corporality.

5   Of course, the disciplines of religious orders often require vows of poverty, chastity and obedience (I have accepted such vows myself).[1] But these oaths are taken as a witness

---

[1]The author is a Paulist priest.

to transcendence; they do not imply a condemnation of the material world. The same church that administers the sacraments has for centuries rejected a dualism between matter and spirit. Rather, Christianity teaches that the body and the spirit are what together make us human. Jesus came to dwell among us, fully divine and fully human, so that eternity could enter time. What better season than Christmas to express our own love of others, in an approximation of God's love for us?

We should remember that the Magi who crossed miles of desert brought the baby Jesus gold (universally desired for monetary purposes and pure decoration), frankincense and myrrh (exotic incense resins reserved mainly for royalty). These were the world's most precious commodities. These gifts might even be called extravagant and superfluous: What would a little baby do with these? Don't they go beyond what is "essential"? Of course. They were, appropriately, the most highly prized symbols of love and awe the three kings had to offer.   6

The anticommercial attitude bespeaks a spiritual elitism—ascetics looking down at the joy common folk experience in giving gifts. Somehow finding the perfect pair of flannel slippers for an uncle or a purple Barney to light the eyes of a youngster is considered false charity and frivolous to boot. One not-for-profit group even sells a poster depicting ancient Bethlehem as it might have looked if the capitalism of today had existed on the first Christmas. They seem to confuse commerce with the invention of electricity.   7

The economic boom experienced during December every year is the best kind of commerce there is. As the Word became flesh, our sentiments become gifts, no matter how humble such expressions may be. Children should be taught to put others before themselves, using allowances or labor to purchase or produce a gift for another. In Advent we are all reminded to focus outward, and take joy in discovering the hidden fancies of family members, friends, and co-workers.   8

Granted, some of the people who profit from this holiday season do not necessarily do so with higher values in mind. Those who hawk their wares are out to make a buck, no doubt. But that in no way takes away from the end result of their business: allowing people to express their generosity of spirit to one another. If early followers of Jesus could take a pagan festival and make it their own, surely Christians should not mind secularists making money by serving good holiday intentions. And surely, spirituality can be discovered in the marketplace, which is, after all, where we spend much of our time.   9

The Christmas season calls us to be thankful for our own prosperity—and to share it with others, including those beyond our circle of family and friends. A huge body of custom has grown up around the celebration of Christmas. It is one of the few religious holidays that is recognized in the secular calendar; and the Christmas tree, yule log, carols, sweetmeats—all commodities to be bought and sold—are all deeply embedded in our culture.   10

In Victorian England, children were given presents at the birth of a brother or sister; during Christmas, the feast of the birth of Jesus, even farm animals were given gifts in celebration of the birthday of the universal little brother. It was customary for a landlord to feed his tenants in exchange for a log that would burn in the fireplace. Advent remains a time for opening our hearts and our homes to those in need. And December is the primary month of charitable giving for reasons other than tax write-offs.   11

12   As for the theological scrooges who want to take commerce out of the season, they should not forget how important this month is for businesses to provide for the public during the rest of the year, when gift giving is not the norm. The jobs and salaries taken for granted during the next 11 months depend in great part on an enterprising holiday season.

13   For Heaven's sake, don't forget the higher meaning of this glorious season. But also for Heaven's sake, and for the sake of generosity and tradition, don't take away the simple pleasure of giving tokens of love and friendship to one another. Love cannot be bought and sold, of course; but it can be expressed and symbolized by material generosity, which is one of the characteristic marks of this beautiful time of the year.

➤ FOR WRITING OR DISCUSSION

1. How important to you is it—or should it be—that this essay was written by a priest rather than by a businessperson? How important is it—or should it be—that the essay was first printed in the *Wall Street Journal* rather than in a religious publication?
2. Summarize in your own words the author's basic defense of buying gifts at Christmas.
3. Is the author fair to the arguments of his opponents? Does he concede any strong points his opponents may have?
4. Referring specifically to at least some of the points raised in this essay, write an argumentative paper either attacking or defending the author's position.

Two Comments on the Megan Kanka Tragedy

THE NEW YORK TIMES

Dealing with Sex Offenders

1   It was a genuine tragedy when 33-year-old Jesse Timmendequas talked 7-year-old Megan Kanka into entering his house in Hamilton Township, N.J., one day last month. Mr. Timmendequas had been convicted twice for sexually assaulting young girls, and had served six years in a facility for sex offenders. Once Megan was in the house he strangled her to death and raped her.

2   Small wonder that the angry residents of Megan's town and much of New Jersey's political leadership want to crack down on sex offenders who have served their time in

jail and been released back into the community. Proposals range from requiring released sex offenders to register with the police departments of the towns they settle in, to requiring that they report their whereabouts every 30 days, to making them spend the rest of their lives in prison unless they can convince officials that they have been rehabilitated. Under one proposal, the police would be alerted and asked to notify neighborhood residents of a sex offender's presence.

The Speaker of the New York Assembly, Sheldon Silver, also plans to introduce a bill calling for community notification; Gov. Mario Cuomo has said he would press for such a law.   3

Those who would impose new stringencies on sex offenders are speaking for millions of Americans. But some proposals could do more harm than good—by triggering outbreaks of vigilantism or by destroying the efforts of thousands of law-abiding former sex offenders to rebuild their lives.   4

Proposals to notify communities of the sex offenders in their midst seem particularly problematic. Why, for instance, should a sex offender be branded when a released drug dealer, armed robber or murderer is not? Some argue that recidivism among sex offenders is so high that "better safe than sorry" should be the rule. But careful studies of sex offenders after release have found that most do not repeat their crimes. Treatment experts claim that recidivism rates are not only exaggerated but depend on a range of factors, including the nature of the crime and whether the offender received treatment. Although several therapies have been shown to lower recidivism rates, the vast majority of jailed sex offenders get no help at all.   5

Community notification laws do little or nothing to prevent a sex offender from striking again; they simply make it more likely that the offender will be hounded from one town to another. Indeed, sex offenders might actually become more dangerous if driven from communities where family and friends help control their behavior.   6

The danger of vigilantism is real. A community notification system in the state of Washington, under which the police can, at their discretion, inform anyone from county officials to local newspapers of a released sex offender's presence, has resulted in arson that destroyed a sex offender's house, death threats, assaults, slashed tires and loss of employment and housing.   7

So how, then, craft a system that will protect a community from those against whom it *must* be protected without stigmatizing those from whom it need not be? Carefully, that is how, and without hysteria. Keeping communities safe should be primarily a matter for the police and the criminal justice system, not for a frightened citizenry.   8

Registration programs that help policy keep track of released sex offenders may well have a place in a careful police program, under court supervision that assures procedures meet constitutional safeguards. After all, police professionals already swap information about the whereabouts of many released criminals. But dissemination of the information can only inflame passions.   9

Penalties for preying on children can be toughened, as they were last week in New Jersey; and juvenile offenders need early counseling and treatment. Those who have   10 spoken for the Megans of this world are speaking from the heart. Now it is time for Americans to use their heads as well.

MIDGE DECTER

Megan's Law and the New York Times

1   Probably there are by now few people who have not heard the story of Megan Kanka of Hamilton Township, New Jersey—or at least some story similar to it. It is the kind of story, indeed, to which we are in danger of becoming inured because of its familiarity: how one day during this past July Megan, seven years old, went missing and after a frantic search was found discarded in some tall grass not far from her house, raped and strangled. Shortly thereafter, a thirty-three-year-old man named Jesse Timmendequas was arrested and then confessed to the crime.

2   Timmendequas had twice before been convicted of sexually assaulting young girls, had spent six years in what the press referred to as a "treatment facility," and had only recently been released and returned, as they say, to the community. Along with two other sexual-offender "rehabilitees," he had been living in the house across the street from Megan's. After he was apprehended, neighbors told reporters, as neighbors in these circumstances so often do, that he had been a quiet man.

3   The citizens of Hamilton Township were naturally outraged—by the crime itself, of course, but almost as much by the fact that no one had informed them of the criminal history of their new neighbors. They quickly organized themselves and began to circulate a petition—which has been signed so far by more than 200,000 New Jerseyans—demanding the passage of a state law that would require correction officials to notify people when a sex offender has moved into their neighborhood. Their crusade is succeeding and has spread to New York, where similar legislation will soon be proposed in the State Assembly.

4   The demand for such notification is not new. In various forms and guises, it has recently figured in numerous proposals to toughen the criminal-justice system and offer more protection to potential victims and less to violent, or potentially violent, criminals.

5   In any event, it seems certain that in many places beyond New Jersey and New York, people are gearing up to initiate referenda or to engage in other forms of public protest against what appears to be the regnant liberal preoccupation with the privacy rights and other privileges of violent criminals, particularly sex offenders.

6   Nowhere has this preoccupation been more in evidence than in an editorial published in the *New York Times* on August 15 under the title, "Dealing With Sex Offenders." What happened to Megan Kanka was a "genuine tragedy," the editorial begins; small wonder that her neighbors, together with much of New Jersey's political leadership, are demanding a crackdown on sex offenders who have been released from jail.

Understandable as is the emotion behind this demand, however, the *Times* would caution everyone not to be too hasty.

It is true, the *Times* acknowledges, that those who wish to have "new stringencies" 7 imposed on sex offenders are speaking for millions of Americans. Nevertheless, the *Times* believes that some of the measures currently being proposed for dealing with these offenders are likely to do more harm than good: for example, that sex offenders be required to register with the police departments of the towns they settle in; or that they be required to report their whereabouts every 30 days; or that the police be required to notify the residents of a neighborhood of a sex offender's presence there; or, most stringent of all, that sex offenders be made to spend the rest of their lives in prison "unless they can convince officials that they have been rehabilitated."

All this, the *Times* fears, could "destroy the efforts of thousands of law-abiding 8 former sex offenders to rebuild their lives."

The demand for notification is, as the *Times* sees it, particularly problematic. "Why, 9 for instance, should a sex offender be branded when a released drug dealer, armed robber, or murderer is not?" It is argued that the rate of recidivism among sex offenders is so high, the editorial continues, that it is better to be safe than sorry. However, "treatment experts" disagree. In the opinion of these experts, says the editorial, not only are the recidivism rates exaggerated, "but [they] depend on a range of factors, including the nature of the crime and whether the offender received treatment." Moreover, although "several therapies have been shown to lower recidivism rates, the vast majority of jailed sex offenders get no help at all."

Be that as it may, "Community-notification laws do little or nothing to prevent a sex 10 offender from striking again; they simply make it more likely that the offender will be hounded from one town to another"—possibly become even more dangerous than he might otherwise be, away from the control of family and friends.

Conversely, the editorial worries, such a system involves the danger of vigilantism. 11 That this danger is real can be seen from the community-notification system in the state of Washington, which has led to incidents of assault, arson, slashed tires, and loss of employment and housing.

How, then, the *Times* asks, can we craft a system that protects a community from 12 those against whom it must be protected without stigmatizing those from whom it need not be protected? The answer is, "Carefully . . . and without hysteria." Registration programs that help the police keep track of released sex offenders, "under court supervision that assures procedures meet constitutional safeguards," may well "have a place in a careful police program." Furthermore, "Penalties for preying on children can be toughened . . . and juvenile offenders need early counseling and treatment."

People who have been speaking for the Megans of this world speak from the heart, 13 concludes the *Times*. "Now it is time for Americans to use their heads as well."

There are, to be sure, very good reasons for sharing the *Times*'s skepticism about the 14 practical value of notification procedures. After all, when it comes down to it, what are the now-informed neighbors of a recently released rapist and/or child molester to do?

Keep their children permanently indoors? Move away? The only really practical step would be to impress upon their new neighbor the advisability of *his* moving on, i.e., "vigilantism"—something most decent people would, if they were capable of it at all, find most repellent. The citizens of Hamilton Township and their fellow petitioners are perhaps focusing what would otherwise be unmanageable rage, fear, and grief on the more manageable demand for notification.

15   The real issue for the residents of Hamilton Township is not that they were left ignorant of Jesse Timmendequas's past but the question of what a man with two prior convictions for sexually assaulting young girls was doing in their, or anybody else's, neighborhood in the first place—after only six years in a "treatment facility." Obviously he had convinced the authorities that he was cured and now ready to become one more of the *Times*'s "thousands of law-abiding former sex offenders" out to rebuild his life.

16   The *Times* relies for its complacency about these people on certain "treatment experts." But there are other experts who strongly doubt that any known programs of rehabilitation can really work to cure violent sex offenders. Thus, the eminent criminologist John J. Dilulio, Jr. of Princeton recently noted in an op-ed piece in the *Wall Street Journal* that in his researches he has come upon no such program that could responsibly be called successful. Readers of the *Times*'s news columns, if not of its editorial page, are provided more than ample anecdotal evidence to support Dilulio. Almost every week, it seems, one rapist-murderer after another turns out to have been on parole or probation after a prior conviction for the same crime or one almost like it.

17   So much for the dismal news about rape in general. Beyond this, we move into the subcategory represented by Megan Kanka.

18   Most people, unconfused by "enlightened" social theories, instinctively understand that a man who is capable of raping a very small child—or a baby in its crib, for we have in these times lived to witness even this—occupies a very special rank of evil, far, far beyond the human territory that is bounded by terms like "rehabilitation" and "law-abiding," or even normal punishment.

19   Such a man is not, as the *Times* would have us believe, in the same class as a drug dealer, or an ordinary murderer, or even, dare one say it?, a rapist of grown women. A person unconfused by fancy social theory might even wonder how someone can commit so unspeakable an act and still find himself worthy to go on living, never mind to be released from incarceration. From whom can he dare to seek understanding, let alone forgiveness—his family, his friends, his therapist? Life imprisonment without parole for the sexual assaulter of a little girl is not only the one truly safe decision from the point of view of society; it might, ironically, be an act of kindness to the rapist as well.

20   It is unlikely that any such thought has ever entered the mind of the author of that *Times* editorial. Partly, no doubt, from a growing habituation to stories like Megan's, but also in no small part out of an unexamined body of pieties about crime and criminals, those who share the *Times*'s views of violent crime have a way of slipping beyond the reality of the criminal behavior they set out to contemplate. Molesters of

children, as we know, were once upon a time shunned even in prison and even by the most brutal of their fellow inmates. They were *special.* But it appears that what was once a point of moral clarity among even the lowest of criminals is now regarded by our leading newspaper as a possibly understandable but nevertheless dangerous form of "hysteria."

Which is why the *Times*'s call to exercise care in crafting a system to deal with this 21 problem is one that it might itself profitably heed in "crafting" its own response to crimes and criminals. Denial, too, is a form of hysteria, and often a very dangerous one. And what but profound denial—especially at a time when Americans are all too justifiably distressed about out-of-control violence—would lead someone to go on reciting that old mantra, "counseling and treatment"?

Vigilantism is certainly not to be taken lightly. Yet anyone thinking seriously about 22 how to forestall it would not, in the year 1994, be worrying about the possible stigmatization of released sex offenders. He would, rather, be worrying about how to restore a little sanity to a criminal-justice system that, when it comes to dealing with really serious crime, has been rendered virtually impotent by a now merely automatic and mindless obsession with the rights of the criminals.

In other words, that the rape-murder of Megan Kanka by a third-time offender 23 should have been seized upon as the occasion for issuing a caution that not all rapists are recidivists, is the sign of something seriously out of whack in the moral understanding of the *Times* and those for whom it speaks.

The treatment for this condition, if there is one, would have to begin with a heavy 24 course of immersion in reality. So far the recidivism rate for perpetrators of mindless piety does not provide much grounds for hope. But who knows what new and effective therapy might one day soon be in the offing?—perhaps the ensconcement of an unannounced two-time rapist in the house across the street.

➤ FOR WRITING OR DISCUSSION

1. Does Midge Decter fairly and fully summarize the contents of the *New York Times* editorial?
2. What does Decter mean by "mindless pieties"?
3. Explain the meaning of Decter's words, "Denial, too, is a form of hysteria."
4. What upsets Decter most about the *Times* editorial?
5. How does Decter think convicted child molesters should be treated?
6. Check your local newspaper, the *New York Times Index,* or *The Readers' Guide to Periodical Literature* for current views and actions on "Megan's law." Where is public opinion on the issue today?
7. Choose one of the following assignments:

   Write your own *Times* editorial replying to Decter.

   Reply to Decter in the role of one of these people: a neighbor or relative of the child, a police officer, a judge, the criminal.

WRITING TOPICS

If you are having difficulty deciding on a topic for your argumentation paper, you might find help simply by choosing one of the following statements and arguing for or against that statement.

1. Get-rich quiz shows on television are bad for the American public.
2. Until adulthood, brothers and sisters are far more likely to be rivals than friends.
3. College students should perform five hours of community service each week.
4. Minimum competence tests should be required before students are granted a high school diploma.
5. The sale of tobacco should be made illegal.
6. Boxing as a sport is an affront to humanity.
7. Among the groups most unfairly discriminated against are fat people.
8. If we require people to pass a driving test before licensing them to operate a car, we should require people to pass some kind of parenting test before allowing them to have children.
9. Marijuana should be legal for medicinal purposes.
10. There are no bad students, only bad teachers.
11. Owning a home makes much better sense than owning an apartment.
12. As an exercise, swimming far exceeds running as a means to health and fitness.
13. Cats make better pets than dogs.
14. The best (or worst) season of the year is _____ .
15. Random drug tests of high school students are a violation of human rights.

CROSSCURRENTS

1. Bernard Sloan's "Old Folks at Home" (page 391) and Betty Rollin's "The Best Years of My Life" (page 308) both deal with the effects of illness and aging. What insights does each selection provide? How are the theses in the two pieces different?
2. Robert A. Sirico in "God's Gift, a Commercial Christmas" (page 400), and Milos Vamos in "How I'll Become an American" (page 184) provide different views of commercialism in America. What point does each essay make about commercialism? Can all three writers be correct? Explain your point of view.

COLLABORATIVE LEARNING

Bring the drafts of your argumentation essays to class. Form groups of three students to discuss the efforts of group members and to make recommendations for the next draft. Use the "Review Checklist: Writing and Revising Your Argumentation Paper" to guide your conversation.

REVIEW CHECKLIST: WRITING AND REVISING YOUR ARGUMENTATION PAPER

- Have I done prewriting to explore ideas for a subject?
- Have I thought carefully about my purpose?
- Have I written for the usual general audience? If I am writing for a special audience, have I made that clear to the reader?
- Have I limited my subject?
- Have I established a clear thesis?
- Do I have enough support for my thesis?
- Have I used a calm, reasonable tone wherever possible and appropriate?
- Have I anticipated objections to my position and refuted them, if possible?
- Have I checked for logical fallacies?
- Have I proofread for grammar, spelling, and mechanics?

Photo courtesy: AP Photo/Bob Jordan

FROM IMAGE TO WORDS: A PHOTO WRITING ASSIGNMENT

The photograph above captures a scene that has stimulated discussion and argument over the last fifteen years or so. Should women participate in what have been tradition-ally male-dominated activities? Use the photograph as a springboard for an essay in which you take one side or the other of this argument. Draw on the principles of solid arguments developed in this chapter.

Special Writing

Special writing situations call for special instructions. Writing on the causes of your decision to go on a diet is far different from writing a paper on the causes of some literary character's actions: Captain Ahab's pursuit of Moby-Dick, for example, or Iago's seemingly motiveless plot against Othello. You may know how to write a well-organized comparison-and-contrast paper, but writing a personal essay on your different reactions to two television sitcoms is far different from writing an essay during a final examination in economics about the arguments for and against lower capital gains taxes.

In Part Three, we provide instruction for dealing with two of the most common kinds of academic writing: literary analysis and essay examinations. In addition, you will find a chapter on business writing, where you will learn about résumés, job application letters, and Internet resources for finding employment.

CHAPTER
15

Literary Analysis

To **analyze** is to study a complex event, thing, or person by examining one or more of its parts and then showing the relationship of each part to the whole. When you are given an assignment such as "Explain the reasons for the disruption of the play in Poston's 'The Revolt of the Evil Fairies' "(pages 311–314) or "Trace the sequence of clues planted by the author so that we have a chance to anticipate the surprise ending in Jackson's 'Charles' " (pages 219–222), you are being asked to write a **literary analysis.** Sometimes instructors assign **explication,** a special form of literary analysis in which short works like poems or stories are examined word by word or paragraph by paragraph to show how each element fits into the general pattern and purpose of the entire work.

Apart from explication, you will find in most cases that literary analysis does not call for any writing skills with which you are unfamiliar. The preceding assignment about "The Revolt of the Evil Fairies," for example, would lead to a cause-and-effect paper. The assignment about "Charles" would lead to a process paper. Likewise, the student who discussed two Shakespeare sonnets in Chapter 10 (pages 235–238) wrote a comparison–contrast paper. However, to write a good literary analysis, you must learn how to read a literary work with analysis in mind.

Many of your instructors have undoubtedly devoted a large portion of their professional lives to analyzing literature. A few classroom sessions with your instructor, digging into specific works without worrying too much about preestablished methods and rules, are probably your best source of learning how to analyze works of literature. However, the following guidelines should also help you to deal with literary works. We can't tell you what to say—that will vary with each assignment. It will depend on the material you are analyzing, and some subjects offer a great deal of leeway for individual interpretation and insight. Still, the following commonsense suggestions should be helpful.

Writing Your Analysis of Literature

■ *Read the material slowly.*   When you need to wade through a pile of junk, fast reading is fine. When you are reading good or great literature, much of which treats complex ideas and emotions, often with complex means of expression, the intelligent approach is to read slowly. Moreover, any analysis involves a close examination of details. Fast reading can give you a general sense of the main points, but it can't prepare you to deal competently with all the concerns of a full-fledged analysis.

■ *Reread.*   When you read a story or poem for the first time, you're unlikely to have any valid notion of what the author is up to. The author knows how the story is going to end, but you don't. And since the author does know in advance what is going to happen on the last page, he or she has been making all sorts of crucial preparations earlier in the story to lead into the ending. On a first reading, those earlier pages cannot mean much to you. They can create interest or suspense, but that's about all, since you don't yet know anything of the author's purpose. Once you do understand what the author has been trying to do, and then *read the story again,* all the ingredients will begin to register in a different way, a way that is emotionally and intellectually impossible to achieve in a first reading. The seemingly separate parts of the story can now come through to you as pieces within a logical pattern. Without a sense of that logical pattern and of how all elements are related to it, your analysis will be weak and incomplete.

■ *Assume that everything is significant.*   In good literature, nothing should be an accident. Each word, each character, each thought, each incident should make a contribution to the total effect the author is trying for. The contribution is sometimes obvious and direct: The author casually mentions that a car is nine years old because later on the car will break down. At other times, the contribution is indirect: The author spends a paragraph describing a glowing fireplace to establish a homey mood that fits in with the story's central idea—the joys of family life. As you think about the material you are going to analyze, as you brood about what you are going to say and how you are going to say it, keep in mind that *nothing is beneath your notice.* Assume that everything serves a purpose and that you have not reached a full understanding of the story, poem, or play until you clearly see the purpose that everything serves. When you come up against elements that serve no purpose, you can safely conclude that the work is imperfect. Read closely, and give serious attention to details. When you get to the writing stage, make liberal use of the details to support your comments. No matter how much actual work you have done, if you do not rely heavily on references to details, your analysis will seem based on vague impressions and snap judgments.

■ *Do not study details out of context.*   Your response to the details of a work—a word, a phrase, a character, an incident—depends on the work as a whole. A sentence like "Mrs. Smythe spent twenty minutes arranging the flowers in the vase" could appear in a satire of a neurotic fussbudget or a moving sketch of a mother preparing the house for her child's return from the army. A diploma may appear in one place as a symbol of hope and in another as a symbol of despair. Your analysis or interpretation of the flower arranging or the diploma must obviously be in harmony with the rest of the work. Keep the intentions of the whole work in mind as you consider the proper approach toward one of its parts.

One more observation: Try not to let your purely personal tastes or prejudices interfere with your responses to the work. If a writer of a short story has a character light a cigarette to show nervousness, fight off any temptation to analyze the character as a stupid person who doesn't know that cigarettes are hazardous to health. If another writer presents a sympathetic and approving study of a couple who decide to stay married for the sake of the children, don't analyze the couple as victims of outmoded bourgeois morality and a repressive society. An analysis explains what is going on in a piece of literature, not what your own philosophy of life may happen to be.

■ *Forget about "hidden meanings."*   A number of people are fond of using the phrase "hidden meanings" when they discuss or write about literature—but it means nothing. No writer who is any good goes around hiding meanings. Writers have enough trouble expressing them openly. The few writers who do play hide-and-seek with their readers are generally pretentious fakes. In any case, avoid the "hidden meanings" approach to literature. Never use the phrase, as many people do, to refer to an idea or emotion that the author had no intention of concealing, but that you just didn't happen to notice on a first reading.

■ *Distinguish between moral and theme.*   Good literature, in general, is not pure art in the sense that a painting of a pretty landscape is pure art. Most literature attempts far more directly than such paintings to make a comment on life. In considering a story like Irwin Shaw's "The Girls in Their Summer Dresses" (page 287), we can and should discuss artistic elements such as plot construction and dialog, but the story is also a comment on human nature. The author has something to say. Our response to the story depends largely on how well that "something" comes through to us. Without artistry, of course, the author's comment has no chance of coming through, but the author obviously has more than artistry alone in mind. For literature to comment on life, the critic needs to understand that comment fully. If a work has something to say, we must ask ourselves what it is saying as well as how it is saying it.

A comment on life, however, is not necessarily a **moral.** In good literature, especially modern literature, it is almost never a moral. This fact confuses many inexperienced readers. For them the question of "what does it mean" or "what does it say" usually implies "what is the moral"—the direct, simple, short statement of a lesson or message to be drawn from the work. When they find no clear moral, they tend to feel cheated or frustrated. Why can't writers just come right out with it and say what they mean? Why are they so fond of hidden meanings (even if the authors of this book state that there aren't such things)? Why do they indulge in these mystifying literary games?

There are two ways of answering these questions, one simple and one not so simple. First, morals have a way of being too tidy, too catchy, and dangerously superficial. They are fine in proverbs. They are fine in children's stories and five-minute sermons. An adult mind, however, can't help being suspicious of truths that are so conveniently packaged. Life is usually too complicated. Literature produced by a thoughtful writer attempts to capture some of the quality of life itself, and the preachy oversimplifications inherent in moralizing spring from distortions of life. *"He who hesitates is lost"; "Life begins at forty"; "It's no use crying over spilt milk"*—this stuff sounds good enough, but we all know that sometimes hesitation is advisable, that a significant life can begin at any age, and that crying over spilt milk has inspired, among many other things, some immortal poetry. When you look for neat little morals in literature, you cheat yourself and you are unfair to the writer. If a writer's comment on life can be summed up in a moral, the odds are that you have wasted your time reading the entire work.

The second reason that people have trouble when they set out to find morals is that a good writer *dramatizes* ideas. The ideas, in other words, are rarely expressed directly, as they would be in a sermon or a philosophy or a sociology textbook. Insofar as the writer has any ideas, they grow out of the characters the writer creates and their responses to the situations the writer devises for them. Thus, because we care about the characters, the ideas register on our emotions as well as our intellects. Writers try to convey life, not merely ideas about life—for if the ideas are all that matter, their works are elaborate shams that should have been sermons, textbooks, or letters to the editor of their local newspapers. Shakespeare does not *tell* us, "Young love can be beautiful, but can create a lot of problems, too"; he writes *Romeo and Juliet.* Granted, we may get this abstract idea about love from the play, along with many other ideas just as significant, but primarily we get a far richer sense of profound concern for two human beings. Ted Poston does not *tell* us "Racial prejudice is harmful" or "African Americans have sometimes tended to accept white values, even when doing so led to self-loathing" or squeeze any number of other morals out of the story; he writes "The Revolt of the Evil Fairies" (page 311) and shows us the results of racial discrimination in action. He dramatizes. Those who read the story as it was meant to be read do not just feel disapproval of discrimination; they cringe with horror at a child's recognition of a terrible truth. How do you put that into a moral?

As readers and critics we are much better off in dealing with a writer's something-to-say if we think not of the moral but the **theme.** A theme in literature is not a moral, a message, or a piece of advice; rather, it is *the underlying issue, the basic area of permanent human experience treated by the author.* A theme does not make a statement; it names a subject. We can say that the theme or themes of *Romeo and Juliet* are love, and family, and fate, and conflicting loyalties, and reason versus passion. We could add to the list, and a good critic could probably then find a way of linking all the separate themes into one theme that covers them all. The author offers comments on these separate themes by creating certain characters who act in certain ways. Are we really entitled to draw general morals from these themes? Almost certainly not. Romeo and Juliet are individuals, not representatives of all young lovers. Their families are feuding, as most families are not. The characters in the play face issues that are permanent ingredients of human life and respond to these issues in their own way—and *that* is why the play has something to say, not because it gives us handy hints on how to live our own lives. Discussing the ideas in literature through the concept of *theme* enables us to escape the tyranny of moralizing. It enables writers to be what they are best at being: writers, not philosophers, prophets, reformers, or know-it-alls.

■ *Learn what a symbol is—and isn't.*   A **symbol** is a person, place, or thing that stands for or strongly suggests something in addition to itself, generally an abstract idea more important than itself. Don't let this definition intimidate you. Symbols are not exotic literary devices that readers have to wrestle with. In fact, the daily, nonliterary lives of readers are filled, quite comfortably and naturally, with more symbols than exist in any book ever written.

A Rolls Royce, for example, is an expensive car manufactured in Britain, but for many people it stands for something else: It is a symbol of success or status or good taste. People do not make sacrifices and sounds of ecstasy over a piece of machinery, but over a symbol. Our lives are pervaded, perhaps dominated, by symbols. Think about the different symbolic meanings everyone gives to the following: a diamond ring, a new house, money, bats, a college diploma, a trip to Europe, a date with a popular and good-looking man or woman, the Confederate flag, Niagara Falls, Watergate, a minivan.

Making symbols and reacting to symbols are such basic ingredients of the human mind that we should hardly be astonished to find symbols in literature. Symbols have an extremely practical value to a writer, however. They enable the writer to communicate abstract concepts with the vitality that can come only from specific details. Just as some people may be indifferent to abstract oratory about freedom's being a good thing but deeply moved by a visit to the Statue of Liberty, a reader may be bored by or antagonistic to philosophical assertions about the passing of time but intensely impressed by the specific symbol—from a novel by Arnold Bennett—of a wedding ring almost totally embedded in the fat flesh on the finger of an elderly woman. Symbols of abstract ideas can often have a dramatic impact that the ideas themselves cannot, and sometimes in the hands of a master, symbols can express what might otherwise be almost inexpressible.

Our comments so far have stressed that symbols in literature are not as difficult and mysterious as they are sometimes imagined to be. Dealing with symbols is nevertheless not child's play, and four major traps lie in wait for critics—professionals no less than amateurs.

First, the symbol stands for or suggests something *in addition to* itself, not *instead of* itself. The symbolic level of a story or poem should never be allowed to dwarf the other levels—especially the basic level of people and plot. The wedding ring on the fat finger not only suggests the sadness of the passing of time but also tells us in a straightforward, down-to-earth, nonsymbolic fashion that the woman eats too much and hasn't taken very good care of herself.

Second, symbols are usually obvious. If a critic has to struggle to establish that something functions as a symbol, it probably was not meant to be one. Excessive ingenuity in symbol hunting is one of the worst of all critical sins. Stick to what the author clearly intends. In Hemingway's *A Farewell to Arms*, one of the characters says repeatedly that she is afraid of the rain because she dreams that it means her death. Then, when she does die and it is indeed raining, we can say that the rain is a symbol of death. This is a deliberately simple example, of course, but the principle is perfectly valid: Real symbols are usually obvious because writers tend to make big productions of them.

Third, symbols should not be confused with ordinary significant details. This confusion can be the main reason a symbol hunter pounces on a nonsymbol. A symbol stands for or suggests something substantially different from itself. Rain may symbolize death. A veil may symbolize isolation. Springtime may symbolize youth, rebirth, longing, hope. If a man in a story, however, wipes his running nose with the back of his hand and doesn't cover his mouth when he coughs, we simply know that he has bad manners (in addition to a cold). The way he wipes his nose is not a symbol of bad manners, nor is the way he coughs; they *are* bad manners, details about the character that reveal something about him. A symbol is a person, place, or thing that bears little concrete resemblance to whatever it stands for or suggests; the reader must make a major mental leap to identify the symbol with its meaning. A significant detail about a person, place, or thing, on the other hand, merely conveys more information about or insight into its subject.

Fourth, nobody who writes about literature should be too eager to make a symbol stand for any one thing in particular. The most effective symbols often are not meant to work that way at all. They *stand for* nothing. They are meant to *suggest*—on an emotional level, at times a virtually subconscious level—a number of different and elusive concepts. That is precisely why symbols can be so valuable. Herman Melville's white whale in *Moby-Dick*, for example, is surely not meant to symbolize any one idea. The whale becomes such a powerful symbol because it suggests so many ideas: evil, humanity's insignificance, the unchanging order of the universe, nature, God's will, and so on. Symbols are often a great writer's imaginative shortcuts for dealing with the imposing and frightening complexity of life as we know it.

■ *Be alert to the use of metaphors and similes.*   Metaphors and similes are the two most common kinds of figurative language or figures of speech. A working definition of **figurative language** is language that cannot be taken literally. In one way or another, figurative language departs from the conventional meaning and expression of words to bring about special effects, usually emotional. Figurative language is a common ingredient of our speech and writing; it is basic to almost all poetry, far more so than rhyme or meter.

A **simile** is a comparison using the word *like* or *as.*

The lecture was *as* dry as the Sahara Desert.

The smokers at the cocktail party drew themselves into a small circle, *like* a wagon train surrounded by Indians.

All through that dreary summer weekend, we felt *as* if life had turned into a slow-motion movie.

A **metaphor** is often defined as a comparison that does without the word *like* or *as,* thus establishing a closer connection between the items compared. It is also helpful, however, to think of a metaphor as a word or phrase that is generally used in one frame of reference but that is shifted to another frame of reference.

The lecture was a Sahara Desert of dryness.

Our lives that dreary summer weekend had turned into a slow-motion movie.

She had ice water in her veins.

Life is a cabaret.

The president told her administrators to stonewall the opposition.

Bill is the spark plug of his team.

We thought the new boss was going to be a tiger, but he turned out to be a pussycat.

As indicated by many of the preceding examples, our daily language is filled with metaphors. A number of them are so familiar that we have to struggle to recognize their metaphorical nature.

the arms of a chair	a wallflower
a clean sweep	the legs of a table
the traffic crawled	the heart of the matter
a green rookie	it's all a whitewash
a poker face	peaches-and-cream complexion

Effective metaphors and similes enable writers to stimulate and direct the emotions of their readers, to communicate their own emotions with concrete images rather than flat, abstract statements, and thus to develop stylistic color and excitement. Readers and critics should pay particular attention to **metaphorical patterns**—metaphors sustained and developed through a whole work rather than dropped after one sentence. Many writers consciously use such patterns to achieve greater unity, consistency, and dramatic power, as you can see in the following example.

ROBERT FROST

Nothing Gold Can Stay

Nature's first green is gold,
Her hardest hue to hold.
Her early leaf's a flower;
But only so an hour.
Then leaf subsides to leaf.
So Eden sank to grief,
So dawn goes down to day.
Nothing gold can stay.

Notice how the term *gold* begins by referring to a color but eventually becomes a metaphor for anything valuable or beautiful. Notice how the blossoms of a flowering shrub that turn into leaves become a lament for all fading glories and for the passing of time.

■ *Avoid plot summary.*   Don't tell the story all over again. Your readers won't be spending time on an analysis of a work with which they are totally unfamiliar. Readers may be unaware of any number of subtleties, but they have read the piece, and they know the names of the characters, who's in love with whom, who lives and dies, and so on. You are writing an analysis, not a book report. Note how the student writer of the essay on Shirley Jackson's "Charles" (pages 421–423) doesn't hesitate to "give away" the surprise ending in her first sentence. Note how all references to events in the story are used to remind readers of the events and to show how they relate to the thesis of the essay, not to inform readers that the events occurred in the first place.

■ *Do not overuse direct quotations.*   Unless you are writing about an author's style or explaining the meaning of some especially difficult lines, you should be cautious about direct quotations. Rely, for the most part, on references in your own words to the work you are discussing. Among other considerations, your instructor needs to evaluate your writing rather than your ability to string together passages of other people's writing. Advising you to be cautious about direct quotations, however, is not the same as prohibiting them altogether. A well-chosen direct quotation can add a strong dramatic touch to your introduction or conclusion. Moreover, direct quotations can sometimes be valuable if you feel your point might be questionable or controversial—"I'm not just making this up or imagining it." A good general principle is to use your own language unless you have a specific, practical reason for using a direct quotation instead.

Student Writing: Literary Analysis

Now let's look at what happens when a student who is a careful reader and competent writer faces a literary work for analysis.

The following paper analyzes a Shirley Jackson short story that appears in an earlier section of this book (page 219). Harriet McKay's assignment was to "Trace the sequence of clues planted by the author so that we have a chance to anticipate the surprise ending in Jackson's 'Charles.' "

Harriet McKay

The Beginning of the End

Until the last sentence of Shirley Jackson's "Charles," 1
I had no idea that Charles, the terror of kindergarten,
was an imaginary person created by Laurie and that Charles's
little monster antics were really Laurie's own antics. The
author fooled me completely, but I have to admit that she
played fair. She gave her readers all the clues they needed
to make a sensible guess about how the story would end.

Laurie's own personality offers one set of clues. Even 2
before classes start, Jackson lets us know that Laurie might
have a lot to overcompensate for. His mother has been dressing him in cute little boy clothes and thinking of him as a
"sweet-voiced nursery-school tot." It is at Laurie's own
insistence that he begins wearing tough-kid blue jeans. In
addition, any boy nicknamed "Laurie" is due for some problems; one doesn't need to be a sexist pig to say that boys
named "Laurence" ought to be called "Larry" and that "Laurie,"
to put it bluntly, is a sissy name. No wonder Laurie goes
overboard. He's not a little boy anymore. He has hit the big
time in kindergarten, and he begins "swaggering" even before
his first class.

Laurie's behavior at home after school starts is another giveaway. Charles may be a monster at school, but Laurie isn't that much better at lunchtime. After only one class, he slams the door, throws his hat on the floor, shouts, speaks "insolently," makes deliberate mistakes in grammar, doesn't look at people when he talks to them but talks to the bread and butter instead, speaks with his mouth full, leaves the table without asking permission and while his father is still talking to him. This is no sweet little tot. His doting parents might try to pin Laurie's behavior on the bad influence of Charles, but that's certainly not the only possible explanation, and that's what doting parents have always tried to do. Besides, it would be stretching things to the limit to imagine that even Charles could have that great an influence after only one morning in the same classroom with him.

4   Still another giveaway is Laurie's explanation for being late. It's impossible to believe that a group of kindergarten kids would voluntarily stay after school to watch a child being punished. Laurie's parents swallow this story so easily that many readers probably didn't notice how fantastic the story really is--but an alert reader would have noticed.

5   The last clue I should have noticed is the way Laurie's parents look forward to the P.T.A. meeting so they can meet Charles's mother. They have been so poised and cool about everything that I really wonder why I did not realize that they would have to be brought down a few pegs at the end of the story. Have they ever made a serious effort to correct their son's bad manners? Have they ever told him to stay away

from a rotten kid like Charles? Heavens no, they're much too enlightened. The parents think Charles is amusing, and they can't wait to meet Charles's mother so they can feel superior to her. In simple justice they deserve what they get, and I should have seen it coming.

Laurie's personality and behavior, his unbelievable   6
explanation for being late, and his parents' complacency
all give readers the clues they need to predict the surprise
ending.

➤ **FOR WRITING OR DISCUSSION**

1. What is the thesis of this paper? Is the thesis stated in one sentence?
2. What personality does the writer present to the reader? Is it appropriate to the subject matter?
3. Does the writer omit details from the story that could have strengthened her case?
4. Should a separate paragraph have been devoted to the issue of Laurie's lateness? If not, how could the issue have been treated more effectively?
5. Is the last paragraph too short? too abrupt? too dull?
6. Write a brief analysis of this student paper, discussing its strengths and making suggestions for any needed improvements.

EXERCISE

Read or reread the student models "Enough Despair to Go Around" (page 61) by Alan Benjamin, "Two Kinds of Love" (page 236) by Julie Olivera, and "We and He" (page 300) by Craig Anders. In what ways do these essays observe the principles of literary analysis that you have studied in this chapter?

Readings for Writing

The five short stories that follow should stimulate you to find topics for your own papers of literary analysis. A checklist for writing and revising your literary analysis (page 445) follows the stories. The checklist will help you review the important points in this chapter.

SAKI (H. H. MUNRO)

The Story-Teller

1   It was a hot afternoon, and the railway carriage was correspondingly sultry, and the next stop was at Templecombe, nearly an hour ahead. The occupants of the carriage were a small girl, and a smaller girl, and a small boy. An aunt belonging to the children occupied one corner seat, and the further corner seat on the opposite side was occupied by a bachelor who was a stranger to their party, but the small girls and the small boy emphatically occupied the compartment. Both the aunt and the children were conversational in a limited, persistent way, reminding one of the attentions of a housefly that refused to be discouraged. Most of the aunt's remarks seemed to begin with "Don't," and nearly all of the children's remarks began with "Why?" The bachelor said nothing out loud.

2   "Don't, Cyril, don't," exclaimed the aunt, as the small boy began smacking the cushions of the seat, producing a cloud of dust at each blow.

3   "Come and look out of the window," she added.

4   The child moved reluctantly to the window. "Why are those sheep being driven out of that field?" he asked.

5   "I expect they are being driven to another field where there is more grass," said the aunt weakly.

6   "But there is lots of grass in that field," protested the boy; "there's nothing else but grass there. Aunt, there's lots of grass in that field."

7   "Perhaps the grass in the other field is better," suggested the aunt fatuously.

8   "Why is the grass in the other field better?" persisted Cyril.

9   The frown on the bachelor's face was deepening to a scowl. He was a hard, unsympathetic man, the aunt decided in her mind. She was utterly unable to come to any satisfactory decision about the grass in the other field.

10   The smaller girl created a diversion by beginning to recite "On the Road to Mandalay." She only knew the first line, but she put her limited knowledge to the fullest possible use. She repeated the line over and over again in a dreamy but resolute and very audible voice; it seemed to the bachelor as though some one had had a bet with her that she could not repeat the line aloud two thousand times without stopping. Whoever it was who had made the wager was likely to lose his bet.

11   "Come over here and listen to a story," said the aunt, when the bachelor had looked twice at her and once at the communication cord.

12   The children moved listlessly towards the aunt's end of the carriage. Evidently her reputation as a story-teller did not rank high in their estimation.

13   In a low, confidential voice, interrupted at frequent intervals by loud, petulant questions from her listeners, she began an unenterprising and deplorably uninteresting story about a little girl who was good, and made friends with everyone on account of her goodness, and was finally saved from a mad bull by a number of rescuers who admired her moral character.

14   "Wouldn't they have saved her if she hadn't been good?" demanded the bigger of the small girls. It was exactly the question that the bachelor had wanted to ask.

"Well, yes," admitted the aunt lamely, "but I don't think they would have run quite   15
so fast to her help if they had not liked her so much."

"It's the stupidest story I've ever heard," said the bigger of the small girls, with   16
immense conviction.

"I didn't listen after the first bit, it was so stupid," said Cyril.   17

The smaller girl made no actual comment on the story, but she had long ago recom-   18
menced a murmured repetition of her favourite line.

"You don't seem to be a success as a story-teller," said the bachelor suddenly from   19
his corner.

The aunt bristled in instant defense at this unexpected attack.   20

"It's a very difficult thing to tell stories that children can both understand and appre-   21
ciate," she said stiffly.

"I don't agree with you," said the bachelor. "There was a little girl called Bertha,   22
who was extraordinarily good."

The children's momentarily-aroused interest began at once to flicker; all stories   23
seemed dreadfully alike, no matter who told them.

"She did all that she was told, she was always truthful, she kept her clothes clean,   24
ate milk puddings as though they were jam tarts, learned her lessons perfectly, and was
polite in her manners."

"Was she pretty?" asked the bigger of the small girls.   25

"Not as pretty as any of you," said the bachelor, "but she was horribly good."   26

There was a wave of reaction in favour of the story; the word horrible in connection   27
with goodness was a novelty that commended itself. It seemed to introduce a ring of
truth that was absent from the aunt's tales of infant life.

"She was so good," continued the bachelor, "that she won several medals for good-   28
ness, which she always wore, pinned to her dress. There was a medal for obedience,
another medal for punctuality, and a third for good behaviour. They were large metal
medals and they clicked against one another as she walked. No other child in the town
where she lived had as many as three medals, so everybody knew that she must be an
extra good child."

"Horribly good," quoted Cyril.   29

"Everybody talked about her goodness, and the Prince of the country got to hear   30
about it, and he said that as she was so very good she might be allowed once a week to
walk in his park, which was just outside the town. It was a beautiful park and no children
were ever allowed in it, so it was a great honour for Bertha to be allowed to go there."

"Were there any sheep in the park?" demanded Cyril.   31

"No," said the bachelor, "there were no sheep."   32

"Why weren't there any sheep?" came the inevitable question arising out of   33
that answer.

The aunt permitted herself a smile, which might almost have been described as   34
a grin.

"There were no sheep in the park," said the bachelor, "because the Prince's mother   35
had once had a dream that her son would either be killed by a sheep or else by a clock
falling on him. For that reason the Prince never kept a sheep in his park or a clock in
his palace."

36   The aunt suppressed a gasp of admiration.

37   "Was the Prince killed by a sheep or by a clock?" asked Cyril.

38   "He is still alive so we can't tell whether the dream will come true," said the bachelor unconcernedly; "anyway, there were no sheep in the park, but there were lots of little pigs running all over the place."

39   "What colour were they?"

40   "Black with white faces, white with black spots, black all over, grey with white patches, and some were white all over."

41   The story-teller paused to let a full idea of the park's treasures sink into the children's imaginations; then he resumed:

42   "Bertha was rather sorry to find that there were no flowers in the park. She had promised her aunts, with tears in her eyes, that she would not pick any of the kind Prince's flowers, and she had meant to keep her promise, so of course it made her feel silly to find that there were no flowers to pick."

43   "Why weren't there any flowers?"

44   "Because the pigs had eaten them all," said the bachelor promptly. "The gardeners had told the Prince that you couldn't have pigs and flowers, so he decided to have pigs and no flowers."

45   There was a murmur of approval at the excellence of the Prince's decision; so many people would have decided the other way.

46   "There were lots of other delightful things in the park. There were ponds with gold and blue and green fish in them, and trees with beautiful parrots that said clever things at a moment's notice, and humming birds that hummed all the popular tunes of the day. Bertha walked up and down and enjoyed herself immensely, and thought to herself: 'If I were not so extraordinarily good I should not have been allowed to come into this beautiful park and enjoy all that there is to be seen in it,' and her three medals clinked against one another as she walked and helped to remind her how very good she really was. Just then an enormous wolf came prowling into the park to see if it could catch a fat little pig for its supper.

47   "What colour was it?" asked the children, amid an immediate quickening of interest.

48   "Mud-colour all over, with a black tongue and pale grey eyes that gleamed with unspeakable ferocity. The first thing that it saw in the park was Bertha; her pinafore was so spotlessly white and clean that it could be seen from a great distance. Bertha saw the wolf and saw that it was stealing towards her, and she began to wish that she had never been allowed to come into the park. She ran as hard as she could, and the wolf came after her with huge leaps and bounds. She managed to reach a shrubbery of myrtle bushes and she hid herself in one of the thickest of the bushes. The wolf came sniffing among the branches, its black tongue lolling out of its mouth and its pale grey eyes glaring with rage. Bertha was terribly frightened, and thought to herself: 'If I had not been so extraordinarily good I should have been safe in the town at this moment.' However, the scent of the myrtle was so strong that the wolf could not sniff out where Bertha was hiding, and the bushes were so thick that he might have hunted about in them for a long time without catching sight of her, so he thought he might as well go off and catch a little pig instead. Bertha was trembling very much at having the wolf

prowling and sniffing so near her, and as she trembled the medal for obedience clinked against the medals for good conduct and punctuality. The wolf was just moving away when he heard the sound of the medals clinking and stopped to listen; they clinked again in a bush quite near him. He dashed into the brush, his pale grey eyes gleaming with ferocity and triumph, and dragged Bertha out and devoured her to the last morsel. All that were left of her were her shoes, bits of clothing, and the three medals for goodness."

"Were any of the little pigs killed?"   49

"No, they all escaped."   50

"The story began badly," said the smaller of the small girls, "but it had a beautiful   51
ending."

"It is the most beautiful story I ever heard," said the bigger of the small girls, with   52
immense decision.

"It is the only beautiful story I have ever heard," said Cyril.   53

A dissentient opinion came from the aunt.   54

"A most improper story to tell to young children! You have undermined the effect of   55
years of careful teaching."

"At any rate," said the bachelor, collecting his belongings preparatory to leaving   56
the carriage, "I kept them quiet for ten minutes, which was more than you were able
to do."

"Unhappy woman!" he observed to himself as he walked down the platform of   57
Templecombe station; "for the next six months or so those children will assail her in
public with demands for an improper story!"

➤ FOR WRITING OR DISCUSSION

1. Saki actually tells two stories in "The Story-Teller." There is the story as a whole about the bachelor, the children, the aunt, and the train ride. Then there is the story within the story—the bachelor's tale about Bertha and the wolf. Designed for children, the bachelor's story has a straightforward moral. What is it?

2. What details in the bachelor's story create an unfavorable impression of Bertha?

3. The wolf had been planning on eating pig and would have settled for pig. What brought about Bertha's doom?

4. How does your answer to question 3 support the moral of the bachelor's story?

5. Does the story as a whole have a similarly straightforward moral? If not, what is its central theme?

6. Write a paper discussing the view of children presented in "The Story-Teller." Or, as an alternative topic, discuss the implications of "The Story-Teller" on the issue of literature and morality. The bachelor's story, for example, is wonderfully well told, but its lesson is "most improper." To what extent is literature obliged to be proper?

JAMAICA KINCAID

Girl

Wash the white clothes on Monday and put them on the stone heap; wash the color clothes on Tuesday and put them on the clothes-line to dry; don't walk barehead in the hot sun; cook pumpkin fritters in very hot sweet oil; soak your little cloths right after you take them off; when buying cotton to make yourself a nice blouse, be sure that it doesn't have gum on it, because that way it won't hold up well after a wash; soak salt fish overnight before you cook it; is it true that you sing benna in Sunday school?; always eat your food in such a way that it won't turn someone else's stomach; on Sundays try to walk like a lady and not like the slut you are so bent on becoming; don't sing benna in Sunday school; you mustn't speak to wharf-rat boys, not even to give directions; don't eat fruits on the street—flies will follow you; *but I don't sing benna on Sundays at all and never in Sunday school;* this is how to sew on a button; this is how to make a buttonhole for the button you have just sewed on; this is how to hem a dress when you see the hem coming down and so to prevent yourself from looking like the slut I know you are so bent on becoming; this is how you iron your father's khaki shirt so that it doesn't have a crease; this is how you iron your father's khaki pants so that they don't have a crease; this is how you grow okra—far from the house, because okra tree harbors red ants; when you are growing dasheen, make sure it gets plenty of water or else it makes your throat itch when you are eating it; this is how you sweep a corner; this is how you sweep a whole house; this is how you sweep a yard; this is how you smile to someone you don't like too much; this is how you smile to someone you don't like at all; this is how you smile to someone you like completely; this is how you set a table for tea; this is how you set a table for dinner; this is how you set a table for dinner with an important guest; this is how you set a table for lunch; this is how you set a table for breakfast; this is how to behave in the presence of men who don't know you very well, and this way they won't recognize immediately the slut I have warned you against becoming; be sure to wash every day, even if it is with your own spit; don't squat down to play marbles—you are not a boy, you know; don't pick people's flowers—you might catch something; don't throw stones at blackbirds, because it might not be a blackbird at all; this is how to make a bread pudding; this is how to make doukona; this is how to make pepper pot; this is how to make a good medicine for a cold; this is how to make a good medicine to throw away a child before it even becomes a child; this is how to catch a fish; this is how to throw back a fish you don't like, and that way something bad won't fall on you; this is how to bully a man; this is how a man bullies you; this is how to love a man, and if this doesn't work there are other ways, and if they don't work don't feel too bad about giving up; this is how to spit up in the air if you feel like it, and this is how to move quick so that it doesn't fall on you; this is how to make ends meet; always squeeze bread to make sure it's fresh; *but what if the baker won't let me feel the bread?;* you mean to say that after all you are really going to be the kind of woman who the baker won't let near the bread?

➤ **FOR WRITING OR DISCUSSION**

1. The author was brought up in the West Indies. What elements in the story suggest that the "action" is taking place in the West Indies, or at least in some place other than the United States?
2. Who is the speaker? To whom is the speaker addressing her remarks?
3. What do the italicized words represent?
4. The speaker can correctly be described as a bossy person, a nag, a scold. What evidence suggests that the speaker also has some redeeming, more praise-worthy characteristics?
5. Write a paper contrasting the methods of bringing up children in "Girl" and "The Story-Teller" (page 424) or in "Girl" and "Doby's Gone" (page 436).

ROALD DAHL

The Landlady

Billy Weaver had travelled down from London on the slow afternoon train, with a change at Reading on the way, and by the time he got to Bath it was about nine o'clock in the evening and the moon was coming up out of a clear, starry sky over the houses opposite the station entrance. But the air was deadly cold and the wind was like a flat blade of ice on his cheeks.   1

"Excuse me," he said to a porter, "but is there a fairly cheap hotel not too far away from here?"   2

"Try the Bell and Dragon," the porter answered, pointing down the road. "They might take you in. It's about a quarter of a mile along on the other side."   3

Billy thanked him and picked up his suitcase and set out to walk the quarter mile to the Bell and Dragon. He had never been to Bath before. He didn't know anyone who lived there. But Mr. Greenslade at the Head Office in London had told him it was a splendid town. "Find your own lodgings," he said, "and then go along and report to the branch manager as soon as you've got yourself settled."   4

Billy was seventeen years old. He was wearing a new navy-blue overcoat, a new brown trilby hat, and a new brown suit, and he was feeling fine. He walked briskly down the street. He was trying to do everything briskly these days. Briskness, he had decided, was *the* one common characteristic of all successful businessmen. The big shots up at Head Office were absolutely fantastically brisk all the time. They were amazing.   5

There were no shops on this wide street that he was walking along, only a line of tall houses on each side, all of them identical. They had porches and pillars and four or five steps going up to their front doors, and it was obvious that once upon a time they had been very swanky residences. But now, even in the darkness, he could see that the paint was peeling from the woodwork on their doors and windows, and that the handsome white facades were cracked and blotchy from neglect.   6

Suddenly, not six yards away, in a downstairs window that was brilliantly illuminated by a street lamp, Billy caught sight of a printed notice propped up against the   7 glass in one of the upper panes. It said, "Bed and Breakfast." There was a vase of yellow chrysanthemums, tall and beautiful, standing just underneath the notice.

8   He stopped walking. He moved a bit closer. Green curtains (some sort of velvety material) were hanging down on either side of the window. The chrysanthemums looked wonderful beside them. He went right up and peered through the glass into the room, and the first thing he saw was a bright fire burning on the hearth. On the carpet in front of the fire, a pretty little dachshund was curled up asleep, with its nose tucked into its belly. The room itself, as far as he could see in the half darkness, was filled with pleasant furniture. There was a baby-grand piano and a big sofa and several plump armchairs, and in one corner he spotted a large parrot in a cage. Animals were usually a good sign in a place like this, Billy told himself, and all in all, it looked as though it would be a pretty decent house to stay in. Certainly it would be more comfortable than the Bell and Dragon.

9   On the other hand, a pub would be more congenial than a boarding house. There would be beer and darts in the evenings, and lots of people to talk to, and it would be a good bit cheaper, too. He had stayed a couple of nights in a pub once before, and he had liked it. He had never stayed in any boarding houses, and to be perfectly honest, he was a tiny bit frightened of them. The name itself conjured up images of watery cabbage, rapacious landladies, and a powerful smell of kippers in the living room. After dithering about like this in the cold for two or three minutes, Billy decided that he would walk on and take a look at the Bell and Dragon before making up his mind. He turned to go.

10   And now a queer thing happened to him. He was in the act of stepping back and turning away from the window when all at once his eye was caught again and held in the most peculiar manner by the small notice that was there. "Bed and Breakfast," it said. "Bed and Breakfast, bed and breakfast, bed and breakfast." Each word was like a large black eye staring at him through the glass, holding him, compelling him, forcing him to stay where he was and not walk away from that house, and the next thing he knew he was actually moving across from the window to the front door, climbing the steps that led up to it, and reaching for the bell.

11   He pressed the bell. Far away in a back room, he heard it ringing, and then *at once*—it must have been at once, because he hadn't even had time to take his finger from the bell button—the door swung open and a woman was standing there. Normally, you ring a bell and you have at least a half-minute wait before the door opens. But this person was like a jack-in-the-box. He pressed the bell—and out she popped! It made him jump.

12   She was about forty-five or fifty years old, and the moment she saw him she gave him a warm, welcoming smile. "*Please* come in," she said pleasantly. She stepped aside, holding the door wide open, and Billy found himself automatically starting forward. The compulsion, or, more accurately, the desire to follow after her into that house was extraordinarily strong, but he held himself back.

13   "I saw the notice in the window," he said.

14   "Yes, I know."

15   "I was wondering about a room."

"It's *all* ready for you, my dear," she said. She had a round pink face and very gentle   16
blue eyes.

"I was on my way to the Bell and Dragon," Billy told her. "But the notice in your   17
window just happened to catch my eye."

"My dear boy," she said, "why don't you come in out of the cold?"   18

"How much do you charge?"   19

"Five and sixpence a night, including breakfast."   20

It was fantastically cheap. It was less than half of what he had been willing to pay.   21

"If that is too much," she added, "then perhaps I can reduce it just a tiny bit. Do you   22
desire an egg for breakfast? Eggs are expensive at the moment. It would be sixpence
less without the egg."

"Five and sixpence is fine," he answered. "I should like very much to stay here."   23

"I knew you would. Do come in."   24

She seemed terribly nice. She looked exactly like the mother of one's best school   25
friend welcoming one into the house to stay for the Christmas holidays. Billy took off
his hat and stepped over the threshold.

"Just hang it there," she said, "and let me help you with your coat."   26

There were no other hats or coats in the hall. There were no umbrellas, no walking   27
sticks—nothing.

"We have it *all* to ourselves," she said, smiling at him over her shoulder as she led   28
the way upstairs. "You see, it isn't very often I have the pleasure of taking a visitor into
my little nest."

The old girl is slightly dotty, Billy told himself. But at five and sixpence a night, who   29
gives a damn about that? "I should've thought you'd be simply swamped with applicants," he said politely.

"Oh, I am, my dear, I am. Of course I am. But the trouble is that I'm inclined to be   30
just a teeny-weeny bit choosy and particular—if you see what I mean."

"Ah, yes."   31

"But I'm always ready. Everything is always ready day and night in this house, just   32
on the off chance that an acceptable young gentleman will come along. And it is such a
pleasure, my dear, such a very great pleasure when now and again I open the door and
I see someone standing there who is just *exactly* right." She was halfway up the stairs,
and she paused with one hand on the stair rail, turning her head and smiling down at
him with pale lips. "Like you," she added, and her blue eyes travelled slowly all the
way down the length of Billy's body to his feet and then up again.

On the second-floor landing, she said to him. "This floor is mine."   33

They climbed up another flight. "And this one is *all* yours," she said. "Here's your   34
room. I do hope you'll like it." She took him into a small but charming front bedroom,
switching on the light as she went in.

"The morning sun comes right in the window, Mr. Perkins. It is Mr. Perkins, isn't it?"   35

"No," he said. "It's Weaver."   36

"Mr. Weaver. How nice. I've put a water bottle between the sheets, to warm them   37
up, Mr. Weaver. It's such a comfort to have a hot-water bottle in a strange bed with clean
sheets, don't you agree? And you may light the gas fire at any time, if you feel chilly."

38   "Thank you," Billy said. "Thank you ever so much." He noticed that the bedspread had been taken off the bed and that the bedclothes had been neatly turned back on one side, all ready for someone to get in.

39   "I'm so glad you appeared," she said, looking earnestly into his face. "I was beginning to get worried."

40   "That's all right," Billy answered brightly. "You mustn't worry about me." He put his suitcase on the chair and started to open it.

41   "And what about supper, my dear? Did you manage to get anything to eat before you came here?"

42   "I'm not a bit hungry, thank you," he said. "I think I'll just go to bed as soon as possible, because tomorrow I've got to get up rather early and report to the office."

43   "Very well, then. I'll leave you now so that you can unpack. But before you go to bed, would you be kind enough to pop into the sitting room on the ground floor and sign the book? Everyone has to do that, because it's the law of the land, and we don't want to go breaking any laws at *this* stage in the proceedings, do we?" She gave him a little wave of the hand and went quickly out of the room and closed the door.

44   Now the fact that his landlady appeared to be slightly off her rocker didn't worry Billy in the least. After all, she not only was harmless—there was no question about that—but she was also quite obviously a kind and generous soul. He guessed that she had probably lost a son in the war, or something like that, and had never got over it. So a few minutes later, after unpacking his suitcase and washing his hands, he trotted downstairs to the ground floor and entered the living room. His landlady wasn't there, but the fire was glowing on the hearth, and the little dachshund was still sleeping soundly in front of it. The room was wonderfully warm and cozy. I'm a lucky fellow, he thought, rubbing his hands. This is a bit of all right.

45   He found the guestbook lying open on the piano, so he took out his pen and wrote down his name and address. There were only two other entries above his on the page, and as one always does with guestbooks, he started to read them. One was a Christopher Mulholland, from Cardiff. The other was Gregory W. Temple, from Bristol.

46   That's funny, he thought suddenly. Christopher Mulholland. It rings a bell. Now where on earth had he heard that rather unusual name before? Was it a boy at school? No. Was it one of his sister's numerous young men, perhaps, or a friend of his father's? No, no, it wasn't any of those. He glanced down again at the book.

Christopher Mulholland, 231 Cathedral Road, Cardiff
Gregory W. Temple, 27 Sycamore Drive, Bristol

47   As a matter of fact, now he came to think of it, he wasn't at all sure that the second name didn't have almost as much of a familiar ring about it as the first.

48   "Gregory Temple?" he said aloud, searching his memory. "Christopher Mulholland? . . ."

49   "Such charming boys," a voice behind him answered, and he turned and saw his landlady sailing into the room with a large silver tea tray in her hands. She was holding it well out in front of her and rather high up, as though the tray were a pair of reins on a frisky horse.

"They sound somehow familiar," he said.   50

"They do? How interesting."   51

"I'm almost positive I've heard those names before somewhere. Isn't that odd?   52
Maybe it was in the newspapers. They weren't famous in any way, were they? I mean,
famous cricketers or footballers or something like that?"

"Famous?" she said, setting the tea tray down on the low table in front of the sofa.   53
"Oh, no, I don't think they were famous. But they were incredibly handsome, both of
them, I can promise you that. They were tall and young and handsome, my dear, just
exactly like you."

Once more, Billy glanced down at the book. "Look here," he said, noticing the   54
dates. "This last entry is over two years old."

"It is?"   55

"Yes indeed. And Christopher Mulholland's is nearly a year before that—more than   56
three years ago."

"Dear me," she said, shaking her head and heaving a dainty little sigh. "I would   57
never have thought it. How time does fly away from us all, doesn't it, Mr. Wilkins?"

"It's Weaver," Billy said. "W-e-a-v-e-r."   58

"Oh, of course it is!" she cried, sitting down on the sofa. "How silly of me. I do   59
apologize. In one ear and out the other, that's me, Mr. Weaver."

"You know something?" Billy said. "Something that's really quite extraordinary   60
about all this?"

"No, dear, I don't."   61

"Well, you see, both of these names—Mulholland and Temple—I not only seem to   62
remember each one of them separately, so to speak, but somehow or other, in some
peculiar way, they both appear to be sort of connected together as well. As though they
were both famous for the same sort of thing, if you see what I mean—like . . .
well . . . like Dempsey and Tunney, for example, or Churchill and Roosevelt."

"How amusing," she said. "But come over here now dear, and sit down beside   63
me on the sofa and I'll give you a nice cup of tea and a ginger biscuit before you go
to bed."

"You really shouldn't bother," Billy said. "I didn't mean you to do anything like that." 64
He stood by the piano, watching her as she fussed about with the cups and saucers. He
noticed that she had small, white, quickly moving hands and red fingernails.

"I'm almost positive it was in the newspapers I saw them," Billy said. "I'll think of it   65
in a second. I'm sure I will."

There is nothing more tantalizing than a thing like this that lingers just outside the   66
borders of one's memory. He hated to give up. "Now wait a minute," he said. "Wait
just a minute. Mulholland . . . Christopher Mulholland . . . wasn't *that* the name of the
Eton schoolboy who was on a walking tour through the West Country and then all of a
sudden—"

"Milk?" she said. "And sugar?"   67

"Yes, please. And then all of a sudden—"   68

"Eton schoolboy?" she said. "Oh, no, my dear, that can't possibly be right because   69
my Mr. Mulholland was certainly not an Eton schoolboy when he came to me. He was

a Cambridge undergraduate. Come over here now and sit next to me and warm yourself in front of this lovely fire. Come on. Your tea's all ready for you." She patted the empty place beside her on the sofa and sat there smiling at Billy and waiting for him to come over.

70   He crossed the room slowly and sat down on the edge of the sofa. She placed his teacup on the table in front of him.

71   "*There* we are," she said. "How nice and cozy this is, isn't it?"

72   Billy started sipping his tea. She did the same. For half a minute or so, neither of them spoke. But Billy knew that she was looking at him. Her body was half turned toward him, and he could feel her eyes resting on his face, watching him over the rim of her teacup. Now and again, he caught a whiff of a peculiar smell that seemed to emanate directly from her person. It was not in the least unpleasant, and it reminded him—well, he wasn't quite sure what it reminded him of. Pickled walnuts? New leather? Or was it the corridors of a hospital?

73   At length she said, "Mr. Mulholland was a great one for his tea. Never in my life have I seen anyone drink as much tea as dear, sweet Mr. Mulholland."

74   "I suppose he left fairly recently," Billy said. He was still puzzling his head about the two names. He was positive now that he had seen them in the newspapers—in the headlines.

75   "Left?" she said, arching her brows. "But my dear boy, he never left. He's still here. Mr. Temple is also here. They're on the fourth floor, both of them together."

76   Billy set his cup down slowly on the table and stared at his landlady. She smiled back at him, and then she put out one of her white hands and patted him comfortingly on the knee.

77   "How old are you, my dear?" she asked.

78   "Seventeen."

79   "Seventeen!" she cried. "Oh, it's the perfect age! Mr. Mulholland was also seventeen. But I think he was a trifle shorter than you are; in fact, I'm sure he was and his teeth weren't *quite* so white. You have the most beautiful teeth, Mr. Weaver, did you know that?"

80   "They're not as good as they look," Billy said. "They've got simply masses of fillings in them at the back."

81   "Mr. Temple, of course, was a little older," she said, ignoring his remark. "He was actually twenty-eight. And yet I never would have guessed it if he hadn't told me—never in my whole life. There wasn't a *blemish* on his body."

82   "A what?" Billy said.

83   "His skin was *just* like a baby's."

84   There was a pause. Billy picked up his teacup and took another sip of his tea, then set it down gently in its saucer. He waited for her to say something else, but she seemed to have lapsed into another of her silences. He sat there staring straight ahead of him into the far corner of the room, biting his lower lip.

85   "That parrot," he said at last. "You know something? It had me completely fooled when I first saw it through the window. I could have sworn it was alive."

86   "Alas, no longer."

"It's most terribly clever the way it's been done," he said. "It doesn't look in the   87
least bit dead. Who did it?"

"I did."   88

"You did?"   89

"Of course," she said. "And have you met my little Basil as well?" She nodded   90
toward the dachshund curled up so comfortably in front of the fire, and Billy looked at
it, and as he did so he suddenly realized that this animal all the time had been just as
silent and motionless as the parrot. He put out a hand and touched it gently on the top
of its back. The back was hard and cold, and when he pushed the hair to one side
with his fingers, he could see the skin underneath, grayish-black, and dry and perfectly preserved.

"Good gracious me," he said. "How absolutely fascinating." He turned away from   91
the dog and stared with deep admiration at the little woman beside him on the sofa. "It
must be most awfully difficult to do a thing like that."

"Not in the least," she said. "I stuff *all* my little pets myself when they pass away.   92
Will you have another cup of tea?"

"No thank you," Billy said. The tea tasted faintly of bitter almonds, and he didn't   93
care much for it.

"You did sign the book, didn't you?"   94

"Oh, yes."   95

"That's good. Because later on, if I happened to forget what you were called, then I   96
could always come down here and look it up. I still do that almost every day with Mr.
Mulholland and Mr. . . . Mr. . . . ."

"Temple," Billy said. "Gregory Temple. Excuse my asking, but haven't there been   97
any other guests here except them in the last two or three years?"

Holding her teacup high in one hand, inclining her head slightly to the left, she   98
looked up at him out of the corners of her eyes and gave him another gentle little smile.

"No, my dear," she said. "Only you."   99

➤ FOR WRITING OR DISCUSSION

1. In what way does Billy's own character contribute to his destruction? Would
   you have left the landlady's house before teatime? Explain.
2. At the start of the story, why does the author bother telling us about the
   weather, Billy's method of transportation, Billy's clothing, and his attitudes
   toward business?
3. How does the hypnotic power of the "BED AND BREAKFAST" sign introduce a
   supernatural element out of keeping with the rest of the story?
4. An effective surprise ending should surprise us, to be sure, but should also be
   logical and believable. Once we reread the story, we should be able to find
   previously overlooked clues and other anticipations of the ending. Write a
   literary analysis tracing the process by which Dahl prepares us for the surprise ending of "The Landlady." (See the student paper "The Beginning of the
   End," page 421.)

ANN PETRY

Doby's Gone

1   When Doby first came into Sue Johnson's life her family were caretakers on a farm way up in New York State. And because Sue had no one else to play with, the Johnsons reluctantly accepted Doby as a member of the family.

2   The spring that Sue was six they moved to Wessex, Connecticut—a small New England town whose neat colonial houses cling to a group of hills overlooking the Connecticut River. All that summer Mrs. Johnson had hoped that Doby would vanish long before Sue entered school in the fall. He would only complicate things in school.

3   For Doby wasn't real. He existed only in Sue's mind. He had been created out of her need for a friend her own age—her own size. And he had gradually become an escape from the very real world that surrounded her. She first started talking about him when she was two and he had been with her ever since. He always sat beside her when she ate and played with her during the day. At night he slept in a chair near her bed so that they awoke at the same time in the morning. A place had to be set for him at mealtime. A seat had to be saved for him on trains and buses.

4   After they moved to Wessex, he was still her constant companion just as he had been when she was three and four and five.

5   On the morning that Sue was to start going to school she said, "Doby has a new pencil, too. And he's got a red plaid shirt just like my dress."

6   "Why can't Doby stay home?" Mrs. Johnson asked.

7   "Because he goes everywhere I go," Sue said in amazement. "Of course he's going to school. He's going to sit right by me."

8   Sue watched her mother get up from the breakfast table and then followed her upstairs to the big front bedroom. She saw with surprise that her mother was putting on her going-out clothes.

9   "You have to come with me, Mommy?" she asked anxiously. She had wanted to go with Doby. Just the two of them. She had planned every step of the way since the time her mother told her she would start school in the fall.

10   "No, I don't have to, but I'm coming just the same. I want to talk to your teacher." Mrs. Johnson fastened her coat and deftly patted a loose strand of hair in place.

11   Sue looked at her and wondered if the other children's mothers would come to school, too. She certainly hoped so because she wouldn't want to be the only one there who had a mother with her.

12   Then she started skipping around the room holding Doby by the hand. Her short black braids jumped as she skipped. The gingham dress she wore was starched so stiffly that the hemline formed a wide circular frame for her sturdy dark brown legs as she bounced up and down.

13   "Ooh," she said suddenly. "Doby pulled off one of my hair ribbons." She reached over and picked it up from the floor and came to stand in front of her mother while the red ribbon was retied into a crisp bow.

14   Then she was walking down the street hand in hand with her mother. She held Doby's hand on the other side. She decided it was good her mother had come. It was

better that way. The street would have looked awfully long and awfully big if she and Doby had been by themselves, even though she did know exactly where the school was. Right down the street on this side. Past the post office and town hall that sat so far back with green lawn in front of them. Past the town pump and the old white house on the corner, past the big empty lot. And there was the school.

It had a walk that went straight down between the green grass and was all brown-yellow gravel stuff—coarser than sand. One day she had walked past there with her mother and stopped to finger the stuff the walk was made of, and her mother had said, "It's gravel." She remembered how they'd talk about it. "What's gravel?" she asked.   15

"The stuff in your hand. It's like sand, only coarser. People use it for driveways and walks," her mother had said.   16

"Gravel." She liked the sound of the word. It sounded like pebbles. Gravel. Pebble. She said the words over to herself. You gravel and pebble. Pebble said to gravel. She started making up a story. Gravel said to pebble, "You're a pebble." Pebble said back, "You're a gravel."   17

"Sue, throw it away. It's dirty and your hands are clean," her mother said.   18

She threw it down on the sidewalk. But she kept looking back at it as she walked along. It made a scattered yellow, brown color against the rich brown-black of the dirt-path.   19

She held on to Doby's hand a little more tightly. Now she was actually going to walk up that long gravel walk to the school. She and Doby would play there every day when school was out.   20

The school yard was full of children. Sue hung back a little looking at them. They were playing ball under the big maple trees near the back of the yard. Some small children were squatting near the school building, letting gravel trickle through their fingers.   21

"I want to play, too." She tried to free her hand from her mother's firm grip.   22

"We're going inside to see your teacher first." And her mother went on walking up the school steps holding on to Sue's hand.   23

Sue stared at the children on the steps. "Why are they looking so hard?" she asked.   24

"Probably because you're looking at them so hard. Now come on," and her mother pulled her through the door. The hall inside was dark and very long. A neat white sign over a door to the right said FIRST GRADE in bold black letters.   25

Sue peered inside the room while her mother knocked on the door. A pretty lady with curly yellow hair got up from a desk and invited them in. While the teacher and her mother talked grown-up talk, Sue looked around. She supposed she'd sit at one of those little desks. There were a lot of them and she wondered if there would be a child at each desk. If so then Doby would have to squeeze in beside her.   26

"Sue, you can go outside and play. When the bell rings you must come in," the teacher said.   27

"Yes, teacher," Sue started out the door in a hurry.   28

"My name is Miss Whittier," the teacher said, "You must call me that."   29

"Yes, Miss Whittier. Good-bye, Mommy," she said, and went quickly down the hall and out the door.   30

"Hold my hand, Doby," she said softly under her breath.   31

Now she and Doby would play in the gravel. Squeeze it between their fingers, pat it into shapes like those other children were doing. Her short starched skirt stood out   32 around her legs as she skipped down the steps. She watched the children as long as she could without saying anything.

33   "Can we play, too?" she asked finally.

34   A boy with a freckled face and short stiff red hair looked up at her and frowned. He didn't answer but kept ostentatiously patting at a little mound of gravel.

35   Sue walked over a little closer, holding Doby tightly by the hand. The boy ignored her. A little girl in a blue and white checked dress stuck her tongue out.

36   "Your legs are black," she said suddenly. And then when the others looked up she added, "Why, look, she's black all over. Looky, she's black all over."

37   Sue retreated a step away from the building. The children got up and followed her. She took another backward step and they took two steps forward. The little girl who had stuck her tongue out began a chant, "Look, look. Her legs are black. Her legs are black."

38   The children were all saying it. They formed a ring around her and they were dancing up and down and screaming, "Her legs are black. Her legs are black."

39   She stood in the middle of the circle completely bewildered. She wanted to go home where it was safe and quiet and where her mother would hold her tight in her arms. She pulled Doby nearer to her. What did they mean her legs were black? Of course they were. Not black but dark brown. Just like these children were white some other children were dark like her. Her mother said so. But her mother hadn't said anyone would make her feel bad about being a different color. She didn't know what to do; so she just stood there watching them come closer and closer to her—their faces red with excitement, their voices hoarse with yelling.

40   Then the school bell rang. And the children suddenly plunged toward the building. She was left alone with Doby. When she walked into the school room she was crying.

41   "Don't you mind, Doby," she whispered. "Don't you mind. I won't let them hurt you."

42   Miss Whittier gave her a seat near the front of the room. Right near her desk. And she smiled at her. Sue smiled back and carefully wiped away the wet on her eyelashes with the back of her hand. She turned and looked around the room. There were no empty seats. Doby would have to stand up.

43   "You stand right close to me and if you get tired just sit on the edge of my seat," she said.

44   She didn't go out for recess. She stayed in and helped Miss Whittier draw on the blackboard with colored chalk—yellow and green and red and purple and brown. Miss Whittier drew the flowers and Sue colored them. She put a small piece of crayon out for Doby to use. And Miss Whittier noticed it. But she didn't say anything, she just smiled.

45   "I love her," Sue thought. "I love my teacher." And then again, "I love Miss Whittier, my teacher."

46   At noon the children followed her halfway home from school. They called after her and she ran so fast and so hard that the pounding in her ears cut off the sound of their voices.

47   "Go faster, Doby," she said. "You have to go faster." And she held his hand and ran until her legs ached.

48   "How was school, Sue?" asked her mother.

"It was all right," she said slowly. "I don't think Doby likes it very much. He likes   49
Miss Whittier though."

"Do you like her?"   50

"Oh, yes," Sue let her breath come out with a sigh.   51

"Why are you panting like that?" her mother asked.   52

"I ran all the way home," she said.   53

Going back after lunch wasn't so bad. She went right in to Miss Whittier. She didn't   54
stay put in the yard and wait for the bell.

When school was out, she decided she'd better hurry right home and maybe the   55
children wouldn't see her. She walked down the gravel path taking quick little looks
over her shoulder. No one paid any attention and she was so happy that she gave
Doby's hand a squeeze.

And then she saw that they were waiting for her right by the vacant lot. She hurried   56
along trying not to hear what they were saying.

"My mother says you're a little nigger girl," the boy with the red hair said.   57

And then they began to shout: "Her legs are black. Her legs are black."   58

It changed suddenly. "Run. Go ahead and run." She looked over her shoulder. A   59
boy was coming toward her with a long switch in his hand. He raised it in a threatening
gesture and she started running.

For two days she ran home from school like that. Ran until her short legs felt as   60
though they couldn't move another step.

"Sue," her mother asked anxiously, watching her try to catch her breath on the front   61
steps, "what makes you run home from school like this?"

"Doby doesn't like the other children very much," she said panting.   62

"Why?"   63

"I don't think they understand about him," she said thoughtfully. "But he loves Miss   64
Whittier."

The next day the children waited for her right where the school's gravel walk   65
ended. Sue didn't see them until she was close to them. She was coming slowly down
the path hand in hand with Doby trying to see how many of the big pebbles they could
step on without stepping on any of the finer, sandier gravel.

She was in the middle of the group of children before she realized it. They started off   66
slowly at first. "How do you comb that kind of hair?" "Does that black color wash off?" And
then the chant began and it came faster and faster: "Her legs are black. Her legs are black."

A little girl reached out and pulled one of Sue's braids. Sue tried to back away and   67
the other children closed in around her. She rubbed the side of her head—it hurt where
her hair had been pulled. Someone pushed her. Hard. In the middle of her back. She
was suddenly outraged. She planted her feet firmly on the path. She started hitting out
with her fists. Kicking. Pulling hair. Tearing at clothing. She reached down and picked
up handfuls of gravel and aimed it at eyes and ears and noses.

While she was slapping and kicking at the small figures that encircled her she   68
became aware that Doby had gone. For the first time in her life he had left her. He had
gone when she started to fight.

69   She went on fighting—scratching and biting and kicking—with such passion and energy that the space around her slowly cleared. The children backed away. And she stood still. She was breathing fast as though she had been running.

70   The children ran off down the street—past the big empty lot, past the old white house with the green shutters. Sue watched them go. She didn't feel victorious. She didn't feel anything except an aching sense of loss. She stood there panting, wondering about Doby.

71   And then, "Doby," she called softly. Then louder, "Doby! Doby! Where are you?"

72   She listened—cocking her head on one side. He didn't answer. And she felt certain he would never be back because he had never left her before. He had gone for good. And she didn't know why. She decided it probably had something to do with growing up. And she looked down at her legs hoping to find they had grown as long as her father's. She saw instead that her dress was torn in three different places, her socks were down around her ankles, there were long angry scratches on her legs and on her arms. She felt for her hair—the red hair ribbons were gone and her braids were coming undone.

73   She started looking for the hair ribbons. And as she looked she saw that Daisy Bell, the little girl who had stuck her tongue out that first day of school, was leaning against the oak tree at the end of the path.

74   "Come on, let's walk home together," Daisy Bell said matter-of-factly.

75   "All right," Sue said.

76   As they started past the empty lot, she was conscious that someone was tagging along behind them. It was Jimmie Piebald, the boy with the stiff red hair. When she looked back he came up and walked on the other side of her.

77   They walked along in silence until they came to the town pump. They stopped and looked deep down into the well. And spent a long time hallooing down into it and listening delightedly to the hollow funny sound of their voices.

78   It was much later than usual when Sue got home. Daisy Bell and Jimmie walked up to the door with her. Her mother was standing on the front steps waiting for her.

79   "Sue," her mother said in a shocked voice. "What's the matter? What happened to you?"

80   Daisy Bell put her arm around Sue. Jimmie started kicking at some stones in the path.

81   Sue stared at her mother, trying to remember. There was something wrong but she couldn't think what it was. And then it came to her. "Oh," she wailed, "Doby's gone. I can't find him anywhere."

➤ FOR WRITING OR DISCUSSION

1. Why does Sue create Doby? Is it normal for a child of Sue's age to create an imaginary playmate, or are we meant to think that Sue may be seriously disturbed mentally?

2. What is Doby a symbol of?

3. Does Miss Whittier know about Doby? Should Miss Whittier have been more aware of the possibilities of Sue's encountering racial prejudice and, if so,

have kept a closer eye on her and the other children? Should Sue's mother have alerted her daughter to the possibilities of racial prejudice?

4. What does Sue have to do before she gets the other children's respect?
5. Exactly when does Doby disappear? Why is he most unlikely to return?
6. Write a paper on the issue of illusion versus reality in "Doby's Gone."

HAVING YOUR SAY

What is the state of race relations in American schools today? Could events like those in "Doby's Gone" occur today? Write an argumentative essay to address the issue. Write a thesis that states your opinion; back it up with specific details.

EDGAR ALLAN POE

The Tell-Tale Heart

True!—nervous—very, very dreadfully nervous I had been and am; but why *will* you say that I am mad? The disease had sharpened my senses—not destroyed—not dulled them. Above all was the sense of hearing acute. I heard all things in the heaven and in the earth. I heard many things in hell. How, them, am I mad? Hearken! and observe how healthily—how calmly I tell you the whole story.   1

It is impossible to say how first the idea entered my brain; but once conceived, it haunted me day and night. Object there was none. Passion there was none. I loved the old man. He had never wronged me. He had never given me insult. For his gold I had no desire. I think it was his eye! yes, it was this! One of his eyes resembled that of a vulture—a pale blue eye, with a film over it. Whenever it fell upon me, my blood ran cold; and so by degrees—very gradually—I made up my mind to take the life of the old man, and thus rid myself of the eye for ever.   2

Now this is the point. You fancy me mad. Madmen know nothing. But you should have seen *me*. You should have seen how wisely I proceeded—with what caution—with what foresight—with what dissimulation I went to work! I was never kinder to the old man than during the whole week before I killed him. And every night, about midnight, I turned the latch of his door and opened it—oh, so gently! And then, when I had made an opening sufficient for my head, I put in a dark lantern, all closed, closed, so that no light shone out, and then I thrust in my head. Oh, you would have laughed to see how cunningly I thrust it in! I moved it slowly—very, very slowly, so that I might not disturb the old man's sleep. It took me an hour to place my whole head within the opening so   3 far that I could see him as he lay upon his bed. Ha!—would a madman have been so wise as this? And then, when my head was well in the room, I undid the lantern cautiously—oh, so cautiously—cautiously (for the hinges creaked)—I undid it just so much that a single thin ray fell upon the vulture eye. And this I did for seven long nights— every night just at midnight—but I found the eye always closed; and so it was impossible to do the work; for it was not the old man who vexed me, but his Evil Eye. And every morning, when the day broke, I went boldly into the chamber, and spoke courageously to him, calling him by name in a hearty tone, and inquiring how he had passed the night. So you see he would have been a very profound old man, indeed, to suspect that every night, just at twelve, I looked in upon him while he slept.

4   Upon the eighth night I was more than usually cautious in opening the door. A watch's minute hand moves more quickly than did mine. Never before that night had I *felt* the extent of my own powers—of my sagacity. I could scarcely contain my feelings of triumph. To think that there I was, opening the door, little by little, and he not even to dream of my secret deeds or thoughts. I fairly chuckled at the idea; and perhaps he heard me; for he moved on the bed suddenly, as if startled. Now you may think that I drew back—but no. His room was as black as pitch with the thick darkness (for the shutters were closed fastened, through fear of robbers), and so I knew that he could not see the opening of the door, and I kept pushing it on steadily, steadily.

5   I had my head in, and was about to open the lantern, when my thumb slipped upon the tin fastening, and the old man sprang up in the bed, crying out "Who's there?"

6   I kept quite still and said nothing. For a whole hour I did not move a muscle, and in the meantime I did not hear him lie down. He was still sitting up in the bed listening;— just as I have done, night after night, hearkening to the death watches in the wall.

7   Presently I heard a slight groan, and I knew it was the groan of mortal terror. It was not a groan of pain or of grief—oh, no!—it was the low stifled sound that arises from the bottom of the soul when overcharged with awe. I knew the sound well. Many a night, just at midnight, when all the world slept, it was welled up from my own bosom, deepening, with its dreadful echo, the terrors that distracted me. I say I knew it well. I knew what the old man felt, and pitied him, although I chuckled at heart. I knew that he had been lying awake ever since the first slight noise, when he had turned in the bed. His fears had been ever since growing upon him. He had been trying to fancy them causeless, but could not. He had been saying to himself—"It is nothing but the wind in the chimney—it is only a mouse crossing the floor," or "it is merely a cricket which has made a single chirp." Yes, he has been trying to comfort himself with these suppositions; but he had found all in vain. *All in vain*; because Death, in approaching him, had stalked with his black shadow before him, and enveloped the victim. And it was the mournful influence of the unperceived shadow that caused him to feel— although he neither saw now heard—to *feel* the presence of my head within the room.

8   When I had waited a long time, very patiently, without hearing him lie down, I resolved to open a little—a very, very little crevice in the lantern. So I opened it—you cannot imagine how stealthily, stealthily, until, at length, a single dim ray, like the thread of a spider, shot from out the crevice and full upon the vulture eye.

It was open—wide, wide open—and I grew furious as I gazed upon it. I saw it with   9
perfect distinctness—all a dull blue, with a hideous veil over it that chilled the very
marrow in my bones; but I could see nothing else of the old man's face or person: for I
had directed the ray as if by instinct, precisely upon the damned spot.

And now have I not told you that what you mistake for madness is but overacute-   10
ness of the senses!—now, I say, there came to my ears a low, dull, quick sound, such as
a watch makes when enveloped in cotton. I knew *that* sound well too. It was the beating of the old man's heart. It increased my fury, as the beating of a drum stimulates the
soldier into courage.

But even yet I refrained and kept still. I scarcely breathed. I held the lantern motion-   11
less. I tried how steadily I could maintain the ray upon the eye. Meantime the hellish
tattoo of the heart increased. It grew quicker and quicker, and louder and louder every
instant. The old man's terror *must* have been extreme! It grew louder, I say, louder every
moment!—do you mark me well? I have told you that I am nervous: so I am. And now
at the dead hour of the night, amid the dreadful silence of that old house, so strange a
noise as this excited me to uncontrollable terror. Yet, for some minutes longer I
refrained and stood still. But the beating grew louder, louder! I thought the heart must
burst. And now a new anxiety seized me—the sound would be heard by a neighbor!
The old man's hour had come! With a loud yell, I threw open the lantern and leaped
into the room. He shrieked once—once only. In an instant I dragged him to the floor,
and pulled the heavy bed over him. I then smiled gaily, to defend the deed so far done.
But, for many minutes, the heart beat on with a muffled sound. This, however, did not
vex me; it would not be heard through the wall. At length it ceased. The old man was
dead. I removed the bed and examined the corpse. Yes, he was stone, stone dead. I
placed my hand upon the heart and held it there many minutes. There was no pulsa-
tion. He was stone dead. His eye would trouble me no more.

If still you think me mad, you will think so no longer when I describe the wise precau-   12
tions I took for the concealment of the body. The night waned and I worked hastily, but in
silence. First of all I dismembered the corpse. I cut off the head and the arms and the legs.

I then took up three planks from the flooring of the chamber, and deposited all   13
between the scantlings. I then replaced the boards so cleverly, so cunningly, that no
human eye—not even *his*—could have detected any thing wrong. There was nothing to
wash out—no stain of any kind—no blood-spot whatever. I had been too wary for that.
A tub had caught all—ha! ha!

When I had made an end of these labors, it was four o'clock—still dark as midnight.   14
As the bell sounded the hour, there came a knocking at the street door. I went down to
open it with a light heart,—for what had I *now* to fear? There entered three men, who
introduced themselves, with perfect suavity, as officers of the police. A shriek had been
heard by a neighbor during the night; suspicion of foul play had been aroused; information had been lodged at the police office, and they (the officers) had been deputed
to search the premises.

I smiled,—for *what* had I to fear? I hade the gentlemen welcome. The shriek, I said,   15
was my own in a dream. The old man, I mentioned, was absent in the country. I took my

visitors all over the house. I bade them search—search *well*. I led them, at length, to *his* chamber. I showed them his treasures, secure, undisturbed. In the enthusiasm of my confidence, I brought chairs into the room, and desired them *here* to rest from their fatigues, while I myself, in the wild audacity of my perfect triumph, placed my own seat upon the very spot beneath which reposed the corpse of the victim.

16   The officers were satisfied. My *manner* had convinced them. I was singularly at ease. They sat, and while I answered cheerily, they chatted familiar things. But, ere long, I felt myself getting pale and wished them gone. My head ached, and I fancied a ringing in my ears: but still they sat and still chatted. The ringing became more distinct:—it continued and became more distinct: I talked more freely to get rid of the feeling: but I continued and gained definitiveness—until, at length, I found that the noise was *not* within my ears.

17   No doubt I now grew *very* pale;—but I talked more fluently, and with a heightened voice. Yet the sound increased—and what could I do? It was *a low, dull, quick sound— much such a sound as a watch makes when enveloped in cotton.* I gasped for breath— and yet the officers heard it not. I talked more quickly—more vehemently; but the noise steadily increased. I arose and argued about trifles, in a high key and with violent ges- ticulations, but the noise steadily increased. Why *would* they not be gone? I paced the floor to and fro with heavy strides, as if excited to fury by the observation of the men— but the noise steadily increased. Oh God! what *could* I do? I foamed—I raved—I swore! I swung the chair upon which I had been sitting, and grated it upon the boards, but the noise arose over all and continually increased. It grew louder—louder—*louder!* And still the men chatted pleasantly, and smiled. Was it possible they heard not? Almighty God!—no, no! They heard!—they suspected!—they *knew!*—they were mak- ing a mockery of my horror!—this I thought, and this I think. But any thing was better than this agony! Any thing was more tolerable than this derision! I could bear those hypocritical smiles no longer! I felt that I must scream or die!—and now—again!— hark! louder! louder! louder! *louder!*—

18   "Villains!" I shrieked, "dissemble no more! I admit the deed!—tear up the planks!— here, here!—it is the beating of his hideous heart!"

➤ FOR WRITING OR DISCUSSION

1. What is the narrator's mental state? How do you know? How does Poe's lan- guage help convey the mental state of the narrator?
2. What does the narrator say is the result of his disease? To whom is he speaking?
3. Sound plays an important part in the telling of this story. What images of sound can you identify here? What claim does the narrator make about sound in the first paragraph?
4. What do the frequent repetitions contribute to this story?
5. Do you trust the narrator? Why, or why not? Are his observations reliable?
6. Edgar Allan Poe, who wrote in the nineteenth century ("The Tell-Tale Heart" was published in 1843), continues to be an extremely popular writer. How do you account for his popularity? Write an essay in which you explain, on the basis of this short story, why Poe continues to have a hold on the American imagination.

REVIEW CHECKLIST: WRITING AND REVISING
YOUR LITERARY ANALYSIS PAPER

- Have I used prewriting to explore ideas for a subject?
- Have I thought carefully about my purpose?
- Have I written for the usual general audience? If I am writing for a special audience, have I made that clear to the reader?
- Have I limited my subject?
- Have I established a clear thesis?
- Do I have enough support for my thesis?
- Have I read the literary work slowly? Have I reread?
- Have I read with the assumption that everything is significant?
- Have I remembered not to interpret details out of context?
- Have I avoided the "hidden meanings" fallacy?
- Have I concentrated on theme rather than moral?
- Have I been aware of any use of symbols?
- Have I been cautious about the dangers of overreading and becoming a symbol hunter?
- Have I been alert to the use of metaphors and similes?
- Have I avoided writing a plot summary?
- Have I been cautious with direct quotations, using them only when they serve a specific, practical purpose?
- Have I proofread for grammar, spelling, and mechanics?

CHAPTER
16

Writing Essay Exams

Essay examinations are an important part of college learning; they provide an excellent gauge of your knowledge of a subject. No doubt you have taken these kinds of tests before: You have one or more questions to answer in an in-class essay of several pages within a defined time frame—usually about an hour.

You may not think writing essay exams is fun, but this type of test does give you a much better opportunity to show the range of your knowledge than other testing measures like short-answer exams of the fill-in-the-blank, true–false, or multiple-choice variety. Essay test questions share a number of qualities that make it possible to generalize about them. This general advice about how to prepare for and take essay exams for all your college courses should help you improve performance.

Preparing for the Exam

To minimize anxiety and to achieve the best results possible on an examination, prepare carefully and well in advance of your test.

If you've paid attention to lectures and class discussions during the semester, you'll have a good sense of your instructor's emphases. Use your lecture notes and review your readings to determine which areas your instructor might target; assume the role of test maker and develop your own essay questions. Use these questions to help you study.

A useful way to begin is to make a table of topics and questions. First, develop a list of the key areas you believe might be covered on the exam. Then alongside the topics, indicate possible questions. Look at this sample prepared by a student studying for a test on child development.

<u>Table of topics and questions</u>

<u>Topic</u>	<u>Possible essay questions</u>
Physical environment of the fetus	1. How does the physical environment of the fetus contribute to the psychological development of the child? 2. Discuss the effects of drugs or alcohol on the fetus and explain some of the noticeable psychological results on the newborn.
Prenatal care	1. Explain the steps a caregiver can take to provide appropriate psychological care for the fetus. 2. Define <u>prenatal</u> and <u>neonatal</u> and give distinguishing characteristics of each.
Psychology of the newborn	1. What can parents do to provide a sound psychological environment for a newborn? 2. What are some possible effects on a child whose basic needs are not met in the first month after birth?

Evaluating the Question

It is very important to know exactly what the exam question is asking so that you can make the required points and provide the necessary detail.

Always read the entire test, and study each essay question carefully. A major complaint from teachers who grade essay exams is that students often do not answer the questions being asked. Read the question with care so that you know precisely what your instructor expects. Essay questions usually contain cue words that signal the specific requirements. You should look for these cue words as you read the question and should develop your responses to address the stated task. The table below lists and explains some cue words and identifies the methods of essay development (explained in Part Two of this book) that you might use to develop your answers. Keep in mind that some essay questions will ask for a combination of these methods.

Cue words	What to do	Method of development
Describe	Give physical characteristics, provide details, indicate sequence, or explain features.	Description
Tell, discuss, trace	Give the history of, state the events, or indicate chronology.	Narration
Explain, illustrate, give examples	Make sense or order of, enumerate, or provide details and examples.	Example
How? Explain how, show how, tell how	Explain a process or indicate chronology.	Process
Compare, contrast, compare and contrast	Indicate similarities and (or) differences.	Comparison–contrast
Analyze, indicate the types, classify	Indicate, explain, and describe the qualities of a group or category.	Classification or division
Why, tell why, analyze, explain the results (or effects) of, tell the consequences of	Show the relation between ideas or events; tell how one event influences, causes, or results from another; or draw conclusions.	Cause and effect
Define, identify, tell the meaning of	Provide extended definitions and explain meanings.	Definition
Agree or disagree, support, evaluate, judge, defend, argue	Provide logical support for your position on a topic; convince a reader that your position is correct.	Argumentation

The following box presents, from courses across the disciplines, typical essay examination questions that use some of these cue words.

Discipline	Essay question
English Literature	Provide examples of Shakespeare's use of animal imagery in *The Tempest* and explain the meaning of several key images.
Biology	Explain the reproductive process of budding in yeast cells.
Sociology	Compare and contrast the conditions in state-run orphanages in California in the nineteenth and twentieth centuries.
Health Care	Terminal illness often has devastating effects on the patient's immediate family. What are some of these effects? How can social service agencies provide support for family members of the terminally ill?
Psychology	Classify abnormal personality patterns in adolescents and identify the key features of the various groups.
History	Trace the rise of the slave trade in America in the eighteenth century.

Planning and Writing the Essay

Once you examine the question carefully and are confident that you understand the task, take time to plan the essay before you begin writing.

■ *Assess the expected length and range of your response.*   From the nature of the questions, determine how much you are expected to write. Some tests do not require essays in the formal sense; these tests may demand a few sentences or a paragraph response to a question. Your teacher may indicate what she expects in the examination questions with statements like "Write a sentence or two" or "Write a paragraph." More often than not, however, you have to infer the length of your expected response. A question worth five or ten points demands a shorter answer—a few sentences or a paragraph, say—than a question worth twenty-five, fifty, or a hundred points.

■ *Use the wording of the essay question to help get you started.*   Essay questions provide information that helps you focus your thinking on the topic. Use some of the language of the question in your response, especially in the introduction to your answer. Often, before the precise task statement on an essay exam, your instructor will include a sentence or two of background information to frame the question or instructions. You can use some of this information as well in your essay.

Let's look again at some of the essay questions from different disciplines just listed and at some possible opening responses to these questions:

Essay question	Opening responses that use elements of the questions
Provide examples of Shakespeare's use of animal imagery in *The Tempest* and explain the meaning of several key images.	In *The Tempest* we find many examples of animal imagery, especially regarding the character Caliban.
Explain the reproductive process of budding in yeast cells.	Yeast plants reproduce by a process of budding in which . . .
Terminal illness often has devastating effects on the patient's immediate family. What are some of these effects? How can social service agencies provide support for family members of the terminally ill?	The effects of terminal illness on patients and their families can be devastating, but social service agencies can help by providing a variety of support for individuals and the family as a whole.

■ *Budget your time.* In an hour's examination, reserve about forty-five minutes for writing and about fifteen to twenty minutes for planning and revising.

■ *Follow the general guidelines for good writing.* The principles of good writing that you have learned in this book are just as important for producing responses on essay exams as for essays you write outside of class. You should express your thesis and purpose clearly and should support your assertions with concrete detail. Accuracy, specificity, completeness, and relevance are essential. You will have to draw most details from your lecture and recitation notes as well as from your readings. Although verbatim citations are difficult unless you have a superb memory, you nevertheless should paraphrase key points carefully, identifying sources whenever you can. For your in-class essay exam, write an introduction and a conclusion—brief as time may require them to be. Connect thoughts with necessary transitions within paragraphs; link paragraphs logically within the essay.

■ *Plan your essay carefully and make any revisions and editorial changes.* Because of time pressures on an essay examination, you certainly will have to condense the steps we recommended that you take as writers. However, do not ignore basic features of the writing process, especially the prewriting and planning strategies.

Even with the clock ticking, take a few moments to plan. Use the margins or the inside or back cover of your exam booklet to jot down ideas and to develop a scratch outline. A few minutes of planning before writing on an essay exam almost certainly will pay dividends in your grade. When you write, consider the effort as somewhere between a first draft and a revised and edited draft. That is, you cannot write your essay exam on scrap paper and expect to return later to make extensive revisions. Certainly, you must reread your first effort, deleting problematic sections, adding words and sentences, as needed, and fixing errors. Write all additions clearly. Your teacher should be able to follow your marks and directional arrows. Many students skip every other line as they write and leave large top and bottom margins to facilitate changes and insertions. Nevertheless, the press of time will prevent you from rewriting your essay entirely. Don't plan on it. Add key elements that you may have omitted; insert definitions or essential detail; correct mistakes. But unless you are sure that you have sufficient time to recopy a draft, or that your instructor expects a second draft, do not rewrite your essay examination.

Business Writing

The principles of good writing that we have advocated throughout the *Student Book of College English* will serve you well in any context that requires writing—from a research paper in advanced college courses to a statement of goals for your environmental group; from a letter to the editor of your local paper to a report on business trends for your department supervisor at the office. Clarity, coherence, unity, specificity, and correctness: These are the hallmarks of all good writing. Yet the writing demands of the business world, newly complicated by widespread use of word processing programs and other computer aids, build on certain formal conventions; and so many misconceptions exist about what constitutes effective writing for a job and on the job that we provide in this chapter what we hope will be useful suggestions as you face business writing tasks.

Writing Inquiry and Complaint Letters

Despite the easy access of E-mail (see page 465) and the availability of office phones, cellular phones, and voice-mail messaging, letters continue to fuel the engine of most businesses, and the preferred mode of communication between businesses and clients is the letter. It is permanent and won't get wiped away by computer glitches and crashes; it provides an accurate record of transactions; it encourages the building of long-term relations among business partners; and it bears a signature that can carry legal weight. (We must note, however, that E-signatures are now as legal as more traditional "wet" ones.) As communications options expand endlessly, it seems, you often can convey the letter instantly through E-mail or fax, which provides quick and easy alternatives to the United States Postal Service and its competitors. Still, you never can go wrong by sending a letter in an envelope with a stamp affixed to it.

It's best to look at a business letter as a letter to do business. That is, your purpose always is to accomplish an objective that you have in mind when you set out to write. In general, business letters fall into one of three categories—an inquiry or request letter, a complaint letter, or an application letter.

If you write a letter to *inquire* about or *request* something—cancellation of your subscription to *People Magazine,* information about the contents of makeup that causes your eyes to tear, or a self-charging mini dust buster that would be great for your dorm room—you want to make your request known as quickly as possible and to back it up with specific and accurate information needed to fulfill your request (see the letter on page 454).

If you write a letter to *complain* about something—incorrect billing for your tuition, the way airline personnel treated you when your flight was cancelled, or the crushed and inedible contents of a box of sourdough pretzels—your objective is to make your complaint known so that the respondent can redress it in some way. Think about what you want in return for your problem and be sure to suggest it in your letter. Your tone in a complaint letter is very important. Be firm and direct but not snide or insulting. Focus on the problem and the resolution; don't condemn the whole company or castigate its leaders. State your charge. Provide all essential details (dates, prices, and place of occurrence as needed) without padding or drama. Remember, you want something in return, and you're writing to someone who may be in a position to give you what you want. Be courteous. Be straightforward. Stick to the facts.

We'll treat *application* letters more directly further on in this chapter, specifically as they relate to applying for a job.

Most business letters follow the **block format,** which word processors now provide automatically as standard, and you can type in information swiftly without worrying about spacing. In the block format, all parts of the letter are flush with the left margin. You separate paragraphs by leaving a blank line between the last line of one paragraph and the first line of the paragraph that comes after it. In the **modified block format**, you indent by 25–30 spaces the inside address, the complimentary close, and the closing instead of placing them flush with the left margin. Note the labeled parts of the block format in the illustration on the following page.

Type your letter on standard, $8\frac{1}{2} \times 11$ inch unlined, heavy bond paper. Unless your letter is really short, use single space, with a blank space between paragraphs. Be sure to proofread your letter very carefully before sending it out.

Margin at least one inch from top of page

318 Walker Street
Boulder, CO 10036   *Heading: your return address (omit if using letterhead staionery) and date*

Comma here April 7, 2001

                          Double space

Mr. Steve Kingsbury, General Manager
Customer Service Division
Bose Corporation   *Inside address*
The Mountain
Framingham, MA 01701

Comma here

                          Double space

Salutation Dear Mr. Kingsbury: *Colon*

Several months ago I received a gift of your Bose Wave radio,
1-1 1/4 inch Model AWR1-1W and have enjoyed using it. But I have encountered
margin   two problems for which I would like to request your help.
                    Double space between body paragraphs   *1 1/4 inch*
First, I have misplaced the Wave radio remote control unit.   *margin*
It is a thin, black, rectangular object measuring approximately
1-1/2 inches by 3 inches. Apparently it has no model or serial
number. Is it possible to replace this item? If so, how much would
it cost—and will you accept a credit card or do you require payment
by check? How long do you think it would take for me to receive the
remote control unit once I place the order? Would there be an extra
charge for rapid delivery service?   *Body*
                    Double space between body paragraphs

Second, I find that the antenna that accompanies the radio is
inadequate for my needs. The antenna is simply a Y-shaped wire
that I have spread and attached to the ceiling of my study, which
is in the basement of my house. Although there are two windows in
the basement, I believe that the radio's location below ground level
weakens the transmission of sound. Could you recommend a more powerful
antenna that would bring better reception to the room? If so, will you
suggest some stores that might carry it? We have a Radio Shack and
a Home Depot nearby.
                    Double space between body paragraphs

I would appreciate a prompt response so that I can enjoy my new
radio more fully.
                    Double space between body paragraphs

Comma here Sincerely,   *Complimentary close*
Quadruple space William Cookson *Signature*

William Cookson *Typed name*

■ **Heading**   Type your full street address flush left on the first line of the heading; your city, state, and zip code on the next; and the date on the last line. Letter conventions require that you avoid abbreviations (like *St., Ave.,* or *Feb.,* to name a few) except for the name of a state, which should appear in the standard two-letter postal code abbreviation—CA, MD, NY, CO, for example. Postal code abbreviations appear on page 458. Do not include your name anywhere in the heading. If you use letterhead stationery—paper that has the company logo and (or) name and the company address printed across the top, bottom, or side—your first typed entry is the date, beneath the letterhead after two or three spaces.

■ **Inside Address**   Space two or three lines (more if you're writing a short letter) beneath the date and type the full name, title, and address of the person you're sending the letter to. Abbreviations such as *Mr., Miss, Mrs., Ms.,* and *Dr.* are acceptable, and you should use them. If you don't know the name of the person you are writing to, it's all right to start the inside address with the person's title or the department you're interested in—for example, *Director of Human Resources* or *Customer Relations Department.* As with the inside address, you want to avoid most abbreviations other than the state, and any abbreviation that appears as part of the company name.

If you want to make reference to previous correspondence or documents that will help the reader relate quickly to the issues in your letter, make reference to it a few spaces below the inside address. Type *Re* (an abbreviation for reference) followed by a colon and then indicate the document:

```
Re: Your letter of December 15, 2000

Re: Invoice Number 67843
```

■ **Salutation**   In your greeting, after the word *dear,* use the appropriate abbreviation for the person's title, followed by the addressee's last name—*Dear Mr. Santiago, Dear Ms. Chin.* If you're writing to more than one person, use the abbreviations from the French, *Messrs.* for the plural of *Monsieur* or *Mmes.* for the plural of *Madame—Dear Messrs. Damon and Afleck, Dear Mmes. Schwartz and Murphy.* If you have not included a name in the inside address, do not use the word *dear* in your salutation. Use *Gentlemen, Ladies,* or the combination *Gentlemen/Ladies.* This last combination has supporters among some letter writers, but it is not used widely.

■ **Body**   The body of the letter is the content, the paragraphs in which you make your point. Keep your correspondence to about one page and your paragraphs short. Your letter will no doubt reach the desk of a busy person, and the shorter the letter, the more quickly your point will get across. Because of this recommended brevity, you must take particular care to make your point concisely and without padding. Civility is essential—the reader of the letter does not have the added advantage of receiving your message with accompanying gestures, intonations, and facial impressions. The words on the page say everything, and you want to be relaxed and informal in your written language (not slangy) but not at the expense of courteous expression. You should avoid stilted (artificially formal and stiff) language and you should prune deadwood carefully (see pages 565–566). Chapters 21 through 22, that is, all of Part Five, Style, in the *Student's Book of College English* can help you develop and sustain appropriate letter language and technique.

■ **Complimentary Close**   Use one of the following forms, which are most appropriate for and typical of business letters. The complimentary close always begins with a capital letter, ends with a comma, and appears on its own line in the letter.

```
Sincerely yours,  Sincerely,  Yours truly,
```

■ **Closing**   Sign the letter and type your name beneath it.

■ **Notations**   Beneath the signature block you can make notations. If you want to indicate that you are enclosing something with the letter, usually a copy of a prior letter, document or other reference material, note it beneath the signature as in the instances below.

```
Enclosures (2)  Encl.: Presbyterian Hospital medical file
```

If you want to indicate that you're sending a copy of the letter to someone, type the abbreviation *c.* (for copy) followed by the other recipient's name:

```
c. Mr. Steven Spielberg  c. Dr. Ramona Leary
```

CHECKLIST: WRITING A BUSINESS LETTER

- Follow an accepted format of business letter writing—block style or modified block style
- Include all essential information in the heading, inside address, salutation, and complimentary close.
- In the body state your point clearly and directly right at the start of the letter.
- Provide all necessary background to the issue you're writing about— exact information you need, dates of former correspondence, invoice numbers, costs, and the names of people you dealt with, for example.
- Always maintain a courteous and civil tone.
- Remember your objective: You want the recipient to do something for you, whether to send you information or a product or to redress a wrong.
- Check the letter carefully for errors in grammar, usage, spelling, and sentence structure.
- If your letter requires more than one page, do not use letterhead stationery on the second and subsequent pages. Instead, use plain white bond paper. In the block style, flush with the left margin, type the page number, the name of the person you are writing to, and the date.

```
2
Mr. Steve Kingsbury
April 7, 2001
```

Unless you're using carbon paper, the abbreviation *cc.* for *carbon copy* is no longer appropriate. Most writers now use a convenient copy machine instead of carbon paper and use *c* instead of *cc* to indicate an enclosed copy.

Addressing an Envelope

Most word processing programs provide an envelope and label option on the toolbar, and produce envelopes in appropriate format for postal delivery, extracting the required addresses for the envelope from the letter itself. You must include a return address in the upper left-hand corner of the envelope (not on the back flap). The address in the center of the envelope is the same as the inside address in the letter.

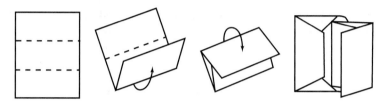

Fold your letter neatly in thirds to fit a number 10 size business envelope.

EXERCISE

Write a letter of inquiry or complaint to address one of the following situations. Figure out whom you would write to and use that information to construct the inside address and salutation.

1. You want information about a graduate program in physical therapy, including deadlines for applications, course requirements, fellowship availability, and any other related matters.
2. You have had your new automobile in the shop four times in the last two months for transmission problems and still it is not working right. You want a new transmission installed now; the existing transmission cannot be repaired, you believe.
3. You have had no success in raising cucumbers in your garden for the last few summers. They start off all right, but the fruits are distorted and not plentiful, and the foliage turns brown toward mid July.
4. The bus that takes you from your dorm to the college building for your first class each morning is never on time. Although a schedule is posted, arrival times at your stop are erratic at best, and you have been late to class several times this semester.
5. The food in your college cafeteria is high in fat and sugar and there are not enough options for people who watch their diet and would choose more healthful foods, such as salads from a salad bar, plain grilled meats or vegetables, and fresh fruit—which seem almost non-existent.

United States				Canada	
Alabama	AL	Missouri	MO	Alberta	AB
Alaska	AK	Montana	MT	British Columbia	BC
American		Nebraska	NE	Labrador	LB
Samoa	AS	Nevada	NV	Manitoba	MB
Arizona	AZ	New Hampshire	NH	New Brunswick	NB
Arkansas	AR	New Jersey	NJ	Newfoundland	NF
California	CA	New Mexico	NM	Nova Scotia	NS
Colorado	CO	New York	NY	Northwest	
Connecticut	CT	North Carolina	NC	Territories	NT
Delaware	DE	North Dakota	ND	Ontario	ON
District		Ohio	OH	Prince Edward	
of Columbia	DC	Oklahoma	OK	Island	PE
Florida	FL	Oregon	OR	Quebec (Province	
Georgia	GA	Pennsylvania	PA	de Quebec)	PQ
Guam	GU	Puerto Rico	PR	Saskatchewan	SK
Hawaii	HI	Rhode Island	RI	Yukon Territory	YT
Idaho	ID	South Carolina	SC		
Illinois	IL	South Dakota	SD		
Indiana	IN	Tennessee	TN		
Iowa	IA	Texas	TX		
Kansas	KS	Utah	UT		
Kentucky	KY	Vermont	VT		
Louisiana	LA	Virginia	VA		
Maine	ME	Virgin Islands	VI		
Maryland	MD	Washington	WA		
Massachusetts	MA	West Virginia	WV		
Michigan	MI	Wisconsin	WI		
Minnesota	MN	Wyoming	WY		
Mississippi	MS				

POSTAL ABBREVIATIONS FOR STATES, TERRITORIES, AND PROVINCES IN THE UNITED STATES AND CANADA

Writing a Letter to Apply for a Job

Whether you're writing for a part-time job after classes, a two- or three-month summer position, or a full-time job after graduation, the job-seeking letter and accompanying résumé are a vital part of the employment process. Particularly for a position advertised in the newspaper or online, a personnel director often receives many responses, and to assure that someone will pay attention to your correspondence, you want to make it stand out from the pack, while still following accepted business writing etiquette.

Start prewriting activity by reviewing your education and job history. Your résumé (look ahead to page 461) will help you here. It's all right to stress key features of your résumé, but you want to be sure not to write a job application letter that merely repeats all the information found there. You'll be including your résumé with the letter, so avoid redundancy. How do you make your letter stand out? Let your personality shine through as you attempt to show the reader your special talents. Use specific examples to indicate relevant experience or to recount an incident that reflects your skills. Avoid the trite and careworn expressions that often infiltrate job letters: "Thank you in advance for your consideration," and "I look forward to hearing from you," and "I would be happy to meet with you at a convenient time," for example. Yes, it's a good idea to try to arrange for an interview, but you gain with a more forceful and direct statement, such as "May I call you next week to set up a meeting?" or "I'll call on Tuesday for an appointment at your convenience." Many people like to indicate their source of information for the position in the first sentence of their job application letter: "I saw your ad in the employment section of the May 15, 2000, issue of the *New York Times*." "A mutual friend, David Stewart, told me that you are looking for an assistant editor."

The sample letter appearing on page 460 is clear and concise, yet forceful and infused with the writer's personality. The writer has chosen the block format.

Writing Your Résumé

A résumé is a summary of your education, job history, and accomplishments. Many students starting to seek employment feel intimidated by producing a résumé: "I haven't done much," they think. Yet a creative view of your past can yield a very interesting résumé. Reflect on your past experiences and make a list of anything that seems relevant to displaying your character or giving any other valuable information about yourself. Think about any full- or part-time jobs you have held. Even if they are not in the field you're seeking to pursue, they can indicate ambition, ingenuity, strength of character, degree of responsibility, and so on. Think about honors and awards in school, on the playing field, or in some extra- or cocurricular enterprise. Even extracurricular work at high school, if it shows your skills in a positive light, can add useful information to your résumé.

Start the résumé with your name, address, and telephone number on the top of the page. Include a fax number and (or) an E-mail address if you have one. Then, you want to establish categories to make it easier for the reader to identify related pieces of information. Some typical categories are *Job Objective, Education, Work Experience, Honors and Awards, Personal,* and *References.* Set off these categories in boldface type or by underlining them and place them at the left margin. Put relevant information beneath the categories, as shown in the Sanchez résumé (page 461). Use sentence fragments to indicate some of your responsibilities and use lively verbs and verb forms. Writing fragments helps you avoid the redundant "I."—*I* studied this, *I* did that, *I* did something else.

201 East 64th Street, Apt. 24J
New York, NY 10021
Phone: (212) 363-9999
E-mail: oscsan@tele.com

All information complete in heading and inside address

Ms. Joyce Haberski, President
Web Designs, Inc.
1520 Commercial Drive
Sacramento, CA 95819

Dear Ms. Haberski: *Salutation: use of Ms. to avoid indicating marital status for woman correspondent*

Purpose of letter stated directly and forcefully

I learned from a mutual friend, Brian O'Malley, that your new company is seeking web designers who can help put together commercial web pages for a variety of companies. I'm the person you are looking for. My interests, education, and experience have prepared me well for the job you are trying to fill.

Source of job announcement stated in first sentence

My parents used to joke that even as a child I had bytes along with gray matter in my brain, so tuned into the possibilities of computers was I from a very early age. The keyboard was (and continues to be) my soul mate. Although I wouldn't exactly call myself a computer nerd—I do like other things such as reading mystery novels and fishing in Folsom Lake not far from our family home in Rancho Cardova—my friends all know that my laptop and I are inseparable. I do love working on the computer and never tire of exploring its potential. In high school I automated the production and design of our school newspaper, <u>Topics Weekly</u>, for which I served as managing editor in my senior year.

Friendly, informal style ("Bytes along with gray matter," "computer nerd"); personal information helps reveal writer's character

Block style followed throughout

After I moved East, I attended Mildred Elley College where I completed the Associate in Occupational Studies in Informational Technology program and received my O.A.S. degree in 1996. Along with courses in computer repair, programming, and software applications, I studied visual programming, Internet design, and electronic commerce. I worked for two years after graduation at the Wiles Corporation as a Help Desk manager before concluding that I liked the creative side of computer work more than the technical side, and I decided to return to college as a communication arts major.

Essential details from résumé highlighted without restating all points

Key courses identified to suggest essential training for position

As a student at Marymount Manhattan College, I now have many more courses in visual design under my belt, and I was fortunate to complete a six-course sequence in the College's Division of Continuing Education, which awarded me a Certificate in Web Design and E-Commerce. As you can see from my enclosed résumé, I will complete my Bachelor of Arts degree this June. I love working with people and, as you can tell, I love working with computers. After an exciting few years in New York City I am eager to return permanently to California, where I was born and reared and where my family lives.

I'll be back home in the Sacramento region after graduation on June 11 and would like very much to meet with you at your convenience soon after. May I call next week to set up an appointment?

Firm yet courteous effort to set up interview

Sincerely yours,

Complimentary close and signature

Oscar Sanchez

Oscar Sanchez

Encl.

RÉSUMÉ

OSCAR SANCHEZ

Home Address
318 Rose Hill Drive
Rancho Cardova, CA 95822
Phone: (916) 851-2345

Complete, relevant addresses for ease of contact

Campus Address
201 East 64th Street, Apt. 24J
New York, NY 10021
Phone: (212) 363-9999

E-mail: oscsan@tele.com   *E-mail address*

Category "Career Objective" set off in boldface

Career Objective   Web Designer/Web Master   *Career objective stated simply and succinctly*

Education
1998–2001

Date ranges indicated in chronologically reverse order

Marymount Manhattan College, New York, NY
Bachelor of Arts in Communication Arts
Degree expected: June 2001
Special courses: Advanced Animation, Desktop Video, The Business of Media Arts, Desktop Publishing, Electronic Newswriting
Gradepoint Average in Major: 3.2

Sanchez highlights GPA in major only because it is higher than his cumulative GPA

1993–1996

Mildred Elley College for Careers, Latham, NY
Associate in Occupational Studies in Information Technology (O.A.S.)
Degree conferred: June 1996
Special courses: Operating Systems, Software Applications, Introduction to Visual Programming, Electronic Commerce, Internet and Web Page Design

Special education suited to the position

Category "Work Experience" includes full- and part-time work

Work Experience
1996–1998

Wiles Corporation, Brooklyn, NY
As Help Desk Manager, answered questions about and repaired computer failures, installed software programs, fixed faulty programs, and offered ongoing workshops to a staff of 35

Sentence fragments with lively verb forms

Summer 1995 and 1996

The Computer Store, Sacramento, CA
Sold computers, did general troubleshooting for repairs, advised on software purchase

Personal Background

Born in California; grew up in Rancho Cardova (near Sacramento). Moved East in 1993. Interests: Fishing, anything high tech, action films, video arcades, mystery novels, moving back West.

"Personal Background" category provides useful information about applicant

"References" category: reader will know how to get needed references

References   Furnished on request

Most people use a *chronological* résumé. Here, you present relevant information about yourself in each category, as appropriate, following reverse time order. That is, you list the most recent item first. Like the business letter, the résumé should follow accepted formatting conventions, although there is no absolute format that requires strict adherence. You should try to keep your résumé to a single page, if possible. To make the page look more attractive, you might want to vary typeface or type size, but you should resist overdoing design elements on your résumé. Look at the sample, on page 461, prepared by Oscar Sanchez and the accompanying annotations.

REVIEW CHECKLIST: PREPARING A RÉSUMÉ

- Establish categories to organize related information—for example, **Education, Work Experience, Personal.** Use underlining, boldface type, or varied font size to set off the categories. Don't be too fancy.
- Try to confine your entries to about a page.
- Leave a $1^1/_2$ inch margin. Type the word *Résumé* on the top line and your name directly beneath it.
- Always enter your full name, address, telephone number, and, if you have one, an E-mail address and (or) a fax number as the first items on your résumé.
- Reflect on your past and include any information relevant to the job you are seeking, including courses of study that show your preparation for the job and previous work experience.
- Use sentence fragments to avoid repeated use of *I.* Use lively verbs and verb forms.
- Remember that character, ambition, and willingness to accept responsibility are qualities that employers look for in potential employees. Indicate key activities that suggest those and other important character traits.
- Use the *Personal* category to highlight special interests and talents.
- Present information in reverse time order, last experiences first.

COLLABORATIVE LEARNING

In groups of three people each, exchange letters and résumés. Assume the persona of a job recruiter and, using the job listing submitted, tell your classmate what you see as the strengths and weaknesses of his or her résumé.

EXERCISE

1. Prepare a résumé that highlights your character, education, and experience. Use the Sanchez résumé and the checklist on page 462 as a guide.

2. Check your local newspaper or familiar web sites for job listings and write a letter applying for some current job that interests you. Attach the job listing with your letter.

Electronic (Digital) Résumés

Your job search may turn up a request for a version of your résumé that an employer can scan into a database. Or, you may wish to send your résumé via E-mail. In these cases, you need to revise your résumé so that it appears in *plain text*. Plain text is text stripped of all special features, such as boldface or italic print, underlining, color, boxes, columns, or graphics of any kind. Only conventional-width type face, like *Times New Roman* or *Courier* in 12–14 point font size, is appropriate. Type all entries in a digital format flush with the left margin. If you want to highlight a particular point, use uppercase letters. Use the space bar on your keypad when you need to separate words and letters; do not use the tab button. Résumés in digital format allow readers to look for key words that match job openings or requirements, so that when you respond to a job announcement, use those key words. For example, words like *web master, help desk manager, supervisor, sales representative,* and *management trainee* are self-descriptors easily keyed into a database.

   If you are sending your résumé electronically, embed it in E-mail. Do not send E-mail with your digital résumé as an attachment. Employers fear viruses in attachments and will be reluctant to open one from an unsolicited source. It's always best to follow up an E-mail application and résumé with hard copy sent through the mail.

   Look at the résumé in digital format on the following page.

EXERCISE

Prepare your own résumé in electronic (digital) format. Use the sample and the annotations as a guide.

Memorandums

The office memorandum (memo, for short) is a vital link between and among workers in an institution and provides a formal record of newly initiated activities and requests for information or action. An office manager may write

SAMPLE OF ELECTRONIC RÉSUMÉ

RÉSUMÉ OF OSCAR SANCHEZ

HOME ADDRESS
318 Rose Hill Drive
Rancho Cardova, CA 95822
Phone: (916) 851-2345

All entries flush left

No italics, underlining, boldface

CAMPUS ADDRESS
201 East 64th Street, Apt. 24J
New York, NY 10021
Phone: (212) 363-9999
E-mail: oscsan@tele.com

Uppercase letters for emphasis

CAREER OBJECTIVE Web Designer/Web Master

Key words

EDUCATION
1993–1996 Mildred Elley College for Careers, Latham, NY. Associate in
Occupational Studies in Information Technology (O.A.S.). Degree conferred:
June 1996. Special courses: Operating Systems, Software Applications,
Introduction to Visual Programming, Electronic Commerce,
Internet and Web Page Design.

Standard width typeface: 12 point Times New Roman

1998–2001 Marymount Manhattan College, New York, NY. Bachelor of Arts
in Communication Arts. Degree expected: June 2001. Special courses:
Advanced Animation, Desktop Video, The Business of Media Arts,
Desktop Publishing, Electronic Newswriting.
Gradepoint Average in Major: 3.2

Category "Work Experience" includes full- and part-time work

WORK EXPERIENCE
Summer 1995 and 1996 The Computer Store, Sacramento, CA. Sold computers,
did general troubleshooting for repairs, advised on software purchase

1996–1999 Wiles Corporation, Brooklyn, NY. As Help Desk Manager, answered
questions about and repaired computer failures, installed software programs,
fixed faulty programs, and offered ongoing workshops to a staff of 35

Key word Help Desk Manager

PERSONAL BACKGROUND Born in California; grew up in Rancho Cardova
(near Sacramento). Moved East in 1993. Interests: Fishing, anything high tech,
action films, video arcades, mystery novels, moving back West.

REFERENCES
Furnished on request

Single column

a memo to all her employees about new safety regulations required by the State; a secretary may write to his boss requesting annual leave over Christmas and New Year; and a sales manager may write to a representative requesting explanations of weakening sales for an important product. Some memos are fairly long, but usually the most effective communication in this medium is brief and to the point—and dealing with an explicit topic. Memos never should go to people outside the organization; for such communication you need to write a letter. Look at the annotated memorandum on the following page.

E-mail

Complementing the paper memorandum and letter as a means of business correspondence, E-mail continues to grow in popularity for good reason. It is quick; it is informal; and it can cover wide geographical territories without problems. Within a business, employees communicate with each other via E-mail because it compresses so many steps required by word-processed memorandums. You don't have to print out a document, put it through office mail, hope it gets there promptly, and wait a long while for a response. From business to business, E-mail also allows speedy messaging in a highly informal context.

E-mail messages should be short and to the point and, despite the informality of the communication, should be error free. Most E-mail providers have built in spell checks, and at the very least you should run your message through a spell check to prevent errors. Don't assume that E-mail is an open field for bad spelling and grammar; mistakes always diminish the impact of your message in any medium. And don't fall into the trap of inappropriate use: business E-mail is for doing business. If you want to pass along or receive jokes, local supermarket sales information, concert dates, and so on, be sure that you use your private E-mail account for such purposes, not the account established where you work. Many companies now monitor their employees' E-mail, and you want to be beyond reproach.

EXERCISE

Write a memorandum or an E-mail on one of the following issues:

1. Announce to members of your class a trip to a local animal sanctuary: include the purpose of the trip, the day and time, the cost, the person in charge, and any other relevant details.
2. Assume that you are the office manager of an employee pool of 25 people and that you are writing to remind your workers of the importance of getting to work and getting to work on time. Sick-day call-ins seem excessive to you. Employees have been clocking in beyond accepted arrival times.
3. Announce to members of your class a series of collaborative study sessions that you're trying to organize in preparation for the biology final.

WALDORF CORPORATION
612 Super Highway
Milwaukee, Wisconsin 53201

MEMORANDUM

Date, including
month, day, and year Date: October 24, 2001

Person receiving
memorandum   To: Midred Greenberg-Stevens, Director of Human Resources

Sender's name and From: Roberta McAlister, Vice President for Administration *(RM)*
handwritten initials
(indicating approval
of the memorandum) Subject: Day Care Center   *Topic of memorandum*

As you know, many of our employees have asked us to establish a day-care center
Purpose and desired for the children of Waldorf Corporation's workers. I think that this is a good idea,
outcome stated in the but we have far too little information to recommend the option to our Board of
first paragraph Directors. I have asked Winifred Rollison and Roger Eggers to work along with *Standard width*
you in developing a preliminary report that will guide a decision. Please address *typeface: 12 poin*
the following issues: *Times New Roman*
Double space between paragraphs

- **Space** Where would be the best place to establish a day-care
  center in our building? What area would serve our employees'
  needs best? How would we create the necessary space?
- **Regulations** What regulations—State, Federal, local—exist
  to guide the construction of a daycare center? For example, are
  we required to reserve a minimum number of square feet; are
  there special restroom facilities requirements or furniture
  requirements for the young children?
- **Cost** What would it cost to establish and maintain the day-care
  center? We need to think about supplies and furniture, but also
  staffing. How much would we have to pay a director? Are
  there other personnel issues that we have to consider?
- **Need** Just how many Waldorf workers would take advantage
  of the Center? How many children would we expect to serve
  each day?

Double space between paragraphs

As you do your research, I'm sure that you will discover other key issues as well; *Deadline for*
feel free to address them in your report. Please finish your work in a month's time. *completion*
of stated task

Thanks very much for agreeing to take this on.

Recipients of copies
of the memorandum c. Winifred Rollison, Director of Personnel
Roger Eggers, Eastern Regional Sales Manager

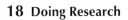

Research

Writing a research paper is a rewarding yet highly demanding task for college writers. Teachers in a variety of courses will expect you to research a topic carefully and present your findings in a well-written paper. Yet a successful research paper is much more than a summary of the books and articles you consulted on a topic—it also makes an assertion that is supported by substantive detail from reliable sources.

The two chapters in Part Four take you through the steps necessary to produce research papers for your college courses. In Chapter 18, you'll learn how to choose a subject, how to develop a thesis, and how to start a preliminary reading for your research paper. You will also learn how to prepare a working bibliography, how to use online sources, and how to take notes on your reading. You will review as well the important uses of an outline in producing a paper.

In Chapter 19, we will point out that necessary to writing a research paper is the ability to document sources accurately and to integrate those sources smoothly with your own writing. You'll see how to quote, summarize, and paraphrase sources. We discuss two major systems of documentation—one developed by the Modern Language Association (MLA style) and the other developed by the American Psychological Association (APA style). Also included is a sample student research paper with annotations that explain the various features of the work. This model paper can help you write your own paper.

18

Doing Research

A research paper (or research essay or library paper or term paper) is a nearly universal assignment in your first-year English course and in many other courses. This is not merely because it's an academic tradition but because it serves a number of worthwhile, practical purposes:

1. The research paper teaches you how to manage substantially longer pieces of writing than does the normal classroom theme. At a minimum, the research paper usually will be five or six typed pages; many papers may be two or three times as long.

2. The research paper teaches you how to use the library. It's probably only a slight exaggeration to state that any adequate library contains most of the information in the world, all accessible and all free. You may not want to know everything, but when you want to know something, it's important to be able to find it.

3. The research paper makes you an expert on your subject. The satisfactions are deep and lasting. Few differences are greater than the difference between the dabbler and the authority.

4. The research paper prepares you for success in other courses. To some extent, teaching how to write research papers is a service the English department performs for other college departments. As you go through college, particularly as you take more and more upper-level courses, you will find the ability to write research papers increasingly important. At the upper levels, instructors require students to demonstrate mastery of course materials—mastery that can come only through intense exploration of a subject and not from a short essay written during a midterm or final exam.

Choosing Your Subject

Often the best subject for a research paper is an unfamiliar one that you are generally interested in and curious about. If you start out knowing everything or thinking that you know everything about your subject, all your research may be boring repetition of the familiar, and, if you are writing a thesis paper (see Chapter 2), you may not be sufficiently open-minded to evaluate fairly any views that conflict with your own. On the other hand, you'll naturally want to avoid subjects that may demand technical knowledge you do not possess. You may be vaguely interested in Einstein's theory of relativity, but that topic would surely be a poor choice for most students.

As you think about formulating a subject, follow some of the prewriting strategies you explored in Chapter 1. Make a rough list. Use free association. Brainstorm on a topic that seems even remotely interesting. Talk at length with roommates, friends, teachers, relatives, employers, co-workers—with anyone who will listen. Watch television talk shows or documentaries related to your subject. Browse in libraries and bookstores. Study newspapers, magazines, and journals: A word or two in a headline or title may catch your eye and get you thinking. Some background reading in a general encyclopedia like the *Encyclopaedia Britannica* may provide a useful overview of your topic. Surf the web to explore a range of approaches to your subject.

Once you have even a vague notion of a topic that interests you, think about it for a while. Consider whether it's too broad. Remember the importance of limiting your subject. "Custer's Last Stand" and "The Lizzie Borden Murder Case" might make good papers, but a good paper of reasonable length could not be written on a topic like "Famous Battles" or "Great Trials" because it's too broad.

One final suggestion: Don't be too eager to settle on any single topic immediately. If you have two or three possibilities in mind, so much the better. There may not be as much information available on your first choice as you had hoped, and it's comforting to have something ready to fall back on.

EXERCISE

For the following broad subjects, indicate how you would limit each one to make it suitable for a research paper. Follow the format of the example.

EXAMPLE

Broad topic	Limited topic
Communication	The importance of regular conversation with children from six weeks to one year old
The solar system	Current theories on the sun's longevity

Broad subjects
1. Poverty
2. Ships
3. Country music

4. Medical cures
5. Immigrants
6. Psychology
7. The French underground in World War II
8. Guns
9. Revolutions
10. Software

EXERCISE

Choose a broad subject on your own and limit it for a research paper.

The Research Paper with a Thesis

Virtually every research paper requires that you gather facts and opinions (sometimes conflicting) from a variety of sources and that you organize and present them in your own words and style through your own hard work. Every research paper also requires that you document whatever sources you have used. When you document a source, you tell the reader where you found information taken from someone else's writing. Typical documentation includes the author's name, the title of the selection, and important publication data. You'll read more about documentation in Chapter 19.

However, the most important kind of research paper does more than cite sources—it has as its basis a **thesis.** True, sometimes you may be asked to write a report in which you present objectively the known facts on an issue without expressing your own point of view. Yet most teachers want students to use research in order to develop opinions of their own and to present those opinions in a carefully documented paper. Hence, in a research paper with a thesis, you do extensive investigation to find facts; but you also interpret those facts and you try to persuade the reader that your interpretation or opinion is correct. Rather than merely stating the facts, you use them to support your opinion. The thesis drives the research you present to your readers.

Of course, you can deal with many subjects either as a report or as a thesis paper. Reports titled "Custer's Last Stand" and "The Lizzie Borden Murder Case" would give the reader information about two colorful episodes of the American past. Thesis papers on the same subjects would give the reader all or most of the same information, but the main purpose would be to argue, for example, that the battle of the Little Big Horn would never have taken place if it had not been for Custer's foolishness and vanity or that Lizzie Borden was really innocent of the murder charge brought against her.

Before you get deeply involved in your research project, make sure you know whether your instructor wants a report or a thesis paper, or if either will be acceptable.

Developing Your Thesis

Developing a thesis is critical to writing a successful research paper. This book pays considerable attention to writing a thesis, and you may wish to review the general steps for developing a powerful thesis in Chapter 2.

Your thesis for a research paper will grow and take shape as you investigate the resources in the library. However, as you conduct library research, you need to keep in mind your purpose and audience. Given the mass of data you're likely to encounter, it's easy to forget the point you intend to make in the paper as well as how much information your readers will need to understand and appreciate your point. Further, your research activities may cause you to change or modify your original thesis as you progress from prewriting to rough draft to final draft.

For the sample paper "The Banning of the Polygraph," which appears in Chapter 19, student writer Elizabeth Kessler arrived at this thesis sentence after conducting some research on her topic.

Thesis 1

```
Many employers have used polygraph testing as a means for

determining the honesty of future employees.
```

She states her topic clearly here—the paper will discuss the use of the polygraph in hiring employees. And Kessler's research supported her point indisputably— many employers had used lie detector tests for making hiring decisions. However, as Kessler considered this thesis sentence, she realized that it makes a simple assertion of fact but offers no opportunity for interpretation or judgment. She then revised her thesis sentence as follows:

Thesis 2

```
Supporters and critics battle the merits and drawbacks of lie

detector tests.
```

Here, too, we see a clear topic statement and, on the surface, what seems to be strong opinions about the topic. Yet the more Kessler thought about the topic, the more she realized that her own opinion was absent from the thesis statement. She again had made an assertion of fact: Some people supported the polygraph test and others opposed it. As she pondered the question "How do I feel about using the polygraph test in job-related situations?" and started shaping an early draft, Kessler wrote this thesis sentence:

Thesis 3

```
My own research indicates that the polygraph test as a condi-

tion of employment is highly unfair.
```

Here Kessler's interpretation of the topic is clear: Required polygraph testing for a job is not fair. As you will see when you examine her paper later in the chapter, as Kessler continued her research, she changed her thesis again.

EXERCISE

Write a tentative thesis for your limited subject. Consider what you will try to assert about your subject. Remember that your thesis may change considerably, especially after you do preliminary (and then sustained) reading and research for your paper.

Preliminary Reading

Once you have an idea of the topic or topics you're interested in, it's time for a trip to the library. Your purpose now is to do some fairly easygoing "reading around." You want to make sure that the subject that seems so interesting when you think about it is still interesting when you read about it. You want to acquire enough of a general perspective on your subject to be able to respond thoughtfully when you begin more serious and detailed reading.

Usually, the most sensible place in which to begin reading is a recent edition of a general encyclopedia, such as the *Encyclopaedia Britannica* or the *Encyclopedia Americana*. No significant research paper is going to use an encyclopedia article as a major source. The entry can offer only a broad survey of its subject, whereas a research paper explores its subject in depth. At this early stage, however, a broad survey is all you want.

In fairness, some encyclopedia articles, especially the longer ones, may be written by leading authorities and contain much useful information. In such cases, you needn't be shy about using the articles as minor sources. If you come across an article that strikes you as potentially usable in your paper, make out a bibliography card for it (see pages 484–487) and take notes (see pages 487–492). Some encyclopedia articles may also be valuable because they conclude with a brief list of important books and articles on the subject. These references can help you decide whether enough material is available for your paper, and they can give you some specific titles to look for immediately.

As good as or better than general encyclopedias for preliminary reading are specialized encyclopedias, dictionaries, and other reference works, many of which are updated and revised regularly. For example, if you are writing about an American who is no longer living, the *Dictionary of American Biography* may have an excellent article. The *Dictionary of National Biography* supplies similar information about British men and women who are no longer living. A list of some other specialized reference works follows; check the latest available edition at your library.

Art

    Britannica Encyclopaedia of American Art

    Encyclopedia of World Art, 15 vols.

    Bernard S. Myers, ed., *Encyclopedia of Painting*

    The McGraw-Hill Dictionary of Art

Business

Douglas Greenwald, *The McGraw-Hill Dictionary of Modern Economics*
Glen G. Munn, *Encyclopedia of Banking and Finance*
Harold S. Sloan and Arnold J. Zurcher, *A Dictionary of Economics*

Education

Encyclopedia of Education, 10 vols.
Encyclopedia of Educational Research

History

Dictionary of American History, 6 vols.
The Cambridge Ancient History, 12 vols.
The Cambridge Medieval History, 8 vols.
The Cambridge Modern History, 14 vols.
William L. Langer, *An Encyclopedia of World History*

Literature

Albert C. Baugh, *A Literary History of England*
John Buchanan-Brown, ed., *Cassell's Encyclopedia of World Literature*
James D. Hart, *The Oxford Companion to American Literature*
Phyllis Hartnoll, *The Oxford Companion to the Theatre*
Paul Harvey, *The Oxford Companion to English Literature*
Robert Spiller and others, *Literary History of the United States*, 2 vols.
Roger Whitlow, *Black American Literature*
Percy Wilson and Bonamy Dobree, *The Oxford History of English Literature*, 12 vols.

Music

The New Grove Dictionary of Music and Musicians, 20 vols.
The New Oxford History of Music, 10 vols.
Percy A. Scholes, *The Oxford Companion to Music*

Philosophy

Frederick C. Copleston, *A History of Philosophy*, 8 vols.
Paul Edwards, ed., *The Encyclopedia of Philosophy*, 4 vols.

Psychology

H. J. Eysenck and others, *Encyclopedia of Psychology*, 3 vols.
Robert M. Goldenson, *The Encyclopedia of Human Behavior*, 2 vols.

Religion

F. L. Cross and Elizabeth A. Livingstone, *The Oxford Dictionary of the Christian Church*

The New Catholic Encyclopedia, 15 vols.

Geoffrey Parrinder, *A Dictionary of Non-Christian Religions*

Encyclopedia Judaica, 16 vols.

Science

The McGraw-Hill Encyclopedia of Science and Technology, 15 vols.

Van Nostrand's Scientific Encyclopedia

Social Science and Politics

John P. Davis, ed., *The American Negro Reference Book*

Barry T. Klein, ed., *Reference Encyclopedia of the American Indian*

E. R. A. Seligman and Alvin Johnson, eds., *Encyclopedia of the Social Sciences*, 15 vols.

David L. Sills, ed., *International Encyclopedia of the Social Sciences*, 19 vols.

Edward C. Smith and Arnold J. Zurcher, eds., *Dictionary of American Politics.*

As the World Wide Web continues to grow in content and complexity, web sites too have become important resources for exploring topics. Go online and call up a variety of web sites that might aid your preliminary thinking on your topic. Search engines like Yahoo and Netscape allow you to search for information via key word or web site address.

The Preliminary Outline

If all goes well in your preliminary reading, you should know enough to feel confident in your choice of subject and perhaps even in your ability to limit that subject further. Best of all, you should be in a position to draw up a **preliminary outline,** or **scratch outline,** indicating the major divisions of your paper. For example, a paper on the Lizzie Borden murder case might have the following headings: "The Crime," "The Trial," "The Controversy." You don't need anything elaborate; you will revise and expand the outline as you go along. In the meantime, the preliminary outline enables you to read and take notes as part of a systematic plan. You'll know what information is relevant and irrelevant, what divisions of the paper you need to work on more thoroughly, and so on.

Here is Elizabeth Kessler's scratch outline for her research paper on lie detector tests:

`Topic/Thesis`: `Polygraph Testing on the Job`

`1. Cost`

`2. Reliability`

`3. Accuracy`

`4. Relation between guilt and physical measures from test`

`5. Consequences of test on person's life`

This outline, based on preliminary reading, guided Kessler's deeper probing into sources related to her topic and her ultimate writing of drafts for the paper. The outline changed many times—compare it with the items in her formal outline on page 531. At this stage, a preliminary outline is a useful guide to further thinking about your topic.

EXERCISE

Check your library for resources, including computer search engines, to use for preliminary reading on your subject. Write the names of three specialized encyclopedias, dictionaries, or other reference works that you use for your preliminary reading.

EXERCISE

Make a scratch outline of the major divisions that you now think will structure your paper. Base the outline on your preliminary readings. (Remember: Your scratch outline will most likely change as your research advances.)

A Working Bibliography

When you complete your preliminary outline, it's time for some serious reading, and that brings us to the subject of the bibliography. When you write the final draft of your research paper, you'll have to include a list of works cited, an alphabetical listing of the books, articles, and other sources that you refer to in the text of your essay. To prepare for that effort, you want to prepare a **working bibliography** by recording the promising resources you consult in the early stages of your research.

Many researchers prepare a working bibliography, a preliminary list of sources that seem helpful. You can accomplish this most efficiently on index cards, where you can record authors' names, titles, and publication data for all promising sources. The final works cited list includes only those sources cited in the paper. Since you cannot know in advance which books or articles will contain useful information, you should prepare bibliography cards (see pages 484–487) for every source that seems useful. As you read, you can eliminate cards for those sources that turn out not to be helpful.

Finding Sources

The two best places to look for titles of books and articles are the book index (or library catalog) and the periodical indexes. Many libraries now list their holdings in automated (computerized) library catalogs. Your pubic library may still rely on card catalogs; these, like the encyclopedias you have already consulted, are located in the reference room of the library.

THE CARD CATALOG

The forms of book catalogs differ from library to library. Until 1960, the most common method of listing books was by means of a **card catalog**, an alphabetical filing system in which a separate card is used to index every book in the library. (A set of sample catalog cards appears below.) Most libraries using card catalogs list each book in three ways: (1) on a subject card, (2) on an author card, and (3) on a title card. Further, the cards in each of the three files are alphabetized by subject, author, and title, respectively. Consider, for example, the sample catalog cards for the book *An American Verdict* by Michael J. Arlen in the accompanying illustration.

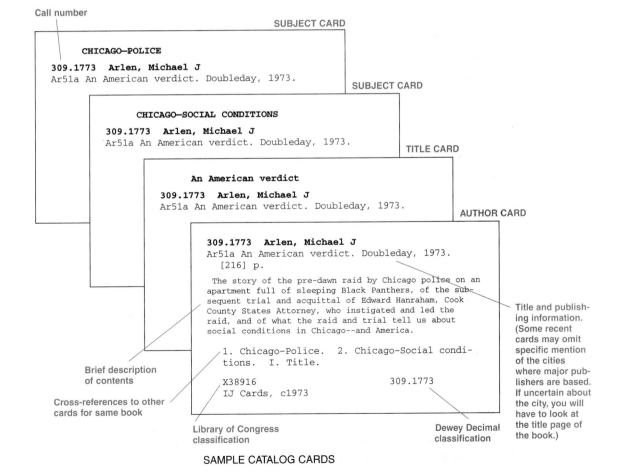

SAMPLE CATALOG CARDS

The book is listed alphabetically under "A" for *American* in the title file (the words *A, An,* and *The* are not used in alphabetizing). The book also appears under "A" (for Arlen, Michael J.) in the author file and under "C" (for "Chicago—Police" and "Chicago—Social Conditions") in the subject file. In addition to listing books by author, title, and subject, some catalogs contain cross-references that suggest other related subject headings for possible consultation.

THE AUTOMATED (COMPUTERIZED) CATALOG

Some libraries continue to use card catalogs, but most have turned to automated cataloging, which provides less expensive and less space-consuming lists of their holdings. Some libraries use computer printouts, which are bound into books. Others list their holdings on microfiche cards, sheets of microfilm about the size of filing cards. Because one microfiche card can list approximately a hundred titles, its use saves a great deal of library space. For the same reason, many libraries have automated their holdings on computer. Sample entries from an automated library system follow.

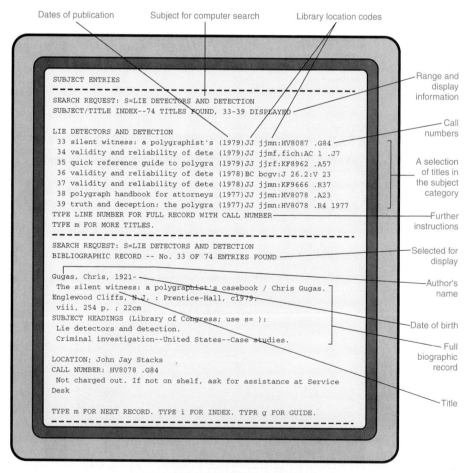

AUTOMATED LIBRARY SYSTEM CATALOG

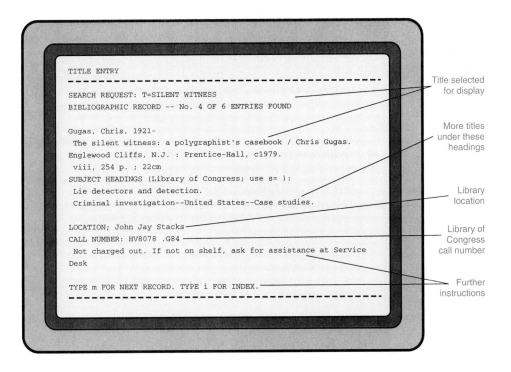

```
TITLE ENTRY
-------------------------------------------------------
SEARCH REQUEST: T=SILENT WITNESS
BIBLIOGRAPHIC RECORD -- No. 4 OF 6 ENTRIES FOUND

Gugas, Chris, 1921-
  The silent witness: a polygraphist's casebook / Chris Gugas.
Englewood Cliffs, N.J. : Prentice-Hall, c1979.
  viii, 254 p. ; 22cm
SUBJECT HEADINGS (Library of Congress; use s= ):
  Lie detectors and detection.
  Criminal investigation--United States--Case studies.


LOCATION; John Jay Stacks
CALL NUMBER: HV8078 .G84
  Not charged out. If not on shelf, ask for assistance at Service
Desk

TYPE m FOR NEXT RECORD. TYPE i FOR INDEX.
-------------------------------------------------------
```

Title selected for display

More titles under these headings

Library location

Library of Congress call number

Further instructions

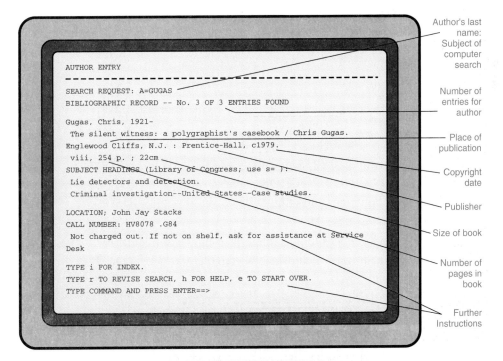

```
AUTHOR ENTRY
-------------------------------------------------------
SEARCH REQUEST: A=GUGAS
BIBLIOGRAPHIC RECORD -- No. 3 OF 3 ENTRIES FOUND

Gugas, Chris, 1921-
  The silent witness: a polygraphist's casebook / Chris Gugas.
Englewood Cliffs, N.J. : Prentice-Hall, c1979.
  viii, 254 p. ; 22cm
SUBJECT HEADINGS (Library of Congress; use s= ):
  Lie detectors and detection.
  Criminal investigation--United States--Case studies.

LOCATION; John Jay Stacks
CALL NUMBER: HV8078 .G84
  Not charged out. If not on shelf, ask for assistance at Service
Desk

TYPE i FOR INDEX.
TYPE r TO REVISE SEARCH, h FOR HELP, e TO START OVER.
TYPE COMMAND AND PRESS ENTER==>
```

Author's last name: Subject of computer search

Number of entries for author

Place of publication

Copyright date

Publisher

Size of book

Number of pages in book

Further Instructions

AUTOMATED LIBRARY SYSTEM CATALOG

PERIODICAL INDEXES

To find magazine or journal articles, you will need to consult **periodical indexes.**
Many of these appear online and many college libraries have discontinued subscriptions to bound indexes for current pieces. Still, many public libraries provide hardcopy indexes. One of the most frequently used is *The Readers' Guide to Periodical Literature,* an index of articles that have appeared in popular American magazines during any given year since 1900. *The Readers' Guide* appears monthly in pamphlet form and is permanently bound every two years. If your subject is a current one, you would, of course, use the most recent *Readers' Guide.* If, however, your subject deals with a particular period in the past, you would want to consult *The Readers' Guide* for the year or years that are appropriate for your subject. If, for instance, your subject is the presidency of Franklin Roosevelt, you would surely want to consult *The Readers' Guide* for the years 1933–1945, in addition to consulting guides of later years to see how Roosevelt's administration was evaluated after his death.

The guide is indexed by both author and subject, but you will probably find it easier to look for subject headings. When you have located the heading or headings you need, you will find listed under the headings all the articles on your subject that have appeared in popular American magazines for the period covered by the particular guide. Because *The Readers' Guide* indexes so much material, the entries must be printed in as little space as possible. That means, for one thing, that many abbreviations appear in each entry. If you do not understand an abbreviation, refer to the keys and explanations of all abbreviations at the beginning of each issue. The need to conserve space also means that the editors do not punctuate titles, dates, and pages. Note the example of a *Readers' Guide* entry below. We've labeled the parts for easy reference.

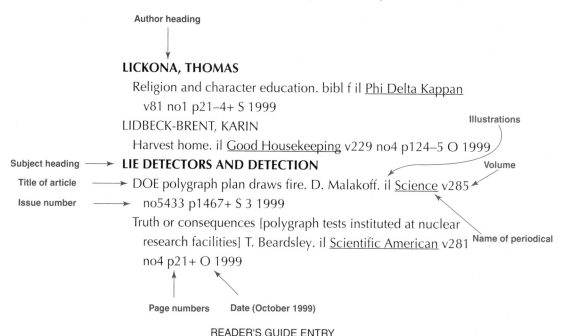

READER'S GUIDE ENTRY

A helpful hint: Don't use *The Readers' Guide* entries as models for entries on your own works cited list (see page 506). Rather, use *The Readers' Guide* to find sources; once you have your sources in hand, copy bibliographic material carefully from the sources themselves and according to the guidelines listed on pages 514–515.

The Readers' Guide is a good place to start, but it does, after all, index only popular American magazines. For most subjects, you will also want to read articles written by scholars in the field in order to get more specialized information. Almost every academic discipline has one or more journals to which specialists in the field contribute, and you would certainly want to look at their articles. To find them, you would consult the special index and abstracts covering your subject. Most indexes are arranged in the same way as the *The Readers' Guide,* so you will have no difficulty using the special indexes if you have mastered the use of *The Readers' Guide.*

Following is a list of some of the specialized indexes you might want to consult. It is by no means complete, but it will give you some idea of the kinds of indexes available. You can find these and other special indexes in the reference room of the library.

Specialized Indexes

Agriculture Index

Applied Science and Technology Index

Art Index

Biological Abstracts

Business Periodicals Index

Chemical Abstracts

Computer Abstracts

Criminal Justice Abstracts

Ecology Abstracts

Education Index

Engineering Index

Environmental Index

Humanities Index, 1974– (called the *Social Science and Humanities Index* from 1965–1973)

Index to Legal Periodicals

Music Index

The Philosopher's Index

Psychological Abstracts

Religion Index

Sociological Abstracts

NEWSPAPER INDEXES

The *New York Times Index* provides a complete listing of every article that has appeared in its newspaper during a given year. The *Times* has been thoroughly indexed since 1913. If you need newspaper articles from local papers, you often must page through or scan on microfilm the newspapers issued during the period your subject covers. *New York Times on the Web* provides articles in an extensive database as does *AP Online* (an electronic source for the Associated Press) and the *Washington Post* web site. Newspaper databases can provide helpful indexes for articles on key topics.

EXERCISE

List four indexes that you could use to find periodical articles related to your subject. Examine two of these indexes carefully and list several articles from them that seem useful to you as you explore your topic.

ELECTRONIC SEARCHES: USING DATABASES

You've already seen how some libraries use computers to catalog their holdings. Like indexes and catalogs, *databases*—reference lists available on computer— provide extensive bibliographic information for topics in a number of disciplines. Essentially, databases are specialized catalog systems. You can retrieve lists of titles and authors in a variety of subjects covered by the database—and with some databases, such as *Infotrac* and *Ebscohost,* you can use the computer to retrieve the works themselves. At your library you may have to pay a fee for using particular databases.

In the fields of humanities, government, education, science, social science, and business, many computerized libraries use other familiar databases like DIALOG, Bibliographic Retrieval Services (BRS), and Academic Search Elite. The Educational Research Information Center (ERIC) provides a wide range of information on education; and the New York Times Information Center (NYTIC) provides summaries (abstracts) of publications in a variety of areas. For legal information, Mead Data Control provides comprehensive listings.

To use a database, you must use a *descriptor,* which is a key word that will signal the computer to locate titles relevant to your topic. Each database provides a set of key words, and you need to identify your research area and match it to a word the electronic program will understand. Spend time choosing the descriptor that most precisely targets your interests; in this way, most of the resources brought up by the computer will serve your research needs. Many beginners use too general a descriptor and have to wade through extensive bibliographic listings that are too broad to be useful. Your librarian will help you connect your research area with an appropriate descriptor.

After you examine the list of resources the computer provides and are satisfied with the citations, print out the list of titles. If you need summaries, you can

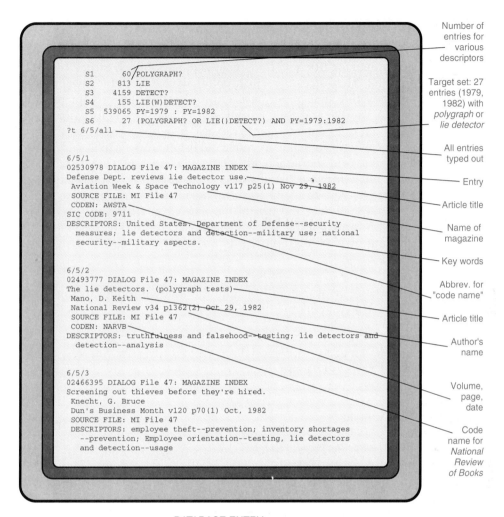

```
      S1      60 POLYGRAPH?
      S2     813 LIE
      S3    4159 DETECT?
      S4     155 LIE(W)DETECT?
      S5  539065 PY=1979 : PY=1982
      S6      27 (POLYGRAPH? OR LIE()DETECT?) AND PY=1979:1982
    ?t 6/5/all


    6/5/1
    02530978 DIALOG File 47: MAGAZINE INDEX
    Defense Dept. reviews lie detector use.
     Aviation Week & Space Technology v117 p25(1) Nov 29, 1982
      SOURCE FILE: MI File 47
      CODEN: AWSTA
    SIC CODE: 9711
    DESCRIPTORS: United States. Department of Defense--security
      measures; lie detectors and detection--military use; national
      security--military aspects.


    6/5/2
    02493777 DIALOG File 47: MAGAZINE INDEX
    The lie detectors. (polygraph tests)
     Mano, D. Keith
     National Review v34 p1362(2) Oct 29, 1982
      SOURCE FILE: MI File 47
      CODEN: NARVB
    DESCRIPTORS: truthfulness and falsehood--testing; lie detectors and
      detection--analysis


    6/5/3
    02466395 DIALOG File 47: MAGAZINE INDEX
    Screening out thieves before they're hired.
     Knecht, G. Bruce
     Dun's Business Month v120 p70(1) Oct, 1982
      SOURCE FILE: MI File 47
      DESCRIPTORS: employee theft--prevention; inventory shortages
       --prevention; Employee orientation--testing, lie detectors
       and detection--usage
```

Number of entries for various descriptors

Target set: 27 entries (1979, 1982) with *polygraph* or *lie detector*

All entries typed out

Entry

Article title

Name of magazine

Key words

Abbrev. for "code name"

Article title

Author's name

Volume, page, date

Code name for *National Review of Books*

DATABASE ENTRY

print those too, but your library and fellow students will appreciate your printing only what you are certain you need. Printing costs money; don't squander your own or your library's resources.

Using DIALOG, Elizabeth Kessler chose to do her search by dates—1979 and 1982—in order to build a historical perspective on lie detector use. She identified *polygraph or lie detector* as the descriptor set most appropriate to her needs with 27 entries. (See Kessler's database entry above.) The descriptor *lie* would provide 813 entries, *detect* 4,159 entries—both of the reference lists available through these descriptors are apparently too extensive to be useful.

Making Bibliography Cards

The most efficient way to prepare your working bibliography is with **bibliography cards.** For each promising title you find, make out a 3 × 5-inch card. Obviously, you will not use all the sources for which you make cards, but it saves time to make cards for any title that might be useful before you begin your reading. Cards are easy to handle, and they permit you to add new sources or delete sources that turn out to be useless. Cards can also be alphabetized easily, which will save you time when you make up your final list of works cited.

Each bibliography card should include all the relevant data that you will need to write a proper entry for your list of works cited. Take time to make complete bibliography cards as you go along because, again, following the appropriate procedure now will save time and frustration when you write your paper later on. Follow the exact format of the following sample cards and on pages 485–486 as you prepare your own bibliography cards.

BIBLIOGRAPHY CARDS FOR BOOKS

Bibliography cards for books should include the following information in the format shown in the accompanying illustration.

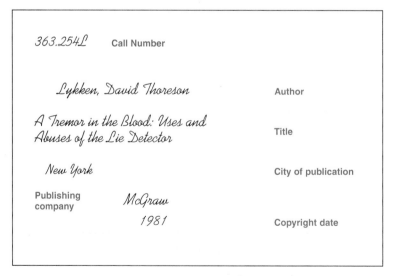

BOOK WITH ONE AUTHOR

1. The author's name.
2. For an essay, poem, short story, or a play in a collection, the title of the relevant selection, enclosed in quotation marks.
3. The title of the book.
4. The city in which the book was published.
5. The name of the publishing company.

6. The copyright date.

7. The complete call number of the book. (See the sample catalog entries on page 477.) If you do not copy the complete call number correctly, you cannot get the book.

Some books require even more information. If the book is edited, the editor's name must also appear on the bibliography card, and if the book is translated, the translator's name must be recorded. If the book has more than one edition or has been revised, that information should appear on your card as well. Finally, if the work contains more than one volume, the number of volumes and the volume number you want should be indicated.

Look ahead to pages 506–515 for the various works cited formats required for a wide variety of books that you might find in your research. These formats tell you what information to include on your bibliography cards.

BIBLIOGRAPHY CARDS FOR PERIODICALS

Bibliography cards for periodicals should include the following information in the format shown in the accompanying sample card.

Shorris, Earl   Author

" *The Last Word: Can the World's*   Title of article
    Small Languages Be Saved?"

Harper's   Name of magazine

Aug. 2000   Date

35–403   Pages

MAGAZINE ARTICLE

1. The author's name, if one is given.

2. The title of the article.

3. The name of the magazine, journal, or newspaper.

4. The publication date.

5. The inclusive page numbers.

6. For a journal article, include the volume and the issue numbers when given.

7. For a newspaper, include the section number or letter and the edition, if one is stated on the masthead.

Pages 509–510 provide examples of the different formats used for citing articles in the list of works cited. Examine these examples carefully as you prepare your bibliography cards.

BIBLIOGRAPHY CARDS FOR INTERNET SOURCES

If you are drawing from the Internet, record this information, using the format in the sample card below.

Webster, Augusta	**Author**
" Circe "	**Title of selection**
Portraits	**Title of book in which selection appears**
1870	**Original publication date of book**
Victorian Women Writers Project	**Title of scholarly project**
Ed. Perry Willett	**Editor**
24 Apr. 1998	**Date of electronic publication or latest update**
Indiana Univ.	**Institutional sponsor**
28 June 2000	**Date of access**
<http://www.indiana.edu/~letrs/vwwp/ webster/portraits.html#p14>.	**Network address (URL)**

INTERNET SOURCE

1. Author's name.
2. Document title.
3. Name of the database, scholarly project, periodical, or other site.
4. Editor of project or database.
5. Electronic publication date (or last update).
6. Name of institution supporting the site.
7. Date you accessed the material.
8. Uniform Resource Locator (URL): network address.

Internet sources are in flux with new sites appearing and others disappearing rapidly. Many sources do not provide all the information you will need to record in your citations list. The Modern Language Association (MLA) recommends that if you cannot find information, cite whatever is available.

An important caution: URLs are complicated in length and use of letters and symbols. Record them carefully and accurately.

EXERCISE

Produce a working bibliography by preparing bibliography cards for your subject. Make at least ten cards for books, periodicals, Internet, or other sources. Your instructor may wish to examine your bibliography cards before you move ahead with your research.

Taking Notes

When you have completed your bibliography cards, you are ready to begin taking notes that provide the evidence and supporting details for the points you will make in your paper. Without good notes, you cannot write a good paper. What, then, are the requirements for taking good notes?

Place for Notes

At one time, style manuals insisted that the only place to write a note was on a 4 × 6-inch **note card**—one note per card—and doing so is still a good idea. When taking notes, you may take many items from the same source, but when you write your paper, you won't present your notes in the order in which you took them. Thus, you will reorganize your notes according to the facts and opinions they contain, not according to the books or magazines the material came from. Since note cards are easy to organize, they are especially useful later on.

However, readily available photocopying machines have caused writers of style manuals to alter their advice. If you are likely to photocopy a number of pages while taking notes, there is another way to take and keep them efficiently. Get a loose-leaf notebook—*not* a folder with pockets—and clip into it half sheets of notebook paper. Write your notes on the half sheets. When you choose to photocopy a page or two, you may want to underline important parts or even write comments in the margin. Then punch holes in the copied sheets and put them into your notebook. Keeping notes this way means you are unlikely to lose any, and it still allows for easy reorganization of the material when you get ready to write your paper.

Rule number one, then, is either take your notes on index cards or take them on half sheets of notebook paper kept in a loose-leaf notebook, adding photocopied pages as you copy them.

Scope of Notes

Rule number two is place only one note on a card or half sheet. One note is one fact, one idea, one opinion. If you put two facts or ideas or opinions on one note, one of them is likely to get buried or lost among your accumulated notes. Either that or, as you organize and reorganize your notes, you may find that you need to recopy that second fact, idea, or opinion, or take the time to cut notes into smaller units—all very inefficient. So put one fact, one idea, or one opinion on a note.

Content of Notes

What do you look for when taking notes? You should look for any fact, idea, or opinion not generally known that appears to relate to your topic. You will, of course, take far more notes than you need for your final paper, but if you plan to do an honest job of research, you should investigate your subject as thoroughly as you can and wait until later to start weeding out the notes you don't actually need. It's easier to take a few extra notes than it is to go back to the library and reread a book or an article when you discover, after you start writing the paper, that you don't have enough evidence to make a point.

Nevertheless, you should not simply take notes at random. You have begun your research with at least a vague idea of what you want to say. The sooner the idea becomes definite, the more directed and less time-consuming your note taking will become. But don't worry if you find yourself taking many notes from the first sources you read. After all, the subject is fairly new to you, and everything about it may seem important. You should soon get a focus on the material, and then you can become more selective in the notes you take.

Consider again the Lizzie Borden example. If you choose such a topic, you might, at first, be so fascinated by the story that you take notes on everything in the accused's life that could possibly have led to the crime: Her mother made her stand in the corner for hours when she was only three; her father made harsh remarks about her appearance; and so on. But soon you may decide that you will not try to provide Lizzie Borden with a motive; you will begin by simply describing the crime: what happened. Once you have made that decision, your reading will be focused. You will look specifically for information about what happened at the scene of the crime.

Similarly, you can restrict the other major topics of the preliminary outline. A complete description of the trial could fill a book, as you soon learn when you begin reading the evidence. You could decide, after some reading, that you will not try to manage the testimony of character witnesses but that you will concentrate solely on physical evidence presented by the prosecution and its rebuttal by the defense. And you may decide to describe the controversy only in terms of Lizzie Borden's legal guilt or innocence, thus eliminating the need to deal with the sociological or psychological arguments that are sometimes raised in discussions of the case. Again, this limiting of your topic will direct your note taking and save you a great deal of time, because you will know exactly what kind of information you are looking for.

When Elizabeth Kessler started taking notes for her paper on polygraph testing (see paper on pages 530–549), she was intrigued at first by the technology of the equipment used to measure physiological changes. Over time this equipment evolved into more and more sophisticated machinery, and Kessler took notes on every aspect of the lie-detecting mechanism itself. But soon she realized that she didn't want to write a paper about the history of lie detector machines. Rather, she wanted to understand the pros and cons of polygraph testing so that she could form her own opinion about the procedure. Kessler's reading and note taking became much more focused at this point. She was able to concentrate on the views of critics and supporters. As her reading advanced further, she discovered that polygraph testing is used in many arenas—police work, government, the armed forces, and job hiring. To manage her subject, Kessler limited it even further by concentrating on lie detector tests and requirements for employment.

Hence, limit your subject and your approach to it as soon as you can, so you can perform the job of note taking efficiently.

Preparing Note Cards

Every note you take should contain two kinds of information: (1) the fact, idea, or opinion and (2) the exact source of the information. (See the sample note cards on page 491.) If you are careful about taking notes accurately and recording citations without fail, you can help avoid **plagiarism.** Plagiarism (see pages 523–525) is using someone else's words and/or ideas without acknowledging their source.

Since you have the complete data for the source on your bibliography card, you need to give yourself just enough information on the note card to refer you to the proper bibliographical reference. Usually, the author's last name and the page number from which you take the information is sufficient. Occasionally, you may have two works by the same author. In this case, use the author's name and an abbreviated form of the title to distinguish one source from the other. If no author is given, use an abbreviation of the title of the book or article. Do not, however, use simply the name of a magazine. You could, for example, be using several articles from various issues of *Time.* If you simply write "*Time,* p. 118" on your note, you won't have enough information to refer you to the bibliography card that lists the particular article from which you are taking notes.

Quotation of Sources

When you **quote** a source, you use the actual wording used in that source to convey facts or ideas contained in it. Quotation marks must enclose the material you quote. It may be a month or more between the time you take the note and the time you write your paper, and you don't want any uncertainty about which words are yours and which are those of the original author. Many researchers use a special mark—an asterisk, a checkmark, an *X*—in the margin to distinguish their own words from the words of the source. Be certain, too, that you copy the quotation *exactly* as it appears in the original. If the original has an obvious error, copy the error and follow it with *sic* (the Latin word for "thus") in brackets.

Occasionally, you may want to quote only parts of an entire passage. If you leave out a whole paragraph or more, indicate the omission by placing spaced dots all the way across the note. If you leave out a part of a sentence or one or two sentences, indicate the omission by placing three spaced dots (an ellipsis) where the sentence or part of the sentence has been omitted. If you omit the beginning of a sentence, place the quotation marks before the ellipsis. If you omit the end of a sentence, place the quotation mark after the ellipsis and the end punctuation (period, question mark, or exclamation point).

A few words of caution about using the ellipsis: Never alter the meaning of the original by using an ellipsis. If the original statement reads, "This is not the most exciting movie of the year," using an ellipsis to omit the word *not* would be dishonest. Second, be sure that you still have a complete sentence when you use the ellipsis. Don't omit from the sentence important elements such as subjects and verbs.

When quoting, you may find it necessary to clarify a word or date in the original quotation because you are taking the words out of context. Pronouns, for example, may need clarification. In context, "He suffered extreme hardships" may be perfectly clear. Isolated on a note, however, the pronoun *he* may need to be explained. If you want to insert a word, phrase, or figure into the quotation, do so by putting the information in brackets: "He [Lincoln] suffered extreme hardships." Or the original might read, "in that year, he faced the greatest crisis of his life." The sentence, taken out of context, does not identify the year. You would want to insert it: "in that year [1839], he faced the greatest crisis of his life."

Summary and Paraphrase of Sources

Despite our advice on how to use quotations in your research and note taking, we urge you to quote sparingly. Most of your notes should be summaries or paraphrases of the original material.

A **summary** is a short restatement of the original source in your own words. A **paraphrase** is a more expanded summary, often contains words taken from the original, and generally follows both the sequence and the logic of the original source. Of course, if you are in a hurry and don't have time to think about the best way to summarize or paraphrase a note, rather than risk plagiarism (see "Plagiarism," pages 523–525), do quote the material and later decide how best to convey it in your own words.

SAMPLE NOTE CARDS

While Elizabeth Kessler researched her topic, she found the following passage useful (from page 132 of *Science vs. Crime: The Hunt for Truth* by Eugene B. Block).

Original Source

In the first part of the nineteenth century, Cesare Lombroso pioneered in experiments with the heartbeat as a means of detecting lying, an interesting forerunner of today's polygraph, which has now advanced far beyond the early concepts of the distinguished Italian, utilizing not only heartbeats but changes in respiration and blood pressure to determine the truth or falsity of an answer.

Proud of his success and certain of the soundness of his theories, Lombroso recorded numbers of effective tests, including one concerning a notorious thief whose heartbeat reactions proved him guilty of one crime and innocent of another. It was on the early Lombroso principle that later criminalists like Vollmer, Keeler, and Larson based their developments of the lie detecting machine, but progress was slow and many methods and theories were tried and abandoned.

The accompanying note cards contain the exact words of the original source enclosed in quotation marks. The ellipsis—the three spaced dots following the word *polygraph*—indicates that Kessler omitted a portion of the quote from the original (the words "which has now advanced far beyond the early concepts of the distinguished Italian"). Further, she uses an asterisk to flag concerns that she will consider later on, when she reviews her note cards.

Block, Science vs. Crime   132

"In the first part of the nineteenth century, Cesare Lombroso pioneered in experiments with the heartbeat as a means of detecting lying, an interesting forerunner of today's polygraph . . . utilizing not only heartbeats but changes in respiration and blood pressure to determine the truth or falsity of an answer."

*Check earlier work on lie detection. 18th century? earlier?

NOTE CARD CONTAINING A DIRECT QUOTATION

Block, Science vs. Crime   132

In the early 1900s, Cesare Lombroso used heartbeats in experiments to detect lies; his work anticipated the modern polygraph, which measures heartbeats as well as "changes in respiration and blood pressure to determine the truth or falsity of an answer."

Lombroso's experiments included one on a thief whose heartbeat showed he had committed one crime but not another. Later developments of the polygraph were based on Lombroso's principle.

NOTE CARD CONTAINING A PARAPHRASE OF THE ORIGINAL MATERIAL

In the previous note card, Kessler paraphrases the original source in her own words but carefully blends Block's words with her own, enclosing them in quotation marks. The note card follows the line of thought of the original. Combining paraphrases and direct quotations is a good note-taking strategy. It allows you to capture the writer's main idea in your own language and to record some of the writer's own words for possible quotation in your paper.

Disagreements: Facts and Opinions

One final warning on note taking: As you take notes, don't assume that just because something is in print, it must be true. Be careful to distinguish between a writer's statement of fact and expression of opinion. There is a world of difference between saying that Aaron Burr was the vice-president of the United States and saying that Aaron Burr was a scoundrel. In rare cases in which you note an outright disagreement among authors on matters of fact, slam on your mental brakes and do some checking. One of the standard reference works or encyclopedias might be a good source for resolving such disagreements or disputes. When you cannot determine which opinion is correct, acknowledge frankly in your paper the difference of opinion and present both opinions as honestly as possible.

EXERCISE

Take notes as you read your sources. Your instructor may wish to examine a set of note cards for one or more of your readings.

Outlining

The research paper must meet the same requirements of good writing as any other paper you have written in your English course. It must have a thesis or purpose. It must support the thesis or purpose by using specific facts presented in specific language. And it must be organized; therefore, you should consider preparing a formal, written outline. The mental outline that may have been enough for a short theme may not be of any use for a research paper. Besides, your teacher may require that you submit a formal outline with your research paper.

Although you may already have written outlines for many papers, we urge you, in case you have forgotten any important rules about outlining, to reread Chapter 3 of this text. A good outline is a good outline—whether it is for a four-paragraph essay or for a ten-page research paper. But we won't try to convince you that writing a good outline for a research paper is as easy as writing one for a four-paragraph paper. The research paper is certainly a long and complex project, and it requires careful planning.

Making a Slug Outline

Start by reading and rereading all your notes carefully. You have accumulated the notes over a period of weeks, and you may not know precisely what material you have gathered.

Read the notes carefully, then. Set aside those that seem irrelevant to your current idea of the paper. Among those you keep you should see a pattern; you may have several groups of notes with each group relating to a particular aspect of your topic. When you are familiar enough with your notes that you can arrange them in piles according to single headings, you are ready to write a **slug**—that is, a brief heading that indicates the content of each note. Don't try to be creative here and write a different heading for each note; you should have several notes with the same slug.

Because you may change your mind about the point that a particular note should support, it is a good idea to write the slugs in pencil at first. That way you can easily change the slugs until you feel secure about the way the notes should be used. Once you have made a final decision, write a slug in ink in the upper right-hand corner of each note so that it can be seen quickly as you shuffle through your notes.

Some of the slugs that Elizabeth Kessler developed for her paper on polygraph testing include mechanical features, training of examiners, accuracy of readings, and legal support for lie detector tests. These and other slugs on her note cards allowed Kessler to classify her ideas and, ultimately, to produce a formal outline for her paper.

Writing a Formal Outline

If you have succeeded in writing slugs on each note, the outline will almost write itself. Either a topic outline or a sentence outline is acceptable (see Chapter 3). However, if you plan to prove a thesis, it is probably wise to make a sentence outline; doing so will force you to state in a complete thought how each section of your paper contributes to the thesis. Observe all the conventions of good outlining as you write, using the slugs on your notes as rough guides for topics and subtopics. (See the outline on page 531 and the sample paper that follows.) For a long and complex paper, it's usually a good idea to add a category labeled "conclusion" to your formal outline.

Look at the topic outline for Elizabeth Kessler's paper, which appears on page 494. After her thesis statement, which is a complete sentence, note the three major divisions, each labeled with a roman numeral—I, II, III. First-level subdivisions appear beside uppercase letters—A, B, C, and so on. Second-level divisions appear beside arabic numbers—1, 2, 3. Note, too, the full-sentence statement of a conclusion here. Readers of this outline see at a glance where Kessler wants to take her topic. For Kessler herself, the outline served as a starting point for the paragraphs she developed in an early draft. Ultimately, she decided to produce a sentence outline for submission along with her paper (see page 531); and she made a number of changes in the order of the elements and in the language of the various outline points. Like your thesis, your outline will change as your thoughts develop on your topic.

Keep in mind that your formal outline should serve as a guide as you develop and refine the various drafts of your paper. As new ideas develop, change your outline as necessary. If you find yourself drifting away from the topic, use your outline to draw you back.

```
         Topic Outline: Polygraph Testing

Thesis: The polygraph test should not be used as part of

employment decisions.

   I. Arguments of polygraph test supporters

      A. Inexpensive and valid way to identify potential

         thieves on the job

      B. Reliable findings

      C. Well-trained examiners

  II. Arguments of those who oppose polygraph tests

      A. "Toothless" laws

      B. Examiners poor

      C. Inaccurate readings

      D. Physiological displays of guilt not measurable

      E. Human rights violations

         1. Loss of employment

         2. Invasion of privacy

         3. Reputations destroyed

 III. Federal legislation against polygraph testing

      A. No polygraph screening for employment

      B. Defined testing procedures

      C. Employee rights

Conclusion--In spite of a recent national law, polygraph test-

ing should be banned in the workplace.
```

EXERCISE

1. Compare the formal topic outline (page 494) with Kessler's preliminary outline on page 476. How are they similar? different?
2. Compare the topic outline (page 494) with the sentence outline (page 531) Kessler ultimately submitted. How are the two outlines alike? different? Why do you think Kessler decided to produce a sentence outline after all?

After you complete your research and note taking, reread your notes carefully and identify a pattern among them. Arrange your notes according to headings and develop a slug outline. (You may find it helpful to review the preliminary outline that you developed for the exercise on page 476.) As you continue planning your paper and writing your drafts, develop a formal outline.

Writing Your
Research Paper

By now you have taken the essential preliminary steps in preparing your research paper. You have selected a subject and developed a thesis; you have done preliminary reading on your topic; and you have produced a scratch outline to track your early thinking. You identified several sources in your library and elsewhere to produce a working bibliography. You prepared bibliography cards for and took notes on the relevant books and articles you thought looked promising. You also examined means for quoting, summarizing, and paraphrasing sources. Finally, you advanced your outline through two more stages—the slug outline and the formal outline.

Using Sources

Think of your outline now as a kind of x-ray of your awaiting paragraphs—only the bare bones showing—and then consider how to flesh out the sentences and develop the paragraphs of your research essay. To support the points made in your paper, you need to quote or paraphrase the information you found in other sources. Most important, however, is to connect your own writing style smoothly with the comments drawn from other writers.

Quoting an Original Source in Your Paper

Following is a quote from Bennett H. Beach's article "Blood, Sweat, and Fears," which appeared in *Time* magazine.

> The FBI uses polygraphs mostly to probe leads and verify specific facts, areas in which, experts concede, the machines are at their best. The agency also employs highly trained examiners, who usually spend half a day on each session (compared with an average of an hour in private industry). Tests given to Jeb Magruder and Gordon Strachan led to evidence of the Watergate cover-up. Right now, Justice Department investigators are using polygraphs extensively in their search for the source of Abscam leaks. Attorney General Benjamin Civiletti has ruled that an "adverse inference" may be drawn if an employee of the FBI or any other part of the Justice Department balks at submitting to the machines.

Assume that you want to use some of this material in your paper. You might want to quote the source exactly—using from one or more phrases to several sentences to even a paragraph or more, depending on your purpose. In the following example, note the smooth connection between the student's words and Beach's words:

```
Agencies of the United States in government have relied

on lie detector tests in important legal matters:

        The FBI uses polygraphs mostly to probe leads and

    verify specific facts. . . . The agency also employs

    highly trained examiners, who usually spend half a

    day on each session. . . . Attorney General Benjamin

    Civiletti has ruled that an "adverse inference" may

    be drawn if an employee of the FBI or any other part

    of the Justice Department balks at submitting to the

    machines. (Beach 44)
```

The writer introduces the long supporting quotation with a sentence of her own. The **block format** is used to set off a quotation of four or more typed lines from the text of the essay. The ellipsis allows the writer to omit a portion of the quotation. Quotation marks are not used in a block quotation; rather, a ten-space indentation at the left margin sets off the quote. However, when quotation marks appear in the original, as in "adverse inference" in the preceding example, the quotation marks are included in the block quotation as well.

In the following example, the writer uses shorter quotations from the same source to support her point. However, here the quotations are carefully integrated with the writer's own words and are in each case enclosed by quotation marks.

> Not only does print industry use lie detectors but the
> federal government does also. "The FBI," reports Beach, "uses
> polygraphs mostly to probe leads and verify specific facts,
> areas in which, experts concede, the machines are at their
> best." To assure a higher degree of accuracy than in other
> testing situations, no doubt, the FBI "employs highly
> trained examiners, who usually spend half a day on each
> session (compared with an average of an hour in private
> industry)" (44).

Paraphrasing an Original Source in Your Paper

You may also choose to paraphrase the source material. In the following example, the writer skillfully expresses Beach's point in her own words. Quotation marks surround the phrase "balks at submitting to the machines" because it is quoted from the original source. Note how the writer of the paraphrase cites the source.

> As Beach points out, the FBI (as might be expected), uses
> polygraph testing to aid in major investigations. Yet employ-
> ees also are expected to take the test. It is clear that the
> FBI views in a negative light any employee who "balks at sub-
> mitting to the machines" (44).

Direct Quotations: How Many?

All the rules of good writing that you have learned so far apply to the research paper. But, as you have seen, the research paper presents a special challenge: You must make borrowed material a part of your own statement. You have spent several weeks now taking notes; you have studied them and have decided how to organize them, and that is half the battle. If, however, you simply string quotations together, you will not be writing a research paper; you will be merely transcribing your notes. The paper must be yours—your idea, your organization, and, for the most part, your words. The notes should be used to support your ideas, which means the notes should be integrated into your statements. Otherwise, you do not have an honest research paper.

In the following excerpt from a student paper, the writer merely strings quotations together:

> W. E. B. DuBois said in Souls of Black Folk that "the
> problem of the twentieth century is the problem of the color
> line" (xiv).
>
> DuBois became aware of racial differences at an early
> age. He related this experience vividly:
>
>> The exchange [of children's calling cards] was
>> merry, till one girl, a tall newcomer, refused my
>> card--refused it peremptorily, with a glance. Then
>> it dawned on me with a certain suddenness that I was
>> different from the other; or like, mayhap, in heart
>> and life and longing, but shut out from this world
>> by a vast veil (16).
>
> DuBois felt that dreams of opportunities and fulfillment
> were reserved solely for whites.
>
>> The shades of the prison-house closed around about us
>> all: the walls strait and stubborn to the whitest,
>> but relentlessly narrow, tall, and unscalable to sons
>> of night who must plod darkly on in resignation, or
>> beat unavailing palms against the stone, or
>> steadily, half hopelessly, watch the streak of
>> blue above (16).
>
> When his infant son died, DuBois was depressed, yet he
> rejoiced because his son would not have to endure life "behind
> the veil" (155).

> All that day and all that night there sat an awful
>
> gladness in my heart--nay blame me not if I see the
>
> world thus darkly through the veil, and my soul
>
> whispers ever to me, saying "not dead, not dead, but
>
> escaped, not bound, but free." No bitter meanness
>
> now shall sicken his baby heart till it die a living
>
> death, no taunt shall madden his happy boyhood. Fool
>
> that I was to think or wish that this little
>
> soul should grow choked and deformed within the
>
> veil! . . . Well sped, my boy, before the world had
>
> dubbed your ambition insolence, had held your ideals
>
> unattainable, and taught you to cringe and bow.
>
> Better for this nameless void that stops my life
>
> than a sea of sorrow for you (155-56).

The student here has simply copied his notes into the paper. The point could be made more clearly if it were phrased largely in the student's own words, as in this example:

> W. E. B. DuBois, who said in Souls of Black Folk that "the
>
> problem of the twentieth century is the problem of the color
>
> line" (xiv), learned as a child that he could be rejected
>
> simply because of the color of his skin. Later, he came to
>
> believe that dreams of opportunities and fulfillment were
>
> reserved solely for whites, and he compared the life of blacks
>
> in America with that of prison inmates (16). Indeed, he grew
>
> so bitter about the plight of blacks that he rejoiced when
>
> his infant son died because the child would never have to
>
> experience the prejudice that he had felt (155-56).

In this version, the writer composed a unified paragraph that makes the point clearly without the overuse of quotations. (A good, safe rule of thumb is, unless the subject of your paper is an author's style, quote no more than ten percent of your paper.) The revised paragraph also avoids overdocumentation—five citations have been replaced by three. This version shows a much greater mastery of the material than does the first version.

EXERCISE

Read the following passage taken from page 26 of Philip Langdon's "Noisy Highways" (*Atlantic Monthly,* Aug. 1997: 26–35). Then write two brief paragraphs. In the first, quote directly from the selection. In the second, paraphrase the source.

> In 1968 California built what are believed to be the first noise barriers along modern federal highways. Walls were erected on Highway 101 in San Francisco and Interstate 680 north of San Jose to shield abutting residential neighborhoods from the sound of heavy traffic. Within four years the federal government followed California's lead, adopting regulations requiring that whenever a state builds, expands, or realigns a federally funded highway, an attempt be made to curtail excessive noise that would otherwise be inflicted on sensitive neighbors, such as schools, hospitals, and residential areas. Since then a total of forty-one states have built highway noise barriers, generally with 75 to 90 percent of the cost paid by the U.S. Department of Transportation. Nineteen of those states, including Colorado, Michigan, and Connecticut, have also voluntarily built noise barriers along existing highways where no widening or relocation of the roadway was taking place. In all, noise barriers have risen along some 1,300 miles of federal highway, and they are being added at the rate of ninety to a hundred miles a year. California still leads the nation, with 438 miles of barriers.
>
> Bruce Donohue, a landscape architect in Westport, Connecticut, is aware of the effects that prolonged exposure to highway noise can bring. "One summer when I was a student," he recalls, "I was painting a house along Interstate 95 in Stamford, and I noticed that I was tense. I noticed that the women in the neighborhood were irritated. They were screeching at the kids, and the kids were raucous. The whole neighborhood was irritable and irritated." Road noise does not damage the hearing of people who live close by, but it seems to cause physiological and psychological stress, with results that include nervousness, difficulty in sleeping, and elevated heart rates.
>
> The effects of stress vary so widely from person to person, however, that transportation departments have avoided basing noise-control programs on them. They have focused on something they can assess more objectively—interference with hearing and speech. Federal regulations say that if a new or expanded road will produce noise approaching sixty-seven decibels (generally measured outdoors, near buildings), the state must try to bring about a "substantial" reduction in the sound level. Sixty-seven decibels is sound so loud that people have to be within three to five feet of each other to hold a conversation without raising their voices.

Documentation in the Humanities: MLA Style

Unless the material you borrow is something as well known as the Gettysburg Address, when you take facts or ideas from someone else, you must credit the source. Such a statement often frightens students because their first assumption is that they will have to credit almost every sentence in their papers. That is not the case.

You should, of course, give a citation for all direct quotations that are not well known. You should also cite all facts and opinions that are not common knowledge—*even when you have put the facts or opinions into your own words*. Two kinds of facts or opinions come under the heading *common knowledge:* (1) facts everyone in our culture is expected to know (George Washington was the first president of the United States, for example), and (2) facts that are common knowledge in the field you are investigating. Suppose you are writing a paper on Custer's last stand. You might not have known, when you began reading, the name of the Indian tribe that fought Custer and his men. If every source you read, however, says that it was the Sioux tribe, you would not need to give a citation for that fact. Your wide reading lets you know the fact is commonly known to historians. Nor would it be necessary to credit the opinion that Custer blundered; most historians agree that he did. But any theories about why Custer led his men into such a trap should be credited.

At this point you may be feeling vaguely disturbed by the fuss being made about apparent trivialities of quoting and crediting sources. Unfortunately, these are the only devices by which your reader will be able to distinguish between the material drawn from other sources and the material that is your own. If you do not pay the most careful attention to the techniques of quoting and crediting sources you run the risk of being accused of plagiarism—taking someone else's thoughts or words and passing them off as your own. We look more closely at the serious issue of plagiarism later in the chapter (pages 523–525).

Parenthetical Documentation

Documenting or **crediting** or **citing** a source simply means letting the reader know where you found another's quotation, fact, idea, or opinion that appears in your paper. In the recent past, the only way to cite a source was to write a footnote or an endnote. Most current style manuals, however, including the influential Modern Language Association's *Handbook for Writers of Research Papers*, Fifth Edition (1999), recommend the much easier and more efficient method of **parenthetical documentation.** In this method, the last name of the author and the page number from which the material is taken are placed within parentheses immediately after the information or quotation. Or, if you can integrate the author's name conveniently in the text itself, only the page number appears in parentheses. (If you refer to a whole work, however, no page reference is necessary.) Readers interested in finding the work cited then consult the bibliography, titled "Works Cited," at the end of the paper for further information about the source. Further, in parenthetical documentation, footnotes and endnotes are used to provide additional information or commentary that might otherwise interrupt the flow of the text.

The following examples of parenthetical documentation reflect MLA style, used widely in the humanities and in other disciplines as well.

A work by one author

The most common citation is for a work written by a single author. It contains the author's last name and the page number from which the material is taken.

```
"The problem of the twentieth century is the problem of the
color line" (DuBois xiv).
```

```
Indeed, he grew so bitter about the plight of blacks that he
rejoiced when his infant son died because the child would
never have to experience the prejudice that he had felt
(DuBois 155-56).
        DuBois shows in dramatic personal terms the effects of
prejudice in America.
```

A work by two or more authors

If the book has two or three authors, use the last names of all the authors. However, if the book has more than three authors, use the last name of only the first author listed on the title page and follow the name with *et al.* (Latin *et alii,* "and others").

```
Millionaires are more like ordinary people than anyone would
expect (Stanley and Danko 8-11).
```

```
Lichter, Lichter, and Rothman see television as a mirror of
American culture (3).
```

```
Teachers in all courses should determine the writing skills

levels of their students (Anderson et al. 4).
```

```
Anderson and her coauthors insist that teachers in all courses

determine the level of writing skills for their students early

in the semester (4).
```

The first example above refers to the book *The Millionaire Next Door* by Thomas J. Stanley and William D. Danko. In the second example, the work cited, *How TV Portrays American Culture*, is by three authors, S. Robert Lichter, Linda S. Lichter, and Stanley Rothman. Anderson and three coauthors wrote *Integrated Skills Reinforcement*. Full references for these books appear on page 507.

Special situations call for different forms of citation, as in the examples that follow.

More than one work by the same author

```
He learned as a child that he could be rejected simply because

of the color of his skin (DuBois, Souls 16).
```

Because more than one work by DuBois is cited in the paper, an abbreviation of the title, *Souls of Black Folks*, is used to distinguish this work by DuBois from other works by the same author.

More than one volume of a work

```
Although he had urged conscientious objection during World War

I, his views changed gradually, and by 1940, he concluded that

he must support the war against the Nazis (Russell 2: 287-88).
```

The Autobiography of Bertrand Russell has more than one volume; thus, the information cited comes from the second volume, pages 287–88.

A title for which no author is given

Frequently, the author of a work is not given or is not known. In such a case, do not use the word *anonymous* or its abbreviation *anon*. Instead, put in parentheses the title or an abbreviated title and the page number, as in this example:

```
Supporters of the polygraph test point out that to help

alleviate possible nervousness, the subject is given access to

the questions he will be asked during the test for as long as

he desires ("What's It Like" 8).
```

Information about a work or author already given in sentence

Many of your sentences may already contain enough information about a work that the parenthetical documentation can be made even shorter than in the examples given so far.

```
W. E. B. DuBois said in Souls of Black Folks that "the problem

of the twentieth century is the problem of the color

line" (xiv).
```

Because the author and title are mentioned in the sentence, only the page number need be put in parentheses.

The following sentence is from a paper that cites more than one work by DuBois. Since the author's name is used in the sentence, you need not repeat it in the documentation. However, an abbreviated title of the book is used to distinguish this work by DuBois from other works by the same author.

```
W. E. B. DuBois, who believed that "the problem of the

twentieth century is the problem of the color line" (Souls

xiv), learned as a child that he could be rejected simply

because of the color of his skin.
```

There are even times when no parenthetical documentation is needed. For example, if a writer says, "DuBois devotes his entire *Souls of Black Folk* to the subject," a reader need simply turn to the bibliography to find the remaining facts of publication. However, if a section of a work—rather than the entire work—should be cited, use one of the following forms:

```
This point has been made before (DuBois 16-156).
```

or

```
DuBois has made this point before (16-156).
```

If the section is in a work of more than one volume, you might write,

```
Russell (2: 3-128) has detailed the kind of opposition to the

war made by pacifists in England.
```

or

```
Russell, in the second volume of his work (3-128), has

detailed the kind of opposition to the war made by pacifists

in England.
```

In other words, the more skillfully you construct your sentences, the less documentation you need.

Parenthetical documentation is both easy to use and less time-consuming since the outdated endnote (or footnote) pages do not have to be added to the paper. The system offers one further advantage: If you decide to use an endnote page, you will use it only for real notes—additional comments on or explanations of material in the text (see pages 515–519).

EXERCISE

Return to the exercise on page 501 and reread the passage. In only one sentence, summarize the passage and provide parenthetical documentation according to the guidelines you just learned.

A List of Works Cited

Parenthetical documentation requires a **list of works cited,** an alphabetical listing of the sources cited in the paper. This list appears on a separate page at the end of the paper and is headed "Works Cited."

All citations in the text are referenced fully in the list of works cited. In making your list, use your bibliography cards; if you prepared them carefully, your cards will contain all the information you need to write correct citations. Further, you should always copy all relevant information from the book or journal itself, *not* from a catalog or an index.

Different types of sources require somewhat different treatment. The examples that follow are typical MLA-style entries for the list of works cited. For entries that do not appear here, consult the *MLA Handbook for Writers of Research Papers,* Fifth Edition, or some other research style manual that your instructor recommends. Social science researchers rely on the *Publication Manual of the American Psychological Association* (APA), Fourth Edition (1994). See p. 519.

STANDARD BOOK ENTRY
FOR THE LIST OF WORKS CITED

A book with one author

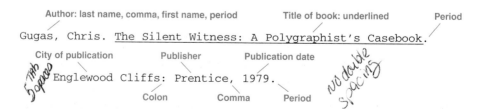

Author: last name, comma, first name, period   Title of book: underlined   Period

Gugas, Chris. The Silent Witness: A Polygraphist's Casebook.

City of publication   Publisher   Publication date

Englewood Cliffs: Prentice, 1979.

Colon   Comma   Period

Double-space the entry. Place a period after the author's name (which is inverted), the title of the book (which is underlined), and the publication date. A colon separates the city of publication and the name of the publisher. A comma separates the publisher's name—written in a shortened form and without *Inc., Company,* and the like and the year of publication. The first line of the entry begins at the left margin and all subsequent lines of the entry are indented five spaces from the left.

OTHER WORKS CITED FORMATS FOR BOOKS

A book with two authors

```
Stanley, Thomas J., and William D. Danko. The Millionaire Next
     Door. Atlanta: Longstreet, 1997.
```

Invert only the name of the first author. The order of the names is the same as that on the title page of the original source.

A book with three authors

```
Lichter, S. Robert, Linda S. Lichter, and Stanley Rothman. How
     TV Portrays American Culture. Washington: Regnery, 1994.
```

A book with more than three authors

```
Anderson, Joann Romeo, et al. Integrated Skills Reinforcement.
     New York: Longman, 1983.
```

Use the name of the first author only, followed by the notation *et al.,* a Latin abbreviation for "and others." The name given is the first name that appears on the title page.

An anthology

```
Cooley, Michael, and Katherine Powell, eds. Making Choices.
     Boston: Houghton, 1997.
```

The editors collected several essays in this book. The editors' names are listed before the title.

A selection in an anthology

```
Finn, Patrick J. "Computer-Aided Description of Mature Word
     Choices in Writing." Evaluating Writing: Describing,
     Measuring, Judging. Ed. Charles R. Cooper and Lee Odell.
     Urbana, IL: NCTE, 1977. 69-89.
```

The page numbers given at the end of the entry indicate where the essay appears in the anthology. The editors' names appear after the abbreviation *Ed.* Note the use of IL for *Illinois* after Urbana; if the city of publication is not well known, the two-letter postal abbreviation for the state is added after the city.

When you use two or more essays from the same collection, you may *cross-reference* them, as in this example:

```
Lloyd-Jones, Richard. "Primary Trait Scoring." Cooper and
    Odell 33-68.
```

The reference "Cooper and Odell" is to the book *Evaluating Writing: Describing, Measuring, Judging.* Since a citation for this book appears in an earlier entry, the abbreviated form is acceptable as a cross-reference.

An edition of an author's work

```
Thoreau, Henry David. Collected Poems. Ed. Carl Bode. Chicago:
    Packard, 1943.
```

Editions other than the first

```
Selzer, Jack. Conversations. 3rd ed. New York: Allyn, 1997.
```

For a revised edition, the abbreviation "Rev. ed." appears after the title.

A translated work

```
Böll, Heinrich. End of a Mission. Trans. Leila Vennewitz. New
    York: McGraw, 1974.
```

A multivolume work

```
Adams, Wallace E., et al., eds. The Western World: To 1770. 2
    vols. New York: Dodd, 1968.
```

A pamphlet

Treat a pamphlet like a book, using the name of the committee or organization that created the pamphlet as the author if no author's name is provided.

A selection in an encyclopedia

```
Kaelunohonoke, Joan W. "Hula." Encyclopedia Americana. 1993 ed.
```

It is not necessary to give full publication information for a well-known reference work. If the article is signed only with the initials of the author, the rest of his or her name—the parts usually included in brackets—can be found by consulting the index volume. In some encyclopedias, the full name of the author can be found in the frontmatter section of the encyclopedia.

```
"Georgetown." Encyclopaedia Britannica: Micropaedia. 1981 ed.
```

When no author is given, the entry begins with the title of the article. *The Encyclopaedia Britannica* has two parts: the *Micropaedia,* which contains short articles on the subject and cross-references to the *Macropaedia,* which contains longer articles on the subject, generally written by important scholars in the field.

An unpublished dissertation

```
Alpern, Gertrude. "Women in Ancient Greek Political Thought."
     Diss. Case Western Reserve U, 1974.
```

STANDARD PERIODICAL ENTRY
FOR THE LIST OF WORKS CITED

An article with one author

Author: last name, comma, first name   Period   Title of selection in quotation marks

```
Busch, Frederick. "Truth, Lies, Fact, Fiction."
```

Title of publication underlined   Volume number   Colon   Period   Period

```
    The American Scholar 69 (2000): 29-35.
```

Publication date in parentheses   Pages on which selection appears

Like the standard entry for a book, the entry for a journal article contains three major divisions: (1) the author's name, (2) the title of the work, and (3) the publication data. However, for journal articles, both the name of the article (in quotation marks) and the name of the journal (underlined) are included.

Many journals use continuous pagination throughout the year—for example, if the January issue ends on page 280, the February issue will begin on page 281. To cite journals that use continuous pagination, place the volume number before the year of publication, which is given in parentheses. A colon precedes the inclusive page numbers on which the selection appears.

OTHER WORKS CITED FORMATS FOR PERIODICALS

An article in a journal that numbers the pages in each issue separately

```
Kominsky, E. A. "Service and Money Rents in the Thirteenth
     Century." Economic History Review 5.2 (1935): 24-45.
```

The issue number is given after the volume number, and a period separates them (5.2 in the preceding example refers to volume 5, issue 2). If only an issue number appears, include it as you would a volume number.

A selection in a monthly (or bimonthly) magazine

```
Shorris, Earl. "The Last Word: Can the World's Small Languages
     Be Saved?" Harper's Aug. 2000: 35-43.
```

The entry includes the month (abbreviated) instead of a volume number. Only the months May, June, and July are not abbreviated.

A selection in a weekly (or biweekly) magazine

```
Wright, Evan. "Porn.com?" Rolling Stone 3 Aug. 2000: 41-48.
```

An unsigned selection in a magazine

> "How to Comply with the Polygraph Law." <u>Nation's Business</u>
>   Dec. 1989: 36-37.

When no author is given, the entry begins with the title of the article. Do not use the word *anonymous* or its abbreviation *anon.*

An article in a daily newspaper

> "Diabetes Rises; Doctors Foresee Harsh Impact." <u>New York Times</u>
>   24 Aug. 2000, late ed.: A1+.

Give the name of the newspaper but omit any introductory article, such as *The* from *New York Times* in the example. If the name of the city is part of the title of the newspaper, as in the <u>New York Times</u>, underline it. However, if the name of the city is not part of the newspaper's title, include the city in brackets and do not underline it: <u>Star-Ledger</u> [Newark]. When the city is not well known, include the two-letter abbreviation in brackets as well: <u>Newsday</u> [Long Island, NY].

Some newspapers print more than one edition a day, and the contents of the editions may differ. In such cases, include the edition you used. In the preceding citation, *late ed.* refers to the late edition of the *New York Times*. In addition, newspapers often indicate section numbers and you should include them in the citation. In the preceding example, A1+ refers to section A, page 1.

The plus sign indicates that the whole article is not printed on consecutive pages. (Here, the piece starts on page A1 and then jumps to page A18, which is not indicated in the citation.) Use a plus sign after the page number when the entire selection does not appear on consecutive pages.

A review in a periodical

> Rev. of <u>The Chief</u>, by David Nasaw. <u>New Yorker</u> 3 July 2000: 83.

> Mallon, Thomas. "A New Social Type Is Born." Rev. of <u>Bobos in
>   Paradise: The New Upper Class and How They Got There</u>, by
>   David Brooks. <u>Atlantic Monthly</u> June 2000: 112-117.

In the first example, the book review is unsigned. In the second, the review is both signed and titled: Mallon's review of the book *Bobos In Paradise: The New Upper Class and How They Got There* is called "A New Social Type Is Born."

WORKS CITED ENTRIES FOR OTHER TYPES OF SOURCES

Recordings, tapes, and compact disks

> Holiday, Billie. <u>Cocktail Hour</u>. Allegro 2000.

The entry includes the name of the artist, the title of the recording, the manufacturer, and the date. The recording is a compact disk and requires no identification as such. If the piece is in another medium, use *LP* (long playing record), *Audiocassette*, or *Audiotape* (reel-to-reel tape) before the manufacturer's name.

Films and television (or radio) programs

> The Perfect Storm. Dir. Wolfgang Petersen. Perf. George
> Clooney, Mark Wahlberg, and Diane Lane. Warner Bros.,
> 2000.

> "Lillian Gish: The Actor's Life for Me." Narr. Eva Marie
> Saint. Prod. and dir. Terry Sanders. American Masters.
> PBS. WNET, New York. 11 July 1988.

Interviews

> Schneider, Pamela. Interview. Seniors: What Keeps Us Going.
> With Linda Storrow. Natl. Public Radio. WNYC, New York.
> 11 July 1988.

> Hilfiger, Tommy. Personal interview. 11 Nov. 2000.

Plays (or other performances)

> A Moon for the Misbegotten. By Eugene O'Neill. Dir. Daniel
> Sullivan. Perf. Gabriel Byrne and Cherry Jones. Walter
> Kerr Theatre, New York. 18 June 2000.

Citing Electronic Sources

The increased popularity of source materials available on the computer warrants special attention to source citation. The *MLA Handbook for Writers*, Fifth Edition, indicates various citation formats for electronic sources.

STANDARD ENTRY FOR AN ONLINE SOURCE

Document within an information database, a scholarly project, or website

Author   Title of selection in quotation marks

Atwood, Margaret. "Ophelia Has a Lot to Answer For."

Name of web site

The Margaret Atwood Information Web Site

Date posted   Date accessed

17 Sept. 1998. 28 June 2000

<http://www.web.net/owtoad/ophelia.html>. —— Period

URL (uniform resource locator, or network address)   Angle bracket

If you must divide the URL at the end of a line, divide it only after a slash mark.

OTHER EXAMPLES

"Circe." Columbia Encyclopedia. 5th ed. 29 June 2000
      <http://cgi-bin/columbia.pl>

Webster, Augusta. "Circe." Portraits. 1870 Victorian Women.
      Perry Willett. 24 Apr. 1998. Indiana U. 28 June 2000
      <http://www.indiana.edu/~letrs/vwwp/webster/
      portraits.html#p14>

An entire online scholarly project, information database, or professional or personal site

Columbia Encyclopedia. 5th ed. 28 June 2000 <http://
      www.ohiolink.edu/db/columbia.html>.

Johnson, James. Home page. 28 June 2000 <http://
      www.wright.edu/~james.johnson/>.

Victorian Women Writers Project. Ed. Perry Willett.
      20 June 2000. Indiana U. 28 June 2000 <http://
      www.indiana.edu/~letrs/vwwp/>.

An online book

Heirich, Max. The Beginning: Berkeley, 1964. New York:
      Columbia UP, 1970. 28 June 2000 <http://
      www.sunsite.berkeley.edu:2020/dynaweb/teiproj/
      fsm/monos/brk0004030358a/@Generic_BookView>.

Hudson, W. H. Tales of the Pampas. 1902. 28 June 2000
      <http://eldred.ne.mediaone.net/whh/ombu.htm>.

Webster, Augusta. Portraits. 1870. Victorian Women Writers
      Project. Ed. Perry Willett. 24 Apr. 1998. Indiana U.
      28 June 2000 <http://www.indiana.edu/~letrs/vwwp/
      webster/portraits.html>.

The Webster example is a book that is part of a scholarly project.

Part of an online book

Hudson, W. H. "Niño Diablo." Tales of the Pampas. 1902.
      28 June 2000 <http://eldred.ne.mediaone.net/whh/
      ombu.htm#nino>.

Webster, Augusta. "Circe." Portraits. 1870 Victorian Women
      Writers Project. Ed. Perry Willett. 24 Apr. 1998. Indiana
      U. 28 June 2000 <http://www.indiana.edu/~letrs/vwwp/
      webster/portraits.html#p14>

The Webster example duplicates the online book for part of a scholarly project.

An article in a scholarly journal

Faubion, James D. "Heiros Gamos: Typology and the Fate of
        Passion." Postmodern Culture 10.3 (2000): 28 pars.
        28 June 2000 <http://www.iath.virginia.edu/pmc/
        current.issue/10.3faubion.html>.

White, Jeff. "Hypersuasion and the New Ethos: Toward a
        Theory of Ethical Linking." Kairos 5.1 (2000). 28 June
        2000 <http://english.ttu.edu/kairos/5.1/
        binder.html?features/white/bridgenw.html>.

An article in an online magazine

Oppenheimer, Todd. "Schooling the Imagination."
        Atlantic Unbound Sept. 1999. 28 June 2000 <http://
        www.theatlantic.com/issues/99sep/9909waldorf.htm>.

An article in an online newspaper

Schiesel, Seth, and David Leonhardt. "Justice Dept. Acts to
        Block Proposed WorldCom-Sprint Deal." New York Times on
        the Web 28 June 2000. 28 June 2000 <http://www.nytimes.
        com/library/financial/62800worldcom-sprint.html>.

A nonperiodical publication on CD-ROM, diskette, or magnetic tape

Mann, Ron. Emile De Antonio's Painters Painting. CD-ROM.
        Irvington: Voyager, 1996.

A selection from a periodically published database on CD-ROM

"Polygraph." Encarta '97. CD-ROM. Redmond: Microsoft, 1997.

An item from an online service

"Circe." Compton's Encyclopedia Online. Vers. 2.0. 1997.
        America Online. 28 June 2000. Keyword: Compton's.

An E-mail communication

Jones, Louise. E-mail to the author. 28 June 2000.

Smith, Johnson C.: "Re: Critique of Marx's Views." E-mail to
        Ramon Vargas-Llosa. 23 June 2000.

The Jones entry illustrates an untitled E-mail message sent directly to the
writer of the paper at hand; the Smith entry illustrates a titled E-mail message
originally sent to some else.

An online posting to an E-mail discussion list

Hinton, Norman D. "Destruction of Archive Averted." Online
        posting. 16 Nov. 1999. Humanist Discussion Group. 28 June
        2000 <http://lists.village.virginia.edu/lists_archive/
        Humanist/v13/0267.html>.

Synchronous communication on a MUD or MOO

```
Online forum for eductional MOO administrators. 6 July 1995.
    LinguaMOO. 28 June 2000 <http:///www.utdallas.edu/
    ~cynthiah/lingua_archive/
```

MUD is the acronym for multiuser domain; MOO is the acronym for multi-user domain, object oriented. These are both forums for posting synchronous communication.

Explanatory Notes

If you need to explain some point or add information but feel that what you want to say really doesn't fit smoothly into the text of your paper, use a footnote or an endnote. Place a raised number (superscript) after the word where you'd like the reader to consider this additional material. Then, on a separate page called "Notes," use the corresponding number and provide the necessary information. If you use a footnote, place it at the bottom of the page on which your superscript appears.

Look at the next example, from the essay "Nathaniel Hawthorne, Una Hawthorne, and *The Scarlet Letter*," by T. Walter Herbert, Jr.

> It would be an oversimplification to say that Una became merely a creature of her father's imagination, no more than the embodiment of his gender conflicts, as projected onto her. Yet her character, like his, was a cultural construction, and it was one in which Hawthorne had a hand.
>
> This is not the occasion for a detailed treatment of the pattern of solicitude and discipline that the Hawthornes organized about their baby daughter,[3] but crucial issues of the selfhood they sought to impart are disclosed in their naming her Una, after Spenser's maiden of holiness. This decision provoked a controversy among family and friends that illuminates the large cultural processes of gender definition that were then taking place.
>
> [3]A discussion of Sophia Hawthorne's role in the formation of Una's mental life lies beyond the scope of this essay. Sophia's exceptional response to the emerging norms of gender, the marriage she made to Nathaniel, and her place in the constellation of family relations are complex subjects that bear on this question, which I will treat in a forthcoming book.

The footnote here discusses Sophia's role in Una's mental life—additional information that the writer chose not to include in the text of his essay.

See page 547 for examples of endnotes in the sample research paper.

Preparing the "Works Cited" List

In preparing your list of works cited, follow these guidelines for the correct format.

1. Prepare the list on a separate page headed "Works Cited," which is placed about an inch from the top and centered. (Do not underline the heading; use uppercase letters only for the first letter in each word.) The Works Cited page appears at the end of the paper.

2. Double-space before typing the first entry. Begin each entry flush with the left margin, and indent all other lines of each entry five spaces. Use double-spacing throughout.

3. Arrange the entries alphabetically, according to the authors' last names. Do not separate books and periodicals. For entries without authors, use the first word in the title (other than *A, An,* or *The*) to determine alphabetical order.

4. When you cite two or more books by the same author, arrange them alphabetically by title and give the author's full name only in the first entry. In subsequent entries, replace the author's name with three spaced hyphens. For example:

```
Geertz, Clifford. The Interpretation of Cultures. New York:
     Basic, 1973.

---. Local Knowledge: Further Essays in Interpretive
     Anthropology. New York: Basic, 1983.
```

Here is an excerpt from the final typed copy of a list of works cited. See page 549 for the complete list.

```
                         Works Cited
Beach, Bennet H. "Blood, Sweat, and Fears." Time 8 Sept. 1980:
     44.

Block, Eugene B. Science vs. Crime: The Evolution of the
     Police Lab. San Francisco: Cragmont, 1979.

Dunn, Donald. "When a Lie Detector Test Is Part of the Job
     Interview." Business Week 27 July 1981: 85-86.
```

EXERCISE

Using two of the bibliography cards you prepared for the exercise on page 487—one for a book and the other for a periodical—write entries for a list of works cited according to the MLA-style system of documentation.

Documenting with Endnotes

Some source material that you consult will follow the older citation system of **footnotes** and **endnotes,** and you should be familiar with this system. In addition, despite the increasing popularity of parenthetical documentation, some journals and presses continue to require endnotes that give the complete source of each work cited. Frequently, the endnote pages replace a list of works cited, or bibliography. Your instructor may, therefore, want you to be familiar with both forms of documentation. If you use endnotes, you will have to consult your bibliography cards to change the brief notations you made on your notes into proper endnote entries. We have reproduced samples of standard endnotes, which follow. For a full range of examples, consult the most recent edition of the *MLA Handbook for Writers of Research Papers.*

Endnotes contain essentially the same information as do works cited entries, but the arrangement and punctuation of that information are somewhat different.

First References

A first endnote reference to a book should include the author, the title, the facts of publication, and the page or pages referred to. The author's name is not inverted in the endnote since endnotes do not appear in alphabetical order. Following are samples of first endnotes for the sources cited in the discussion of the list of works cited (pages 506–511). Notice the differences in punctuation between a list of works cited entry and an endnote entry.

STANDARD ENDNOTES FOR BOOKS
A book with one author

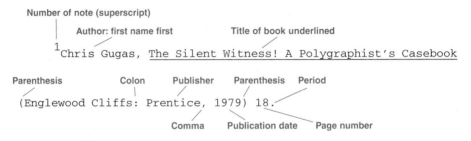

Double-space the entry. Type the number of the note a half space above the line and indent the number five spaces. Second and subsequent lines of the entry are flush left with the margin.

A book with two authors

²Thomas J. Stanley and William D. Danko. <u>The Millionaire Next Door</u>. (Atlanta: Longstreet, 1997) 28.

A book with more than three authors

³Alan T. Seagren et al., <u>Academic Leadership in Community Colleges</u> (Lincoln: U of Nebraska P, 1994) 76.

An anthology

⁴Michael Cooley and Katherine Powell, eds. <u>Making Choices</u> (Boston: Houghton, 1997) 249–51.

A selection in an anthology

⁵Patrick J. Finn. "Computer-Aided Description of Mature Word Choices in Writing," <u>Evaluating Writing: Describing, Measuring, Judging</u>, ed. Charles R. Cooper and Lee Odell (Urbana, IL: NCTE, 1977) 72.

STANDARD ENDNOTES FOR PERIODICALS

An article with one author

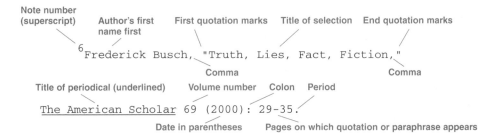

An endnote reference to a magazine should include the author, the title of the article, the name of the magazine, the date, and the page or pages referred to. An endnote reference to a journal should also include the volume and (or) issue number. Endnotes to magazines and journals are almost identical to works cited entries, except that a superscript appears, the author's name is not inverted, commas separate the main elements, and only the specific page or pages referred to are indicated.

An article in a journal that paginates each issue separately

[7]E. A. Kominsky, "Service and Money Rents in the Thirteenth Century," Economic History Review 5.2 (1935): 28.

A selection in a monthly (or bimonthly) magazine

[8]Earl Shorris, "The Last Word: Can the World's Small Languages Be Saved?" Harper's Aug. 2000: 41.

A selection in a weekly (or biweekly) magazine

[9]Evan Wright, "Porn.com?" Rolling Stone 3 Aug. 2000: 46.

An article in a daily newspaper

[10]"Diabetes Rises: Doctors Foresee Harsh Impact," New York Times 24 Aug. 2000, late ed.: A18.

Subsequent References

Although the first reference to a source gives full publication data, subsequent references to the same source include the author's last name and the page number.

[4]Moers 199.

[8]Mizener 21.

[10]Lewis 41.

However, if the reference is to one volume of a multivolume work, the endnote must also include the volume number:

^{6}Adams et al., 2: 78.

In citations of more than one work by the same author, the page number and author's name will not give the reader enough information. A shortened form of the title of the work after the author's last name helps identify the work. After first references, for example, to Ernest Hemingway's *For Whom the Bell Tolls* and *Across the River and into the Trees,* subsequent references would look like this:

^{7}Hemingway, Bell 30.

^{9}Hemingway, River 127.

When the author is unknown or unnamed, subsequent references consist of the title and page number:

^{13}"Thoughts from the Lone Cowboy" 20.

^{17}"Trudeau on Separatism" 22.

^{19}"Massachusetts Bay Company" 1317.

One concluding comment: Footnotes appear at the bottom of the page on which you cite them in the text. Endnotes appear as a list on a separate page or pages immediately after the text. If you use footnotes, be sure to number them sequentially throughout the paper: Do not begin with a footnote number 1 on each page. Check with your instructor about which method of citation you should use. If your instructor has no preference, you will probably find it easier to use endnotes that are typed together on a separate page.

Endnotes: A Sample

> The Lusitania and her sister ship, the Mauretania, were built by John Brown and Company under contract from the British Admiralty for Cunard Lines specifically for the purpose of regaining the Atlantic speed record, then held by German ships.[1] It was feared that Germany would gain control of the seas, leaving England powerless in times of war.[2] The two ships were built to Admiralty warship specifications and were to remain under Admiralty jurisdiction. Cunard was allowed to use the Lusitania and the Mauretania as passenger ships as long as England was not at war. Otherwise, they were to be returned to England and converted into armed cruisers.[3]
>
> The Lusitania sailed on her maiden voyage on June 7, 1906. In 1907, . . .

```
                                                    Homoly 8
                              Notes
     1
      Frank H. Shaw, Full Fathom Five (Boston: Macmillan, 1930) 143.
     2
      Thomas A. Bailey and Paul B. Ryan, The Lusitania Disaster (New
York: Free, 1975) 4.
              3
               Colin Simpson, The Lusitania (Boston: Little, 1972) 18.
```

```
                                                    Homoly 10
                           Works Cited

     Bailey, Thomas A., and Paul B. Ryan. The Lusitania Disaster.
          New York: Free, 1975.

     Shaw, Frank H. Full Fathom Five. New York: Macmillan, 1930.

     Simpson, Colin. The Lusitania. Boston: Little, 1972.
```

Documentation in the Social Sciences: APA Style

Writers in the social sciences use the system of documentation set forth in the *Publication Manual of the American Psychological Association* (APA), Fourth Edition (1994). Since your instructors in psychology, sociology, and other courses may require you to follow APA guidelines, you should be familiar with this system. Like the MLA style, **APA-style documentation** uses parenthetical citations supported by a separate list of sources headed "References," which appears at the end of the research paper.

Parenthetical Citation

A typical APA-style text citation includes the author's name and the date of publication, separated by a comma.

```
Lower species of animals use only a few signs in their

communication systems. For example, the rhesus monkey uses

only about 37 different signals (Wilson, 1972).
```

As with MLA-style documentation, the APA system aims to integrate references smoothly with the text of the paper. Here are some examples:

```
In 1972, Wilson showed that the rhesus monkey uses only about

37 different signals in its communication system.

According to Wilson (1972), rhesus monkeys use only 37

signals. Communication systems that rely on only a few

signs are typical of lower animal species.
```

When quoting a passage from a source, the page number on which the passage appears is given after the publication date. Note the required use of the abbreviations *pp.* for "pages" and *p.* for "page." The date and the page information are separated by a comma.

```
Creative people use divergent thinking to their advantage and

"prefer complexity and some degree of apparent imbalance in

phenomena" (Barron, 1963, pp. 208-09).
```

When citing more than one work by the same author published in the same year, use an *a* after the date for the first publication, a *b* after the date for the second, and so on. The citations on the references list should also include these letters. In the following example, the reference is to the second 1971 article by Schacter, "Some Extraordinary Facts About Obese Humans and Rats." This reference is marked *b* on the references list. Schacter's first 1971 article, "Eat, Eat," would be marked *a* on the references list. (See page 521.)

```
Researchers have identified important similarities for

obesity in rats and humans (Schacter, 1971b).
```

The examples that follow show how to cite multiple authors in the APA system. Note that the ampersand (&) replaces the word *and* between authors' names in the parenthetical citation (see the first example). If the authors' names are not given parenthetically, as in the second example, then the word *and* is used.

```
Famous studies of the chimpanzee Washoe demonstrated that

animals other than humans could learn and use language

(Gardner & Gardner, 1969).

Rumbaugh, Gill, and von Glaserfeld (1973) studied the language

skills of the chimpanzee Pan.
```

When citing works by three or more authors, use all authors' names for the first reference, but in the second and subsequent text references use the abbreviation *et al.* after the first author's name.

Rumbaugh et al. (1973) have documented certain levels of reading

and the ability to complete sentences among chimpanzees.

EXERCISE

Return to pages 502–506. Revise any two MLA-style citations there so that they reflect the APA style of parenthetical citation.

The List of References

APA-style documentation requires that a list of the references cited in the paper appear on a separate page at the end. The heading "References" is typed at the top of the page and is not underlined (see page 522). On the following pages are sample references in the APA format.

SAMPLE APA-STYLE BOOK ENTRIES

Book with one author

Author: last name, comma, initials — Publication date in parentheses; period — Capital letter for only first word in title

Coles, R. (1997). The moral intelligence of

City of publication — Publisher

children. New York: Random House.

Period — Colon — Period

Book with two or more authors

Woodruff, R. A., Jr., Goodwin, D. W., & Guze, S. B. (1974). Psychiatric diagnosis. New York: Oxford University Press.

Lonner, W. J., & Malpass, R. S. (Eds.). (1994). Psychology and Culture. Boston: Allyn & Bacon.

SAMPLE APA-STYLE PERIODICAL ENTRIES

Author's last name, comma, initials — Publication date in parentheses; period — Capital for first letter of first word only

Barkley, R.A. (1999). Behavioral inhibition, sustained

Title of article: no quotation marks or underlining

attention and executive functions: constructing a uniform

Period — Title of journal underlined; all major words capitalized — Comma — Page numbers

theory of ADHD. Psychological Bulletin, 121, 65-94.

Volume number underlined — Comma — Period

An article in a journal that page numbers each issue separately

> Miller, S. M. (1960). Comparative social mobility. Current Sociology, 9(1), 7-80.

The notation 9 (1) refers to volume 9, issue 1.

An article in a monthly (or bimonthly) magazine

> Chase, A. (2000, June). Harvard and the making of the Unabomber. Atlantic, pp. 41-65.

In a monthly or bimonthly magazine, the month of publication is given after the year in parentheses. A comma separates the year and the month. The abbreviation *pp.* for pages is used for magazine and newspaper entries, but not for journals.

An article in a daily newspaper

> Dugger, C.W. (2000, August 24). Cabinet member's death puts spotlight on India's health system. New York Times, p. A7.

                                    References

> Barron, F. (1963). Creativity and psychological health. Princeton: Van Nostrand Reinhold.
>
> Chase, A. (2000, June). Harvard and the making of the unabomber. Atlantic, pp. 41-65.
>
> Gardner, R. A., & Gardner, B. T. (1969). Teaching sign language to a chimpanzee. Science, 165, 664-672.
>
> Schacter, S. (1971a, November). Eat, eat. Psychology Today, pp. 44-47, 78-79.
>
> Schacter, S. (1971b). Some extraordinary facts about obese humans and rats. American Psychologist, 26, 129-144.

Preparing the References List

1. On a separate page that will appear at the end of the paper, type the heading References, centered on the line. Do not underline it; do not enclose it in quotation marks. List all the sources cited in the text. Double-space from the heading References to the first entry.
2. Without separating books from periodicals, arrange all entries alphabetically according to the author's last name (or, according to publication dates—earliest to most recent—for works by the same author).

3. Double-space within and between all entries.
4. Indent the first line of each entry five spaces. Second and subsequent lines of each entry are flush with the left margin.
5. Number the references page.

EXERCISE

Select four bibliography cards (two for books, two for periodicals) that you prepared for your research paper and write an APA-style references list for them.

Plagiarism

As mentioned earlier, without proper attention to documentation of your sources, you run the risk of being accused of plagiarism.

Plagiarism is the use of facts, opinions, and language taken from another writer without acknowledgment. At its worst, plagiarism is outright theft or cheating: A person has another person write the paper or simply steals a magazine article or section of a book and pretends to have produced a piece of original writing. Far more common is plagiarism in dribs and drabs: a sentence here and there, a paragraph here and there. Unfortunately, small-time theft is still theft, and small-time plagiarism is still plagiarism. For your own safety and self-respect, remember the following rules—not guidelines, *rules:*

- The language in your paper must either be your own or a direct quote from the original source.

- Changing a few words or phrases from another writer's work is not enough to make the writing "your own." Remember rule 1: The writing is either your own or the other person's; there are no in-betweens.

- Documentation acknowledges that the fact or opinion expressed comes from another writer. If the language comes from another writer, quotation marks are necessary in addition to documentation.

Now for a detailed example.

Original Passage

In 1925 Dreiser produced his masterpiece, the massively impressive *An American Tragedy.* By this time—thanks largely to the tireless propagandizing on his behalf by the influential maverick critic H. L. Mencken and by others concerned with a realistic approach to the problems of American life—Dreiser's fame had become secure. He was seen as the most powerful and effective destroyer of the genteel tradition that had dominated popular American fiction in the post–Civil War period, spreading its soft blanket of provincial, sentimental romance over the often ugly realities of life in modern, industrialized, urban America. Certainly there was nothing genteel about Dreiser, either as man or novelist. He was the supreme poet of the squalid, a man who felt the terror, the pity, and the beauty underlying the American dream. With an eye at once ruthless and compassionate, he saw the tragedy inherent in the American success ethic; the soft underbelly, as it were, of the Horatio Alger rags-to-riches myth so appealing to the optimistic American imagination. (Richard Freedman, *The Novel* [New York: Newsweek Books, 1975], 104–05)

Student version

Student version	Comment
There was nothing genteel about Dreiser, either as man or novelist. He was the supreme poet of the squalid, a man who felt the terror, the pity, and the beauty underlying the American dream.	Obvious plagiarism: word-for-word repetition without acknowledgment.
There was nothing genteel about Dreiser, either as man or novelist. He was the supreme poet of the squalid, a man who felt the terror, the pity, and the beauty underlying the American dream (Freedman 104).	Still plagiarism. The *documentation alone does not help.* The language is the original author's, and only quotation marks around the whole passage plus documentation would be correct.
Nothing was genteel about Dreiser as a man or as a novelist. He was the poet of the squalid and felt that terror, pity, and beauty lurked under the American dream.	Still plagiarism. The writer has changed or omitted a few words, but by no stretch of the imagination is the student using his or her own language.
"Nothing was genteel about Dreiser as a man or as a novelist. He was the poet of the squalid and felt that terror, pity, and beauty lurked under the American dream" (Freedman 104).	Not quite plagiarism, but incorrect and inaccurate. Quotation marks indicate exact repetition of what was originally written. The student, however, has changed some of the original and is not entitled to use quotation marks.
"Certainly there was nothing genteel about Dreiser, either as man or novelist. He was the supreme poet of the squalid, a man who felt the terror, the pity, and the beauty underlying the American dream" (Freedman 104).	Correct. The quotation marks acknowledge the words of the original writer. The documentation is also needed, of course, to give the reader specific information about the source of the quote.

Student version

By 1925 Dreiser's reputation was firmly established. The reading public viewed Dreiser as one of the main contributors to the downfall of the "genteel tradition" in American literature. Dreiser, "the supreme poet of the squalid," looked beneath the bright surface of American life and values and described the frightening and tragic elements, the "ugly realities," so often overlooked by other writers (Freedman 104).

Comment

Correct. The student writer uses his or her own words to summarize most of the original passage. The documentation shows that the ideas expressed come from the original writer, not from the student. The few phrases kept from the original passage are carefully enclosed in quotation marks.

Writing Your Research Paper: Draft Stages

As you no doubt know by now, writing a research paper requires that you pay attention to a number of complex elements in both form and content. Writing drafts, reading them carefully, and revising what you have written are essential for successful papers. Review what you learned about drafting in Chapters 1 and 2; then consider the additional suggestions that follow.

The First Draft

To remove the temptation of simply stringing notes together, you might try our method of writing a first draft. We suggest that you set your notes aside, put your outline in front of you, and start writing. In this draft, the point is to get your ideas down on paper. Don't worry about grammar or punctuation. Don't try to work in quotations. You should be familiar enough with the contents of your notes by now to remember the general ideas they contain. Just write, perhaps on every third line of a legal pad (leaving the others blank), until you have developed every point in your outline.

If you have really studied your notes, and if you have constructed a reasonable outline, following this procedure should assure that you will develop your own ideas in your own way.

Subsequent Drafts

Now, write the paper again. Consult your notes to add quotations where appropriate and to fill in facts you might not have remembered when writing the first draft. Use the blank lines for your draft additions and changes. You should check your notes, too, to be sure that the facts, ideas, or opinions you have reported are accurate. And, in this second effort, you should make some attempt to correct any grammar or punctuation errors you made in the first draft and to rephrase awkward sentences. Then you should add documentation (see pages 502–506).

Once you have completed this draft, go back through it several times to make certain that you have quoted accurately, that you have documented every source properly, and that you have polished your language as well as you can. Don't hesitate during this process to use scissors and scotch tape to add, delete, or shift passages as you go along. If things look too messy for you to read, do another draft of the offending pages—or of the whole paper if necessary. If you compose your draft on a word processor, moving text around will be easy.

Toward the Final Copy

If you think you have polished the paper as much as you can, make yet another copy, complete with quotations and appropriate documentation (see pages 530–549). Many instructors will not accept a final copy of a paper unless they have seen and approved a draft. If your instructor falls into this category, this draft is the one you should submit. Your instructor will make suggestions, point out stylistic problems, and indicate the parts of your paper that are not developed as fully as they might be. Conscientious students heed their instructors' suggestions and make the appropriate changes on the third draft before typing the final paper.

Also, before typing your final copy, pay attention to editing details. Proofread carefully. By now you should be familiar with your characteristic errors and you should comb your paper to find and correct them before submitting your work for evaluation. (See the checklist on page 528 and the discussion of proofreading on pages 98–99.)

Preparing the Manuscript

The research paper should be typed—or printed if you use a computer. Before you begin to type your final copy, make sure your typewriter or printer has a fresh ribbon or cartridge and is in good working order. Since you have put so much work into writing the paper, you don't want to spoil the final product by presenting your instructor with a hard-to-read, smudged copy. Make certain, too, that the type is elite or pica. Avoid unusual typefaces like script or italic.

Good bond paper gives a more attractive appearance than less expensive types. White, 8½ × 11-inch, twenty-pound bond paper is usually recommended. Avoid using erasable paper because it smudges and will not take corrections made in ink. If you type and do not like to erase or have difficulty erasing neatly, use a correction tab to remove errors. If you use a computer, you'll find corrections easy to make, but don't neglect to reread your paper carefully before you submit it. (Also see pages 27–28 on writing with a computer.) Check for careless errors like unnecessary spaces and repeated words. Follow these guidelines as you prepare the final copy:

1. *Spacing.* Double-space the paper throughout, including long quotations and notes, except as indicated in the following discussion of margins.
2. *Margins.* Leave margins of one inch at the top, bottom, and both sides of the text. If you are not using a title page, type the centered title two inches from the top of the page, and double-space between the title and the first line of the text. Indent the first word of each paragraph five spaces from the left margin. Indent a block quotation ten spaces from the left margin.
3. *Title page.* Although many classroom instructors insist on a title page (see page 530), MLA guidelines call for a heading on the first page instead. The writer's name, instructor's name, course number, and date appear flush left on the first manuscript page, spaced as indicated in the accompanying example.

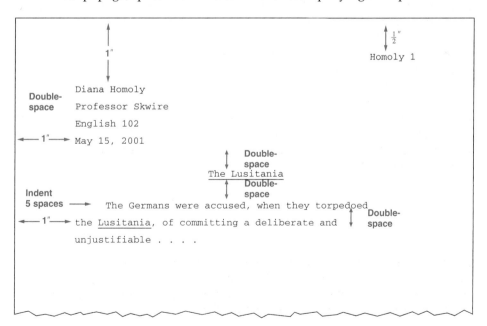

However, most instructors are likely to prefer a title page, especially if an outline or table of contents precedes the first page of text. If your instructor calls for a title page, it should contain the title of your paper, your name, the course name and number, the name of your instructor, and the date. This information should be neatly centered on the page, as in the example on page 530.

Whichever form you use, remember that you should never put your own title in quotation marks, underline it, or capitalize it in full. Underline words in the title only if they would also be underlined in the text.

4. *Pagination.* Number all pages consecutively (except the title page) in the upper right-hand corner. Just type the number; don't punctuate it with a period, hyphens, or parentheses. In addition to putting the number in the upper right-hand corner, you may also want to type your name right before the page number to ensure against misplaced pages. (See the pagination of "The Banning of the Polygraph," page 533, for example.)

REVIEW CHECKLIST: THE RESEARCH PAPER

- Is my thesis clear and appropriately limited? Does it state or suggest an interpretation or judgment on the topic?
- Do I support my assertions with source materials such as quotations and paraphrases?
- Following my instructor's guidelines, have I acknowledged all my sources even when summarizing or paraphrasing? Have I used correct citation format for all sources?
- Are my ideas logically developed and connected with clear transitions?
- Have I listed all my sources on a separate page and included full publication data?
- Have I followed guidelines for correct manuscript preparation? Have I typed my paper according to the format suggested by my instructor?
- If my instructor has read an early draft of my paper and commented on it, have I attended carefully to his or her suggestions?
- Have I edited my paper carefully before submitting it for evaluation, paying particular attention to my own characteristic errors?

EXERCISE

Using your formal outline as your guide, write the necessary drafts of your research paper. Document all sources. Prepare a list of works cited. Be sure to study the student sample and the accompanying commentary on the following pages.

Sample Research Paper

The following sample research paper shows how one student managed to blend a variety of elements successfully. The commentary that appears on the pages facing the paper highlights its key features and calls attention to special issues. The paper uses MLA-style documentation.

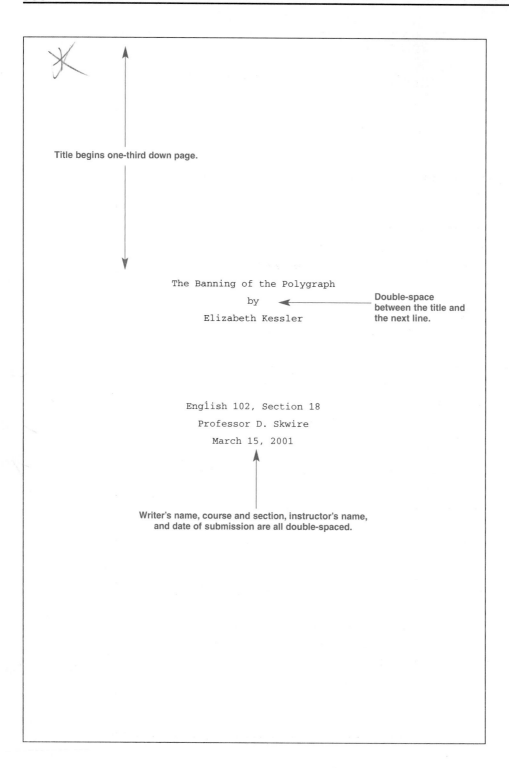

Title begins one-third down page.

The Banning of the Polygraph

by

Elizabeth Kessler

Double-space
between the title and
the next line.

English 102, Section 18

Professor D. Skwire

March 15, 2001

Writer's name, course and section, instructor's name,
and date of submission are all double-spaced.

Kessler 1

Outline

<u>Thesis</u>: The polygraph test as an element in employment decisions
should be banned.

First major division I. Those who argue in favor of the polygraph feel it should
be used as a criterion for employment.

    A. Supporters claim that the examiners are adequately   **First-level subdivision**
trained.

    B. Supporters claim that its findings are reliable.

    C. Supporters argue that it is an inexpensive and effective
method to avoid hiring potential thieves.

  II. Those who oppose the polygraph test correctly believe it
should not be used as a criterion for employment.

    A. Opponents believe the examiners are uneven in quality.

    B. Opponents believe the readings are not accurate.

    C. Opponents believe there is no clear-cut physiological
indication of guilt.

    D. Opponents believe the laws regarding the use of the
polygraph are "toothless."

    E. Opponents believe the test violates basic human rights.

      1. The test can lead to loss of employment and damage
to reputation.   **Second-level subdivision**

      2. The test is an invasion of privacy.

III. The 1988 Polygraph Protection Act restricts lie detector use.

<u>Conclusion</u>: Despite legislation restricting polygraph use
nationally, continuing abuses and potential abuses in the
future argue forcefully against the lie detector test in
the workplace.

a. The page number appears in the upper right-hand corner of each page of the paper. Some writers also include their last name before the page number, as Kessler does. Type the page number (and your name if you choose to include it here) one-half inch from the top of the page.

b. Begin the first paragraph about 2 inches from the top of the page.

c. The raised numeral [1] corresponds to note 1 on page 9 of the research paper.

d. The parenthetical citation (Beach 44) is a standard reference to a work fully named with all the appropriate publishing data in the list of works cited (see page 10). No comma separates the author's name and the page number. No abbreviation for *page* or *pages* is used. The writer of the paper cites Beach because she paraphrased the definition of the polygraph from him.

e. Quotation marks surround the words beginning with *as* and ending with *headache* because Kessler copied the statement word for word from Gugas's book *The Silent Witness* (see page 10 for the complete citation). Here is part of the paragraph as it appears in Gugas; note how Kessler extracted only a small piece that would serve her purpose.

> Business and industry use the polygraph examination widely in screening job applicants and as a means of curbing employee thefts, a multibillion-dollar-a-year headache. Our Army, Navy, Air Force, and Marines all use polygraph testing. I myself set up the lie-detector program for the Criminal Investigation Department of the Marine Corps when I was a Marine Major in 1953. . . .

f. The raised numeral [2] corresponds to note 2 on page 9 of the research paper.

g. Note how the writer briefly introduces the essential argument by calling attention to both supporters and critics of polygraph testing. The paper itself expands on these issues.

h. The citation ("Truth About Lie Detectors" 76) indicates that the quotation appears on page 76 of an unsigned piece. Kessler shortened the full title "The Truth About Lie Detectors, Says David Lykken, Is That They Can't Detect a Lie." See the list of works cited on page 10.

i. The thesis sentence states the topic, following logically from the points raised in the introduction. Kessler's thesis makes a forceful assertion: Keep polygraphs out of the workplace.

j. Kessler cites a quotation from an electronic source. The "Polygraph" piece appears on a CD-ROM called *Encarta*. See page 10 of the research paper for the exact electronic source.

Kessler 2   a

    The polygraph (lie detector) is a machine that   b
monitors a person's physiological changes[1] in blood   c
pressure, pulse rate, breathing, and skin conductivity
(Beach 44). The subject, while attached to the polygraph,   d
is asked a series of questions to measure his or her
honesty. Any great physiological change during a
particular question is said to indicate deception (Inbaw
44). Employers use polygraphs to weed out dishonest
employees or prospective employees and "as a means of   e
curbing employee thefts, a multibillion-dollar-a-year
headache" (Gugas 6). In fact, fifty percent of all retail
employers at one point required that a prospective
employee take a polygraph test. Banks, police
departments, and guard agencies make similar demands
("Tests Untrustworthy" 16). Despite wide use much debate
surrounds polygraph tests. Supporters praise it, it is
true.[2] Yet critics of the polygraph test argue strongly   f
against its use. Merely a machine, the polygraph simply   g
"picks up a person's emotional reactions to questions by
measuring breathing, sweating responses, and blood
pressure." One psychiatrist insists that "there is no
such thing as a lie detector" ("Truth About Lie   h
Detectors" 76). Weighing the evidence, one must agree
with the 1988 Employee Polygraph Protection Act which,
among other provisions, bans the polygraph test as a
criterion for employment. Lie detectors have no place in   i
the work environment.
    Those who for many years have argued in favor of the
polygraph test claim that it is accurate because those who
administer it are adequately trained. Clearly the
examiner's role is important. The examiner "must be
consistently objective and should be thoroughly trained in   j
scientific interrogation to reduce the inherent human
error" ("Polygraph"). In fact, many states demand

a. "In Ohio" is a shortened title for "In Ohio, Anyone May Run Lie Detector," which refers to another unsigned article that Kessler identifies fully in the list of works cited. It is acceptable to abbreviate the title of a long work. The full title appears in the works cited listing.

b. The closing sentence sums up the main issue developed in the paragraph. See also the last sentence of the next paragraph: "Thus, the ability to detect and relieve nervousness should lead to accurate readings." The word *thus* connects the closing sentence logically with the ideas that precede it.

c. Here Kessler uses an important strategy in writing arguments: She presents her opponents' views clearly and fairly. She herself does not approve of polygraph testing, but she does not ignore the issues put forth by those who support the test. The paragraph expands on point I. B. in the writer's outline on page 1.

d. The statistical data are impressive. Even though Kessler is arguing a point opposite to what she believes, she marshalls substantial evidence to show the other side of the issue. To help readers draw thoughtful conclusions on their own, writers should consider opposing arguments thoughtfully.

Kessler 3

education and other requirements for the licensing
of polygraph examiners ("In Ohio" 4). Because nervousness   a
may bring about the same emotional responses as
deception, which may lead to false readings, these
examiners, it is said, are trained extensively in
psychology and physiology. The training supposedly
enables the examiner to distinguish between a person's
nervousness and actual deception during the testing
period ("What's It Like" 8). Supporters of the test   b
believe that the training equips examiners to make
accurate distinctions.

    Advocates of the polygraph also claim that its
findings are reliable. Using control questions during
the testing, an examiner can determine a person's normal
emotional reaction. By establishing a normal response,
the examiner then can detect deception, which reveals
itself in an abnormal response (Inbaw 44). Supporters   c
of the test point out that to help reduce possible
nervousness, the subject is given access to the
questions he will be asked during the test for as long
as he desires ("What's It Like" 8). Thus, the ability to
detect and relieve nervousness should lead to accurate
readings.

    Supporters of the polygraph further argue that it is
"a valuable tool for an employer in screening job
applicants and investigating workplace crime" ("How to
Comply" 36). Each year the total cost of stolen merchandise
and money exceeds twenty billion dollars (Beach 44). To
help decrease this amount, the employers enlist the aid of
the polygraph. According to the National Association of
Convenience Stores, the use of the polygraph reduced
employee theft by 50 percent in 1980 (Flaherty 31).   d
Supporters argue, too, that the polygraph test is much
quicker, more efficient, and less expensive than

a. Here Kessler integrates into her sentence the name of the author from whom she paraphrases. The parenthetical reference (44) tells readers the page number in Beach's article "Blood, Sweat, and Fears." The full citation appears on page 10 of Kessler's paper.

b. Kessler sets off a quotation because it takes more than four lines. Note that the parenthetical citation of Beach comes after the last line of the quotation. See page 497 for the complete paragraph as it appears in Beach's article.

c. The transitional paragraph neatly connects the two major sections of the essay. In the first part of the paragraph, Kessler summarizes the issues advanced by polygraph test supporters. The word *then* in the first sentence connects the ideas expressed here with the preceding paragraphs. With the word *however*, Kessler signals her opposition to the strong arguments put forth by those who support the test. Notice how the last sentence connects to the thesis sentence on page 2 of the research paper.

d. Kessler shows why she believes that the training of polygraph examiners is uneven. Readers must weigh the assertions in this paragraph against the arguments by those who say that examiners are well trained.

e. Kessler has paraphrased the statement for which she credits Beach. Here is the selection exactly as it appears in Beach's article:

> Lie detector tests, either to screen job applicants or to uncover theft by employees, have become big business: hundreds of thousands are given each year, and the number is rising steadily. But despite technical improvements in the equipment, the accuracy of the results is often open to question, and there are persistent reports of browbeating by examiners. . . .

Even though she uses her own language to restate Beach, Kessler attributes the source of her ideas with the page reference (44). The author's name appears in the sentence; hence, it is excluded from the parenthetical citation.

Kessler 4

background checking. As Beach indicates, using the   a
polygraph costs about thirty-five to one hundred fifty
dollars; doing a background check on a potential employee
costs an average of three hundred dollars (44).

And, of course, federal support for polygraph
testing has added validity to their use. Agencies of the
United States in government have relied on lie detector
tests in important legal matters:

> The FBI uses polygraphs mostly to probe leads
> and verify specific facts. . . . The agency also   b
> employs highly trained examiners, who usually
> spend half a day on each session. . . . Attorney
> General Benjamin Civiletti has ruled that an
> "adverse inference" may be drawn if an employee
> of the FBI or any other part of the Justice
> Department balks at submitting to the machines.
> (Beach 44)

The supporters of the polygraph believe its efficiency and
low cost justify its use.

Those who favor the polygraph in the workplace, then,
argue that adequately trained examiners efficiently
produce reliable findings at low cost. These are strong   c
arguments for its use. However, those who oppose the use
of the test question the claims made by its supporters,
and they are right to do so.

Despite assertions that examiners are adequately   d
trained to distinguish accurately among physiological
responses, operators still do not need licenses in half
the states, including New York and California. (No doubt
that will change as a result of new legislation.) Beach
points out that opponents to the test have called   e
attention, also, to regular reports by employees that
examiners browbeat them during polygraph testing (44). And

a. Flaherty and Ward are sources for the paraphrases included in this paragraph.

b. Kessler uses ellipses to indicate that she has left out words in this quotation taken from an editorial, called "Rights Abuse," in the *Christian Science Monitor*. (See reference in Works Cited list, page 10.)

c. This paragraph develops point II. C. in the outline (page 1). The transition "nor" connects the ideas of this paragraph to those in the paragraph before it.

Kessler 5

"about 90% of the damaging reports made to employers
are based not on physiological reactions but on the
examiners' assumptions, or on incriminating confessions
made during an interview" ("Truth About Lie Detectors"
76). These findings suggest that the quality of operators
in the polygraph industry is uneven at best.

There seems, too, to be some reason to doubt the
accuracy of the readings. The test is accurate only 60 to
75 percent of the time, some say, and many variants of the
lie detector test have never been checked for validity
("Tests Untrustworthy" 16). Error is more likely to occur
when a truthful person is shown to be deceptive (Beach
44). The opposition argues that deception is not always
indicated on the readings and that people who do not
believe that the machine can detect deception feel no
stress when lying: Therefore, there will be no great
physiological response indicating deception on the
readings (Flaherty 32). One group claims that clinical   a
tests prove that tranquilizers such as meprobamate reduce
the physiological response that accompanies deception (Ward
et al. 74). And, one must accept the fact that those who
are "really clever... can fool the machines" ("Rights   b
Abuse" 10). Finally, variations in posture during the test
can confuse the physiological responses, leading to false
readings (Flaherty 32). One must question the value of
readings that may be unreliable.

Nor does a clear-cut physiological indication of   c
guilt seem to be as certain as supporters of the test
claim. Often, heightened feelings bring about
physiological responses that are similar to those caused
by deception. According to David Lykken, psychiatrist and
professor of psychology, people who run a special risk
include those who get upset if someone accuses them of
something they did not do, those with short tempers, and
those who tend to feel guilty anyway. Lykken believes that
the polygraph machine detects not only the physiological

a. This paragraph develops point II. D. in the outline.

b. Kessler reflects on her findings, inserting her own opinion on the information she presents. Writers of research papers should do more than simply summarize, paraphrase, or quote acknowledged experts.

c. Kessler smoothly integrates the quote from Block with her own language. Look at the statement from Block, then at the note card Kessler prepared.

> Some sociologists and theologians question the fairness of the lie detector, arguing that it unjustly robs suspects of their innermost secrets, and some courts have held that to some extent it illegally compels defendants to testify against themselves. Yet modern police authorities insist that many baffling cases have been solved only because such a test, taken voluntarily by a suspect, has proved scientifically that he or she lied in answering key questions pertinent to the case.

Block   *Science vs. Crime*   131

"Some sociologists and theologians question the fairness of the lie detector, arguing that it unjustly robs suspects of their innermost secrets, and some courts have held that to some extent it illegally compels defendants to testify against themselves."
    Police say, however, that polygraphs help solve puzzling cases by giving scientific proof of lying.

*Focus here is on criminal cases.

Kessler has copied one paragraph exactly and has enclosed it in quotation marks on her note card. She also has paraphrased a portion of the original paragraph—the sentence starting with the words *Police say* on the note card. In addition, she has written a brief note to herself on the card—the sentence beginning with the word *Focus*. She uses an asterisk to highlight the statement as her own, so that she will not mistakenly attribute it to Block when she reviews the note cards later on and chooses information to include in her essay.

When Kessler draws on the material from this note card to make her point in the paper, she uses only one part of the quotation from Block. Kessler paraphrases the portion of the quote that reads "and some courts have held that to some extent it illegally compels defendants to testify against themselves." In her paper, this part of the quote becomes "Courts have ruled that the test illegally forces a person to testify against himself (Block 131)." The parenthetical documentation tells readers that both the quote and the paraphrase are from Block.

Kessler 6

responses that accompany lying but also the nervousness people feel when strapped to a machine. The polygraph confuses the emotions of guilt with fear, anger, and many other emotions that can alter heart rate, breathing, and perspiration. Each person varies in his or her physiological response to these emotions ("Truth About Lie Detectors" 79).

Moreover, until now, laws regarding the polygraph   **a** tended to be "toothless." For example, some laws prohibit requiring present or prospective employees to submit to a polygraph; however, businesses are still free to make the request (Flaherty 34). If an employee or prospective employee refuses to take the test at an employer's request, his refusal may be interpreted as an admission of guilt ("Truth About Lie Detectors" 79). In fact, his   **b** refusal may mean the loss of a job (Beach 44). Certainly, this is unfair: the burden lies entirely on the employee's shoulders. Further, some state or city laws free only present employees from a polygraph test but not prospective employees. Finally, the fines and jail terms prescribed for violating these laws rarely have risen above the misdemeanor level. These fines, which seldom exceed one thousand dollars, do not hinder "deep-pocketed" employers from using the polygraph (Flaherty 34). Such laws, opponents of the test rightly argue, have not protected employees.

One must also consider the problem of violating basic human rights ("In Ohio" 4). Especially in regard to   **c** criminal cases, some sociologists and experts in theology say that polygraph testing "unjustly robs suspects of their innermost secrets." Courts have ruled that the test illegally forces a person to testify against himself (Block 131). Several experts claim that the lie detector, with all its apparatus, constitutes a "modern third degree" and may

a. This paragraph develops point II. E. 2. in the outline.

b. Kessler draws to a close by bringing the topic up to date in light of current law. She treats fairly the positive provisions of the new bill, even though they might challenge her own position. This paragraph expands on point III in Kessler's outline.

Kessler 7

intimidate a subject into blurting out a false confession
before the test begins (Beach 44). They argue, also,
that an unfavorable reading, whether accurate or
not, could result in the loss of a job, damage to an
employee's reputation, and the inability to obtain new
employment, especially since, in many states, a person
before taking the test must sign a form that allows any
individual access to the test results ("Personal Rights
Issue" 7). On the basis of a questionable test, then, one
can, in effect, be found guilty and be punished--having
committed no crime--without the traditional protections of
presumption of innocence until guilt is proved, trial by
jury, and the right to confront accusers. Oddly enough,
even police may be called on to take lie detector tests in
order to "make it more difficult for police officers to
perjure themselves" ("Curb Police Perjury" 13). Finally,
many employers see in the polygraph an opportunity to
force their values and ideas on employees (Flaherty 30).
The polygraph test, then, can be an infringement on
individual rights.

    A further infringement on individual rights,   a
according to opponents of the test, is an unwarranted
invasion of privacy. Many examiners have probed into
personal affairs of those being tested (Beach 44). The
examiners ask questions pertaining to political, sexual,
and union matters. Mike Tiner of the Union of Food and
Commercial Workers reported that in the 1980s questions
involving political, sexual, and union matters were
definitely on the increase (Beach 44). Such invasions of
privacy may be seen as violations of constitutional rights
and should not be tolerated.

    It is heartening to report that, to a large degree,   b
the government apparently heeded the chorus of voices
against the lie detector over the years. In 1988, Congress

a. Note punctuation with ellipsis at the end of a sentence. Three spaced periods indicate an omission at the end of the *Nation's Business* quote. The parenthetical reference here follows the quotation mark after the ellipsis; a sentence period follows the final parenthesis.

b. The opening sentence of the conclusion reestablishes one of the basic themes of the paper—the ongoing debate about polygraph testing. Kessler here states strongly her own opinions, raising again what she sees as the key issues in the dispute—the test's unreliability and its encroachment on civil rights. Her conclusion does not simply restate the essential points of the paper, nor is it a shorter version of the introduction. Rather, Kessler uses the conclusion to reassert her own beliefs sharply and clearly.

Kessler 8

passed the Polygraph Protection Act, which, according
to an article called "How to Comply with the Polygraph
Law" in <u>Nation's Business</u>, finally "prohibits the use
of polygraphs to screen job applicants or investigate
employees . . ." (36). The law defines proper testing   **a**
procedures and gives employees a wide range of rights,
including written notification at least 48 hours in
advance of the time and place of the examination, its
scope, and the reasons the employer has for suspecting
participation of the employee in some specific incident
"involving economic loss or injury to the business" (36).
In addition, the law spells out "procedural requirements"
for testing, and it establishes guidelines for the
qualifications of examiners. Some good sense seems to
have prevailed here; workers now have protection against
some abuses in polygraph testing in the workplace.

Yet despite the restrictive provisions of the 1988   **b**
law, many civil rights advocates are still unhappy. The
legal system in the past has not protected employees
adequately against abusive polygraph testing, and one must
reserve judgment about how long-term enforcement will
support the federal law. The Polygraph Protection Act
allows too many exceptions, particularly the "reasonable
suspicion" feature. Without much difficulty, employers
bent on using the test no doubt can develop charges of
suspicion against employees they dislike. Additionally,
several private-sector employers are exempt from the law,
including security companies and many pharmaceutical
companies. Finally, the poor accuracy record of the tests
in general condemns them, no matter how much they are
restricted. As a result of these weaknesses in the law and
of other major issues, polygraphs should have no place in
any employee judgments.

a. This note refers to the superscript [1] on page 2 of Kessler's paper. It adds information that is not essential to the paper but that nonetheless is instrumental in helping readers understand how the polygraph equipment may be used. Kessler does not want to focus on the mechanical features of the polygraph in the text of her paper, which concentrates on the unfairness of using the device.

   Type the note number as a superscript; indent five spaces and double-space all lines of the note. Place the notes on a separate page headed "Notes," typed one inch from the top and centered. The Notes page appears directly before the Works Cited page. (Your instructor may prefer that you type footnotes at the bottom of the page on which the superscript appears in the text.)

b. This note refers to the superscript [2] on page 2 of the paper.

Kessler 9

Notes

[1] These physiological changes in body functions are   a
measured by the use of special apparatus: a rubber tube
placed around the chest, a pressurized cuff around one
arm, and several sensors taped to the skin (Dunn 85).
[2] Although efforts to detect lies go back to ancient   b
times, the modern history of polygraph testing starts with
Cesare Lombroso and his experiments with human heartbeats.
After him, Hugo Munsterberg, "Harvard's pioneer in
criminal psychology" (Block 132), advanced efforts to
develop a reliable lie detector. In 1920, criminologists
August Vollmer, John A. Larson, and Leonardo Keller
developed a machine that could record "on paper with up-
and-down lines a subject's changes in heartbeat, blood
pressure, and respiration under steady questioning" (134).

a. The references appear on a separate page headed "Works Cited" and are listed alphabetically by the authors' last names (or, if the work is unsigned, by the first key word in the title). The heading "Works Cited" is typed about an inch from the top of the page and centered. Do not separate entries for books and periodicals.

b. The reference is to an article from a weekly periodical.

c. This is an entry for a book with one author.

d. If a reference runs to a second line, it is indented five spaces. In other words, the first letter of the second and subsequent lines is printed at space six.

e. This is another standard entry for a book. *Prentice* is an acceptable abbreviation for Prentice-Hall, the publisher.

f. Because the article is unsigned, it is alphabetized according to the word *In*, the first word in the title. The item *F4* means that the article appears in section F, page 4 of the newspaper.

g. In this entry for an article in a daily newspaper, the notation *late ed.* after the date indicates the particular edition in which the article appeared. (Different editions of a newspaper often contain different material.) Note the comma before the specified edition.

h. In using an editorial, Kessler indicates it as such with the word *Editorial* right after the title of the selection.

i. This article from a weekly magazine appears on interrupted pages; the selection starts on page 75 and continues on pages 76 and 79. The pages on which the selection continues do not appear in the citation.

j. Since there are more than three authors for this magazine article—William Ward, Emily Carota Orne, Mary R. Cook, and Martin T. Orne—the citation names only the first author, followed by the Latin abbreviation *et al.*, meaning "and others." However, you may choose to give all names in full in the order in which they appear. Invert only the names of the first author, placing the last name first. For all other authors in a multiple author citation, place the first name before the surname.

Kessler 10

Works Cited   **a**

Beach, Bennet H. "Blood, Sweat, and Fears." Time 8 Sept.   **b**
      1980: 44.

Block, Eugene B. Science vs. Crime: The Evolution of the   **c**
      Police Lab. San Francisco: Cragmont, 1979.   **d**

Dunn, Donald. "When a Lie Detector Test Is Part of the Job
      Interview." Business Week 27 July 1981: 85-86.

Flaherty, Francis. "Truth Technology." Progressive June
      1982: 30-35.

Gugas, Chris. The Silent Witness: A Polygraphist's   **e**
      Casebook. Englewood Cliffs: Prentice, 1979.

"How to Comply with the Polygraph Law." Nation's Business
      Dec. 1989: 36-37.

Inbaw, Fred. "Polygraph Test." Encyclopedia Americana.
      1993 ed.

"In Ohio, Anyone May Run Lie Detector." Dayton   **f**
      Daily News 31 Mar. 1982: F4.

"Lie Detectors Could Curb Police Perjury." USA Today Aug.
      1996: 13-14.

"Lie Detectors Raise Personal Rights Issue." Dayton [OH]
      Daily News 29 Mar. 1982: F6-8.

"Lie Detector Tests Untrustworthy." USA Today Feb. 1981: 16.

"Lie Detector Use on Jobs Growing." New York Times 7 Aug.   **g**
      1980, late ed.: B5.

"Polygraph." Encarta '97. CD-ROM. Microsoft: 2000.

"Rights Abuse." Editorial. Christian Science Monitor 20 Oct. **h**
      1999:10.

"The Truth About Lie Detectors, Says David Lykken, Is That
      They Can't Detect a Lie." People 11 May 1981: 75+.   **i**

Ward, William, et al. "Meprobamate Reduces Accuracy of
      Physiological Detection of Deception." Science 3 Apr.   **j**
      1981: 73-74.

"What's It Like to Take a Lie Detector Test?" Law and
      Order [Columbia, SC] 5 July 1981: F7-8.

Style

Writing a well-organized theme is one thing. Writing a well-organized *good* theme is another, more complicated thing. Thousands of rusty filing cabinets and dusty shelves are filled with perfectly well-organized writings that got their authors nothing but bored and irritated readers—not to mention poor grades. These writings all had a thesis; they all supported the thesis; they all had an introduction, a body, and a conclusion. The paragraphs in these writings all had topic sentences, and the topic sentences were all connected to the thesis. In short, these writings followed all the directions and advice that this book has given so far. So what went wrong?

The answer to that begins with another question. Do we waste time praising a relative's remodeled home because the sofa is in the living room and the stove in the kitchen? We all know that if the sofa had been in the bathroom and the stove on top of the coffee table, we'd be faced with a disaster, but we generally take logical organization for granted. In a reasonably well-organized piece of writing the reader simply assumes the struc-ture is satisfying and then concentrates on other matters. The reader is right, too. Few homeowners have ever received compliments for putting the bed in the bedroom, and few writers have ever been praised for their superb mastery of topic sentences.

When we do praise writers, we generally praise them because they know how to work with words. We may think we liked a particular story or article because its ideas were powerful and interesting, but it was the words that *made* the ideas powerful and interesting. Good writers can fascinate us with instructions on how to use automobile directional signals. Poor writers can bore us with passionate love letters. Bear in mind, too, that good writers are almost never just born that way. Their writing skill is the result of intelligent tinkering and careful revision, not of magic.

Part Five, then, discusses ways of refining your use of language. We concentrate here not on grammar and organization but on **style**—not just how to write correctly but how to write well.

CHAPTER

20

Proper Words
in Proper Places

Jonathan Swift, the author of *Gulliver's Travels*, once defined good style as "proper words in proper places." Gustave Flaubert, the great French novelist, felt that the writer's craft was embodied in the quest for *le seul mot juste*, the single right word. On one level or another, everyone who writes is involved in the same quest. Total success, if it has ever been achieved, may depend ultimately on such vital but indefinable qualities as sensitivity, perceptiveness, creativity, and dozens of others. Fortunately, few people expect or demand total success. Nearly all writers can learn to hit the right word more often simply by becoming more alert to the possibilities of language and the need for thoughtful revision.

Denotation and Connotation

Traditionally, the most logical way to begin thinking about right and wrong words is through the distinction between denotation and connotation. The **denotation** of a word is its explicit, surface meaning, its bare "dictionary meaning." The **connotation** of a word is its implicit meaning, the meaning derived from the emotions associated with the word in people's minds. Words like *Las Vegas* or *Ireland*, for example, simply denote a particular city or country—a mere geographical location—but for many people, they also have an emotional significance that has nothing to do with geography. The connotative meanings of a word are not always included in the dictionary, but they are as vital a part of the word's full meaning as are denotations.

Let's take a simple example. Suppose you are the head of a successful advertising agency, and a major motor corporation wants you to handle the campaign introducing a new car. Would you recommend calling the car the Giraffe, the Porcupine, or the Hawk? Whatever name you suggest will denote the same mechanical device with set wheelbase and rear headroom measurements, fuel tank capacity, engine size, and so on. But an advertising agency that thinks only of the denotations of words will soon go out of business.

We all probably agree that among Giraffe, Porcupine, and Hawk, the last name is the only reasonable choice for the new car. For most people, the idea of a hawk carries with it connotations of power, speed, and perhaps freedom and beauty. These are concepts that motivate people who buy cars, no matter how loudly they may claim that their sole interests are economy and "just transportation." Consider the animal names in use for car models and notice how many connote power, speed, or both: Cougar, Mustang, Jaguar, Colt, Skylark, Thunderbird, Firebird, Eagle. The name Hawk, then, has certain connotations that might be helpful in marketing the car.

What are the connotations of the name Giraffe? Most of us would probably think of tremendous—even absurd—size, and of something that basically looks funny. Zoologists may tell us that giraffes are actually capable of running extremely fast, but the average person associates the animals far more with awkwardness than with speed. What about Porcupine? When the average person bothers to think about porcupines at all, the connotations are likely to be of pesky creatures that sensible folks try to stay away from. People respond to the connotations of words, and it is hard to conceive of finding many car buyers for the Giraffe or the Porcupine. "A rose by any other name would smell as sweet," Shakespeare once wrote. From a strictly scientific point of view, he was undoubtedly correct. In all other respects, though, he was dead wrong.

Developing a sensitivity to the connotations of words, then, is an invaluable asset for all writers. A dozen different words may have the same, or almost the same, denotation. But the right word will be the one with the right connotations—the connotations that most precisely reflect the writer's intended meaning and produce the desired reaction from the writer's audience. Was the person who had too much to drink *inebriated, intoxicated, drunk, looped, smashed, tipsy, high, crocked, pickled, loaded,* or *blotto*? Was the overweight person *plump, fat, pudgy, obese, chubby, portly, chunky, corpulent, stout,* or *stocky*? Few greater compliments can be paid to writers than to say that they have a knack for choosing the right words. That knack does not come simply from having a large vocabulary. Rather, it comes mainly from thinking about the fine distinctions in connotation that separate words with similar denotation. It comes from never automatically assuming that the first word that springs to mind is the right one. And it comes from careful revision and never being too happy with one's choice of words too soon.

EXERCISE

Rearrange each group of words by connotation, from the least favorable term to the most favorable. In many cases, opinions will differ; there are few purely right and purely wrong answers.

1. unromantic, realistic, pragmatic, hardheaded
2. thin, skinny, slender, bony, emaciated
3. teach, educate, drill, train
4. weep, cry, blubber, bawl
5. squabble, disagreement, quarrel, brawl
6. knowledgeable, bright, shrewd, smart, brainy
7. laugh, chuckle, giggle, guffaw, snicker
8. pretty, gorgeous, lovely, stunning, beautiful
9. drink, cocktail, booze, rotgut, alcoholic beverage
10. look, ogle, stare, glower, gaze
11. sweltering, hot, sultry, blistering
12. strut, swagger, stride, pace
13. friendly, gushy, approachable, cordial
14. gripe, complain, squawk, bellyache
15. talkative, articulate, gabby, loquacious
16. toss, fling, throw, hurl
17. garbage, trash, filth, pollutants, waste
18. strict, rigid, authoritarian, fascistic
19. pungent, fragrant, smelly, scented
20. beg, appeal, request

EXERCISE

All the words in parentheses make sense in the sentences that follow. How does the meaning of the sentence change, depending on which word is used?

1. The minister strikes me as (an idealist, a dreamer).
2. The criticisms of the new health care proposal are mostly (uninformed, foolish, idiotic).
3. We have (loud, raucous, noisy) neighbors.
4. The salesperson at the bookstore seemed (reserved, aloof).
5. The astronauts' mission was (challenging, laborious).
6. I was (apprehensive, terrified) about beginning a new career.
7. My father says that as a young man he (loved, adored) Marilyn Monroe.
8. He was as smart as (a fox, a trained dog in a circus, Albert Einstein).
9. Congresswoman Saunders is a gifted (speaker, talker, orator).
10. Sometimes (solitude, loneliness, isolation) can be good for the soul.
11. The football team was (beaten badly, humiliated).
12. Meeting people from other countries can be (broadening, educational).
13. Dinner had been delayed, and I felt truly (famished, hungry, ravenous).
14. Next to the little boy, the Great Dane looked (huge, immense).

15. The brush fires (damaged, devastated) much of the landscape.
16. Though we tried to convince her, she remained (resolute, obstinate).
17. The engineers outlined the details of their (intricate, complicated, elaborate) plans for the building.
18. Alex has a great fondness for (fashionable, trendy) clothing.
19. Ravioli and potato chips is a (deplorable, revolting) dinner combination.
20. He (quickly, hastily, expeditiously) prepared dinner for his unexpected guests.

Abstract Writing and Concrete Writing

Although the distinction between denotation and connotation is valuable to writers, it is sometimes easier to see the immediate, practical consequences to a writer's quest for the right word in the distinction between abstract writing and concrete writing. **Abstract writing** is writing that lacks specific details and is filled with vague, indefinite words and broad, general statements. **Concrete writing** is characterized by specific details and specific language. Every piece of writing needs generalizations, of course, and vague words such as *nice* and *interesting* can be useful. But writing that is dominated by such words is abstract writing, and abstract writing is the main cause of bored readers. It is often a reflection of lazy or careless thinking. It can interfere with full communication of meaning. It prevents many students from developing their themes adequately ("I've already said all I have to say. How am I supposed to get 300 more words on this subject?").

Consider the following examples of abstract and concrete writing.

Abstract	Concrete
Too much poverty exists in this country.	I see one-third of a nation ill-housed, ill-clad, ill-nourished.
Mr. Jones is a tough grader.	Mr. Jones flunked 75 percent of his class and gave no higher than a C to the students who passed.
Computers now execute many of the tasks that only humans could do many years ago.	Today's technology allows computers to perform tasks like processing banking transactions, obtaining research from thousands of sources, and sending information overseas.
The story is quite amusing in places, but basically is very serious.	Underneath the slapstick humor, the story presents a bitter attack on materialism and snobbishness.

Abstract

Religious faith is important,
but practical considerations are
also important.

Concrete

Trust in God, and keep your powder dry.

Nothing is technically wrong with all these examples of abstract writing, but we need only compare them to the rewritten concrete versions to see their basic inadequacy. They convey less information. They are less interesting. They have less impact. There is nothing wrong with them except that they could be much better.

Specific Details

The use of specific details is the most direct way to avoid abstract writing. We tend to get irritated with a politician—or college dean—who, when confronted by a crucial issue, releases a press statement declaring, "We will give this matter our careful consideration." We get irritated not because the matter doesn't require careful consideration, but because the abstractness of the statement makes us suspect that we have just received a strong whiff of hot air. That suspicion will probably decrease significantly if the statement goes on to tell us the names of the people who will confer on this issue next Monday under orders to present recommendations within two weeks, those recommendations to be acted on inside of forty-eight hours. In this case, the specific details have served to support the generalization, have given us a clear notion of what the generalization means, and have helped create an impression of seriousness and sincerity.

Politicians and college deans are not the only people who sometimes seem too fond of hot air. Much of the material we read every day is abstract: flabby, dull, vague, and essentially meaningless. Like hot air, it lacks real body, real substance. The sports columnist writes, "The team should do better this year," and leaves it at that, instead of adding, "It should finish in third or fourth place and even has a fighting chance for the pennant." The teacher writes an angry letter saying, "This school ignores all vital needs of the faculty," and sounds like just another crank unless the letter goes on and points to *specific* needs that have in fact been ignored.

Student writing—from essay exams to themes in composition courses— could be vastly improved if more attention were paid to eliminating excessive abstractions and adding specific details. The more specific details, the less chance of hot air. Students should not tolerate the same things in their own writing that antagonize them in someone else's. Our use of language, not to mention our level of thought, would probably improve a hundredfold if we established an informal rule *never* to make an unsupported general statement, a general statement not backed up by specific details.

This rule sounds easy enough, but it means what it says. It means a writer should never try to get by with sentences such as, "The day was too hot"; "The hero of the story was very ambitious"; "The administration is corrupt"; "The Industrial Revolution brought about many changes." These sentences are neither ungrammatical nor necessarily incorrect in what they say, but if they are not backed up by specific details they are worthless. "The day was too hot" is uninteresting and unpersuasive. *Back it up.* The reader should know that the temperature was 93 degrees, that Bill's sweaty glasses kept slipping off his nose, that even the little children who usually filled the street were inside trying to keep cool, that a cocker spaniel who had managed to find a spot of shade was too exhausted and miserable to bother brushing away the flies. Whatever the piece of writing—a letter of application for a job, an analysis of a short story, a final exam in history—specific details give the writing life and conviction that abstractions alone can never achieve.

One more point about specific details: within reason, *the more specific the better.* As long as the detail is relevant—as long, that is, as it supports the generalization and is not instantly obvious as too trivial for consideration—the writer is unlikely to go wrong by being too specific. On a history exam, a student may generalize, "In the Revolutionary War, the Americans had many difficulties." As specific support for that statement, the student may go on to write, "The number of Tories was quite large." But better in all respects would be, "Tories numbered as much as 30 percent of the population." The more specific the better, and one can almost always be more specific. Eventually, it is true, one can defeat one's purpose; it would be a mistake to give the reader the names and addresses of all the Tories during the Revolutionary War. The writing would then become so overwhelmed by specifics that the major point would be lost. Elementary common sense is usually the best guide in preventing that kind of mistake, and in actual practice few student writers run up against the problem of being too specific.

To summarize: Support all your generalizations with relevant, specific details. Remember that, within reason, the more specific the details, the better the writing.

Abstract (weak)

The telephone is a great scientific achievement, but it can also be a great inconvenience. Who could begin to count the number of times that phone calls have come from unwelcome people or on unwelcome occasions? Telephones make me nervous.

More specific (better)

The telephone is a great scientific achievement, but it can also be a great pain. I get calls from bill collectors, hurt relatives, salespeople, charities, and angry neighbors. The calls always seem to come at the worst times, too. They've interrupted my meals, my baths, my parties, my sleep. I couldn't get along without telephones, but sometimes they make me a nervous wreck.

Still more specific (much better)

The telephone is a great scientific achievement, but it can also be a great big headache. More often than not, that cheery ringing in my ears brings messages from the Ace Bill Collecting Agency, my mother (who is feeling snubbed for the fourth time that week), salespersons of encyclopedias and magazines, solicitors for the Police Officers' Ball and Disease of the Month Foundation, and neighbors complaining about my dog. That's not to mention frequent wrong numbers—usually for someone named "Arnie." The calls always seem to come at the worst times, too. They've interrupted steak dinners, hot tubs, Friday night parties, and Saturday morning sleep-ins. There's no escape. Sometimes I wonder if there are any telephones in padded cells.

EXERCISE

Invent two or three specific details to back up each of the following generalizations. Use your imagination. Remember, the more specific the better. Don't settle for a detail like "He reads many books" to support the statement "My teacher is very intellectual."

1. Some television commercials are extremely entertaining.
2. Some television commercials are extremely irritating.
3. Basketball is a very fast-paced sport.
4. Most people are foolish about their own health.
5. Our society systematically discriminates against left-handed people.
6. After enough time goes by, anything can become a bore.
7. Bill is a sloppy eater.
8. It's hard to keep up with Gretchen.
9. Readers cannot evaluate essay examinations fairly.
10. When it comes to driving, slowpokes are as bad as speed demons.
11. Uncle George is a born loser.
12. I have no mechanical ability at all.
13. A photograph can capture the emotions of a moment.
14. Going on a picnic is asking for trouble.
15. Being in love is worse than having the flu.
16. Movies have become too violent.
17. Having children isn't all fun and games.
18. Jackie Robinson changed the game of baseball.
19. Convertibles are my favorite cars.
20. I'll never understand men!

Specific Words and Phrases

Writers who take seriously our "the-more-specific-the-better" rule will find not only that their writing has more impact and meaning but also that their style as a whole—their use of language—has started to change significantly. Specific details in themselves are not a guarantee of good writing. Something has to happen to the language, too. The words with which a specific detail is presented must *themselves* be specific. In fact, through using **specific words,** a good writer can make even the most tiresomely familiar abstractions take on new life.

For most writers, the biggest challenge is learning to recognize when a particular word or phrase is not specific enough, and why. Often the first word that pops into our heads doesn't really work as effectively as it should. "He smiled," for example, may seem the natural way to describe a common facial expression. What rational person could complain about such a straightforward phrase? But have we truly conveyed the exact expression we are trying to write about or have we just settled for a fuzzy approximation? Wouldn't our readers get a clearer picture of the face we have in mind if we tried to pin down the word that best describes *this* smile: He grinned? Smirked? Sneered? Leered? Simpered? Turned up the corners of his mouth? Smiled half-heartedly? Smiled broadly? Once we develop the habit of checking our original word choices carefully, making sure we've come as close to our precise meaning as possible, our style will become at once more specific and more colorful. Revision, then, is not an inconvenience; it's an essential tool of the trade.

Nobody, it is true, will ever be ridiculed or exposed to public disgrace for writing, "She went to the door." But surely our readers deserve to be told, and surely we should want them to know, if she ran or walked or strolled or strutted or shuffled or limped or stumbled or sauntered or trotted or tiptoed to that door. Only one abstract word needs to be changed here, but the person who habitually recognizes that abstract word, refuses to let it pass, and selects a specific word to replace it is no longer just someone who writes, but a *writer.*

Using specific words is a different matter from supporting generalizations with details, though specific words may sometimes help give us a more detailed picture. Selecting specific words is primarily a means of expression, a way of putting things, a style. "He wore a hat" becomes, "His top hat was tilted jauntily over one eyebrow." We are not backing up a previous statement about someone's clothing preferences here—we are making a statement that has a specific meaning in and of itself. Together, specific details and specific words are the primary means of eliminating boring and dreary abstractions from our writing.

EXERCISE

In the sentences that follow, the italicized words or phrases are abstract and dull. Find a specific word or short phrase that can substitute for the abstract one without changing the meaning of the sentence.

1. His *family* took a *long vacation* last year.
2. The *pet* was *poorly trained.*
3. My aunt *made a nice profit* on *that investment.*
4. Sam *behaved rudely* at the *party.*
5. The *local savings institution* has just *readjusted its interest rates.*
6. Amy brought a *small gift* for the party's *host.*
7. My parents gave me a *nice watch* for the *great event.*
8. *Certain tests* revealed that the *athlete* had a *serious injury.*
9. The articles in that *publication* discussed very *timely issues.*
10. We *spent some time* in the park because it was such a *nice day.*
11. Her *spiritual advisor* gave her a good suggestion about her *problem.*

12. *Local dignitaries* attended the *ceremony.*
13. Unless you make *payment promptly,* we will take *legal action.*
14. Some *members of the class* presented *severe disciplinary problems.*
15. The *school official* commented that *technology* is a valuable tool in education.
16. *Traveling by air* makes me *slightly uncomfortable.*
17. We have *received instructions* and will *attempt to remedy the situation.*
18. I planted some *beautiful flowers outside.*
19. The home team *won the game.*
20. Gus *did well* in school and *did nicely* in business, too.

Comparisons

Another way of avoiding abstract writing and increasing the liveliness of concrete writing is to use effective figures of speech, particularly **comparisons** (see pages 418–421) for a discussion of metaphors and similes). Sometimes a writer may have a hard time coming up with a forceful substitute for a humdrum expression like "it was very easy." There are plenty of synonyms for "very easy," of course, but the writer's best bet might be a comparison: "It was as easy as (*or* It was so easy it was like) drinking a second glass of beer," or "splattering toothpaste on the bathroom mirror," or "forgetting the car keys." Good comparisons are attention-getters. They provide a legitimate opportunity to show off a bit. They can demonstrate a writer's imagination or sense of humor. They can add a helpful spark to otherwise pedestrian writing.

Two cautions are in order. First, use comparisons in moderation. The more comparisons a piece of writing contains, the less impact each one is likely to have. Second, and more important, avoid the routine, trite comparisons with which our language is filled. Don't write "it was as easy as pie" or "It was as easy as taking candy from a baby." Try to be fresh and different. Rather than be trite, avoid comparisons altogether.

Make sure, too, that you phrase your comparisons correctly, whether you are using them for lively specific detail or as a simple means of making a point—"Alice is smarter than Sally," for example. Often, there is no problem, and we can do what comes naturally. But sometimes, through careless phrasing, we can appear to be comparing things that we had no intention of comparing, things that can't be compared because no relationship exists between them. None of us would think of writing "Eyebrows are better than hubcaps," but many of us have probably tossed off illogical sentences like those that follow.

Incorrect

Some of these horror stories are very similar to Edgar Allan Poe. [Intending to compare the horror stories of one author to the horror stories of another author, the writer instead compares the horror stories of one author to another author.]

Improved

Some of these horror stories are very similar to Edgar Allan Poe's.

or

Some of these horror stories are very similar to those of Edgar Allan Poe.

Incorrect	Improved
His appetite was as huge as a pig.	His appetite was as huge as a pig's.
	or
	His appetite was as huge as that of a pig.
	or
	His appetite was as huge as a pig's appetite.
The new supermarket's prices are higher than the competition.	The new supermarket's prices are higher than the competition's.
	or
	The new supermarket's prices are higher than those of the competition.

Another kind of illogical comparison unintentionally excludes an item of comparison from the group that it belongs to through the omission of the word *other.*

Incorrect	Improved
Lincoln had more detailed knowledge of the Bible than any American president.	Lincoln had more detailed knowledge of the Bible than any other American president.
My high school paid less attention to sports than any school in the city.	My high school paid less attention to sports than any other school in the city.

Sometimes, too, improper phrasing can result in confusion. What did the writers of these sentences want to say?

I like him more than you.	Did the writer mean "I like him more than you like him" or "I like him more than I like you"?
Hemingway is more indebted to Mark Twain than anyone else.	Did the writer mean "Hemingway is more indebted to Mark Twain than to anyone else" or "Hemingway is more indebted to Mark Twain than anyone else is"?

EXERCISE

Make up *two* phrases to complete each of the following comparisons. Be prepared to tell which of your phrases is better and why.

1. I have no more chance of passing this course than . . .
2. The imposing leader stood as stiff and straight as . . .

3. This dreary novel has all the dramatic interest of . . .
4. My brother is more dependable than . . .
5. As she left the job interview, she felt the calm, cool confidence of . . .
6. The congressman's explanation was as plausible as . . .
7. The dentist looked at me like . . .
8. If you'd buy an insurance policy from him, you're the kind of person who . . .
9. I haven't had a more hectic day since . . .
10. A tender glance from my sweetheart is more precious to me than . . .
11. I am as likely to date him as I am to . . .
12. The National Parks are as majestic as . . .
13. The police officers chased the speeding car like . . .
14. In my hands the newborn robin felt as fragile as . . .
15. If you would believe that thug's alibi, you would . . .
16. The burning sun made my skin feel like . . .
17. Waiting in line is more boring than . . .
18. This book is even heavier than . . .
19. After his dunk in the lake, my golden retriever was as wet as . . .
20. I trust her so much that I would . . .

EXERCISE

Rephrase the following sentences where necessary.

1. The judge was less harsh on me than my friend.
2. Whitman's beard was more impressive than Tennyson.
3. Legalized abortions arouse stronger emotions than any controversial issue.
4. His gift for sarcasm is like my boss.
5. I owe the IRS more than my friend Rosa.
6. I prefer 7-Up commercials to Coke.
7. Hillary Rodham Clinton's travels have included more countries than Barbara Bush's.
8. Our gross national product is substantially larger than Germany.
9. She was as delightful a sight as the first crocus of spring.
10. *A Chorus Line* had a longer run than any Broadway musical.
11. The incumbent's campaign is more radical than her opponent.
12. This soap opera has more agony per character than any show on television.
13. The fans swarmed around the rock star like bees to honey.
14. His strength was like a lion, his figure like a hippo.
15. The administration's proposal for reducing the deficit is less drastic than the opposition.
16. Howard's kitchen floor was as clean as a whistle.
17. Andrew, I love you more than any man.
18. Fran wanted to see the movie more than her cousin.
19. The leopard is more beautiful and more powerful than any animal.
20. My medical plan is better than my sister's.

21

Effective Sentences

The stylistic considerations we have discussed so far—denotation and connotation, specific details, specific language—require decisions about individual words. In this chapter we consider elements of style more closely related to entire sentences and groups of sentences than to single words.

Wordiness and Economy

Many human individuals use more words in their sentences than are absolutely necessary and essential to express the thoughts and ideas that they (the human individuals) are attempting to communicate. They repeat the same thing constantly and say the same thing over and over again. Sometimes instead of actually repeating themselves they merely substitute various and sundry long phrases for a simple word due to the fact that it is their opinion that readers will be impressed by this writing method of procedure. But in the modern contemporary world of today, good writing should never be wordy. It should be economical; that is, it should say what it has to say, and then stop, cease, and desist.

In case you haven't noticed, the sentences you just read violate all of their own good advice. They contain numerous examples of wordiness: "human individuals" instead of "people," "thoughts and ideas" instead of "thoughts" *or* "ideas," "due to the fact that" instead of "because," "it is their opinion" instead of "they think." The sentences could be cut to half their length without losing anything but a mass of nonfunctioning words:

> Many people use more words than are necessary to express their thoughts. They repeat the same things constantly or substitute long phrases for a simple word because they want to impress their readers. But good writing should never be wordy: It should say what it has to say, and then stop.

Wordiness is a major writing problem. It is hard to avoid because it can turn up for any number of reasons, and writers usually don't realize that they are being wordy. Nobody wants to be a windbag, yet unneeded words sneak into nearly everyone's writing.

Before discussing the different kinds of wordiness, we should clear up one point: Wordiness results from using words that don't do anything—it has no direct connection to the number of words. A poor writer can produce a wordy paragraph on the meaning of freedom; a good writer can produce a whole book on the same subject that is not wordy. If the words contribute to the effect the author wants, if eliminating any of them would sacrifice something valuable, then the author is *not* being wordy. Many pieces of writing with lots of specific details are longer than abstract versions of the same pieces would be, but getting rid of the details would mean a loss of interest and clarity. Only when words can be eliminated without any harm being done do we find real wordiness.

There are four major sources of wordiness: deadwood, pointless repetition of meaning, inadequate clause cutting, and delay of subject.

Deadwood

Some words are like dead wood on a tree or bush—unless they are removed, they sap the strength of the healthy words around them. Moreover, **deadwood** can be removed with little or no tampering with the rest of the sentence, as in the examples that follow.

Deadwood	Improved
His hair was red in color.	His hair was red.
Pollution conditions that exist in our cities are disgraceful.	Pollution in our cities is disgraceful.
The building has a height of 934 feet.	The building rises 934 feet.
She was in a depressed state of mind.	She was depressed.
Disneyland struck us as a fascinating kind of place.	Disneyland struck us as fascinating.
In this day and age we live in, people seem totally apathetic about everything.	People today seem totally apathetic.
The hero of the story was an individual in the high-income bracket.	The hero of the story was wealthy.

Deadwood	Improved
The validity of such statements should not be adhered to.	Such statements are invalid.
He spoke to her in a harsh manner.	He spoke to her harshly.
I am going to major in the field of sociology.	I am going to major in sociology.
The character had a hard type of decision to make.	The character had a hard decision to make.
Because of the fact that my teacher disliked me, he gave me a bad grade.	Because my teacher disliked me, he gave me a bad grade.
Sometimes the moral of a story is a very important factor.	Sometimes the moral of a story is very important.
The story "Silent Snow, Secret Snow," written by the author Conrad Aiken, is a story with an unhappy ending.	"Silent Snow, Secret Snow" by Conrad Aiken is a story with an unhappy ending.

The wise writer is always on the lookout for deadwood, especially during revision. Deadwood infiltrates nearly everyone's first draft, but there is no room for these tiresome words-without-purpose in a finished composition. As a general rule, it is safe to assume that if words can be removed without harming anything—as in the preceding examples—they should be removed.

Pointless Repetition of Meaning

Pointless repetition of meaning is a special kind of deadwood. Aside from adding useless words, such repetition reflects writers' lack of confidence in themselves—their fear that their point will not be clear unless they make it twice. Unfortunately, this overemphasis usually suggests sloppy thinking to the reader, rather than a desire for accuracy.

Pointless repetition	Improved
The film was very interesting and fascinating.	The film was fascinating.
Our streams are filthy and dirty.	Our streams are filthy.
This approach could end in a catastrophic conclusion.	This approach could end catastrophically.
The author gives examples of different and varied criticisms of the novel.	The author gives examples of different criticisms of the novel.
To begin with, in the first place, the story has terrific suspense.	In the first place, the story has terrific suspense.
Some early critics of Jonathan Swift called him an insane madman suffering from the symptoms of mental disease.	Some early critics of Jonathan Swift called him insane.

Pointless repetition	Improved
There is no question about the worth and value of an education.	There is no question about the value of an education.
He has no emotional feelings.	He has no feelings.
Each and every person ought to read a newspaper.	Everyone ought to read a newspaper.
The new administration will make the exact same mistake as the old one.	The new administration will make the same mistake as the old one.

EXERCISE

Point out any instances of deadwood and pointless repetition in the following sentences.

1. At this point in time, we have no travel plans.
2. Depression is a terrible kind of illness.
3. Shari spent many numerous hours perfecting her chess game.
4. We have ignored and neglected the basic fundamental essentials for too long a period of time.
5. Senior citizens, elderly people, get frequent discounts for travel and entertainment expenditures.
6. The name of the game was blackjack, and the name of the dealer was Big Sam.
7. Men and women of both sexes must join the combat to fight for a better world.
8. Rebecca Lobo is an individual who excels in the area of basketball.
9. The man her mother married was a cruel and unkind stepfather to her.
10. All day long, he took forever to make up his mind.
11. A healthful lifestyle can help prevent many different kinds of diseases and illnesses.
12. The class situation stimulates interpersonal communication between students.
13. At the end of the program, the two competing contestants were tied.
14. As far as jewelry is concerned, my favorite jewelry is a simple string of pearls.
15. He disliked me due to the fact that I spoke to him in a sarcastic way.
16. With bright, vivid colors and hues, Georgia O'Keefe made American modern painting a beautiful kind of art.
17. His boorish and unmannerly behavior was condemned by every single individual person.
18. I pledge to oppose the forces of godless atheism and disloyal treason.
19. The documentary was an interesting, fascinating account of one soldier's experience during a time of war.
20. My fellow colleagues and I intend to make a final decision on this tax levy once and for all.

Inadequate Clause Cutting

One of the most effective ways of reducing wordiness is to cut a cumbersome dependent or independent clause into a shorter phrase or, if possible, a single word. This **clause cutting** can result in a tighter, more economical structure, with the phrase or word more firmly incorporated into the sentence than the original clause ever was. Sometimes, of course, a writer may choose to leave the clause alone for a perfectly valid reason, such as emphasis. But more often than not, such clauses are tacked on awkwardly and add unnecessary words; they should always be examined with a critical eye.

Wordy clause	Improved
The woman who had red hair was afraid.	The red-haired woman was afraid.
Some of the students who were more enthusiastic wrote an extra paper.	Some of the more enthusiastic students wrote an extra paper.
The story was very exciting. It was all about ghosts.	The ghost story was very exciting.
Alexander the Great was a man who tried to conquer the world.	Alexander the Great tried to conquer the world.
The applause, which sounded like a thunderclap, shook the auditorium.	The applause shook the auditorium like a thunderclap.
No one who has a child of his or her own can fail to appreciate the charm of this poem.	No parent can fail to appreciate the charm of this poem.
Passionate love is a feeling that has inspired many great writers and artists.	Passionate love has inspired many great writers and artists.
He is an extremely ambitious man; he is scheming to replace his boss.	Extremely ambitious, he is scheming to replace his boss.
The two main characters in the play have similar attitudes toward other people and the way in which each feels about the conventions of society.	The two main characters in the play have similar attitudes toward other people and social conventions.

Delay of Subject

The phrases *there is, there has, it is,* and *it has*—in all tenses—are frequent causes of wordiness. Nothing is wrong with these phrases in themselves; they are necessary parts of the language, and some thoughts might be inexpressible without them. Too often, however, they are used carelessly and delay a sentence or clause from getting down to business. In the following examples, the original sentences begin with words that have no more purpose than the throat-clearing noises made by a speaker before a talk. The revised sentences begin with important words, words that communicate the central concern of each sentence.

Wordy delay	Improved
There are too many people who care only for themselves.	Too many people care only for themselves.
It has often been commented on by great philosophers that philosophy solves nothing.	Great philosophers have often commented that philosophy solves nothing.
There have been a number of conflicting studies made of urban problems.	A number of conflicting studies have been made of urban problems.
It was on December 7, 1941, that the Japanese attacked the U.S. fleet at Pearl Harbor.	On December 7, 1941, the Japanese attacked the U.S. fleet at Pearl Harbor.
It is a fact that there has been a great increase in sensationalism in the theater.	Sensationalism in the theater has greatly increased.

EXERCISE

Rewrite these sentences to make them more economical, cutting clauses and eliminating wordy delay of subject wherever possible.

1. The man who lives next door to me walks his two poodles every morning that it is cool and sunny.
2. The colors of the sunset, which were red, orange, and a rich purple, gave her a feeling that moved her to the brink of tears.
3. There have been many complicated plans that have been proposed to reduce the number of nuclear weapons that are stationed in Europe.
4. Citizens who are both liberal and conservative generally agree that the court system that exists in the United States today needs to be streamlined.
5. Many people who frequently travel by plane may experience some delays, which are caused by new airport security measures.
6. The idea of a guaranteed annual wage is a notion that conflicts with many traditional middle-class values.
7. New crayons, which are made from soybeans, are more environmentally sound than crayons that are made from wax.
8. The painting which Picasso created that is called *Guernica* commemorates the destruction of that city which was caused by Nazi air raids.
9. Recently there have been many opportunities for consumers to make purchases that are good values.
10. Another time, when he was shown the list of the names of the officers who had been appointed to serve under him at the Battle of Waterloo, the Duke commented, "I don't know if they will frighten the French, but, by Gad, they terrify me!"

11. People who do not know any better unthinkingly use chemicals that can be harmful to health on their backyard flowers and vegetables.
12. Emerson had an optimistic philosophy. It probably reflected the spirit of mid-nineteenth-century America.
13. There has been much disagreement among people who produce television programs about giving shows ratings to tell audiences which are programs that contain violence and explicit subject matter.
14. People who play practical jokes are people who are basically insecure.
15. Cars that are made in Germany do not have the reputation for good workmanship that they used to have.
16. It was an agonizingly difficult decision to make.
17. Those arcades where you can find all those computer games are far from being mere teenage hangouts. Many middle-aged gentlemen also spend hours there.
18. There was an eruption for the first time in over seventy years from the Popocatépetl Volcano, which is in Mexico.
19. The team of people who worked at NASA to send the space rover to Mars is celebrating; their mission was a success.
20. On the old television shows and movies of *Star Trek*, Mr. Spock was played by an actor whose name was Leonard Nimoy. Mr. Spock was characterized as a completely rational being.

Passive Verbs

In most English sentences, the subject performs an action.

John likes this poem.

The critic saw the movie.

The senator is going to vote for the bill.

The verb in such sentences is said to be in the **active voice.** The active voice is direct, clear, and concise; in most sentences, it is what we expect.

Too often, however, instead of using the active voice, writers substitute the more stilted **passive voice.** A verb in the passive voice combines a form of *to be* with the past participle of the verb: *is given, has been delivered, was mailed.* Thus, instead of *acting,* the subject of the sentence is *acted upon.*

This poem is liked by John.

The movie was seen by the critic.

The bill is going to be voted for by the senator.

Compared to the active voice, the passive is generally awkward, exceedingly formal, and wordy. It is better to write "This theme will analyze the story" than "The story will be analyzed in this theme." It is better to write "My sociology teacher offered some challenging insights into contemporary problems" than

"Some challenging insights into contemporary problems were offered by my sociology teacher."

On occasion, the passive voice doesn't sound bad, of course. Such occasions may arise when the actor is unknown, insignificant, or nonexistent, or when a deliberately impersonal tone is required. Don't be afraid of the passive when it seems normal and unforced—as in the last part of the preceding sentence—but always be alert to its dangers. Here are a few examples of perfectly acceptable passives:

The game was delayed because of rain.

The eighteenth century has been called the Age of Enlightenment.

Your prompt attention to this request for payment will be appreciated.

The building will be finished in a few months.

We have been victimized time after time.

EXERCISE

Change the passive voice to the active voice wherever appropriate in the following sentences.

1. Six pumpkin pies were devoured in six minutes by Steve.
2. At the corner restaurant, all of the pastries are freshly made each day.
3. The director was convicted of embezzling funds and using the money for herself.
4. The generous check was given to the Democratic National Committee by a small real estate firm.
5. The doctor was advised to get malpractice insurance.
6. The doctor was advised to get malpractice insurance by his lawyer.
7. Don't believe everything that you are told.
8. The victim was pronounced dead on arrival.
9. The victim was pronounced dead on arrival by the coroner.
10. A good time was had by all who attended the cocktail party.
11. The causes of food poisoning are being studied by researchers at Procter and Gamble.
12. Her wicked actions will eventually be punished.
13. Your child should be hugged and kissed by you frequently.
14. Marriages are made in heaven.
15. Legislation to raise taxes is being considered in a joint meeting of the House and Senate.
16. The young couple was married by their favorite minister.
17. Two suspects were interrogated by Officer Wesley.
18. The ball was hit into the bleachers, where it conked an unsuspecting hot dog vendor on the head.
19. The course syllabus was handed out by Professor Sharp and was read by all of the students.
20. Cassie's punishment is being discussed by her parents.

Faulty Parallelism

Essentially, **parallelism** means expressing ideas and facts of equal (or coordinate or "parallel") importance in the same grammatical form. We do it all the time, almost unconsciously.

The store was filled with *chairs, tables, sofas,* and *lamps.*	(a group of four nouns)
He came *home, ate dinner,* and *went to bed.*	(three verb phrases)
You can get there by *car, bus,* or *plane.*	(three nouns)
I thought the climactic episode in the story was *shocking, offbeat,* and *amusing.*	(three adjectives)

Parallel grammatical structure reinforces a writer's thoughts by stressing the parallel importance of the various sentence elements, and so makes life easier for the reader. Many of the most famous phrases in our language draw strength in part from effective use of parallelism:

. . . *life, liberty,* and the *pursuit* of happiness.	(group of three nouns)
. . . *of the people, by the people,* and *for the people.*	(three prepositional phrases)
Love me or *leave me.*	(two imperatives)
Early *to bed* and early *to rise* / Makes a man *healthy,* and *wealthy,* and *wise.*	(two infinitives/three adjectives)
To be or not *to be.*	(two infinitives)
Friends, Romans, countrymen . . .	(three nouns)
I come *to bury Caesar,* not *to praise him.*	(two infinitives with objects)
I came, I saw, I conquered.	(three independent clauses)
Better be *safe* than *sorry.*	(two adjectives)
. . . *the land of the free* and *the home of the brave.*	(two nouns, each with a prepositional phrase)

Now notice how faulty parallelism or lack of parallelism can sabotage a sentence.

You can get there by *car, bus,* or *fly.*	(two nouns, and suddenly a verb)
I thought the climactic episode in the story was *shocking, offbeat,* and *I found it very amusing.*	(two adjectives, coupled with an independent clause)
The teacher told us *to work fast* and *that we should write on only one side of the paper.*	(shift from infinitive to clause)
She *liked* people and *was liked* by people.	(shift from active to passive voice)

| Bill was a *good husband*, a *loving father*, and *worked hard*. | (adjective–noun, adjective–noun, verb–adverb) |

Descriptive words added to some of the parallel elements do not break the basic parallelism and can be valuable in avoiding monotony.

Judith had *brains*, *talent*, and an extremely charming *personality*.	(still parallel: a group of three nouns, even though one is modified by an adjective, and the adjective is modified by an adverb)
The man owned a *mansion* and a fine *collection* of modern etchings.	(still parallel: two nouns, even though one of them is modified by an adjective and followed by a prepositional phrase)
The baby has now learned how to *whimper*, *shriek*, *yell* loudly, and *cry* its head off.	(still parallel: four infinitives, even though one is modified by an adverb and one is followed by an object)

Parallelism, then, is an indispensable aid to style and meaning, but keep in mind that its value is limited to cases in which the various elements are of equal importance. If we try to parallel unequal elements, we can wind up with startling calamities, unless we are being intentionally humorous:

She had wealth, vitality, sophistication, and a short nose.

The story offers a profound message of inspiration and hope to humanity and occupies pages 152 to 170 of our textbook.

My friend John is a revolutionary activist and a former Cub Scout.

We must all work together to eliminate war, disease, hunger, and dirty movies.

EXERCISE

Which of the following sentences use faulty parallelism? Which use parallelism correctly? Which use inappropriate parallelism? Make corrections in the sentences that need them.

1. He enjoys cooking, writing, and antique stores.
2. Some day I will go mountain climbing, parasailing, and buy a boat.
3. Clothing with some fashionable brand name or symbol on the outside is tasteless and a ridiculous expense.
4. The principal said the main issues were discipline, academic achievement, and good attendance at the pep rally.
5. The book *The Joy Luck Club* was insightful, poignant, and appealed to many audiences.
6. Percy Bysshe Shelley wrote some of the greatest poems in the English language, lived a spectacularly scandalous private life, and had a weird middle name.

7. The trip sounds expensive, exhausting, and a truly enjoyable experience.
8. Steven Yip's résumé shows that he is hardworking, responsible, and an experienced manager.
9. Alfred Hitchcock had a nearly unbroken record of directing films that were suspenseful, original, and great successes.
10. The assignment was difficult but a great challenge.
11. Magazines, newspapers, and reading books are some waiting-room pastimes.
12. I need a break, and a break is needed by Ann, too.
13. Jean's kitten is scrawny, dirty, and bites other cats.
14. I believe in hard work and getting fair compensation.
15. Children's cartoons rot the brain, create violence, and produce eyestrain.
16. I have always thought Chad was cute, funny, and a good person to have around.
17. My sister's doctor told her to eat a lot of leafy vegetables, fruits, and not to smoke.
18. Faith, hope, and charity are three classic virtues.
19. Julia Child's cookbook contains recipes for elaborate hors d'oeuvres, delicious entrées, and exquisite desserts.
20. The dress was shockingly expensive, but an exquisite creation.

Faulty Subordination and Sentence Combining

Which of the following observations on that great new epic movie, *The Return of the Hideous Vampire*, is likely to be most significant?

It was produced by Paramount Brothers.

It is one of the best horror movies of the last ten years.

It was filmed in Technicolor.

Which of these facts about Earnest N. Dogood deserves the most emphasis?

He is a Republican.

He has announced his candidacy for president of the United States.

He is a senator.

The answers are obvious; in both cases, the second item is the one you should have chosen. Neither set of statements would be appropriate as a list of parallel thoughts—because ideas and facts are not all created equal. This simple truth has tremendous consequences for our writing.

If we tried to present all the information we have as if it really were of equal, parallel importance, we would probably wind up with a form of baby talk. At one time or another, many of us have probably had to suffer through a young child's account of a movie or television show. To the child, everything is supremely fascinating. Distinctions between major and minor episodes mean nothing, and the child can easily make a plot summary seem to last as long as the show itself:

> First the cowboy woke up and he got dressed and then he went downstairs and he got on his horse and his horse's name was Big Boy and then he rode off on his horse to fight the bad guy.

Note that the child gives equal emphasis to all the facts by expressing each one as an independent clause, a unit that can stand alone as a separate sentence: "the cowboy woke up, he got dressed, he ate," and so on. This equality is further stressed by the use of *and* to tie the clauses together. The word *and* simply links new ingredients to a sentence or phrase—it doesn't help the reader decide which ingredient is more significant ("ham and eggs," "boys and girls," "war and peace," for example). Essentially, the problem with the cowboy story is that important facts are forced to compete for our attention with relatively trivial ones.

Instead of giving equal weight to each fact, then, and creating a monotonous stream of unfiltered data, a skillful writer will **subordinate** some of those facts, arranging the sentence or paragraph so that some parts are clearly secondary to others. This process is sometimes called **sentence combining.**

> After waking up, eating, going downstairs, and getting on his horse, Big Boy, the cowboy rode off to fight the bad guy.

We certainly have no specimen of prize-winning prose here, but we don't have the total mess we started out with either. This revision contains only one independent clause—"the cowboy rode off to fight the bad guy"—and that clause contains the most important fact. None of the other independent clauses in the original sentence survives. They have all been subordinated grammatically and no longer clamor for the reader's primary attention.

Look again at the beginning of this section on subordination. We have three pieces of information about a movie. The writer with no sense of subordination merely smacks down each point as it comes to mind, without attempting to differentiate between major and minor items, giving each item a sentence to itself.

> *The Return of the Hideous Vampire* was produced by Paramount Brothers. It is one of the best horror movies of the last ten years. It was filmed in Technicolor.

By contrast, with proper subordination the writer collects the three related observations, reserves the independent clause for the most important one, and tucks away the rest in a less conspicuous place.

> *The Return of the Hideous Vampire,* a Technicolor film produced by Paramount Brothers, is one of the best horror movies of the last ten years.

We can see the same principle at work with the sentences about Earnest N. Dogood that begin this section.

Unsubordinated	Subordinated
Earnest N. Dogood is a Republican. He has announced his candidacy for president of the United States. He is a senator.	Senator Earnest N. Dogood, a Republican, has announced his candidacy for president of the United States.

Remember that related ideas can often be combined in a way that shows their relationships more clearly. Remember, too, that an independent clause, whether it stands alone as a single sentence or is incorporated into a complex sentence, is a loud cry for attention and should generally be saved for matters of importance.

Here are a few examples of how subordination can improve writing:

Unsubordinated	Subordinated
Jane is a wonderful person. She is very shy. She is extremely kind to everybody.	Although very shy, Jane is a wonderful person who is extremely kind to everybody.
	or
	Although she is a wonderful person who is extremely kind to everybody, Jane is very shy.
This play explores the fate of love in a mechanized society. It is highly symbolic, and it has two acts.	This highly symbolic play of two acts explores the fate of love in a mechanized society.
Professor Jones is terribly sarcastic. He is also a tough grader. It is true that he knows his subject. Most students dislike him, however.	Despite Professor Jones's knowledge of his subject, most students dislike him because of his terrible sarcasm and tough grading.

EXERCISE

Rewrite the following sentences, making effective use of subordination.

1. Some scientists are skeptical about life on other planets. Astronomers calculate that there are many Earth-like planets. Some evidence exists that microbes once survived on Mars.
2. He is an ignorant young man. He is boorish. He is ugly. He is cheap. Why did I say "yes" when he asked me to go to the party?
3. Cape Cod is crowded. It's overcommercialized. It's expensive. I love it.
4. Maine is nicer than Cape Cod in many ways. It is much farther away, however. The water is also too cold for swimming.
5. *Contact* is a movie about an astronomer who communes with extraterrestrial life. Jodie Foster plays the astonomer. The movie is based on a book by Carl Sagan.

6. Jill was going up the hill to fetch a pail of water, and Jack was helping her. Then Jack fell down.

7. Bicycle riding is an exhilarating and challenging sport. It is also great exercise. It tones muscles. It builds stamina.

8. Some people don't like the city. I enjoy the great variety of restaurants. I also enjoy strolling down busy sidewalks. I like to watch the sea of faces bobbing past me.

9. It was sad to hear him say such harsh things about poor people. He had once been poor himself.

10. My uncle will never give up his dream of making a killing on the stock market. All his investments have been bad so far, and people laugh at him constantly.

11. Good writing does not happen by accident. Inexperienced writers believe in inspiration. Professionals know that good writing requires hard work.

12. Everything I like to eat is fattening. Everything I like to eat is also unhealthy. I know I should eat more salads and fresh vegetables. I hate them, however. I don't think I will ever be able to change.

13. "Ping-pong" is a childish name for a real sport. It shows that most Americans look down on it. The grown-up name is "table tennis." It is a sport that is taken seriously almost everywhere else in the world, and it is played with great skill and ferocity.

14. Late September is a great time to go apple picking in the Northeast. Driving to the orchards is beautiful. The foliage is spectacular. The apples are sweet and juicy.

15. My mother is a bundle of nerves. My mother is afraid of dark rooms. She also fears insects. Some of her other fears are directed toward heights, dogs, door-to-door salespeople, and doctors.

16. Watching golf on television is silly. You can't see anything. The tiny golf balls are invisible as they fly through the air. It's boring, too.

17. Most Texans know what to do in case of a tornado. They have endured more tornadoes in the last forty years than any other state.

18. People are always mocking my dream of being a star of the NBA. I'm five feet tall. I can't dribble. I am determined to succeed.

19. Cinderella went to the ball. Her coach turned back into a pumpkin at midnight. She danced with a prince. She lost a shoe.

20. Sara just got a golden labrador retriever. He is the color of honey. He is just ten weeks old. He is not yet trained. Sara thinks he knows his name already since he comes when she calls, "Tyler!"

Sentence Monotony and Variety

Readers frequently find themselves struggling to concentrate on a string of sentences even though nothing obvious seems to be wrong. Sentence by sentence, in fact, the author may be writing perfectly well. Put the sentences together, though, and monotony sets in. The monotony can usually be attributed either to a series of sentences that are all, or nearly all, of the same *length* or the same *structure.*

Sentence Length

Sentences come short, medium, and long—and the simple principle for effective writing is to try for variety. Don't take this principle more rigidly than it's intended. Don't assume, for instance, that every single short sentence must be followed by a long one, and vice versa. A string of short or long sentences can sometimes be effective, providing that it is eventually followed by a sentence that varies the pattern. Common sense and alertness will tell you when variety is needed. Just remember that too many sentences of the same length bunched together can create a monotonous style and a restless reader.

Monotonous	Improved
He told us the car got good mileage. He said the tires were excellent. The engine was supposed to be quiet. The transmission was supposed to be smooth. He stressed that the brake linings still had plenty of wear. Everything he said was a lie.	He told us the car got good mileage and that it had excellent tires, a quiet engine, a smooth transmission, and sound brake linings. In other words, he lied.
I thought the course was going to be easy, but I was wrong, because after a two-week sickness early in the term I could never find the time to catch up with the assignments, and I kept getting poor grades. I wish I had had the foresight to see what was coming and had taken the initiative either to drop the course or to ask the teacher for an incomplete, but pride or vanity kept me plugging away, and nothing did any good.	I thought the course was going to be easy, but I was wrong. After a two-week sickness early in the term, I could never find the time to catch up with the assignments, and I kept getting poor grades. Why didn't I drop? Why didn't I ask for an incomplete? If I'd known for sure what was coming, I probably would have done one or the other. Pride or vanity kept me plugging away, however, and nothing did any good.

Sentence Structure

Regardless of sentence length, a group of sentences can become monotonous because each sentence uses the same basic structure. All the sentences may begin with a present participle (*-ing* endings), for example, or the first word of each sentence may always be the subject of the sentence, or the first word may never be the subject. Perhaps every sentence turns out to be a compound sentence (two or more independent clauses) or a complex sentence (one independent clause and one or more dependent clauses). Now forget about the grammatical terms. Remember only that there are many different ways of structuring a sentence, and wise writers never limit themselves to one method. Variety is again the key.

Monotonous	Improved
Entering the personnel manager's office, Bill wanted to make a good impression. Smiling, he shook hands. Sitting down, he tried not to fidget. Answering the questions politely, he kept his voice low and forced himself not to say "uh." Being desperate for a job, he had to be at his best. Wondering if his desperation showed, he decided to risk a little joke.	Entering the personnel manager's office, Bill wanted to make a good impression. He smiled, shook hands, and tried not to fidget when he sat down. He answered questions politely, keeping his voice low and forcing himself not to say "uh." Bill was desperate for a job. He had to be at his best. Wondering if his desperation showed, he decided to risk a little joke.
Red wine goes best with meat, and white wine goes best with fish. Red wine should be served at room temperature, and white wine should be chilled. Red wine should usually be opened about a half hour before serving, and the accumulated gases should be allowed to escape from the bottle. These rules are not meaningless customs, but they are proven by centuries of experience, and they improve the taste of the food as well as the wine.	Red wine goes best with meat, and white wine goes best with fish. Unlike white wine, which should be served chilled, red wine should be served at room temperature. Red wine also benefits from being opened about a half hour before serving to allow the accumulated gases to escape from the bottle. Proven by experience, these rules improve the taste of the food as well as the wine. They are not meaningless customs.

EXERCISE

The following groups of sentences are monotonous. Rewrite them to add greater variety in sentence length and structure.

1. I tried to bake a cheesecake using my father's recipe, but it came out terrible, probably because I didn't have all the ingredients I needed so I substituted some things I had in the house. I should have realized that when a recipe calls for sugar, honey may not serve the same purpose, but unfortunately this did not occur to me until after my cheesy mess came out of the oven, and by that time it was too late to make another dessert before my dinner guests arrived.
2. Tired and bored, I gazed vacantly out the window. Energetic and powerful, a robin dug for worms. Cheerful and bright, a cardinal chirped melodiously in a treetop. Ashamed and humbled, I watched their total involvement in life.

3. Certificates of deposit from local banks are insured by a federal agency, so they are extremely safe investments, but your money is tied up in them for long periods of time unless you are willing to accept stiff penalties for early withdrawal, and they also do not always pay particularly high rates of interest. You may find it more beneficial to invest in a conservative mutual fund specializing in government bonds, which will give you great safety, too, but it also offers excellent returns on your money and permits you to withdraw money by check any time you wish.

4. I love Christmas, but it can be a nerve-racking experience. The tree is gorgeous, but getting it to stand up straight is always a struggle. Gift-giving and gift-getting are great, but Christmas shopping can be a terrible chore. The festive spirit is great, too, but excessive eating and drinking gets me down after a while. Visits from long-lost relatives can also be fun, but I confess that I'm always glad to see them go.

5. Eager to begin their vacation, the family loaded the station wagon. Filled with enthusiasm, they drove for twenty-five minutes. Shocked by the sudden failure of the engine, they pulled the car to the side of Interstate 90. Horrified at their poor planning, they realized they had forgotten to fill the tank with gas.

6. The Nelsons' living room reflects their love of antiques. Hanging on the wall is a portrait from nineteenth-century England. Lying on the couch is a patchwork quilt from the 1700s. Standing in the corner is a Queen Anne's style chair. Resting on the table is a mother-of-pearl box from Mrs. Nelson's great-grandmother.

7. Going shopping with my sister is lots of fun. Walking around the mall, we go into almost every store. Making decisions is easier with her along, too. Keeping each other from buying useless or silly items is part of our game plan.

8. If you mow the lawn, I will plant some flowers. If I plant some flowers, Maurice will stake the tomatoes. If Maurice stakes the tomatoes, Shannon will prune the roses. If Shannon prunes the roses, Brad will weed the vegetable patch.

9. Recycling cans, glass, paper, and plastic is very important for the human race because if we keep making more trash we will run out of places to put it, and then we will suffocate ourselves and our planet under piles of junk. Don't let this happen because it would be a terrible tragedy, and all we have to do to prevent it is remember to recycle.

10. Esteban's phone rings constantly. Sometimes it is his friends. Sometimes it is his colleagues. Sometimes it is his softball teammates. Sometimes it is telephone marketing salespeople.

CHAPTER
22

Additional Notes on Style: Problems and Solutions

We discussed individual word choices in Chapter 20 and effective sentences in Chapter 21. In a sense, style has to be a matter of words and sentences, of course, but some issues are best approached from a wider perspective. Writers who frequently use trite expressions or sexist language, for example, are not merely creating ineffective sentences but are creating an image of themselves in the reader's mind that can have a far more devastating impact than a wordy phrase or an error in parallelism. Writers who overindulge themselves in showing off large vocabularies or familiarity with current slang can antagonize a reader and risk ruining a whole essay. In this chapter, we define and describe these problems and others that are most likely to arise so that you can either avoid them completely or recognize and correct them if they do appear in your writing. We also explain which of these stylistic elements can serve a valid purpose when used consciously and carefully.

Triteness

A **trite expression,** or **cliché,** is a word or phrase that has become worn out through overuse. Many trite expressions may once have been original and even brilliant, but through constant repetition they have lost whatever impact they once had. If a writer uses many trite expressions, a reader may be tempted to assume that the thoughts are as secondhand as the language.

Triteness generally calls attention to itself in some way. Words like *the, a, man, woman, come, go* are not trite even though they are used all the time, because they are simple, direct, and unself-conscious. Trite expressions are pretentious. They seem, on the surface, to convey a thought or feeling particularly well, and people who haven't read enough to recognize them sometimes think them clever, or elegant, or lively. Experienced readers, however, interpret them for what they usually are—evidence of a writer's laziness and lack of imagination.

The best way to handle triteness is to eliminate it. Apologetic little quotation marks do not help. If the writer has been trite, quotation marks call more attention to the fault and let the reader know that the triteness was no accident.

The following list contains a number of trite expressions. Avoid them. Choose ten from the list and try to think of original and effective ways to express the same ideas.

Trite expressions

more fun than a barrel of monkeys	dumb as an ox
worth its weight in gold	meaningful dialog
over the hill	turned on
stop on a dime	red as a rose
fresh as a daisy	tired but happy
happy as a lark	a good time was had by all
hard as nails	white as snow
have someone in a corner	black as pitch
make a long story short	put it in a nutshell
no use crying over spilled milk	Mother Nature
a penny saved is a penny earned	Father Time
cool as a cucumber	spread like wildfire
pretty as a picture	the crack of dawn
in the pink	spring chicken
hale and hearty	dog-eat-dog
apple-pie order	survival of the fittest
under the weather	every cloud has a silver lining
devil-may-care attitude	sick as a dog
go at it tooth and nail	work like a dog
generation gap	easy as pie
broaden one's horizons	sweet as sugar
peer pressure	quick as a wink
do unto others	quick as a flash
flat as a pancake	greased lightning

Trite expressions (continued)

tender loving care	a matter of life and death
sly as a fox	male chauvinist pig
stubborn as a mule	a bolt from the blue
rat race	father of his country
Old Glory	signed, sealed, and delivered
trial and error	open-and-shut case
struggle for existence	flash in the pan
the bigger they are the harder they fall	babe in the woods
sad but true	not a cloud in the sky
south of the border	feathered friends
armed to the teeth	slow as molasses
lean and lanky	do your own thing
flattery will get you nowhere	last but not least

In addition to these phrases, some familiar—and important—ideas have been expressed in the same language so often that the ideas themselves seem trite unless they are worded differently. No matter how much we believe in the need for stable human relationships, we are not going to get very excited when someone tells us "People must learn to get along with one another." If we are presenting one of these ideas, we must express it in a dramatic, forceful way, or at least show that we do not regard it as a profound new insight. Here is a partial list of such potentially trite ideas:

The older generation has made a mess of things.

A good marriage involves more than sex.

Getting to know people of different backgrounds is a good thing.

College is more difficult than high school.

Pollution is a major problem in the United States.

Education is necessary for many jobs.

We live in a technological society.

This problem could have been avoided by better communication.

This problem will be solved by better communication.

We need to think more about people who are less fortunate.

It is possible to have different opinions about a poem.

Nature is beautiful.

Adults have more responsibilities than children.

This issue is very complicated.

Euphemisms

A **euphemism** is a word or phrase used as a polite substitute for a more natural but less refined word or phrase. Euphemisms can be handy to have around, especially in social situations. Chances are that the parents of Suzy or Jerry will be more comfortable to hear that their child is "not working up to full capacity" than to be told that their child is "lazy." Chances are that a widow will find her grief easier to bear if we say, "I was so sorry to hear about Fred," and thoughtfully omit the unpleasant medical details.

As a rule, though, euphemisms should be avoided, especially in writing. They generally seem pretentious, fussy, and old-fashioned. They can make writers appear afraid to face facts or to say what they mean. The natural, honest word is usually the best one, so long as honesty is not confused with exhibitionistic crudeness or vulgarity. In most cases, then, avoid writing both "He passed on to a better world" and "He croaked." Try instead "He died."

Euphemisms	Honest terms
low-income individual	poor person
urban poverty area	slum
sanitation worker	trash collector
custodian *or* superintendent	janitor
mortician *or* funeral director	undertaker
conflict	war
distortion of the facts	lie
casualties	dead and wounded
senior citizen	old person
powder one's nose	go to the bathroom
financially embarrassed	in debt
reconditioned	used
to pass on	to die

EXERCISE

Locate the trite expressions and euphemisms in the following sentences and suggest alternatives.

1. He had once established a meaningful relationship with a member of the fair sex, but time flies, and she moved on to greener pastures.
2. Finally realizing that life was not a bowl of cherries, he decided to get down to business.

3. When the senior citizen stepped into the street and began walking as slow as molasses, I had to stop my car on a dime to avoid an unfortunate incident.
4. The male chauvinist pig said that a woman's place is in the home.
5. Excessive ingestion can significantly increase adipose tissue.
6. To get to the bottom line, Boris was informed that he would have to remit payment or face incarceration.
7. The army executed a strategic withdrawal.
8. It made my blood boil to hear that officers of the law were accused of assaulting an unarmed gentleman who was as helpless as a kitten.
9. The powder room at the gas station was a sight for sore eyes.
10. Mr. Fong's immediate superior told him that his services would no longer be required.
11. Many years of substance abuse had made the former star of stage and screen as helpless as a newborn baby.
12. We live in a dog-eat-dog world.
13. Feeling sick as a dog, I thumbed through a weekly publication and waited to see my health care professional.
14. In order to broaden her horizons and achieve her goals, Victoria decided to enter an institution of higher learning.
15. After eating enough to feed an army, Miguel suffered from stomach distress.
16. Mrs. Chung's recent generous donations to various philanthropic organizations suggested that she was rolling in dough.
17. The unruly child screamed like a banshee and ran around like a bull in a china shop, his face turning beet red and his hair sticking up in all directions.
18. The adolescent male's parental units told him to shape up or ship out.
19. Gina's hair is jet black, her skin is smooth as silk, and her evening gown fits her like a glove, but she doesn't hold a candle to my betrothed.
20. The firms need some new blood, so they will employ several up-and-coming young lawyers.

Repetition, Good and Bad

Repetition can help or hurt your writing depending on how it is used. When used to add clarity or dramatic impact, repetition is a major stylistic resource. At other times, however, repetition can interfere with good style, and writers need to be aware of its dangers.

Repetition for Clarity

Repetition can help to clarify meaning and get the writer and reader from one sentence or clause to another. One of the simplest and most valuable transitional devices for a writer is the repetition of a key word or phrase, sometimes in slightly altered form, from a preceding sentence or clause:

> Five drug *companies* have been accused of misleading advertising. The first of these *companies* is. . . .

> Critics tend to make too much of a fuss about *symbols*. *Symbols* are not obscure artistic tricks. Our own daily lives are filled with *symbols*.

> Few people want to be thought of as extremely *conventional*, but respect for *conventions* of some sort is necessary for any society to function adequately.

Repetition for Impact

Repetition can often add effective dramatic impact, as in the following examples.

> We've shrugged at scandals. We've shrugged at violence. We've shrugged at overpopulation and pollution and discrimination. Now it's time to stop shrugging.

> When she lost her husband, she lost her friend, lost her lover, lost her confidant. She lost everything that had given meaning to her life.

> The decision must be made this week—not this year, not this month, not early next week, but this week.

If not handled skillfully and tastefully, repetition for impact can also lead to foolish emotionalism or unnecessary stress on the obvious:

> Must cruel developers have their way forever? What of the flowers? What of the trees? What of the grass? What of the homeless birds and squirrels and bunnies?

> There is too much violence on television. Bang, bang, bang, bang, bang—that's all we ever hear. Bang, bang, bang.

Undesirable Repetition of Meaning

Avoid restating a point that is already sufficiently clear. For example:

> The American flag is red, white, and blue *in color.*

> She was remarkably beautiful. *She was, in fact, quite exceptionally good-looking.*

> The effect *and outcome* of all this was most unfortunate.

> In today's *modern contemporary* world . . . .

(See the discussion of wordiness in Chapter 21, pages 564-570.)

Undesirable Repetition of the Same Word

Although repetition of a word or word form can help to clarify a point or serve as a transitional device, if used too often it can become monotonous and irritating.

This is especially true if the word itself is not crucial to the meaning of the passage; words such as *very, really,* and *interesting* are major offenders.

> I am *very* pleased to be here on this *very* distinguished occasion. Your *very* kind remarks and your *very* generous gift have left me *very* much at a loss for words, but *very* deeply appreciative.

> I *really* enjoyed reading this story. It was a *really* exciting story with *real* people in *real* situations. The suspense was *really* terrific.

> We had a *wonderful* time in Florida. During the day we went swimming, and at night we saw some *really interesting* shows. The weather was great, the food was *really* just *wonderful,* and the sights were *very interesting.*

Beware of using different forms of the same word through carelessness. The result can be an awkward and confusing sentence.

> We had a *wonderful* time seeing the *wonders* of Florida.

> The *beauties* of Shakespeare's sonnets are outstandingly *beautiful.*

> People must be made more *aware* of the need for increased *awareness* of our environment.

One more menace to watch out for is repetition of words in the same sentence, or otherwise close together, if there is a change in the meaning of the word. Never commit this particular crime unless you are trying to be intentionally humorous.

> Only a perfect *dope* would experiment with *dope.*

> If I *run* hard, my nose will *run.*

> Our weekly games of *bridge* have helped to build a friendly *bridge* of understanding between our two families.

Undesirable Repetition of Sounds

Save rhymes for poetry. Avoid horrors like these:

> The condemnation of the administration was brought about by its own lack of ability and student hostility.

> The church is reexamining its position on the condition of the mission.

> The Allied troops' defensive stance stopped the German advance into France.

Go easy on **alliteration,** the repetition of sounds at the beginning of words. Every once in a while, alliteration can be effective, but when a writer is obviously pouring it on, the results are silly at best.

> We must toss these sneering, snickering, swindling swine out of office.

> The orchestra's bold blowing of the brasses thrilled me to the bottom of my being.

> The main piece of furniture in the room was a dirty, damaged, dilapidated, and dreary old desk.

EXERCISE

Point out any undesirable repetition in the following sentences and make the necessary corrections.

1. Endless streams of tourists threaten to ruin our state's rivers, brooks, and streams.
2. Henry's mother stated that the state of his room was terrible.
3. Let's not bring up that argument anymore. Let's never discuss it again.
4. Despite efforts to forget, I find that the mind will remind us of our errors.
5. I am sure that avarice adds fuel to his already active aspirations for advancement.
6. I asked her to marry me, and she said yes. She said yes!
7. A burglar stole Mrs. Plutocratz's jewelry and mink stole.
8. The tragic death of Princess Diana—a truly extraordinary figure—truly shocked the world and made us truly cherish the memory of all that she truly was.
9. Too many pollutants now pollute our air and water.
10. The carpenter has such energy and drive that it's a pleasure just to watch him drive a nail into a piece of wood.
11. At this point in time I am looking for an assistant.
12. Bill Hawkins was a tragic figure—tragic in school, tragic in business, tragic in marriage, tragic in life.
13. Angela Donaldson's dreadful, disastrous decision still depresses and dismays her devoted fans.
14. The president squandered and foolishly spent the company's money until he had to declare bankruptcy.
15. The invitation to the afternoon seminar sounded so inviting that Mr. and Mrs. Keating decided on treating themselves to another meeting.
16. I love you, my love, with a love that surpasses the love of all the greatest lovers in history.
17. The fantastic fragrance of the field filled with wildflowers made me feel faint.
18. It seems that Professor Reames had great dreams.
19. Miles Davis is a jazz musician with great musical talent.
20. The food was vile, and the company was violent.

Slang

A carefully chosen, appropriate **slang** expression can sometimes add interest and liveliness to writing. It can be helpful in establishing a humorous or casual tone. More significantly, in a few cases, it can suggest an attitude or a shade of meaning that a more conventional expression could not. By and large, however, slang is inappropriate for the comparatively formal, analytical writing that college courses most often demand. But when you feel sure that a slang expression can genuinely communicate something you would not otherwise be able to convey as well, don't be afraid to use it. When you do use it, avoid the coy quotation marks that some writers put around slang to show that they are really sophisticated people who could use more formal language if they wanted to. Good slang should seem natural, and if it is natural, it doesn't need quotes.

> Once thought of as the intellectual leader of a generation, Thompson turned out to be just another jerk with the gift of gab.
>
> Billed as a luxury resort, the hotel was a high-priced dump.
>
> I don't think I'll ever be able to forget the creepy old busybody who used to live next door to us.

Be careful about using slang, however. Don't use it to show how up-to-date you are; slang changes so fast that what seemed current yesterday is often embarrassingly old-fashioned tomorrow. Don't use slang to show your reader what a folksy person you are; that technique almost always fails. Avoid crude sentences like these:

> In *Hamlet,* Hamlet's girlfriend, Ophelia, goes nuts.
>
> This profound political allegory really turned me on.
>
> Albert Einstein was one of the big brains of the twentieth century.

Fancy Writing

For every writer who uses slang to show off, there are probably a dozen who show off by habitually using big or unfamiliar words. A large vocabulary is an asset for any writer, of course, but that fancy word or phrase should be used only when it adds something valuable to tone or meaning that a more familiar word or phrase could not add. If the familiar word will do the job as well, use it; the unfamiliar word will seem stilted and pretentious. (See the discussion of jargon on page 596.)

Fancy	Improved
Many of our new buildings suffer from inadequate fenestration.	Many of our new buildings have too few windows.
Some of the water we drink is insalubrious.	Some of the water we drink is unhealthy.
They raised their hands in the time-honored gesture of respect to the emblem of their nation's sovereignty.	They saluted their country's flag.

Fancy	Improved
Charles Dickens's novelistic achievements are veritably unrivaled in English letters.	Charles Dickens wrote better novels than any other English writer.
We require an augmentation of interpersonal communications on substantive issues.	We need to talk more to each other about important issues.

Be particularly careful about mixing slang and fancy writing unless you are deliberately trying for a humorous effect. Tuxedos and sweatshirts are both wearable articles of clothing, but they do not go well together.

Poor mix	Improved
Also listed as available options on this formidable contender for car-of-the-year honors are cruise control, power sunroof, tape deck, and zillions of other gizmos.	Also listed as available options on this formidable contender for car-of-the-year honors are cruise control, power sunroof, tape deck, and a host of other luxuries.
With its vulgarity masquerading as wit, its tired stereotypes masquerading as characters, and its disjointed episodes masquerading as plot, this new play is totally yucky.	With its vulgarity masquerading as wit, its tired stereotypes masquerading as characters, and its disjointed episodes masquerading as plot, this new play is a dismal failure.

EXERCISE

Correct any inappropriate use of slang or fancy writing in the following sentences.

1. The cacophony emanating from the foyer indicated to us an altercation among our offspring.
2. Good writers eschew prolixity.
3. Through all the vicissitudes of life, Benjamin Franklin kept his cool.
4. Alcoholism is manifestly a serious sociological phenomenon, but, hey, a few snorts now and then don't do any harm.
5. Little Billy became lachrymose when his mother turned off the boob tube.
6. Formidable though his contributions be to British letters, D. H. Lawrence sometimes acted like an airhead.
7. My antiquated automobile may appear dilapidated, but this baby's going to last.
8. Many liberal policy makers concur with welfare recipients who express sentiments indicating their desire to obtain employment as long as it isn't flipping burgers at some burger joint.
9. Eben is feeling positively leonine.
10. Off the concert stage, Artur Rubinstein was not above indulging in some nutty shenanigans.

11. The mobster's hortatory remarks were intended to placate his minions but only exacerbated long-simmering tensions.
12. Anthony Trollope's novels are generally distinguished by tough-minded realism, but even Trollope gets corny sometimes.
13. The team's preseason Herculean exertions to establish a running game have proven ephemeral.
14. If the object of your scrutiny is not in need of remediation, it is not desirable to activate remedial modes of operation.
15. My previous employer was a birdbrain.
16. My colleague's perpetual obsequiousness makes me want to toss my cookies.
17. *Vanity Fair* is a wicked cool novel.
18. The vocalist's melodious utterances lulled me into a slumber.
19. After I have performed my matutinal ablutions, we can promenade on the greensward.
20. Geometry is difficult, but interesting. Algebra is the pits.

Sexist Language

Sexist language is language that displays prejudice and stereotyped thinking about the roles, character, and worth of both sexes, though women have most frequently been its victims. Avoiding sexist language is a moral issue, of course — the sexist bigot is no more appealing than the racial, religious, or ethnic bigot. It is also a stylistic issue because language reflects social realities, and habits of language may continue long after the social realities have changed. Sexist language is sometimes more the product of habit than of intention.

To prevent or eliminate sexist language, pay particular attention to the following suggestions.

■ *Avoid stereotypes in occupations.* The notion of distinctive man's work and woman's work has by and large become outdated.

Sexist language	Improved
A nuclear physicist needs to take his environmental responsibilities seriously.	Nuclear physicists need to take their environmental responsibilities seriously.
Adele is hoping to become a policeman.	Adele is hoping to become a police officer.
Carla Rodriguez is an outstanding lady doctor.	Carla Rodriguez is an outstanding doctor.
Our file clerk quit yesterday, and we need a new woman for the job.	Our file clerk quit yesterday, and we need to find someone new for the job.

■ *Avoid stereotypes in character and social behavior.* Not all women giggle, gossip, and want to have babies any more than all men swear, drink beer, and overdose on football.

Sexist language	Improved
A good cook always seems to have a secret recipe for her Thanksgiving stuffing.	A good cook always seems to have a secret recipe for Thanksgiving stuffing.
The wise shopper can save real money by remembering to use her coupons.	The wise shopper can save real money by remembering to use coupons.
Her woman's heart melted when she saw her new grandson.	Her heart melted when she saw her new grandson.

■ *Avoid insulting and condescending language.* Some sexist words are obvious insults and easy enough to recognize: *babes, dames, dolls, broads,* and the like. Other words and phrases masquerade as affectionate tributes or compliments but can, in fact, be extremely patronizing: *the fair sex, the gentle sex, my better half, girl* (when used to describe a grown woman), and so on. Avoid both types.

Sexist language	Improved
When Jenny left the company, it was hard to find another girl to replace her.	When Jenny left the company, it was hard to find anyone to replace her.
My aunt was thoughtful, helpful, and compassionate—a truly gracious lady.	My aunt was thoughtful, helpful, and compassionate—a truly outstanding person.
President Clinton said that his wife Hillary had been his main source of strength.	President Clinton said that Mrs. Clinton had been his main source of strength.

■ *Avoid using* man, men, *and* mankind *as synonyms for* humanity, people, *and* the human race.

Sexist language	Improved
Man's future is uncertain.	Humanity's future is uncertain.
Men must first learn to love themselves before they can love anyone else.	People must first learn to love themselves before they can love anyone else.
Are you telling me that mankind is on the brink of doom? What else is new?	Are you telling me that the human race is on the brink of doom? What else is new?

■ *Avoid using the pronoun* he *when sex is unknown or irrelevant.*

Sexist language	Improved
We need a person who can offer a few hours of his time each week.	We need a person who can offer a few hours of time each week.
Everyone wants to feel that he is esteemed.	All people want to feel that they are esteemed.
A liar needs to make sure that he has a good memory.	Liars need to make sure that they have good memories.

(For a more detailed discussion of nonsexist pronoun use, see pages 647–648 of the Handbook and page 700 of the Glossary.)

EXERCISE

Rewrite the following sentences to eliminate sexist language.

1. After moving from her neighborhood of the past twenty-five years, Julie most missed the girls' nights out every Tuesday.
2. Anyone who owns an ATM card, an EZ-pass, or a computer may have his right to privacy violated.
3. A collegiate athlete must be able to manage his time well.
4. Marjorie Small is a fully ordained lady minister.
5. A parent concerned about her child's progress in school should first arrange for a conference with her child's teacher.
6. With both of them working, they thought they were at last in a position to pay for a cleaning lady.
7. Forget about elections and wars. The fate of man is determined more by climate than by anything else.
8. After the wedding, Annette's great lover turned out to be just another loud-mouthed, beer-guzzling slob of a man.
9. Alan urgently needs a father to enforce discipline and teach him right from wrong.
10. She shouldn't let these disappointments bother her pretty little head. All she really needs is a good cry.
11. Schoolwork thrives on parental interest. Make sure to keep in touch with your children's teacher and show her that you care.
12. Every company should have a day for fathers to bring their daughters to work with them.
13. I'm tired of waiting in the hospital waiting room for a doctor to make time in his busy schedule to see me!
14. A student athlete must take special pains to achieve balance between his activities in class and in sports.
15. Stand by your man, little lady.

16. Anyone contemplating cosmetic surgery needs to question her doctor carefully about possible health problems, not just about expenses.
17. Our postal service has become most erratic. I'm not sure that mailmen still take pride in their work.
18. Almost no young clerk at a malfunctioning supermarket cash register nowadays seems capable of figuring out for herself how to make change.
19. Mothers who attend PTA meetings may feel more involved in their children's education.
20. To cite an old expression, a teenager needs to be allowed some freedom to sow his wild oats.

Miscellaneous Do's and Don'ts

Some special stylistic problems common to classroom writing don't fit conveniently under any of the main labels, so we've included brief comments about them here. Our comments are based on the assumption that you are writing for an audience of intelligent nonspecialists who have not yet made up their minds about your subject. You may argue that you're really writing for your instructor alone, but most English instructors have worked hard at training themselves to dismiss purely personal quirks and preferences from their reading of student themes. Despite the red pens or pencils in their hands, when they look at themes, they mentally turn themselves into an imaginary general reader—the intelligent, uncommitted nonspecialist just mentioned.

■ *Don't write a personal letter to your instructor.*

> This assignment at first confused me, but after several cups of coffee, I began to get an idea: I remembered that last week you said something about certain kinds of literature depending on formal patterns, and I think I've come up with an interesting notion about the two stories we just read. See what you think.

If that paragraph were read by anyone other than the teacher or the members of the class in which the stories were discussed, it would make almost no sense. What difference does it make to a general reader—or teacher—how much coffee the student drank? What assignment does the student refer to? What stories did the class just read?

■ *Don't make formal announcements of what you are going to do.*

> In this paper I am going to prove that, far from being ignored, the elderly have received special privileges for decades.

> The thesis that I shall attempt to establish in this paper is that crime rates have gone down because of broad social patterns, not because of better police work.

It's distracting and unnecessary to begin a paper with a trumpet fanfare. Don't tell the reader what you are going to do. Get down to business and do it.

> Far from being ignored, the elderly have received special privileges for decades.

Crime rates have gone down because of broad social patterns, not because of better police work.

■ *Avoid a speechmaking tone.*

In conclusion, let me simply say that. . . .

With your permission, I'd like to make a few observations on that point.

Such sentences introduce an irritating artificial quality into written English.

■ *Don't shilly-shally.*

In my opinion, the Industrial Revolution was a major chapter in the history of civilization.

I think that Dr. Watson is childishly impressed by Sherlock Holmes.

Go easy on terms such as *in my opinion, I think,* and the like. Of course you think, and the paper *is* your opinion, your interpretation of the material—backed up by all the facts necessary to support it. An apologetic or uncertain tone suggests that you do not have faith in your ideas, and if you do not believe in what you say, your audience probably won't either. Of course, you would not state a personal theory as a universal truth; but don't weaken solid ideas by shilly-shallying, and don't expect an *in my opinion* to make a shaky idea more acceptable.

■ *Don't bluster.*

Anyone but an idiot can see that Hughes's poem protests against the treatment of African Americans.

Legalized prostitution is opposed mainly by neurotic hypocrites and religious nuts.

Blustering is the opposite of shilly-shallying. Its effect on an intelligent audience is just as negative.

■ *Be careful about using* you *as an indefinite pronoun.*

Even though you are a drug addict, you are not necessarily an evil person.

Your constant arguments with your parents are part of the process of growing up.

You is the pronoun of direct address. In this book, for example, we, the authors, write to you, the students in a composition course, and thus address you directly. But in writing aimed at a general audience, it is preferable to use the indefinite pronouns *anyone, one, each, either, neither, another, anybody, someone, somebody, everyone, everybody,* and *nobody.* And *you* cannot be substituted for *the speaker, the character, the average citizen, people, the student, the author, the reader,* and so on. Since you cannot be sure of the age, class, sex, or living conditions of your readers, you will not want to chance offending or unintentionally amusing them by attributing to them attitudes, strengths, vices, or talents they may not possess.

Drug addicts are not necessarily evil.

Constant arguments with parents are part of the process of growing up.

■ *Define unfamiliar terms.*   This advice is especially important in any paper on technical subjects. An audience of nonspecialists can be expected to have the general knowledge of educated citizens, but nothing more. Avoid **jargon**—the special language of particular professions and activities—whenever you can. When you can't, see to it that your reader understands you. A paper on automobile repairs, for instance, would need to define terms such as *universal joint* and *differential.* A paper on legal problems would need to define *tort* and *writ of mandamus.* A paper on finance would need to define *cash flow* and *price-earnings ratio.*

EXERCISE

Comment on the stylistic problems in each of the following sentences, and rewrite the sentences where necessary.

1. If you'll allow me another moment, I would like to expand on this point.
2. Your ugly buck teeth can now be corrected more quickly and economically than was once the case.
3. This paper will demonstrate that Scott Joplin tried to impose the forms of classical music on the raw materials of ragtime.
4. Cobalt treatment engendered remission.
5. In conclusion, I feel strongly that parents need quality time with their children each day.
6. Writing this comparison–contrast paper involved less drudgery than I first thought it would.
7. The morons and gangsters who oppose the death penalty ought to be exposed once and for all.
8. Any intelligent person knows that seatbelt laws violate your right to privacy.
9. Recent government funding cuts mean that you may no longer be able to feed your hungry children.
10. Thus the poem clearly shows, in my humble opinion, that Dickinson was a shrewd observer.
11. I feel that it will be many years before experts know exactly how anesthetics operate on the body.
12. It is patently obvious that radicals of any sort are lunatics.
13. Assuming that you are still with me, I will continue to explain my point of view.
14. The focus of this paper will be the explanation of the pros and cons of nuclear power.
15. The caesura in the fourth stanza of the sestina is effected by the poet's scrupulous diction.
16. You will be pleased to know that the White House will now focus many of its proposals on children's health and well-being.
17. Sitting here, crouched before my typewriter, I wonder how to begin this theme.
18. A Shakespearean sonnet is, I think, easier to write than a Petrarchan.
19. This novel, in my mind, is a very important work of fiction, and I'm sure you will agree.
20. Only tyrants and fascist oppressors could support this new law.

Handbook
and Glossary

Part Six is a quick guide to basic writing skills. Use it to check up on grammatical points, to answer simple questions that may occur to you while writing or revising, and to correct any mechanical errors that your instructor finds in your work. Most English instructors assume that you have already mastered the basics. For the most part, you probably have—but even skilled professional writers sometimes need to use a reference book. Your instructor, at any rate, will probably devote only limited classroom time to mechanics; it is your responsibility, then, to make your papers grammatically correct. This Handbook and Glossary can help you do that.

Both the Handbook and the Glossary are arranged alphabetically. The Handbook discusses the most common areas of trouble: comma splices, fragmentary sentences, and so on. A number of exercises on more difficult points are provided so that you can test your understanding of these points. The Glossary of Problem Words explains specific words and phrases that are a frequent source of confusion to writers. After you complete the exercises to

measure your success in mastering these skills, take the Self Tests as they appear throughout Part Six. Check your answers to the Self Tests on pages 721–730.

We have tried to keep this material as straight-forward as possible. In general, we have taken a direct yes-or-no, right-or-wrong approach, even though that approach may sometimes seem to oversimplify complex and controversial issues. Our purpose is to give reasonable answers to common questions—not to write a dissertation on obscure grammatical details.

We have also tried to keep our explanations as free as possible of specialized grammatical terminology. When such terminology is necessary, we have strived to make our explanations self-contained. For example, in our treatment of adjective–adverb confusion, definitions of adjectives and adverbs are worked into the discussion. Some separate definitions have proven essential, however—it's wasteful to define overwhelmingly common terms such as *subject, noun,* and *verb* every time they are mentioned, and definitions of such common terms appear in alphabetical order in the Handbook.

Handbook

Abbreviations.   As a rule, avoid abbreviations.

Wrong	Right
The financial ills of N.Y.C. and other municipalities can be cured only by aid from the federal gov't.	The financial ills of New York City and other municipalities can be cured only by aid from the federal government.
Thanksgiving comes on the fourth Thurs. of Nov.	Thanksgiving comes on the fourth Thursday of November.
I had trouble finding the proper st. & had to ask a taxi driver for directions.	I had trouble finding the proper street and had to ask a taxi driver for directions.

Even when abbreviations are permissible, it is nearly always acceptable in standard English to spell a word in its entirety; therefore, when in doubt, spell it out.

However, in cases like the following, abbreviations are required or preferred.

A. *Standard forms of address.* Before a person's name, it is standard usage to write *Mr., Mrs., Ms., Dr.,* or *St.* (for Saint, not street).

B. *Titles.* If both a person's surname (last) and given name (first) or initials are used, then it is acceptable to write *Rev., Hon., Prof., Sen.*

Rev. John Rice, Prof. A. J. Carr (but not Rev. Rice or Prof. Carr)

C. *Degrees.* After a name, abbreviate academic degrees, *Jr.,* and *Sr.* Academic degrees may also be abbreviated when used by themselves.

Thomas Jones, M.D.

He is now studying for a B.A.

D. *Organizations.* The names of many organizations and some countries are commonly abbreviated, often without periods.

NATO   NAACP   OPEC   UN   USA   AFL-CIO   MLA

E. *Other.* Traditional footnote references and bibliographical terms (many no longer in common use) are nearly always abbreviated, as are a few familiar words.

etc.	pp. 137–40
ibid.	vol.
et al.	TNT
p. 23	DNA

EXERCISE

Replace unnecessary abbreviations in the following sentences.

1. Last Jan. my dr. vacationed in TX.
2. Many U.S. airlines have flights from L.A. to N.Y.
3. Mr. Dowd always complains that there is nothing to watch on t.v. on Tues. nights.

Self Test: **ABBREVIATIONS**

Replace unnecessary abbreviations in the following sentences.

1. Dr. Rauch's daughter got her M.B.A. at a university in PA.
2. The firm's offices moved last Dec. from Spring St. to Valley Rd.
3. The FBI raided his co.'s quarter in L.A., Calif.
4. By bro. & sister left town on Thurs.
5. The rev. worked for the NAACP & held a special Xmas service for gov't workers.

ad

Adjective–adverb confusion.   Adjectives modify nouns.

Getting a diploma takes *hard* work.

The boxer's *left* jab is his *strongest* weapon.

The *better* team won.

The porridge was *hot.*

Adverbs modify verbs, adjectives, or other adverbs.

We walked *carefully.*

Foolishly, we kept arguing until midnight.

The porridge was *very* hot.

The doctor had to cut *quite* deeply.

Most adverbs are formed by adding *-ly* to adjectives:

Adjective	Adverb
nice	nicely
strong	strongly
poor	poorly

When an adjective already ends in *y* or *ly*, the *y* may sometimes have to be changed to an *i* before the adverbial *-ly* ending is added. A few of the resulting adverbs may sound so awkward that an adverbial phrase is the preferred form.

Adjective	Adverb
pretty	prettily
messy	messily
nasty	nastily

but

Adjective	Adverb
friendly	in a friendly way
lovely	in a lovely way
heavenly	in a heavenly way

A few adjectives and adverbs are identical in form:

Adjective: He is a *better* person for the experience.

Fast drivers are dangerous drivers.

Adverb: He did *better* than I.

I can type *fast*.

Some words are adverbs in themselves—adverbs to start with—and do not spring from adjectives: *very, quite, rather, somewhat*. Other adverbs are irregular; the adjective *good*, for example, is expressed as an adverb by the word *well*.

Adjective: He was a *good* worker.

Adverb: He did the work *well*.

Confusion of adjectives and adverbs is among the most common grammatical errors and is likely to turn up from one of the following causes.

A. *Misuse of an adjective to modify a verb.*

Wrong	Right
I wish she acted *different*.	I wish she acted *differently*.
Bill did *good* on his examination.	Bill did *well* on his examination.
Let's speak *direct* to each other.	Let's speak *directly* to each other.

B. *Misuse of an adjective to modify an adverb or other adjective.*

Wrong	Right
The price was *sure* very expensive.	The price was *surely* very expensive.
The patient is *considerable* worse today.	The patient is *considerably* worse today.
My teacher is *real* strict.	My teacher is *really* strict.

C. *Misuse of an adverb after a linking verb.* The correct modifier after a linking verb is an adjective. The single most common linking verb is *to be (am, is, are, was, were, will be,* and so on). Verbs dealing with the senses—sight, touch, taste, smell, hearing—are often used as linking verbs: *feel, look, sound, taste, appear.* Other verbs frequently serving as linking verbs are *get, seem, remain, become.* (See also *good, well* in the Glossary.)

Wrong	Right
The music sounds *beautifully*.	The music sounds *beautiful*.
The food tastes *badly*.	The food tastes *bad*.

Some verbs, including many of those just listed, may be used as transitive or intransitive verbs, as well as linking verbs. In such cases, note how an adjective or adverb determines meaning.

I smell bad. (I need to buy deodorant.)
I smell badly. (My sinuses are stuffed up.)
He looks evil. (He looks like a wicked person.)
He looks evilly. (His glances are frightening.)
I feel terrible. (I am depressed or in ill health.)
I feel terribly. (My sense of touch has deserted me.)

EXERCISE

Choose the correct adjective or adverb in the following sentences.

1. If you act (quick, quickly), you will receive a free bonus gift.
2. Rifle fire rattled (angry, angrily) from the hills.
3. Some frozen foods are (real, really) tasty.
4. The international news sounds (explosive, explosively).

5. If you speak (hasty, hastily), you may repent (hasty, hastily).

6. Feeling (thirsty, thirstily), he drank (noisy, noisily).

7. Driving too (slow, slowly) can cause as many accidents as driving too (fast, fastly).

8. Writing (concise, concisely) helps to prove a point more (effective, effectively).

9. Though he appeared (calm, calmly) his heart thumped (rapid, rapidly).

10. My sister looks (splendid, splendidly) in her new three-piece suit.

EXERCISE

Find the errors in the following paragraphs.

1. My Florida vacation went terrible! It rained the entire time I was there. I had planned to get a suntan, go snorkeling, and maybe see some dolphins, but all my plans went sour. Instead, I wandered unhappy through the hotel hallways, wishing I had stayed at home. The worst part of all was that the sun shone down brilliant as I boarded the plane to go home.

2. Linguine with clam sauce is made much more easy than you might expect. Prepare the linguine as you would normally. Then, fry some onions and garlic in butter. Add the juice from a can of clams and a little parsley and simmer the mixture gentle. Add the clams and, after they have heated, mix the linguine in real good. This dish tastes great with a little Parmesan cheese.

3. A curving path wound through the forest. Bob and Martha walked down it slow, admiring the scenery and enjoying the cool shade. They spotted a doe and her fawn hiding among the trees. They moved closer, but the animals ran away too quick to follow.

Self Test: CORRECT ADJECTIVES AND ADVERBS

Select the correct word from parentheses.

1. Speaking (personal, personally), I think the coach is the only real problem the team has.

2. All our products are (fresh, freshly) baked each day.

3. Juan drove home (quick, quickly) to see if his son was still not feeling (good, well).

4. As (near, nearly) as I can determine, the first job offer seems the best.

5. Far from being a snob, Frank is a (real, really) fine person once you get to know him.

6. The cat burglar scaled the wall of the building as (quick, quickly) as she could.

7. She is an excellent teacher and writes (beautiful, beautifully), too.

8. The twins always looked (similar, similarly) in their matching clothes.

9. Tara's supervisor felt (bad, badly) about snapping at Tara for no reason.

10. The fans hollered so (loud, loudly) that the gym echoed.

Adjectives, comparative and superlative forms. See *Comparative and superlative forms.*

Adjectives, coordinate. See *Comma, E.*

Adverbs. See *Adjective–adverb confusion.*

Adverbs, comparative and superlative forms. See *Comparative and superlative forms.*

Agreement. See *Pronoun agreement; Subject–verb agreement.*

Antecedent. The noun or pronoun to which a pronoun refers.

> *John* left *his* lunch at home.
> Here, the pronoun *his* refers to its noun antecedent, *John.*

Apostrophe. The apostrophe is used to form contractions, plurals, and possessives.

A. *Contractions.* In contractions, the apostrophe indicates that a letter or letters have been left out.

it is = it's	she is = she's	who is = who's	you will = you'll
let us = let's	you are = you're	do not = don't	she would = she'd

B. *Plurals.* The *'s* is used to form the plural of letters: *a's, x's, B's, C's.* Only an *s* is used to form the plurals of abbreviations and numbers.

the 1930s	the &s (*or* the &'s)
DAs	POWs

C. *Possessives.* An apostrophe is used to form the possessive of nouns and indefinite pronouns. The first task is to determine whether a possessive apostrophe is needed. If one is needed, the second task is to use it correctly.

   Difficulties for many people begin with the confusion of speaking with writing. In speech, *cats, cat's,* and *cats'* all sound identical. The meanings are all different, however, and in writing, those differences show up immediately. *Cats* is a simple plural—*s* is added to the singular and no apostrophe is used.

The cats howled all night.

Purring is a way cats have of showing affection.

Liver is a favorite food for many cats.

Cat's is a possessive singular, another way of expressing the thought *of the cat. Cats'* is a possessive plural, another way of expressing the thought *of the cats.* Note the simplicity of determining whether a word with a possessive apostrophe is singular or plural: just look at the part of the word *before the apostrophe.*

Singular	Plural
cat's claws	cats' claws
machine's speed	machines' speed
Mr. Smith's home	the Smiths' home

Note, too, that in a phrase like *of the cats,* the word *of* takes care of the idea of possession, and no apostrophe is used.

Possessives with *of* (no apostrophe)	Possessives with apostrophes
The claws of a cat are sharp.	A cat's claws are sharp.
The name of my cat is Tigger.	My cat's name is Tigger.
The hunting abilities of cats are well known.	Cats' hunting abilities are well known.
The mysterious glow in the eyes of cats can be frightening.	The mysterious glow in cats' eyes can be frightening.

One more observation is necessary. Possessive pronouns—*my, mine, our, ours, your, yours, his, her, hers, its, their, theirs*—are already possessive in themselves and *never take apostrophes.*

When a possessive apostrophe is required, the rules are relatively simple.

1. Singular or plural nouns that do not end in *-s* form their possessives by adding *'s.*

Ivan's car	Arlene's book	Women's Liberation
the teacher's notes	New York's mayor	children's games

2. Plural nouns that end in *-s* form their possessives by adding only an apostrophe:

the students' teacher	Californians' freeways
oil companies' profits	the two boys' mother
automobiles' engines	the two teachers' classes

3. Singular nouns that end in *-s* ordinarily form their possessives by adding *'s.* Some writers make exceptions of words that already have so many *s* or *z* sounds in them (for example, *Massachusetts, Jesus*) that pronunciation of a final *'s* could create awkward hissings and buzzings. The possessive of such words can be formed by adding only an apostrophe. Both methods are correct, and writers can use their own judgment as long as they are consistent.

the octopus's tentacles	the press's responsibilities
Dickens's novels	the business's profits
Charles's bowling ball	Jesus's disciples (*or* Jesus' disciples)
Mr. Jones's new roof	Moses's journey (*or* Moses' journey)

4. Indefinite pronouns form their possessives by adding *'s:*

nobody's fool   someone's knock

anyone's guess   everybody's business

5. In the case of joint possession—possession by two or more—the possessive is formed by adding an apostrophe or *'s,* as appropriate, to the last noun:

the girls and boys' school   Jill and Bob's car

NOTE: To show individual possession, write "Jill's and Bob's cars" and "the girls' and boys' schools." Here Jill has a car and Bob has a car, the girls have a school and the boys have a school.

EXERCISE

Rewrite the following phrases to form possessives, using only an apostrophe (') or an apostrophe plus the letter *s* (**'s**) as appropriate.

1. The wail of the saxophone.
2. The wail of the saxophones.
3. The president of the country.
4. The presidents of the countries.
5. The checking account of Mr. James.
6. The checking account of the Jameses.
7. The manager of the team.
8. The managers of the teams.
9. The suspense of the story.
10. The suspense of the stories.
11. The leaves of the birch tree.
12. The leaves of the birch trees.
13. The choice of the person.
14. The choice of the people.
15. The mother of Sarah and Jess.
16. The mothers of Sarah and Jess. (*two mothers—individual possession*)
17. The title of the book.
18. The desire of one to excel.
19. The debt of our company.
20. A notice of a moment.

EXERCISE

In the following sentences, decide which of the italicized words ending in *-s* are simple plurals or verbs and which are possessives. Then make the necessary corrections and be prepared to explain them.

1. *Managements problems* with the *unions* are based more on *misunderstandings* than on genuine *conflicts* of interest.

2. The Post *Offices* commemorative *stamps* are much sought after by some *members* of the public.

3. The *prison guards* ignored the *inmates complaints* about their *cells* filthy *conditions*.

4. *Joggings* appeal *eludes* me. There must be *less* boring *exercises*.

5. That ancient *trees* gnarled *branches* only add to *its* beauty.

6. *Ballplayers* contractual *disputes* have achieved the impossible; they have aroused the *publics* sympathy for the *owners*.

7. Your behavior is worse than *theirs; yours* can't be excused by your *fathers* neglect.

8. The *Smiths* went to the *Joneses* house for dinner.

9. The *Devils* Triangle refers to a region in the Atlantic Ocean of many unexplained *accidents*.

10. The *actors* constant bickering forced the *shows producers* to choose which one of them would leave.

11. The *ships* arrival assured the rescue of the *survivors*.

12. After *years* of happiness, *Frances* and *Roberts* marriage seems to be on the *rocks*.

13. Many of our *universes* greatest *mysteries*, like the *causes* of aging and the *reasons* we need sleep, have baffled the *worlds scientists* for *centuries*.

14. *Hundreds* of *customers complaints* filled the *companys* mail room.

15. The *decisions* were *ours*, but Mr. *Ross* misleading *documents* were also responsible.

Self Test: APOSTROPHE USE

Correct any errors.

1. The girls hat's are more colorful than your's.

2. Investors' began to worry that the company's stock price's would fall dramatically.

3. Our neighbors houses are much more modern than our's.

4. Clinical trial's of the pharmaceutical company's new vaccine begin next week.

5. Sheet's and towel's are on sale this week.

6. The boy's basketball rolled under their Uncle Manuels' van.

7. Before we move in, we will decide which room will be our's, which will be your's, and which will be Miguel's.

8. My brothers ferocious German shepherd tore a hole with his sharp teeth in the mail carriers' bag.

9. David's sisters wedding is in two weeks, but most of the bridesmaid's dresses' are still not ready.

10. Five of the student's test scores were misplaced, but your's and Giovanni's were not among them.

[ ]

cap

Appositive. See *Comma, F.*

Block quotations. See *Quotation marks, A, 1.*

Brackets. Use brackets ([ ]) to enclose comments or added information that you have inserted into a direct quotation. Do not use parentheses instead of brackets because the reader will assume that the inserted material is part of the original quotation.

> "While influenced by moral considerations, Lincoln signed it [the Emancipation Proclamation] primarily to further the war effort."

> "The music column had the altogether intimidating title of *Hemidemisemiquavers* [sixty-fourth notes]."

Capital letters. Use a capital letter for the first word of a sentence or direct quotation, the first word and all important words of titles, the first word and all nouns of a salutation, the first word of a complimentary close, some pronouns, and all proper nouns—the names of particular persons, places, or things.

A. *The first word of a sentence or direct quotation.*

> A popular early television show featured a detective whose most characteristic line was, "We just want the facts, ma'am."

B. *The first and all important words of titles of books, movies, radio and television programs, songs, magazines, plays, short stories, poems, essays, and chapters.* Unimportant words (for example, *a, an, and, the*) and prepositions (e.g., *of, in, to, with, about*) are not capitalized.

A Streetcar Named Desire	"Ode to a Nightingale"
Time	"Such, Such Were the Joys"
Roget's College Thesaurus	"Basin Street Blues"

C. *The first word and all nouns of a salutation.*

> Dear Sir: My dear Ms. Hunt: Dear Bill,

D. *The first word of a complimentary close.*

> Sincerely yours,   Yours truly,

E. *Some pronouns.*

1. First-person singular: *I.*
2. References to the Judeo-Christian Deity, where necessary to avoid confusion:

> God told Moses that he must carry out His commandments.

F. *Proper nouns.*

1. Names and titles of persons and groups of persons:
   a. Persons: James Baldwin, Gloria Steinem, President Clinton.
   b. Races, nationalities, and religions: Caucasian, Chinese, Catholic (but *black, white*).
   c. Groups, organizations, and departments: League of Women Voters, Ford Motor Company, United States Senate, Department of Agriculture.
   d. Particular deities: God, Allah, Buddha, Zeus.

2. Names of particular places:
   a. Cities, counties, states, and countries: Cleveland, Cuyahoga County, Ohio, United States of America.
   b. Particular geographical regions: Europe, Pacific Northwest, the South.
   c. Streets: East Ninth Street, El Cajon Avenue.
   d. Buildings: Empire State Building, Union Terminal.
   e. Heavenly bodies (except the sun and moon): Mars, Milky Way, Andromeda, Alpha Centauri.

3. Names of particular things:
   a. Days and months: Friday, August.
   b. Holidays: Easter, May Day.
   c. Historical events and periods: the Civil War, the Middle Ages.
   d. School courses: Biology 101, History 102 (but "a *history* course").
   e. Languages: English, Russian.
   f. Schools: Cornell University, Walt Whitman High School (but "I graduated from *high school*").
   g. Brands: Buick, Peter Pan Peanut Butter (but "I had a *peanut butter* sandwich for lunch").

EXERCISE

Add capital letters as needed in the following sentences.

1. my best subject in high school was mathematics, but my tenth grade english teacher really taught me to enjoy classics like *jane eyre* and *the grapes of wrath.*
2. every saturday in july the arthur taylor jazz quartet performs concerts in grant park.
3. my friend suzy yip has adopted bart simpson's saying: "don't have a cow, man!"
4. ellen hasn't decided whether to spend christmas in chicago with her grandparents or in seattle with her aunt felice and uncle gregg.
5. mr. tanner's third graders at pine street elementary school planted daffodils in the park in honor of mother's day.

6. according to the food and drug administration, genetically altered crops are entirely safe.
7. drive south on sumpter street and park across from home depot, the largest store in our town.
8. director michael blakemore won tony awards both for the musical *kiss me kate* and for the play *copenhagen.*
9. have you seen the two-headed turtle at the nature museum in charlotte, north carolina?
10. painting 101 will meet on tuesdays and thursdays beginning this fall.

Self Test: **CAPITAL LETTERS**

Replace lowercase letters with capital letters as needed in the following sentences.

1. please park your car on marquette lane.
2. the carson middle school's marching band raises money each year for a trip to montreal.
3. some doctors feel that taking fever reducing medicines like tylenol is unnecessary, and that low fevers can be helpful to the body.
4. when juanita traveled to the south, she tasted crawfish for the first time.
5. do you think that the new jersey devils could win the stanley cup?
6. we'll leave for florida on the friday after thanksgiving.
7. anika speaks four languages: english, french, german, and spanish.
8. the golden retriever darted back and forth from the water's edge to his owner, wagging his tail playfully and barking at the sunbathers on crawford beach.
9. we will have our next cub scout meeting at the springfield civic center.
10. the portrait of princess diana at the national portrait gallery in london seems to attract more viewers than any other picture in the gallery.

Clause. A group of words with a subject and predicate. A clause can be independent or dependent. An *independent clause* stands alone as a separate sentence.

Maria went home.

A *dependent clause* cannot stand alone; rather, it must depend on an independent clause to complete its meaning.

After I came home, I took a nap.

The man *who lived next door* died.

Collective nouns. See *Subject–verb agreement, E.*

Colon. A colon (:) commonly appears after a clause introducing a list or description, between hours and minutes, in the salutation of a formal letter, between biblical chapter and verse numbers, and between the title and subtitle of a book. Less commonly, a colon may separate independent clauses and appear before quotations.

A. *List.* A colon appears between a general statement and a list or description that follows:

We shall never again find the equals of the famous three *B's* of music: Bach, Beethoven, and Brahms.

He plans to take five courses: history, English, psychology, French, and physical education.

NOTE: A colon should appear after a complete statement. A colon should not be used after a form of the verb to be (be, am, is, are, was, were, been, etc.) or after a preposition.

Wrong	Right
Perennial contenders for the NFL championship are: San Francisco, Dallas, and Buffalo.	Several teams are perennial contenders for the NFL championship: San Francisco, Dallas, and Buffalo.
	or
	Perennial contenders for the NFL championship are San Francisco, Dallas, and Buffalo.
F. Scott Fitzgerald is the author of: *This Side of Paradise, The Beautiful and Damned, The Great Gatsby,* and *Tender Is the Night.*	F. Scott Fitzgerald wrote the following books: *This Side of Paradise, The Beautiful and Damned, The Great Gatsby,* and *Tender Is the Night.*
	or
	F. Scott Fitzgerald is the author of *This Side of Paradise, The Beautiful and Damned, The Great Gatsby,* and *Tender Is the Night.*

B. *Time.* When recording a specific time in numerals, use a colon between hours and minutes:

8:00 p.m.   8:10 a.m.

C. *Salutation.* In formal letter writing, use a colon after the salutation:

Dear Ms. Johnson: Dear Sir:

D. *Biblical references.* To separate chapter from verse, use a colon:

Genesis 1:8 (chapter 1, verse 8)

E. *Title and subtitle.* A colon separates the title and subtitle of a book:

Johnson's Dictionary: A Modern Selection

F. *Independent clauses.* A colon may appear between independent clauses when the second clause explains the first:

They raised their children on one principle, and one principle only: Do unto others what they would like to do unto you—and do it first.

G. *Quotations.* A colon sometimes introduces a short quotation and often introduces a long block quotation:

Whenever I try to diet, I am reminded of the bitter truth of Oscar Wilde's epigram: "I can resist everything but temptation."

In commenting on his function as a writer, Joseph Conrad put every writer's dream into words:

> My task which I am trying to achieve is, by the power of the written word to make you hear, to make you feel—it is, before all, to make you *see*. That—and no more, and it is everything. If I succeed, you shall find there according to your deserts: encouragement, consolation, fear, charm—all you demand—and, perhaps, also that glimpse of truth for which you have forgotten to ask.

EXERCISE

Correct any errors by adding or removing colons.

1. The conference will resume at 200 p.m.
2. My heroes have always been: Albert Einstein and Martin Luther King, Jr.
3. We brought several board games Monopoly, Scrabble, and Sorry.
4. Professor Barkley's voice was calm and her eyes were kind, but her message was clear if you don't take the class seriously, you will get a poor grade.

Self Test: COLONS

Add or remove colons to make the sentences correct.

1. The *Wall Street Journal's* front page story about Amazon.com did two things it introduced Amazon to new customers, and it caught the attention of rival companies not yet online.
2. Karl's new job brought him to cities he had never visited like: Milan, London, Santiago, and Tokyo.
3. Because my father is always looking at his watch, for Father's Day I bought him the book *Keeping Watch A History of American Time.*
4. Gina's delectable brownies are the perfect dessert: sweet, rich, gooey, and chocolatey.
5. I hate to admit it, but my mother's favorite saying was true "Give some people an inch, and they'll take a mile."

Comma.   Using a comma correctly is almost never a matter of taste or inspiration. It is even less a matter of following the ancient junior high school formula of tossing in a comma "to indicate a pause." Different people pause for breath and emphasis in different places and nearly *every* mark of punctuation indicates some kind of pause—periods, semicolons, and dashes no less than commas. When errors in comma usage occur, they are most often the result of the writer's being comma happy—putting in too many commas. Our basic rule, then, is *never use a comma unless you know it is necessary.* It is necessary in the following cases:

- Between elements in a list or series
- Between independent clauses joined by *and, but, yet, for, or, nor, so*
- After introductory elements
- Before and after interrupting elements
- Between coordinate adjectives
- Before and after nonrestrictive elements
- Before and after phrases that express a contrast
- Before and after words of direct address, interjections, and *yes* and *no*
- Between certain words to prevent misreading
- In conventional elements such as dates, numbers, addresses, titles, correspondence, and direct quotations

A. *Series.* Three or more items in a list or series must be separated by commas for the sake of clarity.

The potential buyer should take special care to inspect the roof, basement, and ceilings.

Make sure you read parts one, two, and three before completing the assignment.

The three novels in Dos Passos's *USA* trilogy are *The 42nd Parallel, Nineteen Nineteen,* and *The Big Money.*

NOTE: In all three examples, the comma before *and* is optional. Most experienced writers use the comma, however, because it reinforces the idea of a series in the reader's mind.

B. *Independent clauses.* An independent clause—a group of words that can stand alone as a complete sentence—that is joined by a coordinate conjunction—*and, but, for, yet, or, nor, so*—requires a comma *before* the conjunction:

Connotations are not usually entered next to a word in a dictionary, but they still exist in people's minds.

Each writing assignment requires a different kind of organization, and each may be a different length.

No comma would be used if the preceding sentences were rewritten to have only one independent clause:

Connotations are not usually entered next to a word in a dictionary but still exist in people's minds.

Each writing assignment requires a different kind of organization and may be a different length.

EXERCISE

Add or remove commas as necessary in the following sentences. Some sentences may be correct as written.

1. I decided against taking the new job yet I suspected I would always be grateful for the offer.
2. Marie knew that the book would sell but never dreamed of its record-breaking success.
3. I have traveled extensively throughout the U.S. but I have never been abroad.
4. The division heads were told that they must all work together or they would all be fired separately.
5. Sheila came home from a hard day at the office, and went straight to bed.
6. Nothing made any sense in my income tax forms so I decided I needed to consult an accountant.
7. Laughter is the best medicine and frowns make me sick.
8. Martin was restless and he thought about giving Pamela a call.
9. Martin was restless and thought about giving Pamela a call.
10. The Spanish Armada was partly destroyed by the English, but the weather played an even larger destructive role.

Self Test: COMMAS IN SERIES AND CLAUSES

Add or remove commas as needed in the following sentences.

1. I continue to receive the newspaper yet I never have time to read it.
2. We did not use our video camera but we did scan our vacation photos onto the computer.
3. Doug went to the mall, and then to the movies.
4. José, ran fifteen yards, and scored a touchdown.
5. Ice cream is better than nothing, but a hot fudge sundae is better than anything.
6. Marry me, for I love you.
7. College is lots of fun and lots of work.
8. Becoming a pilot was George's dream yet he was afraid to fly.
9. The head of this department must have creativity ingenuity and reliability.
10. Ruth read *Interview with a Vampire* and watched *Dracula* on television so she was too scared to sleep.

C. *Introductory elements.* A comma generally should be used after an introductory element:

Because the students were having trouble with commas, they read the section on punctuation.

In good writing, there are few punctuation errors.

The italicized parts of these two sentences are introductory elements. When the introductory element is extremely short—one word, for example—the comma can sometimes be omitted if the meaning remains clear: *"Soon* the term will end."

Poor	Correct
Because this is an introductory element it should have a comma after it.	Because this is an introductory element, it should have a comma after it.
Despite the best efforts of both parties no agreement was reached.	Despite the best efforts of both parties, no agreement was reached.
Never having seen her before I expected the worst.	Never having seen her before, I expected the worst.
As soon as he had showered he went straight to bed.	As soon as he had showered, he went straight to bed.

However, if the introductory element is moved so that it appears *after* the independent clause (and thus no longer introduces anything), no comma should be used:

No agreement was reached despite the best efforts of both parties.

He went straight to bed as soon as he had showered.

EXERCISE

Insert a comma after the introductory element where necessary.

1. Finished at last with work she looked forward to an evening on the town.
2. Because Carmela forgot to set her alarm she missed her nine o'clock appointment.
3. Having decided that both sides had presented excellent cases I then concluded that my only reasonable vote was an abstention.
4. We frequently find lost objects only after we have stopped looking for them.
5. After a long introductory clause or phrase use a comma.
6. As any vacationer knows it is easy to get lost.
7. Now I feel better prepared.
8. Considering my shortcomings I have been luckier than I deserve.
9. Bored and disgusted with the ball game I thought bitterly that there were some peanut vendors in the stands who were better athletes than anyone on the field.
10. Whenever I hear someone suggest that love is the answer to our problems I wonder why love has usually made me miserable.

Self Test: COMMAS AT INTRODUCTORY ELEMENTS

Insert commas as needed in the following sentences.

1. At the Land Rover Driving School students learn to control their four-wheel drive vehicles on unpaved roads.
2. Our eyes were bleary, and our knees were shaky after we spent the entire day watching cartoons.
3. During the past twenty years Emily has learned many things.
4. Watching the circus, eating cotton candy, and drinking lemonade Freddy was happier than he had ever been.
5. Soon recycling will be so much a part of our lives that we will not even notice its minor inconveniences.
6. Having prepared the fish perfectly Julia Child tossed several sprigs of parsley on top of it for decoration.
7. Tomorrow Evan will be ready for work.
8. After a long, difficult day at work Natalie enjoyed a five-mile jog.
9. You must do some research on the company before you go there for an interview.
10. Having finished the whole assignment he suddenly realized he'd done the wrong exercises.

D. *Interrupting elements.* A comma should be used before and after an interrupting element. Interrupting elements, while often needed for clarity and continuity, are those that break the flow of words in the main thought of a sentence or clause. In the previous sentence, *while often needed for clarity or continuity* is an interrupting element. Some writers find it helpful to think of interrupting elements as asides to the audience or parenthetical insertions. Interrupting elements may be words such as *indeed, however, too, also, consequently, therefore, moreover, nevertheless* and phrases such as *as the author says, of course, after all, for example, in fact, on the other hand.*

Wrong	Right
Suppose for example that you decide to write about your own life.	Suppose, for example, that you decide to write about your own life.
We must bear in mind too that even the best system is imperfect.	We must bear in mind, too, that even the best system is imperfect.
Punctuation as we can see is not exactly fun.	Punctuation, as we can see, is not exactly fun.
The only thing wrong with youth according to George Bernard Shaw is that it is wasted on the young.	The only thing wrong with youth, according to George Bernard Shaw, is that it is wasted on the young.
His pledges for the future however could not make me forget his broken promises of the past.	His pledges for the future, however, could not make me forget his broken promises of the past.

E. *Coordinate adjectives.* A comma is used to separate coordinate adjectives—adjectives of equal rank—that come before the nouns they modify.

Wrong	Right
This poet uses concrete believable images.	This poet uses concrete, believable images.
Her warm enthusiastic energetic behavior was often mistaken for pushiness.	Her warm, enthusiastic, energetic behavior was often mistaken for pushiness.

Coordinate adjectives can be identified in two ways: (1) the word *and* may be used to join them (concrete *and* believable, warm *and* enthusiastic *and* energetic) or (2) they may be reversed (believable, concrete; enthusiastic, energetic, warm). Compare these examples to "This poet uses several concrete images." We cannot say "several and concrete" or "concrete several." Therefore, we do not use a comma between them. Note, too, that if the coordinate adjectives had originally been joined by *and*, no commas would have been necessary: "Her warm *and* enthusiastic *and* energetic behavior was often mistaken for pushiness."

EXERCISE

Add commas as needed around the interrupting elements and between the coordinate adjectives in the following sentences. Also remove any commas that have been incorrectly placed. Some sentences may be correct as written.

1. The student's sincere deep apology fell on deaf ears.
2. The teacher's apology I am sorry to say seemed less sincere.
3. Protracted, municipal efforts to expand the airport are at a standstill.
4. The mayor keeps insisting however that efforts will continue.
5. Drinking a glass of cool refreshing water can energize you.
6. Always make certain, in addition, to check your manuscript for careless errors.
7. Dogs too can get sunburns.
8. The so-called, good, old days were often actually bad, old days.
9. Turner's theory to put it bluntly was wrong.
10. Her inherent bad vertebral structure inhibited her career as a gymnast.

Self Test: COMMAS AND INTERRUPTING ELEMENTS

Insert commas as required in the following sentences. Remove any unnecessary commas.

1. The wild days of stupid, educational gimmicks thank goodness seem to be behind us.
2. Preventative care for an automobile to be sure is worthwhile.
3. Don't let those sweet meaningless smiles deceive you.

4. The administration's basic, economic problem is fair taxation.
5. The outlook for the future, according to Secretary Miller, is not as bad as most columnists seem to think.
6. Teenagers' bedrooms tend to be chaotic, rumpus rooms in short pig sties.
7. There are effective ways I believe to perform better under pressure.
8. My fundamental, monetary difficulty is that I'm broke.
9. The cat in Dad's opinion is nothing but a sweet cuddly pain in the neck.
10. Early Gothic novels are basically silly overwritten romances.

F. *Nonrestrictive elements.* A comma should be used before and after a nonrestrictive element.

Nonrestrictive modifiers. Commas are used before and after nonrestrictive modifiers. A nonrestrictive modifier gives additional information about the noun it modifies but is not necessary to identify or define that noun:

The Empire State Building, *which I visited last year,* is a most impressive sight.

My father, *who has worked in a steel foundry for thirty years,* has made many sacrifices for me.

A *restrictive modifier* is not set off by commas. It is a necessary part of the meaning of the noun it modifies:

A person *who is always late for appointments* may have serious psychological problems.

The novel *that Professor Higgins praised so highly* is very disappointing.

People *who live in glass houses* shouldn't throw stones.

Many jobs *for highly skilled technicians* are still available.

Proper punctuation of restrictive and nonrestrictive modifiers often can affect meaning:

The sofa, with those huge armrests, is an eyesore.	(The writer sees just one sofa. The nonrestrictive modifier merely conveys more information about it.)
The sofa with those huge armrests is an eyesore.	(The writer sees more than one sofa. The restrictive modifier is necessary to distinguish this sofa from the others.)

A special type of nonrestrictive element is called the *appositive*—a word or group of words that means the same thing as the element that precedes it. In the sentence, "Joseph Terrell, *mayor of Greenville,* will speak at graduation," the italicized phrase is an appositive; that is, it has the same basic meaning as the first element, *Joseph Terrell*. The rules governing the punctuation of modifiers also govern the punctuation of appositives.

Nonrestrictive appositives. Commas are used before and after nonrestrictive appositives. A nonrestrictive appositive gives additional information about the noun it follows but is not necessary to identify that noun:

Ms. Susan Swattem, *my high school mathematics teacher,* was the meanest person in town.

Thomas Jefferson, *third president of the United States,* also founded the University of Virginia.

A *restrictive appositive* is not set off by commas. It is necessary to identify the noun it follows:

The expression *hitch your wagon to a star* was first used by Emerson.

He spoke to Susan *my sister,* not Susan *my wife.*

As with modifiers, proper punctuation of nonrestrictive and restrictive appositives often can affect meaning.

My brother, George, is a kindly soul.	(The writer has only one brother, so the word *brother* is sufficient identification. *George* is nonrestrictive.)
My brother George is a kindly soul.	(The writer has more than one brother, so the name of the specific brother is a necessary part of the meaning. *George* is restrictive.)

EXERCISE

Add commas where necessary to set off the nonrestrictive elements in the following sentences. Also remove any commas that have been incorrectly placed. Some sentences may be correct as written.

1. A person who is not in medical school cannot imagine the amount of time and effort it involves.
2. The Smurfs, elflike blue creatures of spectacular cuteness, won the hearts of America's children during the early 1980s.
3. Nobody who cares about the future can be indifferent to the proliferation of nuclear weapons.
4. The highway repair project, which was scheduled to be finished in two years, now will need double that time to be completed.
5. My sister Sonya has four children. My sister Judith has none.
6. Albert Einstein that legendary figure of modern science was a notable underachiever during his school days.
7. Exxon which is the largest oil company in the world used to be known as Standard Oil Company of New Jersey.

8. The man who picked up the packages for the old woman had his wallet stolen when he bent over.
9. Harold Arlen who wrote such songs as "Stormy Weather" and "Let's Fall in Love" also composed the classic score for the film *The Wizard of Oz*.
10. The baseball player who has the highest lifetime batting average in the history of the game is Ty Cobb.

Self Test: **COMMAS AND NONRESTRICTIVE ELEMENTS**

Set off nonrestrictive elements with commas in the following sentences. Remove any unnecessary commas. Some sentences are already correct.

1. A college student, who doesn't have the sense to study, may not have the sense to belong in college.
2. The Republican candidate who promised to cut taxes defeated the Democrat in last night's election.
3. Nobody who dislikes bubble gum can be trusted.
4. A person, who dislikes dogs and children, can't be all bad.
5. Bill Gates the founder and CEO of Microsoft is considered one of the most intelligent people in America.
6. People, who are early to bed and early to rise, may be healthy, wealthy, and wise, but they certainly are dull!
7. Some women feel that a skirt, which is too short, is uncomfortable and embarrassing.
8. People who are lonely may seem aloof and proud.
9. Maya Angelou who wrote *I Know Why the Caged Bird Sings* is quite eloquent.
10. That which we most desire may be that which we least require.

G. *Contrast.* Commas should be used to set off phrases expressing a contrast.

She told him to deliver the furniture on Wednesday, not Tuesday.

Hard work, not noble daydreams, is what I believe in.

The money did not bring hope, but anxiety.

NOTE: The comma can sometimes be omitted before contrasting phrases beginning with *but*: "We have nothing to fear *but* fear itself."

H. *Direct address, interjections,* yes *and* no. Commas separate words and phrases of direct address, interjections, and the words *yes* and *no* from the rest of the sentence.

1. *Direct address:*

I tell you, ladies and gentlemen, that this strategy will not work.

Jim, you're still not following the instructions.

2. *Interjections:*

Well, it appears that the committee has finally issued its report.

Oh, I'd say the new car should arrive in about three weeks.

Although commas are generally used with mild interjections, more dramatic interjections may take exclamation points:

Well! It was the worst mess I'd ever seen.

Oh! How could she have made such a contemptible remark?

3. *Yes* and *no:*

Yes, I plan to vote for Ruppert.

I have to tell you plainly that, no, I cannot support your proposal.

I. *Misreading.* Apart from any more specific rules, commas are sometimes necessary to prevent misreading. Without commas, the following examples would be likely to stop readers in midsentence and send them back to the beginning.

Confusing	Correct
High above the trees swayed in the wind.	High above, the trees swayed in the wind.
High above the trees an ominous thundercloud came into view.	High above the trees, an ominous thundercloud came into view.
At the same time John and Arnold were making their plans.	At the same time, John and Arnold were making their plans.
Hugging and kissing my half-smashed relatives celebrated the wedding.	Hugging and kissing, my half-smashed relatives celebrated the wedding.

J. *Conventions.* Commas are used in such conventional elements as dates, numbers, addresses, titles, correspondence, and direct quotations.

1. *Dates.* Commas separate the day of the month and the year:

April 24, 1938   January 5, 1967

If only the month and year are used, the comma may be omitted:

April 1938   *or*   April, 1938

If the year is used in midsentence with the day of the month, it should be followed by a comma. With the month only, the comma may be omitted:

World War II began for the United States on December 7, 1941, at Pearl Harbor.

World War II began for the United States in December 1941 at Pearl Harbor.

World War II began for the United States in December, 1941, at Pearl Harbor.

2. *Numbers.* Commas are used to group numbers of more than three digits to the left of the decimal point:

$5,280.00   751,672.357   5,429,000   5,280

However, commas are not used for page numbers, addresses, or years:

page 4233   1236 Madison Ave.   1989

3. *Addresses.* Commas are used to separate towns, cities, counties, states, and districts:

Cleveland, Ohio

Brooklyn, Kings County, New York

Washington, D.C.

NOTE: A comma is not used to separate the zip code from the state.

Pasadena, California   91106

4. *Titles.* A comma often separates a title from a name that precedes it:

Harold Unger, M.D.   Julia Harding, Ph.D.

5. *Correspondence.* A comma is used after the salutation in informal letters and after the complimentary close:

Dear John,   Dear Jane,

Respectfully yours,   Sincerely yours,

6. *Direct quotations.* See *Quotation Marks, A.*

EXERCISE

Insert commas as needed in the following sentences. Remove any unnecessary commas.

1. My mother, was born in Salt Lake City Utah on September 8 1948.
2. Yes I do hope that my activism will help change government policies.
3. Emily is this your sweater?
4. At the moment, we are compiling, a guest list for our New Year's Eve bash.
5. Savoring each delicious bite she wanted the meal to go on forever.
6. Take it from me no one is immune to Andrew's outrageous accusations.
7. Apply sunscreen liberally and spend your summer romping in the sun not indoors cringing from the discomfort of sunburn.
8. Susan's reaction, was one not of outrage but of resignation.
9. Beginning July 12 2001 we will accept applications for the position of Assistant Director of the Milton School.
10. You must understand my friend that this is not easy for me.

Self Test: COMMAS: OTHER USES

Insert commas as needed in the following sentences. Remove any unnecessary commas. One sentence is correct.

1. Yes dear I did call your sister yesterday.
2. A preschooler's spinning of tall tales is part of the development of intellect not a purposeful attempt to deceive.
3. The keynote speaker at Memorial Hospital's next benefit dinner will be Sidney Johnson M.D.
4. No, there are not any written instructions for these next two projects.
5. My letter dated March 17 1998 explains in detail my strategies for expanding our human resources department.
6. Facing the crowd together the band members felt confident and self-assured.
7. Annette when do you plan to return to Detroit?
8. Oh I am beginning to feel so frustrated by your selfishness.
9. A song from the Broadway show *Rent,* refers to a year as 525600 minutes.
10. Kent Hoffman Ph.D. is an associate professor at Thomas Jefferson University in Philadelphia Pennsylvania.

Comma splice.   Often considered a special kind of *run-on sentence* (for which the Handbook provides a separate entry), a *comma splice* is a punctuation error that occurs when two independent clauses are joined only by a comma. A comma splice may be corrected by (1) using both comma and a coordinating conjunction or (2) replacing the comma with a semicolon or a period.

CS

There are only seven coordinating conjunctions: *and, but, or, nor, for, yet,* and *so.* When these are used between independent clauses, they should be preceded by a comma:

Wrong	Right
The boy had been crippled since infancy, he still tried to excel in everything he did.	The boy had been crippled since infancy, but he still tried to excel in everything he did.
	or
	The boy had been crippled since infancy; he still tried to excel in everything he did.
	or
	The boy had been crippled since infancy. He still tried to excel in everything he did.

Wrong	Right
Each writing assignment requires a different kind of organization, each may be a different length.	Each writing assignment requires a different kind of organization, and each may be a different length.

or

Each writing assignment requires a different kind of organization; each may be a different length.

or

Each writing assignment requires a different kind of organization. Each may be a different length.

It is often tempting to use words such as *however, therefore, nevertheless, indeed,* and *moreover* after a comma to join independent clauses. Don't! The only words following a comma that can join two independent clauses are the seven coordinating conjunctions.

Wrong	Right
We started with high hopes, however, we were disappointed.	We started with high hopes; however, we were disappointed.
She had been hurt many times, nevertheless, she always seemed cheerful.	She had been hurt many times; nevertheless, she always seemed cheerful.

Although any choice among coordinating conjunctions, semicolons, and periods will be technically correct, the best choice often depends on complex issues of style and thought. If the independent clauses under consideration are surrounded by long sentences, for example, the writer might choose to break the monotony with a period, thus creating two short sentences. If the independent clauses are surrounded by short sentences, the writer can sometimes achieve variety by creating a long sentence with a coordinating conjunction or semicolon. in addition, the more closely connected the thoughts in two independent clauses, the more likely the writer will be to show that connection by using a coordinating conjunction or semicolon. in such cases, two separate sentences would indicate too great a separation of thought. Obviously, no easy rules work here, and the writer's intentions have to be the main guide.

A somewhat more sophisticated way to correct a comma splice is often the best way: Since the comma splice is created by connecting two independent clauses with a comma, change one of the independent clauses into a phrase or dependent clause. Notice how this technique works with the preceding sample sentences.

Crippled from infancy, the boy still tried to excel in everything he did.

Although he had been crippled from infancy, the boy still tried to excel in everything he did.

While each writing assignment requires a different kind of organization, each may be a different length.

We started with high hopes but were disappointed.

Despite her being hurt many times, she always seemed cheerful.

> *NOTE:* Comma splices can be acceptable in standard English when each clause is unusually short and when the thought of the whole sentence expresses an on-going process.

I came, I saw, I conquered.

Throughout the interview, she squirmed, she stammered, she blushed.

EXERCISE

Rewrite the following sentences, correcting the comma splices where necessary.

1. General Electric is a widely diversified company, it makes everything from light bulbs to airplane engines, refrigerators to medical scanning devices.
2. It is allergy season again, the pollen and ragweed always aggravate my asthma.
3. Trash talk is a disgrace to professional sports, it should be outlawed.
4. Although I am no cook myself, I love to study the gourmet recipes.
5. Fear can prevent a person from acting, hate, on the other hand, will often cause action.
6. She was a human being: she was born, she lived, she suffered, she died.
7. Nothing matters more than your own personal integrity, never surrender your principles.
8. Most daytime talk shows allow people to air their dirty laundry in public, however Oprah Winfrey's program contains relevant topics for intelligent viewers.
9. Do not join two sentences with just a comma, use a comma and a conjunction, a semicolon, or a period to separate sentences.
10. Loyalty is rarely rewarded as much as it should be in the business world, therefore, do not be afraid or ashamed of changing jobs.

EXERCISE

Correct the comma splices in the following paragraphs.

1. Desperately searching the kitchen for something to eat, I found nothing. A little milk, some leftover macaroni, and one beet were the only things in the refrigerator. The situation was hopeless, I knew I would starve. In my anguish I thought about competing with the puppy for his food, but that seemed a little extreme. There was no escape, I would have to shop.
2. Air travel seems to be getting more and more expensive and less and less comfortable. In order to give travelers in first class more room, airlines

have moved the less expensive seats even closer together. This change leaves travelers almost no leg room at all, it's ridiculous. Even a short flight leaves one with numb feet and aching knees. Unless airlines make considerable improvements, they may find that people are choosing slower, but more comfortable, ways to travel.

3. The children ran wild through the neighborhood that summer. They chased each other up and down the streets on roller skates, skate boards, and bicycles. Their games of tag engulfed block after block in the town. It was glorious. It seemed as if the long, sunny days would never end, school would never start. But the weather began to cool, and the leaves began to change. Back to school they went. The streets were quiet and a little lonely without them.

Self Test: **COMMA SPLICES**

Correct the comma splices in the following sentences. Some sentences are already correct.

1. Some appetite-suppressing pills are now off the market, research found that they can cause heart problems.
2. The Olympic Games are supposed to promote international harmony, but they often appear to do the opposite.
3. Nothing can make Arthur change his mind, he can make a mule look cooperative.
4. Many mail-order companies sell their customer lists, then we receive hundreds of unsolicited offers each year.
5. After fifty pages, the book had failed to interest me, therefore, I finally decided to give up.
6. I used to write comma splices all the time, Dad taught me how to find and correct them.
7. Lawrence and Paolo spent too many nights at the bars, they looked tired and ill, they were a real mess.
8. She is a fantastic driver and a good mechanic; however, she can never remember where she parked her car.
9. Teenage Mutant Ninja Turtles were silly, childish, and too violent, nevertheless, the kids loved them.
10. Last winter we went sledding, we ice skated, and we went on sleigh rides.

Comparative and superlative forms. Comparative forms of adjectives and adverbs are used to compare or contrast groups of two—and only two. The comparative form of regular adjectives is formed by adding *-er* to the ending of the adjective or by using the word *more* before the adjective: *nicer, sweeter, more dramatic, more beautiful.* (Some adjectives are irregular: The comparative of *good* is *better*; the comparative of *bad* is *worse*.) The comparative form of adverbs is formed by using *more* before the adverb: *more nicely, more sweetly, more dramatically, more beautifully.*

Superlative forms of adjectives and adverbs are used to compare or contrast groups of three or more. The superlative form of regular adjectives is formed by adding *-est* to the ending of the adjective or by using the word *most* before the adjective: *nicest, sweetest, most dramatic, most beautiful.* (Some adjectives are irregular: The superlative of *good* is *best;* the superlative of *bad* is *worst.*) The superlative form of adverbs uses *most* before the adverb: *most nicely, most sweetly, most dramatically, most beautifully.*

In summary, comparative forms apply to two and superlative forms apply to more than two.

Wrong	Right
If I had to choose between Meryl Streep and Emma Thompson, I would have to say that Thompson is the *best* actor.	If I had to choose between Meryl Streep and Emma Thompson, I would have to say that Thompson is the *better* actor.
The high school girl and the junior high school girl competed on the parallel bars. The junior high school girl was given the *highest* scores.	The high school girl and the junior high school girl competed on the parallel bars. The junior high school girl was given the *higher* scores.
I like many people, but I like Betsy *more.*	I like many people, but I like Betsy *most.*
Although my first and second themes both required hard work, I wrote the second *most* easily.	Although my first and second themes both required hard work, I wrote the second *more* easily.

EXERCISE

Correct any errors in comparative and superlative forms.

1. Comparing travel by cars to travel by planes, I enjoy cars most.
2. Rockefellers and Kennedys are both rich, but Rockefellers are probably richer.
3. Phillip has to be the most charming man I have ever met.
4. Jenny won first prize for her watercolor landscape, but Elizabeth's painting was better.
5. One needs both love and friendship in marriage. Friendship could easily be the most important.
6. Among all my friends, I believe Karen is the one more likely to help in a crisis.
7. Though I adore both chocolate and strawberry ice cream, I enjoy strawberry the most.
8. At the moment, I feel more inclined toward a career in medicine than in law.

9. Most complicated choices depend on luck as well as on intelligence.
10. Dreiser was a great writer in many respects but of all the giants of American literature he probably had less basic talent.

EXERCISE

Correct the comparative–superlative errors in the following paragraphs.

1. Hansel and Gretel stopped just outside the gingerbread house. It was the most wonderful thing they had ever seen. Every bit of the house was made out of something delicious: candy, cookies, or cake. The children were very hungry, and the house smelled very good. They decided to break off small pieces to eat. Hansel was oldest, so he went first.
2. My mother and father shop very differently. Mom goes out for an entire day, looks in every store, and sometimes comes home with nothing. She shops to see what is available and to think about what she might want to buy. Dad goes out for twenty minutes, shops in one place, and always brings home what he set out to buy. He shops for one reason: He needs something. Dad is certainly more efficient, but Mom probably has the most fun.
3. Writing business letters can be very difficult. It is a real challenge to find the appropriate tone. One must be formal yet friendly, brief yet thorough. Even the more experienced writers may have great trouble composing a really good business letter. Perhaps this widespread difficulty is the reason that form letters have become so popular.

Self Test: COMPARATIVES AND SUPERLATIVES

Correct any errors in comparative and superlative forms. Not all sentences have errors.

1. She said that if she had to choose between Tom Cruise and Kevin Costner, she would be the most luckiest woman alive.
2. I have visited many national parks, and Bryce Canyon is the more spectacular.
3. Which of the seven dwarfs do you think is the more amusing?
4. He is most at home in front of an audience than alone in his room.
5. Whitney Houston is a talented musician but Mariah Carey is the best of the two.
6. This has been the worst trip ever.
7. Orange may be the less flattering of the two colors, but it is the more cheapest.
8. Good nutrition requires balanced meals and self-control. Which is hardest?
9. My grandmother's quilt is one of her most prized possessions.
10. At this point, it would be more better to run away than to fight.

Comparisons.   Comparisons must be both logical and complete.

A. *Logical.* Do not compare items that are not related. For example, you would not compare horses to safety pins because they have nothing in common. Not all illogical comparisons are this obvious, however, since it is usually the phrasing rather than the thought behind it that is at fault.

comp

Wrong	Right
His appetite is as huge as a pig. (Here the comparison is between *appetite* and *pig*.)	His appetite is as huge as a pig's. *or* His appetite is as huge as a pig's appetite. *or* His appetite is as huge as that of a pig.
Mark Twain is more amusing than any American writer. (Here Mark Twain is excluded from the group that he belongs to.)	Mark Twain is more amusing than any other American writer.

B. *Complete.* A comparison must be complete; that is, the items being compared must be clear, and both items must be stated.

   1. Clarity:

   Poor: I like him more than you.

   Right: I like him more than I like you.

   or

   I like him more than you like him.

   2. Both items stated:

   Poor: Old Reliable Bank has higher interest rates. (Higher than it had before? Higher than other banks have? Higher on deposits or higher on loans?)

   Right: Old Reliable Bank has higher interest rates on savings accounts than any other bank in the city.

(For further discussion of comparisons, see Chapter 20, pages 561–563.)

EXERCISE

Correct any faulty comparisons in the following sentences.

1. Dan Rather's presentation of the news is more lively than Tom Brokaw.
2. *The Sixth Sense* was the most frightening movie.
3. I like meeting strangers more than my husband.
4. Her marks were higher than anyone in the class.
5. My new television's reception is better than my old TV.
6. *Hamlet* is more interesting than any play ever written.
7. His great big sad eyes are like a cocker spaniel.
8. Curious, bouncy, and not too bright, he was as out of place at the meeting as a kangaroo.
9. Wah Lee's kitchen is cleaner than his sister.
10. Thomas Edison is more famous than any inventor in history.

Self Test: FAULTY COMPARISONS

Revise the faulty comparisons in the following sentences. One sentence is correct.

1. Carmella says she likes you better than any of her friends.
2. Cal Ripkin Jr.'s record for consecutive games played is better than any other baseball player in history.
3. The graceful line of neck and throat resembles a swan.
4. Nobody's acting is better than Jack Nicholson.
5. Miss Rochester had the best rating.
6. Dr. Raj is better with children than any pediatrician.
7. My feet are bigger than my sister.
8. His hand felt as cold and flabby as a week-old fish.
9. This poetry is better than any of Lord Byron.
10. McDonald's hamburgers are better than Burger King.

Complement. Usually a noun, pronoun, or adjective that follows a linking verb and is necessary for logical completion of the predicate.

Marilyn Monroe was an *actor.*

Who are *you*?

That proposal seems *sensible.*

Compound subjects. See *Subject–verb agreement, A.*

Conjunction. A word used to join parts of sentences or clauses. *Coordinating conjunctions* (joining words or clauses of equal importance) are *and, or, but, for, nor, yet, so; subordinating conjunctions* (linking dependent and independent clauses) are *because, while, when, although, until, after,* and so on.

Conjunctions, coordinating.   See *Comma, B; Comma splice.*

Conjunctions, subordinating.   See *Fragmentary sentences, C.*

Coordinating adjectives.   See *Comma, E.*

Coordinating conjunctions.   See *Comma, B; Comma splice.*

Dangling modifier.   See *Modifiers, A.*

Dash.   A dash (—) is used primarily to emphasize a parenthetical or otherwise nonessential word or phrase. It can also highlight an afterthought or separate a list or series from the rest of the sentence. An introductory list or series may be separated by a dash from the rest of the sentence if it is summarized by a word that serves as the subject of the sentence.

A. *Parenthetical word or phrase.*

Only when politicians are exposed to temptation—and rest assured they are almost always so exposed—can we determine their real worth as human beings.

B. *Afterthought.*

The only person who understood the talk was the speaker—and I have my doubts about her.

C. *List or series.*

The great French Impressionists—Manet, Monet, Renoir—virtually invented a new way of looking at the world.

The Scarlet Letter, Moby-Dick, Walden, Leaves of Grass, Uncle Tom's Cabin—these American classics were all published during the incredible five-year span of 1850–1855.

NOTE: Use dashes sparingly, or they lose their force. Do not confuse a dash with a hyphen (see *Hyphen*). In typing, indicate a dash by striking the hyphen key twice (--), leaving no space between the dash and the two words it separates.

Dependent clause.   See *Clause.*

Direct object.   See *Object.*

Double negative.   Always incorrect in standard English, a double negative is the use of two negative terms to express only one negative idea. Remember that in addition to obvious negative terms such as *no, not,* and *nothing,* the words *hardly* and *scarcely* are also considered negatives.

Wrong	Right
I don't have no memory of last night.	I don't have any memory of last night.
	or
	I have no memory of last night.
For truly religious people, money cannot mean nothing of value.	For truly religious people, money cannot mean anything of value.
	or
	For truly religious people, money can mean nothing of value.
His mother could not hardly express her feelings of pride at his graduation.	His mother could hardly express her feelings of pride at his graduation.
Our troubles had not scarcely begun.	Our troubles had scarcely begun.

Ellipsis.   An ellipsis (. . .) shows omission of one or more words from quoted material. If the ellipsis occurs at the end of a sentence, four spaced dots are used; one dot is the period for the sentence.

Original	Use of ellipsis
"The connotation of a word is its implicit meaning, the meaning derived from the atmosphere, the vibrations, the emotions that we associate with the word."	"The connotation of a word is its implicit meaning, . . . the emotions that we associate with the word."
"We had a drought in 1988 and major floods in 1989. Statistics can be deceptive. The two-year statistics for rainfall look totally normal, but the reality was wildly abnormal."	"We had a drought in 1988 and major floods in 1989. . . . The two-year statistics for rainfall look totally normal, but the reality was wildly abnormal."

End marks.   The three end marks are the period, question mark, and exclamation point.

A. *Period.* A period is used at the end of complete sentences, after abbreviations, and in fractions expressed as decimals.

1. *Sentences.* If a complete sentence makes a statement, use a period at the end:

Please give unused clothing to the Salvation Army.

Place pole *B* against slot *C* and insert bolt *D*.

The class wants to know when the paper is due.

2. *Abbreviations.* A period is used after some abbreviations:

Mr. R. P. Reddish   Mt. Everest   p.m.

NOTE: A period is not used in abbreviations such as UNESCO, NAACP, FCC, MLA, and AARP. See Abbreviations.

3. *Decimals.* A period is used before a fraction written as a decimal.

$^1/_4 = 0.25$ $^1/_{20} = 0.05$

NOTE: If a decimal is used to indicate money, a dollar sign is also necessary: $5.25.

B. *Question mark.* A question mark is used to indicate a direct question or a doubtful date or figure.

1. *Direct question.* Use a question mark at the end of a direct question. Do not use a question mark with indirect questions such as "They asked when the paper was due."

When is the paper due?

Did the teacher say when the paper is due?

A question mark is also used when only the last part of a sentence asks a question, and when a quotation that asks a question is contained within a larger sentence.

I know I should go to college, but where will I get the money for tuition?

The student asked, "When is the paper due?"

After asking, "When is the paper due?" the student left the room.

NOTE: In the last example, the question mark replaces the usual comma inside the quotation.

2. *Doubtful date or figure.* After a doubtful date or figure, use a question mark in parentheses. This does not mean that if you are giving an approximate date or figure you should use a question mark. Use it only if the accuracy of the date or figure is doubtful.

The newspaper reported that the government said it cost $310(?) to send a person to the moon. (Here a question mark is appropriate because it is doubtful if $310 is the figure. Perhaps there has been a misprint in the paper.)

Chaucer was born in 1340(?) and died in 1400. (Here historians know when Chaucer died but are doubtful of exactly when he was born, even though most evidence points to 1340. If historians were completely unsure, they would simply write, "Chaucer was born in the mid-1300s and died in 1400.")

A question mark in parentheses should never be used to indicate humor or sarcasm. It is awkward and childish to write, "He was a good(?) teacher," or, "After much debate and cynical compromise, the legislature approved a satisfactory(?) state budget."

C. *Exclamation point.* An exclamation point is used at the end of emphatic or exclamatory words, phrases, and sentences. In formal writing, exclamation points are rare. They most often occur in dialog, and even there they should be used sparingly lest their effect be lost.

1. *Word or phrase:*

   My God! Is the paper due today?

   No! You cannot copy my exam.

2. *Sentence:*

   The school burned down!

   Stop talking!

   NOTE: Comic book devices such as !?! or !! should be avoided. Words, not the symbols after them, should carry the primary meaning.

EXERCISE

Add periods, question marks, and exclamation points as needed in the following sentences.

1. Every newspaper delivery driver must have dependable transportation and a reliable backup driver
2. Who will volunteer to coach the varsity basketball team this fall
3. Ling wondered if her fax machine was malfunctioning again
4. Last May I got a job with a nonprofit consumer advocacy organization based in Washington, D.C.
5. Did you know that the most desirable ratio for salad vinaigrettes is four parts oil to one part vinegar
6. The receptionist asked when I could come in for an interview
7. "Why do you insist on taking my things without asking" she demanded angrily
8. I believe that we must hold HMOs accountable for any decisions that affect patients' health
9. The candidate claims that he favors hate-crimes legislation, but why did he never propose such legislation when he was a congressman
10. Don't you think it's time you moved into your own apartment

Self Test: END MARKS

Correct any mistakes in the use of end marks in the following sentences. Some sentences contain more than one mistake.

1. "How can you write an essay on a book you've never read," she asked?
2. Elba wondered why it took six months for her new sofa to arrive?
3. The climate at the summit of Mt. Washington is extremely volatile and unpredictable!
4. I know that my petunias get plenty of sun, so why are they dying.
5. Oh, no. I've lost my keys again.
6. Clive asked himself how much he really enjoyed golf?
7. The city bus will take you to the ML Grieg Library.
8. The speakers asked the state, local, and federal governments to cooperate with private organizations on environmental preservation?
9. Get me out of here right now.
10. Why can't we all just get along.

Exclamation point.   See *End marks, C.*

Fragmentary sentences.   A fragmentary sentence is a grammatically incomplete statement punctuated as if it were a complete sentence. It is one of the most common basic writing errors.

To avoid a sentence fragment, make sure that your sentence contains at least one independent clause. If it does not contain an independent clause, it is a fragment.

Here are some examples of sentences with the independent clause italicized; sometimes the independent clause is the whole sentence, and sometimes the independent clause is part of a larger sentence.

Jack and Jill went up the hill.

He sees.

If you don't stop bothering me, *I'll phone the police.*

Tomorrow at the latest, *we'll have to call a special meeting.*

He straightened his tie before he entered the room.

Discovering that she had lost her mother, *the little girl started to cry.*

An *independent clause* is a group of words that contains a subject and verb and expresses a complete thought. This traditional definition is beyond criticism except that it can lead to messy discussions about the philosophical nature of a complete thought. Such discussions can usually be avoided by concentrating on the practical reasons for a missing independent clause. There are three major reasons: omission of subject or verb, confusion of verb derivatives (verbals) with verbs, and confusion of a dependent clause with an independent clause.

frag

A. *Omission of subject or verb.* This is the simplest kind of fragment to spot:

There are many events that take place on campus. *Such as plays, concerts, and innumerable other things.*

My father finally answered me. *Nastily and negatively.*

Mr. Jones has plenty of activities to keep himself busy. *Nagging, scolding, snooping, and drinking.*

The new department head had a brand new pain in the neck. *In addition to the old ones.*

We had many blessings. *Like love, nature, family, God, and television.*

These fragments should be obvious even without the italics, and the remedies should be just as obvious. Simple changes in punctuation will solve the problems. Here are the same sentences with the fragments eliminated:

There are many events that take place on campus, such as plays, concerts, and innumerable other things.

My father finally answered me nastily and negatively.

Mr. Jones has plenty of activities to keep himself busy: nagging, scolding, snooping, and drinking.

The new department head had a brand new pain in the neck in addition to the old ones.

We had many blessings, like love, nature, family, God, and television.

B. *Confusion of verb derivatives (verbals) with verbs.* Verbals are words derived from verbs. Unlike verbs, they cannot function by themselves as the predicate of a sentence. Infinitive forms are verbals (*to do, to see, to walk*). So are gerunds and present participles (-*ing* endings: *doing, seeing, walking*). Study the italicized sentence fragments that follow.

I decided to take her to the game. *Susan enjoying football a lot.*

Nobody ought to vote. *The government being corrupt.*

We should take pleasure in the little things. *A boy petting his dog. Lovers holding hands. Soft clouds moving overhead.*

To make the world a better place. To help people be happy. These are my goals.

In the last example, the fragments lack subjects as well as verbs and can readily be identified. Inexperienced writers, however, looking at the fragments in the first three examples, see a subject and what appears to be a verb. They assume, consequently, that the words make up an independent clause. They are wrong. A present participle by itself cannot serve as a verb, and an independent clause must have a verb. Study these corrected versions of the fragments.

I decided to take her to the game. Susan has been enjoying football a lot.

Nobody ought to vote. The government is corrupt.

We should take pleasure in the little things: a boy petting his dog, lovers holding hands, soft clouds moving overhead.

I want to make the world a better place. I want to make people happy. These are my goals.

C. *Confusion of a dependent (subordinate) clause with an independent clause.* All clauses contain a subject and a verb. Unlike an independent clause, however, a *dependent* or *subordinate clause* does not express a complete thought and therefore cannot function as a sentence. A subordinate clause at the beginning of a sentence must always be followed by an independent clause. A subordinate clause at the end of a sentence must always be preceded by an independent clause. Fortunately, subordinate clauses can be readily identified if you remember that *they always begin with subordinating conjunctions*—a much easier approach than trying to figure out whether your sentence conveys a complete thought. Here, in alphabetical order, is a list of the subordinating conjunctions you are most likely to encounter. Whenever one of these words immediately precedes a clause (subject + verb), that clause becomes a subordinate clause and cannot stand alone as a complete sentence.

after	as soon as	even though	provided that	unless
although	as though	how	since	until
as	because	if	so that	whenever
as if	before	in order that	than	wherever
as long as	even if	once	though	while

NOTE: Except when used as question words, who, which, when, and where also introduce a subordinate clause.

In the left-hand column below, examples of subordinate clauses used as sentence fragments are italicized. In the right-hand column, italics indicate corrections to repair these sentence fragments.

Fragments	Corrected
If I ever see home again.	If I ever see home again, *I'll be surprised.*
Keats was a great poet. *Because he was inspired.*	*Keats was a great poet* because he was inspired.
I will never apologize. *Unless you really insist.*	*I will never apologize* unless you really insist.
Provided that the contract is carried out within thirty days.	Provided that the contract is carried out within thirty days, *we will not sue.*
This is the person who will be our next governor. *Who will lead this state to a better tomorrow.*	*This is the person who will be our next governor,* who will lead this state to a better tomorrow.

The major difficulty anyone is likely to have with sentence fragments is in identifying them. They are usually easy to correct. Sentence fragments occur, in many cases, because of a misunderstanding of complex grammatical issues, but they can almost always be corrected with elementary revisions in punctuation.

Sentence fragments should nearly always be avoided. In rare situations, they can sometimes be justified, especially if the writer wants a sudden dramatic effect.

I shall never consent to this law. Never!

Oh, God!

Scared? I was terrified.

Lost. Alone in the big city. Worried. The boy struggled to keep from crying.

EXERCISE

Some of the following are sentence fragments. Rewrite them to form complete sentences.

1. As long as we continue to follow traditional ways of thinking.
2. After majoring in English at the University of Southern California.
3. Who will send the invitations?
4. Although I admired her greatly and thought she deserved a chance.
5. The managing editor, an excellent journalist and former reporter.
6. Because the senator planned to pursue some other interests.
7. Although improving many people's appearance, contact lenses are far less convenient than traditional eyeglasses.
8. From muffins and rolls to cakes and breads.
9. To make a long story short.
10. Before long, the fire died down.
11. Shuffling papers and looking busy are the only requirements of the job.
12. Sobered by the costly ordeal.
13. To mention just a few items of relatively minor importance.
14. A person who can approach problems with a unique combination of vision and practicality.
15. Unless we all work together for a better world, we may have no world at all.
16. If American airports follow the overseas model.
17. Who was that masked man?
18. Until the orchestra plays more popular selections.
19. Angry and screaming at the top of their lungs.
20. In addition to dwindling market share, mounting losses, and falling stock prices.

EXERCISE

Find and correct the sentence fragments in the following paragraphs.

1. Yu-lin had several errands to run that afternoon. Going to the shoe repair store, stopping off at the bank, and dropping off a few books at the library. He had no idea if he could finish in time. Thinking carefully, he made a plan. He would stop at the bank, then pick up his shoes. And then drive all the way across town to the library. If he drove quickly and didn't get stopped by any red lights, he could be home in time to start supper and do a few loads of laundry.

2. Scrabble is a game that requires intelligence, skills, and almost infinite patience. A single game can take as long as three hours and can get very dull at times. While you wait for your opponent to think of a word. There isn't much for you to do but look at the ceiling, try to remember how to spell *syzygy,* and hope that your opponent doesn't play a word in the space you hope to use. Beyond these few diversions, all you can do is wait. And wait.

3. My favorite way to spend an evening is to curl up on the couch with a big bowl of popcorn and watch old movies. Black-and-white movies are best. I munch my popcorn and let myself get pulled into a world where people have doormen, where everyone wears hats and gloves, where chivalry is not dead. Romance, too. I love the movies where the hero and heroine fall desperately and hopelessly in love. Films like that are always wonderfully sad and romantic, and if I cry, the popcorn just gets a little extra salt. Of course, I also like the old comedies and suspense thrillers. There's just no way for me to go wrong with a night filled with comfort, snack food, and entertainment.

Self Test: FRAGMENTS

Find and correct the fragments in the following sentences. More than one option exists for correcting the fragments.

1. Americans celebrate Flag Day on June 14. To salute a flag that was stitched in 1776. And has bound the nation together ever since.

2. After Celeste's five-year-old daughter split her lip. On a metal shovel at the playground. The distraught mother decided that playgrounds are just too dangerous.

3. Barking and wagging her tail furiously. My golden retriever welcomed me home. After a grueling day at the office. I really needed her affection.

4. It was the perfect day for a barbeque. Sunny, breezy, and warm.

5. Living on a farm isn't easy. So much work to do beginning at dawn. Milking cows. Collecting eggs. Caring for all the animals.

6. Mrs. Scott always acts aloof towards us. If she even acknowledges us at all. As if we aren't good enough. Because our home isn't as large as hers.

7. A spokesperson for Chevrolet says that the company's new pickup combines several important attributes. Ruggedness, versatility, and personal comfort.

8. The panelists at the business symposium wrestled with a difficult question. Whether technology and the Internet have left small businesses behind.

9. Wind gusts can cause serious problems for firefighters. Struggling to keep a fire under control.

10. When you make your own car payments. When you pay rent. And when you earn a paycheck. That's when I will consider you a responsible adult.

Fused sentence. See *Run-on sentence.*

Hyphen. A hyphen (-) is used to form some compound words and to divide words at the end of a line.

A. *Compound words.*

   1. As a general rule, you should consult a recent dictionary to check the use of the hyphen in compound words. Many such words that were once hyphenated are now combined. The following are some compound words that are still hyphenated:

     mother-in-law   court-martial

     knee-deep   water-cooled

   2. All numbers from twenty-one to ninety-nine are hyphenated:

     forty-three   one hundred fifty-six

   3. A hyphen joins two or more words that form an adjective before a noun:

     a well-known teacher   a first-rate performance

     but   *but*

     The teacher is well known.   The performance was first rate.

B. *Divided words.* Divide words at the end of a line by consulting a dictionary and following accepted syllabication. A one-syllable word cannot be divided. In addition, a single letter cannot be separated from the rest of the word; for example, *a-bout* for *about* would be incorrect. The hyphen should come at the very end of the line, not at the beginning of the next line.

Independent clause. See *Clause.*

Indirect question.   See *End marks, B, 1.*

Infinitive.   Simple form of a verb preceded by the word *to,* for example, *to come, to go.*

Intransitive verb.   See *Verb.*

Italics (underlining).   In manuscript form—handwriting or typing—under-lining represents printed italics. The rules for underlining and italics are the same. Underline titles of complete works; most foreign words and phrases; words used emphatically; and letters, words, and phrases pointed to as such.

NOTE: When a word or phrase that would usually be italicized appears in a section of text that is already italicized, the word or phrase is typed or written with no italics.

A. *Titles of complete works.*

    1. Books: *The Great Gatsby, Paradise Lost, Encyclopaedia Britannica, Webster's New Collegiate Dictionary*

    2. Newspapers and magazines: *New York Times, Chicago Tribune, Newsweek*

    3. Plays: *Raisin in the Sun, Macbeth*

The titles of poems are enclosed in quotation marks, except for book-length poems such as Milton's *Paradise Lost* or Homer's *Iliad.* The titles of small units contained within larger units—such as chapters in books, selections in anthologies, articles or short stories in magazines, and individual episodes of a television series—are also enclosed in quotation marks. (See *Quotation marks, B.*)

B. *Foreign words and phrases not assimilated into English.*

vaya con Dios   *paisano*   *auf Wiedersehen*

but

cliché   genre   laissez-faire   taco

C. *Words used emphatically.*

Ask me, but don't *tell* me.

Under *no* circumstances can this be permitted to happen.

Except in special situations, good word choice and careful phrasing are far more effective than underlining to show emphasis.

D. *Letters, words, and phrases pointed to as such.*

Words such as *however* and *therefore* cannot be used as coordinating conjunctions.

The letter *x* is often used in algebra.

The phrase *on the other hand* anticipates contrast.

Linking verb.   See *Verb; Adjective–adverb confusion.*

Misplaced modifier.   See *Modifiers, B.*

Modifiers.   The most frequent errors involving modifiers are dangling modifiers and misplaced modifiers.

dm

A. *Dangling modifiers.* A *dangling modifier* is a group of words, often found at the beginning of a sentence, that does not refer to anything in the sentence or that seems to refer to a word to which it is not logically related. Dangling modifiers usually include some form of a verb that has no subject, either implied or stated. This construction results in statements that are often humorous and always illogical. To correct a dangling modifier, either change the modifier into a subordinate clause, or change the main clause so that the modifier logically relates to a word in it. On occasion, it may be necessary to change both clauses.

Incorrect	Correct
Climbing the mountain, the sunset blazed with a brilliant red and orange. (This sentence says that the sunset is climbing the mountain.)	As we were climbing the mountain, the sunset blazed with a brilliant red and orange. (Subordinate clause)
	or
	Climbing the mountain, we saw the sunset blazing with a brilliant red and orange. (Main clause)
After looking in several stores, the book was found. (In this sentence, the book is looking in several stores.)	After looking in several stores, we found the book.
To become an accurate speller, a dictionary should be used. (In this sentence, the dictionary is becoming an accurate speller.)	If you want to become an accurate speller, you should use a dictionary.
	or
	To become an accurate speller, you should use a dictionary.
While talking and not paying attention, the teacher gave the class an assignment. (This sentence says that the teacher is talking and not paying attention while giving an assignment. If that is what the writer meant, then this sentence is correct. If, however, the writer meant that the class was talking and not paying attention, then it is incorrect.)	While the class was talking and not paying attention, the teacher gave an assignment.
	or
	While talking and not paying attention, the class was given an assignment by the teacher.

B. *Misplaced modifiers.* Since part of the meaning of the English language depends on word order—some other languages depend mostly on word endings—you must make sure that phrases serving as modifiers and adverbs such as *only, always, almost, hardly,* and *nearly* are placed in the position that will make the sentence mean what you intend. *Misplaced modifiers,* unlike dangling modifiers, can almost always be corrected simply by changing their positions.

mm

1. Phrases serving as modifiers:

   The teacher found the book for the student in the library.

   This sentence indicates that the student was in the library. If, however, the writer meant that the book was found in the library, then the modifier *in the library* is misplaced. The sentence should read:

   The teacher found the book in the library for the student.

   The writer of the following sentence seems to be saying that the college is near the lake:

   His parents met his friend from the college near the lake.

   If, however, the writer meant that the meeting took place near the lake, the modifier is misplaced and the sentence should read:

   Near the lake, his parents met his friend from the college.

2. Adverbs like *only, always, almost, hardly* and *nearly* usually qualify the word that comes after them. Therefore, the position of these words depends on what the writer wishes to say.

   The adverb *only* is a notorious troublemaker. Observe how the sentence *"I want a son"* changes meaning significantly with the change in position of *only:*

I *only* want a son.	(I don't yearn for or long for a son; I only want one.)
I want *only* a son.	(I have no other wants.)
I want an *only* son.	(One son is as many as I want.)
I want a son *only*.	(I do not want a daughter.)

EXERCISE

Rewrite the following sentences as necessary to correct any dangling or misplaced modifiers.

1. Racing down the street, our books fell out of the bag.
2. My history professor spoke passionately about the evils of cheating on Tuesday.
3. Carve the roast after standing at room temperature for a few minutes.
4. I baked special cookies for the minister with chocolate chips.
5. The quarterback was removed from the game before he was permanently injured by the coach.

6. Speaking in a moderate tone, the lecture was more successful.
7. Erica bikes well on the mountain trails with powerful leg muscles.
8. Running toward second base, we saw the runner make a daring slide.
9. Juan wants Judy to love him badly.
10. While driving through Yosemite, a bear stopped our car.

Self Test: DANGLING AND MISPLACED MODIFIERS

Correct the misplaced modifiers in the following sentences. One sentence is correct.

1. Nailed to the fence, Walter noticed a "NO TRESPASSING" sign.
2. My parrot landed gracefully on my shoulder with ruffled feathers.
3. Barking wildly and nipping at an old woman's heels, I thought the dog had gone mad.
4. Plucking the delicate petals, the children smiled secretly as they felt the autumn breeze.
5. Watching the horror film, Esteban got a terrible pain from the gruesome scene in his stomach.
6. Chomping loudly and belching, we were appalled at Uncle Ray's terrible table manners.
7. Sam grabbed the milk and drank it from the fridge.
8. I like to watch television doing my ironing.
9. Michelle was told never to speak to strangers by her mother.
10. Golden brown and juicy, I thought the turkey looked fantastic.

EXERCISE

Correct any dangling or misplaced modifiers in the following paragraphs.

1. The weather was beautiful that day, and it seemed as if everyone was making the most of it. The park was filled with people playing catch, flying kites, or simply lying in the grass and soaking up the sun. Chirping happily in the trees, numerous picnickers were entertained by choruses of birds. Swimming was a popular way to spend the day, too. The river overflowed with kids of all ages taking their last summer swim.
2. Everyone knew the house was haunted. Looming ominously in the distance, it overshadowed the whole town. No one had been inside for years. Everyone had been afraid since that fateful day when, shrieking and hollering, the house was rapidly vacated by the family that owned it. They all said they had seen a ghost. No one believed them, not at first. Then, the noises began.
3. Football fans sometimes seem a little crazy to the rest of the world. They love their teams so much and want them to win so badly that these fans will do just about anything. Cleveland is just one example. Wearing dog masks, barking, and throwing dog bones at the opposition, the town goes wild. All of this silliness springs not from insanity, but from love and devotion. It's just the fans' way of saying, "We're behind you all the way. Win one for us!"

Modifiers, nonrestrictive.   See *Comma, F.*

Modifiers, restrictive.   See *Comma, F.*

Nonrestrictive modifiers.   See *Comma, F.*

Noun.   Traditionally defined as the name of a person, place, thing, or concept, nouns are generally used as the subject, object, or complement of a sentence: *Roosevelt, Bill, accountant, California, Lake Ontario, Boulder Dam, desk, car, freedom, love.*

Numerals.

A. *Numerals are used to indicate dates, times, percentages, money, street numbers, and page references.*

On January 21, 1994, at 5:00 a.m., a fire broke out at 552 East 52nd Street, and before the Fire Department brought the flames under control, 75 percent of the building had been destroyed.

B. *In other cases, if a number is one or two words, spell it out; if it is over two words, use the numeral.*

In the big contest yesterday, forty-five young boys were able to eat 152 hot dogs in two minutes.

C. *Spell out all numbers that begin a sentence.*

Four thugs assaulted an old woman last night.

Three hundred thirty-one deaths have been predicted for the Labor Day weekend.

Object.   The person, place, or thing that receives the action of a verb, or the noun or pronoun after a preposition.

George shot *Joe.*

Florence kissed *him.*

All motives are suspect to *them.*

You'll find your *gloves* in the car.

Parallelism.   Ideas and facts of equal importance should be expressed in the same grammatical form:

Incorrect	Correct
You can get there by *car, bus,* or *fly.* (noun, noun, verb)	You can get there by *car, bus,* or *plane.* (noun, noun, noun)
I thought the climactic episode in the story was *shocking, offbeat,* and *I found it very amusing.* (adjective, adjective, independent clause)	I thought the climactic episode in the story was *shocking, offbeat,* and very *amusing.* (adjective, adjective, adjective)

//

Incorrect	Correct
She *liked* people and *was liked* by people. (active voice, passive voice)	She *liked* people and people *liked* her. (active voice, active voice)
The teacher told us *to work* fast and *that we should write on only one side of the paper.* (infinitive, clause)	The teacher told us *to work* fast and *to write* on only one side of the paper. (infinitive, infinitive)

(For fuller treatment of parallelism, see Chapter 21, pages 572–573.)

Parentheses.   Parentheses can enclose incidental comments, provide explanatory details, and sometimes set off numerals that accompany the points of a paper. Parentheses are also used in footnotes. In many cases, parentheses serve to mark afterthoughts that should have been incorporated into the writing elsewhere. Therefore, use parentheses sparingly.

A. *Incidental comments.*

The movie *The Killers* (its plot had little resemblance to Hemingway's short story) won an award.

B. *Explanation of details.*

The cornucopia (the horn of plenty) is a Thanksgiving symbol.

C. *Enumerated points.*

This essay has four main pieces of advice: (1) know your professors as people, (2) attend college-sponsored events, (3) attend student-sponsored events, and (4) use the library.

D. *Footnotes.*

[1]Peter Straub, *Shadowland* (New York: Coward, McCann & Geoghegan, 1980), 10.
[2]Straub 10.

Passive voice.   See *Voice.* Also see Chapter 21, pages 570–571.

Period.   See *End marks, A.*

Person.   The form of pronouns and verbs that indicates the speaker (*first person*), the person or thing spoken to (*second person*), or the person or thing spoken about (*third person*).

	Pronoun	Verb
First person	I, we	go
Second person	you	go

	Pronoun	Verb
Third person	he, she, it	goes
	they	go

Possessives.   See *Apostrophe, C.*

Predicate.   The part of a clause that tells what the subject does, or what is being done to the subject.

Sal *went home.*

The child *will be punished.*

Also see *Subject.*

Preposition.   A connecting word such as *in, by, from, on, to,* or *with* that shows the relation of a noun or a pronoun to another element in a sentence.

The man *with* the gun shot the deer.

Pronoun.   A word that takes the place of a noun. It may be personal (*I, you, he, she, it, we, they, me, him, her*), possessive (*my, mine, your, yours, his*), reflexive or intensive (*myself, yourself, herself*), relative (*who, which, that*), interrogative (*who, which, what*), or indefinite (*anyone, somebody, nothing*).

Pronoun agreement.   A pronoun must agree with its antecedent both in gender (masculine, feminine, or neuter) and number (singular or plural). The antecedent of a pronoun is the word or words to which the pronoun refers. For example, in the sentence "Jason lost his book," the pronoun *his* refers to the antecedent *Jason.* Another example is "Jason could not find his book. He had lost it." In the second sentence, there are two pronouns—*he* and *it.* The antecedent of *he* is *Jason,* and the antecedent of *it* is *book.* With the exception of constructions such as *it is nearly eight o'clock,* in which *it* has no antecedent, all pronouns should have antecedents.

agr

A. *Gender.* When the gender of a singular antecedent is unknown, irrelevant, or general (as in *student* or *person,* for example), be sure to avoid sexist language. The traditional rule calling for the masculine pronoun to take precedence in such situations is now outdated and has been rejected by all or nearly all publishers of books, magazines, and newspapers as well as English instructors.

sexist

If the singular antecedent is retained, sexist language can be avoided by using a form of *he or she,* though this phrasing can often be awkward and excessively formal.

A student needs to turn in his or her work on time.

A person who truly likes others will find that others will like him or her.

machine. Then there are the kids who have never done laundry before. They wash their socks and their underwear with their blue jeans and complain when their whites get dingy. The rest of us have to wait while these fools relaunder all their clothes. I am so tired of it all that I just might start doing my laundry in my dishwasher.

Self Test: PRONOUN AGREEMENT

Correct pronoun agreement errors in the following sentences. Some sentences are correct.

1. Everyone must have their passport and birth certificate if they want to cross the border.
2. The screaming citizenry shouted rude slogans at their disgraced former ruler.
3. Either Delia or her sisters will have to give up her turn in the front seat.
4. One of the Marlowe brothers leaned back casually, carefully straightening their shirtsleeves.
5. No one but Fred will have their license revoked.
6. Neither Greg nor Marcia can find her textbook.
7. Every chef knows they must work with extremely sharp knives.
8. None of it was finished, so they were set aside for a while.
9. A patient with damage to the part of the brain called the hippocampus may remember only events from before his injury.
10. Emma and John opened the champagne and poured some into their glasses.

ca

Pronoun case.   *Pronoun case* refers to the change in form of pronouns that corresponds with their grammatical function. There are three cases, and their names are self-explanatory: *subjective* (when the pronoun acts as a subject), *objective* (when the pronoun acts as an object), and *possessive* (when the pronoun acts to show possession). Following is a list of case changes for the most common pronouns:

Subjective	Objective	Possessive
I	me	my, mine
you	you	your, yours
he	him	his
she	her	her, hers
it	it	its
we	us	our, ours
they	them	their, theirs
who	whom	whose

Case rarely presents problems for native speakers. Nobody says or writes, "He gave I the album," or, "Me like she." Complications turn up in relatively few situations.

A. *Compound subjects and objects (subjects and objects connected by* and*).* Do not be misled by a compound subject or object. Use the pronoun case that shows the pronoun's grammatical role.

Wrong	Right
My father scolded Jim and *I*.	My father scolded Jim and *me*.
Betty and *her* had many good times.	Betty and *she* had many good times.

A simple test for getting the right word is to eliminate one of the compound terms and see which pronoun works better. No one would write "My father scolded I"—so "My father scolded me" is correct. No one would write "Her had many good times"—so "She had many goods times" is correct.

B. *Object of a preposition.* In a prepositional phrase, any pronoun after the preposition always takes the objective case.

Wrong	Right
This match is just between you and *I*.	This match is just between you and *me*.
I went to the movies with *she*.	I went to the movies with *her*.
This present is for John and *he*.	This present is for John and *him*.

C. *After forms of* to be *(is, am, are, was, were, has been, had been, might be, will be, etc.).* A pronoun after forms of *to be* is always in the subjective case. This rule still applies rigorously in formal written English. It is frequently ignored in informal English and has all but disappeared from most conversation.

It was she.

This is he.

The winners will be they.

D. *After* as *and* than*.* In comparisons with *as* and *than*, mentally add a verb to the pronoun to determine which pronoun is correct. Should you write, for example, "Bill is smarter than I," or, "Bill is smarter than me"? Simply complete the construction with the "understood" verb. You could write, "Bill is smarter than I am," but not, "Bill is smarter than me am." Therefore, "Bill is smarter than I" is correct.

Wrong	Right
I am just as good as *them*.	I am just as good as *they*.
Her mother had more ambition than *her*.	Her mother had more ambition than *she*.

Wrong	Right
Bill liked her more than *I*.	Bill liked her more than *me*. (Meaning *Bill liked her more than he liked me*.)
Bill liked her more than *me*.	Bill liked her more than *I*. (Meaning *Bill liked her more than I liked her*.)

E. We *or* us *followed by a noun*. Use *we* if the noun is a subject, *us* if the noun is an object. If ever in doubt, mentally eliminate the noun and see which pronoun sounds right. Should you write, for example, "The professor had us students over to his house" or "The professor had we students over to his house"? Mentally eliminate *students*. No one would write "The professor had we over to his house," so *us* is correct.

Wrong	Right
After the final exam, *us* students were exhausted.	After the final exam, *we* students were exhausted.
The company's reply to *we* consumers was almost totally negative.	The company's reply to *us* consumers was almost totally negative.

F. *Gerunds*. A gerund is an *-ing* verb form that functions as a noun. In "Swimming used to be my favorite sport," *swimming* is a gerund. A pronoun before a gerund takes the possessive case.

Wrong	Right
Us nagging him did no good.	*Our* nagging him did no good.
His parents do not understand *him* reading so poorly.	His parents do not understand *his* reading so poorly.
Them believing what she says does not mean that she is telling the truth.	*Their* believing what she says does not mean that she is telling the truth.

G. *Who and whom*. See the Glossary, pages 717–719.

EXERCISE

Choose the correct pronoun in each of the following sentences. Be prepared to explain your choice.

1. He cared about money every bit as much as (I, me), but he was a more successful hypocrite than (I, me).
2. For (he and she, him and her), divorce might have been the only practical choice.
3. Will you accompany Sally and (I, me) to the movies?
4. (She, Her) and I took the same courses last semester.
5. (Him, His) lying has become part of his character.

6. (He and I, Him and me) decided that we would adopt a beagle from our local shelter.

7. I honestly don't know what he expects (we, us) poor students to do.

8. The judge then assessed an additional fine for (them, their) resisting arrest.

9. The winning contestants were no brighter or quicker than (I, me).

10. Bennett hated Stephen and (she, her) with a jealous passion.

EXERCISE

Find and correct any errors in pronoun case in the following paragraphs.

1. Jack Fitzwilliam, master thief, walked calmly down the street. In his pockets were the diamonds and pearls that, until recently, had been the sacred treasure of the Montgomery family. Now they were Jack's. He knew the police were only moments behind him. However, with his false beard and moustache, he had no fear of being recognized, and if he ran from the police they might think of him running as an admission of guilt.

2. Just between you and I, I've never been very fond of Ann Pickett. It's not that she's cruel or nasty; we just have so little in common. For some reason, we are always expected to be best friends and exchange cozy confidences. To me, that is unthinkable. We just never have anything to talk about.

3. We are tired of this abuse, and we just won't take it any longer. Us poor kids do all the work around here. We mow the lawn, take out the trash, do the dishes, feed and walk the dogs, fold the laundry, and wash windows. You adults just sit around and do nothing. When are you going to start taking some responsibility for yourselves? When are you going to become mature and capable? We're tired of waiting. Us kids are on strike.

Self Test: PRONOUN CASE

Select the correct pronoun in the following sentences.

1. (She, Her) and her three cats boarded the plane.

2. There's no question that I'm taller than (she, her).

3. Discouraged and crestfallen, Brett and (I, me) slowly returned home.

4. Our aged music professor, a once-famous contralto, can still sing better than any of (we, us) students.

5. He gave the money to Woo Chai and (I, me).

6. (Us, we) consumers are tired of being tricked by false advertising.

7. I know so little about politics that (me, my) running for political positions makes no sense.

8. It was a secret between (he and she, him and her), but the whole world knew about it by sunset.

9. The attorney best suited for this complicated case is (she, her).

10. The people who are latest to the party will be (they, them).

ref

Pronoun reference. A pronoun must not only agree with its antecedent, but that antecedent must be clear as well. An ambiguous antecedent is as bad as no antecedent at all. Generally, two types of ambiguity occur: a pronoun with two or more possible antecedents, and one pronoun referring to different antecedents.

A. *Two or more possible antecedents.* In the sentence, "When Stanton visited the mayor, he said that he hoped his successor could work with him," the pronouns *he, his,* and *him* can refer to either the mayor or Stanton. This problem can be avoided by making the antecedent clear: "When Stanton visited the mayor, Stanton said that he hoped his successor could work with the mayor." Here the pronouns *he* and *his* clearly refer to Stanton. Be particularly careful of the potential ambiguity in vague use of the word *this.*

Ambiguous	Improved
I received an *F* in the course and had to take it over again. This was very unfair. (Was the *F* unfair or having to take the course again? Were both unfair?)	I received an *F* in the course and had to take it over again. This grade was very unfair.
Young people are unhappy today and are demanding change. This is a healthy thing. (What is healthy—being unhappy, demanding change, or both?)	Young people are unhappy today and are demanding change. This demand is a healthy thing.

B. *One pronoun referring to different antecedents.* "Mark received an *F* on his term paper and had to write a revision of it. It took a long time because it had many errors." In these sentences, the first *it* refers to the paper, the second to the revision, and the third to the paper. A reader could easily become confused by these sentences. In that case, simply replacing the pronouns with their antecedents would solve the problem: "Mark received an *F* on his term paper and had to write a revision of it. The revision took a long time because the paper had many errors."

EXERCISE

Rewrite the following sentences by correcting any errors in pronoun reference.

1. Scuba diving and snorkeling are very popular in Palau, but it can be dangerous.
2. The fans cheered the performers hysterically, and they didn't leave the hall for another hour.
3. The students left the rooms in their usual order.
4. Jim told his father that he ought to put his funds into a money-market account.
5. Anita inspected the carburetor and distributor. It needed several adjustments.
6. Emma's coach told her that she needed to see some more plays before she could leave for the day.

7. Charlotte received her citizenship papers and registered to vote. This made her very happy.

8. The animals clawed and rattled their cages. They were filthy and their stench was horrifying.

9. The prosecutor disagreed with the judge. He felt he was guilty.

10. Phil's final grades were an *A* and an incomplete. This really saved him.

EXERCISE

Find and correct the pronoun reference errors in the following paragraphs.

1. The old Road Runner and Coyote cartoons are popular with just about all children. The shows have no plot to speak of, just lots of random silliness. This is what makes them so much fun for kids to watch. It's always amazing to see the endless schemes the Coyote will use to try to catch the Road Runner, and it's even more fun to try to guess how it will fail. These cartoons certainly aren't edifying or educational, but it's so much fun that no child really minds.

2. Sir William Gilbert and Sir Arthur Sullivan are famous for writing some of the greatest operettas in the history of music. Although the two men never got along personally (perhaps because of his infamous temper), their words and music blended harmoniously. Extremely popular, if slightly shocking in their time, Gilbert and Sullivan's operettas are just as popular today. Everyone from the Met to the smallest community theater has a Gilbert and Sullivan show in their repertoire. *Topsy Turvey*, a recent film, made the two writers come alive for audiences. They still dazzle with their words and music.

3. A three-year-old's idea of the perfect lunch is a peanut butter and jelly sandwich. Do not, however, make the mistake of thinking you can slap a little PB and J on some bread, toss it to a kid, and be left in peace. Three-year-olds are picky. They must be made to precise specifications or they won't eat them. Use white bread, the squishier the better. Little kids don't eat whole wheat. Use creamy peanut butter, not chunky. Little kids don't like food with texture. Use grape jelly. Don't mess with exotic alternatives. Little kids can't say *marmalade* and won't eat it. Cut the sandwich into four triangles; remove the crusts; serve; and breathe a sigh of relief.

Self Test: PRONOUN REFERENCE

Correct errors in pronoun reference in the following sentences. One sentence is correct.

1. The novelist admitted to plagiarizing his rival's work, but all he said was that he was very upset by his actions.

2. The cold wind seemed to give life to the newspaper as it swept along the street and skimmed the pavements.

3. The stuffed Cornish hens annoyed the weekly patrons. They were dry and unappealing.
4. Even the most talented performers can practice for years and still make mistakes. This can be discouraging.
5. Leigh told Anne that her stocking had a run.
6. Sandy and Bill attempted to read the signs, but they were too mixed-up.
7. George Washington supposedly chopped down a cherry tree and never told a lie. Can this be true?
8. The teachers had the students get ready for recess. They couldn't wait to get out to the playground.
9. This examination is an absolute outrage.
10. The musicians carefully cleaned their instruments, and then they were stored in their cases for the night.

Question marks.   See *End marks, B.*

Questions, indirect.   See *End marks, B, 1.*

" "

Quotation marks.   Quotation marks are used to indicate material taken word for word from another source; to mark the title of a poem, song, short story, essay, and any part of a longer work; and to point out words used in a special sense—words set apart for emphasis and special consideration, slang and colloquial expressions, derisively used words.

A. *Direct quotations.* Quotation marks indicate what someone else has said in speech or writing:

> The mayor said, "The city is in serious financial trouble if the new city income tax does not pass."

> "No man is an island," John Donne once wrote.

If there is a quotation within a quotation, use single marks for the second quote:

> The mother commented wryly, "I wonder if Dr. Spock and the other great authorities on bringing up kids have ever seen one look at you, calm as can be, and say, 'I don't wanna.'"

The following rules must be observed in punctuation of direct quotations.

1. *Block quotation.* If a direct quotation other than dialog is more than four lines long, it should be blocked. Block quotations *do not* take quotation marks and are indented ten spaces from the left margin. The traditional practice of single-spacing between the lines of a block quotation has now been replaced by double-spacing.

In the section of the text on quotation marks, the
authors make the following observation:

> Quotation marks are used to indicate material
> taken word for word from another source; to mark
> the title of a poem, song, short story, essay,
> and any part of a longer work; and to point out
> words used in a special sense--words set apart
> for emphasis and special consideration, slang and
> colloquial expressions, derisively used words.

2. *Periods and commas.* Periods and commas at the end of quotations always go inside the quotation marks.

"The city will be in serious financial trouble if the city income tax does not pass," said the mayor.

Although the producer used the word "art," the film was widely considered to be pornographic.

3. *Other punctuation.* An exclamation point or question mark goes inside the quotation marks if it is part of the quotation. If it is part of a longer statement, it goes outside the quotation marks.

The student asked, "Is this paper due Friday?"

Did Robert Frost write "Mending Wall"?

A colon or a semicolon always goes outside the quotation mark.

The text says, "A colon or a semicolon always goes outside the quotation marks"; this rule is simple.

B. *Titles.* Use quotation marks to indicate the title of a work—a poem, a song, a short story, a chapter, an essay—that is part of a larger whole, or a short unit in itself.

John Collier wrote the short story "The Chaser."

The chapter is called "Stylistic Problems and Their Solutions."

C. *Words used in a special sense.* Quotation marks are sometimes put around words used in a special sense, but these quotation marks are often overused. Pay close attention to the cautionary statements that accompany the following examples.

EXERCISE

Correct the following run-on sentences by using a comma and a coordinating conjunction (*and, but, or, nor, for, yet, so*), a semicolon, or a period.

1. I was terribly upset at my boss's insensitivity I had a debilitating illness that kept me out of work she never called.
2. Microwave cooking has come into its own the convenience to working couples, in particular, is outstanding.
3. It is possible to "zap" almost anything in a microwave roasts, though, should still be cooked conventionally.
4. The roller coasters at Cedar Point in Ohio may be the nation's best for some people, I'm told, a cross-country tour trying the roller coasters at major parks is the ideal vacation.
5. The fear of being buried alive is universal the fear may first have been expressed in writing by Poe.
6. Make sure you separate sentences with a conjunction, a semicolon, or a period never just run them together.
7. When the movie *101 Dalmatians* came out, many people rushed out to buy live dalmatians now those people realize dalmatians are high-strung and difficult to care for.
8. Drunk drivers are dangerous they killed thousands of people last year.
9. Many houses have hidden defects for example, the plumbing may be bad.
10. Medical literature lists more than three hundred causes for hiccups so-called everyday hiccups can result from inhaling too much air, eating spicy foods, and drinking too rapidly, among other causes.
11. It's all very well to say that we need new carpeting the trouble is that we don't have the funds.
12. The little engine steadfastly pulled itself over the ridge as it did it chanted over and over, "I think I can."
13. Your new sweater is lovely the color is perfect.
14. Waking early has never agreed with me it leaves me sulky and disagreeable.
15. A knowledge of classical mythology is a valuable part of anyone's educational background it can not only add a spark to one's own writing but can enable one to get more out of one's reading.
16. I don't know how anyone can possibly dislike chocolate it's my favorite food.
17. My sister can't sit still for more than a few minutes she can barely sit through her favorite sitcom she certainly can't concentrate on a novel.
18. He can't decide if he should go or not he thinks she might have some advice.
19. They boarded the airplane with a sense of fear and trepidation they noticed the pilot was reading an instruction book.
20. Spinach is the best vegetable Popeye claimed it gave him his incredible strength.

Self Test: RUN-ON SENTENCES

Insert the appropriate punctuation to correct the following run-on sentences.

1. Hundreds of bicyclists will participate in an exciting event this Sunday it is the county's fourth annual Mountain Bike Festival cyclists begin and end at the county park in Kent.
2. My aunt has a recipe for delicious chocolate chip cookies the secret ingredient is oatmeal.
3. The candidate is considering very carefully his pick for vice president a crucial consideration is to find a reliable team player.
4. This dorm room is tiny how can anyone expect two people to cohabitate here?
5. Many of America's river communities face a common challenge they must balance the search for prosperity with the need to preserve their natural resources.
6. Darryl walked the dog then he fed her.
7. I love to go to the movies I often like the popcorn better than the films.
8. Immigrants continue to make our country great they take many jobs that businesses cannot fill.
9. I saw *The Patriot* it was bloodier than I had thought.
10. Phish began to play suddenly the audience jumped up and cheered.

;

Semicolon.   A semicolon can be used between two independent clauses when the coordinating conjunction has been left out and between separate elements in a list or series when the elements contain punctuation within themselves.

A. *Between independent clauses.*

Stating the problem is simple enough; solving it is the tough part.

Roberta wasn't precisely sure what the bearded stranger wanted; all she knew was that he made her nervous.

Observe that in both of these cases a coordinating conjunction preceded by a comma could be used to replace the semicolon. Under no circumstances could a comma alone be used between these independent clauses. In order to use a comma, you must also have a coordinating conjunction (*and, but, or, nor, for, yet, so*) between independent clauses. (See *Comma splice.*)

B. *Between separate elements in a list or series.*

The following American cities have grown enormously in recent years: Houston, Texas; Dallas, Texas; Phoenix, Arizona; and Denver, Colorado.

Sentence.   A group of words beginning with a capital letter and ending with a period, question mark, or exclamation point that contains at least one independent clause.

Birds sing.

Do birds sing?

Shut up, all you birds!

(See *Clause; Subject; Predicate.*)

shift

Shifts in time and person.   Do not unnecessarily shift from one tense to another (past to present, present to future, and so on) or from one person to another (*he* to *you, one* to *I*).

A. *Tense shifts.* If you begin writing in a particular tense, do not shift to another unless a change in time is logically necessary. The following paragraph breaks this rule:

In William Carlos Williams's "The Use of Force," a doctor *was called* to examine a young girl. The doctor *was concerned* about diphtheria and *needs* to examine the girl's throat. The girl *is* terrified and *begins* to resist. As her resistance *continues,* the doctor *is compelled* to use more and more physical force. Though he *knows* the force *is* necessary, the doctor, to his horror, *found* that he *enjoyed* it and really *wanted* to hurt the girl.

Here the writer starts in the past tense (*was called, was concerned*), shifts to the present tense (*needs, is, begins, continues, is compelled, knows, is*), and then shifts back to the past tense (*found, enjoyed, wanted*). Why? There is no reason. No change in time is needed. If writers view the events of a story as happening in the present, they should use the present tense consistently. Writers could also view the events as past actions—over and completed—and write entirely in the past tense. In either case, writers should decide which view they prefer and stick to it throughout.

All verbs in present tense

In William Carlos Williams's "The Use of Force," a doctor *is called* to examine a young girl. The doctor *is concerned* about diphtheria and *needs* to examine the girl's throat. The girl *is* terrified and *begins* to resist. As her resistance *continues,* the doctor *is compelled* to use more and more physical force. Though he *knows* the force *is* necessary, the doctor, to his horror, *finds* that he *enjoys* it and really *wants* to hurt the girl.

All verbs in past tense

In William Carlos Williams's "The Use of Force," a doctor *was called* to examine a young girl. The doctor *was concerned* about diphtheria and *needed* to examine the girl's throat. The girl *was* terrified and *began* to resist. As her resistance *continued,* the doctor *was compelled* to use more and more physical force. Though he *knew* the force was necessary, the doctor, to his horror, *found* that he *enjoyed* it and really *wanted* to hurt the girl.

B. *Shifts in person.* Write from a consistent point of view, making sure that any change in person is logically justified. If, for example, you begin expressing your thoughts in the third person (*he, she, it, they, one, the reader, the student, people,* and so on), avoid sudden shifts to the first person (*I, we*) or to the second person (*you*). Similarly, avoid sudden shifts from third- or first-person singular to third- or first-person plural.

Poor	Improved
Most *average citizens* think *they* are in favor of a clean environment, but *you* may change *your* mind when *you* find out what it will cost. (Shift from third person *average citizens* and *they* to second person *you, your.*)	Most *average citizens* think *they* are in favor of a clean environment, but *they* may change *their* minds when *they* find out what it will cost.
The teenager resents the way *he* is being stereotyped. *We're* as different among *ourselves* as any other group in the population. *They* are tired of being viewed as a collection of finger-snapping freaks who say "cool" all the time. (Shift from third-person singular *teenager* and *he* to first-person plural *we* to third-person plural *they.*)	*Teenagers* resent the way *they* are being stereotyped. *They* are as different among *themselves* as any other group in the population. *They* are tired of being viewed as a collection of finger-snapping freaks who say "cool" all the time.
Readers will find this suspense-filled mystery irresistible, just as *they* have found P. D. James's previous efforts. *You* should have a real battle keeping *yourself* from looking ahead to the last page. (Shift from third-person *readers* and *they* to second-person *you, yourself.*)	*Readers* will find this suspense-filled mystery irresistible, just as *they* have found P. D. James's previous efforts. *They* should have a real battle keeping *themselves* from looking ahead to the last page.
One wonders what is going on at City Hall. *We* have put up with flooded basements and lame excuses long enough. (Shift from third-person *one* to first-person *we.*)	*We* wonder what is going on at City Hall. *We* have put up with flooded basements and lame excuses long enough.

EXERCISE

Correct any illogical shifts in tense or person in the following sentences.

1. One rarely sees your own worst faults.
2. Chapter 1 introduces us to a scientist who is devoted to making the world a safer place. In Chapter 2, the scientist turned into a werewolf.
3. Teenage parents get the worst of both worlds. We didn't have the temperament or finances for adulthood, and we had too many responsibilities to enjoy what remained of our youth.

4. The two thugs drive up to the door of the diner. They walk in, sit down, and pick up a menu. They look at Nick coldly. "What's the name of this dump?" they asked.

5. You need to be careful about shopping at discount stores. First, a person needs to check the quality as well as the price. Even cheap is too expensive if your purchase self-destructs after a few days.

6. Many of John Grisham's books involve a lawyer who became disillusioned with the judicial system or who is forced to give up his or her position as an attorney.

7. The snow is falling, and we were getting ready for another winter.

8. The company is going to introduce its new line of luxury cars this weekend. We decided two years ago that we would have to be represented at the high end of the market to stay fully competitive.

9. A person who is contemplating buying a new washing machine must take into account your types of clothing and your washing habits.

10. Alex was in another dilemma. His parents want him to go camping with them, but he wants to stay in town with Joyce.

Self Test: **SHIFTS IN PERSON OR TENSE**

Change any inappropriate shifts in tense or person in the following sentences.

1. Switching tenses was a big problem. It is not an easy habit to break.

2. Mark Twain said, "Be good, and you will be lonesome." He also says that the reports of his death are greatly exaggerated.

3. Thousands of registered voters forget to cast their votes at election time. You should be proud of your voice and proud to use it.

4. Verb tenses make me tense. They made my best friend cranky, too.

5. My pen is running out of ink, and I will get another when the ink was completely gone.

6. Contact lenses are less convenient than glasses, but many people thought that contacts were more attractive.

7. Karin crept softly up the stairs, then she peers around the corner to see if the coast is clear.

8. The tennis champion raced across the court and with a desperate sweep of his outstretched racket, he slams the ball out of his opponent's reach.

9. One has no choice but to square your shoulders and clean the oven.

10. Learning to write well takes time and practice and took lots of hard work.

sp

Spelling.   Poor spelling can seriously damage an otherwise fine paper. Faced with any significant number of spelling errors, readers cannot maintain their original confidence in the writer's thoughtfulness and skill.

The one spelling rule every writer needs to know is very simple: *Use the dictionary.* Rules for spelling specific words and groups of words almost always have exceptions and are difficult to learn and remember. Good spellers, almost without exception, turn out to be people who read a great deal and who have the dictionary habit, not people who have memorized spelling rules. The most important spelling rule, then, as well as the quickest and easiest one, is use the dictionary.

Despite this good advice, it can sometimes be handy to have available a list of frequently misspelled words. For quick reference, we include such a list. Note that words spelled the same as parts of longer words are not usually listed separately: for example, the list has *accidentally* but not *accident*, *acquaintance* but not *acquaint*.

Frequently misspelled words

absence	business	dormitory	hoping
accidentally	calendar	effect	humorous
accommodate	candidate	eighth	hypocrisy
accumulate	category	eligible	hypocrite
achievement	cemetery	eliminate	immediately
acquaintance	changeable	embarrass	incidentally
acquire	changing	eminent	incredible
acquitted	choose	encouragement	independence
advice*	chose	encouraging	inevitable
advise*	coming	environment	intellectual
all right	commission	equipped	intelligence
amateur	committee	especially	interesting
among	comparative	exaggerate	irresistible
analysis	compelled	excellence	knowledge
analyze	conceivable	exhilarate	laboratory
annual	conferred	existence	laid
apartment	conscience*	existent	led
apparatus	conscientious*	experience	lightning
apparent	conscious*	explanation	loneliness
appearance	control	familiar	lose
arctic	controversial	fascinate	losing
arguing	controversy	February	maintenance
argument	criticize	fiery	maneuver
arithmetic	deferred	foreign	manufacture
ascend	definitely	formerly	marriage
athletic	definition	forty	mathematics
attendance	describe	fourth	maybe
balance	description	frantically	mere
batallion	desperate	generally	miniature
beginning	dictionary	government	mischievous
belief	dining	grammar	mysterious
believe	disappearance	grandeur	necessary
beneficial	disappoint	grievous	Negroes
benefited	disastrous	height	ninety
boundaries	discipline	heroes	noticeable
Britain	dissatisfied	hindrance	occasionally

*See the Glossary.

Frequently misspelled words (continued)

occurred	preferred	repetition	technique
occurrence	prejudice	restaurant	temperamental
omitted	preparation	rhythm	tendency
opinion	prevalent	ridiculous	than, then*
opportunity	principal*	sacrifice	their, there,
optimistic	principle*	sacrilegious	they're*
paid	privilege	salary	thorough
parallel	probably	schedule	through
paralysis	procedure	seize	to, too, two*
paralyze	proceed*	sense	tragedy
particular	profession	separate	transferring
pastime	professor	separation	tries
performance	prominent	sergeant	truly
permissible	pronunciation	severely	tyranny
perseverance	prophecy (noun)	shining	unanimous
personal*	prophesy (verb)	siege	undoubtedly
personnel*	pursue	similar	unnecessary
perspiration	quantity	sophomore	until
physical	quiet*	specifically	usually
picnicking	quite*	specimen	village
possession	quizzes	stationary*	villain
possibility	recede	stationery*	weather
possible	receive	statue	weird
practically	receiving	studying	whether
precede*	recommend	succeed	woman, women
precedence	reference	succession	writing
preference	referring	surprise	

*See the Glossary.

EXERCISE

Correct the misspelled words in the following sentences. Numbers in parentheses indicate the number of incorrectly spelled words.

1. In February he generaly feels disatisfied with the whether. (4)
2. When you are referring to the commission on attendance, don't exagerate their excellence. (1)
3. You can succeed at writting if you persue your goal to elimenate grammar errors. (3)
4. Ocasionally a beleif can controll your existance and sieze your good sense. (5)
5. I usualy recomend that you truely seperate the salery issue from the more intresting challanges you will face by working in a foreign country. (7)

Self Test: SPELLING

Find the incorrectly spelled word in each of the following groups. Write the word correctly on the line.

_____	**1.** atheletic	advice	too	quantity	statue
_____	**2.** marriage	opinion	village	lose	changable
_____	**3.** wisdom	prefered	belief	surprise	convince
_____	**4.** fortunate	friend	seperation	distance	again
_____	**5.** minute	opposite	interruption	sargeant	people
_____	**6.** offended	assured	exellent	neither	encouragement
_____	**7.** reccommend	coming	height	villain	beyond
_____	**8.** maybe	niece	breakfast	ambulance	fourty
_____	**9.** cemetery	jewlery	among	losing	succeed
_____	**10.** president	balance	recede	tries	agruement

Subject.   A word, phrase, or clause that names the person, place, thing, or idea that the sentence is about. (See *Predicate.*)

> *Sal* went home.
>
> The president's *speech* was heard by 100,000 people.

Subject–verb agreement.   A verb must agree with its subject in number and person. This rule has most practical meaning only in the present tense; in other tenses, the verb forms remain the same regardless of number or person. (The single exception is in the past tense of *to be;* in that one instance the verb forms do change: *I was, you were, he was, we were, they were.*)

In the present tense, the third-person singular verb usually differs from the others—most often because an *-s* or *-es* is added to the verb stem. A third-person singular verb is the verb that goes with the pronouns *he, she,* and *it* and with any singular noun.

to dream

	Singular	Plural
First person	I dream	we dream
Second person	you dream	you dream
Third person	he she } dreams it	they dream

agr

The lovers *dream* of a long and happy future together.

The lover *dreams* of his sweetheart every night.

People often *dream* about falling from great heights.

Jennifer *dreams* about being buried alive.

to miss

	Singular	Plural
First person	I miss	we miss
Second person	you miss	you miss
Third person	he she it } misses	they miss

The children *miss* their father more than they thought they would.

The child *misses* her friends.

The commuters *miss* the bus almost every morning.

The left fielder *misses* more than his share of easy fly balls.

Even with highly irregular verbs, the third-person singular in the present tense takes a special form (always with an *-s* at the end).

to be

	Singular	Plural
First person	I am	we are
Second person	you are	you are
Third person	he she it } is	they are

to have

	Singular	Plural
First person	I have	we have
Second person	you have	you have
Third person	he she it } has	they have

The clowns *are* happy.

Erica *is* sad.

The Joneses *have* a lovely new home.

Mr. Jones *has* a lot to learn.

The few cases in which a present tense verb in the third-person singular has the same form as in the other persons come naturally to almost every writer and speaker: *he can, he may, he might,* and so on.

Once a writer realizes the difference between third-person singular and other verb forms, the only problem is likely to be deciding which form to use in a few tricky situations.

A. *Compound subjects.* If the subject is compound (joined by *and*), the verb is plural unless the two words function as a single unit—"Pork and beans *is* an easy dish to prepare," for example—or unless the two words refer to a single person, as in "My cook and bottle washer *has* left me" (one person performed both jobs).

Wrong	Right
Writing and reading *is* necessary for success in college.	Writing and reading *are* necessary for success in college.
The introduction and conclusion *does* not appear in an outline.	The introduction and conclusion *do* not appear in an outline.

B. *Neither . . . nor, either . . . or, nor, or.* If two subjects are joined by any of these terms, the verb agrees with the closer subject.

Wrong	Right
Neither the students nor the teacher *are* correct.	Neither the students nor the teacher *is* correct.
Either the supporting details or the thesis statement *are* wrong.	Either the supporting details or the thesis statement *is* wrong.
Snowstorms or rain *cause* accidents.	Snowstorms or rain *causes* accidents.
Rain or snowstorms *causes* accidents.	Rain or snowstorms *cause* accidents.

C. *Time, money, weight.* Words that state an amount (time, money, weight) have a singular verb when they are considered as a unit even if they are plural in form.

Wrong	Right
Two semesters *are* really a short time.	Two semesters *is* really a short time.
Five dollars *are* a modest fee for credit by examination.	Five dollars *is* a modest fee for credit by examination.
Five kilos of soybeans *are* about eleven pounds.	Five kilos of soybeans *is* about eleven pounds.

D. *Titles.* Titles of songs, plays, movies, novels, or articles always have singular verbs, even if the titles are plural in form.

Wrong	Right
The Wings of the Dove were made into a movie.	*The Wings of the Dove was* made into a movie.
"The Novels of Early America" *were* published in *American Literature.*	"The Novels of Early America" *was* published in *American Literature.*

E. *Collective nouns.* Collective nouns such as *family, audience, jury,* and *class* have singular verbs when they are considered as a unified group. If the individuals within the unit act separately, the verb will be plural.

Wrong	Right
The family *plan* a vacation.	The family *plans* a vacation.
The jury *is* divided on the verdict.	The jury *are* divided on the verdict.
The audience *are* going to give this show a standing ovation.	The audience *is* going to give this show a standing ovation.
The audience *is* divided in their opinion of the show.	The audience *are* divided in their opinion of the show.

F. *Indefinite pronouns.* Indefinite pronouns such as *one, no one, someone, everyone, none, anyone, somebody, anybody, everybody, each, neither,* and *either* take singular verbs:

Wrong	Right
None of the ideas *are* correct.	None of the ideas *is* correct.
Each of the students *have* the time to study.	Each of the students *has* the time to study.
Either *are* a valid choice.	Either *is* a valid choice.

G. *Intervening elements.* No matter how many words, phrases, or clauses separate a subject from its verb, the verb must still agree with the subject in number.

  1. Separated by words:

   Wrong: Many state capitals—Carson City, Augusta, Jefferson City, Olympia—*is* only small towns.

   Right: Many state capitals—Carson City, Augusta, Jefferson City, Olympia—*are* only small towns.

  Here the plural *capitals,* not the singular *Olympia,* is the subject.

2. Separated by phrases:

Wrong: A crate of oranges *are* expensive.

Right: A crate of oranges *is* expensive.

Here *crate,* not *oranges,* is the subject.

Wrong: Agreement of subjects with their verbs *are* important.

Right: Agreement of subjects with their verbs *is* important.

Here *agreement,* not *subjects* or *verbs,* is the subject.

3. Separated by clauses:

Wrong: Reading well, which is one of the necessary academic skills, *make* studying easier.

Right: Reading well, which is one of the necessary academic skills, *makes* studying easier.

Here *reading,* not *skills,* is the subject.

H. *Reversed position.* If the subject comes after the verb, the verb must still agree with the subject.

1. *There.* If a sentence begins with *there* and is followed by some form of *to be* (*is, are, was, were,* etc.), the number of *be* is determined by the subject. *There* is never the subject (except in a sentence like this one).

Wrong: There *is* five students in this class.

Right: There *are* five students in this class.

Here *students* is the subject, and it is plural. Therefore, the verb must be plural.

2. *Prepositional phrases.* Sometimes a writer begins a sentence with a prepositional phrase followed by a verb and then the subject. The verb must still agree with the subject.

Wrong: Throughout a grammar book *appears* many helpful writing hints.

Right: Throughout a grammar book *appear* many helpful writing hints.

Here *hints,* not *book,* is the subject.

EXERCISES

Correct any subject–verb agreement errors in the following sentences.

  1. *Days of Wine and Roses* are among several serious films starring Jack Lemmon, known mostly for his comic roles.

  2. The twists and turns of international espionage are the main themes of the novels of John Le Carré.

  3. Tomorrow I must deal with the towering stack of papers that are on my desk.

4. My school, as well as hundreds of others all over the country, are trying to tighten academic standards.

5. Disagreement among highly trained economists about budgetary deficits of hundreds of millions of dollars are causing the public to become more confused every day.

6. Neither John nor Bill have enough money to buy textbooks.

7. Peeling all of those nasty carrots are making me sick.

8. Compositions of this one special type requires a detailed knowledge of logical fallacies.

9. Each of the celebrities' houses are more extravagant than the next.

10. Federal judges and the president constitutes the judicial and executive branches of government.

11. The heavenly fragrance of the roses and gardenias were my reward for having coaxed them into bloom.

12. The sound of raindrops plays a musical pitter-patter on the roof.

13. Although I can't see the bells, their clanging and chiming rouses me from my idle daydreams.

14. The shooting pains from her sprained back keeps her awake every night.

15. Everyone except those of you with more than ten demerits are permitted to attend the social.

16. Fixing dinner, especially those darned pork chops, was his primary concern.

17. Five pounds of apples are enough for several pies.

18. Every pair of glasses Rosa owns are missing.

19. Cars, bars, and women were Chris's primary focus in life.

20. The vacuum cleaner was broken, and so was the carpet sweeper.

EXERCISE

Find and correct any subject–verb agreement errors in the following paragraphs.

1. Lobsters are great eating, but you have to work for what you eat. You'll need to crack the claws of your lobster with a pair of nutcrackers, which are the only tool for the task. Once the claws are cracked, you can pull out the meat with a nutpick. After consuming the claws, you will want to attack the tail, the smaller legs, and the actual body of the lobster. Proper consumption requires an expertise gained only through years of experience. So, if you're a first-timer, bring a veteran along for guidance.

2. Balancing checkbooks aren't really very difficult. Problems arise only because of carelessness or inattention. Forgetting to note the amount and number of each check that has been written, neglecting to write down automatic teller transactions, and assuming that bank statements are always correct are major causes of checkbook imbalances. All that are required for balanced checkbooks is attention. Pay attention to every transaction, and

write everything down immediately. Assuming that things can be taken care of later will result in checkbook chaos.

3. In fairy tales, the beautiful princess was always locked up in some high stone tower. She didn't do much. She didn't say much. She just waited to be rescued. I want to know why the princesses never bothered to try to escape. Were they too stupid? Were they too weak? I bet that half of the tower doors were left unlocked, and that those two dragons guarding the gate was no more than baby dragons. Any princess worth her salt would have tried to escape. Why didn't a single one even consider it?

Subjunctive mood.   Once far more common English than it is now, the subjunctive mood is still sometimes used to express "conditions contrary to fact"—hypothetical conditions, conditions not yet brought about, suppositional ideas, and the like. In the subjunctive, the verb form is usually plural even though the subject is singular.

She wished she *were* here.

If I *were* you, I would turn down the latest offer.

I move that the chairperson *declare* the meeting adjourned.

He looked as if he *were* going to be sick.

Self Test: **SUBJECT–VERB AGREEMENT**

Correct the errors in subject–verb agreement in the following sentences.

1. Neither the train nor the bus are air conditioned.
2. There is many ways to catch fish.
3. A meal of rice and beans are quite nutritious.
4. Each of the game show contestants are required to answer twelve questions correctly.
5. The winning team plan to celebrate their victory at the local pizza parlor.
6. *The Sound and the Fury* are among Fauklner's most complex novels.
7. Three days were too long for me to be apart from my daughters.
8. Seven dollars are all you spent on your date?
9. Every family in those apartment buildings are living in squalor.
10. None of the wildfires are showing any sign of abating.

Subordinating conjunctions.   See *Fragmentary sentences, C.*

Subordination.   The most important idea in a sentence should be in an independent clause. Lesser ideas, explanations, qualifying material, and illustrations should be in subordinate clauses or phrases. (See also Chapter 21, pages 574–577.)

sub

Poor	Improved
John is a wonderful person. He is very shy. He is extremely kind to everybody.	Although very shy, John is a wonderful person who is extremely kind to everybody. (The main idea is that John is a wonderful person.)

or

	Although he is a wonderful person who is extremely kind to everybody, John is very shy. (The main idea is that John is very shy.)
Professor Jones is terribly sarcastic. He is also a tough grader. It is true that he knows his subject. Most students dislike him, however.	Despite Professor Jones's knowledge of his subject, most students dislike him because of his terrible sarcasm and tough grading.
I am going to start on my new job and I am very optimistic.	I am very optimistic about starting on my new job.

Superlative forms.   See *Comparative and superlative forms.*

Tense shifts.   See *Shifts in time and person, A.*

Titles, punctuation of.   See *Italics, A; Quotation marks, B.*

Transitive verb.   See *Verb.*

Underlining.   See *Italics.*

vb

Verb.   A word that expresses an action, an occurrence, or a state of being. Verbs may be divided into three classes: *transitive verbs,* which require objects to complete their meaning (Mary *admires* him); *intransitive verbs,* which are complete in themselves (John *trembled*); and *linking verbs,* which join a subject to its complement (Phyllis *is* a beauty; Their actions *were* cowardly).

Verbs: principal parts.   The form of most verbs changes according to which tense is being used, and to get the correct form a writer needs to know the principal parts of each verb. There are generally considered to be three principal parts: the *stem* or *infinitive* (the stem is the present tense form of the verb, and the infinitive is the stem preceded by *to*), the *past tense,* and the *past participle.* The past participle is the form used in perfect tenses (*I have seen, I had seen, I will have seen*) and in the passive voice (*I am seen, I was seen, I will be seen, I have been seen*).

The principal parts of *regular verbs* are formed by adding *-ed* or *-d* to the stem: *rush, rushed, rushed; love, loved, loved; drag, dragged, dragged*. The past tense and past participle of regular verbs are always the same.

The principal parts of *irregular verbs* need to be learned separately—and even for the most experienced writer sometimes require checking in a dictionary or handbook. For quick reference, here is an alphabetical list of the principal parts of the most common irregular verbs.

Stem	Past tense	Past participle
arise	arose	arisen
be	was	been
bear	bore	borne, born
begin	began	begun
bind	bound	bound
blow	blew	blown
break	broke	broken
bring	brought	brought
burst	burst	burst
buy	bought	bought
catch	caught	caught
choose	chose	chosen
come	came	come
creep	crept	crept
deal	dealt	dealt
dig	dug	dug
dive	dived, dove	dived
do	did	done
draw	drew	drawn
drink	drank	drunk
drive	drove	driven
eat	ate	eaten
fall	fell	fallen
flee	fled	fled
fly	flew	flown
forbid	forbad, forbade	forbidden
freeze	froze	frozen
give	gave	given
go	went	gone
grow	grew	grown
hang	hung	hung
hang (execute)	hanged	hanged
know	knew	known
lay	laid	laid
lead	led	led
lend	lent	lent
lie	lay	lain

Stem	Past tense	Past participle
lose	lost	lost
mean	meant	meant
ride	rode	ridden
ring	rang	rung
rise	rose	risen
run	ran	run
see	saw	seen
seek	sought	sought
send	sent	sent
shake	shook	shaken
shine	shone, shined	shone, shined
shrink	shrank	shrunk
sing	sang	sung
sink	sank, sunk	sunk
sleep	slept	slept
speak	spoke	spoken
spin	spun	spun
spit	spat	spat
spread	spread	spread
steal	stole	stolen
stink	stank	stunk
swear	swore	sworn
swim	swam	swum
swing	swung	swung
take	took	taken
teach	taught	taught
tear	tore	torn
thrive	thrived, throve	thrived, thriven
throw	threw	thrown
wear	wore	worn
weep	wept	wept
write	wrote	written

Confusion of the past tense and past participle of irregular verbs is a frequent cause of writing errors. Remember that the past participle is the correct form after *has*, *have*, and *had*.

Wrong	Right
The mountaineers *had froze* to death.	The mountaineers *had frozen* to death.
The sprinter *has* just *broke* another track record.	The sprinter *has* just *broken* another track record.
I *begun* the book yesterday.	I *began* the book yesterday.
We *seen* that movie when it first came out.	We *saw* that movie when it first came out.

EXERCISE

Correct any errors in verb form in the following sentences.

1. Gus was finally apprehended. He had stole his last Ferrari.
2. They flown nonstop around the world. Now they begun nonstop appearances on television.
3. I have wrote on this painful subject before, but your negligence has drove me to distraction.
4. The phone must have rang thirty times last night.
5. I have swore on the altar of the gods to do my duty even unto death.
6. Yesterday Priscilla swum thirty laps. Her recovery seems complete.
7. We have sang and sang this carol until we are too tired to go on.
8. The quarterback thrown the ball at least fifty yards down the field.
9. The wide receiver had blew another great opportunity.
10. My mother insisted that she had wore that threadbare winter coat for the last time.

EXERCISE

Find and correct any errors in verb form in the following paragraphs.

1. Ella loved watching her older sisters get ready to go out at night. It was always fun to watch women who were working all day transform themselves into beautiful butterflies. They were so quick to change, too! Off came the dingy work clothes and the everyday shoes and socks and on went the delicate dresses, tiny dance slippers, and silky stockings. Suddenly, her sisters weren't the people she fighted with over the telephone and the bathroom. They were beautiful, elegant, sweet-smelling strangers.

2. Every once in a while, monks who worked on transcribing manuscripts couldn't resist adding their own words to the books they were copying. Because transcribing was hard, dull, and tiring work, the words the monks added were often words of complaint. Scribbled in the margins of some old books are messages praying that the work day would end soon, or saying that the monks would have froze to death without a miracle. Sometimes these marginal notes are more interesting than the books that hold them. The notes are a window into the monks' lives and a way for modern readers to personalize the Middle Ages.

3. It was a creepy kind of night. The wind blown fiercely through the streets. We shivered in our flimsy Halloween costumes. We weren't scared, of course. We were too old to be scared. If we walked a little more quickly and clung more closely than usual, it was for warmth, not protection. The moon shined down from behind the clouds. It gave a softened light. We admired it, picked up our candy bags, and continued down the block.

Self Test: VERB FORM

Correct any verb form errors in the following sentences. Not all sentences have mistakes.

1. Angela would've went to the park if she hadn't arose feeling sick.
2. They couldn't possibly have stole that much money.
3. The whale had spat Jonah out onto dry land.
4. Sharon swore she had lain the photographs on the table.
5. Joe had drank too much and felt ill for the rest of the night.
6. Honey, I shrunk the kids!
7. The movie *The Ox-Bow Incident* is about a group of men who have hung three innocent people.
8. I fell in love, and it seemed the sun shined brighter than before.
9. J. C. swum until her fingers begun to wrinkle from the water.
10. Alice had fell down the rabbit hole for a long time before she began to worry.

Verbs: tenses. What is the difference between *I eat* and *I am eating*? What is the difference between *I passed* and *I have passed*? Most verbs can be expressed in any tense, and the many different tenses enable the writer to present fine shades of meaning with great accuracy.

There are six tenses. Most verbs can take either the *active voice* or the *passive voice* in any tense (see pages 570–571). To make matters even more varied, *progressive constructions* can be used for all tenses of active verbs and some tenses of passive verbs.

to save

Tenses	Active voice	Progressive
Present	I save	I am saving
Past	I saved	I was saving
Future	I will (*or* shall) save	I will be saving
Present perfect	I have saved	I have been saving
Past perfect	I had saved	I had been saving
Future perfect	I will (*or* shall) have saved	I will have been saving
	Passive voice	
Present	I am saved	I am being saved
Past	I was saved	I was being saved
Future	I will (*or* shall) be saved	
Present perfect	I have been saved	
Past perfect	I had been saved	
Future perfect	I will (*or* shall) have been saved	

to drive

Tenses	Active voice	Progressive
Present	I drive	I am driving
Past	I drove	I was driving
Future	I will drive	I will be driving
Present perfect	I have driven	I have been driving
Past perfect	I had driven	I had been driving
Future perfect	I will have driven	I will have been driving

	Passive voice	
Present	I am driven	I am being driven
Past	I was driven	I was being driven
Future	I will be driven	
Present perfect	I have been driven	
Past perfect	I had been driven	
Future perfect	I will have been driven	

A. *Present tense.* The present tense indicates present action, of course, especially continuing or habitual action:

I *save* ten dollars every week.

I *eat* a good breakfast each morning.

She *drives* carefully.

The present is also used to express permanent facts and general truths, and is usually the preferred tense for discussing literary actions:

The speed of light *is* faster than the speed of sound.

Truth *is* stranger than fiction.

In *The Great Gatsby,* all of the events *take* place during the 1920s.

Nick Carraway *is* the only character in the novel who *understands* Gatsby.

The present can even be called upon to deal with future action.

Tomorrow she *drives* to the convention.

The *present progressive* indicates actions occurring—actions "in progress"—at the specific instant referred to.

I *am eating* a good breakfast, and I do not want to be interrupted.

She *is driving* too fast for these icy roads.

The same principle of action in progress at the time applies to all progressive tenses:

Past Progressive: The criminal *was shaving* when the police arrested him.

Future Progressive: At this time next week, I *will be surfing* in Hawaii.

B. *Past tense.* The past tense describes previous actions, generally actions over and done with.

The lifeguard *saved* two children last week.

She *drove* to Florida three years ago.

C. *Future tense.* The future tense describes actions after the present:

From now on, I *will save* fifteen dollars every week.

Marlene says that her in-laws *will drive* her to drink.

D. *Present perfect tense.* The present perfect tense (*have* or *has* plus the past participle) refers to past actions, generally of the fairly recent past, that still go on or have bearing on the present:

I *have saved* over one thousand dollars so far.

She *has driven* this short route to work many times.

The preceding sentences expressed in the simple past would suggest different meanings. "I saved over one thousand dollars" would suggest that the saving has now stopped. "She drove this short route to work many times" would suggest that some other route is now being used.

E. *Past perfect tense.* The past perfect tense (*had* plus the past participle) is employed for actions previous to the simple past—"more past than past."

The lifeguard saved two children last week and *had saved* three adults the week before.

She *had driven* to Florida three years ago, so she felt quite confident about making the trip again.

F. *Future perfect tense.* The future perfect tense (*will have* or *shall have* plus the past participle) expresses action that will be completed before some future time.

By this time next year, I *will have saved* two thousand dollars.

When she gets to Florida, she *will have driven* through three time zones.

The proper sequence of tenses within a sentence or series of sentences when different verbs refer to different time periods is an important consideration for all writers. The simple rule that verb tenses need to express precisely the intended period of time is not always simple to apply to one's own writing.

Improper sequence	Correct sequence
The witness *told* [past] the court that on the night of the crime he *saw* [past] the accused break the window of the liquor store.	The witness *told* [past] the court that on the night of the crime he *had seen* [past perfect] the accused break the window of the liquor store. (The past perfect *had seen* refers to events "more past than past.")
When I *will get* [future] to the lake, you *will* already *be* [future] there for two weeks.	When I *will get* [future] to the lake, you *will* already *have been* [future perfect] there for two weeks. (The future perfect *will have been* refers to events that will be completed before some future time.)
Although the coach *has set* [present perfect] new curfew hours, the players still *have refused* [present perfect] to comply.	Although the coach *has set* [present perfect] new curfew hours, the players still *refuse* [present] to comply. (The coach's rules were set a while ago. The present tense *refuse* is necessary to show that the players' refusal to follow the rules is current.)

EXERCISE

Make any necessary corrections in verb tenses in the following sentences.

1. The candidate had promised that she will never increase taxes, but she did.
2. The doctor says that when he first saw the patient, the patient was suffering for two weeks with severe migraine headaches.
3. When the book will be released, the competition will already be on sale for a month.
4. Lei Feng saved half of each paycheck for two years, but then he had blown it all on one trip to the casino.
5. Joan has taken all the abuse she can. She felt a legal separation was the only course open to her.
6. Brian still says that he really loves her, but Joan had declared that he has said that many times before.
7. The long-awaited report is going to be printed next week. It will have shown a long pattern of misappropriation of public funds.
8. At the hearings, the admiral insisted he did not receive any warning of the enemy attack.
9. When I will finally visit England, all my friends will be there dozens of times.
10. I did not want my nephew to play that horrible music again. I heard it many times before.

Self Test: VERB TENSE

Correct the verb tense errors in the following sentences. Two sentences are correct.

1. If only she had admitted her guilt at the beginning her sentence would be reduced.
2. David did not do it anymore. He did it too many times for too many years.
3. By the time the party had begun we will have just left our house.
4. When you slowpokes will have arrived, we will have been there for hours.
5. If you took the high road, and I took the low road, who would get to Scotland first?
6. Pedro combed his hair, brushed his teeth, and went to bed.
7. We had not tasted the main course before our plates have been whisked away.
8. Simone always knows all the news. She knows it all tomorrow, too.
9. When this machine is in working order, it will have enabled Dr. Doom to control the planet.
10. When Carlos and Marsha first met, Marsha had been crossing the street.

Voice.   The quality of a verb that tells whether the subject *acts* or is *acted upon*. A verb is in the *active voice* when its subject does the acting, and in the *passive voice* when its subject is acted upon.

Active:	The Senate passed the new law.
Passive:	The new law was passed by the Senate.

wordy

Wordiness.   *Wordiness* means using more words than are necessary. Wordiness never makes writing clearer, more convincing, more interesting, or more graceful—just longer. Be sure to examine your work for wordiness before turning it in. Brief examples of the most common types of wordiness follow. (For exercises and more detailed information, see Chapter 21, pages 564–571.)

A. *Deadwood.*

Wordy writing	Economical writing
Her hair was red in color.	Her hair was red.
Pollution conditions that exist in our cities are disgraceful.	Pollution in our cities is disgraceful
In this day and age we live in, people seem totally apathetic to everything.	People today seem totally apathetic.

B. *Pointless repetition.*

Wordy writing	Economical writing
The film was very interesting and fascinating.	The film was fascinating.
The author gives examples of different and varied criticisms of the novel.	The author gives examples of different criticisms of the novel.
Some early critics of Jonathan Swift called him an insane madman suffering from symptoms of mental disease.	Some early critics of Jonathan Swift called him insane.

C. *Delay of subject.*

Wordy writing	Economical writing
There are too many people who care only for themselves.	Too many people care only for themselves.
It is a fact that there has been a great increase in sensationalism in the theater.	Sensationalism in the theater has greatly increased.

D. *Inadequate clause cutting.*

Wordy writing	Economical writing
The woman who has red hair was afraid.	The red-haired woman was afraid.
Some of the students who were more enthusiastic wrote an extra paper.	Some of the more enthusiastic students wrote an extra paper.

Glossary
of Problem Words

A, an.   Use *a* when the next word begins with a consonant sound. Use *an* when the next word begins with a vowel sound.

a book	a horror film
a rotten apple	a use of soybeans
an element	an urgent request
an honest man	an added attraction

Note that it is the sound that counts, not the actual letter.

a hasty decision	an unusual picture
an hour	a usual routine

Accept, except.   *Accept* is a verb meaning "to receive, to agree to, to answer affirmatively." *Except* is usually a preposition meaning "excluding." It is also used infrequently as a verb meaning "to exclude."

I accepted the parcel from the mail carrier.

Senator Jones hoped they would accept his apology.

Should she accept that rude invitation?

I liked everything about the concert except the music.

I except you from my criticism.

Adapt, adept, adopt.   *Adapt* means "change or adjust in order to make more suitable or in order to deal with new conditions." *Adept* means "skillful, handy, good at." *Adopt* means "take or use as one's own" or "endorse."

The dinosaur was unable to adapt to changes in its environment.

The new textbook was an adaptation of the earlier edition.

Bill has always been adept at carpentry.

They had to wait six years before they could adopt a child.

The Senate adopted the new resolution.

Adolescence, adolescents. *Adolescence* refers to the teenage years. *Adolescents* are teenagers.

My adolescence was marked by religious questioning, parental snooping, and skin problems.

Adolescents pay outrageous rates for automobile insurance because, as a group, they have outrageous numbers of accidents.

Adverse, averse to. *Adverse* means "hostile, difficult, unfavorable." *Averse to* refers to someone's being unwilling or reluctant.

Adverse weather conditions have tormented farmers for the past decade.

John has always been averse to accepting other people's ideas.

Advice, advise. *Advice* is a noun. *Advise* is a verb.

My advice to you is to leave well enough alone.

I advise you to leave well enough alone.

Affect, effect. If you are looking for a noun, the word you want is almost certainly *effect*, meaning "result." The noun *affect* is generally restricted to technical discussions of psychology, where it means "an emotion" or "a stimulus to an emotion." If you are looking for a verb, the word you want is probably *affect*, meaning "impress, influence." The verb *effect* is comparatively uncommon; it means "bring about, accomplish, produce."

Many of our welfare programs have not had beneficial effects.

This song always affects me powerfully.

The crowd was not affected by the plea to disband.

We hope this new program will effect a whole new atmosphere on campus.

Affective, effective. The word you are after is almost certainly *effective*, meaning "having an effect on" or "turning out well." *Affective* is a fairly technical term from psychology and semantics meaning "emotional" or "influencing emotions."

Only time will tell if Federal Reserve policy is effective.

The affective qualities of sound are difficult to evaluate in laboratory conditions.

Aggravate. The original meaning of *aggravate* is "worsen" or "intensify." The more common meaning of "irritate" or "annoy" is also acceptable in all but the fussiest formal writing.

Ain't.   *Ain't* should never be used in written English except in humor or dialog. Use of the phrase *ain't I,* when asking a question in conversational English, is undesirable, as is the supposedly elegant but totally ungrammatical *aren't I. Am I not* is grammatically correct, but awkward and stuffy. The best solution to the problem is to avoid it by expressing the thought differently.

All ready, already.   *Already* means "previously" or "by the designated time." *All ready* means "all set, all prepared."

> Professor Wills has already told us that twice.

> The plane is already overdue.

> The meal was all ready by six o'clock.

All right, alright.   *Alright* is often considered nonstandard English. It is good policy to use *all right* instead.

All together, altogether.   *All together* means "joined in a group." *Altogether* means "thoroughly" or "totally."

> For once, the citizens are all together on an important issue.

> The character's motivations are altogether obscure.

Allusion, illusion.   An *allusion* is "an indirect mention or reference," often literary or historical. The verb form is *allude.* An *illusion* is "an idea not in accord with reality."

> In discussing our problems with teenage marriages, the speaker made an allusion to *Romeo and Juliet.*

> The nominating speech alluded to every American hero from Jack Armstrong to Neil Armstrong.

> The patient suffered from the illusion that he was Napoleon.

> At the end of the story, the character loses her pleasant illusions and discovers the harsh truth about herself.

A lot of.   This phrase is more appropriate in conversation than in general written English. Use it sparingly. Remember that *a lot* is *two* words. Do not confuse it with *allot,* meaning "to give out" or "apportion."

Alright.   See *All right, alright.*

Altogether.   See *All together, altogether.*

A.M., P.M. (*or* a.m., p.m.).   Either capitals or lowercase letters are acceptable, but you should not alternate between the two in any one piece of writing. These abbreviations must be preceded by specific numbers.

Wrong: We expect her sometime in the a.m.

Right: Her appointment is for 10:30 a.m.

Among, between. Use *between* when dealing with two units. Use *among* with more than two.

Wrong: The company president had to make an arbitrary decision among the two outstanding candidates for promotion.

Tension has always existed among my parents and me.

Tension has always existed between my mother, my father, and me.

Right: The company president had to make an arbitrary decision between the two outstanding candidates for promotion.

Tension has always existed between my parents and me.

Tension has always existed among my mother, my father, and me.

Amount, number. Use *amount* to refer to quantities that cannot be counted. Use *number* for quantities that can be counted.

No amount of persuasion will convince the voters to approve the new levy, though the mayor has tried a number of times.

An. See *A, an.*

And etc. *Etc.* is an abbreviation of *et cetera,* meaning "and so forth" or "and other things." Using the word *and* in addition to *etc.* is therefore repetitious and incorrect. See *Etc.*

Anxious, eager. *Anxious* suggests worry or fear as in anxiety. *Eager* suggests enthusiasm.

I waited anxiously for the telephone to bring me news of Joan's safe arrival.

The whole town waited eagerly to greet the triumphant hockey team.

Anyone, any one. Use *anyone* when you mean anybody at all. Use *any one* when you are considering separately or singling out each person or thing within a group.

Anyone can learn how to do simple electrical wiring.

Any one of these paintings is worth a small fortune.

The same principle applies to *everyone, every one* and *someone, some one.*

Anyways. Not standard written English. Use *anyway.*

As. Do not use *as* as a substitute for *because* or *since.*

Poor: I was late for my appointment as I missed the bus.

As I am a shy person, I find it hard to make new friends.

Better: I was late for my appointment because I missed the bus.

Since I am a shy person, I find it hard to make new friends.

As far as.   This phrase should be followed by a noun and a verb. Without the verb, it is incomplete.

Poor: As far as religion, I believe in complete freedom.

Better: As far as religion is concerned, I believe in complete freedom.

Askance.   This word is an adverb meaning "suspiciously, disapprovingly"— used for looks, glances, and the like. It should never be used as a noun.

Wrong: The sportswriters looked with askance at the coach's optimistic prediction.

Right: The sportswriters looked askance at the coach's optimistic prediction.

Aspect.   An overused, pseudoscholarly word. Try to avoid it wherever possible. Where you feel you must use it, try to preserve the concept of *looking* as part of the implicit meaning of the word.

We viewed the problem in all its aspects.

As to.   Stuffy. Change to *about*.

Poor: We need to talk more as to our late deliveries.

Better: We need to talk more about our late deliveries.

Averse to.   See *Adverse, averse to.*

Awful.   The original meaning of *awful* is "awe-inspiring, arousing emotions of fear." Some people insist that this is still its only valid meaning. We see nothing wrong, however, when it is also used to mean "extremely bad, ugly, unpleasant." The word *dreadful* has evolved in the same way, and we know of no objections to that word. See *Awfully.*

Awfully.   Does not mean "very."

Poor: He's an awfully nice person.

I'm awfully impressed by what you said.

Jim felt awfully bad.

A while, awhile.   *A while* is a noun. *Awhile* is an adverb.

I thought I saw her a while ago.

Take it easy for a while.

Success comes only to those who are prepared to wait awhile.

Bad, badly. *Bad* is the adjective, *badly* the adverb. In some sentences, the verbs *look, feel,* and *seem* function as linking verbs and must be followed by the adjectival form.

> I play badly.
>
> *but*
>
> I feel bad.
>
> She looks bad.
>
> The idea seems bad.

Watch the location of *badly* when you use it to mean "very much." It can often be misread as having its more familiar meaning, and comic disaster can occur.

> *Incorrect:* I want to act badly.
>
> He wanted her to love him badly.

Be. Not standard written English in constructions like *I be going* and *They be ready.* Use *I am going* or *They are ready* instead.

Being as, being as how, being that. Not standard written English. Use *because* or *since.*

Beside, besides. *Beside* means "alongside of." It can also mean "other than" or "aside from."

> He pulled in beside the Buick.
>
> Your last statement is beside the point.

Besides means "in addition to" or "moreover."

> I'm starting to discover that I'll need something besides a big smile to get ahead.
>
> Besides, I'm not sure I really liked the dress in the first place.

Between. See *Among, between.*

Brake, break. *Brake,* whether a verb or noun, has to do with stopping a vehicle or other piece of machinery. For additional meanings, see a dictionary.

> Frantically, he slammed on the brake.
>
> She braked her car to a complete stop.

Break, whether a verb or noun, has many meanings, most commonly "to destroy, damage, exceed, interrupt." The simple past is *broke;* the past participle is *broken.*

> Porcelain can break, so be careful.
>
> Her left arm was broken.

Henry Aaron broke Babe Ruth's home-run record.

The committee took a ten-minute break.

The attempted jail break was unsuccessful.

The brake of the school bus has been broken.

Breath, breathe.   *Breath* is a noun. *Breathe* is a verb.

His statement is like a breath of fresh air.

The soprano drew a deep breath.

In some cities it can be dangerous to breathe the air.

The soprano breathes deeply.

But however, but nevertheless, but yet.   All these phrases are guilty of pointless repetition of meaning. Rewriting helps the logic and eliminates wordiness.

Poor: Inflation is horrible, but however, the remedies are sometimes even more horrible.

She loved her husband, but yet she feared him.

Failure may be inevitable, but nevertheless we will do our best.

Better: Inflation is horrible, but the remedies are sometimes even more horrible.

Inflation is horrible; however, the remedies are sometimes even more horrible.

She loved her husband, yet she feared him.

Failure may be inevitable, but we will do our best.

But that, but what.   Not standard written English. Use *that.*

Wrong: I don't question but that you have good intentions.

I don't question but what you have good intentions.

Right: I don't question that you have good intentions.

Can, may.   In formal English questions, *can* asks if the ability is there, and *may* asks if the permission is there.

Can your baby speak yet?

May I intrude on your conversation? (Not *can*—anyone with a voice has the ability to intrude.)

Outside of formal contexts, few people worry about the distinction.

Can't hardly.   A double negative. Use *can hardly.*

Can't help but.   Wordy and repetitious. Avoid this phrase in written English.

> *Poor:*   I can't help but worry about what winter will do to my old car.

> *Better:*   I can't help worrying about what winter will do to my old car.

Capital, capitol.   *Capital* refers to money, uppercase letters, and cities that are seats of government. A *capitol* is a building in which major legislative bodies meet. With an uppercase *C, Capitol* refers to the building in Washington, D.C.

> Investments in Compucorp, though highly speculative, offer excellent opportunities for capital gains.

> The poet e. e. cummings had an aversion to capital letters.

> Madison is the capital of Wisconsin.

> Madison's capitol closely resembles the Capitol in Washington, D.C.

Casual, causal.   These look-alike words are often misread. *Casual* means "informal" or "unplanned." *Causal* means "having to do with a cause," "constituting a cause," and so on.

> Wear casual clothes to the party.

> Bill is entirely too casual about his financial future.

> Karen understands the causal connection between cigarettes and lung disease, but she keeps smoking anyway.

Censor, censure.   *Censor,* as a verb, means "to examine mail, art, etc., to see if it should be made public," or "to cut out, ban." As a noun, *censor* means "a person engaged in censoring." *Censure* can be a verb or noun meaning "condemn" or "condemnation," "criticize adversely" or "adverse criticism."

> Parts of the movie have been censored.

> The prison censor examines all mail.

> The Citizens Committee recently censured the mayor.

> Dickens's deathbed scenes have long been singled out for censure.

Center around.   Since a center is a single point in the middle of something, *center around* is an illogical phrase. Use *center on* instead.

> The discussion centered on ways to increase productivity in the coming year.

Cite, site.   *Cite,* a verb, means "mention." *Site,* a noun, means "location."

> He cited many examples to prove his point.

> The site of a new housing project has been debated for more than a year.

Climactic, climatic.   *Climactic* is the adjectival form of *climax.*

> The hero's death is the climactic moment of the story.

Climatic is the adjectival form of *climate.*

> Climatic conditions in the Dakotas go from one extreme to the other.

Complected.   Not standard English. *Complexioned* is preferable, but it's better to reword your sentence so you can avoid using either term.

> *Acceptable:* He was a light-complexioned man.
>
> *Better:*   He had very fair skin.

Complement, compliment.   The verb *complement* means "to complete" or "bring to perfection." The noun *complement* means "the full amount." *Compliment* means "praise" (noun or verb).

> A string of pearls elegantly complements a black dress.
>
> Cheese and wine complement each other.
>
> The ship had its required complement of officers.
>
> I don't appreciate insincere compliments.
>
> Don't compliment me unless you mean it.

Compose, comprise.   *Compose* means "to make up, to constitute."

> Thirteen separate colonies composed the original United States.

Comprise means "to be made up of, to encompass."

> The original United States comprised thirteen separate colonies.

If the distinction between these two words gives you trouble, forget about *comprise* and use *is composed of* instead.

Conscience, conscientious, conscious.   *Conscience* is the inner voice that tells us right from wrong. *Conscientious* means "painstaking, scrupulous, ruled by conscience," as in *conscientious objector. Conscious* means "aware."

> No one should ask you to act against your conscience.
>
> I've tried to do this work as conscientiously as possible.
>
> Jerry became conscious of a subtle change in Mary's attitude.

Console, consul, council, counsel.   *Console:* As a verb (accent on second syllable)—"to sympathize with, to comfort." As a noun (accent on first syllable)—"a radio, phonograph, or television cabinet, usually a combination, resting directly on the floor"; also "a small compartment, as found in an automobile between bucket seats"; for other meanings see a dictionary.

Consul: A representative of a nation, stationed in a foreign city, whose job is to look after the nation's citizens and business interests.

Council: A governing body or an advisory group.

Counsel: As a verb—"to advise, to recommend." As a noun—"advice, recommendation, exchange of ideas."

> I could find no words to console the grieving widow.
>
> I've lived with this portable stereo too long. I want a console.
>
> The French consul will answer any of your questions on import duties.
>
> The council met last week in a special emergency session.
>
> The tax expert counseled him on medical deductions.
>
> Sarah knew she could rely on her father's friendly counsel.

Contemptible, contemptuous.   Use *contemptible* to describe something or someone deserving of scorn. Use *contemptuous* to describe the expression of scorn.

> Few crimes are more contemptible than child abuse.
>
> Instead of shaking hands, she thumbed her nose and stuck out her tongue. Her contemptuous attitude was clear.

Continual, continuous.   *Continuous* means "completely uninterrupted, without any pause."

> The continuous noise at the party next door kept us awake.
>
> The patient received continuous round-the-clock care.

Continual means "frequently repeated, but with interruptions or pauses."

> He had a bad cold and blew his nose continually.
>
> She changed jobs continually.

Costume, custom.   *Costume* refers to style of dress. *Custom* refers to conventional practice. See a dictionary for other meanings.

> He decided to wear a pirate's costume to the masquerade.
>
> Trick or treat is an old Halloween custom.

Could care less.   See *Couldn't care less.*

Couldn't care less.   Means "utterly indifferent to." The phrase *could care less* is sometimes mistakenly used to mean the same thing. It does not mean the same thing; it makes no sense at all.

> *Wrong:*   I could care less about her opinion of me.
>
> *Right:*   I couldn't care less about her opinion of me.

Couldn't hardly.   See *Can't hardly* and *not hardly.*

Could of, should of, would of.   Not standard written English. Use *could have, should have, would have.*

Council.   See *Console, consul, council, counsel.*

Counsel.   See *Console, consul, council, counsel.*

Credible, creditable, credulous.   *Credible* means "believable." *Creditable* means "worthy of praise." *Credulous* means "gullible, foolishly believing."

> Their lame excuses were not credible.
>
> Adam's behavior since his parole has been creditable.
>
> She's so credulous she still believes that the stork brings babies.

Criterion.   This word (plural: *criteria*) is overused and frequently stuffy. Use *standard,* instead.

Cute.   An overused word. Avoid it wherever possible in written English.

Data.   Technically, a plural word, the singular form of which is *datum.* The word's Latin origins, however, have nothing to do with its current usage. We believe that *data* can be treated as singular in all levels of English—and probably should be.

> *Correct:*   This data is accurate and helpful.
>
> *Correct (but very formal):*   These data are accurate and helpful.

Decompose, discompose.   *Decompose* means "to rot or break into separate parts." *Discompose* means "disturb, fluster, unsettle."

> When the police found the body, it had already begun to decompose.
>
> His drunken foolishness discomposed all of us.

Definitely.   Nothing is wrong with this word except that it is used far too often to add vague emphasis to weak thoughts and weak words.

Detract, distract.   *Detract* means "belittle." *Distract* means "divert, confuse."

> Almost everyone tries to detract from television's real accomplishments.
>
> A mosquito kept distracting her attention.

Device, devise.   *Device* is a noun meaning, among other things, "mechanism" or "special effect." *Devise* is a verb meaning "to invent" or "to plot."

> The safety pin is a simple but extraordinarily clever device.
>
> The person who devised the safety pin is one of humanity's minor benefactors.

Dialog. Alternative spelling for *dialogue.* In general, save this word for references to conversation in literary works.

> No creative writing class can give a writer an ear for good dialog.
>
> Proper punctuation of dialog requires knowledge of many seemingly trivial details.
>
> Some critics assert that Eugene O'Neill's plays have many great speeches but almost no believable dialog.

Martin Buber, the great twentieth-century theologian, expanded the meaning of *dialog* to refer to an intense, intimate relationship that can sometimes take place between God and human beings. Buber's influence, unfortunately, has led many people who should know better to corrupt the term into a pretentious, sometimes self-serving, synonym for normal conversation. Avoid this usage.

> *Poor:*   At its meeting last week, the committee engaged in effective dialog.
>
> The Singles Club provides its members with many opportunities for meaningful dialog.

As if corruption were not enough, the word has been virtually destroyed through its faddish use as a verb. *Dialog* is not a verb in standard written English. Never use it that way.

> *Wrong:* We dialogued about politics until two in the morning.
>
> Professor Biggs said that she enjoyed dialoging with her students after class.

Different than. *Different from* is preferable in all circumstances.

Discompose. See *Decompose, discompose.*

Discreet, discrete. *Discreet* means "tactful," "reserved." *Discrete* means "separate," "distinct."

> Discreet silence is sometimes the most effective reply to an insult.
>
> Rising interest rates have several discrete effects on the economy.

Disinterested, uninterested. Don't confuse these words. *Disinterested* means "impartial, unbiased." *Uninterested* means "bored, indifferent." An audience is uninterested in a poor play. A disinterested judge is necessary for a fair trial.

Disorientate, disorientated. Awkward variations of *disorient* and *disoriented.*

Distract. See *Detract, distract.*

Each. Takes a singular verb and a singular pronoun. See *He, his, him, himself.*

> Each breed of dog has its own virtues.

Each actress was told to practice her lines.

Each of the Cleveland Indians is taking his turn at batting practice.

Eager.   See *Anxious, eager.*

Economic, economical.   Use *economic* for references to business, finance, the science of economics, and so on. *Economical* means "inexpensive" or "thrifty."

We need to rethink our entire economic program to avert a recession.

Economic conditions are improving in the textile industry.

The economical shopper looks hard for bargains.

It's economical in the long run to use first quality oil in your car.

Effect.   See *Affect, effect.*

Effective.   See *Affective, effective.*

Either.   Use *either* only when dealing with two units.

Wrong: Either the Republican, the Democrat, or the Independent will be elected.

Right: Either Elaine or Tom will get the job.

When *either* is the subject, it takes a singular verb and pronoun.

The men are both qualified. Either is ready to give his best.

See *Neither.*

Elicit, illicit.   *Elicit* means "to draw out." *Illicit* means "improper" or "prohibited."

The interviewer was unable to elicit a direct answer.

Where would our modern novelists turn if they were suddenly prohibited from writing about illicit romance?

Eminent, imminent.   *Eminent* means "distinguished" or "noteworthy." *Imminent* means "about to happen."

The eminent speaker delivered a disappointing address.

After years of frustration, a peace treaty is imminent.

Ensure, insure.   Both words are often used interchangeably, but use *insure* for references to financial guarantees against loss of life, health, and property.

The new screens should ensure that insects stay outside where they belong.

Authorities say that if you insure your home or apartment, you should take photographs of all your most valuable possessions.

Our state has just made it mandatory for motorists to insure their own vehicles.

Equally as.   Not a standard English phrase. Eliminate the *as* or substitute *just as.*

Poor: My grades were equally as good.

The style was equally as important as the plot.

Better: My grades were equally good.

The style was just as important as the plot.

Etc.   Except where brevity is a major concern, as in this glossary, avoid *etc.* It tends to convey the impression that the writer doesn't want to be bothered with being accurate and specific. See *And etc.*

Every.   This adjective makes the noun it modifies take a singular verb and a singular pronoun. See *He, his, him, himself.*

Every businesswoman needs to learn how to deal with the prejudices of her male counterparts.

Every Denver Bronco is required to report his weight upon arrival at training camp.

Every idea has been put into its proper place in the outline.

Every day, everyday.   *Every day* is the common phrase used for references to time.

He loved her so much that he wanted to see her every day.

Every day that we went to the pond that summer, we saw new signs of pollution.

Everyday is an adjective meaning "normal, ordinary, routine."

After the interview, Bill looked forward to changing into his everyday clothes.

The everyday lives of many everyday people are filled with fears, tensions, and the potential for tragedy.

Everyone, every one.   See *Anyone, any one.*

Except.   See *Accept, except.*

Expand, expend.   *Expand* means "to increase, enlarge, fill out." *Expend* means "to spend, use up."

The company needs to expand its share of the market.

The speakers will soon expand on their remarks.

Taxes must not be expended on visionary projects.

The student fell asleep during the final examination because he had expended all his energy in studying.

Explicit, implicit.   *Explicit* means "stated or shown directly." *Implicit* means "implied, not stated or shown directly."

> Cheryl's mother gave explicit instructions to be home before dark.
>
> Even by current standards, the movie goes to extremes in its explicit presentation of sex.
>
> My wife and I have an implicit understanding that the first one who can't stand the dirt any longer is the one who does the dishes.
>
> The diplomatic phrasing does not hide the implicit threat of war.

Facet.   An overused, pseudoscholarly word. Avoid it wherever possible.

Farther, further.   Use *farther* for geographic distance, *further* for everything else.

> Allentown is five miles farther down the road.
>
> Further changes need to be made in the curriculum.
>
> Jim kissed her, but they were further apart than ever.
>
> We need to go further into the subject.

Faze, phase.   *Faze* means "disconcert, fluster."

> No great artist is fazed by critical sneers.

Phase means "a stage in development." It is an overused word. Limit it to contexts in which the passage of time is especially significant.

> *Poor:*   One phase of the team's failure is poor hitting.
>
> *Better:*   The history of the team can be divided into three phases.

Fellow.   As an adjective, *fellow* means "being in the same situation" or "having the same ideas." Make sure you do not use it to modify a noun that already implies that meaning.

> *Wrong:*   My fellow colleagues have been hasty.
>
> *Right:*   My fellow workers and I voted to strike.

Fewer, less.   Use *fewer* for references to amounts that can be counted individually, item by item. Use *less* for general amounts or amounts that cannot be counted or measured.

> Fewer students are taking the course this term than last.
>
> The company's advertising is less crude than it used to be.
>
> Joe earned fewer dollars this year than he did five years ago.
>
> Joe made less money this year than he did five years ago.

Figurative, figuratively.   See *Literal, literally.*

Flaunt, flout. *Flaunt* means "show off arrogantly or conspicuously." *Flout* means "treat scornfully, show contempt," mostly in attitudes toward morality, social customs, traditions.

> They lost no opportunity to flaunt their newfound wealth.

> Those hoodlums flout all the basic decencies and then complain that we misunderstand them.

Foreword, forward.   A *foreword* is a preface or introduction. *Forward* is the opposite of backward. It can also mean "bold" or "impertinent."

> The only interesting part of the entire book was the foreword.

> Our mistakes are part of history. We must now look forward.

> Amy's old-fashioned grandfather told her that she was a forward hussy.

Formally, formerly.   *Formally* means "in a formal manner." *Formerly* means "in the past."

> We were asked to dress formally.

> People formerly thought that the automobile would turn out to be just another fad.

Former.   Means "the first of two." Don't use *former* when dealing with more than two items or persons.

> *Wrong:*   Grant, McKinley, and Harding were poor presidents. The former was the poorest.
>
> *Right:*   Grant, McKinley, and Harding were poor presidents. The first was the poorest.
>
> Grant and McKinley were poor presidents. The former was the poorer.

See *Latter.*

Further.   See *Farther, further.*

Good, well.   The adjective *good* modifies a noun. The adverb *well* modifies a verb, adjective, or other adverb.

> Mary was a *good speaker.*

> She *spoke well.*

> The speech *went well.*

After a linking verb, always use *good.* Common linking verbs are *to be* (in all forms and tenses—*am, is, are, was, were, have been, has been, had been, would be, will be,* and so on), *feel, look, sound, taste, appear, smell,* and the like.

> Her voice sounded good.

The speech was good.

Mary felt good.

See the discussion of adjective–adverb confusion, pages 600–604.

Hanged, hung.   Both are past participles of *hang;* technically, they are inter-changeable. Traditionally, however, *hanged* is reserved for references to execu-tions and *hung* is used everywhere else.

The spy was hanged the next morning.

All the pictures hung crookedly.

He, his, him, himself.   English has no distinct singular pronoun to refer to both sexes. In the past, the masculine pronoun was used to refer to a singular subject of either sex or when sex was irrelevant or unknown.

The used-car buyer needs to be careful. In fact, *he* can hardly be too careful, for many dealers are waiting for the opportunity to swindle *him.*

Each citizen can make *his* choice known on Election Day.

Everybody should protect *himself* from the dangers of alcoholism.

However, increased sensitivity to sexist language (see pages 591–593) has caused this usage to disappear from contemporary published writing. The easiest and most common way to avoid sexist language is to change singular phrasing to plural whenever possible.

Used-car buyers need to be careful. In fact, *they* can hardly be too careful, for many dealers are waiting for the opportunity to swindle *them.*

All citizens can make *their* choice known on Election Day.

People should protect *themselves* from the dangers of alcoholism.

Sentences that do not lend themselves to a plural approach should be rephrased. See *He/she, his/her, him/her, he or she, his or hers, him or her.*

He/she, his/her, him/her, he or she, his or hers, him or her.   Though often con-venient and sometimes indispensable, these efforts to achieve sexual equality in language are usually best saved for legal contracts. The phrasing is generally strained and pompous. Use a plural subject and pronoun whenever possible, or recast the sentence to eliminate sexist language (see pages 591–593).

Poor: Everyone needs to make early plans for his/her career.

            In cases of fatal illness, should a patient be told the truth about what is wrong with him or her?

Better: People should make early plans for their careers.

            In cases of fatal illness, should patients be told the truth about what is wrong with them?

Hoard, horde. *Hoard* is a verb meaning "amass" or a noun meaning "a large, hidden supply." *Horde* is a large throng or crowd.

> As rumors of war increased, some citizens began to hoard food.

> The old man's hoard of gold was concealed beneath the floorboards.

> The horde of locusts totally destroyed last year's grain crop.

Hopefully. *Hopefully* is an adverb, which means that it modifies and usually appears next to or close to a verb, adjective, or another adverb.

> The farmers searched hopefully for a sign of rain.

> Hopefully, the children ran down the stairs on Christmas morning.

Hopefully does *not* mean "I hope, he hopes, it is hoped that. . . ." Avoid using it in sentences like the following:

> Hopefully, we can deal with this mess next weekend.

> The new driver's training program, hopefully, will cut down on traffic fatalities.

In fairness, so many educated writers and speakers mishandle *hopefully* that the incorrect usage is likely to worm its way into standard English someday.

Human, humane. *Humane* means "kind, benevolent."

> Humane treatment of prisoners is all too rare.

I, me. *I* functions as the subject of a sentence or clause, and as a complement in the extremely formal but grammatically correct *It is I. Me* is the object of a verb or preposition.

> He gave the book to me.

> He gave me the business.

> For me, nothing can beat a steak and French fries.

> Why does she like me so much?

To determine which word to use in sentences like "Nobody is more enthusiastic than I" or "Nobody is more enthusiastic than me," simply complete the sentences with a verb, and see which makes sense.

> *Wrong:*   Nobody is more enthusiastic than me (am).

> *Right:*   Nobody is more enthusiastic than I (am).

Idea, ideal. An *idea* is a concept or notion. An *ideal* is a model of perfection. As an adjective, *ideal* means "perfect."

> A new idea for solving the problem suddenly occurred to Linda.

> Lofty ideals need to be tempered by common sense.

> Ideal children exist only in books.

Illicit.   See *Elicit, illicit.*

Illusion.   See *Allusion, illusion.*

Imminent.   See *Eminent, imminent.*

Implicit.   See *Explicit, implicit.*

Imply, infer.   To *imply* means "to suggest or hint at something without specifically stating it."

> The dean implied that the demonstrators would be punished.

> The editorial implies that our public officials have taken bribes.

To *infer* means "to draw a conclusion."

> I inferred from her standoffish attitude that she disliked me.

> The newspaper wants its readers to infer that our public officials have taken bribes.

Incredible, incredulous.   *Incredible* means "unbelievable." *Incredulous* means "unconvinced, nonbelieving."

> The witness gave evidence that was utterly incredible.

> I was incredulous at hearing those absurd lies.

Indict.   To *indict* means "to charge with a crime." It does not mean to arrest or to convict.

> The grand jury indicted Fields on a gambling charge.

Individual.   Often contributes to stuffiness and wordiness.

> *Bad:*   He was a remarkable individual.

> *Better:*   He was a remarkable man.

> *Best:*   He was remarkable.

Infer.   See *Imply, infer.*

Inferior than.   Not standard English. Use *inferior to.*

Ingenious, ingenuous.   *Ingenious* means "clever." *Ingenuous* means "naive, open."

> Sherlock Holmes was an ingenious detective.

> Nothing could rival the ingenuous appeal of the little child's eyes.

The noun forms are: *ingenuity, ingenuousness.*

In reference to.   Stuffy business English. Use *about.*

In spite of.   *In spite* is two separate words.

Insure.   See *Ensure, insure.*

Inter-, intra-.   *Inter-* is a prefix meaning "between different groups." *Intra-* is a prefix meaning "within the same group."

> Ohio State and Michigan fought bitterly for intercollegiate football supremacy.
>
> The English faculty needs a new department head who can control intradepartmental bickering.

Irregardless.   Not standard English. The proper word is *regardless.*

Irrelevant, irreverent.   *Irrelevant* means "not related to the subject." *Irreverent* means "scornful, lacking respect."

> Your criticisms sound impressive but are really irrelevant.
>
> America could use some of Mark Twain's irreverent wit today.

Confusion of these words may be responsible for the frequent mispronunciation of *irrelevant* as *irrevelant.*

Its, it's.   *Its* is the possessive of *it. It's* is the contraction for *it is.*

> The cat licked its paws. It's a wonderfully clean animal.

Its' is not a word. It does not exist in current usage, and it never has.

Job.   Frequently overused in student writing. *Job* is probably most effective when reserved for simple references to employment for wages.

> *Poor:*   Shakespeare does a great job of showing Hamlet's conflicting emotions.
>
> *Better:*   Our economy needs to create more jobs.

Kind of.   Means what it says—"a type of, a variety of." It does *not* mean "somewhat" or "rather" except in the most informal writing.

> *Poor:*   She was kind of eccentric.
>
> I was kind of curious about his answer.
>
> *Better:*   He suffered from an obscure kind of tropic fever.
>
> She had a kind of honest stubbornness that could be very appealing.

Latter.   Means "the second of two." Don't use *latter* when dealing with more than two items or people.

Wrong: Washington, Jefferson, and Lincoln were great presidents. The latter was the greatest.

Right: Washington, Jefferson, and Lincoln were great presidents. The last was the greatest.

Washington and Lincoln were great presidents. The latter was the greater.

See *Former.*

Lay, lie. *Lay* is a transitive verb. It always takes an object *or* is expressed in the passive voice.

Present	Past	Past participle	Present participle
lay	laid	laid	laying

Lie is an intransitive verb. It never takes an object and never is expressed in the passive voice. This problem-causing *lie,* by the way, means "recline," not "fib."

Present	Past	Past participle	Present participle
lie	lay	lain	lying

Now I lay my burden down.

The hen laid six eggs yesterday.

The mason has laid all the bricks.

Our plans have been laid aside.

The porter is laying down our suitcases.

Now I am going to lie down.

Yesterday he lay awake for five hours.

The refuse has lain there for weeks.

Tramps are lying on the park benches.

Lead, led. As a noun, *lead* has various meanings (and pronunciations).

The student had no lead for his pencil.

The reporter wanted a good lead for her story.

Which athlete is in the lead?

The past of the verb *lead* is *led.*

The declarer always leads in bridge.

I led an ace instead of a deuce.

Is it possible to lead without making enemies?

Grant led the Union to triumph at Vicksburg.

Leave, let. *Let* means "to allow, permit." *Leave* means "to depart."

Wrong: Leave us look more closely at this sonnet.

Right: Let us look more closely at this sonnet.

Lend, loan.   *Lend* is a verb; *loan* is a noun.

Jack was kind enough to lend me ten dollars.

High interest rates have interfered with loans.

Less. See *Fewer, less.*

Liable, libel.   *Liable* means "likely to" or "legally obligated." *Libel* is an unjust written statement exposing someone to public contempt.

After a few drinks, that man is liable to do anything.

The owner of the dog was liable for damages.

Senator Green sued the newspaper for libel.

Libel, slander.   *Libel* is written. *Slander* is spoken.

Like, as.   In agonizing over whether to use *like* or *as* (sometimes *as if*), look first at the words that follow. If the words make up a clause (subject plus verb) use *as;* if not, use *like.*

Even philosophers can sometimes act like fools.

Even philosophers can sometimes act as fools would act.

The painting made the sunset look like a double-cheese pizza.

The painting made the sunset look as if it were a double-cheese pizza.

My boss treated me like dirt.

My boss treated me as if I were dirt.

This rule is not foolproof, but it will solve most practical problems. *Like* in place of *as* is now fairly well accepted outside of formal written English.

Literal, literally.   These terms mean "in actual fact, according to the precise meaning of the words." Some people use *literal, literally* when they mean the opposite: *figurative, figuratively.*

Wrong: He literally made a monkey of himself.

Some of our councilmen are literal vultures.

I literally fly off the handle when I see children mistreated.

Right: The doctor said Karen's jealousy had literally made her ill.

We were so lost that we literally did not know north from south.

A literal translation from German to English rarely makes any sense.

Loan.   See *Lend, loan.*

Loath, loathe.   *Loath* is an adjective meaning "reluctant." *Loathe* is a verb meaning "hate."

> I am loath to express the full intensity of my feelings.

> I loathe people who use old-fashioned words like *loath.*

Loose, lose.   *Loose* is the opposite of *tight. Lose* means "to misplace."

Mad.   Use *mad* in written English to mean "insane," not "angry." Also, avoid it in its current slang senses of unusual or wild.

> *Poor:*   Please don't be mad at me.
>
> She wore a delightfully mad little hat.
>
> *Better:*   Shakespeare tends to be sympathetic to his mad characters.
>
> The current trade policy is utterly mad.

Majority, plurality.   A candidate who has a *majority* has more than half of the total votes. A candidate who has a *plurality* has won the election but received less than half the total votes.

Masochist.   See *Sadist, masochist.*

Massage, message.   A *massage* makes muscles feel better. A *message* is a communication.

May.   See *Can, may.*

May be, maybe.   *May be* is a verb form meaning "could be, can be." *Maybe* is an adverb meaning "perhaps."

> I may be wrong, but I feel that *Light in August* is Faulkner's finest novel.

> Maybe we ought to start all over again.

Me.   See *I, me.*

Medal, metal, mettle.   A *medal* is awarded to heroes and other celebrities. *Metal* is a substance such as iron or copper. *Mettle* refers to stamina, enthusiasm, vigorous spirit.

> The American team won most of its Olympic medals in swimming.

> Future metal exploration may take place more often beneath the sea.

> Until the Normandy invasion, Eisenhower had not really proved his mettle.

Medium.   An overused word in discussing communications. The plural of *medium* is *media*. See a dictionary for its many meanings.

Mighty.   Use *mighty* to mean "powerful" or "huge." Do *not* use it as a substitute for *very*.

    Poor: I was mighty pleased to meet you.

Moral, morale.   *Moral,* as an adjective, means "having to do with ethics" or "honorable, decent, upright." As a noun, it means "lesson, precept, teaching." *Morale* refers to one's state of mind or spirit.

    Not all moral issues are simple cases of right and wrong.

    The story has a profound moral.

    The new coach tried to improve the team's morale.

More, most.   Use *more* when two things are being compared. For any number over two, use *most*.

    Between Sally and Phyllis, Sally was the more talented.

    Of all my teachers, Mr. Frederic was the most witty.

Never use *most* as a synonym for *almost*.

    Wrong: Most everyone showed up at the party.

             I'll be home most any time tomorrow.

Mr., Mrs., Miss, Ms.   These titles should not be used in referring to figures from the historical, cultural, and scientific past. With living figures, the titles should be used in moderation; the better known the person, the less need for the title.

    Poor: Mr. John Adams was the second president of the United States.

           The Scarlet Letter was written by Mr. Nathaniel Hawthorne.

           Mr. Yeltsin's speech received worldwide press coverage.

    Better: John Adams was the second president of the United States.

           The Scarlet Letter was written by Nathaniel Hawthorne.

           Yeltsin's speech received worldwide press coverage.

Ms.   Now standard usage as a title for women, though *Miss* and *Mrs.* are still used.

Myself.   Use *myself* to reinforce and stress the pronoun *I*, not as a replacement for it or the word *me*.

    Wrong: Make an appointment with José and myself next week.

    Right: I myself made that fudge.

Natural.   Means "unartificial," among other things. It is overused as a term of vague praise. It might be applied to someone's voice or manner, but it sounds absurd in a sentence like this:

> Brand X eyelashes will give you that natural look.

Neither.   Use only when dealing with *two* units.

> *Wrong:* I like neither collies nor poodles nor dachshunds.
>
> *Right:* I like neither dogs nor cats.

When *neither* is the subject, it takes a singular verb and pronoun.

> Both nations are responsible. Neither is doing its best for the environment.

See *Either.*

Nice.   An overused word, generally too vague in meaning to have much value. Try to find more specific substitutes.

None.   Means "no one" or "not one" and takes a singular verb and pronoun.

> None of these women understands that she is a public servant.
>
> None of those men is willing to accept his responsibilities.

Not hardly.   A double negative. Not standard English. Use *hardly.*

> *Wrong:* He couldn't hardly see his hand in front of his face.
>
> *Right:* He could hardly see his hand in front of his face.

Number.   See *Amount, number.*

Oftentimes.   Wordy and pointless version of *often.*

Only.   A tricky word in some sentences. Make sure that it modifies what you really want it to.

> *Poor:* I only felt a little unhappy. (Only *felt?* Are we meant to assume that the writer did not consciously *think* this way?)
>
> I only asked for a chance to explain. (Are we meant to assume that the writer did not insist on or strongly desire that chance?)
>
> *Better:* I felt only a little unhappy.
>
> I asked only for a chance to explain.

Orientate, orientated.   Awkward variations of *orient* and *oriented.*

Passed, past.   *Passed* is the past participle of pass. *Past* is used mainly as an adjective or a noun. Never use *passed* as an adjective or noun.

> We passed them on the highway.

> Valerie had a mysterious past.

> History is the study of past events.

Patience, patients.   *Patience* has to do with not being in a hurry. *Patients* are people seeking medical care or under medical attention.

> We expect the delivery tomorrow; our patience is almost at an end.

> The patients nervously waited in the doctor's office.

Perpetrate, perpetuate.   *Perpetrate* means "to commit an evil, offensive, or stupid act." *Perpetuate* means "to preserve forever."

> He perpetrated a colossal blunder.

> We resolved to perpetuate the ideals our leader stood for.

Persecute, prosecute.   *Persecute* means "to oppress or pick on unjustly." *Prosecute* means "to carry forward to conclusion or bring court proceedings against."

> Persecuting religious and racial minorities is an ongoing folly of the human race.

> The general believes that the war must be prosecuted intensely.

> We must prosecute those charged with crimes as rapidly as possible.

Personal, personnel.   *Personal* is an adjective meaning "private, individual." *Personnel* is a noun referring to the people employed in an organization. It can also refer to a department in the organization that oversees employee-based issues such as hiring and firing, morale, and processing of claims for benefits.

> My love life is too personal for me to discuss.

> There is no point to arguing about matters of personal taste.

> The company's personnel increased more than 10 percent in the past year.

> Address all inquiries to the Personnel Department.

Perspective, prospective.   *Perspective* has various meanings, most commonly "the logically correct relationships between the parts of something and the whole" or "the drawing techniques that give the illusion of space or depth." *Prospective* means "likely to become" or "likely to happen."

> Inflation is not our only problem; we need to keep the economy in perspective.

> Medieval painting reveals an almost complete indifference to perspective.

> The prospective jurors waited nervously for their names to be called.

> None of the prospective benefits of the merger ever materialized.

Phase.   See *Faze, phase.*

Phenomenon.   Singular; the standard plural form is *phenomena.*

Plurality.   See *Majority, plurality.*

Plus.   Do not use *plus* between clauses as a substitute for *and.*

Poor: I had to buy groceries, plus I had to study for a test.

Better: I had to buy groceries, and I had to study for a test.

Precede, proceed.   *Precede* means "to go before." *Proceed* means "to go on." See a dictionary for other meanings.

Years of struggle and poverty preceded her current success.

Let us proceed with our original plans.

Prejudice, prejudiced.   *Prejudice* is ordinarily used as a noun. *Prejudiced* is an adjective.

Wrong: John is prejudice.

The neighborhood is filled with prejudice people.

Right: John is prejudiced.

Legislation alone cannot eliminate prejudice.

Prescribe, proscribe.   *Prescribe* means "to order, recommend, write a prescription." *Proscribe* means "to forbid." See other meanings in a dictionary.

The committee prescribed a statewide income tax.

The authorities proscribe peddling without a license.

Prescription.   *Prescription* is often misspelled "perscription"—there is no such word.

Principal, principle.   As an adjective, *principal* means "foremost, chief, main." As a noun, it can refer to a leading person (as of a school) or the amount owed on a loan exclusive of interest. For other meanings see a dictionary. *Principle* is a noun meaning "a fundamental doctrine, law, or code of conduct."

The principal conflict in the novel was between the heroine's conscious and subconscious desires.

For the third time that week, Jeff was summoned to the principal's office.

The interest on a twenty-five- or thirty-year mortgage often exceeds the principal.

Be guided by one principle: "Know thyself."

The candidate is a woman of high principles.

Prioritize.   This overused word is often a pretentious and awkward substitute for *set up priorities.*

Pronunciation.   Note the spelling. There is no such word as *pronounciation.*

Quiet, quite.   *Quiet* means "silence, to become silent, to make silent." *Quite* means "rather" or "completely," in addition to its informal use in expressions like "quite a guy."

> The parents pleaded for a moment of peace and quiet.
>
> The crowd finally quieted down.
>
> Throughout the concert, I tried to quiet the people behind me.
>
> April was quite cold this year.
>
> When the job was quite finished, Mary felt like sleeping for a week.

Raise, rise.   *Rise* is an intransitive verb and never takes an object. *Raise* is a transitive verb.

> I always rise at 8:00 a.m.
>
> The farmer raises corn and wheat.

Rationalize.   This word is most effective when used to mean "think up excuses for." It can also mean "to reason," but in this sense it is just a stuffy word for a simple idea. The noun form is *rationalization.*

> The gangster tried to rationalize his behavior by insisting that his mother had not loved him.
>
> All these rationalizations conceal the unpleasant truth.

Really.   An overused word. It is especially weak in written English when it serves as a synonym for *very* or *extremely.*

> *Poor:*   We saw a really nice sunset.
>
> That was a really big show.

When you do use *really,* try to preserve its actual meaning, stressing what is *real* as opposed to what is false or mistaken.

> The noises were really caused by mice, not ghosts.
>
> He may have been acquitted through lack of evidence, but everyone knew that Bronson was really guilty.

Reason is because.   Awkward and repetitious. Use *reason is that.* Even this phrase is awkward and should be used sparingly.

Poor: His reason for jilting her was because his parents disapproved of older
               women.

Better: His reason for jilting her was that his parents disapproved of older
               women.

Even better: He jilted her because his parents disapproved of older women.

Relevant.   An overused word, frequently relied on to express shallow thought:
"Literature is not relevant to our needs," for example. See *Irrelevant, irreverent* for
note on pronunciation.

Respectfully, respectively.   *Respectfully* means "with respect." *Respectively* means
"each in the order named."

Everyone likes to be treated respectfully.

The speaker discussed education, medical research, and defense spending,
 respectively.

Sadist, masochist.   A *sadist* enjoys hurting living creatures. A *masochist* enjoys
being hurt.

Seeing as how.   Not standard English. Use *since* or *because*.

Seldom ever.   *Ever* is unnecessary in this phrase. Avoid it.

Poor: He was seldom ever angry.

Better: He was seldom angry.

Sensual, sensuous.   *Sensuous* is the usually positive word referring to physical
pleasure. The negative word is *sensual*, suggesting gross overindulgence in
physical sensations.

Jane felt that a hot tub and a cold martini were among life's great sensuous delights.

Two years of unlimited sensual abandon were directly responsible for Ben's early
death.

Set, sit.   To *set* means "to place" or "to put." The dictionary gives dozens of
other meanings as well. Our main concern is that *set* does not mean *sit* or *sat*.

Set the table.

We sat at the table. (*Not* "We set at the table.")

Set down that chair.

Sit down in that chair. (*Not* "Set down in that chair.")

Shall, will.   Elaborate rules differentiate between these words. Few people understand the rules, and no one remembers them. Our advice on this subject is to use *will* all the time except when *shall* obviously sounds more natural, as in some questions and traditional phrases. Examples: "Shall we dance?" "We shall overcome."

Share.   *Share* is an excellent word to indicate what generous children do with candy bars and what generous adults do with their last five dollars. In recent years, the word has sometimes been abused as a pretentious and sentimental synonym for *show* or *tell about*.

> *Poor:*   Joan shared her snapshots of her summer vacation with us.
>
> *Better:*   Joan showed us her snapshots of her summer vacation.
>
> *Poor:*   I asked him to share his innermost thoughts with me.
>
> *Better:*   I asked him to tell me his innermost thoughts.

Shone, shown.   *Shone* is the alternate past tense and past participle of *shine*. Same as *shined*. *Shown* is the alternate past participle of *show*. Same as *showed*.

> The sun shone brightly.
>
> More shocking films are being shown than ever before.

Should of.   See *Could of, should of, would of.*

Sic.   Means *thus* or *so* in Latin. *Sic* is used in brackets within quoted material to indicate that an obvious error or absurdity was actually written that way in the original.

> The author tells us, "President Harold [sic] Truman pulled one of the biggest political upsets of the century."

Site.   See *Cite, site.*

Slander.   See *Libel, slander.*

So.   When *so* is used for emphasis, the full thought often needs to be completed by a clause. See *Such.*

> *Poor:*   The coffee was so sweet.
>
>   My sister is so smart.
>
> *Right:*   The coffee was so sweet that it was undrinkable.
>
>   My sister is so smart that she does my homework for me every night.

So-called.   This word has a specific meaning. Use *so-called* to complain about something that has been incorrectly or inaccurately named. Do not use it as a simple synonym for *undesirable* or *unpleasant*.

Wrong: These so-called jet planes make too much noise.

  She wore a so-called wig.

Right: Many of our so-called radicals are quite timid and conservative.

  These so-called luxury homes are really just mass-produced bungalows.

Someone, some one.   See *Anyone, any one.*

Somewheres.   Not standard English. Use *somewhere.*

Sort of.   Means "a type of, a variety of." Do not use as a substitute for *somewhat* or *rather.* See *Kind of.*

Stationary, stationery.   *Stationary* means "unmoving, unchanging." *Stationery* is paper for letter writing.

Story.   A *story* is a piece of short prose fiction. Do not use the word when referring to essays and articles, poems, plays, and novels. Remember, too, that the action in any work of literature is *plot,* not story.

Such.   When *such* is used for emphasis to mean "so much" or "so great," the full thought usually needs to be completed by a clause. See *So.*

Poor: He was such a wicked man.

  We had such fun at the picnic.

Right: He was such a wicked man that everyone feared him.

  We had such fun at the picnic, we had to force ourselves to go home.

Supposed to.   Don't forget the *d* in *supposed.*

This poem is supposed (not *suppose*) to be one of the greatest ever written.

The students are supposed (not *suppose*) to have a pep rally tomorrow night.

Sure and.   *Sure to* is preferable in writing.

Poor: Be sure and cancel newspaper deliveries before leaving for vacation.

Better: Be sure to cancel newspaper deliveries before leaving for vacation.

Than, then.   *Than* is the word for expressing comparisons and exceptions. *Then* is the word for all other uses.

> Florida is more humid than California.
>
> John has nothing to worry about other than his own bad temper.
>
> At first Roberta thought the story was funny. Then she realized its underlying seriousness.
>
> We must work together, then, or we are all doomed.

Their, they're, there.   *Their* is the possessive form of *they*.

> They took their seats.

They're is the contraction of *they are*.

> The defensive linemen say they're going to do better next week.

For all other situations, the correct word is *there*.

They.   Often used vaguely and meaninglessly, as in "They don't make things the way they used to," or "They really ought to do something about safety." Nowhere is the use of they more meaningless and weird than when applied to an individual writer. *Never* write:

> This was an excellent mystery. They certainly fooled me with the solution.
>
> I think it was sad that they had Othello die at the end of the play.

This, these.   Frequent problem-producers when used imprecisely. Make certain that no confusion or vagueness is possible. To be on the safe side, many writers make a habit of following *this* and *these* with a noun that clarifies the reference: "this idea, these suggestions, this comment."

Through, thru.   *Through* is the standard spelling except, perhaps, on road signs where space and reading time merit special consideration.

> We drove straight through to Buffalo.
>
> Thru Traffic Keep Left.

Thusly.   Not standard English. Use *thus*.

To, too, two.   *To* is the familiar preposition used in diverse ways. *Too* means "also" or "excessively." *Two* is the number.

Try and.   Acceptable in conversation, but undesirable in print. Use *try to*.

> *Poor:*   We must all try and improve our environment.
>
> *Better:*   We must all try to improve our environment.

Type of.   This phrase frequently contributes to wordiness.

Wordy: He was an interesting type of artist.

I enjoy a suspenseful type of novel.

Better: He was an interesting artist.

I enjoy a suspenseful novel.

Under way.   Two words, except in special technical fields.

Uninterested.   See *Disinterested, uninterested.*

Unique.   This word means "one of a kind"; it cannot be made stronger than it already is, nor can it be qualified. Do not write "very unique, more unique, less unique, somewhat unique, rather unique, fairly unique."

Used to.   Don't forget the *d* in *used.*

I used (not *use*) to like the tales of Jules Verne.

We are used (not *use*) to this kind of treatment.

Vain, vane, vein.   *Vain* refers to vanity or futility. *Vane* is most commonly another word for "weathervane." *Vein* is a blood vessel but has many other figurative meanings.

Jim is so vain that he dyes the gray hairs on his chest.

Betty's efforts to control her temper were mostly in vain.

You can recognize the house by the rooster vane near the chimney.

The vein carries blood to the heart.

Beneath the teasing runs a vein of deep tenderness.

At first the miners thought they had found a vein of gold.

Very.   One of the most overused words in the language. Try to find one *exact* word for what you want to say instead of automatically using *very* to intensify the meaning of an imprecise, commonplace word.

very bright	*could be*	radiant
very bad	*could be*	terrible
very sad	*could be*	pathetic
very happy	*could be*	overjoyed, delighted

Weather, whether.   *Weather* has to do with climate. *Whether* has to do with choices and alternative possibilities.

The dark clouds indicate that the weather may soon change.

Anita needs to decide whether to accept the most recent job offer.

I can never recall whether the bank is closed on Monday or Wednesday.

When.   In using this word, make sure it refers to *time,* as in "It was ten years ago when we first fell in love."

Wrong: Basketball is when five men on opposing teams . . .

Right: Basketball is a game in which five men on opposing teams . . .

Wrong: New York is when the Democratic Convention was held.

Right: New York is where the Democratic Convention was held.

Where.   In using this word, make sure it refers to *place,* as in "This is the house where I used to live."

Wrong: I am interested in seeing the movie where the motorcycle gang takes over the town.

Right: I'm interested in seeing the movie in which the motorcycle gang takes over the town.

Wrong: The class is studying the time where the Industrial Revolution was beginning.

Right: The class is studying the time when the Industrial Revolution was beginning.

Where . . . at, where . . . to.   The *at* and the *to* are unnecessary. They show how wordiness can often sneak into our writing almost subconsciously.

Poor: Where are you staying at?

            Where is he going to?

Better: Where are you staying?

            Where is he going?

Whether or not.   The one word *whether* means the same as *whether or not,* and is therefore preferable.

Poor: We wondered whether or not it would snow.

Better: We wondered whether it would snow.

Who, that, which.   Use *who* or *that* for people, preferably *who,* never *which.* Use *which* or *that* for things, preferably *that,* never *who.*

Keats is one of many great writers who died at an early age.

There's the woman that I was telling you about.

Podunk is a town that people always ridicule.

The play which we are now studying is incredibly difficult.

Who, whom.   Although the distinction between *who* and *whom* is no longer a major issue in the conversation of many educated speakers and in much informal writing, formal English still fusses about these words—and perhaps your instructor does, too. We first discuss the traditional rules; then we consider more casual approaches.

A. Formal English requires *who* to serve as the *subject* of verbs in dependent clauses:

He is a fine man who loves his family.

She is a person who should go far in this company.

I dislike people who can't take a joke.

Formal English uses *whom* as the *object* in dependent clauses:

The drunk driver whom Officer Jerome had ticketed last night turned out to be Judge Furness.

The teacher whom I feared so greatly last term has now become a good friend.

Note that it is the role played by *who* or *whom* in the *dependent clause* that determines which word is right; don't be distracted by the connections that *who* or *whom* may appear to have with other parts of the sentence. In cases of doubt, a sometimes effective tactic is to substitute *he, she, they* or *him, her, them* for the word in question and see which makes better sense. If *he, she, they* works, use *who.* If *him, her, them* works, use *whom.*

I dislike people (who, whom) can't take a joke.

Take the dependent clause (*who, whom*) *can't take a joke.* Clearly, *they can't take a joke* works, and *them can't take a joke* does not work. Use *who.*

The drunk driver (who, whom) Officer Jerome had ticketed last night turned out to be Judge Furness.

Take the dependent clause (*who, whom*) *Officer Jerome had ticketed last night. Officer Jerome had ticketed him last night* makes sense; *Officer Jerome had ticketed he last night* does not make sense. Use *whom.*

Special problems pop up when words intervene between *who* or *whom* and its verb. Don't be misled by expressions like *I think, they say, it seems, she feels,* and so on. These expressions should be thought of as interrupting words and do not affect the basic grammar of the clause.

The minority leader is the man who I think should be the next president. (*Who* is the subject of *should be.*)

No artist who he said was brilliant ever impressed us. (*Who* is the subject of *was.*)

B. Through the years, the complex traditional rules have confused many people, and we've tried to explore only the most frequent complexities. As teachers, we confess that we feel distinctly uncomfortable when the old rules are broken. We also confess, however, that Theodore Bernstein, late stylist-in-chief of the *New York Times,* makes a strong case in declaring that the rules are more trouble than they are worth. Check with your own instructor, and then consider the following guidelines and shortcuts:

1. Immediately after a preposition, use *whom.*

   He asked to whom I had been speaking.

   This is the person in whom we must place our trust.

2. At other times, use *who.*

   In my home, it's the man who does the cooking.

   Fred Smiley is the man who Ethel chose.

3. If *who* sounds "wrong" or unnatural, or if you are in a situation that demands formal writing and feel uncertain about the formal rules (the sample sentence about Fred and Ethel breaks the rules), try to eliminate the problem with one of these techniques:

   a. Change *who* or *whom* to *that.*

      Fred Smiley is the man that Ethel chose.

   b. Remove *who* or *whom.*

      Fred Smiley is the man Ethel chose.

Who's, whose.   *Who's* is a contraction of *who is* or *who has. Whose* is the possessive form of *who.*

   Who's going to get the promotion?

   Fenton is a man who's been in and out of jail all his life.

   Whose reputation shall we attack today?

   Kennedy was a president whose place in history is still in doubt.

Will.   See *Shall, will.*

Would of.   See *Could of, should of, would of.*

Your, you're.   *You're* means "you are." *Your* is the possessive form of *you.*

   You're certain to get caught in rush-hour traffic.

   All of your suggestions are excellent.

   Your attitude shows that you're not truly interested.

EXERCISE

Make any changes necessary to correct the following sentences containing problem words. Numbers in parentheses refer to the number of errors in each item.

1. She should of left the cite earlier but refused to except her own advise. (4)
2. Miss Chien was unaccustomed to receiving complements on her wardrobe from her kindergarten students, but however, she excepted this complement gracefully anyways. (5)
3. Given a choice between chicken, fish, or beef, I usually pick fish, being that its so healthful. (3)

4. My nephew literally drives me up a wall when he repeatedly asks whether or not we're going to the park. (3)
5. The whether this winter has been awfully bitter, so I'm glad I bought alot of wool sweaters, heavy pants, and etc. (4)
6. The cable television network announced that it's restructuring now underway would center around integrating its t.v. and Internet operations to insure quality service. (2)
7. Maria was all together alright this a.m. but by evening she felt so badly she couldn't hardly breath. (6)
8. I could care less as to her advise anyways. (4)
9. The reason she disliked him was because he was equally as vein as his boss, the principle. (4)
10. Hopefully next year there will be less people sent to prison seeing as how the nation's prison population is so high. (3)

Self Test: **PROBLEM WORDS**

Correct any incorrect words in the following phrases and sentences.

1. can't hardly talk
2. an exciting type of film
3. drive thru the park
4. a more unique idea
5. Did you except her suggestion?
6. between you, Chung Woo, and me
7. mighty tasty enchilada
8. Pedro and myself made a crumb cake
9. I like neither dogs, cats, nor birds as pets
10. suppose to leave early
11. keep quite in the church
12. over their
13. disinterested in the speaker's lecture
14. ate less M & Ms
15. hung the murderer
16. leave us study the homework
17. laid in the sun at the pool
18. a lose knot
19. paid her a complement
20. different than her friend

Answer Key to Self Tests

ABBREVIATIONS, PAGES 599–600

1. Dr. Rausch's daughter got her M.B.A. at a university in Pennsylvania.
2. The firm's offices moved last December from Spring Street to Valley Road.
3. The FBI raided his company's quarters in Los Angeles, California.
4. My brother and sister left town on Thursday.
5. The reverent worked for the NAACP and held a special Christmas service for government workers.

ADJECTIVES AND ADVERBS, PAGES 600–604

1. personally
2. freshly
3. quickly, well
4. nearly
5. really
6. quickly
7. beautifully
8. similar
9. bad
10. loudly

APOSTROPHE USE, PAGES 604–607

1. girls' hats; yours
2. Investors; company's prices
3. neighbors'; ours
4. trials

5. Sheets; towels
6. boys'; Manuel's
7. ours; yours; Miguel's
8. brother's; carrier's
9. sister's; bridesmaids' dresses
10. students'; yours

CAPITAL LETTERS, PAGES 608–610

1. Please park your car on Marquette Lane.
2. The Carson Middle School's marching band raises money each year for a trip to Montreal.
3. Some doctors feel that taking fever-inducing medicines like Tylenol is unnecessary, and the low fevers can be helpful to the body.
4. When Juanita traveled to the South, she tasted crawfish for the first time.
5. Do you think that the New Jersey Devils could win the Stanley Cup?
6. We'll leave for Florida on the Friday after Thanksgiving.
7. Anika speaks four languages: English, French, German, and Spanish.
8. The golden retriever darted back and forth from the water's edge to his owner, wagging his tail playfully and barking at the sunbathers on Crawford Beach.
9. We will have our next Cub Scout Meeting at the Springfield Civic Center.
10. The portrait of Princess Diana at the National Portrait Gallery in London seems to attract more viewers than any other picture in the gallery.

COLONS, PAGES 610–612

1. The Wall Street Journal's front page story about Amazon.com did two things: it introduced Amazon to new customers, and it caught the attention of rival companies not yet online.
2. Kar's new job brought him to cities he had never visited, like Milan, London, Berlin, and Paris.
3. Because my father is always looking at his watch, for Father's Day I bought him the book *Keeping Watch: A History of American Time.*
4. Correct.
5. I hate to admit it, but my mother's favorite saying was true: "Give some people an inch, and they'll take a mile."

COMMAS IN SERIES AND CLAUSES, PAGES 613–614

1. I continue to receive the newspaper, yet…
2. We did not use our video camera, but…
3. Doug went to the mall and…
4. Jose ran 15 yards and scored a touchdown.
5. Correct.
6. Correct.
7. Correct

8. Becoming a pilot was George's dream, yet…
9. …creativity, ingenuity, and reliability.
10. Ruth read *Interview with a Vampire* and watched Dracula on television, so…

COMMAS AT INTRODUCTORY ELEMENTS, PAGES 614–616

1. At the Land Rover Driving School, students learn to control their four-wheel drive vehicles on unpaved roads.
2. Our eyes were bleary and our knees were shaky (no commas needed)
3. During the past twenty years, Emily has learned many things.
4. Watching the circus, eating cotton candy, and drinking lemonade, Freddy was happier than he had ever been.
5. Acceptable.
6. Having prepared the fish perfectly, Julia Child tossed several sprigs of parsley on top of it for decoration.
7. Acceptable.
8. After a long, difficult day at work, Natalie enjoyed a five-mile jog.
9. Acceptable.
10. Having finished the whole assignment, he suddenly realized he'd done the wrong exercises.

COMMAS AND INTERRUPTING ELEMENTS, PAGES 616–618

1. The wild days of stupid educational gimmicks, thank goodness, seem to be behind us.
2. Preventative care for an automobile, to be sure, is worthwhile.
3. Don't let those sweet, meaningless smiles deceive you.
4. The administration's basic economic problem is fair taxation.
5. Correct.
6. Teenagers' bedrooms tend to be chaotic rumpus rooms, in short, pig sties.
7. There are effective ways, I believe, to perform better under pressure.
8. My fundamental monetary difficulty is that I'm broke.
9. The cat, in Dad's opinion, is nothing but a sweet, cuddly pain in the neck.
10. Early Gothic novels are basically silly, overwritten romances.

COMMAS AND NONRESTRICTIVE ELEMENTS, PAGES 618–620

1. A college student who doesn't have the sense to study may not have the sense to belong in college.
2. The Republican candidate, who promised to cut taxes, defeated the Democrat in last night's election.
3. Nobody who dislikes bubble gum can be trusted.
4. A person who dislikes dogs and children can't be all bad.
5. Bill Gates, the founder and CEO of Microsoft, is considered one of the most intelligent people in America.

6. People who are early to bed and early to rise may be healthy, wealthy, and wise, but they certainly are dull!
7. Some women feel that a skirt which is too short is uncomfortable and embarrassing.
9. Correct.
10. Maya Angelou, who wrote *I Know Why the Caged Bird Sings,* is quite eloquent.
11. Correct.

COMMAS: OTHER USES PAGES 620–623

1. Yes, dear, I did call your sister yesterday.
2. A preschooler's spinning of tall tales is part of the development of intellect, not a purposeful attempt to deceive.
3. The keynote speaker at Memorial Hospital's next benefit dinner will be Sally Johnson, MD.
4. Correct
5. My letter, dated March 17, 1998, explains in detail my strategies for expanding our human resources department.
6. Facing the crowd together, the band members felt confident and self-assured.
7. Annette, when do you plan to return to Detroit?
8. Oh, I am beginning to feel so frustrated by your selfishness.
9. A song from the Broadway show Rent refers to a year as 525,600 minutes.
10. Kent Hoffman, Ph.D., is an associate professor at Thomas Jefferson University in Philadelphia, Pennsylvania.

COMMA SPLICES, PAGES 623–626

1. Some appetite suppressing pills are now off the market because research found that they can cause heart problems.
2. Acceptable.
3. Nothing can make Arthur change his mind; he can make a mule look cooperative.
4. Many mail-order companies sell their customer lists, so be wary about buying mail-order items.
5. After fifty pages, the book had failed to interest me; therefore, I finally decided to give up.
6. I used to write comma splices all the time, but Dad taught me how to find and correct them.
7. Lawrence and Paul spent too many nights at the bars. They looked tired and ill; they were a real mess.
8. She is a fantastic driver and a good mechanic; however, she can never remember where her car is parked.
9. Teenage Mutant Ninja Turtles were silly, childish, and too violent. The kids loved them.
10. Correct.

COMPARATIVES AND SUPERLATIVES, PAGES 626–628

1. She said that if she had to choose between Tom Cruise and Kevin Costner, she would be the luckiest woman alive.
2. I have visited many national parks, and Bryce Canyon is the most spectacular.
3. Which of the seven dwarfs do you think is the most amusing?
4. He is more at home in front of an audience than alone in his room.
5. Whitney Houston is a talented musician, but Mariah Carey is the better of the two.
6. Correct.
7. Orange may be the less flattering of the two colors, but it is the cheaper.
8. Good nutrition requires balanced meals and self-control. Which is harder?
9. Correct.
10. At this point, it would be better to run away than to fight.

FAULTY COMPARISONS, PAGES 629–630

1. Carmella says she likes you better than she likes any of her other friends OR Tiffany says she likes you better than any of her friends do.
2. Cal Ripkin Jr.'s record for consecutive games played is better than any other baseball player's in history.
3. The graceful line of neck and throat resembles that of a swan.
4. Nobody's acting is better than Jack Nicholson's.
5. Miss Rochester had the best rating of all the contestants.
6. Dr. Raj is better with children than any other pediatrician.
7. My feet are bigger than my sister's OR My feet are bigger than those of my sister.
8. Correct.
9. This poetry is better than any of Lord Byron's.
10. McDonald's hamburgers are better than Burger King's OR McDonald's hamburgers are better than those of Burger King.

END MARKS, PAGES 632–635

1. "How can you write an essay on a book you've never read?" she asked.
2. Elba wondered why it took six months for her new sofa to arrive.
3. The climate at the summit of Mt. Washington is extremely volatile and unpredictable.
4. I know that my petunias get plenty of sun, so why are they dying?
5. Oh, no! I've lost my keys again.
6. Clive asked himself how much he really enjoyed golf.
7. The city bus will take you to the M.L. Grieg Library.
8. The speakers asked the state, local, and federal governments to cooperate with private organizations on environmental preservation.
9. Get me out of here right now!
10. Why can't we all just get along?

FRAGMENTS, PAGES 635–640

1. Americans celebrate Flag Day on June 14 to salute a flag that was stitched in 1776 and has bound the nation together ever since.
2. After Celeste's five-year-old daughter split her lip on a metal shovel at the playground, the distraught mother decided that playgrounds are just too dangerous.
3. Barking and wagging her tail furiously, my golden retriever welcomed me home. After a grueling day at the office, I really needed her affection.
4. It was the perfect day for a barbeque: sunny, breezy, and warm.
5. Living on a farm isn't easy because there is so much work to do. Beginning at dawn we are milking cows, collecting eggs, and caring for all of the animals.
6. Mrs. Scott always acts aloof towards us, if she even acknowledges us at all. It's as if we aren't good enough because our home isn't as large as hers.
7. A spokesperson for Chevrolet says that the company's new pickup combines several important attributes: ruggedness, versatility, and personal comfort.
8. The panelists at the business symposium wrestled with a difficult question: Have technology and the Internet have left small businesses behind?
9. Wind gusts can cause serious problems for firefighters struggling to keep a fire under control.
10. I will consider you a responsible adult when you make your own car payments, when you pay rent, and when you earn a paycheck.

DANGLING AND MISPLACED MODIFIERS, PAGES 642–644

1. Walter noticed a "No Trespassing" sign nailed to the fence.
2. With ruffled feathers, my parrot landed gracefully on my shoulder.
3. I thought the dog that was barking wildly and nipping at an old woman's heels had gone mad.
4. Acceptable.
5. Watching the horror film, Esteban got a terrible pain in his stomach from the gruesome scene.
6. Hearing him chomping loudly and belching, we were appalled at Uncle Ray's terrible table manners.
7. Sam grabbed the milk from the fridge and drank it.
8. I like to watch television while doing my ironing.
9. Michele was told by her mother never to speak to strangers.
10. I thought the golden brown and juicy turkey looked fantastic.

PRONOUN AGREEMENT, PAGES 647–650

1. All the tourists must have their passport and birth certificate if they want to cross the border OR To cross the border, everyone must have a passport and birth certificate.
2. Acceptable.
3. Either Delia or her sisters will have to give up their turn in the front seat.

4. One of the Marlowe brothers leaned back casually, carefully straightening his shirtsleeves.
5. Only Fred will have his license revoked.
6. Correct.
7. All chefs know they must work with extremely sharp knives.
8. None of it was finished, so it was set aside for a while.
9. Correct.
10. Correct.

PRONOUN CASE, PAGES 650–653

1. She
2. she
3. I
4. Us
5. me
6. We
7. My
8. him and her
9. she
10. they

PRONOUN REFERENCE, PAGES 654–656

1. The novelist admitted to plagiarizing his rival's work but all the guilty man said was that he was very upset by his own actions. OR The novelist admitted to plagiarizing his rival's work, but all his rival said was that he was very upset by his competitor's actions.
2. Sweeping along the street and skimming the pavements, the cold wind seemed to give life to the newspaper OR The cold wind seemed to give life to the newspaper that swept along the street and skimmed the pavement.
3. Condescendingly, the patrons complained about the dry and unappealing stuffed Cornish hens.
4. Even the most talented performers can practice for years and still make discouraging mistakes OR Even the most talented performers can be discouraged by the way they can practice for years and still make mistakes.
5. Leigh told Anne that Anne's stocking had a run OR "My stocking has a run," Leigh said to Anne.
6. Sandy and Bill attempted to read the signs but the wording was too mixed-up.
7. George Washington supposedly chopped down a cherry tree and never told a lie. Can these things be true?
8. The teachers had the students get ready for recess. The kids couldn't wait to get out to the playground.
9. No change.
10. The musicians carefully cleaned their instruments and then stored them in their cases for the night.

QUOTATION MARKS, PAGES 656–659

1. Our local children's theater group is doing a choral reading of "The Raven," by Edgar Allan Poe.
2. "I'm sure the referee said, 'Strike,'" Ginger said.
3. How many times a day do you think your mother said, "In a minute!" when you were a child?
4. "I'm out of the Olympics," the disappointed skater announced after her third foot injury.
5. My financial planner urged me to read a pamphlet called "Your Guide Through Life's Financial Decisions."
6. The student asked anxiously, "Will we have some time to review the material before the exam?"
7. "Kids should work very hard during the year and then have a break for time with their parents and activities like camps and jobs," the former Education Secretary stated.
8. I can never leave a party until I hear Donna Summer's song "Last Dance."
9. "Spider venom is a gold mine of pharmacological tools," the neuroscientist explained.
10. "Have you chosen a running mate?" the reporters asked the presidential candidate.

RUN-ON SENTENCES, PAGES 659–661

1. Hundreds of bicyclists will participate in an exciting event this Sunday. It is the county's fourth annual Mountain Bike Festival. Cyclists begin and end at the county park in Kent.
2. My aunt has a recipe for delicious chocolate chip cookies, and the secret ingredient is oatmeal.
3. The candidate is considering very carefully his pick for vice president. A crucial consideration is to find a reliable team player.
4. This dorm room is tiny. How can anyone expect two people to cohabitate here?
5. Many of America's river communities face a common challenge. They must balance the search for prosperity with the need to preserve their natural resources.
6. Darryl walked the dog, and then he fed her.
7. I love to go to the movies, but I often like the popcorn better than the films.
8. Immigrants continue to make our country great; they take many jobs that businesses cannot fill.
9. I saw *The Patriot*, and it was bloodier than I had thought.
10. Phish began to play suddenly, and the audience jumped up and cheered.

SHIFTS IN PERSON OR TENSE, PAGES 662–664

1. Switching tenses is a big problem. It is not an easy habit to break either.
2. Mark Twain said, "Be good, and you will be lonesome." He also said that the reports of his death were greatly exaggerated.

3. Thousands of registered voters forget to cast their votes at election time. They should be proud of their voices and proud to use them.
4. Verb tenses make me tense. They make my best friend cranky, too.
5. My pen is running out of ink, and I will get another when the ink is completely gone.
6. Contact lenses are less convenient than glasses, but many people think that contacts are more attractive.
7. Karin crept softly up the stairs, then she peered around the corner to see if the coast was clear.
8. The tennis champion raced across the court and, with a desperate sweep of his outstretched racket, he slammed the ball out of his opponent's reach.
9. One has no choice but to square one's shoulders and clean the oven.
10. Learning to write well takes time and practice and a lot of hard work.

SPELLING, PAGES 664–667

1. athletic
2. changeable
3. preferred
4. separation
5. sergeant
6. excellent
7. recommend
8. forty
9. jewelry
10. argument

SUBJECT-VERB AGREEMENT, PAGES 667–673

1. Neither the train nor the bus is air conditioned.
2. There are many ways to catch fish.
3. A meal of rice and beans is quite nutritious.
4. Each of the game show contestants is required to answer twelve questions correctly.
5. The winning team plans to celebrate its victory at the local pizza parlor.
6. *The Sound and the Fury* is among Faulkner's most complex novels.
7. Three days was too long for me to be apart from my daughters.
8. Seven dollars is all you spent on your date?
9. Every family in those apartment buildings is living in squalor.
10. None of the wildfires is showing any sign of abating.

VERB FORM, PAGES 674–678

1. Angela would've gone to the park if she hadn't woken up feeling sick.
2. They couldn't possibly have stolen that much money.
3. Correct.
4. Sharon swore she had laid the photographs on the table.

5. Joe had drunk too much and felt ill for the rest of the night.
6. Mom's grandfather clock had broken years ago.
7. The movie *The Ox-Bow Incident* is about a group of men who have hanged three innocent people.
8. Correct.
9. J.C. swam until her fingers began to wrinkle from the water.
10. Alice had fallen down the rabbit hole for a long time before she began to worry.

VERB TENSE, PAGES 678–682

1. If only she had admitted her guilt at the beginning her sentence would have been reduced.
2. David did not do it any more. He had done it too many times for too many years.
3. By the time the party has begun we will have just left our house.
4. When you slowpokes arrive, we will have been there for hours.
5. Correct.
6. Correct.
7. We had not tasted the main course before our plates had been whisked away.
8. Simone always knows all the news. She will know it all tomorrow, too.
9. When this machine is in working order, it will enable Dr. Doom to control the planet.
10. When Carlos and Marsha first met, Marsha was crossing the street.

PROBLEM WORDS, PAGE 721

1. can
2. an exciting film
3. drive through the park
4. a unique idea
5. Did you accept her suggestion?
6. among you, Chung Woo, and me
7. very tasty enchilada
8. Pedro and I
9. I do not like dogs, cats, or birds as pets. OR I like neither dogs nor cats as pets.
10. supposed to leave early
11. keep quiet in the church
12. over there
13. uninterested in the speaker's lecture
14. ate fewer M&Ms
15. hanged the murderer
16. let us study the homework
17. lay in the sun at the pool
18. a loose knot
19. paid her a compliment
20. different from her friend

Credits

Index

Guide to Planning, Writing, and Revising

Consult these sections of *Student's Book* to help you plan, write, and revise your essays and papers. Useful checklists on important topics appear throughout the book and are listed here.

Planning

Writing

Revising